Social Alternatives in Southern Europe and Latin America

AF763481

This book deals with the evolution of initiatives connected to the social and solidarity economy and their political cultures and educational implications in the south of Europe and in Latin America.

Employing a comparative perspective, the contributors present 11 studies of these trajectories in Argentina, Chile, Portugal, France, Italy, Spain, and Catalonia in order to engender familiarity with social tributary practices and projects in the Latin world. As the cyclical crises of capitalism and their resulting inequalities have created proposals of reform and brought them into action, certain shared ideological influences and policies have emerged across these societies. Faced with the interpretative schemes used for the Anglo-Saxon sphere, which have been the usual reference in international research, this volume's geographical and cultural matrix of analysis helps fill a longstanding gap in this field.

The book will be of interest to scholars, educators, and students specialising in the history and political science of the social and solidarity economy sectors, as well as professionals involved in cooperatives, mutual aid societies, and associations.

Montserrat Duch-Plana is a professor at Rovira i Virgili University. Her main areas of research are the social history of the 20th century, memory policies, and the public uses of history and the history of women.

Josep M. Pons-Altés is a professor at Rovira i Virgili University. His main areas of research are contemporary history of Catalonia and didactics of the social sciences.

Routledge Studies in Modern History

Transnationalism and Migration in Global Korea
History, Politics, and Sociology, 1910 to the Present
Edited by Joanne Miyang Cho, Lee M. Roberts, and Sang Hwan Seong

Longing for the Future
Mal D'Afrique and Afro-Optimism in Perspectives on Somalia
Edited by Rosetta Giuliani Caponetto, Giusy Di Filippo and Martina Di Florio

Class War or Race War
The Inner Fronts of Soviet Society during and after the Second World War
Tamás Kende

Carlo di Rudio and the Age of Revolution
Nick Ridley

History and Psychoanalysis in the Columbus Centre
The Meaning of Evil
Danae Karydaki

Science, Religion and Nationalism
Local Perceptions and Global Historiographies
Edited by Jaume Navarro and Kostas Tampakis

How the World Hunger Problem Was not Solved
Christian Gerlach

Social Alternatives in Southern Europe and Latin America
Solidarity, Mutual Aid, and Cooperation in Comparative Perspective (19th–21st Centuries)
Edited by Montserrat Duch-Plana and Josep M. Pons-Altés

For more information about this series, please visit: www.routledge.com/Routledge-Research-in-Modern-History/book-series/MODHIST

Social Alternatives in Southern Europe and Latin America

Solidarity, Mutual Aid, and Cooperation in Comparative Perspective (19th–21st Centuries)

Edited by Montserrat Duch-Plana and Josep M. Pons-Altés

Routledge
Taylor & Francis Group
NEW YORK AND LONDON

First published 2024
by Routledge
605 Third Avenue, New York, NY 10017

and by Routledge
4 Park Square, Milton Park, Abingdon, Oxon, OX14 4RN

Routledge is an imprint of the Taylor & Francis Group, an informa business

© 2024 selection and editorial matter, Montserrat Duch-Plana and Josep M. Pons-Altés; individual chapters, the contributors

The right of Montserrat Duch-Plana and Josep M. Pons-Altés to be identified as the authors of the editorial material, and of the authors for their individual chapters, has been asserted in accordance with sections 77 and 78 of the Copyright, Designs and Patents Act 1988.

All rights reserved. No part of this book may be reprinted or reproduced or utilised in any form or by any electronic, mechanical, or other means, now known or hereafter invented, including photocopying and recording, or in any information storage or retrieval system, without permission in writing from the publishers.

Trademark notice: Product or corporate names may be trademarks or registered trademarks, and are used only for identification and explanation without intent to infringe.

ISBN: 978-1-032-57481-3 (hbk)
ISBN: 978-1-032-57480-6 (pbk)
ISBN: 978-1-003-43955-4 (ebk)

DOI: 10.4324/9781003439554

Contents

Figures

Tables

Acknowledgements

This book is part of the research project *Historia de la Catalunya Subalterna Contemporánea: alternativas solidarias y cooperativas* (History of Contemporary Subaltern Catalonia: Solidarity and Cooperative Alternatives), PID2019-109560GB-I00, funded by the Ministry of Science, Innovation and Universities of the Government of Spain.

MINISTERIO
DE CIENCIA, INNOVACIÓN
Y UNIVERSIDADES

AGENCIA
ESTATAL DE
INVESTIGACIÓN

Introduction

Montserrat Duch-Plana and Josep M. Pons-Altés

In the current context, in which we have to face up to major challenges such as the increase in social inequality, environmental sustainability, or the questioning of human rights, it becomes vital to understand the historical trajectory and potential of projects which are committed to the common good.[1]

Expressed in other terms, the pernicious effects of a certain evolution of capitalism, which is increasing the levels of social segregation, make initiatives linked to social and solidarity economy more necessary than ever. 'Social and solidarity economy' is, however, a concept of diffuse limits (consisting of entities such as cooperatives, mutual societies, foundations, or associations) which we address using the following definition: 'Group of socioeconomic initiatives whose members, via association or cooperation, collectively or individually, democratically create, organize and develop [...] processes of production, interchange, management, distribution of surplus, money, of consumption and financing of goods and services which satisfy needs, guided by a relationship of solidarity, cooperation, donation, reciprocity and self-management, defending natural and cultural commonwealth and the egalitarian transformation of economy and society with the objective of living well and the reproduction and sustainability of the general population'.[2]

It is important to stress that terms such as 'social economy' and 'solidarity economy' have hazy limits and with different traditions in every country. While they are well-used concepts in Latin languages, in English 'social economy' and 'solidarity economy' are not habitual terms, despite the growth in their use: the Anglo-Saxon world tends to prefer 'non-profit economy' or 'sharing economy'. The terminological differences are indicative of different cultural traditions which have made it difficult for the experience of Latin-culture countries to be incorporated into the Anglo-Saxon literature.

The historiography has often avoided the presences and absences in the transmission of a long and dense history of initiatives rising from below

DOI: 10.4324/9781003439554-1

that address radical needs via cooperativism (in production, consumption, housing ...), mutual societies (unemployment, retirement, illness ...), self-management, and the emergence of social and solidarity economy projects. But the social and solidarity economy, cooperation, and the common good have gained more and more presence as concepts and valid analytical parameters in the study of social history, obliging us to revisit the historiography and take a new, kaleidoscopic look at the analysis of the past also including many aspects of how the working class has tried, collectively and democratically, to resolve its material and immaterial needs (work, life, culture, leisure, security, protection ...) as much in terms of social transformation of the capitalist order as in a reform of capitalism itself. In two previous research projects, centred on the Catalan case, we already explored the importance of popular sociability and its memory as ambits of construction of citizenry: *Los espacios y la memoria de la sociabilidad popular en la Cataluña contemporánea* (The spaces and memory of popular sociability in contemporary Catalonia) (HAR-2011-28123) and *Sociabilidades: espacios de construcción de la ciudadanía en Catalunya* (1868–1938) (Sociabilities: spaces of construction of the citizenry in Catalonia) (HAR-2014-54230-P).[3]

The social sciences, and especially history, have been formalised and have advanced by analysing conceptual categories which have been used to formulate hypotheses and better interpret the reality of the present and indicate future options. Concepts such as social class, popular culture, social capital, class hegemony, and so on have been useful as ways of examining and picking apart facts and processes of the past in historical-economic terms, seeking to resolve dynamics and doubts, fomenting debate, and offering new interpretations. In this way, a superficial narrative has been avoided, given that interpretive contact, despite not always leading to progress, in many cases has generated doubts which in turn have created new questions, then leading to novel interpretations.

In this way, new cultural history assumes daily practice, material bases, and representations of the world as created by the community, turning them into decisive agents of change or of resistance of transformation. If in the German tradition one talks about the history of daily life, British Marxist historiography considers more the subaltern groups, as well as marginalised or historically silenced groups.

One has to keep in mind that industrialisation and the creation of new capitalist and liberal societies changed the social classes and their most traditional tensions throughout the 19th century. The protagonism and visibility of a new working class would grow. Working-class activism, perpetuated in a more selfish liberal economy dedicated to capitalist profit, raised the flag of a moral economy in defence of solidarity and collective interest. This came from the condemnation of the expropriations carried out in the interests of the dominant elites and the biased and restrictive interpretations of social rights which were being imposed by the new liberal legislation. In addition, during the first decades of the 19th century, the affirmation of associationism, and in particular mutualism and cooperativism, was an international phenomenon.

Cooperativism and mutual help are becoming basic elements of an analysis of history conducted from the base of society, aiming to listen to 'the lower voices in history'.[4] In this way, detailed analysis of concrete entities is demonstrating the ambiguity of denominations and the diversity of functions which they developed beyond the specific name adopted.

It is in this context that the framework of the history of social and solidarity economy must be amplified, and many questions must be reconsidered. The associative context has to be connected with diverse national contexts, with a variety of political cultures, with diverse political and cultural practice, and with diverse elements of memory. Social alternatives must be analysed in confrontation or union with the dominant political cultures, widening the radius of action, so as to visualise the whole picture that has generated a given situation, its organisation, direction, and in many cases disappearance. From special and comparative studies, connections will be sought between these social alternatives and their inclusion, or not, in popular and class-based movements.

The book deals, therefore, with the evolution of initiatives connected to the social and solidarity economy, and its political cultures and educational implications, in the south of Europe and in Latin America. We employ a comparative perspective and present studies on Argentina, Chile, Portugal, France, Italy, Spain, and Catalonia.

Faced with the interpretative schemes used for the Anglo-Saxon sphere, which are the usual reference in international research, our geographical and cultural matrix of analysis is the Latin world. And in this area, certain convergences emerge in the evolution of associationism, cooperativism, and mutualism, with ideological influences and shared policies, and organisations often characterised by functional polyvalence.

The cyclical crises of capitalism with their corollary of inequalities have created, in peripheral societies such as those studied, proposals of reform accompanied by solid practice, the knowledge of which is now functional. The scarcity of previous comparative works in this field gives more relevance to our contribution.

This book brings together contributions from diverse geographical areas, innovative and necessary works. We aim to deal with those experiences which, perhaps, because they run against the grain of the majority or winning social and economic dynamics in every historical moment, don't fit neatly into the epistemological schemes of human and social sciences because it is more difficult to perceive and think about them historically.

The conceptual axes of the contributions refer to the common good, associationism, cooperativism, mutualism, and the political cultures that have promoted these phenomena, as well as to educational proposals associated therewith. These axes, studied as a whole, allow us to see the reasons for the visibility or invisibility of unions in the vertexes of class: in social aspects of self-help, resistance for subsistence, the search for response to the market, etcetera.

Eleven studies of these trajectories at the European and South American levels are presented so as to observe similarities and differences and engender familiarity with social tributary practices and projects within the concept of the social and solidarity economy. As Jordi Estivill and Rogério Roque explain in the case of the south of Europe, some common elements of their historical trajectories are the expansion of the popular associative movement connected to the social economy, organisational transversality, and its functional polyvalence, with a criticism of the dominant political economy in the academic ambit.[5]

Jordi Estivill is the author of the first chapter of the book, an ambitious text which presents a comparative discussion of the history of the social and solidarity economy in Latin Europe, with brief visits, where appropriate, to Latin America. The geographical and cultural context of the analysis is the Latin world in which certain convergences seem to emerge, affecting the development of associationism, cooperativism, and mutualism. A preliminary working hypothesis is that the conceptual category of the social and solidarity economy helps to better understand substantial aspects of social history. A second hypothesis is that this new view is part of the current crisis in critical thinking in the social sciences. The text ends by suggesting some questions and opening some fields of research which will spur on future work.

Pedro Hespanha revisits the long historical trajectory of common lands in Portugal to strengthen the successive threats they had to face from various antagonists and how this historical process affected the bonds of internal cohesion and the autonomy of communities. In Portugal, the *baldios* (the most common designation today for communal lands) have survived to this day, despite the attacks against them mainly from the second half of the 18th century onwards by an adverse state inspired by liberal thought and by a fierce and powerful rural bourgeoisie who eagerly wanted to appropriate these lands. The fact that the communities faced attacks from different antagonists (feudal nobility, landlords, landed bourgeoisie, physiocratic, liberal, and positivist thinkers, modern state administration) strengthened the bonds of cohesion and identity among commoners.

Joana Dias Pereira also centres her work on Portugal and seeks to provide an overview of the first social economy organisations' origin and evolution in Portugal – the mutual societies and cooperatives – in the transition to modernity. The process has been observed from two perspectives: the emergence of voluntary associations in the continuity of premodern institutions and their involvement in political massification during the liberalism crisis. However, the connections between the two processes are rarely considered. By analysing institutional evolution and social mobilisation, Joana Dias Pereira explains how locally based and professional associations' changes relate to the social movements' jump of scale and politicisation. This long duration and connected perspective reveal that the advent of social economy results from the intersection of a bottom-up movement, the resilience and adaptation of traditional grassroots reciprocity, with top-down innovations determined by the circulation of new associative models among the literate elites and European States.

According to the prevailing interpretation, adding the term 'solidarity' only marginally changes the social economy. Contradicting this interpretation, Jean-Louis Laville argues that the advent of the social and solidarity economy is not insignificant, but offers the opportunity for a practical and theoretical overhaul of the field as it stands. Analysis of the shifts in the mid-19th century and at the end of the 20th century reveals two contrasting scenarios, one in which the solidarity economy is simply an appendage on the margins of a social economy that is still seen as a grouping together of collective enterprises, and another whereby the social and solidarity economy calls for a new interpretation more appropriate to the challenges of the 21st century in which it is a matter of moving on from the grouping together of enterprises to create a solidarity social economy.

Patrizia Battilani presents the Italian example and, specifically, analyses the evolution with which the cooperative movement has been experimenting in recent decades. She provides an overview of the variegated Italian cooperative movement by focusing on the hybridisation of large cooperative groups as well as on the emergence of new types of undertaking, such as the social (dating back to the 1970s) and the community cooperatives. The development of these cooperatives was the consequence of a double movement: a bottom-up process activated by residents in marginal areas who wanted to improve the quality of life of the entire community; a top-down process started by cooperative apex organisations and public administrations which accompanied the residents' attempts by providing a legal framework as well as capacity building and financial support.

The Chilean case is studied by Fernando Venegas, with the aim of presenting the historical trajectory of mutualism. A new interpretation is proposed, emphasising cultural, social, and economic factors which explain both its moments of expansion and crisis. The central hypothesis is that the most critical moments of mutualism in the 20th century were those linked first to the Great Depression (1929 onwards) and the economic crisis of 1982. The latter has turned out to be even more difficult to overcome due to sociocultural changes that were promoted during the Civic-Military Dictatorship, which exacerbated individualism instead of collectivism.

Mirta Zaida Lobato analyses the formation of worker cooperatives in the 1960s in greater depth based on two case studies from the province of Buenos Aires. One is the Berisso textile cooperative, and the other is the Martín Fierro de Zárate Cooperative. The purpose here is to reflect on the different ways workers reacted to the problem of their company shutting down. Unlike the cooperative movement in general, this initial period of work-related cooperatives has remained almost entirely unstudied. When producing a history of solidarity in the working world, especially in relation to the phenomenon of unemployment, it is also important to compare these earlier experiences with those arising after Argentina's critical year of 2001.

In turn, the evolution of Spanish mutualism is dealt with by Santiago Castillo. He presents a general overview of studies related to the period 1836–1936. The evolution of the proposals and contributions made with respect to some of the most relevant topics in the field are then addressed, emphasising both achievements and failures, breaking these down into considerations regarding the current state of research and possible future lines of investigation. A summarised framework is also established regarding the particular characteristics of Spanish mutualism, compared to other manifestations in various nearby countries.

The specific case of Catalonia is studied by Montserrat Duch and Ramon Arnabat. Their article analyses the foundations and functions of the associationism created by the working classes during the major expansion of capitalism and bourgeois society, as well as their geographical extension and relationships with other economic, social, political, and cultural elements. The fundamental absences that affected the working classes during Catalonia's contemporary history are a key explanatory factor for proliferation of the mutual insurance societies, as well as for expansion of solidarity culture.

In the final two chapters, we wanted to introduce a question which is often absent in reflections about social and solidarity economy, or more specifically about cooperativism: the educational proposals inspired by its values. In this light, Sylvain Connac defines cooperation as a relational behaviour determined by three characteristics: concerted action, intentionality, and individual benefit. Cooperation between students corresponds to the set of situations where students are encouraged to act and learn by, with and for others, in order to gain personal benefit. France has been a rich territory for cooperative educational practices. The chapter traces the evolution of these conceptions of pedagogy (some of which originated in countries other than France) first and then draws up a brief inventory of the cooperative organisations currently observed, making it possible to think about didactics of cooperation.

Finally, Albert Irigoyen, Josep M. Pons-Altés, and Carole Gauthié explain how, in recent decades, the proposals of the implementation of cooperative learning in educational centres have seen a substantial increase in many countries, but the dominant factor is the disconnection from projects of social change. Within this general framework, they then reflect on the conceptualisation and impact of the Anglo-Saxon concept of 'cooperative learning', which clearly predominates in Spanish and Italian schools that apply cooperation between pupils, and contrast it with the francophone concept of 'pédagogies coopératives'. To conclude, they examine areas in which cooperative learning could converge with the social and solidarity economy.

To conclude this introduction, as coordinators of the book we would like to acknowledge the collaboration of our colleagues in the ISOCAC (*Història, Societat, Política i Cultura des de Catalunya al món*) research group at the Universitat Rovira i Virgili, and, in particular, Júlia Cuadrat and Sara Masalias for their revisions of texts. We would also like to thank the implication and generosity of all the experts who participated in a working seminar, held in Tarragona in April 2022, and who then accepted our invitation to participate in the creation of the book. A seminar and a publication which form part of our research project *Historia de la Catalunya Subalterna Contemporánea: alternativas solidarias y cooperativas* (History of Contemporary Subaltern Catalonia: Solidarity and Cooperative Alternatives), PID2019-109560GB-I00, funded by the Ministry of Science and Innovation of the Government of Spain.

Notes

1 From another perspective, we might find common elements with the prioritisation of those sectors of the economy whose mission is the defense of life (Jacques ATTALI: *La economía de la vida. Prepararse para lo que viene*, Buenos Aires, Libros del Zorzal, 2021).

2 Jordi ESTIVILL and Ivan MIRÓ: *L'Economia Social i Solidària a Catalunya. Fonaments teòrics i reptes estratègics*, Barcelona, Icaria, 2020, p. 169.

3 Among the publications generated as a result of these two projects, we would point out Montserrat DUCH, Ramon ARNABAT and Xavier FERRÉ (eds.): *Sociabilitats a la Catalunya contemporània. Temps i espais en conflicte*, Barcelona, Publicacions de l'Abadia de Montserrat, 2015; Montserrat DUCH, Ramon ARNABAT and Antoni GAVALDÀ (eds.): *La Catalunya associada (1868–1938)*, Valencia, Universitat de València, 2020.

4 Montserrat DUCH: "El mutualismo catalán: la construcción desde abajo de la ciudadanía social", *Historia Contemporánea*, 61 (2019), pp. 793–833.
5 Jordi ESTIVILL: "Catalunya associada i solidària", *L'Avenç*, 483 (2021), pp. 36–43; and Rogério ROQUE AMARO: "Similituds i diferències entre els enfocaments de l'economia social i solidària en diferents països de l'Europa del Sud (Catalunya, França, Itàlia, Portugal)", in Jordi ESTIVILL and Jean Louis LAVILLE (eds.): *Economia solidària i història social*, Barcelona, Icaria, 2020, pp. 193–223.

References

ATTALI, Jacques: *La economía de la vida. Prepararse para lo que viene*, Buenos Aires, Libros del Zorzal, 2021.

DUCH, Montserrat: "El mutualismo catalán: la construcción desde abajo de la ciudadanía social", *Historia Contemporánea*, 61 (2019), pp. 793–833.

DUCH, Montserrat; ARNABAT, Ramon and FERRÉ, Xavier (eds.): *Sociabilitats a la Catalunya contemporània. Temps i espais en conflicte*, Barcelona, Publicacions de l'Abadia de Montserrat, 2015.

DUCH, Montserrat; ARNABAT, Ramon and GAVALDÀ, Antoni (eds.): *La Catalunya associada (1868–1938)*, Valencia, Universitat de València, 2020.

ESTIVILL, Jordi: "Catalunya associada i solidària", *L'Avenç*, 483 (2021), pp. 36–43.

ESTIVILL, Jordi and MIRÓ, Ivan: *L'Economia Social i Solidària a Catalunya. Fonaments teòrics i reptes estratègics*, Barcelona, Icaria, 2020, p. 169.

ROQUE AMARO, Rogério: "Similituds i diferències entre els enfocaments de l'economia social i solidària en diferents països de l'Europa del Sud (Catalunya, França, Itàlia, Portugal)", in Jordi ESTIVILL and Jean Louis LAVILLE (eds.): *Economia solidària i història social*, Barcelona, Icaria, 2020, pp. 193–223.

1 Comparative Notes on the History of the Social and Solidarity Economy in Latin Europe

Jordi Estivill

Fruitful encounters

This chapter is a comparative discussion of the history of the social and solidarity economy in Latin Europe, with brief incursions into Latin America where appropriate. The geographical and cultural context of the analysis is the Latin world, in which certain convergences seem to emerge which impact the evolution of associationism, cooperativism, and mutualism. The paucity of previous work on this subject means that these observations, ranging from 1830 to the 1930s, have a provisional, hypothetical, and often adventurous character. They attempt to pose some questions and open up some fields of research to encourage future work.

A preliminary working hypothesis is that the concept of the social and solidarity economy serves to better interpret substantive dimensions of social history.[1] It provides an overarching and cross-cutting perspective and a set of values and viewpoints to offer insights into the origins and development of socioeconomic initiatives emerging from the popular and working classes and the political culture that surrounds them.

A second hypothesis is that this new view reflects some of today's emerging currents in critical thinking in the social sciences. Some economic scientists are very critical of the quantitative measurements and indicators (gross national product, per capita income, etc.) used to weight and, in their view, conceal economic activity and development.[2] The recent pandemic forces further reconsideration of the implications of unlimited growth, which degrades nature and creates enormous inequalities. A growing number of economists are now turning to value in use rather than exchange value, and taking an interest in common goods, local and community development,[3] platform cooperativism, and the ecological transition, and accepting the plurality of economic forms (reciprocity, distribution, benefit) already highlighted by Polanyi.[4] It may be no coincidence that Polanyi and Mauss[5] were among the theoretical founders of the solidarity economy and anthropologists, since they set out from this sphere to reflect on giving, the

DOI: 10.4324/9781003439554-2

daily lives of those at the bottom, otherness, and the logic of domestic life and reproductif work. Furthermore, new sociological approaches incorporate feminist theories, the notion of common and community spaces, general and collective interest and social capital, and emerging forms of participatory democracy and governance. Critical geography also draws us closer to a new view of the city and regional inequalities. These renewals of the human and social sciences are occasions for exchange and cross-fertilisation concerning the issues involved in the social and solidarity economy.

However, perhaps it is in social history that these exchanges are most fruitful, since social history, following in the footsteps of English heterodox Marxist historians like Thompson and Hobsbawm and the workshops, has revealed a moral economy of the masses, a reconsideration of popular revolts and uprisings, and of autonomy and mediation, in the long process of building working-class awareness and organisations. In France, numerous new studies have challenged more traditional approaches. The revamping of the journals *Annales* and *Mouvement Social*, the important contribution of Foucault, the nebulous but intriguing notion of sociability from Agulhon, Castel's categories of affiliation and precariousness, the contributions of the *Révoltes Logiques* group led by Rancière, Laville's new interpretation of the role of associationism, and the supposedly utopian thinking of Abensour are all changing views of the social scenario of the nineteenth century.

Undeniably, in Italy, the research of Ginzburg, Levi, Grandi, and others in microhistory has shaken up historiography by showing how general trends can be drawn from the study of certain people, events, and local networks. One thing this approach has led to is a flourishing of historical research[6] into the proliferation of small local workers' mutual aid societies. Portugal is also taking part in this change. Social history is keeping up with the latest developments there, and interest in it is growing.[7] Publications are also being produced on developments in social economics,[8] mutualism,[9] associationism,[10] and their structures and doctrines. In Catalonia, which has a long tradition of studies of the culture of popular association[11] and cooperativism,[12] there have been some considerable advances. The publications of a group of historians from the University of Rovira i Virgili in Tarragona,[13] using a database of about 23,154 records, make it possible to produce findings on the quantitative development of popular associationism stretching from 1868 to 1980, as well as a detailed regional account. Research by the Ciutat Invisible team on cooperativism in three Barcelona neighbourhoods,[14] in line with previous work by Oyón[15] and Ealham,[16] shows the way in which forums for collective identity construction and socialisation in the city's working-class neighbourhoods originated and evolved[17] and the social struggles they generated. This phenomenon can also be observed in many county towns and industrial cities in Catalonia.

In many Latin American countries, a similar change is taking place in the reappraisal of social history, largely paralleling the emergence and spread of the solidarity economy.[18] Studies of the Latin American workers' movement by Abad de Santillan, Alba, Rama, Godio, Capelletti, and Max Netlau in 1927[19] – now considered classics – have been followed by numerous studies and publications on research from Mexico[20] to Argentina, which reappraise the approach to immigrants and exiles from Catalonia, Spain, Italy, and France, highlighting their role in the spread of libertarian and socialist ideas on the continent, as well as its autochthonous capacity to create specific organisations and practices and international Pan-American networks.[21] The search for the uniqueness of the Latin American framework is a matter of concern for Latin American historians, who denounce, on the one hand, the ideological impositions of the Soviet communist party and, on the other, the attempts of US trade unionism to penetrate the continent. The new Latin American social history is very interested in the role of 'ethnic communities'[22] and the creation of mutual aid societies as well as cultural, sports, and recreational associations. Historians of the continent ask to what extent they have or have not shaped the national identities of individual countries.

A remarkable tradition of cooperatives, associations, and social, cultural, and sporting centres emerges, sometimes more directly, as in the works of Grez[23] and Venegas[24] on mutualism, or more indirectly, as in the study of anarchist ideology and organisations – of particular importance from 1880 to 1920[25] – and in more specific studies, such as those on the first general strike in Uruguay[26] and the initiatives of workers outside work in Colombia.[27] This involves circles of fellowship, forums for education and discussion, cultural production and publications, organisation through collective action, and often mutual assistance. The organisation and promotion of these types of initiatives would be more the preserve of artisans, tradespeople, and skilled workers than urban and industrial workers, who are a minority in many countries and would be more likely to organise through trade unions. Nor should we fail to recognise that the richness of indigenous forms of self-organisation and the satisfaction of collective needs,[28] attitudes to nature and the land, and the historical significance of the informal and popular economy[29] are areas that invite new approaches to social history in the context of the solidarity economy.

In the shadow of social history

However, there is no shortage of obstacles in this new panorama. The first is that the very definition of the social and solidarity economy is subject to debate and is continually being constructed in response to thousands of experiences around the world. Its boundaries are often blurred. For example, the different concepts of social economy that were widely used in nineteenth-century Europe are not so widely used, or much less so, in many Latin American countries. So, when a set of grassroots initiatives that did not seek to follow the criteria of the market or depend on the state gained visibility in the second half of the twentieth century, several new notions emerged in these countries. In their efforts to establish a definition for these notions, they were able to more openly consider what to call them.[30] They did not have to distinguish them from the social economic perspective and its historical, symbolic, and real weight, as was the case in Latin Europe, although it is important to remember that this perspective has carried little weight in Italian history, as the concept of civil economy[31] has been more widely used, as has that of the third sector economy[32] more recently, and the economy of solidarity[33] for the last 20 years or so.

Conversely, social history has long shown greater interest in social and political organisations that emulate the established powers and whose logic is to access them, occupy them, or negotiate with them. Hence, workers' parties and trade unions and the conflicts they generated[34] were given preferential treatment, while initiatives and collectives that did not explicitly follow this approach and were not the main protagonists in struggles were considered subordinate or even as deviating from revolutionary goals and therefore of little interest. Mutual aid and resistance societies, cooperatives, and popular associations have thus remained in the shadows of social history. With a few exceptions, they were considered to be part of the prehistoric or primitive stages of a workers' movement that went beyond them teleologically[35] and constituted a class, a homogeneous bloc.[36] Perhaps the current loss of the central role of the factory and the industrial proletariat has promoted the emergence and visibility of other forms of sociability. At the same time, the heterogeneity of social groups and a certain interclassism have been present in facets of the social economy and have enjoyed relative continuity, with ups and downs that don't align well with the concept of social progress and its necessarily upward movement, as much of previous social history has presupposed.

Similarly, the short-term struggles of the labour movement and the well-known names of prominent figures attracted the attention of social historians, often to the detriment of long-term social movements. This fixation on short-term conflicts and big names made it difficult to analyse the everyday lives of ordinary people, on the one hand, and, on the other, deeper processes that are more hidden but no less important, since they shape awareness and identity among the popular classes. The various forms of expression and organisation are like a river that meanders and does not always flow into the sea. So, the riverbanks take on greater importance. Resistance associations, mutual aid societies, popular associations of all kinds, athenaeums, cooperatives, etc., become a backwater.

Water rests, is filtered, and creates new channels through which it can run and become free, although it does not always reach the main stream.

Another obstacle to an all-round overview arises from the structuring of the various families of the social economy, which has been diversifying in Central European countries since the nineteenth century and has followed courses that often do not converge. This parallel evolution, to which the compartmentalisation of public administration has contributed, has meant that those who have studied it have followed individual courses and only exceptionally built bridges between them or conducted generalised studies. So, all four countries have specific histories of cooperativism,[37] associationism, and mutualism. It is only since the 1980s that these three movements have been recognised and brought together again, and the term 'social economy' has re-emerged as an umbrella term for all three. In the same decade, the vision of the solidarity economy[38] appeared in Brazil, France, and the Azores. In the European sphere, this has largely been in a context of, and often in opposition to, excessive institutionalisation, corporatism, and complicity with the established powers of the more traditional social economy.

Another source of confusion is that for many, the concepts of 'social' and 'solidarity' often evoke a positive dimension, of helping the most disadvantaged. All economies are social, so using the two words together is a tautology. Many associate the world of associations, and more specifically the 'third sector', with combatting poverty. They also think that if the economy must be solidarity-based, it is essentially because it must address poverty and arises from it. This is the case for many current Latin American authors. This has led to associating both perspectives with welfarism and, historically, with public and private charity. However, it bears repeating that the social and solidarity economy and a large proportion of associations are not concerned with the reduction and alleviation of poverty but with combating its structural causes.

Despite these obstacles and areas of confusion, there has recently been practical and theoretical conciliation that encourages dialogue. On the one hand, it is becoming more common at the international level to refer to the thousands of experiences around the world that are people-centred and not-for-profit, that practice economic democracy, participation, and gender equality, that respect the environment, and seek social and economic change as 'social and solidarity economies'. On the other hand, intellectual output in relation to these ideas has increased considerably, so much so that it has a sufficient foundation to tackle controversies and engage in debate with the new approaches to the human and social sciences and social history.

Transnational comparative analyses: some background

Taking stock of comparative analyses of the social and solidarity economy would be quite a task in itself. Therefore, we have tried to give an overview of the most important publications dealing with its history from both near and far.

When Sombart compares Germany and the United States, with the aim of answering the question of why socialism has not been implemented in the latter,[39] he states that comparative studies help us to better understand the realities of each country. Learning and sharing would be a secondary objective of this type of study. A third would be to improve one's own actions by including the lessons of others, and a fourth could be setting the stage for joint strategies and activities.

However, it is not a question of explaining the potential of comparative analyses of a historical nature but of explaining that there are some precedents. The most direct of these was the conference held in Barcelona in 2019, a meeting of French, Portuguese, Italian, and Catalan historians and sociologists. Rogério Roque Amaro presented an initial comparative study there.[40] He set out by warning that there is a tendency in this type of research to find homogeneity and convergence: the origins of the social economy would tend to be Eurocentric and Francophone, while those of the solidarity economy would be polycentric and multicultural. There is, therefore, no need to seek a kind of forced syncretism.

International comparative analyses are often presented in the form of an introduction to present the theme, followed by a series of national monographs addressing it, and concluding with an epilogue reflecting on similarities and differences. Some authors have called this 'methodological nationalism'.[41] This is the case for most work on social enterprises carried out by the EMEs group[42] and the latest research by Selusi and Seforis. Most of these publications do not include a historical analysis. However, there are some interesting exceptions in comparisons of the conceptual characteristics of European social enterprises and those in North America,[43] or the social economy of the South and the North,[44] which manage to define some sufficiently specific and unique features. However, this type of comparison necessitates the definition of common characteristics in very broad geopolitical frameworks (Europe and Latin America), which have very different internal situations. This is, for example, the main problem with Jeantet's book,[45] which, moreover, covers the short chapter on history from an exclusively French perspective. However, when the geographical scope is restricted, it is easier to conduct a more in-depth comparative analysis.[46]

Another approach that fails to advance transnational analyses to any great extent is taking the matrix of a single country and basing a comparison on that.[47] This is a frequent issue, since it is difficult to leave aside the implicit features of one's own culture. To a large extent, this drawback is evident in Jean Louis Laville's early works, which are heavily tinged with the French tricolour.[48] He then corrects this by including and integrating transnational aspects and providing some improvements on bilateral analysis, as in his book co-authored with Genauto de França Filho, in which they compare the solidarity economy in Brazil and France.[49] However, the matrix of the latter country continues to dominate,[50] and they conclude that both countries share a plurality and hybridisation of economic forms as well as the challenge of establishing another public forum, while the enormous historical and current importance of Brazil's informal and popular economy and their diverse approach to social exclusion stand out as two differentiating factors. Laville also offers two good examples of integrated transnational historical analysis in the first chapter of his book on the association movement[51] and in the chapter *For an Economic Sociology Nourished by History* in his work *L'économie solidaire: une perspective internationale* (The Solidarity Economy: An International Perspective).[52] His book also has another fruitful approach: a transnational sectoral analysis. In this case, it is applied to local services, fair trade, feminist economics, and the political dimension of the solidarity economy, an approach also applied in other works of interest.[53] This is also the case of the book edited by Peter Utting[54] – who organised an international conference at the United Nations in Geneva in 2014 on the social and solidarity economy – the second part of which revolves around analysis by sector and thematically and nationally significant aspects. It is a pity that the first part, devoted to more conceptual and theoretical reflections, includes only one article devoted to history by Laville.

An argument in favour of a certain unity in Latin Europe is provided by the similar responses of authors from these countries regarding the important international comparative research by Americans Lester Salomon and Helmut Anheier on the third sector in 12 countries and later in 32 others. Archambault for France,[55] Barbetta for Italy,[56] Franco for Portugal,[57] and Ruiz de Olabuenaga for Spain[58] all agree that they must modify some general research criteria and adapt them to their specific situations, and they all devote substantial parts of their work to the historical evolution of the third sector, including the paths taken by associations, cooperatives, mutual aid societies, and other forms of collective organisation.

It is precisely in the evaluation of the historical paths of the different families of the social and solidarity economy that some transnational comparative research can be found, regarding which, however, many paths remain to be discovered.

One exception is the Turin Conference of 1988, where associationism in Italy and France in the eighteenth and nineteenth centuries was compared. This is a rare example of bilateral historical comparison in the field of associationism.[59]

One can continue with the work on mutualism by Dreyfus[60] and Solà,[61] and, above all, with the conference held in Paris in 1992, which led to the publication edited by Van der Linden.[62] It contains monographs on the historical development of mutual systems in 29 countries and is a considerable compendium of information covering all 5 continents. Earlier comparative research,[63] in contrast, only compared the United States with Europe and focused on increasing public intervention. This approach broke new ground and led to a multitude of studies[64] on the origin and evolution of the 'welfare states', but it is far removed from the subject and period covered here.

The world of cooperativism enjoys more comparative historical research and a greater number of authors who bridge the different domains than the world of mutualism. This is probably because it is viewed as the most comprehensive expression of associationism, which has led to it being treated by renowned authors in the history of economic and political thought,[65] such as Marx, Walras, Stuart Mill, Pareto, Sismondi, Lassalle, Gide, etc. Their studies are not comparative, strictly speaking, but analytical discourses on the economic system and the role of cooperativism, but they influence the development of cooperative thought on an international scale. This thinking on cooperativism is largely nourished by comparative learning. There is no doubt that Holyoake's short book telling the story of the Rochdale pioneers has crossed many borders and become an international instruction manual.

Other types of comparative research use history to demonstrate the cooperative model's greater efficiency and resilience. It is a new production model[66] that survives better than traditional companies,[67] even over long periods of time,[68] that adjusts wages instead of destroying jobs,[69] that does not relocate, and that adds value to the territory.

Perhaps because of the quality of the authors and the European approach, some of the most interesting comparative works on the history of cooperativism are those edited by Degli Innocenti.[70] They are the result of two conferences: the first, held in Genoa in 1985, and, above all, the second, held a year later in Florence. The latter included a paper by Desroche, one of the driving forces behind the re-emergence of the concept of the social economy in France, and a section on historiography, which included papers on the evolution of cooperativism in England, France, Italy, Belgium, and Hungary. Finally, one cannot ignore the somewhat uneven collection of essays on the global history of consumer cooperation since 1850.[71]

The origins of the use of the concept of social economy in Latin Europe

A first comparative examination shows that origin of the use of the concept of the social economy is shared among the countries of Latin

Europe. Although until recently it was thought that France had a certain monopoly, stemming from the treatise of the liberal Dunoyer[72] in 1830 and continued by socialist theoreticians Pecqueur[73] (1837 and 1842) and Vidal (1846),[74] this is less and less the case. A play written in 1806 and published in 1823[75] was discovered in Portugal, which offers advice, much of it moral, on individual and collective economic behaviour for the 'proper' functioning of the political and economic life of the country. In the dialogues between the characters in the play, precepts are periodically presented, attacking monopolies, excessive luxury, the ostentatiousness of the idle and the wealthy, speculation and embezzlement, and criticising foreign plundering of the country's resources. The piece advocates austerity, work, and state intervention to limit the ravages of overconsumption, which creates poverty among the people. It is a document – a pioneering one for its time – on the use of the social economy in which a moral perspective similar to Portuguese arbitrism is implicit.[76]

The Portuguese surprises do not end there. In 1840, the same year that the Galician Ramon de la Sagra published his treatise in Madrid,[77] the magazine *Litteraria de Porto* reported on it, publishing two chapters of the work.[78] Four years later, Alves Martins, the future Bishop of Viseu, published a book in which 'social economy' appeared in the title.[79] It presented the theories of Chitti (an Italian economist and lawyer who in 1834 published in French the course on social economy[80] he gave at the Museum of Arts and Industry in Brussels, a course he later repeated at the Faculty of Law of the secular university of that city), as well as those of the polemic heterodox French theologian Lamennais.[81] Also worthy of mention are Pinheiro Ferreira,[82] a follower of Proudhon, and the interesting manual by Brandao.[83] A year later, in Great Britain, the cradle of classical political economics, Scottish Victorian reformer Samuel Smiles used the expression 'social economy' in his book *Thrift*[84] in opposition to economic policy in his view of self-help. In Italy, in 1837, Neapolitan jurist and moderate liberal Matteo de Augustinis, perhaps in a continuation of the moral and civic spirit of Genovesi,[85] criticised mercantilism and physiocracy and, while insisting on its moral and social character, warned in *Istituzioni di economia sociale*[86] that, although knowledge of social economy had advanced, there were still many unresolved issues that remained to be clarified and understood. Augustinis was right in 1837, and what he said is still valid 150 years later. Much remains to be discovered.

So, the four countries of Latin Europe agree substantially on the initial use of the basic concept of social economy, as a science that aims to take different and often contrary paths to those of classical economics, even if their content has nuances that sometimes differ.

The importance of three families: the weight of the law

An initial observation that draws the social economy as a whole in the four countries closer together is that it has to struggle to exist within a capitalist system that has a different logic for how it operates and different criteria for assessment. By putting work first, by not seeking profit and not aiming to remunerate capital, by introducing democracy in economic activity, the social economy of the nineteenth century not only confronts capitalism but also dominant values and ethics (individualism, competition, hierarchy, etc.). In this struggle, and in seeking to make a place for itself between the market and the state, the social economy has gone from modest, subaltern, and marginal – even semi-clandestine – origins to periods of greater affirmation and recognition. For a long time, its fate was linked to that of the workers and popular movement and so to the balance of power the movement struck with the wealthy classes. It was not until well into the twentieth century that the social economy scaled back its ambitions and became an intermediary, and, to some extent, an accomplice of the established powers. Logically, this process followed different paths and took different forms in the four countries.

All four countries share the historical importance of the claiming for associationism and the association movement. The right to associate and to find loopholes in the repressive nineteenth-century legal system was a constant concern of the workers and popular movement and a determining factor in its ability to organise and grow stronger. In fact, democratic associationism became an ideal project for social organisation.

The volume of popular associations was dependent to a large extent on the political situation and the different phases of the transition towards democracy. Workers' organisations were forced to undergo periods of secrecy, semi-legality, relative tolerance, and legal permissiveness. Up until 1848, workers' societies in **France** demanded that the betrayed ideals of the Revolution be put into practice. And after the revolt, legislation was tightened. The revolt and the Paris Commune of 1871 showed not only their capacity for self-organisation but also their distance from the dominant political apparatus. It was not until 1901 that the right to form associations was fully recognised. Other legislative milestones reflected the backwardness of a Jacobin state: 1884 for trade union organisations, 1898 for mutual aid societies. The despotic and anachronistic **Spanish state** did not recognise the right to organise until 1887, and workers' organisations had to camouflage themselves and rely on an 1839 Decree that allowed for mutual benefit societies. The fact that one of the banners at the demonstration during the general strike in Barcelona in 1855 bore the slogan 'association or death' is significant. This represented a major opposition, which, to a certain extent, permeated the associationists' struggle and its achievements in Catalonia.[87] In **Portugal**, meanwhile, the repression did not seem to be as harsh. Political oscillations, the relative strength of the right-wing liberals, and the role of Freemasonry and urban sociability would tend to explain this.[88] Patriotic and professional societies and those linked to the interests of employers[89] opened a path that was later followed by workers' and popular organisations. Legal milestones along this path were reached in 1864, 1867, and 1890 and include the regulations of 1891 and 1896. In **Italy**, the Catholic Church[90] (*opere pie*) and the factor of localism dominated the association scene until the constitution of Italy in 1861. The liberal oligarchy that controlled it tried to centralise and secularise society. In this struggle, the Crispi Law (1890) was significant because it allocated healthcare to the state and charity to the Church, thereby regulating a facet of associationism. Another component came from the northern middle class, which aided in the unification of Italy. But little by little, mutual societies and cooperatives became more autonomous and were focal points of worker resistance. Their origins and development help to explain the sensitivity towards the possibility of state interference, as evidenced by the refusal of the mutual benefit societies to be recognised by the National Congress in 1855 and their response[91] to the 1886 law that sought to discipline them.

To what extent do the four countries share a lack of institutional channels for demands for greater freedom of association? Perhaps this is indicative of the lack of political inclusion of the working classes and the role of their associations, which became more politicised, radicalised, and diversified as the century progressed. In none of the four countries was there an English-style Chartist movement of mass popular demand for civic and political rights.

A second comparative interpretation of this is to try to weigh the importance of the three families that comprise the social and solidarity economy. In this regard, comparative research in Latin Europe reveals a number of similarities and differences.

In Italy and Catalonia, the cooperative movement grew towards the end of the nineteenth century and became one of the backbones of the workers' movement and a symbol of their autonomy to a certain extent. Portugal had a pioneering law on cooperativism (1867) but the cooperative movement, which was promoted from the 1860s onwards, did not expand as much as in the other two countries. In none of the four countries was there a willingness to wait for the introduction of a legal statute to create associations that would meet the most pressing civil and social needs and demands. When the time came to enact legislation on cooperatives, the debate centred on whether they should be governed by civil law or commercial law. In Italy (1874) and Portugal (1888), cooperatives were placed under the commercial code, which emphasised business and market considerations, relegating the association aspect to a secondary role. Another specific law, the Catalan Law of 1934, constituted a quantitative leap for cooperatives. However, not all legal regulations were positive. One should remember the regulatory systems enacted in the dictatorial periods (the 1944 laws and regulations in Spain, and the *Lei do Garrote* in Portugal).

Mutual aid societies were abundant in Italy and Portugal, where earlier guild structures and the strength of the trades and craftsmanship still persisted. They increased in number until the 1920s, which was also the case in Catalonia. Meanwhile, in France, their rapid institutionalisation under Napoleon III gave strength and continuity to mutualism, which from 1884 onwards moved away from trade unionism[92] and other more assertive forms.

Interestingly, Latin American historians note that mutualism also lost ground in the second decade of the twentieth century. The interpretation given to date is that this loss was due to the gradual introduction of subsidies for public social welfare. It is possible that other factors also played a role,[93] such as competition from private insurance, the lack of foresight and limited size of local mutual societies, the growing heterogeneity of mutualists, improvements in health, longer life expectancy, etc., and, most probably, the radicalisation of the workers' movement after the Soviet revolution of 1917. This, together with the Mexican Revolution of 1910,[94] also shaped the Latin American labour movement. Everything seems to indicate that in this case, and from then on, cooperativism and mutualism were to a certain extent anchored in a reformist vision, which is also the case to a large extent in Portugal.[95]

Some ideological and political influences: functional polyvalence

From its beginnings, and throughout much of the nineteenth century, one can find under the concept of social economy in the four countries: 1) an opposition to welfare mechanisms and policies and proposals to modify them; 2) a critique of the dominant science of political economics, which focuses on the wealth of nations, and the will to create another scientific approach more committed to labour and the distribution of its output; 3) plural expressions of cooperativism, associationism, and mutualism; and 4) ideological formalisations oscillating between operational pragmatism and an alternative to capitalist society.

The influence of the Catholic Church is very much present, especially in associationism in Portugal and Italy. This is underscored by the presence of the charitable *misericordias*, coming to represent a major current, which was affirmed after *Rerum Novarum* in 1891 and continues to this day. To a certain extent, the different expressions of the social economy in

France, Italy, and Portugal are influenced by the historical struggle between State and Church, between clericalism and anticlericalism, which was also important in Catalonia, where churches were burned in multiple episodes of unrest, culminating in the popular revolt of 1909.[96]

Against this background, Catholic and conservative sociologist Le Play marks a turning point in the terrain of the social economy in France in the second half of the nineteenth century. His disciples would extend his influence throughout the Latin domain, from Belgium[97] to Portugal[98] via Italy[99] and Catalonia.[100] Le Play was an important sociologist, who, in 1856, founded the *Société Internationale des études pratiques d'économie sociale* as well as the journal *La Réforme Sociale*. He is known for his monographs on the working-class world and for applying the direct survey and participant observation method. Le Play favoured the creation of cooperatives, commissaries, and other social tools with a vision of patronage that was beginning to be practised in the large factories of Northern France, and which developed in Catalonia's industrial colonies and in Belgium's *charbonnages*.[101] This system of exercising employer power was also applied in certain large factories in Portugal and in factories in northern Italy.

For Robert Castel,[102] reformist attempts to tackle pauperism and improve working-class living conditions in France can be seen in the work of Frédéric Ozanam, Armand de Melun, Gérando, and Villeneuve Bargémont.[103] They lent substance to a social economy with Catholic roots that was critical of traditional charity and proposed establishing savings banks and popular credit institutions to provide social welfare, improve the housing situation of workers on a regional scale, offer factory welfare, and provide company stores, dispensaries, occupational training schools, some subsidies, and sports grounds. This could even be positive for mutual benefit societies, as long as they did not turn into resistance societies. They even allow for production cooperatives, as long as they are led by an 'eminent director and members are from the elite'.[104]

Jean Louis Laville's interpretation[105] complements Castel's in that he suggests that the move towards a moralising and paternalistic social economy that addresses poverty is a condition for neutralising democratic solidarity based on equality and the capacity of the initial grassroots association movement to make demands.

If with Le Play the social economy came in through the back door of the Paris Universal Exposition[106] of 1855 and 1867, with Gide[107] it came in through the front door at the 1900 World's Fair. Gide, a Protestant professor who founded the *École de Nîmes* cooperative movement, sought to give the social economy a scientific and academic identity and to raise awareness of it. In a lecture he gave at the University of Geneva in 1880, he distinguished four schools of economic thought:[108] Christian, liberal, socialist, and the new ideology, based on cooperation and solidarity.[109] In 1905, he published a book in which he outlined this new science, which he named 'social economics'. Gide was also a theorist and a staunch defender of the cooperative movement, especially consumer cooperatives, which he believed could serve to reform the economic system as a whole, to move towards a cooperative republic. Gide had considerable international influence[110] and a notable impact in Catalonia,[111] Italy,[112] and Portugal.[113]

However, utopian socialism, republicanism – very often driven by Freemasonry – and anarchism were the foremost currents in the different forms of the social economy. In all four countries, the different expressions of republicanism play a role in the origins of the social economy that remains to be explained. Associationism and much of cooperativism and mutualism draw on the ideas of King, Owen, Fourier, Saint Simon, Proudhon, and their followers.

In the spread of anarchism, Catalonia seems to be an exception, since, on the one hand, it shares with the other countries the importance of libertarian ideas up to the First World War and the peak of social struggles around 1917–1920, and, on the other hand, it is distinguished by its continuity and the strength of anarcho-syndicalism in the 1930s, after the repressive period of Primo de Rivera, when anarchism was losing strength in the other three countries for various reasons.

Not all Catalan anarchists were cooperativists and mutualists, nor were all cooperativists and mutualists anarchists. The most radical anarchists rejected cooperativism and accused it of desensitising the working class and taking on the role of master. But their earlier misgivings faded as the twentieth century progressed. The 1930s saw an intense debate between cooperativists and collectivists.[114] During the civil war, workers managed to gain some power and applied the ideals they had previously advocated, collectivising not only a large part of the economy (industry, services, agriculture) but also the health, education, and housing systems. It was a quite unprecedented experience, during which Felipe Alaiz used the expression 'solidarity economy' for the first time.[115] It lasted for three years. The war and internal struggles hampered and limited it, but it has lived on in the collective memory, and interest in it reappears cyclically, providing a backdrop for current expressions of the solidarity economy.

In the general comparative analysis, a second exception is France.[116] This is not only due to its greater economic power, which shares many characteristics with Central European countries, or the effect of public intervention, as advocated by the solidarity school, but also because there were no long periods of fascist dictatorships, as was the case in Italy, Portugal, and Spain, where expressions of the social economy were persecuted, controlled, and integrated into state corporate structures. This period has been researched relatively little from the point of view of the social and solidarity economy.[117] It also raises a number of questions. To what extent were the repressive and inclusive measures taken by the dictatorships towards the different advocates of the social and solidarity economy similar? How did these figures respond when defending the cause of democracy? What degree of complicity did they have with the political system? How did the corporate system impact them? And what consequences did these dictatorships have for the revival of the social and solidarity economy with the subsequent advent of parliamentary democracy?

Another discovery from the transnational comparative analysis of the solidarity economy is organisational diversity and multifunctionality. Vicens Vives[118] highlighted this in 1840 when he described the early Asociación Mutua de Obreros de la Industria Algodonera de Barcelona (Mutual Association of Cotton Industry Workers of Barcelona), which combined trade union advocacy, mutual aid, a cooperative factory, and employment for the unemployed. Likewise, new works by French historians[119] show that until the revolt of 1848, workers' associations not only demanded and fought for an alternative implementation of the ideals of the revolution,[120] but also tried to intervene in the labour market and support each other. Then, in France, vertical solidarity replaced horizontal solidarity[121] and the different families (associationism, cooperativism, mutualism, syndicalism) diversified and took parallel paths.[122] Perhaps one of the few exceptions is the experience of the Fraternelle de Saint Cloud, which was created in 1881 and followed the Belgian model of *maisons du peuple* (houses of the people), sharing a single social fund. In a single building, it combined a consumer cooperative, a mutual society, and social and cultural activities.[123] In contrast, there are many examples in the other three countries of the persistence of a more generalist and holistic vision and practice. We can see three specific examples in the wide range of actions of the Centro Promotor del Melhoramento de las Clases Laboriosas (Centre for the Improvement of the Working Classes) of 1850 in Portugal,[124] the Fratellanza Artigiana of 1861 in Italy,[125] and the Catalan Law of 1934, which covers cooperatives, mutual societies, agricultural cooperatives, and trade unions.

In Catalonia,[126] it was very common for workers' athenaeums devoted to educational, cultural, and recreational activities to take a stand on citizens' issues, to set up aid mechanisms for their most disadvantaged members, or to form consumer cooperatives. They would organise cultural and leisure initiatives, provide shelter for repressed comrades, and show solidarity with workers' strikes. Mutual societies would set up small libraries on their premises or organise sporting or choral events. Often in small towns and districts of cities, these organisations were run by the same activists. To a large extent, this multifunctional approach can be explained by the need to address different kinds of urgent needs at the same time and by the lack of public social welfare, which was only created at the beginning of the twentieth century and was then very limited. One could hypothesise that the multifunctional approach in Catalonia, Italy, and Portugal was also a tangible demonstration of the desire to create autonomous, often local, systems to address all needs[127] in order to begin to build an alternative world of their own. At the same time, it is not surprising that organisational forms based on economic democracy and emancipatory ideals were similar.

Recent Latin American studies show many workers' organisations share this multifunctionality, although the 'social centres' have attracted the most attention. These centres focused on awareness-raising and social and trade union activism, but in some cases, they created mechanisms for mutual aid, finding and creating employment, defending the rights of their members, and organising cultural outreach and leisure time.

Argentinian mutualist Benjamin Castillo offers an interesting overview of European popular collective organisations at the beginning of the twentieth century. It offers an example of an international analysis of European cooperativism and mutualism seen from a Latin American point of view.[128] He came to Europe at the invitation of the French Mutualité Française, whose president, also the director of the Social Museum of Paris,[129] Mabilleau,[130] had visited Argentina in 1912 and 1913. Castillo, a social Catholic, connected with the Social Museum of Buenos Aires, advisor of Argentine mutual societies, and promoter of the Spanish Federation of Mutual Aid Societies[131] in Argentina, examined in detail the cooperative and mutualist experiences of Germany, France, Italy, Spain, Belgium, and Portugal and related them to the beginnings of public social welfare. He concluded that the best example for Argentina to follow would be Italy, not only because the societies in Italy had a million members but also because they were independent of the state and because they were able to cover a range of health needs, build housing, set up evening and Sunday schools, establish libraries, provide aid for the families of members who had to do military service, and contribute to popular culture with recreational activities and festivals.

Mutual aid and economic cycles

It should be noted that there is a whole field of research devoted to the role of the domestic and reproductive economy, where care for the weakest (the elderly, children, the disabled, etc.) rests on the shoulders of women, as evidenced in the growing number of studies on the invisible history of women[132] and the primary mechanisms of solidarity: horizontal solidarity among equals, who also organise themselves to meet needs that exceed the capacity of families. The work of sowing and harvesting, problems related to poor health and death, and external natural dangers (fires, avalanches, floods, etc.) or more far-reaching causes (wars, epidemics, etc.) lead to processes of collective and democratic organisation.[133] The management and protection of common goods (forests, water, collective lands, etc.) should also be mentioned here, as demonstrated by the *badius*, which are still important in Portugal, Galicia, and the high valleys of the Pyrenees and the Alps, as well as some cooperative communal exchange schemes and productive activities.

Two examples of this type of activity in Portugal are offered by Campos Lima in his 1905 book on the workers' movement.[134] In the section on the association movement, he mentions that in Trás-os-Montes there is a cooperative system applied when agricultural work requires more workers. At that time, people who live in the same village would come together to work on different plots, one by one, receiving 'a meal all of them would happily feast on' in exchange, which allowed communal work to replace money.[135] The second example is of tile making in the regions around the Minho and Douro rivers, where a small number of people could together buy some clay and rent a piece of land on which to build a kiln and a cabin. Once the tiles were made, with everyone taking part, they would sell them. The profit was then distributed among the participants, and the society was dissolved. The author comments that these groups were ephemeral. They would emerge intuitively and reflected a traditional notion of cooperativism.[136]

It is likely that throughout the nineteenth century and much of the twentieth century, various forms of mutual aid based on reciprocity and cooperation, with differing degrees of formality and informality, were common in working-class neighbourhoods and especially in rural societies, which were predominant in Italy and the Iberian Peninsula, and even in France. Unfortunately, this terrain remains largely unexplored at present.

Another area that has not been investigated much is the influence of economic development on initiatives related to the social and popular economy, especially the effect of economic crises. To what extent do economic cycles condition their expansion or recession? What degree of resilience do they offer?

It is also increasingly clear that economic globalisation, although it has accelerated in recent times, is a phenomenon that has deep roots. This should encourage and facilitate transnational historical comparisons insofar as it is possible to identify transborder processes. The crisis of 1929 is a good example of economic globalisation because it had repercussions in numerous countries,[137] especially those that were most industrialised and financially connected. It shook economic systems, increased unemployment, and poverty, especially in cities and ports, and strengthened welfare mechanisms. Some of those in the labour movement interpreted it as the end of capitalism. To what extent did it affect the different families of the social economy?

A priori, one can suggest that their number would have decreased as a result of the crisis. This does not seem to have been the case in France, where only the cooperative banks faltered,[138] nor is it the case for the Galician mutual society in Buenos Aires, which saw an increase in membership as public health coverage failed to improve while healthcare worsened.[139] Although Chile was one of the countries most affected by the crisis,[140] the number of mutual aid societies does not seem to have decreased in the early 1930s, as they were in the midst of diversifying their services and experiencing a significant period of expansion. In Catalonia, Valencia, and the Balearic Islands, the decline in mutualism began in the 1920s. However, cooperativism and associationism underwent periods of expansion in the effervescent climate of the Second Republic and Catalan autonomy in the 1930s. This expansion and maturation led to the application of the concept of the new social economy in 1936.[141] In Italy, mutual aid societies and workers' cooperatives were the object of attacks by fascist groups prior to the 1930s. In Portugal, a mainly agricultural country with weak foreign trade, the 1929 crisis did not seem devastating and had less impact on mutualism and cooperativism than Salazar's corporatist measures, which started in 1933.[142]

Circulation, circuits, and transnational 'circumventions': a happy night

If one were to propose priorities for future transnational comparative historical studies, the first would be an analysis of how men and women moved, their circuits and networks,[143] how their ideas circulated, and by what means. It would be a way of verifying to what extent the Latin world is a separate entity, a shared source of ideas and practices, and a common domain of exchanges and relationships.[144]

Despite the many difficulties involved in travelling from one place to another, many different types of circulation took place in the nineteenth century: migration, exile, banishment, deportation, and international meetings were commonplace. Every time the repressive boot crushed one nest, the worker ants fled and sought refuge elsewhere. The revolt of '48 and the Paris Commune in France created a diaspora of activists[145] as well as great interest in what happened. Portuguese leaders and thinkers went into exile in France and England time and time again.[146] Catalans, many of whom fled to France in the most repressive periods, visited Rochdale in 1862 and started writing about cooperativism. Along with the Andalusians somewhat earlier, they echoed French utopian thinkers.[147]

Some embarked on Icarian adventures in the United States. People like Garrido[148] and Sixto Càmara,[149] who took refuge in Portugal, campaigned to organise an Iberian expedition to help Garibaldi. French and Italian activists are also known to have passed through Barcelona, where some stayed and encountered Mazzini and Luzzatti.

The 1860s saw the beginning of a process of economic and political migration by Portuguese, French, Italians, Catalans, and Spaniards to Latin America, which increased in subsequent decades. Those travelling to the Americas took with them concepts of liberation as well as specific practices (mutual and resistance societies, centres for study, and activism) of the workers' movement in these countries. Flora Tristan,[150] an outspoken Peruvian, would be the exceptional figure who travelled in the opposite direction, from Latin America to Europe. If one digs, one may find other examples[151] similar to this pioneer of labour and feminist activism.

It is undeniable that the First International was a generator of meetings and exoduses, exchanges of ideas, and a gathering point for the more or less incipient workers' groups of the time. It marks a turning point in the transnational circuits, setting specific objectives and raising hopes for closer international relationships. Although it had its vicissitudes, there was a significant presence of members from Latin European countries, including Belgian Socialists and the powerful Jura Federation. At the same time, its subsequent significant influence in some Latin American countries should be taken into account.[152] Marx's debates with Proudhon and Bakunin forced workers' associations to align themselves, and often they were divided. Reclus (French), Fanelli (Italian), and Lafargue (Cuban) came to the Iberian Peninsula, and their opinions and writings became compulsory reading along with those of Kropotkin. Everything seems to indicate that Proudhon came first and took hold more in Portugal than Marx, and that the ideas of the First International were conveyed by Anselmo Lorenzo, Francisco Mora, and Gonzalez Morago to the Portuguese Antero de Quental, José Fontana, and Jaime Batalha, when they went out on the Tagus River in a boat to escape the police one 'happy night'.[153] The year was 1871. A year earlier, Catalan workers had drawn up a manifesto of solidarity with the Portuguese. After that, relationships in the Iberian Peninsula grew closer, with more frequent exchanges. But not only in the Iberian Peninsula, since the networks created with the Italians and French were numerous and long-lasting as, of course, were those with Argentina, Uruguay, Cuba, and Mexico,[154] and those of Portugal with Brazil.

Towards the end of the nineteenth century, cooperative and mutualist federations began to structure themselves on different regional scales. As such, they also took on the role of representation and convening international congresses and conferences.[155] At these meetings, the participants, who were the heads of regional organisations, got to know one another, shared ideas and information about their respective situations, and tried to devise common strategies. These 'circumventions' were frequent. The ICA (International Cooperative Alliance)[156] was founded in 1895, and, in 1900, the International Mutualist Congress was held, which culminated six years later in the creation of the Fédération Internationale de la Mutualité. Representatives from Latin European countries, especially the French and Italians, were very active in it.

Although Barcelona had already played a role in raising international awareness,[157] at the beginning of the twentieth century, it became known as the 'Rose of Fire', casting a spotlight on the workers' movement everywhere, especially in Latin America.[157] The execution by firing squad of instructor Ferrer i Guardia, arbitrarily accused of being the instigator of the 1909 revolt, sparked a wave of protest throughout Europe and Latin America. His innovative teaching methods were followed in many places, while the restructuring of the Confederación Nacional del Trabajo (National Confederation of Labour, or CNT) at the Sants Congress and the introduction of the eight-hour day following the La Canadenca strike attracted the attention of activist workers everywhere. The celebration of May Day and the annual remembrance of the Chicago martyrs were also occasions for international awareness-raising.

The role of workers' publications and libraries as an example of cultural influence, where exchange and reciprocity were basic values, should not be overlooked either. In Latin America, Belgium, Portugal, Italy, France, and Spain were the preferred sources of publications from Europe. Barcelona is mentioned six times in the list of cities publishing magazines and newspapers read by workers' associations in Chile between 1899 and 1904.[158] More or less everyone read the same authors that were being translated: Bakunin, Grave, Kropotkin, Reclus, Malatesta, Gorki Zola, Tolstoy, etc ... The circuit is opened and closed.

Some final reflections

If our original hypothesis was that there are common convergences in the history of social and solidarity economies in Latin Europe, the reasoning in this chapter would not seem to refute it. While it is true that in the four countries the importance of mutualism, cooperativism, and associationism differs, that they have differing development, timelines, and roles vis-à-vis the state and the market, and that they have diversified in different ways, some common features do seem to prevail. To a certain extent, the evolution of each country's context conditioned the paths of the social and solidarity economy. However, looking beyond state borders, shared characteristics emerge that shape social history and, more specifically, the social and solidarity economy.

In the early 1840s, the concept of the social economy emerged in the four countries with very similar content and visions. To a certain extent, the renewal of the social sciences and social history, which also took place in Latin America, has created new perspectives that reveal similar issues and contents. The importance of the Catholic Church and struggles with anticlericalists influenced some forms of the social economy, especially after *Rerum Novarum*. But it was utopian socialism, republicanism, and anarchism that had the greatest influence on its theoretical and practical expression. The importance of Freemasonry became increasingly significant in the origins and development of the social economy in the four countries. Although the countries shared the traits of organisational universality and multifunctionality, at least in their beginnings, France would later break with this trend, with greater specialisation and diversification of the three families. Although the issue has not been the focus of much inquiry, informal initiatives also played a greater role in the Italic and Iberian peninsulas. These circumstances could be explained largely by the inability of the market to meet needs and the slowness of public social welfare in responding to them. Similarly, there is a lack of studies on the influence of the economic structure and situation on the development of the social economy. The crisis of 1929 is an example of economic globalisation, but it does not provide definitive conclusions for comparison, nor is its role clear in the emergence of the three fascist dictatorships of the twentieth century. The impact of legislation was felt in all four countries. It oscillated between repression, in the nineteenth century and in the dictatorial periods, and protection. In the four countries, popular and workers' associations did not wait for the creation of a legal framework to establish themselves. They went through periods of clandestinity, illegality, and institutional permissiveness. The laws made the cooperative world swing towards commercial regulatory frameworks and impeded the expansion of associationism until the end of the nineteenth century. Ultimately, in the four countries, the social economy emerged and developed as the rearguard of the labour and popular movement in a hostile capitalist system. In some cases, it pragmatically adapted to it, while in others it attempted to reform it or offered transformative alternatives.

Another interesting point in the comparative analysis is to contrast the specific characteristics of the social and solidarity economy in Latin America and Europe, a question that should be pursued in greater depth. This chapter merely seeks to offer a few clues about the relationships in which, as a result of migration and repression, the conglomerate of Latin European countries appears to be fairly homogeneous in terms of the ideas and practices that had an influence in the Americas.

In order to further substantiate the common foundation of the social and solidarity economy in Latin Europe, it would be necessary to compare it with the paths it has taken in other European countries. It is very likely that there is a Scandinavian matrix, a Germanic matrix, an anglophone matrix, and a Slavic and Central European matrix, each with similar traits and differences when compared with the others. But this comparative study remains a task to be undertaken in future work.

Notes

1 Some initial notes can be found in Jordi ESTIVILL: "La economía solidaria, ¿categoría conceptual para la historia?", in Enrique SANTAMARÍA, Laura C. YUFRA and Juan de la HABA (eds.): *Investigando economías solidarias*, Barcelona, ERAPI Ed. Pol·len, 2019. A second version is Jordi ESTIVILL: "Catalunya associada i solidària", *L'Avenç*, 483 (2021), p. 36.
2 Manfred MAX NEEF and Philip B. SMITH: *La economia desenmascarada*, Barcelona, Icària, 2014.
3 Jordi ESTIVILL and Casimiro BALSA (eds.): *Economia local, comunitària e solidaria. O desenvolvimento visto de baixo*, Famalicâo, Ed. Humus, 2022.
4 Karl POLANYI: *La Gran transformación*, Madrid, La Piqueta, 1989.
5 Marcel MAUSS: "Essai sur le don. Forme et raison de l'échange dans les sociétés primitives", *L'Anné Sociologique*, second series (1923); and ÍD: *Essai sur le don*, Paris, P.U.F., 2001.
6 Alberto GROHMAN: *Perugia e la sua Società di mutuo soccorso 1861–1939*, Perugia, Volumnia Editrice, 2000; Erminio FONZO: *L'unione fa la forza. Società di mutuo soccorso e altre organizzazioni dei lavoratori a Napoli dall'Unità alla crisi di fine secolo*, Rubbettino, Soveria Mannelli, 2010; Alberto SOAVE: *Breve storia della società Operaie di muto soccorso*, 2015; Nazario GALASSI: *Società Operaie di Mutuo soccorso: origine della Cooperazione generale e bancarie*, Imola, Bachilega, 2008.
7 VV. AA.: *Atlas do primeiro congreso de historia do movimento operaio e dos movimentos sociais em Portugal*, vol. II, Pes no Chao, Lisbon, IHC Universidade Nova de Lisboa, 2016.
8 Álvaro GARRIDO: *Uma história da economia social*, Lisbon, Tinta da China, 2016; ÍD: *A economia social em movimento. Uma història das organizações*, Lisbon, Tinta da China, 2018; Jordi ESTIVILL: "Os primordios da economia social em Portugal. Contributos de Ramon de la Sagra", *Sociologia*, 33 and 34 (2017).
9 Joana DIAS PEREIRA: *Origens do mutualismo em Portugal*, Lisbon, Uniao das Mutualidades Portuguesas, 2021.
10 Joana DIAS PEREIRA: *Associativismo Livre. Uma historia de fraternidade e progresso (1824–1926)*, Coïmbra, Almedina, 2020.
11 Pere SOLÀ: *Cultura popular a Catalunya (1900–1939)*, Barcelona, La Magrana, 1978. And the works of Pere Gabriel, especially Pere GABRIEL: "Sobre la cultura popular i obrera a Catalunya en el segle XIX", *Cercles*, 8 (2005).
12 Jordi ESTIVILL: *'Cooperativisme a Ictineu': Diccionari de les Ciències de la Societat als Països Catalans*, Barcelona, Edicions 62, 1979, pp.126–130; Jordi ESTIVILL and Marc DALMAU: "L'estat de la qüestió. Balanç bibliogràfic sobre l'economia social i solidària a Catalunya", in Jordi ESTIVILL and Jean-Louis LAVILLE (eds.): *Economia solidària i historia social*, Barcelona, Icaria, 2020, pp. 123 and 192.

13 Montserrat DUCH: *Micaela Chalmeta*, Barcelona, Roca i Galès Foundation, 2009; Ramon ARNABAT and Montserrat DUCH (coords.): *Historia de la sociabilitat contemporanea*, Valencia, PUV, 2014; Montserrat DUCH, Ramon ARNABAT and Xavier FERRÉ (eds.): *Sociabilitats a la Catalunya contemporània. temps i espais en conflicte*, Barcelona, Publicacions Abadia de Montserrat, 2015; Montserrat DUCH, Ramon ARNABAT and Antoni GAVALDÀ: *La Catalunya associada (1868–1938)*, València, PUV, 2020.

14 Marc DALMAU and Ivan MIRÓ: *Les cooperatives obreres de Sants. Autogestió proletària en un barri de Barcelona. 1870–1939*, Barcelona, La Ciutat Invisible, 2010; Marc DALMAU: *Un barri fet a cops de cooperació. El cooperativisme obrer al Poble Nou*, Barcelona, La Ciutat Invisible and Arxiu Històric del Poblenou, 2015; Emma ALARI, Santiago GOROSTIZA and Marc DALMAU: *La forja solidària d'un barri portuari, La Barceloneta obrera i cooperativa*, Barcelona, Montaber, 2016.

15 José Luis OYÓN (ed.): *Vida obrera en la Barcelona d'entreguerres,1918–1936*, Barcelona, CCCB, 1998.

16 Chris EALHAM: *La lucha por Barcelona. Clase, cultura y conflicto, 1898–1937*, Madrid, Alianza, 2005.

17 See the work on the neighbourhoods of Barcelona by Ivan MIRÓ: *Ciutats Cooperatives*, Barcelona, Ed. Icaria, 2018. In the case of a working-class neighbourhood of Buenos Aires, see Mirta Zaida LOBATO: *La vida en las fábricas, trabajo, protesta y política en una comunidad obrera, Berisso. 1904–1970*, Buenos Aires, Ed. Prometeo, 2001. Especially the first chapter.

18 Pablo GUERRA: "Economía de la Solidaridad. Construcción de un camino a veinte años de las primeras elaboraciones", III Jornadas en Historia económica, Montevideo, 2003.

19 Max NETLAU: *Contribución a la bibliografía anarquista en América Latina*, Buenos Aires, La Protesta, 1927.

20 John LEAR: "Del mutualismo a la resistencia: las organizaciones laborales en la Ciudad de Mexico desde fines del porfiriato a la Revolución", in Carlos ILLADES and Ariel RODRIGUEZ KURI (eds.): *Ciudad de México: instituciones, actores sociales y conflicto político, 1774–1931*, México, Universidad Autónoma Metropolitana-El Colegio de Michoacan, 1996.

21 José Julián LLAGUNO THOMAS: "Acçào local e audiència global na America Central segondo suas fontes documentais (1910–1930)", *Verve*, 31(2017). See accounts in the Mexican publication *Regeneración with Tierra y Libertad and Solidaridad Obrera de Barcelona*. Jacinto BARRERA BASSOLS: *La biblioteca sociológica. Regeneración y la red internacional anarquista*, México, Universidad Autónoma de Méjico.

22 Ronaldo MUNCK: "Mutual Benefit Societies in Argentina. Workers, Nationality, Social Security and Trade Unionism", *Journal of Latin American Studies*, 30, 3 (1998), pp. 573–590.

23 Sergio GREZ: "La trayectoria histórica del mutualismo en Chile (1853–1990)", *Mapocho: Revista de Humanidades y Ciencias Sociales*, 35 (1994), pp. 293–315.

24 Fernando VENEGAS and Sergio GREZ: "Historiografía del mutualismo chileno, 1853–1990: análisis crítico y nuevas perspectivas", *Izquierdas*, 50 (2021), pp. 1–30.

25 See also Jorell MELENDEZ VADILLO: *Voces libertarias. Los orígenes del anarquismo en Puerto Rico*, Santurce, Ed. C. C. C., 2013, pp. 68–69; José Julián LLAGUNO THOMAS: *Anarquismo, sociabilidad obrera y redes*

intelectuales en Costa Rica, Un estudio de cultura política, Tesis doctoral, Universidad de Costa Rica, 2015.

26 Mauricio ARCHILA: *Cultura e identidad obrera en Colombia 1910–1945*, Bogotá, G.R.C., 2010.

27 Pascual MUÑOZ: *La Primera Huelga General en el Uruguay*, Montevideo, La Turba Ediciones, 2011, pp. 9–13.

28 Alberto ACOSTA: *El buen vivir, Sumak Kawsay*, Barcelona, Ed. Icaria, 2013.

29 Luis RAZETO: *Desafíos y proyectos de la economía solidaria*, Santa Fe, Universidad Nacional del Litoral, 2010; Luiz I. GAIGER: "Da informalidade a economia popular: distinguindo realidades e conectando abordagens", *Ciencias Sociais Unisinos*, 55, 1 (2019).

30 See the debate in the first edition of the publication *Otra Economia* published by RILESS.

31 Stefano ZAMAGNI: *L'economia civile*, Bologna, Il Mulino, 2004.

32 Carlo BORZAGA, Manlio CALZARONI, Eddi FONTANARI and Lori MASSIMO: *L'Economia Sociale in Italia*, Trento Istat, Euricse, 2021, p. 5.

33 TAVOLO PER LA RETE ITALIANA DI ECONOMIA SOLIDALE: *Un'economia nuova, dai Gas alla zeta. L'economia solidale e le sue reti: Gruppi d'acquisto solidali, Distretti di economia solidale, filiere corte. Per cambiare il sistema economico con le relazioni e il consumo critico*, Milan, Altra Economia, 2013.

34 Michel DREYFUS: "Mutualité et coopération: une histoire par trop méconnue", *Cahiers d'histoire*, 133 (2016).

35 Miguel GARAU: "Los estudios sobre cooperativismo en la historiografía española: un estado de la cuestión", *Bulletin d'Histoire Contemporaine de l'Espagne*, 54 (2020).

36 Stefano MUSSO: *Gli operai nella storiografia contemporannea a Tra fabbrica e società – Mondo operai nell'italia del novecento*, Milan, Feltrinelli, 1999.

37 For example, the analysis of only cooperativism in Italy by Fabio FABBRI: *L'Italia cooperativa. Centocinquant' anni di storia e di memòria (1861–2011)*, Rome, Ediesse, 2011. For Portugal, José Hipólito DOS SANTOS: *Maneiras cooperativas de pensar e agir. Contributo para a história do Cooperativismo*, Lisbon, Ediçoes Universitárias Lusófonas, 2009. For France, Henri DESROCHE: *Le projet coopératif*, Paris, Ed. Ouvrières, 1976. And for Catalonia, Albert PEREZ BARÓ: *Historia de la cooperación catalana*, Barcelona, Ed. Nova Terra, 1974.

38 Jordi ESTIVILL: *Invitació a l'economia solidària*, Barcelona, Ed. Pol·len, 2018; Jean Louis LAVILLE: *L'économie solidaire. Une perspective internationale*, Paris, Pluriel, 2010.

39 Werner SOMBART: *¿Porque no hay socialismo en los Estados Unidos?*, 1st. published in 1905, Madrid, Capitan Swing, 2009.

40 Rogério Roque AMARO: "Similituds i diferències entre els enfocaments de l'economia social i solidària en diferents països de l'Europa del Sud", in Jordi ESTIVILL and Jean Louis LAVILLE: *Economia solidària i història social*, Barcelona, Ed. Icaria, 2020.

41 Maria MIGUELAÑEZ: "Diego Abad de Santillan. 1897–1983. Los Viajes doctrinarios de un anarquista transnacional", in Manuel PEREZ LEDESMA (ed.): *Trayectorias transatlanticas (siglo xx) Personajes y redes entre España y América*, vol. II, Madrid, Polifemo, 2013.

42 Jordi ESTIVILL: "Empresas, emprendedurismo y empresariado social", *Economia solidaria*, 8 (2015).

43 Jacques DEFOURNY and Marthe NYSSENS: "Conceptions on Social Entrepreneurship in Europe and the United States, Convergences and Divergences", *Journal of Social Entrepreneurship*, 1, 1 (2009), pp. 32–53.
44 Jacques DEFOURNY, Patrick DEVELTERE and Bénédicte FONTENEAU (eds.): *L'économie sociale au Nord et au Sud*, Bruxelles, De Boeck, 1999.
45 Thierry JEANTET: *L'économie sociale européenne*, Paris, CIEM, 1999.
46 Isabelle DARMON and Jordi ESTIVILL: *L'économie sociale en Belgique, en France et en Italie: essai comparatif*, Barcelona, GES-Fondation MACIF, 1999, pp. 17–29; Ramon ARNABAT, Montserrat DUCH and Josep M. PONS-ALTÉS: "El asociacionismo popular en la construcción de la ciudadanía en Catalunya y en la Emilia Romagna contemporáneas", *Historia Social*, 95 (2019), pp. 61–83.
47 This is the critique made by Henri Desroche of his own "Movimento cooperativo ed economia sociale", in Maurizio DEGLI INNOCENTI: *Il movimento cooperativo nella storia d'Europa*, Milan, Franco Angeli, 1988, p. 52. For an example of the genesis of mutualism with Spain as the matrix, see Rafael MORENO: "La génesis del mutualismo moderno en Europa", *REVESCO*, 72 (2000).
48 For some constructive criticism, see Jordi ESTIVILL: "Espacios públicos y privados, construyendo diálogos en torno a la economía solidaria", *Critica de Ciencias Sociais*, 84 (2009).
49 Jean Louis LAVILLE and Genauto Carvalho de França FILHO: *Economia Solidária, Uma abordagem internacional*, Porto Alegre, Editora de UFRGS, 2004.
50 This is evidenced in the 148 pages on France of a total of 189 pages.
51 Jean Louis LAVILLE: *Asociarse para el bien común. Tercer sector, Economía Social y Economía solidar*ia, Barcelona, Ed. Icaria, 2015, pp. 47–66.
52 Jean Louis LAVILLE (dir.): *L'économie solidaire, une perspective internationale*, Paris, Hachette, 2007.
53 Such as Claude AUROI and Isabel YEPEZ DEL CASTILLO: *Economie solidaire et commerce équitable. Acteurs et actrices d'Europe et d'Amérique Latine*, Louvain, Presses Universitaires de Louvain, 2006.
54 Peter UTTING (ed.): *Social and Solidarity Economy. Beyond the Fringe.* London, Zed Books-UNRISD, 2015. Practically the only article of a historic nature is from Laville.
55 Edith ARCHAMBAULT: *Le secteur sans but lucratif; Associations et Fondations en France*, Paris, Ed. Economica, 1996.
56 Gian Paolo BARBETTA: *Senza scopo di lucro*, Bologna, Il Mulino, 1996.
57 Raquel FRANCO *et al.*: *O sector ñao lucrativo portuguès numa perspectiva comparada*, Porto. Universidade Catolica Portuguesa, 2005.
58 José Ignacio RUIZ DE OLABUENAGA (dir.): *El sector no lucrativo en España*, Bilbao, Fundación BBVA, 2000.
59 Maria Teresa MAIULLARI: *Storiografia francese ed italiana a confronto sul fenomeno associativo durante XVIII e XIX secolo*, Torino, Einaudi, 1990.
60 Michel DREYFUS and Bernard GIBAUD (dirs.): *Mutualité de tous les pays, un passé riche d'avenir*, Paris, Mutualitè Française, 1995.
61 Pere SOLÀ: "El mutualismo y su función social: sinopsis histórica", *CIRIEC-España*, 44 (2003).
62 Marcel VAN DER LINDEN (coord.): *Social Security Mutualism. The Comparative History of Mutual Benefit Societies*, New York, Lang Ed., 1996.

63 Abram SWAAN: *In Care of the State, Health Care, Education and Welfare in Europe and USA in the Modern Era*, New York, OUP, 1988. For non-Latin countries, see also Bernard HARRIS and Paul BRIDGEN (eds.): *Charity and Mutual Aid in Europe and North America since 1800*, New York, Routledge, 2012. See especially chapter four in which Daniel Weinbren relates early mutual societies to philanthropy and English friendly societies.
64 In France, François Ewald traced the path from the first social insurance schemes to the welfare state. François EWALD: *L'état Providence*, Paris, Editions Grasset, 1986.
65 José Luís MONZÓN: "El Cooperativismo en la historia de la literatura económica", *CIRIEC-España*, 44 (2003).
66 Bruno JOSSA: "Cooperative Firms as a New Mode of Production", *Review of Political Economy*, 24 (2012).
67 Udo STABER: "Age-dependence and Historical Effects on the Failure Rates Of Worker Cooperatives: An Event-history Analysis", *Economic and Industrial Democracy*, 10 (1989).
68 Virginie PÉROTIN: "Workers Cooperatives: Good, Sustainable Jobs in the Community", *Journal of Entrepreneurial and Organisational Diversity*, 2, 2 (2014).
69 Ben CRAIG and John PENCAVEL: "The Behavior of Worker Cooperatives: The Plywood Companies of the Pacific Northwest", *American Economic Review*, 82, 5 (1992); Gabriel BURDÍN and Andrés DEAN: "New Evidence on Wages and Employment in Worker Cooperatives Compared With Capitalist Firms", *Journal of Comparative Economics*, 37 (2009).
70 Maurizio DEGLI INNOCENTI (ed.): *Le imprese cooperative in Europa (la storia)*, Pisa, Nistri Lischi, 1986; and ÍD: *Il movimento cooperativo nella storia d'Europa*, Milan, Franco Angeli, 1988.
71 Mary HILSON, Silke NEUNSINGER and Greg PATMORE (Comp.): *Global History of Consumer Co-operation since 1850*, Leiden, Brill, 2017.
72 Charles DUNOYER: *Nouveau traité d'économie sociale*, Vol. II, Paris, A. Santelet Librairie éditeurs, 1830.
73 Constantin PECQUEUR: *Economie sociale. Les intérêts du commerce, de l'industrie et de l'agriculture et de la civilisation*, París, 1837; ÍD: *Théorie nouvelle d'économie sociale et politique*, Paris, Capelle, 1842.
74 François VIDAL: *De la répartition des richesses ou de la justice distributive en économie sociale, ouvrage contenant l'examen critique des théories exposées soit par les économistes, soit par les socialistes*, Paris, Capelle, 1846.
75 UNKNOWN AUTHOR: *Economia Social, Verdades interesantes a o Reino e a o estado e a todas classes de gentes: Antidotos contra os luxos aparatozos e faustos escuzados. Remedios para curar os males das uzuras e monopólios*, Lisbon, Typografia de Joze Baptista Morando, 1823. I am grateful for the information provided by Martins Pereira.
76 António ALMODÓVAR and José Luís CARDOSO: *A History of Portuguese Thought*, London, Routledge, 1998.
77 Ramón de la SAGRA: *Lecciones de economía social*, Madrid, Imprenta de Ferrer y Compañía, 1840.
78 Jordi ESTIVILL: "Os primordios da economia social … ".
79 António, ALVES MARTINS: *Grandes questòes de economia social tratadas by M. Chitti* and *La Mennais postas en vulgar e precedidas de uma introdução*, Porto, Typografia La Revista, 1844.

80 Louis CHITTI: *Cours d'économie sociale (Discours d'ouverture prononcé le 14 décembre 1833, Bruxelles, Jobert, 1834; 2e Lecture, 21 décembre 1833, Bruxelles, Ode et Wodon, 1834; 3e et 4e Lecture, 4 et 11 janvier 1834)*, Bruxelles, Ode, 1834.

81 Lamennais had considerable influence on the Iberian Peninsula. See Daniel Henri PAGEAUX: "Lamennais en péninsule ibérique: Note sur la diffusion des idées Ménarcissiennes en Espagne et au Portugal (1834–1840)", in VV.AA.: *Utopie et socialisme au Portugal au XIX siècle*, Paris, Gulbenkian Foundation, 1982, pp. 121–152.

82 Silvestre Pinheiro FERREIRA: *Projecto de um Banco de Socorro e Seguro Mutuo*, Paris, Rey et Gravier, 1836; ÍD: *Projecto de associaçào para o Melhoramento das classes industriosas*, Paris, Fain et Thunot, 1840.

83 Francisco Maria de SOUSA BRANDAO: *Economia Social, part I, O Trabalho*, Lisbon, Progresso, 1857.

84 Samuel SMILES: *Thrift*, London, John Murray, 1875, p. 31. Chapter 7 on cooperative and friendly societies. In 1859 he had already published a book on self-help.

85 Adrian PABST: "Political Economy Virtue: Civil Economy. Happiness and Public Trust in the Thought of Antonio Genovesi", *European Journal of the History of Economic Thought*, 1, 25 (2016).

86 Mateo de AUGUSTINIS: *Istituzioni di economia sociale*, Naples, Tipografia dei Porcelli, 1837.

87 Montserrat DUCH, Ramon ARNABAT and Antoni GAVALDÀ: *La Catalunya associada …*

88 Joana DIAS PEREIRA: *Assocativismo livre …*

89 Joao FREIRE: *Associaçoes profesionais em Portugal*, Oeiras, Celta Editora, 2009.

90 Sergio ZANINELLI: "Gli sviluppi storici Barbetta", in Gian Paolo BARBETTA (ed.): *Senza scopo di lucro. Dimensioni economiche, legislazione e politiche del settore nonprofit in Italia*, Bologna, Il Mulino, 1996, pp. 119–125.

91 Massimo PACI: "Il sistema di welfare italiano tra tradizione clientelare e prospettive di riforma", in Ugo ASCOLI (ed.): *Welfare State all'italiana*, Rome, Laterza, 1984, p. 312.

92 Edith ARCHAMBAULT: *Le secteur sans but lucratif* …p. 31.

93 Fernando LARGO and Josep PUJOL-ANDREU: "Desarrollo y crisis del mutualismo de los trabajadores en España en el siglo XX: Nueva aproximación desde el capital social", *Scripta Nova. Revista Electrónica de Geografía y Ciencias Sociales*, 20, 540 (2016).

94 Jordi ESTIVILL: "Introducción. Aportaciones mexicanas a la Economía solidaria" in Boris MARAÑON-PIMENTEL and Dania LÓPEZ CÓRDOBA: *Solidaridad Económica, Buenos vivires, descolonialidad del poder. Aproximaciones desde México*, Barcelona, Ed. Icaria, 2023.

95 Thiago SILVA LEMOS: *O dia a dia do movimento operàrio impresso em crònica: O sindicalismo revolucionario Portuguès a partir da trajetoria de Neno Vasco*, Uberlandia, UFU, 2012, p. 11.

96 Jordi ESTIVILL and Gustau BARBAT: "L'anticlèricalisme populaire en Catalogne", *Social Kompass*, 27, 2/3 (1980), pp. 215–230.

97 In Belgium in 1881, following the teachings of Le Play, the Société Belge de l'Économie Sociale (Belgian Society of the Social Economy) was formed.

98 The Catholic economist Tamagnini, who published a manual of political

economics and a book defending cooperativism in 1916, drew from the teachings of Le Play.

99 Maria Rosa PROTASI: "Tra scienzia e riforma sociale. Il pensiero e il metodo d'indagine sociale di F. Le Play e dei suoi continuatori in Italia (1857–1914)", *Studi Storici*, Anno 37, 3(1996), pp. 813–845.

100 Jacques Valdour, a disciple of Le Play who applied the same method of participant observation, came to Catalonia in 1912 and published two books, one dedicated to explaining his experiences as a manual worker in Badalona and Barcelona Jacques VALDOUR: *L'ouvrier espagnol. Tome I- Catalogne*, Paris, René Giard, Arthur Rousseau, 1919.

101 Alain DEWIER: *Mémoire en images. Le bassin Charbonnier du Centre*, Agora, 2010.

102 Robert CASTEL: *Les métamorphoses de la question sociale*, Paris, Fayard, 1995, pp. 245–259.

103 Some of these authors have a clear influence on social Catholicism in Portugal and Spain.

104 UNKNOWN AUTHOR: *Bulletin de l'économie sociale*, 36 (1898), p. 127.

105 Jean Louis LAVILLE: *Asociarse para el bien común* ...pp. 59–61.

106 In the 19th century, the Universal Exhibitions, launched by the London Exhibition of 1851, were a kind of competitive showcase for the technological and industrial advances of the major European countries and their 'social virtues'. At the Paris expositions of 1855 and 1867, the Emperor chose Frederic Le Play as coordinator and author for Group 10 on social issues. At the 1900 exhibition, the Ministry of Trade and Industry of the new French government appointed Gide as coordinator of the pavilion and author of the report for Group 16 on the social economy.

107 Marc PÉNIN: *Charles Gide (1847–1932): L'esprit critique*, Paris, L'Harmattan, 1997.

108 Charles GIDE: *Quatre écoles d'économie sociale*, Geneva, Librairie Stapelmohr, 1880. Lecture given at the University of Geneva under the aegis of the Swiss Christian Social Economy Society.

109 One hundred years later Desroche again systemised this classification. Henri DESROCHE: *Pour un traité d'économie sociale*, Paris, CIEM, 1983.

110 His work *Principles of Political Economy* was in its 20th edition in 1919 and had been translated into 15 languages. The Spanish translation is from 1896.

111 A detailed study of their influence remains to be done. Gide came to Barcelona in 1929.

112 See, for example, the controversy with Pantaleoni in Luca MICHELINI: *Marginalismo e socialismo: Maffeo Pantaleoni (1882–1904)*, Milan, Franco Angeli, 1998, pp. 134–135.

113 Fernando FERREIRA DE COSTA: *Doutrinadores cooperativistas portugueses*, Lisbon, Libros Horizonte, 1978, p. 23.

114 This debate took place in *Solidaridad Obrera* and *Acción Cooperatista*.

115 It was in the middle of the civil war that Felipe Alaiz first used the expression 'solidarity economy' in a booklet. Felipe ALAIZ: *Economía solidaria entre el campo y la ciudad*, Barcelona, Ed. CNT, 1937; Jordi ESTIVILL: *La economía solidaria según Felipe Alaiz y la economía colectiva en Catalunya*, unpublished, 2020.

116 See, for example, Michel DREYFUSS: *Histoire de l'économie sociale de la grande guerre á nos jours*, Rennes, Presses Universitaires de Rennes, 2017.

117 Tito MENZANI: *Il movimento cooperativo fra le due guerre. Il caso italiano nel contesto europeo*, Rome, Carocci Ed., 2009; F. CÓRODOVA: *Cooperazione e fascismo nella crisi dello stato liberale*; Giulio SAPELLI: "La Cooperazione e il fascismo: organizzazione delle masse e dominazione burocratica" in Fabbio FABBRI: *Il movimento cooperativo nella storia di Italia*, Milano, Feltrinelli, 1979.
118 Jaume VICENS i VIVES and Montserrat LLORENS: *Industrials i polítics, al segle XIX*, Barcelona. Ed. Vicens Vives, 1961, pp. 154–156.
119 Michèle RIOT-SARCEY: *Le procès de la liberté. Une histoire souterraine du XIX siècle en France*, Paris, Éditions la Découverte, 2016.
120 Jacques RANCIERE: *La nuit des prolétaires*, Paris, Fayard, 1981.
121 Jean Louis LAVILLE: *Contre la Société du mépris. Réinventer l'Association*, Paris, Desclèe de Brouwer, 2019.
122 André GUESLIN: *L'invention de l'économie sociale. Le XIX siècle français*, Paris, Ed. Economica, 1987.
123 This extraordinary experience in the French scene drew the attention of Charles Gide, who dubbed it the 'School of Saint-Claude'. Charles GIDE: "L'école de Saint Claude", *Le Jura socialiste*, 43 (1902). See presentation in Michel DREYFUS: "Charles Gide, L'école de Saint Claude et la Fraternelle", *RECMA*, 275–276 (2000)
124 Joao LAZARO: *Despontar do movimento operario portuguès na esfera pública. Das prácticas a o debate parlamentar (1850–1870)*, Lisbon, Chiado, 2018.
125 Anna PELLEGRINO: "Solidarité sociale et identité nationale lors de l'unification de l'Italie: l'exemple de la solidarité artisanale", *RECMA*, 329 (2013), pp. 52–64.
126 Jordi ESTIVILL and Ivan MIRÓ: *L'economia Social i Solidaria a Catalunya*, Barcelona, Ed. Icaria, 2020.
127 Luigi TOMASSINI: "L'associacionismo operaio: aspettie problemi della difusione del mutualismo nel'Italia Liberale" in Stefano MUSSO (ed.): *Tra fabbrica e società: mondi operai nell'Italia del Novecento*, Milan, Feltrinelli, 1999, pp. 24–26.
128 Benjamin CASTILLO: *Mutualidad, Cooperativismo y Previsión*, Valencia, Ed. Sempere, 1913. Editorial Sempere in Valencia together with Marucci and *La Presa de Barcelona* played an important role in increasing the visibility of socialist and anarchist authors and ideas in Latin America.
129 Janet HORNE: *Le Musée Social. Aux origines de l'Etat providence*, Paris, Belin, 2004. Social museums played an important role in international social and labour relations.
130 The thinking of Gide, Bourgeois, and Duguit (who gave a series of lectures at the University of Buenos Aires in 1911) is also well known.
131 Pilar GONZALEZ BERNALDO DE QUIRÓS: "El momento mutualista en la formulación de un sistema de protección social en Argentina: socorros mutuos y prevención subsidiada a comienzos del siglo XX", *Revista de Indias*, 73, 257 (2013), pp. 175–177. The author stresses the importance of mutual societies created by Spanish, Catalan, Italian, and French immigrants. Interestingly, in 1907, the Galician mutual aid society was founded, which went on to become one of the most important mutual aid societies in Spain.
132 A comparative historical work on the role of women in Catalonia and Italy: Ginés PUENTE PÉREZ: "Al margen del feminismo. Las vindicaciones de las anarquistas y españolas por la liberación de las mujeres (1868–1939)",

Chronica Mundi, 12, 1(2017), pp. 38–72. The article focuses on Teresa Mañè i Miravent.

133 Algarra recalls this. David ALGARRA: *El comú català. La història dels que no surten en la història*, Barcelona, Potlach, 2015.

134 Joao LIMA CAMPOS: *O movimento operario em Portugal*, Porto, Ed. Afrontamentos, 1972.

135 Joao LIMA CAMPOS: *O movimento operario em Portugal* ... p. 75.

136 Joao LIMA CAMPOS: *O movimento operario em Portugal* ... p. 76.

137 For Latin America, see Javier MORENO, Eduardo MARTIN and Agustina VENCE: *El crack del 29 en Iberoamerica. Perspectivas. Enfoques locales y regionales*, Paris, AHILA, 2021.

138 Michel DREYFUSS: *Histoire de l'économie sociale de la grande guerre* ... p. 95.

139 Maria Liliana DA ORDEN: "Salud, Inmigración y ayuda mutua en Argentina. El Centro Gallego de Buenos Aires, Entre la crisis y la emergencia de un nuevo sistema sanitario (1930–1950)", *Revista de Indias*, 80, 280 (2020), p. 952.

140 Fernando VENEGAS and Sergio GREZ: "Historiografía del mutualismo chileno ... ".

141 Jordi ESTIVILL and Ivan MIRÓ: *L'economia Social i Solidaria* ... p. 118.

142 See the consequences of the crisis of 1929 on the primary Portuguese mutual benefit society Montepio Geral in José Eduardo FRANCO and António CASTRO HENRIQUES (coords.): *Historia do Montepio Geral. Sob o signo do pelicano.1840–2015*, Lisbon, INCM, 2015, pp. 297–298.

143 Latin American historians insist on applying the concept of networks to explain the many different relationships between workers' organisations, such as relationships between Argentina and Mexico in the previous century or relationships in Central America and the Caribbean.

144 Pierre Yves SAUNIER: "Les régimes circulatoires du domaine social (1840–1940). Projets et ingénerie de la convergence et la différence", *Genèse*, 71 (2008), pp. 4–25. This article examines the North Atlantic area.

145 Communards such as Paul Brousse, Emmanuel Fournier and Charles Alerini took refuge in Barcelona.

146 Rogério Roque AMARO: "Similituds i diferències entre els enfocaments ... ".

147 Josep Maria OLLÉ: *Introducció del socialisme utòpic a Catalunya (1835–1837)*, Barcelona, Ed. 62, 1969; ÍD: *El moviment obrer a Catalunya, (1840–1843)*, Barcelona, Nova Terra, 1973.

148 One of the first authors to systematically examine cooperativism was Fernando GARRIDO: *La cooperación. Estudio teórico practico sobre las cooperativas de consumo y de producción en Inglaterra y otros países y especialmente en Cataluña*, Barcelona, Imp. De Oliveros, 1879. See the biography by Pere GABRIEL: *Fernando Garrido Tortosa. Agitació i escriptura política. La pulsió cooperativista*, Barcelona, Fundació Roca i Galès, 2009.

149 Sixto SAENZ DE LA CÁMARA: *La Unión Ibèrica, 1859*, Lisbon, Typographia Universal, 1859. Republished in two languages in Madrid – Badajoz, Ediciones 19, 2014.

150 Flora TRISTAN: *La Unión obrera*, 1843. Republished in Barcelona, De Barris 2005

151 One example is Peruvian worker and anarchist Fidel de la Sota who was expelled in 1919 and found refuge in Barcelona.

152 Max NETLAU: *Contribución a la bibliografía anarquista* ...; Diego ABAD DE SANTILLAN: *El anarquismo en el movimiento obrero*, Barcelona, Cosmos, 1925; ÍD: *El movimiento anarquista en Argentina desde sus comienzos hasta 1910*, Buenos Aires, Argonauta, 1930.
153 For the Spanish side, see Anselmo LORENZO: *El proletariado militante, Memorias de un internacional*, Toulouse, Ediciones MLE-CNT, 1947, pp. 165–185. For the Portuguese side, see Carlos da FONSECA: *Origens da Internacional. (1871–1873)*, Lisbon, Ed. Estampalhadores, 1973. See also Joao LAZARO: "Associaçao Internacional de Trabalhadores em Portugal", *Revista Mundos do Trabalho*, 11, (2019), pp. 1–19.
154 For a detailed description of the communist anarchist international relations from 1882 to 1896, see Fran FERNANDEZ GOMEZ: *Origenes del anarquismo comunista en España* 1882–1896, Sabadell, Bells Vells Temps, 2017, pp. 118–126.
155 Patricia R. TURNER: "Hostile Participants? Working-Class Militancy, Associational Life, and the Distinctiveness of Pre-War French Labor Movement", *The Journal of Modern History*, 71/1 (1999), pp. 34–35.
156 William P. WATKINS: *The International Co-operative Alliance. 1895–1970*, London, ACI, 1971; and Laura GÓMEZ: *La Alianza Cooperativa Internacional y su desarrollo como institución y en especial como instrumento transformador de la sociedad*, Vitoria-Gasteiz, Consejo Superior de Cooperativas de Euskadi, 1998.
157 Álvaro GIRÓN: *De redes informales e historias cruzadas. Barcelona-Buenos Aires y la gestión libertaria del conocimiento científico Hacia 1900*, Madrid, IMF-CSIC, 2017.
158 Manuel LAGOS MIERES: *Lecturas subversivas*, Santiago, Centro de Estudios Sociales, 2014, pp. 31–34.

References

ABAD DE SANTILLAN, Diego: *El anarquismo en el movimiento obrero*, Barcelona, Cosmos, 1925.

ABAD DE SANTILLAN, Diego: *El movimiento anarquista en Argentina desde sus comienzos hasta 1910*, Buenos Aires, Argonauta, 1930.

ACOSTA, Alberto: *El buen vivir, Sumak Kawsay*, Barcelona, Ed. Icaria, 2013.

ALAIZ, Felipe: *Economía solidaria entre el campo y la ciudad*, Barcelona, Ed. CNT, 1937.

ALARI, Emma; GOROSTIZA, Santiago and DALMAU, Marc: *La forja solidària d'un barri portuari, La Barceloneta obrera i cooperativa*, Barcelona, Montaber, 2016.

ALGARRA, David: *El comú català. La història dels que no surten en la història*, Barcelona, Potlach, 2015.

ALMODÓVAR, António and CARDOSO, José Luís: *A History of Portuguese Thought*, London, Routledge, 1998.

ALVES MARTINS, António: *Grandes questòes de economia social tratadas by M. Chitti and La Mennais postas en vulgar e precedidas de uma introdução*, Porto, Typografia La Revista, 1844.

AMARO, Rogério Roque: "Similituds i diferències entre els enfocaments de l'economia social i solidària en diferents països de l'Europa del Sud", in Jordi

ESTIVILL and Jean Louis LAVILLE (eds.): *Economia solidària i història social*, Barcelona, Ed. Icaria, 2020.
ARCHAMBAULT, Edith: *Le secteur sans but lucratif; Associations et Fondations en France*, Paris, Ed. Economica, 1996.
ARCHILA, Mauricio: *Cultura e identidad obrera en Colombia 1910–1945*, Bogotá, G.R.C., 2010.
ARNABAT, Ramon and DUCH, Montserrat (coords.): *Historia de la sociabilidad contemporánea*, Valencia, PUV, 2014.
ARNABAT, Ramon; DUCH, Montserrat and PONS-ALTÉS, Josep M.: "El asociacionismo popular en la construcción de la ciudadanía en Catalunya y en la Emilia Romagna contemporáneas", *Historia Social*, 95 (2019), pp. 61–83.
AUGUSTINIS, Mateo de: *Istituzioni di economia sociale*, Naples, Tipografia dei Porcelli, 1837.
AUROI, Claude and YEPEZ DEL CASTILLO, Isabel: *Economie solidaire et commerce équitable. Acteurs et actrices d'Europe et d'Amérique Latine*, Louvain, Presses Universitaires de Louvain, 2006.
BARBETTA, Gian Paolo: *Senza scopo di lucro*, Bologna, Il Mulino, 1996.
BARRERA BASSOLS, Jacinto: *La biblioteca sociológica. Regeneración y la red internacional anarquista*, México, Universidad Autónoma de Méjico, 2011.
BORZAGA, Carlo; CALZARONI, Manlio; FONTANARI, Eddi and MASSIMO, Lori: *L'Economia Sociale in Italia*, Trento Istat, Euricse, 2021, p. 5.
BURDÍN, Gabriel and DEAN, Andrés: "New Evidence on Wages and Employment in Worker Cooperatives Compared with Capitalist Firms", *Journal of Comparative Economics*, 37 (2009), 517–533.
CASTEL, Robert: *Les métamorphoses de la question sociale*, Paris, Fayard, 1995.
CASTILLO, Benjamin: *Mutualidad, Cooperativismo y Previsión*, Valencia, Ed. Sempere, 1913.
CHITTI, Louis: *Cours d'économie sociale (Discours d'ouverture prononcé le 14 décembre 1833, Bruxelles, Jobert, 1834; 2e Lecture, 21 décembre 1833, Bruxelles, Ode et Wodon, 1834; 3e et 4e Lecture, 4 et 11 janvier 1834)*, Bruxelles, Ode, 1834.
CÓRODOVA, F.: *Cooperazione e fascismo nella crisi dello stato liberale*.
CRAIG, Ben and PENCAVEL, John: "The Behaviour of Worker Cooperatives: The Plywood Companies of the Pacific Northwest", *American Economic Review*, 82, 5 (1992), 1083–1105.
DA ORDEN, Maria Liliana: "Salud, Inmigración y ayuda mutua en Argentina. El Centro Gallego de Buenos Aires, Entre la crisis y la emergencia de un nuevo sistema sanitario (1930–1950)", *Revista de Indias*, 80, 280 (2020), 842–880.
DALMAU, Marc: *Un barri fet a cops de cooperació. El cooperativisme obrer al Poble Nou*, Barcelona, La Ciutat Invisible and Arxiu Històric del Poblenou, 2015.
DALMAU, Marc and MIRÓ, Ivan: *Les cooperatives obreres de Sants. Autogestió proletària en un barri de Barcelona. 1870–1939*, Barcelona, La Ciutat Invisible, 2010.
DARMON, Isabelle and ESTIVILL, Jordi: *L'économie sociale en Belgique, en France et en Italie: essai comparatif*, Barcelona, GES-Fondation MACIF, 1999.

DEFOURNY, Jacques; DEVELTERE, Patrick and FONTENEAU, Bénédicte (eds.): *L'économie sociale au Nord et au Sud*, Bruxelles, De Boeck, 1999.
DEFOURNY, Jacques and NYSSENS, Marthe: "Conceptions on Social Entrepreneurship in Europe and the United States, Convergences and Divergences", *Journal of Social Entrepreneurship*, 1, 1 (2009), pp. 32–53.
DEGLI INNOCENTI, Maurizio (ed.): *Le imprese cooperative in Europa (la storia)*, Pisa, Nistri Lischi, 1986.
DEGLI INNOCENTI, Maurizio: *Il movimento cooperativo nella storia d'Europa*, Milan, Franco Angeli, 1988.
DESROCHE, Henri: *Le projet coopératif*, Paris, Ed. Ouvrières, 1976.
DESROCHE, Henri: *Pour un traité d'économie sociale*, Paris, CIEM, 1983.
DESROCHE, Henri: "Movimento cooperativo ed economia sociale", in Maurizio DEGLI INNOCENTI (ed.): *Il movimento cooperativo nella storia d'Europa*, Milan, Franco Angeli, 1988.
DEWIER, Alain: *Mémoire en images. Le bassin Charbonnier du Centre*, Bois de Luc, Agora, 2010.
DIAS PEREIRA, Joana: *Associativismo Livre. Uma historia de fraternidade e progresso (1824–1926)*, Coïmbra, Almedina, 2020.
DIAS PEREIRA, Joana: *Origens do mutualismo em Portugal*, Lisbon, Uniao das Mutualidades Portuguesas, 2021.
DOS SANTOS, José Hipólito: *Maneiras cooperativas de pensar e agir. Contributo para a história do Cooperativismo*, Lisbon, Ediçoes Universitárias Lusófonas, 2009.
DREYFUS, Michel and GIBAUD, Bernard (dirs.): *Mutualité de tous les pays, un passé riche d'avenir*, Paris, Mutualitè Française, 1995.
DREYFUS, Michel and GIBAUD, Bernard: "Charles Gide, L'école de Saint Claude et la Fraternelle", *RECMA* (2000), 1, pp. 275–276.
DREYFUS, Michel and GIBAUD, Bernard: "Mutualité et coopération: une histoire par trop méconnue", *Cahiers d'histoire*, 133 (2016), pp. 169–180.
DREYFUS, Michel and GIBAUD, Bernard: *Histoire de l'économie sociale de la grande guerre á nos jours*, Rennes, Presses Universitaires de Rennes, 2017.
DUCH, Montserrat: *Micaela Chalmeta*, Barcelona, Roca i Galès Foundation, 2009.
DUCH, Montserrat; ARNABAT, Ramon and FERRÉ, Xavier (eds.): *Sociabilitats a la Catalunya contemporània. Temps i espais en conflicte*, Barcelona, Publicacions Abadia de Montserrat, 2015.
DUCH, Montserrat; ARNABAT, Ramon and GAVALDÀ, Antoni: *La Catalunya associada (1868–1938)*, València, PUV, 2020.
DUNOYER, Charles: *Nouveau traité d'économie sociale*, Vol. II, Paris, A. Santelet Librairie éditeurs, 1830.
EALHAM, Chris: *La lucha por Barcelona. Clase, cultura y conflicto, 1898–1937*, Madrid, Alianza, 2005.
ESTIVILL, Jordi: *'Cooperativisme a Ictineu': Diccionari de les Ciències de la Societat als Països Catalans*, Barcelona, Edicions 62, 1979, pp. 126–130.
ESTIVILL, Jordi: "Espacios públicos y privados, construyendo diálogos en torno a la economía solidaria", *Critica de Ciencias Sociais*, 84 (2009), pp. 101–113.

ESTIVILL, Jordi: "Empresas, emprendedurismo y empresariado social", *Economia solidaria*, 8 (2015), pp. 18–50.
ESTIVILL, Jordi: "*Os primordios da economia social em Portugal. Contributos de Ramon de la Sagra*", *Sociologia*, 33 and 34 (2017).
ESTIVILL, Jordi: *Invitació a l'economia solidària*, Barcelona, Ed. Pol·len, 2018.
ESTIVILL, Jordi: "La economía solidaria, ¿categoría conceptual para la historia?", in Enrique SANTAMARÍA, Laura C. YUFRA and Juan de la HABA (eds.): *Investigando economías solidarias*, Barcelona, ERAPI Ed. Pol·len, 2019.
ESTIVILL, Jordi: *La economía solidaria según Felipe Alaiz y la economía colectiva en Catalunya*, unpublished, 2020.
ESTIVILL, Jordi: "Catalunya associada i solidària", *L'Avenç*, 483 (2021), p. 36.
ESTIVILL, Jordi: "Introducción. Aportaciones mexicanas a la Economía solidaria", in Boris MARAÑON-PIMENTEL and Dania LÓPEZ CÓRDOBA: *Solidaridad Económica, Buenos vivires, descolonialidad del poder. Aproximaciones desde México*, Barcelona, Ed. Icaria, 2023.
ESTIVILL, Jordi and BALSA, Casimiro (eds.): *Economia local, comunitària e solidaria. O desenvolvimento visto de baixo*, Famalicâo, Ed. Humus, 2022.
ESTIVILL, Jordi and BARBAT, Gustau: "L'anticlèricalisme populaire en Catalogne", *Social Kompass*, 27, 2/3 (1980), pp. 215–230.
ESTIVILL, Jordi and DALMAU, Marc: "L'estat de la qüestió. Balanç bibliogràfic sobre l'economia social i solidària a Catalunya", in Jordi ESTIVILL and Jean-Louis LAVILLE (eds.): *Economia solidària i historia social*, Barcelona, Icaria, 2020.
ESTIVILL, Jordi and MIRÓ, Ivan: *L'economia Social i Solidaria a Catalunya*, Barcelona, Ed. Icaria, 2020.
EWALD, François: *L'état Providence*, Paris, Editions Grasset, 1986.
FABBRI, Fabio: *L'Italia cooperativa. Centocinquant' anni di storia e di memòria (1861–2011)*, Rome, Ediesse, 2011.
FERNANDEZ GOMEZ, Fran: *Origenes del anarquismo comunista en España 1882–1896*, Sabadell, Bells Vells Temps, 2017, pp. 118–126.
FERREIRA, Silvestre Pinheiro: *Projecto de um Banco de Socorro e Seguro Mutuo*, Paris, Rey et Gravier, 1836.
FERREIRA, Silvestre Pinheiro: *Projecto de associação para o Melhoramento das classes industriosas*, Paris, Fain et Thunot, 1840.
FERREIRA DE COSTA, Fernando: *Doutrinadores cooperativistas portugueses*, Lisboa, Libros Horizonte, 1978.
FONSECA, Carlos da: *Origens da Internacional. (1871–1873)*, Lisboa, Ed. Estampalhadores, 1973.
FONZO, Erminio: *L'unione fa la forza. Società di mutuo soccorso e altre organizzazioni dei lavoratori a Napoli dall'Unità alla crisi di fine secolo*, Rubbettino, Soveria Mannelli, 2010.
FRANCO, José Eduardo and CASTRO HENRIQUES, António (coords.): *História do Montepio Geral. Sob o signo do pelicano.1840–2015*, Lisbon, INCM, 2015.
FRANCO, Raquel *et al.*: *O sector ñao lucrativo portuguès numa perspectiva comparada*, Porto, Universidade Catolica Portuguesa, 2005.

FREIRE, Joao: *Associaçoes profesionais em Portugal*, Oeiras, Celta Editora, 2009.
GABRIEL, Pere: "Sobre la cultura popular i obrera a Catalunya en el segle XIX", *Cercles*, 8 (2005), pp. 15–42.
GABRIEL, Pere: *Fernando Garrido Tortosa. Agitació i escriptura política. La pulsió cooperativista*, Barcelona, Fundació Roca i Galès, 2009.
GAIGER, Luis I.: "Da informalidade a economia popular: distinguindo realidades e conectando abordagens", *Ciencias Sociais Unisinos*, 55, 1 (2019), pp. 97–110.
GALASSI, Nazario: *Società Operaie di Mutuo soccorso: origine della Cooperazione generale e bancarie*, Imola, Bachilega, 2008.
GARAU, Miguel: "Los estudios sobre cooperativismo en la historiografía española: un estado de la cuestión", *Bulletin d'Histoire Contemporaine de l'Espagne* 54 (2020).
GARRIDO, Álvaro: *Uma história da economia social*, Lisbon, Tinta da China, 2016.
GARRIDO, Álvaro: *A economia social em movimento. Uma història das organizações*, Lisbon, Tinta da China, 2018.
GARRIDO, Fernando: *La cooperación. Estudio teórico practico sobre las cooperativas de consumo y de producción en Inglaterra y otros países y especialmente en Cataluña*, Barcelona, Imp. De Oliveros, 1879.
GIDE, Charles: *Quatre écoles d'économie sociale*, Geneva, Librairie Stapelmohr, 1880.
GIDE, Charles: "L'école de Saint Claude", *Le Jura socialiste*, 43 (1902).
GIRÓN, Álvaro: *De redes informales e historias cruzadas. Barcelona-Buenos Aires y la gestión libertaria del conocimiento científico Hacia 1900*, Madrid, IMF-CSIC, 2017.
GÓMEZ, Laura: *La Alianza Cooperativa Internacional y su desarrollo como institución y en especial como instrumento transformador de la sociedad*, Vitoria-Gasteiz, Consejo Superior de Cooperativas de Euskadi, 1998.
GONZALEZ BERNALDO DE QUIRÓS, Pilar: "El momento mutualista en la formulación de un sistema de protección social en Argentina: socorros mutuos y prevención subsidiada a comienzos del siglo XX", *Revista de Indias*, 73, 257 (2013), pp. 175–177.
GUERRA, Pablo: "Economía de la Solidaridad. Construcción de un camino a veinte años de las primeras elaboraciones", III Jornadas en Historia económica, Montevideo, 2003.
GUESLIN, André: *L'invention de l'économie sociale. Le XIX siècle français*, Paris, Ed. Economica, 1987.
GREZ, Sergio: "La trayectoria histórica del mutualismo en Chile (1853–1990)", *Mapocho: Revista de Humanidades y Ciencias Sociales*, 35 (1994), pp. 293–315.
GROHMAN, Alberto: *Perugia e la sua Società di mutuo soccorso 1861–1939*, Perugia, Volumnia Editrice, 2000.
HARRIS, Bernard and BRIDGEN, Paul (eds.): *Charity and Mutual Aid in Europe and North America since 1800*, New York, Routledge, 2012.
HILSON, Mary; NEUNSINGER, Silke and PATMORE, Greg (Comp.): *Global History of Consumer Co-operation since 1850*, Leiden, Brill, 2017.

HORNE, Janet: *Le Musée Social. Aux origines de l'Etat providence*, Paris, Belin, 2004.
JEANTET, Thierry: *L'économie sociale européenne*, Paris, CIEM, 1999.
JOSSA, Bruno: "Cooperative Firms as a New Mode of Production", *Review of Political Economy*, 24 (2012), pp. 339-416.
LAGOS MIERES, Manuel: *Lecturas subversivas*, Santiago, Centro de Estudios Sociales, 2014.
LARGO, Fernando and PUJOL-ANDREU, Josep: "Desarrollo y crisis del mutualismo de los trabajadores en España en el siglo XX: Nueva aproximación desde el capital social", *Scripta Nova. Revista Electrónica de Geografía y Ciencias Sociales*, 20, 540 (2016), pp. 1–25.
LAVILLE, Jean Louis and FILHO, Genauto Carvalho de França: *Economia Solidária, Uma abordagem internacional*, Porto Alegre, Editora de UFRGS, 2004.
LAVILLE, Jean Louis and FILHO, Genauto Carvalho de França (dir.): *L'économie solidaire, une perspective internationale*, Paris, Hachette, 2007.
LAVILLE, Jean Louis and FILHO, Genauto Carvalho de França: *L'économie solidaire. Une perspective internationale*, Paris, Pluriel, 2010.
LAVILLE, Jean Louis and FILHO, Genauto Carvalho de França: *Asociarse para el bien común. Tercer sector, Economía Social y Economía solidaria*, Barcelona, Ed. Icaria, 2015.
LAVILLE, Jean Louis and FILHO, Genauto Carvalho de França: *Contre la Société du mépris. Réinventer l'Association*, Paris, Desclèe de Brouwer, 2019.
LAZARO, Joao: *Despontar do movimento operario portuguès na esfera pública. Das prácticas a o debate parlamentar (1850–1870)*, Lisbon, Chiado, 2018.
LAZARO, Joao: "Associaçao Internacional de Trabalhadores em Portugal", *Revista Mundos do Trabalho*, 11 (2019), pp. 1–19.
LEAR, John: "Del mutualismo a la resistencia: las organizaciones laborales en la Ciudad de México desde fines del porfiriato a la Revolución", in Carlos ILLADES and Ariel RODRIGUEZ KURI (eds.): *Ciudad de México: instituciones, actores sociales y conflicto político, 1774–1931*, México, Universidad Autónoma Metropolitana-El Colegio de Michoacán, 1996.
LIMA CAMPOS, Joao: *O movimento operario em Portugal*, Porto, Ed. Afrontamentos, 1972.
LLAGUNO THOMAS, José Julián: *Anarquismo, sociabilidad obrera y redes intelectuales en Costa Rica, Un estudio de cultura política*, Tesis doctoral, Universidad de Costa Rica, 2015.
LLAGUNO THOMAS, José Julián: "Acçào local e audiència global na America Central segondo suas fontes documentais (1910–1930)", *Verve*, 17 (2016), pp. 33–51.
LOBATO, Mirta Zaida: *La vida en las fábricas, trabajo, protesta y política en una comunidad obrera, Berisso. 1904–1970*, Buenos Aires, Ed. Prometeo, 2001.
LORENZO, Anselmo: *El proletariado militante, Memorias de un internacional*, Toulouse, Ediciones MLE-CNT, 1947.
MAIULLARI, Maria Teresa: *Storiografia francese ed italiana a confronto sul fenomeno associativo durante XVIII e XIX secolo*, Torino, Einaudi, 1990.

MAUSS, Marcel: “Essai sur le don. Forme et raison de l’échange dans les sociétés primitives”, *L’Anné Sociologique*, second series (1923).

MAUSS, Marcel: *Essai sur le don*, Paris, P.U.F., 2001.

MAX NEEF, Manfred and SMITH, Philip B.: *La economia desenmascarada*, Barcelona, Icària, 2014.

MELENDEZ VADILLO, Jorell: *Voces libertarias. Los orígenes del anarquismo en Puerto Rico*, Santurce, Ed. C. C. C., 2013.

MENZANI, Tito: *Il movimento cooperativo fra le due guerre. Il caso italiano nel contesto europeo*, Rome, Carocci Ed., 2009.

MICHELINI, Luca: *Marginalismo e socialismo: Maffeo Pantaleoni (1882–1904)*, Milan, Franco Angeli, 1998.

MIGUELAÑEZ, Maria: “Diego Abad de Santillan. 1897–1983. Los Viajes doctrinarios de un anarquista transnacional”, in Manuel PEREZ LEDESMA (ed.): *Trayectorias transatlánticas (siglo XX) Personajes y redes entre España y América*, vol. II, Madrid, Polifemo, 2013.

MIRÓ, Ivan: *Ciutats Cooperatives*, Barcelona, Ed. Icaria, 2018.

MONZÓN, José Luís: “El Cooperativismo en la historia de la literatura económica”, *CIRIEC-España*, 44 (2003), pp. 9–34.

MORENO, Javier; MARTIN, Eduardo and VENCE, Agustina: *El crack del 29 en Iberoamerica. Perspectivas. Enfoques locales y regionales*, Paris, AHILA, 2021.

MORENO, Rafael: “La gènesis del mutualismo moderno en Europa”, *REVESCO*, 72 (2000), pp. 199–214.

MUNCK, Ronaldo: “Mutual Benefit Societies in Argentina. Workers, Nationality, Social Security and Trade Unionism”, *Journal of Latin American Studies*, 30, 3 (1998), pp. 573–590.

MUÑOZ, Pascual: *La Primera Huelga General en el Uruguay*, Montevideo, La Turba Ediciones, 2011, pp. 9–13.

MUSSO, Stefano: *Gli operai nella storiografia contemporannea a Tra fabbrica e società – Mondo operai nell’italia del novecento*, Milan, Feltrinelli, 1999.

NETLAU, Max: *Contribución a la bibliografía anarquista en América Latina*, Buenos Aires, La Protesta, 1927.

OLLÉ, Josep Maria: *Introducció del socialisme utòpic a Catalunya (1835–1837)*, Barcelona, Ed. 62, 1969.

OLLÉ, Josep Maria: *El moviment obrer a Catalunya, (1840–1843)*, Barcelona, Nova Terra, 1973.

OYÓN, José Luis (ed.): *Vida obrera en la Barcelona d’entreguerres,1918–1936*, Barcelona, CCCB, 1998.

PABST, Adrian: “Political Economy Virtue: Civil Economy. Happiness and Public Trust in the Thought of Antonio Genovesi”, *European Journal of the History of Economic Thought*, 1, 25 (2016), pp. 524–530.

PACI, Massimo: “Il sistema di welfare italiano tra tradizione clientelare e prospettive di riforma”, in Ugo ASCOLI (ed.): *Welfare State all’italiana*, Rome, Laterza, 1984.

PAGEAUX, Daniel Henri: “Lamennais en péninsule ibérique: Note sur la diffusion des idées Ménarcissiennes en Espagne et au Portugal (1834–1840)”, in *VV.AA.:*

Utopie et socialisme au Portugal au XIX siècle, Paris, Gulbenkian Foundation, 1982, pp. 121–152.

PECQUEUR, Constantin: *Economie sociale. Les intérêts du commerce, de l'industrie et de l'agriculture et de la civilisation*, París, 1837.

PECQUEUR, Constantin: *Théorie nouvelle d'économie sociale et politique*, Paris, Capelle, 1842.

PELLEGRINO, Anna: "Solidarité sociale et identité nationale lors de l'unification de l'Italie: l'exemple de la solidarité artisanale", *RECMA*, 329 (2013), pp. 52–64.

PÉNIN, Marc: *Charles Gide (1847–1932): L'esprit critique*, Paris, L'Harmattan, 1997.

PEREZ BARÓ, Albert: *Historia de la cooperación catalana*, Barcelona, Ed. Nova Terra, 1974.

PÉROTIN, Virginie: "Workers Cooperatives: Good, Sustainable Jobs in the Community", *Journal of Entrepreneurial and Organisational Diversity*, 2, 2 (2014), pp. 34–47.

POLANYI, Karl: *La Gran transformación*, Madrid, La Piqueta, 1989.

PROTASI, Maria Rosa: "Tra scienzia e riforma sociale. Il pensiero e il metodo d'indagine sociale di F. Le Play e dei suoi continuatori in Italia (1857–1914)", *Studi Storici, Anno*, 37, 3 (1996), pp. 813–845.

PUENTE PÉREZ, Ginés: "Al margen del feminismo. Las vindicaciones de las anarquistas y españolas por la liberación de las mujeres (1868–1939)", *Chronica Mundi*, 12, 1 (2017), pp. 38–72.

RANCIERE, Jacques: *La nuit des prolétaires*, Paris, Fayard, 1981.

RAZETO, Luis: *Desafíos y proyectos de la economía solidaria*, Santa Fe, Universidad Nacional del Litoral, 2010.

RIOT-SARCEY, Michèle: *Le procès de la liberté. Une histoire souterraine du XIX siècle en France*, Paris, Éditions la Découverte, 2016.

RUIZ DE OLABUENAGA, José Ignacio (dir.): *El sector no lucrativo en España*, Bilbao, Fundación BBVA, 2000.

SAENZ DE LA CÁMARA, Sixto: *La Unión Ibèrica, 1859*, Lisbon, Typographia Universal, 1859. Republished in two languages in Madrid – Badajoz, Ediciones 19, 2014.

SAGRA, Ramón de la: *Lecciones de economía social*, Madrid, Imprenta de Ferrer y Compañía, 1840.

SAPELLI, Giulio: "La Cooperazione e il fascismo: organizzazione delle masse e dominazione burocratica" in Fabbio FABRI (ed.): *Il movimento cooperativo nella storia di Italia*, Milano, Feltrinelli, 1979.

SAUNIER, Pierre Yves: "Les régimes circulatoires du domaine social (1840–1940). Projets et ingénierie de la convergence et la différence", *Genèse*, 71 (2008), pp. 4–25.

SILVA LEMOS, Thiago: *O dia a dia do movimento operàrio impresso em crònica: O sindicalismo revolucionario Portuguès a partir da trajetoria de Neno Vasco*, Uberlandia, UFU, 2012.

SMILES, Samuel: *Thrift*, London, John Murray, 1875.

SOAVE, Alberto: *Breve storia della società Operaie di mutuo soccorso*, 2015. https://storiachepassione.wordpress.com/

SOLÀ, Pere: *Cultura popular a Catalunya (1900–1939)*, Barcelona, La Magrana, 1978.

SOLÀ, Pere: "El mutualismo y su función social: sinopsis histórica", *CIRIEC-España*, 44 (2003), pp. 175–198.

SOMBART, Werner: *¿Porque no hay socialismo en los Estados Unidos?*, 1st. published in 1905, Madrid, Capitan Swing, 2009.

SOUSA BRANDAO, Francisco Maria de: *Economia Social, part I, O Trabalho*, Lisboa, Progresso, 1857.

STABER, Udo: "Age-Dependence and Historical Effects on the Failure Rates of Worker Cooperatives: An Event-History Analysis", *Economic and Industrial Democracy*, 10 (1989), pp. 59–80.

SWAAN, Abram: *In Care of the State, Health Care, Education and Welfare in Europe and USA in the Modern Era*, New York, OUP, 1988.

TAVOLO PER LA RETE ITALIANA DI ECONOMIA SOLIDALE: *Un'economia nuova, dai Gas alla zeta. L'economia solidale e le sue reti: Gruppi d'acquisto solidali, Distretti di economia solidale, filiere corte. Per cambiare il sistema economico con le relazioni e il consumo critico*, Milan, Altra Economia, 2013.

TOMASSINI, Luigi: "L'associacionismo operaio: aspetti problemi della difusione del mutualismo nel'Italia Liberale" in Stefano MUSSO (ed.): *Tra fabbrica e società: mondi operai nell'Italia del Novecento*, Milan, Feltrinelli, 1999, pp. 24–26.

TRISTAN, Flora: *La Unión obrera*, 1843. Republished in Barcelona, De Barris 2005.

TURNER, Patricia R.: "Hostile Participants? Working-Class Militancy, Associational Life, and the Distinctiveness of Pre-War French Labor Movement", *The Journal of Modern History*, 71/1 (1999), pp. 34–35.

UNKNOWN AUTHOR: *Economia Social, Verdades interesantes a o Reino e a o estado e a todas classes de gentes: Antidotos contra os luxos aparatozos e faustos escuzados. Remedios para curar os males das uzuras e monopólios*, Lisbon, Typografia de Joze Baptista Morando, 1823.

UNKNOWN AUTHOR: *Bulletin de l'économie sociale*, 36 (1898), p. 127.

UTTING, Peter (ed.): *Social and Solidarity Economy. Beyond the Fringe*, London, Zed Books-UNRISD, 2015.

VALDOUR, Jacques: *L'ouvrier espagnol. Tome I- Catalogne*, Paris, René Giard, Arthur Rousseau, 1919.

VAN DER LINDEN, Marcel (coord.): *Social Security Mutualism. The Comparative History of Mutual Benefit Societies*, New York, Lang Ed., 1996.

VENEGAS, Fernando and GREZ, Sergio: "Historiografía del mutualismo chileno, 1853–1990: análisis crítico y nuevas perspectivas", *Izquierdas*, 50 (2021), pp. 1–30.

VICENS i VIVES, Jaume and LLORENS, Montserrat: *Industrials i polítics, al segle XIX*, Barcelona, Ed. Vicens Vives, 1961.

VIDAL, François: *De la répartition des richesses ou de la justice distributive en économie sociale, ouvrage contenant l'examen critique des théories exposées soit par les économistes, soit par les socialistes*, Paris, Capelle, 1846.

VV. AA.: *Atlas do primeiro congreso de historia do movimento operaio e dos movimentos sociais em Portugal*, vol. II, Pes no Chao, Lisbon, IHC Universidade Nova de Lisboa, 2016.

WATKINS, William P.: *The International Co-operative Alliance. 1895–1970*, London, ACI, 1971.

ZAMAGNI, Stefano: *L'economia civile*, Bologna, Il Mulino, 2004.

ZANINELLI, Sergio: "Gli sviluppi storici Barbetta", in Gian Paolo BARBETTA (ed.): *Senza scopo di lucro. Dimensioni economiche, legislazione e politiche del settore nonprofit in Italia*, Bologna, Il Mulino, 1996, pp. 119–125.

2 The Old and New Uses of Communal Lands[1]

How to Escape Commodification?

Pedro Hespanha

Introduction

In almost all societies in pre-modern Europe, there was land intended for cultivation or pasture, gathering wood or stone for construction, bushes for fuel or fertilising, or producing honey, which was used in common by the population of one or more nearby communities, taking on different designations, one of the most frequent being communal or people's lands. The activities carried out in them were the result of a collective organisation of the peasants to face common needs, including the fight against excessive taxes and rents, and to self-regulate their conflicts, either through collective deliberation or through elected agents with mediation capacity. What happens is that these rules that governed the life of agrarian communities were completely ignored by jurists and ruling classes, as they were alien to codes and written law. That is why they were designated as the right of the rustics, that is, of rude and uneducated people, incapable of understanding the subtleties of the law.

In Portugal, the *baldios* (the most common designation for communal lands) have survived to this day, despite the attacks against them mainly from the second half of the 18th century onwards by an adverse state inspired by liberal thought and by a fierce and powerful rural bourgeoisie who eagerly wanted to appropriate these lands. It is not easy to estimate the area occupied by common lands in the most distant past, but we know that, in 1937, the survey carried out by the Junta de Colonização Interna recognised the existence of a total area of 490,000 hectares occupied by common lands, which represented about of 5.3% of the surface of mainland Portugal.[2] A few decades earlier, in 1874, the uncultivated area, including *baldios* and *charnecas*,[3] was estimated at four million hectares, or 45% of the national surface.[4] However, taking into account what is known about the policy of collective tenure used in medieval times to fix populations in the reconquered territories, the commons had a period of great expansion that lasted until the second half of the 18th century, when this trend was

DOI: 10.4324/9781003439554-3

reversed and the depreciation of commons was started.[5] The most recent and in-depth work on common areas in Portugal results from a survey carried out in 2000 by the Instituto Superior de Agronomia de Lisboa, but which is limited to the North Region of the country,[6] where it can be seen that of the 3,754 *baldios* surveyed in 1938, occupying 3,710 hectares, only 820 remained, with an area of 675 hectares; that is, they suffered a reduction of 21.8% in number and of 18.2% in the area.

The recognition of community ownership of *baldios* by the Portuguese Political Constitution of 1976, immediately after the Carnation Revolution, became an opportunity for local communities to recreate new ways of using their common land more suited to contemporary realities.

Since then, however, much has changed in Portuguese rural areas, as the economy of rural families is no longer dependent, as in the past, on agricultural production and land ownership. Today, people who remained in the rural villages combine agriculture with other forms of economic activity and combine income from cultivating the land with other sources of non-agricultural income. The occupational trajectories of peasant families show that most of the children who got married and live in the same community resume their parents' agriculture, despite having a non-agricultural profession. They manage to do so under different conditions, generally less dependent on physical labour and using resources that come, in part, from mutual help in their communities and in part from the market (machinery, seeds, fertilisers).

Where the lack of jobs forced emigration to urban centres or even abroad, we find the same attraction for the communities of origin, expressed by the physical presence at local festivities and holidays, by the remote management of heritage (investment in improving housing, purchase of land, or collective goods), and, finally, by the return to the community after the reform, so often postponed but always desired. These facts confirm that small family farming and the social spaces that surround it are being recreated in new ways, in a process dependent on other sectors of society. For example, public and social policies in areas as diverse as urban planning, encouraging SMEs, promoting tourism, health, and social security are gradually reducing community self-sufficiency by eroding those institutions that produced it, such as mutual aid, collective action, oral tradition, folk medicine, and intergenerational skills.

Thus, the use of *baldios* is increasingly shifting from the individual economy of neighbours to the economy of the community as a whole, which has seen its income increase through the renting of some parcels of common land to large companies interested in installing windmills and photovoltaic stations for the production of electricity, or antennas for telecommunications and radio broadcasting, in investing in the forest to supply those new industries based on wood to produce pulp, textile fibre or cross-laminated timber (CLT), in exploring mineral water or in extracting mineral resources, like lithium or ornamental stone, for industrial purposes, in developing leisure, recreation, and environmental enjoyment activities, radical sports or photo safaris, oriented to increasing demand of urban consumers.

In short, if some of the new uses of the commons are promoted by the community members themselves and allow for its revitalisation through collective action and investment in material and social capital, with a wide margin of decision by the community's neighbours, others, however, involve a high degree of commodification of common land and its opening to outside users with very different consumption habits.

When realising this change in the uses of *baldios* that is taking place before our eyes, two questions arise: the first is whether they will be able to survive in the face of the growing subordination of the use of those lands to a market logic that threatens to erode its identity as a collective institution; and the second is to know how, in the past, communities of *baldios* faced other similar challenges without dissolving. The following section deals with this second question.

The long historical trajectory of communal land in Portugal

In this section, we will summarise the literature on the historical origin of common lands and the main transformation milestones of this institution throughout its existence, with particular emphasis on the period since the advent of economic liberalism.

The term *baldio* is currently used in Portuguese legal-administrative language to mean communal land. *Baldios* are areas of land traditionally used and managed by local communities for numerous activities, as mentioned above.

Etymologically *baldio* means vacant, idle, or uncultivated land, but this is not the meaning that communities associate with the term. First of all, because traditionally the *baldios* had a clear productive use – cattle raising – and, even today, when the number of herds has greatly decreased, three-quarters of the *baldios* in Portugal produce forest, timber for civil construction, firewood or heating, and bushes for soil fertilisation. If there are areas of uncultivated land, they are largely (about 70%) in private hands and not in the hands of the commoners.[7]

The designation of *baldio* was only generalised in the 18th century, although there are references to this designation at least since the middle of the 15th century.[8] The current designation at the time was "maninhos" or "matos maninhos"[9] which designated the uncultivated land that was used in common by the neighbours of a village to pasture their cattle or to collect bush, firewood, and wood for their homes and as fertilisers. The different households took turns leading the herds to the common lands;

sometimes there was even a collective herd, but this did not mean the existence of a community economy, as each household used their own plots for cultivation.

The origin of communal land is lost in people's memory

Regardless of the more or less remote origin that historians recognise to communal lands, in the Iberian Peninsula, their expansion is strongly related to the policy of settling peasant communities on lands that were being reconquered by the Christian kings from the Muslims who occupied them in the 8th century.[10] Consisting as a rule of a royal concession through "cartas de foral",[11] this policy benefited both these peasant communities incited to populate abandoned territories, as well as the Mozarabic communities that remained in the reconquered territories after conversion to Christianity, benefiting from great administrative and judicial autonomy according to their traditional rules.

Rebelo da Silva, a Portuguese historian of the second half of the 19th century, recognises that the first kings of Portugal, following the Christian reconquest, used different processes of settlement and incentives to agriculture in the reconquered territories, through collective leases which were associated with the right to use and enjoy land held in common.[12] According to the same author, King Dinis (1279–1325) used three distinct regionally based systems: in the south (region of Alentejo), a system based on large donations to secular or religious landlords who, in turn, allocated land to small peasants[13]; in the northwest (region of Entre Douro e Minho), a system based on "casais" distributed by a reduced number of families[14]; and in the northeast (region of Trás-os-Montes) a system based on collective "foros", with the land being commonly owned by the village.[15] This difference became more accentuated, especially from the 19th century onwards. On the coastal zone where the population was concentrated, the common lands suffered a strong reduction due to the clearing of land for the cultivation of corn and potatoes in response to demographic growth.[16] Later, the historian Alberto Sampaio reported on the transformations that had taken place in the agrarian landscape of Minho due to the distribution of common land to neighbours, considering that a process of transition from community property to individual property was taking.[17]

To allow the subsistence of the settlement communities, the kings often endowed the peasants of each "casal", hamlet, or village with lands commonly owned and not individually appropriated for grazing or obtaining firewood, at the same time that they prevented the powerful from seizing these lands.[18] Abundant royal concessions thus promoted the installation of peasant families on reconquered land, attributing them some perks so that they could prosper in self-managed communities.

From an early age, a distinction was made between "property of the county" and "common goods of the county": the former are, in current terminology, "the rustic and urban assets owned and leased by the county"; the second are "goods that were used collectively by the neighbours, including the common land, roads, watermills, ovens, rivers, streams, lakes, and so on".[19]

But this expansion was not without difficulties. In the 14th century, a proto-bourgeoisie of wealthy merchants and gentlemen farmers emerged, claiming access to uncultivated fields and communal lands with the argument that they were not producing for the market. Abusive appropriations of communal lands have become more and more frequent from then onwards, along with complaints from the communities against these abuses.

Later, in the 18th century, the population growth and the pressure on the "unproductive landowners", associated with the influence of physiocratic doctrines, placed the communal property in front of new threats. Several studies and proposals published in the Memoirs of Economics of the Lisbon Academy of Sciences, at the turn of the 19th century, advocated a more intensive use of land and the transformation of common land into an individual property. The common property was increasingly seen as a holdover from feudal rule to be abolished.[20]

Another controversial issue concerns how one should classify the type of property that the common use of land represents. Shortly, it can be said that there are two main positions over the legal framework for the use of *baldios* by their communities: one that identifies this relationship with a Germanic type of property right and another one that identifies it with a Roman type of property right.

In Portugal, the first position is widely accepted.[21] Oliveira Martins argues that "the principles of the Roman law influenced the individualisation of property throughout the Celtic-Germanic area, leaving the Slavic area, less affected by Latin influence, as a historical representative of primitive collectivism".[22] Even so, he recognises that it is not rare to find cases of periodic division of land into temporary lots, a situation that was very common in the Middle Ages but which had almost disappeared. In turn, the jurist Rogério Soares defended the Roman origin of the commons, arguing that Roman law was favourable to the free use of land intended for the supply of urban centres of firewood and pasture.[23] For the historian Oliveira Marques, the origin of the commons is more complex. The Roman principle of private property prevailed in almost the entire Celto-Germanic area, except in areas less affected by Latin influence where primitive collectivism prevailed.[24]

In Spain, there is a vast bibliography on this subject, since the inspiring contribution of Joaquin Costa (1983) on the customary law in Spain and, more generally, since the debate he opened on collectivism and individualism in land ownership in Spain.[25] Other seemingly inspiring contributions came from Eduardo de Hinojosa who rooted the common land use in the Germanic mark, that is, an area around the villages that was intended for common use,[26] and from Rafael Altamira, to whom we owe the most in-depth theorisation on the Germanic genesis of the communal land.[27] He argues that for Roman law the limitations to individual property (such as co-ownership or undivided property) were exceptional; clarity and precise definition of rights were preferred to the relativity of the community of goods. Beyond the Roman Empire and in the Roman provinces of the north,[28] the Germanic people had very different ideas and customs about the property. This is the case of the unlimited communal property of land and other resources which can be individually used, but not alienated or destroyed, because it is intended to guarantee the needs of all its members, current and future. The model of the unlimited communal property has long since disappeared, but it allows a better understanding of the current property regimes that result from its transformation over time. Mobile goods were the first to emancipate from their communal condition, leaving intact the commonality of immobile goods (land, irrigation channels, threshing floors, people's ovens, shelters, etc.). Later, it is the immobile goods - mainly houses and farmland - that lose their community status, although limitations on private use of farmland may still persist for a longer period of time.[29] Brought to the Iberian Peninsula after the fall of the Roman Empire, the communal property had to adapt to adverse contexts, enduring pressure and changes before its disappearance in many territories in our days. Some authors emphasise the hybrid character of many communal lands whose ownership belongs "to all or a to a good part of the neighbours, as a community, either Germanic or Roman, without such lands having the condition of communal" (Guaita Martorell cited by José-Cândido Paz ARES: *Régimen de los Llamados Montes de Vecinos em Galicia*, Vigo, Editorial Galaxia, 1966, p. 20). If during the Muslim presence in the Iberian Peninsula, there were no major changes, with the reconquest, the feudal appropriation of land and the settlement policies implied a generalised division of the property rights through emphyteutic contracts: the direct domain (*dominium directum*) to the landlord with the obligation of respecting the land use permanently or temporarily by those who cultivated the land, and the useful domain (*dominium utile*) of the land, with the obligation for those who cultivated the land to pay a feudal tribute – the "foro" – to the landlord.[30] This consisted of the tenure regime that expanded a lot not only in the feudal period but also later.[31] As a rule, only the uncultivated lands surrounding the communities would maintain their communal uses despite the greed of the landlords (nobles and Church) who pressed as much as possible for the "desamortização"[32] of the common land, similar to what happened with the land owned by monasteries. A different situation, but sometimes intertwined with this one, was that of the land belonging to municipalities and parishes, entities that also benefited from the granting of "cartas de foral".

To conclude this point, it is also important to address the issue of agro-pastoral communitarianism. This concept is used to describe the forms of cooperation among neighbours for the use of common goods (either physical resources, such as the soil, its arboreal covering and its geological and mineral richness and the waters in its multiple uses, but also the constructions for common use such as the mills, the people's ovens, the threshing floors, and the irrigation channels; or other resources that are the result of human cooperation such as the herds, the "ox of the community", or the wild animals). As Luís Polanah points out, in the mountain hamlets where an agro-pastoral economy developed, "the community formed by a group of families, more or less linked by a strong sense of local identity" and "sharing the same desire for individual and family survival" constituted itself as "a self-sufficient and self-managed unit, with autonomy to others of the same type, although not excluded from the legal and economic system of the country".[33] For this reason, "collective control over the use of communal goods has never curbed individual competition": "no one interferes with the individual work of families on their properties, or with the destination intended to their crops. Individual interest prevails above everything else, but the satisfaction of basic needs necessarily involves the defence of the common heritage, which enjoyment cannot be left to the free will of anyone, because selfishness is seen as a threat for the existence of most families and, consequently, the cohesion of the parish".[34]

The process of de-communalisation of baldios: strengths and resistances

If the orientation expressed in the Ordenações Régias[35] was to preserve the uses of the *baldios* by the communities, since the 18th century this orientation had to face increasing pressure in the opposite direction, that is, towards its privatisation.[36]

During the 18th century, population growth and pression to promote free access to land, associated with the influence of physiocratic doctrines, placed the communal property in the face of new threats. Private interest was seen as the best motivation for wealth production, private property as the best instrument to increase the value of any natural resource, and individual freedom of trade (impeded by corporations and other banal rights) as the essence of life in society. The *baldios*, like the land owned by religious corporations, were considered dead property – "bens de mão morta" – due its status of goods that were maintained out of the market.

In Portugal, several reformist proposals published in the *Memórias Economicas* of the Royal Academy of Sciences of Lisbon, at the turn of the 19th century, advocated the physiocratic ideas of a more intensive use of the land and, therefore, the transformation of common land into an individual property.[37] Common property is increasingly seen as a remnant of the feudal regime to be abolished.[38] The legal culture of the late 18th century, more marked by the French Revolution, also had an indisputable individualist footprint, finding its foundation and focus on individual private property, considered the most valuable guarantee of the individual's freedom. For this reason, any collective dimension of ownership was rejected as subversive of the political order, especially if it were applied to land ownership.[39] For his part, the Venetian geographer Adrien Balbi, who spent a few months in Lisbon in 1819, writes in his Essay on Portugal that one of the causes of the decline of agriculture is due to the immense extension of uncultivated land, including the *baldios* that, not being legally able to be sold, remain uncultivated or reduced to miserable pastures, in careless hands, instead of passing, if they were susceptible of sale, to the hands of industrious people, who would know how to make them profitable.[40]

The opposition of the commoners to these threats was fierce. Protest actions appeared throughout the country invoking the most diverse reasons for the most diverse reasons: annual allocation of the lots of common lands in favour of the more powerful, abuses in the collection of "foros", occupation or enclosure of parts of the *baldios* against the will of the people, invasion of *baldios* by herds strange to the community, legislation that allowed local authorities to sell or lease parcels of common land for specific purposes, frequent coexistence, in the same municipality, of land owned by the municipality and communal land for common enjoyment, which favoured the abusive appropriation of municipalities against the will of the people.[41]

Throughout the 19th century, the process of incorporation of agriculture into the universe of capitalist relations accelerated and with it increased pressure for the extinction of collective forms of property. This is the meaning of the new legislation, published between 1804 and 1815, which allows for the division of the common land by commoners ("compartes") or for the transfer of management of common lands from communities to local administration (municipalities). Soon afterwards, the liberal revolution of 1820 showed itself to be militantly anti-feudal and anti-community, identifying the community agro-pastoral system with backwardness and ignorance,[42] as one of its epigones would later express: "the existence of common pastures, is one of the most serious obstacles to the progress of agriculture among us".[43] The arguments that supported the division and alienation of the commons were basically the following:

first, the rapid population growth during the 18th century and the first decades of the 19th century provoked a great deficit in the cereal production and, thus, forced to an increase in the cultivated area; the commons became a preferred target for these proposals, particularly those in less mountainous regions; second, knowing that when *baldios* were divided equally, the lots that fell to the poor were sooner or later bought by the rich, then alienation was preferable to division;[44] third, the lack of preparation of commoners to choose the most suitable crops or animal species or to introduce improvements able to increase production; and fourth, the variety of forms of use of common land throughout the country and the uncertainty of the rules based on customs, make it difficult to judge conflicts and monitor abuses.

In 1867, the Civil Code recognised the legitimacy of the *baldios*, expressly defining them as "common things" that are "not individually appropriated and from which only individuals included in certain administrative limits are allowed to take advantage" (article no. 381). Nevertheless, the ownership of the *baldios* is attributed to municipalities and parishes which will prove disastrous for communities in the future, although at the time the ethnologist Rocha Peixoto ensured that everything will be deliberated, not by the parish councils but by the suffrage of the assemblies of commoners.[45]

The clarification of the legal status by a broad-spectrum law such as the Civil Code did not prevent or limit the impetus to privatise the *baldios*. Two years later, in 1869, a new law intended to extend to them the same regime of "desamortização" that had already been applied in 1834 to the "mão-morta" institutions, only preserving those which the communities proved to be essential for common use. The strong popular reaction against this threat prevented the widespread implementation of this law.

Later, it is the positivist idea of bringing "progress" to agriculture that will inspire the new legislation attacking the commons. This time, the argument is the potential of the production of wood that is being lost on the *baldios*. The lack of interest in forests in Portugal had already been pointed out by different reformists, such as Andrade e Silva who published, in 1815, a Memoir on the benefits of planting forests in Portugal, where he recognised that "the trees in the *baldios* and public domains were abandoned to the destroying ax of the peasants, to the teeth of the rodent animals, and to the fire of the clearings made by the shepherds".[46] In 1886, the Forest Services were created and in 1888 a report on the generalised afforestation was published, which reported that about 60% of the national territory is uncultivated land. Still, in 1888, the afforestation of 60,000 hectares of *baldios* was decreed which immediately triggered a strong reaction from the communities, in some places destroying the plantations and seedbeds by the state.[47]

In 1887, Oliveira Martins, a socialist member of the Chamber of Deputies and an influential economic thinker, presents his project for a law on rural progress in which he advocated a protectionist policy that would open up new opportunities for national production. Under the motto "today we need to implant men and implant trees: give the earth to those who make it fruitful", an ambitious economic reformist plan was drawn up, based on the "internal colonisation" of delimited areas of baldios,[48] the incentive for cereal production,[49] some measures to prevent the excessive reduction in the size of farms in the north, and the afforestation of land, in particular uncultivated and common land. Despite never having been discussed in the Parliament, this project had an enormous impact on reformist public policies for agriculture practically until the Carnation Revolution.[50]

The overthrow of the Monarchy, in 1910, did not change this process of "amortização"/privatisation of the baldios, and, on the contrary, it become more strong due to an accelerated demographic growth in the first two decades of the 20th century. Once again, it was the scarcity of food, experienced especially during the First World War, which led governments, through successive laws, to encourage an increase in areas for agriculture at the expense of communal lands. This is the case of new laws, in 1920 and 1921, that authorised the state, city councils, and parish councils to divide those *baldios* that have not been cultivated into plots of land to be alienated, in whole or in part, to former commoners or other interested farmers. For this purpose, the common lands are considered property of the respective municipal councils, so that they can give them productive use.

The policy of nationalisation of the commons

The most serious attack on common lands, from this perspective, was triggered during the Salazar dictatorship (1926–1974) and operated on several fronts: i. reinforcement of the measures that, since the 18th century, promoted the division of common lands; ii. attributing to the municipalities the power to dispose of *baldios*, while usurpation went unpunished; iii. settlement of peasant families in the *baldios* under the framework of "internal colonisation")[51] without the consent of the commoners; and iv. imposition of a reserve of 400,000 hectares for afforestation (about 80% of the number of *baldios* at that time), in which the traditional use by the commoners was prohibited, thus promoting the substitution of livestock for wood production.[52]

Generally speaking, the division, made by the state, of common lands into "glebes" and their afforestation created resentment and revolt. Afforestation was seen by the communities as a "theft" and not as a "gift", and the arrogant attitude of the forest guards, the abusive intrusion of the Forestry Services in the common areas, and the planting of forest species very vulnerable to fires incited a generalised popular resistance. However, the government systematically reacted to this resistance with intimidation, repression, and fines.

On a different scale, the pressure to afforest the commons cannot be dissociated from the increase in the world market prices for wood since the 19th century due to a very sharp expansion of wood industries in different branches, from civil construction and paper pulp to furniture and shipbuilding, coupled with the expansion resin industries and with an increasing demand for firewood and timber to the railways.[53] More recently, the European Union itself, grappling with surplus agricultural production, promotes non-agricultural land uses, including forestation, through its structural funds.[54]

The late restitution of baldios to their communities of origin

In 1974, the democratic regime that emerged from the Carnation Revolution recognised the communities of "compartes" as the legitimate owners of the *baldios* with full autonomy in deciding what to do with them. Immediately after the fall of the dictatorship, the communities had created commissions to claim the common lands back and to regain autonomy in deciding how to manage the land and the forest that had been installed on them. Although communal ownership was constitutionally guaranteed from 1976 onwards, the communities of "compartes" still had to remove many obstacles to recover full control of their lands, through mass demonstrations and other forms of protest.[55]

In 1976, two government decrees had come to regulate the use and management of the baldios and to entitle the communities dispossessed by the state's afforestation plan to claim their commons back to create a true democracy of "compartes". The first[56] defined the categories of *baldio*[57] and *comparte*[58] and allowed the assemblies of "compartes" to decide between one of two management modalities: a) the modality of exclusive management by a directive board of five "compartes" elected by their peers; b) the modality of associative management with the state by a directive board composed of four elected "compartes" and a fifth member appointed by the state. The second[59] establishes the legal procedures for the restitution to the "compartes" of the *baldios,* or part of them, that have been abusively appropriated by private persons or entities.

The general orientation of this legal framework aimed to preserve the communitarian forms of using and managing the *baldio* and to recognise the maximum autonomy to the communities of "compartes". However, several circumstances occurred in the meantime that forced the directive boards of the *baldios* to introduce changes in the traditional uses and forms of management. Those circumstances are related to different interconnected aspects of economic life such as the loss of economic relevance of agriculture and the use of the land for the income of the families, the increasing occurrence of forest fires that destroy the forest as a source of income, the increasing migration flows out of the community, and the external pressure for the access to new uses of the *baldio* upon payment of rent.

In 1976, the Political Constitution recognised the communitarian means of production as part of the public sector (and later, in 1982, as part of the cooperative and social sector). However, this new orientation was not peacefully accepted, first of all by the local authorities – parishes and municipalities, which lost their status as legal owners of the *baldios* accorded by the Civil Code of 1867 and, hence, the rents from forest exploitation. It is not surprising, therefore, that many Parish Councils delayed the elaboration of the census of commoners as much as they could to maintain those rents.[60] This dead-lock was only resolved in 1989, when the norms approved by the Assembly of the Republic that made the common lands part of the "public domain of the parish" and "transferred to the parish bodies the management of *baldios*" were considered unconstitutional.[61]

Strong opposition came also from those political forces that, in the liberal tradition, insisted to claim against the bad use of common lands. The divergence of views regarding the future of common lands has always been evident in the political debate and has manifested itself particularly sharply in these almost 50 years of the democratic regime. Over this time, dozens of proposals of law on *baldios* were presented and debated in the Parliament which, step by step, demarcated the positions of left-wing parties that supported the laws of 1976 and the Constitutional law that reassert the autonomy of commoners in the use the *baldios* from those of right-wing parties that advocate a tight regulation of the boards of "compartes" and the prediction of situations that lead to the extinction of *baldios* or the granting of their use to private persons or entities. It is important to bear in mind that the fate of projects has always depended heavily on the composition of political forces in Parliament.

Traditional and new uses of communal lands

Like other forms of popular resources that remained ignored for a long time, communal lands recently became the spot of state and market ambition. Both the regulatory regime designed by the state to frame the common land governance and the web of bondage ties engendered by the market to force communities to negotiate the lease of common lands came to reduce the room for manoeuvre and the ability of executive boards to maintain community freedom of decision. At the same time that the commons are being framed by legislation on forest management, fire prevention, or nature protection, private businesses offer tempting counterparts for the use of portions or all of the communal land for activities that have nothing to do with the economies of the commoners.

The leasing of parcels of common land for eucalyptus production to paper pulp companies, the access of strangers to areas of common land where they are allowed to hunt or to practice radical sports, the permission to install long-distance transmission antennas, wind farms, or photovoltaic panels for electricity generation,[62] and the concession to explore quarries to private companies are all examples of activities that transform the productive function of the commons into a mere rentier function.[63]

History allows us to look at these changes in a different way. Over time, communities had to adapt to new vicissitudes such as food shortages, increasing outmigration, the decline of the farming for subsistence system, imposition of intensive afforestation, or extracting the mineral from the soil. Therefore, we can find throughout the national territory a wide variety of ways of appropriating and managing common land, without, however, removing the communal nature of that land.

It is true that history also shows us that in many cases internal dissensions arise in communities, somehow resulting from the double face of communities mentioned by Paz Moreno Feliu (1996), pressing for privatisation of common land. Dissensions that, in part, were instigated from outside by those interested in individually appropriating the commons and, in part, came from within the communities themselves by those members who were more subject to ideological, political, and social forces that came from outside.[64] Today, when this pressure to use the *baldios* as the support for-profit activities is coming from everywhere, it is not surprising that those most disinterested, unmotivated, or even sceptical about the use of the *baldios* by the community feel attracted by the tempting offers coming from the outside.

Conclusions

This seems to be the more serious threat that the common land and commoners face today. The difficult compromise between the market and the community in terms of management options raises the question of knowing to what extent the strategic objectives assumed by the executive boards of *baldios* are recognised and legitimised by the different interest groups around the commons and, in particular, by the universe of the commoners. The National Confederation of Baldios addressed this question in these terms: "It is necessary to discuss the issues that divide commoners and use the greatest transparency (...) to overcome the conflicts" (Director of BALADI).

For the commoners, good management of common land is one that, in addition to protecting the community heritage, allows for life improvements that everybody may benefit from: the opening or maintenance/rehabilitation of roads, bridges, fountains, churches, and others; civic centres for recreational or cultural activities; social facilities aimed especially at children and the elderly; sports and leisure equipment; awards and incentives for community students; and distribution of firewood by the population.

Experience has shown that, where villagers have few direct benefits from the use of their commons, this pro-community strategy of the executive boards keeps people concerned with the commons and ensures a relatively high level of social cohesion. In many places, parties or activities that involve the population as a whole are organised, such as an "emigrant day", a "traditional music or dance festival", or an "assembly of the mountain peoples".

In many places, the executive boards of *baldios* use a communitarian strategy based on a) the exploitation of the commons resources, either directly or mediated through market agents in terms that make it possible to satisfy the main social needs of the community, through the investment of the earned rents on physical and social infrastructures; b) on the development of activities that make it possible to create local jobs, qualify skills, and fix the population; c) on the use of public policies, national or European, oriented towards the sustained development of local communities; and d) on cooperation with other similar or complementary organisations, benefiting from economies of scale to strengthen the position of common land before the state and the market.

The need to recover the legitimacy of the communal system implies in principle also a reinforcement of the social and solidarity economy inside the community[65] in different ways: first, by creating joint management of the *baldios* owned by different but close communities for increasing the scale (e.g. to use European structural funds for forestation or to reduce the costs of investment in infrastructure for tourism and recreation); second, by promoting initiatives that increase the participation and civic involvement of the commoners.

The future of the communitarian system will largely depend on the ability of neighbours to maintain their identity as commoners and to consider the *baldios* as an extension of their private ownership. If this is the case, the processes of change designed and conducted by the community itself and oriented, as in the past, towards improving the livelihood of residents will be accepted without any dramatic episodes of conflict. Otherwise, it will be very difficult to curb the commercial use of common lands and the total loss of autonomy of communities to avoid their degradation. The new common land uses that have been generated recently in Portugal are dominated by large corporations that do not care about the effects of their extractive action on the environment or respect the way of life and dignity of communities. And these effects, in the form of soil or landscape degradation, depletion of resources, noise and stress, and unsanitary conditions, are already taking place in many *baldios* through mining projects, wind farms or radio antennas, intensive eucalyptus plantations, radical sports, and mass tourism, with or without the agreement of communities.

Thus, where the processes of change are marked by a mercantile logic and the individual interests of the commoners overlap the collective interest, the sense of community vanishes or takes on imprecise contours, allowing the market dynamics tend to go beyond those traditional rules that seek to safeguard the aptitudes of common land. Where, on the contrary, those processes enlarge the opportunities to enhance the material and social capital of the community, then the diversity of skills and aspirations of neighbours will be absorbed and a high degree of autonomy in the use of communal land will be maintained.

Notes

1 This text is an extension of the author's work on the research project "Economías Transformadoras en un Contexto de Urgencia Ecosocial" coordinated by the Complutense University of Madrid (PID2019–106757GA-I00 // ECOEMBEDDEDNESS).
2 JCI (Junta da Colonizacao Interna): *Reconhecimento dos Baldios do Continente*, Lisboa, Ministério de Agricultura, 1939.
3 This designation covers barren and arid lands where there is only undergrowth.
4 Gerardo PERY: *Geographia e Estatistica Geral de Portugal e Colonias com um Atlas*, Lisboa, Imprensa Nacional, 1875, p. 107.
5 Armando de CASTRO: "Baldios", in Joel SERRÃO (org.): *Dicionário da História de Portugal*, vol. 1, Lisboa, Iniciativas Editoriais, 1971, pp. 277–282, esp. p. 280.
6 Fernando Oliveira BAPTISTA: *O Espaço Rural. Declínio da Agricultura*, Oeiras, Celta, 2010.
7 Roland BROUWER: *Planting Power: The Afforestation of the Commons and State Formation in Portugal*, Delft, P&L, 1995.
8 The etymology of the word baldio is controversial. The authors are divided into those who advocate an Arabic origin – "Baladi" which means arid, uncultured, useless – (Joaquim VITERBO: *Elucidário das palavras, termos e frases que em Portugal antigamente se usaram*, Lisboa, A. J. Fernandes Lopes, 1865; JCI: *Reconhecimento dos Baldios* ...) and those who advocate a Germanic origin - "bald" which still means in English bald, naked (Henrique da Gama BARROS: *História da Administração Pública em*

Portugal nos Séculos XII a XV, vol. IV, Lisboa, Tipografia Castro Irmão, 1922; Francisco José VELOSO: *Baldios, maninhos e exploração silvo-pastoril em comum. Estudo económico, histórico e jurídico*, Braga, Livraria Cruz, 1953).

9 Alexandre HERCULANO: "Breves reflexões sobre alguns pontos de economia agrícola. 1849", *Opúsculos*, VII, pp. 23–46.

10 Gumersindo de AZCARATE: *Ensayo sobre la Historia del Derecho de Propiedad*, vol. 2, Madrid, Imprenta de la Revista de Legislación, 1880, p. 88; Henrique da Gama BARROS: *História da Administração Pública em Portugal nos Séculos XII a XV*, vol. III, Lisboa, Tipografia da Academia Real das Sciencias, 1896, p. 22.

11 These "cartas de foral" were royal documents that granted the use and fruition of the lands temporarily or perpetually to settlers who agreed to cultivate them and keep them productive upon payment of retribution usually in kind: the "foro". Over time, this contractual device that jurists call emphyteusis was extended to secular or religious landlords who, being owners of the land, did not directly cultivate it.

12 Luís REBELO DA SILVA: *História de Portugal nos séculos XVII e XVIII*, vol. 3, Lisboa, Imprensa Nacional, 1867.

13 In Alentejo, the aim was, first, to settle as many villages as possible and to give each neighbour family its plot; second, to forbid the powerful landlords from enclosing large tracts of uncultivated land, and to order that those that have been enclosed become common pastures to be used by village neighbours; third, to divide uncultivated domains among those who want to cultivate it; fourth, to demarcate to each landlord the adequate portion of land necessary to support the cattle he/she had, or needed to have and to order the rest of the area to be removed of their domain (Luís REBELO DA SILVA: *História de Portugal* ... , p. 105).

14 In Entre Douro e Minho, the system adopted consisted of dividing the land into "casais" and distributing them to 10, 20, or 30 peasant settlers, each "casal" usually paying its "foro" in cereals, chickens, and money in addition to the "direituras" (small fix retribution), the personal services, the "lutuosa" (a payment to the landlord on the death of the cultivator), and often to the harvest. The "casal" was the basic unit for agriculture production composed of a dwelling house with land attached to it. Each "casal" corresponded to a sufficient portion of land for culture, plus some portion to be cleared for cultivation, "baldios" for pasture, and weeds for organic manure (Luís REBELO DA SILVA: *História de Portugal* ... , pp. 108–109).

15 In Trás-os-Montes, the system adopted was based on the granting of collective tenure to the neighbours of a rural community, who shared the costs of the "foro" among themselves. "The lands should remain commonly owned, and as soon as the number of neighbours increased, the general interest prevented anyone of them from appropriating the smallest part and considered almost as spoliation the land given to someone outside, or individually used by the neighbours" (Luís REBELO DA SILVA: *História de Portugal* ... , pp. 110–111).

16 Margarida SOBRAL NETO: "Biens et usages communaux au Portugal (1750–1950)", in Marie Danielle DEMELAS and Nadine VIVIER (orgs.): *Les Propriétés Collectives face aux Attaques liberales (1750–1914)*, Rennes, Presses Universitaires, 2003, p. 185.

17 Alberto SAMPAIO: "Estudos de economia rural do Minho. A apropriação da terra e as classes que constituem a população campestre", *Revista de Guimarães*, 4 (1) Jan.–Mar. 1887, pp. 21–38.

18 The baldios or "people's backyards" are distinguished from those uncultivated lands that are privately owned by the municipalities. There are still parcels of land inside the "baldios" that do not belong to all neighbours, but only to some of them and are transmitted by inheritance that results from an abusive appropriation of community lands by richer or more powerful neighbours (Armando de CASTRO: "Baldios" ..., p. 277).

19 António HESPANHA: *História das Instituições. Épocas medieval e moderna*, Coimbra, Livraria Almedina, 1982, p. 137.

20 According to liberal economic theory, common goods are non-exclusive use goods, i.e. goods whose access cannot be conditional, where two or more people may compete for the use of the same good. In the case of "baldios" the sustainability of their use became controversial until our days. It is worth remembering that 50 years ago, Garrett Hardin came to update the same argument: "The tragedy of the commons develops in this way. Picture a pasture open to all. It is to be expected that each herdsman will try to keep as many cattle as possible on the commons. Such an arrangement may work reasonably satisfactorily for centuries because tribal wars, poaching, and disease keep the numbers of both man and beast well below the carrying capacity of the land. Finally, however, comes the day of reckoning, that is, the day when the long-desired goal of social stability becomes a reality. At this point, the inherent logic of the commons remorselessly generates tragedy. As a rational being, each herdsman seeks to maximize his gain" and rationally concludes that "the only sensible course for him to pursue is to add another animal to his herd. And another; and another ... ", since "the negative effects of overgrazing are shared by all the herdsmen" (Garrett HARDIN: "The Tragedy of the Commons", *Science, New Series*, 162, 3859 (1968), p.1244). To avoid this tragedy, the coercive establishment of rules has been suggested: on the one hand, rules mutually agreed upon by most affected people; on the other hand, rules instituted by an "external agent" to whom individuals delegate this power (typically, the State, since Hobbes) and which may well lead to a policy of compulsive distribution of common areas in the name of market efficiency. However, this argument was debunked a few years later by those who recognised that there was an institutional dimension in the use of common goods, consisting of land use practices embedded use in belief systems, values, norms, and roles of the community that prevented overgrazing and other negative effects (Robert WADE: "The Management of Common Property Resources: Collective Action as an Alternative to Privatisation or State Regulation", *Cambridge Journal of Economics*, 11, 1987, pp. 95–106; Elinor OSTROM: *Governing the Commons: The Evolution of Institutions for Collective Action*, Cambridge, Cambridge University Press, 1990.b; Peter WAGNER: "Enablement and Constraint. Understanding Modern Institutions", *A Sociology of Modernity*, Pt. II, London, Routledge, 1994, pp. 19–33).

21 Jorge DIAS: *Rio de Onor - Comunitarismo Agropastoril*, Porto, Instituto de Alta Cultura, 1953; Antonio BICA: *Baldios. Quadro Histórico e Legal*, S. Pedro do Sul, Empresa Jornalística da Gazeta da Beira, 2010.

22 Joaquim OLIVEIRA MARTINS: *Quadro das Instituições Primitivas,* Lisboa, Guimarães e Cª Editores, 1953 [1883], p. 112.

23 Rogério Erhardt SOARES: "Sobre os baldios", *Separata da Revista de Direito e Estudos Sociais*, 14,1967, pp. 259–313.

24 A. H. de OLIVEIRA MARQUES: *Introdução à história da agricultura em Portugal: a questão cerealífera durante a Idade Média*, Lisboa, Cosmos, 1978.

25 Joaquin COSTA: *Colectivismo Agrario en España*, 2 vols., Zaragoza, Guara Editorial, 1983. The theme would be, in Portugal, treated by Oliveira Martins in the following terms: "Society, in its dynamism, moves between the two poles of individual property and collective property, more or less perfect: and the exclusive theories of communism and individualism are nothing more than utopian generalizations. Communism is the chimaera child of equality and solidarity, and individualism the chimaera child of the idea of freedom" (Joaquim OLIVEIRA MARTINS: *Quadro das Instituições* ..., p. 88).

26 Eduardo de HINOJOSA: *El régimen señorial y la cuestión agraria en Cataluña, durante la edad media*, Madrid, V. Suárez, 1905.

27 Rafael ALTAMIRA: *História de la Propriedad Comunal*, Pamplona, Analecta, 2018.

28 The people integrated into the Roman Empire who had a tribal organisation regime maintained their right to collective property, until the third century, when they began to have a fully agricultural-based economy; then, Roman law was extended to all provinces of the empire by Emperor Caracalla (Antonio BICA: *Baldios* ...).

29 For example, a) the work in the fields is done in common but the products are divided; b) plots are divided periodically between neighbours for individualised production (albeit frequently through mutual aid); c) the division of the parcels becomes permanent, but they cannot be individually sold (Antonio BICA: *Baldios* ..., p. 32.).

30 Rosa CONGOST and Pablo LUNA (eds.): *Agrarian Change and Imperfect Property: Emphyteusis in Europe (16th to 19th Centuries)*, Turnhout, Belgium, Brepols, 2018.

31 This property regime was abolished in 1976, immediately after the Carnation Revolution, having the direct domain transferred to the holder of the useful domain.

32 "Bens de mão-morta" or mortmain assets were those goods that escape the rules of transference by death because their owner has an indefinite existence. With the end of the Ancien Régime, these goods, including the rich land patrimony of religious congregations, were subject to the laws of "desamortização" or, in other words, were removed from their "mão-morta" status and sold at public auction.

33 Luís POLANAH: "Espírito do Comunitarismo", *Trabalhos de Antropologia e Etnologia*, 30, (1990), p. 65.

34 *Ibid.*, p. 69.

35 The *Ordenações* were compilations of laws ordered by the kings Afonso V in 1446–1448, Manuel I in 1521, and Filipe I in 1608, the latter being in force until the publication of the first Portuguese Civil Code in 1867.

36 Francisco José VELOSO: *Baldios, maninhos e exploração* ...

37 Carlos BASTIEN: "A divisão da história do pensamento económico português em períodos", *Working paper do Gabinete de História Económica e Social*, 16 (2000).

38 In his "Agronomic Memoir about the Municipality of Chaves", José Inácio da Costa, aware of people's opposition to the allocation of *baldios* for private use, proposes the mandatory cultivation of species valued by the market, such as flax and hemp, planting mulberry trees or other "yielding" trees on the edges of the land. In another memoir about agriculture in the Alentejo, António Henrique da Silveira proposes that, instead of the traditional system of annual allocation of parcels to the poorest neighbours, a definitive allocation to those more able to fully cultivate the land. Finally, in a Memoir on the *baldios* of Vila Nova de Ourém, Tomás de Villa-Nova Portugal advocates the definitive

distribution, by all residents, of the parts of the *baldios* that can be used for cultivation or for planting trees, leaving the rest of the land that is not suitable for agricultural or forestry production to the communitarian regime (PORTUGAL, Tomás de Villa-Nova: "Memória sobre a cultura dos terrenos baldios que há no termo da Vila de Ourém". In *Memórias Económicas da Academia Real das Ciências de Lisboa (1789–1815)*. Tomo II. Lisboa, Banco de Portugal, 1991 [1790], pp. 295–306).

39 Paolo GROSSI: "Le Proprietà Collettive Ieri, Oggi e Domani", in Claudia BERNARDI, Frencesco BRANCACCIO, Daniela FESTA and Bianca Maria MENNINI: *Fare Spazio. Pratiche del comune e diritto alla città*, Milano, Mimesis Edizioni, 2014, pp. 37–50.

40 Adrien BALBI: Essai Statistique sur le Royaune de Portugal et d'Algarve, Paris, Rey et Gravier Libraires, 2004, p. 162.

41 Adriano J. CARVALHO: *O Regime Florestal em Serpins: Exposicão e Critica*, Coimbra, Imprensa da Universidade, 1911; Armando de CASTRO: "Baldios" ...; Manuel RODRIGUES: *Os baldios*, Lisboa, Caminho, 1987; A. da Rocha PEIXOTO: "Formas de vida comunitária em Portugal", in VV.AA: *Notas sobre Portugal*, vol. I, Lisboa, Imprensa Nacional, 1908; Francisco José VELOSO: *Baldios, maninhos e exploração* ...; Albert SILBERT: "O colectivismo agrário em Portugal. História de um problema", Economia e Finanças, XXVIII, (1960), pp. 987–1057; ÍD: *Le problème agraire portugais au temps des premières Cortès libérales (1821–1823)*, Paris, Fondation Calouste Gulbenkian/Presses Universitaires de France, 1968; João Arriscado NUNES and Rui Graça FEIJÓ: "As Transformaçães dos "Incultus" no Noroeste (1750–1900). Uma Proposta de Reapreciação", *Cadernos de Ciências Sociais, 8/9* (1990), pp. 45–90; José TENGARRINHA: *Movimentos Populares Agrários em Portugal*, Lisboa, Publicações Europa-América, 1994.

42 A relevant source of information, worked on by the historian Albert Silbert, are the petitions presented to the Liberal Cortes (1821–1823) and which the Committee on Agriculture of these Cortes dealt with. Among these innumerable petitions, he identified 28 of them concerning communal lands ("maninhos" or *baldios*) throughout the country: some complaining about the abusive appropriation of the common land by landlords who hold the direct dominium, demanding from the users retribution for their use or alienating them, others complaining about the abusive occupation of the commons by the powerful ones with the complacency or connivance of the municipalities or of the local judges ("corregedores"). But the Cortes, dominated by the liberals, not only did not respond to complaints but also opened the way for the loss of autonomy of common lands by confirming the competence of the municipalities to promote the planting of trees in the common lands.

43 Alexandre HERCULANO: "Breves reflexões sobre ... ", p. 35.

44 Gerardo PERY: "Estatística Agrícola do Concelho de Barrancos", *Boletim da Direcção Geral de Agricultura*, 1 (1893), pp. 1–2.

45 A. da Rocha PEIXOTO: "Formas de vida comunitária ... ".

46 José B. de ANDRADE E SILVA: *Memoria sobre a necessidade e as utilidades do plantio de novos bosques em Portugal*, Lisboa, Academia Real das Ciências, 1815, p. 19.

47 Maria C. RADICH and António Alberto MONTEIRO-ALVES: *Dois Séculos de Floresta em Portugal*, Lisboa, Celpa, 2000.

48 Internal colonisation is a public policy oriented to the settlement of landless peasant families in areas removed from the use of the commoners, hoping to

increase the production of food for the market instead of just subsisting (Elisa L. da SILVA: "O Território da Colonização: Oliveira Martins e a Ordem Imaginada da Nação", *Actas del XII Congreso de la Asociación de Historia Contemporánea,* UAM Ediciones, 2015).

49 Through the clearing and cultivation of land that has not yet been cultivated, transforming uncultivated areas, cork forests, or pastures into cereal lands.

50 And also in other reformist thinkers such as Basilio Teles, Ezequiel de Campos, Quirino de Jesus, A. Lino Neto, E. A. Lima Basto, A. de Oliveira Salazar, Mário de Azevedo Gomes, Mário de Castro, Rafael Duque, Henrique de Barros, Mário Pereira and Eugénio de Castro Caldas (José Amado MENDES: "Portugal Agrícola ou Industrial? Contornos de urna polémica e suas repercussões no desenvolvimento (Sécs. XIX-XX)", *Revista de História das Ideias*, 18, (1996), p. 191.).

51 The official census of common land completed in July 1938 showed that there were 7,638 *baldios* at the time, with an estimated area of 407,543 hectares; 181 of them, with a total area of 79,451 hectares, susceptible to be used for internal colonisation (SNI: *Colonização Interna*, s/d., p. 76).

52 Roland BROUWER: "Changing Name-tags. A Legal Anthropological Approach to Communal Lands in Portugal", *Journal of Legal Pluralism,* 31, 1999, pp. 1–30.

53 José ESTEVÃO: "A florestação dos baldios", *Análise Social,* XIX, (1983), pp. 1157–1260.

54 Roland BROUWER: *Planting Power: The Afforestation of the Commons and State Formation in Portugal*, Delft, P&L, 1995.

55 Manuel RODRIGUES: *Os baldio ...*, p. 63.

56 The Decree-Law no. 39/76, of January 19.

57 "Baldios are those lands communally used and enjoyed by residents of a certain parish or parishes, or part of them".

58 "The residents who carry out their activity on the site and who, according to the uses and customs recognised by the community, have the right to enjoy it are part of the vacant land".

59 The Decree-Law n° 40/76, of January 19.

60 Antonio BICA: *Baldios ...*, p. 95.

61 Constitutional Court Decision No. 325/89, of April 4.

62 After the political decision taken in the late 1970s not to use nuclear energy in Portugal, massive public financial and tariff aid was invested to encourage other forms of renewable energy, namely wind energy and solar energy. In the case of wind energy, the installation of generators has tended to be in peripheral rural areas – mountainous, declining population and economically disadvantaged areas; often "baldios" – which function as market solutions for ecological modernisation and as accumulation zones for the "electric oligarchy" made up of large multinational corporations (Jaume FRANQUESA: *Molinos y Gigantes*, Madrid, Errata Natura, 2023.). This is despite unfavourable arguments regarding generators' impacts on the health of local populations, the lack of transparency of risk assessment procedures, as well as the visual intrusion into the landscape (Beatriz CHITO y Raúl CAIXINHAS: "A participação do público no processo de avaliação do impacte ambiental", *Revista Critica de Ciências Sociais*, 36 (1993), pp. 41–55.). In the case of photovoltaic energy, the process is more complex, since there are very relevant environmental aspects that condition its use. The main problem is the location of these photovoltaic plants, because the need to be located in large areas close

to the access points to the electricity network, can lead to conflicts about the type and size of the occupied land or the sensitivity in terms of landscape or nature conservation (Alexandra COSTA: "Energia: porque não aproveitamos o sol?", *Jornal de Negócios*, 14 (2021). Retrieved from the internet (https://www.jornaldenegocios.pt/sustentabilidade/ambiental/detalhe/20210414-1022-energia-porque-nao-aproveitamos-o-sol).

63 Fernando Oliveira BAPTISTA: *O Espaço Rural. Declínio da Agricultura*, Oeiras, Celta, 2010, pp. 58 and ss.

64 Paz MORENO FELIU: "Las dos caras de la Comunidad", in José Antonio FERNÁNDEZ DE ROTA Y MONTER (dir.): *Las Diferentes Caras de Espana Perspectivas de Antropologos Extranjeros Y Espanoles*, A Coruña, Universidad de A Coruña Servizo de Publicacións, 1996.

65 Fernando Oliveira BAPTISTA: *O Espaço Rural* ..., p. 82; Armando da Silva CARVALHO: *Baldio. Do Regime Florestal e Co-Gestão à Economia Local e Solidária*, Vila Real, BALADI; s/d.

References

ALTAMIRA, Rafael: *História de la Propriedad Comunal*, Pamplona, Analecta, 2018 [1890].

ANDRADE E SILVA, José B. de: *Memoria sobre a necessidade e as utilidades do plantio de novos bosques em Portugal*. Lisboa, Academia Real das Ciências, 1815.

ARES, José-Cândido Paz: *Régimen de los Llamados Montes de Vecinos em Galicia*, Vigo, Editorial Galaxia, 1966

AZCARATE, Gumersindo de: *Ensayo sobre la Historia del Derecho de Propiedad*, vol. II, Madrid, Imprenta de la Revista de Legislación, 1880.

BALBI, Adrien: *Essai Statistique sur le Royaune de Portugal et d'Algarve*, Paris, Rey et Gravier Libraires, 2004.

BAPTISTA, Fernando Oliveira: *O Espaço Rural. Declínio da Agricultura*, Oeiras, Celta, 2010.

BAPTISTA, Fernando Oliveira: "Prefácio à obra de Armando de Carvalho", *Baldio: Do Regime Florestal e Co-Gestão à Economia Local e Solidária*, Vila Real, BALADI, 2010.

BARBOUZE, Alain and RUBINO, Roberto (eds.): *Terres collectives en Mediterranee. Histoire, legislation, usages et modes d'utilisation par les animaux*, Roma, FAO, 1992. Retrieved from the internet (http://agris.fao.org/agris-search/search.do?recordID=XF19940094086)

BARROS, Henrique da Gama: *História da Administração Pública em Portugal nos Séculos XII a XV*, vol. III, Lisboa, Tipografia da Academia Real das Sciencias, 1896.

BARROS, Henrique da Gama: *História da Administração Pública em Portugal nos Séculos XII a XV*, vol. IV, Lisboa, Tipografia Castro Irmão, 1922.

BASTIEN, Carlos: "A divisão da história do pensamento económico português em períodos", *Working Paper do Gabinete de História Económica e Social*, 16 (2000).

BICA, Antonio: *Baldios. Quadro Histórico e Legal*, S. Pedro do Sul, Empresa Jornalística da Gazeta da Beira, 2010.

BROUWER, Roland: *Planting Power: The Afforestation of the Commons and State Formation in Portugal*, Delft, P&L, 1995.
BROUWER, Roland: "Changing Name-Tags. A Legal Anthropological Approach to Communal Lands in Portugal", *Journal of Legal Pluralism*, 43 (1999), pp. 1–30.
CABRAL, Manuel Vilaverde: *O Desenvolvimento do Capitalismo em Portugal no séc. XIX*, Porto, A Regra do Jogo, 1996.
CARVALHO, Adriano J.: *O Regime Florestal em Serpins: Exposicão e Critica*, Coimbra, Imprensa da Universidade, 1911.
CARVALHO, Armando: *Sobre a importância do Associativismo nas áreas comunitárias*, Vila Real, BALADI, 2020.
CASTRO, Armando de: "Baldios", in Joel SERRÃO (org.): *Dicionário da História de Portugal*, vol. 1, Lisboa, Iniciativas Editoriais, 1971, pp. 277–282.
CHITO, Beatriz and CAIXINHAS, Raúl: "A participação do público no processo de avaliação do impacte ambiental", *Revista Critica de Ciências Sociais*, 36 (1993), pp. 41–55.
CONGOST, Rosa and LUNA Pablo (eds.): *Agrarian Change and Imperfect Property: Emphyteusis in Europe (16th to 19th Centuries)*, Turnhout, Brepols, 2018.
COSTA, Alexandra: "Energia: porque não aproveitamos o sol?", *Jornal de Negócios*, 14 (2021). Retrieved from the internet (https://www.jornaldenegocios.pt/sustentabilidade/ambiental/detalhe/20210414-1022-energia-porque-nao-aproveitamos-o-sol)
COSTA, Joaquin: *Colectivismo Agrario en España*, 2 vols., Zaragoza, Guara Editorial, 1983.
DELICADO, Ana *et al.*: "Ambiente, paisagem, património e economia: Os conflitos em torno de parques eólicos em Portugal", *Revista Crítica de Ciências Sociais*, 100 (2013), pp. 11–36.
DIAS, Jorge: *Rio de Onor - Comunitarismo Agropastoril*. Porto, Instituto de Alta Cultura, 1953.
DIAS, Jorge: *Vilarinho da Furna. Uma Aldeia Communitária*, Lisboa, Imprensa Nacional/Casa de Moeda, 1983 [1948].
ESTEVÃO, José: "A florestação dos baldios", *Análise Social*, XIX (1983), pp. 1157–1260.
FRANQUESA, Jaume: *Molinos y Gigantes*, Madrid, Errata Natura, 2023.
GROSSI, Paolo: "Le Proprietà Collettive Ieri, Oggi e Domani", in Claudia BERNARDI, Frencesco BRANCACCIO, Daniela FESTA and Bianca Maria MENNINI: *Fare Spazio. Pratiche del comune e diritto alla città*, Milano, Mimesis Edizioni, 2014, pp. 37–50.
HARDIN, Garret: "The Tragedy of the Commons", *Science, New Series*, 162, 3859 (1968), pp. 1243–1248.
HERCULANO, Alexandre: "Breves reflexões sobre alguns pontos de economia agrícola. 1849", *Opúsculos*, VII (1898), pp. 23–46
HINOJOSA, Eduardo de: *El régimen señorial y la cuestión agraria en Cataluña, durante la edad media*, Madrid, V. Suárez, 1905.

JCI (Junta da Colonizacao Interna): *Reconhecimento dos Baldios do Continente*, Lisboa, Ministério de Agricultura, 1939.

LOPES, Elisa: "O território da colonização: Oliveira Martins e a ordem imaginada da Nação", in Pilar FOLGUERA *et al.* (coords.): *Actas del XII Congreso de la Asociación de Historia Contemporánea. Pensar con la historia desde el Siglo XXI*, Madrid, UAM Ediciones, 2015, pp. 6261–6276.

MENDES, José Amado: "Portugal Agrícola ou Industrial? Contornos de urna polémica e suas repercussões no desenvolvimento (Sécs. XIX–XX)", *Revista de História das Ideias*, 18 (1996), pp. 187–230.

MORENO FELIU, Paz: "Las dos caras de la Comunidad", in José Antonio FERNÁNDEZ DE ROTA Y MONTER (dir.): *Las Diferentes Caras de Espana Perspectivas de Antropologos Extranjeros Y Espanoles*, A Coruña, Universidad de A Coruña Servizo de Publicacións, 1996.

NUNES, João Arriscado and FEIJÓ, Rui Graça: "As Transformaçães dos "Incultus" no Noroeste (1750–1900). Uma Proposta de Reapreciação", *Cadernos de Ciências Sociais*, 8/9 (1990), pp. 45–90.

OLIVEIRA MARTINS, Joaquim: *Quadro das Instituições Primitivas*, Lisboa, Guimarães e Cª Editores, 1953 [1883].

OSTROM, Elinor: *Governing the Commons: The Evolution of Institutions for Collective Action*, Cambridge, Cambridge University Press, 1990.

PEIXOTO, A. da Rocha: "Formas de vida comunitária em Portugal", in VV.AA.: *Notas sobre Portugal*, vol. I, Lisboa, Imprensa Nacional, 1908.

PERY, Gerardo: *Geographia e Estatistica Geral de Portugal e Colonias com um Atlas*, Lisboa, Imprensa Nacional, 1875.

PERY, Gerardo: "Estatística Agrícola do Concelho de Barrancos", *Boletim da Direcção Geral de Agricultura*, 1 (1893), pp. 1–2.

POLANAH, Luís: "Espírito do Comunitarismo", *Trabalhos de Antropologia e Etnologia*, 30 (1990), pp. 63–82.

PORTUGAL, Tomás de Villa-Nova: "Memória sobre a cultura dos terrenos baldios que há no termo da Vila de Ourém". In *Memórias Económicas da Academia Real das Ciências de Lisboa (1789–1815)*. Tomo II. Lisboa, Banco de Portugal, pp. 295–306, 1991 [1790].

RADICH, Maria C. and MONTEIRO-ALVES, António Alberto: *Dois Séculos de Floresta em Portugal*, Lisboa, Celpa, 2000.

REBELO DA SILVA, Luis: *História de Portugal nos séculos XVII e XVIII*, 3 vols., Lisboa, Imprensa Nacional, 1867.

RODRIGUES, Manuel: *Os baldios*, Lisboa, Caminho, 1987.

SILBERT, Albert: "O colectivismo agrário em Portugal. História de um problema", *Economia e Finanças*, XXVIII (1960), pp. 987–1057.

SILBERT, Albert: *Le problème agraire portugais au temps des premières Cortès libérales (1821–1823)*, Paris, Fondation Calouste Gulbenkian/Presses Universitaires de France, 1968.

SIMÕES, Sara and CRISTÓVÃO, Artur: "Baldios no norte de Portugal: o papel da propriedade comunitária no desenvolvimento local", *Comunicação ao VII Congresso Português de Sociologia de 2012*. Retrieved from the internet (http://www.aps.pt/vii_congresso/papers/finais/PAP1190_ed.pdf).

SNI: *Colonização Interna*, Lisboa, Cadernos do Ressurgimento Nacional, 1945.

SOARES, Rogério Erhardt: "Sobre os baldios", *Separata da Revista de Direito e Estudos Sociais*, 14 (1967), pp. 259–313.

SOBRAL NETO, Margarida: "Biens et usages communaux au Portugal (1750–1950)", in Marie Danielle DEMELAS and Nadine VIVIER (orgs.): *Les Propriétés Collectives face aux Attaques liberales (1750–1914)*, Rennes, Presses Universitaires, 2003.

TENGARRINHA, José: *Movimentos Populares Agrários em Portugal*, Lisboa, Publicações Europa-América, 1994.

VELOSO, Francisco José: *Baldios, maninhos e exploração silvo-pastoril em comum. Estudo económico, histórico e jurídico*, Braga, Livraria Cruz, 1953.

VITERBO, Joaquim: *Elucidário das palavras, termos e frases que em Portugal antigamente se usaram*, Lisboa, A. J. Fernandes Lopes, 1865.

WADE, Robert: "The Management of Common Property Resources: Collective Action as an Alternative to Privatisation or State Regulation", *Cambridge Journal of Economics*, 11 (1968), pp. 95–106.

WAGNER, Peter: "Enablement and Constraint. Understanding Modern Institutions", *part II, A Sociology of Modernity*, London, Routledge, 1994, pp. 19–33.

3 Mutuality and Cooperation in the Transition to Modernity (Portugal, 1834–1934)

Joana Dias Pereira

Introduction

This chapter seeks to provide an overview of the first social economy organisations' origin and evolution in Portugal – the mutual societies and cooperatives – in the transition to modernity. It seeks to understand the historical relationship between continuous evolution and innovation within the institutions for collective action since the Ancient Regime's end and the social mobilisation process developed from 1890 until the imposition of corporatism in 1933. A joint analysis of these two processes is rare, despite their transversality to the different social economy organisations. This chapter argues that, from a historical perspective, they are closely related.

As we shall seek to demonstrate, the institutions for collective action evolution during the transition to modernity progressively substituted communal and corporative practices of reciprocity with regular and standardised practices of cooperation and mutuality. Furthermore, among this period's innovations stands out the grassroots associations' articulation of national and international movements and the inauguration of a new repertoire, the associational congresses. These meetings, joining popular strata, literate elites, and statemen, gave rise to innovations, such as clinical services federation, social pharmacies, or regional and national supply warehouses for cooperatives. There were also calls for public recognition and support for new organisations and social reform proposals based on a partnership between the State and civil society.

The institutional innovations allowing the expansion and translocal articulation of voluntary associations drew the attention of political elites, who were increasingly concerned with the emerging social question. Since the 1860s, multiple surveys on the phenomenon were developed to inform public policies. The collective perception of this opportunity to influence state intervention gave rise to an unprecedented civic participation and

DOI: 10.4324/9781003439554-4

social mobilisation process with the irruption of popular layers and claims into the public and political spheres.

This chapter thus crosses two distinct fields of research within the scope of which it is possible to observe the origin and nature of the social economy: the long-term institutional analysis and the process of social mobilisation survey. Concerning the first, renewed attention has been paid to institutionalised collective action in recent decades, with leading authors from distinct disciplines examining the nature and evolution of associations. It is worth highlighting the work of the Nobel prize winner Elinor Ostrom who consecrated the concept of *Institutions for Collective Action*, highlighting institutional details as determinants for common resources sustainability.[1]

Inspired by this model, historians have analysed and compared the norms that regulated the most enduring institutions.[2] In this field, the medieval commons and guilds have been the subject of numerous studies on an international scale, proving that they were institutions that spread globally and fostered technical and institutional innovation while ensuring social protection based on mutuality.[3] More recently, Tine de Moor analysed the evolution of the commons norms across Europe, arguing that periodic manufacture and sanctions-related rule innovation ensured this institution's resilience over the centuries.[4] Research on enduring mutual practices also highlights their adaptability to social, legal, and economic change in the contemporary period.[5]

In Spain, Fernando Largo Jiménez applied this theoretical model to the transition period in which the premodern brotherhoods gave way to the first mutual aid associations in the 19th century. The author underlines the importance of the institutional design inherited from the former for the latter's success, namely the small scale and the members' involvement in the production and distribution of services, which allowed costs to be reduced. In the first decades of the 20th century, larger institutions with more bureaucratised management overcame this model based on proximity and member participation.[6] Rafael Moreno Ruiz also analysed the transition between the institutions of the Ancient Regime and the 19th-century mutual aid associations. The author describes premodern reciprocity practices as an activity of social assistance rather than true welfare since subsidies were often of an indeterminate amount and granted only to poor confreres. In the 19th century, mutual assistance associations were substantially different, with consistent benefits predominating in sickness allowances, often accompanied by medical and pharmaceutical assistance and funeral services.[7]

The genealogical study of different mutual institutions in Portugal also suggests a direct relationship between the confraternal and mutualist movements.[8] Although institutional innovation in the transition to modernity has not been analysed transversally, as a past article has shown,[9] 19th-century cooperatives also provide new institutional arrangements to replace part of the old guilds' functions as quality control and price setting.

Social economy studies concerning this historical period gave much less attention to rural institutions than urban or industrial ones. Moreover, rarely are both contexts compared, like in Tine de Moor's survey on medieval commons and guilds.[10] While much literature attributes the ascendancy of modern mutualism to confraternities, there need to be more studies on the relationship between premodern and contemporary rural associations. However, the origins of the mutualist movement within peasant communities show the variety of mutual aid mechanisms based on reciprocity, created to share the risks associated with agricultural activities.[11] Modern associations, such as livestock mutuals,[12] were also related to premodern practices.[13] Tapia even argues that the pre-existence of commons facilitated the emergence of agricultural cooperatives in Spain.[14]

This process intersects another phenomenon of distinct but related nature, the process of social mobilisation during the liberalism crisis. Although rarely analysed together, some historians opted for distinguishing two periods, the *associative social moment* and the *associative political moment,* which enabled them to analyse the germination of the associative phenomenon in close relation to ancestral and informal forms of association and its subsequent politicisation under the impact of the modern state-building.[15] Literature exclusively on the latter is abundant, although focusing more on labour movement agency than other types of institutionalised collective action.[16]

According to this trend, in the 19th century last decades, recognition and government intervention boosted and encouraged the strengthening of social movements, what Eric Hobsbawm called the "democratisation of politics" – laws favouring association, surveys on living and working conditions, social regulations such as restricting the working hours of women and children, or protective measures against social risks, such as insurance against accidents at work, concessions which were inseparable from the international concertation of the labour movement in demand for social reforms.[17] The need for legal recognition and state support drove the federation of grassroots structures. As Craig Calhoun argues, although it is empirically proven that workers' solidarity is rooted in face-to-face relations, the State's growing intervention in the economic and social sphere forced workers to organise themselves on a broader basis.[18]

Some analyses focused on this process in Portugal, despite the need for more historical surveys. For example, António Costa Pinto and Pedro Tavares de Almeida argue that the expansion of the associative movement in this period is closely linked to industrialisation and urbanisation, concomitant with the rise of democratic movements like Republicanism and Socialism. They also argue that the lower middle classes and industrial workers played a crucial role in this process, with the mutualist associations, trade unions, and strikes, alongside civic movements such as the anticlerical or nationalist, being the most visible face of civil society emergence in Portugal.[19]

This chapter is divided into two sections that analyse the institutional evolution of grassroots associations and their translocal articulation and politicisation. The first reveals that modern associations arose from the incremental progression of communalist and corporative institutions, adapting to modern economic and social change. The second exposes how, in parallel with the State interventionist turn, the associational life expanded, assembled itself nationally and internationally, and drew up proposals for unprecedented social reform with significant political impact. For the institutional analysis, the institutions for collective action commitments, agreements, and bylaws dating from the transition to modernity were used. In addition, the associative press and the minutes of associative congresses were considered to explore the process of social mobilisation.

Institutional innovation in the transition to modernity

Rural communities' self-management experience dates back to the High Middle Ages, based on shared uses and resources (grazing land, water channels, among others) managed by informal institutions, such as neighbourhood councils.[20] Testimonies on these institutions include ethnographic observations of their survival in the mountainous areas during the 19th and 20th centuries. The diary of Father Manuel José Martins Capela, dated between 1891 and 1913, points to institutions with strict rules of cooperation and mutuality, although based on oral tradition. It described the presence of various common resources and shared working practices in which joint herding stands out.[21] Despite the evidence of their resilience, little is known concerning these practices' evolution during the transition to modernity. Written norms, formalised in the 18th and 19th centuries, were preserved in some parishes in Gerês, proving the existence of fixed norms regarding the frequency of assemblies, different governing bodies, elective processes, tasks performed in common, and sanctions applied in non-compliance. These rules also contemplate financial compensation for livestock losses.[22]

In parallel with this tendency to formalise the traditional customs of communal villages, an increasing number of agreements were formalised specifically concerning mutual livestock insurance. According to the agricultural engineer Bugalho Pinto, in communities where land and herding were shared when it was necessary to make deliberations or open the chest for livestock losses compensation, "the chief would summon the inhabitants by playing the Carrapita (shell), and soon everyone, men and women, would gather in the usual place in the open air".[23] However, from the end of the 18th century, written agreements began to spread in mountain areas with small and medium-sized properties, giving rise to mutual cattle associations.

Surveys are partial, but according to existing data, in the first decades of the 20th century, there were around 2,000 of these institutions in Portugal. Their proliferation occurred mainly in the north and centre of the country, in mountainous regions, and mainly among small peasants, i.e. in areas where the common property was divided.[24] The transcribed rules show institutional details demonstrating the commitment to common risks management, rigorously defined insured objects, compensation amounts and their gradations, verification procedures by elected members, and graded sanctions for non-compliance. It also outlined administrative positions and elective processes, their powers, and procedures for accountability. It was also foreseen that the funds raised would be monetary or in-kind, with the society responsible for selling them and lending them to members. Considering these clauses, Bugalho Pinto claims that mutual cattle associations pioneered mutual agricultural credit "when the Raiffeisen institutions had not yet set up mutual agricultural credit".[25]

One of the most relevant continuities in managing these societies of participation, as Fernando Largo Jiménez points out for the mutual aid societies of the 19th century, was the small scale and the participation of stakeholders in the regulation, supervision, and resolution of conflicts. As in the confraternities, the "visitors" were responsible for visiting the oxen and informing the management of their condition. The "andadores" (the ones who walk) were responsible for collecting the quotas and deciding whether or not the animal, through veterinary treatment given at the owner's expense, would recover from the disability resulting from the catastrophe.[26] Financial penalties were also foreseen for members who did not assume the positions to which they were elected without justifiable reason, not being obliged to "serve two years".[27] Moreover, it previews the expulsion of those who "behave recklessly against the indications of the present articles". The analysis of the various bylaws published by Bugalho Pinto reveals relevant innovations compared to the casuistic practice of compensating the loss through collections in assemblies convened for this purpose. The contributions could already be graduated according to the "fair value" of the insured oxen and the corresponding indemnities defined.[28]

Still, if in most societies the contributions were fixed and constant, in some, the losses could be shared "equally by all members, except for the those whose ox died", and the values could "decrease or increase according to the season, the general assembly being open to discussion and decision".[29] These variations show a process of transition from traditional customs to modern norms.

In short, as has been shown, communal customs in rural environments, which according to national historiography, date back to the High Middle Ages,[30] included practices of mutualism present in managing the risks inherent to herding. Comprising broader regulations of the so-called communalist societies, specific practices were formalised in cattle mutuals in the 18th century. Written formalisation of these customs of oral tradition points to the need for official commitments, with their subscription by participants and local authorities' recognition. This innovation may be related to the increasing privatisation of grazing land and rural exodus, which increased default risks.[31]

In the same period, we observe a process with significant parallels in the urban confraternal movement, linked to the corporate regime of arts and crafts, also threatened by the advance of industrialisation and capital markets.[32] Since medieval times, these institutions inserted different collective management bodies, such as the "Cabidos" (assemblies) and the "Mesas" (direction boards), with regulated competencies and functioning, together with the rights and duties of the confraternity members. As in community villages, members' management participation was valued, and heavy sanctions were foreseen in case of non-compliance. Confraternities had welfare functions associated with making suffrages, accompanying the deceased, and supporting brothers who fell into poverty through "alms". This support, however, was not detailed in the bylaws, nor were the nature and values of mutual help specified. Furthermore, they were exclusively aimed at the brothers who "fell into poverty", the support depending on the institution's financial situation, without guaranteeing the members.[33]

At the end of the Ancient Regime, these institutions revised various formalised norms in their commitments. A growing regularisation in the attribution of "alms" moved these practices away from charity to bring them closer to mutuality. The Brotherhood of the Blessed Saint Eloy case is emblematic since having reformed its bylaws in 1750 and again in 1793; it reveals that successive institutional innovations in granting aid were made during this period. The 1750 Compromise assumed mutual help in different circumstances of vulnerability in which confreres might find themselves but did not discriminate the nature or amount of this support. The same compromise, reformed in 1793, provided procedures of a modernising nature, making explicit the nature and value of the help given in a graduated way. Aid was no longer seen as alms for the "poor". Furthermore, it should be noted that the procedure for accessing confraternity aid depended in this latter compromise on medical opinion rather than on the discretion of the governing bodies.[34]

It is in this framework that the first modern mutualist associations emerged. Although the first "montepios" had an official initiative.[35] These previous innovations prove that this was not a top-down movement. Moreover, simultaneously with these providence institutions promoted by the State, new locally based and professional associations were emerging within the old premodern institutions.[36] Some of these *Montepios* were founded within the old brotherhoods, but the relief to which the brothers were entitled was statutorily discriminated, with fixed values depending on the different insured adversities.[37] These new institutions spread in Lisbon in the 1840s, reaching an expressive associative mass, as evidenced by the printed card of the Montepio de S. António de Lisboa, founded in 1843 and which in 1844 already had over 1800 members.[38]

At the dawn of the 19th century, the first professionally based mutualist experiences were recorded. The first normative document identified dates back to 1822. The rules regulating the workers' montepio at the Army Arsenal point to the formalisation of occasional mutual aid practices between work colleagues – when a member was incapacitated, each member contributed a fixed amount for four weeks. According to the conditions of admission, the new institution was open to masters, officers, apprentices, porters, and guards, showing a new trend contrary to corporate exclusivism, revealing a process of adaptation to the new industrial reality.[39]

From the 1850s onwards, the mutualist associations, both locally based and professional, spread across the territory, reaching almost 70,000 people associated with around 300 associations in 1876.[40] If, in the two main cities, the different trades tended to organise themselves autonomously, in the smaller agglomerations, the trend was towards creating associations open to "all individuals of both sexes when they met the conditions required by the bylaws",[41] which is not to say that exclusion factors were not present, namely those of gender.[42] Male exclusivism reveals itself above all in retained member relationships because the statutory rules tend to create possibilities for female participation, generally based on the family unit.[43] The main factor excluding women's participation was related to the membership fee value, which, when of equal value, became unaffordable for the female with lower salaries, which led women to found their associations.[44]

Statutory rules presupposed democratic administration, with the general assembly as the sovereign body[45] and the idea of equality in the individuals' relationship, establishing, alongside the duties, the same rights for all participants.[46] The former reinforced the collective commitment to democratic management, foreseeing the obligation to "serve the positions for which they were elected free of charge".[47] Moreover, members were compelled to participate in assemblies and elections, subject to sanctioning rules ranging from fines to expulsion. Effectively, members' participation was valued by avoiding what, in institutional theory, is called *free-riders*, i.e. those who benefit from collective action without getting involved in it.[48] The bylaws analysed also reveal a strong influence of the Enlightenment tradition in positivist practices, with costs and benefits being statistically calculated[49] but also expressive continuities concerning the confraternal movement. Among these is the maintenance of the *visitors* whose *noble task consists of visiting the sick members,*[50] as well as the *receivers, to receive members' weekly dues and jewels*[51] stands out.

The primary purpose of montepios and mutual aid associations was to provide for sickness and death.[52] They envisaged helping those who enroled "with a surgeon, apothecary and a pecuniary subsidy in their illnesses",[53] ensuring burial and support for widows and orphans.[54] They also included in their purposes economic cooperation, namely to "provide work for members"[55] and create mutual credit funds to "avoid ruinous usury".[56] In September 1854, the Centre for the Promotion of the Improvement of Working Classes (the first federation of mutualist associations in Lisbon) carried out a diagnosis of workers' associations.[57] Among the reported cases, the first attempts at economic cooperation, led by the Lisbon Tailors Association, stand out: a special fund was created for the "purchase of the trims necessary for the making of works on a small scale and in proportion to consumption"; by the Fraternal Association of Shoemakers, the largest association in the capital which ensured work for unemployed members; by the Working Association for Silk Manufacturers, which acquired three looms and started a "social industry"; or by the Fraternal Association of Manufacturers of Fabrics and Related Arts, to help the "unemployed comrades" produce towels, napkins, cotton strips, skirts, and woollen blankets.[41]

After the cooperative founding law was promulgated on 2 July 1867, the first bylaws submitted for legal approval reflected the craft community's tendency to build multi-functional institutions that would respond articulately to their different needs. The first cooperatives simultaneously sought to: "1° Contract with the appropriate establishments to supply the members with their work; 2° Buy raw materials from each member's industry to sell to the members; 3° Sell, on behalf of the members, the products of their work; 4° Loan money to members to build houses; 5° Carry out credit operations to the members benefit; 6° Create commercial kitchens on behalf of the society or by auction; 7° Buy a headquarters".[58]

These purposes reflect the artisan reaction to production, trade disarticulation, and the consequent loss of market control. They wanted to ensure the distribution of raw materials and goods, which the corporative rules precisely regulated, avoiding competition. They also sought to perpetuate the indissoluble union between the worker and his means of production, something that the corporative regulations prevented by limiting the number of officers that each master could employ.[59] In order to give up mercantile capital, investment in cooperatives was "formed by subscriptions and contributions, from individuals and associations".[60] It is not uncommon for the bylaws to define the objective of "Supporting new social industries".[61]

Cooperative societies founded in a rural context sought to support the production and sale of members' products by resisting the advance of capital markets. In regions where small property dominated, this associative formula was most used, providing family economies with new tools to acquire credit, raw materials, and tools, and the possibility of disposing of their surplus. The cooperatives in rural areas proposed to: "rent machinery to members with less capital and sell seeds"[62] and "supply machinery, raw materials, seeds and agricultural fertilisers".[63]

Among the maritime trades, the new associations that emerged to replace the old compromises sought to ensure that control over the means of production was maintained, facilitating access to credit and insurance. The Montepio dos Pescadores da Vila do Seixal, whose bylaws date back to 1851, had its purposes, in addition to "assisting in illnesses and convalescence, for themselves and their families, to make loans on pledges for the repair and manufacture of boats".[64] In other cases, in addition to helping in cases of disability, compensation was provided for material losses in shipwrecks.[65]

Although the first experiences were aimed at the productive sphere, the main typology disseminated from 1880 onwards among the emerging urban proletariat was consumer cooperativism "in order to cheapen as much as possible the respective products".[66] The models disseminated were inspired by the Rochdale pioneers and induced by legislation and promotion by the elites.[67] Nevertheless, during the liberalism crisis, the increasing cost of living induced the widespread of this institution for collective action both in urban and rural areas.

Like mutual societies, all cooperatives had democratic management. Positions were elected by secret ballot, with the general assembly being the highest governing body, in which all members who fulfilled their obligations could participate and vote, with restrictions on their eligibility usually relating to gender, age, or literacy. The elected bodies were the management and the supervisory board, who managed the society's activity and reported to the general assembly. Cooperatives were equal to mutual aid associations in terms of democratic management practices but with one specificity that should be underlined: they were divided concerning the distribution or application of profits, which could be divided according to the capital invested, consumption made in a mixed manner or committed to the progress of the society.

In summary, the analysis of institutional evolution since the end of the 18th century reveals incremental innovations at the heart of the pre-modern institutions with a local and professional base which gave rise to new associative typologies. These innovations were related to the need for greater formalisation and regularisation of welfare practices due to the advance of private property, the rural exodus in the countryside, and the progressive dissolution of corporative ties in the cities, calling into question the old agreements and commitments based on casuistic reciprocity. In the production sphere, innovations suggest a close relationship with the loss of control over the means of production by artisans, the advance of the monetarised economy and the process of urbanisation, and the consequent need for credit and consumption.

National and international networking

Alongside grassroots associations' institutional evolution, it is necessary to consider the top-down influences which implied other fundamental innovations in these social movements. In parallel with the incremental change of premodern institutions for collective action, new associative typologies, such as the scientific academies, emerged. Between the end of the 17th century and the beginning of the 18th century, these scholars' corporations proliferated in Portugal and the then colonies, launching a new positivist and developmental perspective and densifying transnational networks and transfers.[68]

The academic movement influenced the germination of new association types and practices of civic participation, such as patriotic societies and those dedicated to economic development. The former proliferated above all during the revolutionary process, mobilising the intermediate social strata – traders, military men, men of law, civil servants, intellectuals, and artisans.[69] The economic societies – agricultural, commercial, and industrial associations – emerged at the dawn of the 19th century, initially seeking to involve all sectors, including the working classes.

This movement was the first civil society movement to achieve a national and international scale, with the foundation in 1860 of the Royal Central Association of Portuguese Agriculture (RACAP) and its participation in transnational debates and institutions. The economic societies also inaugurated the creation of their communication organs in which they reported on associative progress and disseminated new knowledge through the reproduction of foreign articles sent by the corresponding members.[70] Of particular note was the purpose of providing a consultancy service to the government regarding the diagnosis of the national economy and the drafting of legislative proposals.[71]

Despite their predominant elitist composition, these institutions assimilated the new practices of mutuality and cooperation germinating among the popular grassroots associations. One example is the Portuense Industrial Association, in which the 1849 bylaws envisaged industrial design and technical training but also "the mutual aid that our nascent industry needs so much" and "the establishment of machines and instruments of common utility".[72]

Within this framework, the first translocal alliance of popular associations was founded, the *Centre for the Promotion of the Improvement of Working Classes* (CPMCL), federating the Lisbon artisans associations. The initiative came from philanthropists and reformers, men of science and public administration who saw in the new mutualist experiences a privileged field of observation and experimentation to elaborate new doctrines and policies of welfare and social assistance. The CPMCL *newspaper* developed the debate on the private initiative legal regulation and State's intervention in the social sphere.[73] Elites' interest in the institutional innovations forged among the artisanal and rural communities is also patent in abundant literature from the 19th century, describing the emergent practices of mutuality and cooperation, still serving as a source for studies on the history of the social economy.[74]

The economic societies also played a unique role in the Portuguese participation in the universal exhibitions and congresses movement.[75] Particularly after the 1848 popular mobilisations, the debates addressing the social question stood out in the international penitentiary, statistical, or charitable congresses. Within these forums, the grassroots institutional innovations described above had a prominent place.[76] Furthermore, the popular associations actively participated in this process. In 1862, CPMCL was invited to organise information on workers' associations to present at the Berlin Statistical Congress of 1863 (Rosendo, 1996, 466). In the same year, a CPMCL delegation went to the Universal Exhibition, where the III Congress of Beneficence was held.[77]

States' unprecedented attention to the institutional innovations forged within local-based and professional associations is verified alongside this process. The first official survey on the phenomena was developed in 1860, aiming to quantify and categorise membership and insurance.[78] The questionnaires and statistical analyses were repeated in 1866 and 1869, increasing the sample but not the general conclusions. The societies' financial equilibrium was precarious. The accumulated capital was small, requiring extraordinary funding mechanisms to meet fixed expenses. The problems of unsustainability were attributed to the lack of statistical knowledge, and it was recommended to draw up specific legislation to promote the organisation of associations on a "scientific basis".[79] This unprecedented interest in developing popular associations was perceived as a political opportunity to claim their recognition and public support.

The need to influence State's interventionist turn gave rise to a new typology of institutionalised collective action described by Cristian Topalov as machines manufacturing consensus.[80] In Portugal, an era of congresses[81] would be launched by the CPMCL, with the organisation of the first associative congress in Portugal, the *Social Congress*. Held between October 1865 and February 1866, it brought together 71 mainly mutual aid institutions. In addition to their delegates, various personalities linked to the regenerative movement were present.[82]

Innovation in collective action allowed for the circulation of new institutional models. The weekly session minutes analysis, published in *A Federação*, indicates that the central question concerning the congress members was their associations' sustainability and development. The chief proposal debated was the creation of a federation of mutual aid associations to boost economies of scale. Moreover, the relationship between the associative movement and the State was not neglected, being demanded a special law to regulate and promote mutual aid associations and the creation of a central committee in charge of "monitoring and proposing measures tending towards social improvements".[83]

The expectations created by State's interest were met with the launch of a new period of enquiries and diagnosis on associations and debates on the public policies that should frame them. In November 1866, two commissions were created by royal decree, one in Lisbon and the other in Porto, bringing together a broad set of politicians, academics, and activists to assess mutual aid societies' development and to propose the necessary official measures for their sustainability.[84] In the report published in the *Diário de Governo of* 31 March 1869, the Lisbon Commission diagnosed the movement and sought to outline the requested public policy guidelines. The diagnosis was not auspicious concerning the accumulated experience in the late quarter of the century since the mutualist associations had sprouted. A significant part of them was struggling with severe difficulties, and those that presented positive balances and capitalised funds were almost always due to the product of extraordinary receipts. According to the commissioners, the cause of the associations' unsustainability was that they were not organised on a scientifically studied base. The bases adopted for calculating the contributions were hypothetical or null and repeated in many societies, imitating the bylaws of others, thus multiplying the organisational defects. These calculations were particularly flawed as regards the average duration of pensions. The commission recommended that the associations submit their bylaws to government approval and that the State only provide tax and other benefits to those following scientific sustainability rules. It also argued that these societies should have refrained from paying pensions in old age or survival cases.[85]

In addition to the tendency to shape mutual aid associations' internal norms, the State promoted other institutional models. In 1867 the fundamental law of Portuguese cooperatives was promulgated, and associationism was enshrined as an original right of citizens by the Civil Code of 1867. The former legislator, Andrade Corvo, was part of the philanthropists' elites who advocated welfare following the 19th-century liberal spirit and gathered around the CPMCL.[86] These reformers aimed for social progress but feared social unrest and trusted workers' associations' effectiveness, specifically in the model inaugurated by the Rochdale pioneers. This was expressed in the opinion given by the *Committees on Commerce and Arts and Legislation*, meeting on the proposed law on cooperative societies: "We have come to cherish the hope that the working man, through his activity, foresight and moderation, will manage to satisfy his principal needs, and in this way not be burdensome to his fellow citizens".[87] The diploma's fiscal provisions demonstrate the real intention of favouring.[88] This intention was reflected in other government initiatives, such as the edition and distribution via CPMCL of an official collection of documents on cooperative societies, including Andrade Corvo's speech on the 1867 draft law, the commissions' opinion and a model of bylaws.[89]

The 1880s saw the resumption of the 1865 debates with the organisation of four *Portuguese Associations' Congresses* from 1882 to 1885. The organising committee had the objective of revisiting the 1865 proposals relating to the progression of associations, namely the idea of creating a federation of mutual aid associations' clinical and administrative services. The mobilisation for this forum was unprecedented, with 380 circular letters and advertisements published in the capital and provincial newspapers, ensuring the participation of 150 mutual aid, educational, recreational, agricultural, commercial, industrial, scientific, and charity associations. The creation of a permanent council was foreseen, in charge of the future congresses' organisation, including a commission to make up for the absence of official statistics that would enable the movement's progress on a scientific basis. The *Portuguese Associations' Congresses* also discussed the creation of other associative typologies necessary for economic and social progress, such as cooperative societies, a bank of associations, particular associations for disability, and school savings banks. These meetings meant a leap in scale for the movement, favouring the circulation of more associative models. Two departmental juntas, the North and the South, were created for the first time, with the former being represented at the International Scientific Congress of Welfare Institutions in Paris in 1883.[90]

As across borders, the 18th-century last decade and the first of the 19th century were marked by an unprecedented expansion and diversification of associational life and congress activity. The first associative typology to organise an autonomous meeting was the trade union one, in 1885, gathering 16 class associations and 2 cooperatives.[91] This was followed by mutual societies in 1890, bringing together 92 delegates from 46 associations and cooperatives in 1894, bringing together 18 cooperatives and 4 class associations. Despite this specialisation, the close relationship between the movements is ensured by the participation of the Portuguese Socialist Party, founded in 1875, in the three new associative branches.

Portuguese class associations' representation at the possibilist congress of 1889 in Paris[92] decisively influenced the mutualist movement, which took on a more demanding attitude as regards effective state intervention in the social sphere. At the 1890 Congress of Mutual Aid Associations, there were calls for a regulatory law, an arbitration court, tax exemptions, and support in the event of an epidemic crisis.[93] The congress resolutions also recommended a more significant public intervention in social assistance and welfare, creating a tax to subsidise the associations helping disabled people. As we shall see, this heralded a more expressive evolution of the international mutualist doctrine in the following decades. The congress conclusions also argued for the regulation of labour relations, namely the establishment of the eight-hour working day and the weekly rest period, the protection of female and child labour, and the employers' liability for accidents at work.[94]

This meeting demands political impact was reflected in the promulgation, during the congress itself, of the Decree of 10 February 1890, according to which the government was authorised to regulate the organisation of the mutual aid associations, to exercise a "beneficial" administrative supervision over them and facilitate as much as possible their "development" and "free expansion". Responding directly to the congress's demands, the decree sets out the following guidelines for the respective regulation: that the mutual aid associations were to be exempted from the house rent contributions; that the State would grant an accessible building for their headquarters; that pecuniary aid would be granted to the associations on the occasion of epidemics. Provision was also made for the creation of an arbitration court to regulate matters of mutual aid associations, with arbitrators elected by the associations themselves to sit on its organisation, as well as the regulation of work by minors and women in industrial establishments and hygiene and safety in workshops.[95]

At the dawn of the 20th century, official studies on mutualism development were deepened, maintaining the evaluation relative to the movement's precarious sustainability. Detailed surveys focused on the Lisbon case in 1901, the Oporto district in 1904, and Braga, Viana, Vila Real, and Bragança districts in 1907, recommending the adaptation of the quota and contribution regimes (Santa-Rita, 1901). In parallel, the mutualist associations put into practice the strategy debated since 1865 to mitigate the threat of unsustainability. Among the main resolutions of the mutualist congress of

September 1904 in Porto, the creation of Mutualist Pharmacy Leagues stands out.[96] The congress decided to organise with their pecuniary reserves the League of Mutualist Relief Associations of Oporto, opening in 1906 four pharmacies, one in each of the city's popular areas.[97] Vila Nova de Gaia associations also created their own League. According to the report presented in 1911, the pharmaceutical class tried to prevent the approval of their bylaws, which, however, were given the go-ahead in May 1906 and made good progress in the following years, bringing together six local associations. In July 1910, the League inaugurated its new headquarters, which included the League's pharmacy, consulting rooms, and a savings bank.[98]

In the 20th century first decade, international relations were deepening within the mutualist movement through the organisation of international congresses, in which Portugal has been represented since the second edition, in Liège in 1905. The central debate in these international forums was between the defence of an individual and a free welfare system, keeping the principle of freedom, or the adhesion to the German example of a compulsory system. The evolution was towards the principle of compulsory insurance and State subsidy.

The mutual aid movement's capacity to cover risks such as long-term illness or invalidity was also at the heart of international debates. At the last congress before the Great War and the first organised by the International Federation of Mutual Societies, in Roubaix in 1911, various national models were presented, being concluded that the State should be made responsible and that a public system should be organised, as provided for in the French law of 5 April 1910 on pensions. The mutualists argued that making the associations responsible for administering the public insurance system, whether against the invalidity or to ensure retirement, was the best guarantee of effectiveness and stakeholders' participation and supervision.[99] It should be remembered that this debate around state intervention was contemporary with the international congresses on accidents at work and social insurance, organised from 1889 to 1914 through the Permanent International Committee for Social Insurance (CPIAS), in which the reflections on the international harmonisation of social protection legislation were also deepened.[100]

With the Republic's implementation in 1910, one of the political trends influencing and mobilising social economy organisations in the previous decades came to power. Chaired by the first president of the Portuguese Republic, Teófilo Braga, and with the participation of various new executive members, the 1911 National Congress of Mutual Societies, in which cooperatives were also represented, with a total of 304 associations, took on an almost official nature. Álvaro Garrido and David Pereira argue that in the Republican period, the significant advances in social reform resulted, above all, from proposals conveyed by the mutualist movement due to the intense cooperation and overlap between the Republican political leaderships and the mutualists.[101]

The congress resolutions were the corollary of all the reflections developed in this period of mutualism emergence and met the international trends. Congress members defended the creation of disability and retirement funds, with compulsory contributions, management by the associations, States, and employers subsidisation. It is worth highlighting that although explicitly demanding State intervention, the mutualists did not neglect the process of democratic control by the mutual societies. They proposed the creation of elected commissions to manage the insurance funds and the creation of a "general board, which will be in charge of preparing all social legislation and directly supervising its compliance". They did not fail to stress the need to respect "the good principles of a pure and healthy democracy".[102]

In addition to social protection, the consumers' defence was also undertaken in the National Congress of Mutual Societies in 1911 by defending the annulment of consumption taxes and their replacement with direct taxes on assets and incomes. The same thesis highlighted the cooperative movement's role in combating the mill lobbying and food quality falsification and proposed the federation of cooperative societies.[103]

The social economic movement's institutional innovations profoundly impacted Modern State-building in the following years. The National Federation of Mutual Aid Associations (FNASM) was founded at this congress to promote the defence of all rights concerning federated associations enshrined in the laws and to study "all questions of interest to mutuality in our country".[104] The federation's existence was deeply linked to republican social doctrine and policies. In 1916 the Ministry of Labour and Social Welfare was created, to which several FNASM leaders were co-opted, and the National Welfare Council, where the federation was represented. In the same year, FNASM organised a second national congress attended by the President of the Republic and several government members. The memoir "The Creation of Compulsory Social Insurance"[105] was presented at this congress, announcing the law of May 1919.[106]

According to this later, compulsory social insurance covered illness and disability, accidents at work, old age, and survival. At the same time, the Institute of Compulsory Social Insurance and General Provident Insurance (ISSOPG) was created, the coverage for work-related disasters was extended, and social labour exchanges were created. The ISSOPG, for which once again several mutualist and cooperative leaders had been co-opted, had as its first mission the propaganda of a compulsory social insurance system among mutual societies, given that the law aimed to complete the coverage of free associations, which were planned to assume a prominent role in the new regime.[107] This propaganda was intended to convert the free mutual societies into compulsory mutual societies and create new associations in the municipalities where these did not exist. The latter was created through civic mobilisation by creating local installation commissions.[108]

It is noteworthy that the post-war period, in addition to the increasing politicisation, was also when the mutualist and cooperative movements reached their climax in terms of membership, with mutual-aod societies exceeding 600,000[109] members and cooperatives 120,000 members,[110] associates. On the other hand, internationally, social protection was at the centre of post-war policies, with the Peace Treaty imposing on the International Labour Organisation the task of improving living conditions and listing some of the risks that should be covered by social insurance: "the protection of the worker against illness, accident and invalidity arising out of his employment; (...) provision for old age and invalidity". Public social insurance systems were being built or strengthened throughout Europe. The ILO published several studies on the different models in different national contexts, and recommendations were approved on protection for unemployment (1919 and 1920), industrial accidents (1921 and 1924), and maternity (1919 and 1924).[111]

At the same time, in 1920, the idea of organising a National Federation of Cooperatives that could regulate the markets, as proposed by the 1911 Congress, took shape through the direct intervention of the ISSOPG. The cooperative movement had "illustrious and dedicated co-operators" within the State apparatus and namely in the Ministry of Labour, such as Andrade de Saraiva.[112] He proposed to the ISSOPG Board of Directors the creation of a federation of cooperatives "not only to lift the national economy but also to defend it against speculation". To this end, all consumer cooperatives were notified of the advantages and convenience of forming a federation and invited to submit their suggestions on the best way to set up the federation mentioned above.[113]

The new associative network emerged in a heightened livelihood crisis and intense social polarisation, reflected in the theses approved at the *1st Cooperative Congress in* June 1921. Concerning internal organisation, FNC was meant to function as a great central warehouse allowing the cooperatives to compete with the "large capitalist organisations". The cooperative movement intervention in solving the housing problem and in support of small peasants was also foreseen.[114] Tax exemption stood out among the co-operators political demands.[115]

Congress approved, however, a set of theses that go far beyond these purposes. In the thesis, *The FNC in Its Relations with the Current Situation of Portuguese Society,* the President of the new organisation defended: "war contribution to the newly rich, progressive direct taxes, reduction of unproductive expenses, use of German indemnities for a large work of material and moral promotion (...) de-commercialise and demonopolise the necessities, socialise some factories and agriculture".[116]

In January 1922, *A Acção Cooperativa (Cooperative Action)* appeared as the *organ of the National Federation of Cooperatives* to lead a "national movement" against the "foreign-owned oligarchies" responsible for "the current serious crisis". *Cooperative action* invites "class associations, universities, schools, scientific and literary societies" to collaborate in a "redemptive national action" in which cooperatives should have a central role – "alongside its intense propaganda, it will promote the foundation of new cooperatives and seek to give birth to a true cooperative movement, and with all these elements thus excited and conjugated the FNC will strengthen and develop both under the aspect of economic defence against the famine of life, and under that of moral defence and progress".[117]

State's increasingly interventionist orientation escorted the movement's radicalisation to combat speculation riffing in this period. The *Social Welfare Bulletin*, an organ of the Ministry of Labour, condemned the rise in prices, denouncing it as a speculative manoeuvre organised by the preponderant elements in commerce and industry.[118] In response to this situation, the Minister of Agriculture invited the "FNC President to set up an autonomous body with sufficient resources to combat the high cost of living", together with the President of the Agricultural Unions and the Director of Military Maintenance. According to *Ação Cooperativa*, however, "the difficulties arising on the part of the lively hoarding forces, which intrigued and manoeuvred with terror", managed to "finally abort it completely", as well as the government itself.[119]

In effect, the conservative reaction prevented the post-war social reforms implementation, which the governments of the Republican left had sought to implement in partnership with the social economy organisations. In addition to the inflation concertation maintenance, the industrial, commercial, and agricultural associations also articulated themselves on a national scale to promote joint political intervention. In their congresses, which they also organised prolixly during this period, was defined a common strategy of refusal to comply with the new social legislation, such as the eight-hour working day or the contribution to the Compulsory Social Insurance.[120] In this sequence, the 1926 military coup signified the inflexion of the long-lasting process. The social economy experiences and social reformers' debates and proposals allowed the consensus and testing of Portugal's first public social protection system.

In short, the top-down institutional innovations, namely national articulation and political intervention, ensured unprecedented organisational resources for popular strata civic participation and the collective construction of impactful proposals for social reform. As a result, social mobilisation started in the mid-19th century, deepened from 1890 onwards, and reached its climax in the post-war period. However, the conservative reaction determined an unfavourable outcome to the reforms proposed by social economy organisations.

Conclusion

This chapter was intended to cross two research tendencies on the social economy origin, institutional analysis, and the social mobilisation process. It was expected that the long-term enquiry allowed to highlight the connexions between two historical processes that market the transition to modernity – the emergence of new forms of institutionalised collective action – namely modern associational life – and what Eric Hobsbawm called the "democratisation of politics" – the conversion of an oligarchical liberal regime into mass politics. The results of the first section align with the studies cited above concerning the premodern institutions for collective action resilience and institutional adaptability. The second section confirms the analyses of the process of political democratisation preceding and succeeding the First World War.

The long-term analysis of the social economy origin and development revealed that institutional innovation was determined by the intersection of bottom-up and top-down movements during this period. The innovations illustrated were distinguished between those forged within premodern institutions at a grassroots level and those disseminated among transnational academic networks, the economic elites, and the State. Among the first, new norms assuring reliable insurance and cooperation stood out. Within the second associations national and international coalition, the movement's intervention in the public sphere, primarily through the press and in the political arena, namely through the organisation of congresses, were the main innovations.

The long-term analysis also revealed a close relationship between institutional evolution and the process of social mobilisation. Connections between the two were surprisingly more significant than expected. The literate and political elites debated incremental innovation at the grassroots level, namely in congresses focusing on the social issue. In turn, these meetings and the overall academic networks favoured the circulation of new institutional models. State intervention in the social sphere first addressed institutional innovations by creating special commissions to study the new associations' norms and propose accurate legal regulations to improve the institutional design. In turn, State attention to innovative experiences at the grassroots level, reflected in surveys and legislative proposals, boosted the movement's national articulation to demand recognition and public support.

Moreover, the grassroots associations' national and international federations allowed for the debate and experimentation of other relevant innovations, such as the federation of clinical and administrative services of mutual societies or the cooperative supply warehouses. Finally, these experiments denounced the limitations of private initiative in the universalisation of social protection, the regulation of markets, and the redistribution of wealth. Without neglecting the war economy's impact, revealing the available legal instruments, the evolution of mutualist and cooperative experiences was fundamental in broadening the consensus around State interventionist the economic and social spheres.

These results should be interpreted cautiously because some profound transformations in this period appear only as background due to analytical options. For example, more research is needed to address the relationship between institutional innovation in rural communities, agricultural and food market transformations, artisan guilds, and industrialisation progress. Another gap in this chapter, filled in previous studies, is the relationship between social economy organisations and the emerging labour movement.

Nevertheless, its results suggest that the transition to modernity was a period of intense institutional innovation, deeply related to the origin and rapid expansion of the modern social economy and its emergence in the public and political sphere. Moreover, these results show that institutional evolution in this period has to be assessed at different scales and considering the political process. These new insights into the relationship between the social economy grassroots, national and international developments, and its relationship with the State intend to stimulate the dialogue between two separate research trends. Future studies should deepen these connections to further the intelligibility of the overall historical process.

Notes

1 Elinor OSTROM: *Governing the Commons: The Evolution of Institutions for Collective Action*, 1st. ed., Cambridge, Cambridge University Press, 1990. Retrieved from the internet (https://www.cambridge.org/core/product/identifier/9780511807763/type/book).

2 Tine DE MOOR: "The Silent Revolution: A New Perspective on the Emergence of Commons, Guilds, and Other Forms of Corporate Collective Action in Western Europe", *International Review of Social History*, 53, S16 (2008), pp. 179–212.

3 Jan LUCASSEN, Tine DE MOOR and Jan Luiten VAN ZANDEN: "The Return of the Guilds: Towards a Global History of the Guilds in Pre-industrial Times", *International Review of Social History*, 53, S16 (2008), pp. 5–18. Retrieved from the internet (https://www.cambridge.org/core/product/identifier/S0020859008003581/type/journal_article).

4 Tine DE MOOR et al.: "Taking Sanctioning Seriously: The Impact of Sanctions on the Resilience of Historical Commons in Europe", *Journal of Rural Studies*, 87 (2021), pp. 181–188. Retrieved from the internet (https://linkinghub.elsevier.com/retrieve/pii/S0743016721002333).
5 Marco H. D VAN LEEUWEN: *Mutual Insurance 1550–2015: From Guild Welfare and Friendly Societies to Contemporary Micro-Insurers.*, Palgrave Macmillan, 2017.
6 Fernando larGO JIMÉNEZ: "Institutional Factors in the Decline of Spanish Workers' Mutualism. The Case of Barcelona in the First Third of the 20th Century", *International Journal of the Commons*, 10, 2 (2016), p. 642.
7 Rafael MORENO RUIZ: "La génesis del mutualismo moderno en Europa", *Revesco: Revista de Estudios Cooperativos*, 72 (2000), pp. 199–214.
8 Vasco ROSENDO: *O mutualismo em Portugal: dois séculos de história e suas origens*, Lisboa, Montepio Geral, distribuição, Multinova, 1996; Álvaro garrido and David pereira: *A economia social em movimento: uma história das organizações*, 1st. ed., Lisboa, Tinta da China, 2018.
9 Joana Dias PEREIRA: "Resilient Alliances: Portuguese Cooperative Movement in the Transition to Modern Times (1867–1933)", *REVESCO: Revista de Estudios Cooperativos*, 128 (2018), pp. 59–75.
10 Tine DE MOOR, "The Silent Revolution ... ", pp. 179–212.
11 Alan R. H BAKER: *Fraternity among the French Peasantry: Sociability and Voluntary Associations in the Loire Valley, 1815–1914*, Cambridge, Cambridge University Press, 2004.
12 Stephen MATTHEWS: "Insurance and Plague in the Mid-Nineteenth Century", *The Agricultural History Review*, 2, 53 (2005), pp. 192–211.
13 Jerònia PONS-PONS and Juan CARPIO-ELÍAS: "Evolución de la gestión del riesgo en el sector agrario español: De la economía preindustrial a los seguros", *Historia Agraria Revista de agricultura e historia rural*, 2020. Retrieved from the internet (http://www.historiaagraria.com/FILE/articulos/RHA81_pons-carpio.pdf).
14 Francisco J. BELTRAN TAPIA: "Commons, Social Capital, and the Emergence of Agricultural Cooperatives in Early Twentieth Century Spain", *European Review of Economic History*, 16, 4 (2012), pp. 511–28.
15 Franco RAMELA: *Storiografia francese e italiana a confronto sul fenomeno associativo durante XVIII e XIX secolo. Atti delle giornate di studio promosse dalla Fondazione Luigi Einaudi (Torino, 6 e 7 maggio 1988)*, Turim, Fondazione Luigi Einaudi, 1990, pp. 171–178.
16 Robert S. ALEXANDER: *Europe's Uncertain Path, 1814–1914: State Formation and Civil Society*, Chichester, John Wiley and Sons, 2012; Benjamin ZIEMANN and Thomas MERGEL (eds.): *European Political History 1870–1913*, Aldershot, Burlington, VT, Ashgate, 2007.
17 E. J. HOBSBAWM: *A era dos impérios: 1875–1914*, São Paulo, Paz e Terra, 2010.
18 Craig J. CALHOUN: *The Roots of Radicalism: Tradition, the Public Sphere, and Early Nineteenth-century Social Movements*, Chicago; London, University of Chicago Press, 2012.
19 António COSTA and Pedro TAVARES: "On Liberalism and Civil Society in Portugal", in Nancy Gina BERMEO and Philip G. NORD (eds.): *Civil Society Before Democracy: Lessons from Nineteenth-century Europe*, Lanham, MD, Rowman & Littlefield Publishers, 2000, pp. 3–21.

20 Margarida SOBRAL NETO: *O universo da comunidade rural: época moderna*, Coimbra, Palimage, 2010.
21 Tude SOUSA: "Comunalismo na Serra", *Terra portuguesa: revista ilustrada de arqueologia artística e etnografia*, 32–33 (1922), pp. 99–100.
22 Tude SOUSA: *Costumes e Tradições Agrícolas do Minho: Regímen Pastoril dos Povos da Serra do Gerês*, Porto, Imprensa Portuguesa, 1908.
23 Virgilio Bugalho PINTO: *Do seguro mútuo de gado: estudo monográfico, estatístico e crítico das associações mútuas locais encontradas no distrito de Viana do Castelo em 1915*, Coimbra, Imprensa da Universidade, 1920, p. 454.
24 Miguel Maria BELO: "Associações de Seguros de Gado", *Boletim do Ministério da Agricultura*, 1931.
25 Virgilio Bugalho PINTO: *Do seguro mútuo de gado: estudo monográfico, estatístico e crítico das associações mútuas locais encontradas no distrito de Viana do Castelo em 1915*, p. 76.
26 Antazude Oxen Agreement of 29 June 1895 (Inquiry into Mutual Cattle Insurance Associations, 1936: 52–54).
27 Agreement of the Association belonging to the Associated Farmers of the Parish of Santa Cristina de Meadela founded on 23 January 1865.
28 Bylaws of the Agricultural Society of the Parish of Santa Maria de Portuzelo from 1885.
29 Agreement of the Farmers of the Parish of Santa Cristina de Meadela Association, founded on 23 January 1865.
30 Margarida SOBRAL NETO: *O universo da comunidade rural: época moderna*, Coimbra, Palimage, 2010.
31 Margarida SOBRAL NETO: "As estruturas agrárias: a força da tradição", *Revista de História*, X (1990), pp. 129–135; ÍD: "Propriedade e usos comunitários em Portugal", in Márcia MOTTA and Mónica PICCOLO (orgs.): *Domínio de outrem: Posse e propriedade na era moderna (Portugal e Brasil)*, S. Luís do Maranhão, São Luís, Guimarães: Editora UEMA (Universidade Federal do Maranhão) & Nós Por Cá Todos Bem, 2017, pp. 13–30. Retrieved from the internet (http://hdl.handle.net/10316/84810); ÍD: "A população de mira e a desamortização dos baldios na segunda metade do séc. XIX", *Revista Portuguesa de História*, 19 (1982), pp. 15–58.
32 Miriam HALPERN PEREIRA: *Do estado liberal ao estado-providência: um século em Portugal*, Bauru, SP; Lisboa, EDUSC; FCT, CEHC-IUL, 2012.
33 Ana Catarina SIMÃO: "Introdução ao Estudo das Confrarias Corporativas do Porto", unpublished Mestrado, Porto, Faculdade de Letras da Universidade do Porto, 1996. Retrieved from the internet (https://ler.letras.up.pt/uploads/ficheiros/2462.pdf).
34 Ministry of the Kingdom, Ecclesiastical Affairs, Brotherhoods' Bylaws and Commitments, Ministry of the Kingdom, book 197, fl. 13v–14. National Archives, Torre do Tombo.
35 The first montepio created in Portugal was an official one, among the military, on 16 December 1790. It was followed by the montepios of the Companhia da Porta do Terreiro da Cidade de Lisboa (1803), the Secretarias de Estado (1835), and the Alfândega das Sete Cidades (1836), also under state supervision. The exceptions in the organisation of these institutions within the public administration, due to their voluntary nature and private initiative, were undoubtedly the Montepio Literário (1816), founded by official or private teachers, and the Montepio Geral (1840), by civil servants

and later extended to the general population, offering pensions to members and families, mutual life insurance, and pawnbroking loans.
36 Vasco ROSENDO: *O Mutualismo em Portugal ...*
37 Bylaws of the Montepio da Irmandade do Santíssimo Sacramento.
38 Bylaws of Montepio de S. António de Lisboa of 1843.
39 José COSTA GOODOLPHIM: *A Previdência: Associações de Socorros Mútuos, Cooperativas, Caixas de Pensões e Reformas, Caixas Económicas*, Lisboa, Imprensa Nacional, 1889.
40 José COSTA GOODOLPHIM: *A Associação*, Lisboa, Imprensa Nacional, 1876.
41 Bylaws of the Associação de Socorros Mútuos Humanitária das Classes Laborariosas do Porto e Funeral Familiar Montepio of 1877.
42 Bylaws of the mutual aid and funeral association of the working classes of the municipality of Valongo of 1899.
43 Historical Archive of the Directorate-General for Trade and Industry. Process of Montepio Artístico Tavirense, 1858–1904.
44 Virginia BATISTA: "As Mulheres e o Mutualismo – do final da Monarquia ao Estado Novo", in Eduarda ferreira *et al.* (ed.): *Percursos Feministas: Desafiar os Tempos,* Lisboa, UMAR, 2014.
45 Bylaws of the Montepio Firmeza of 1849.
46 Bylaws of the Montepio da Nossa Senhora da Caridade da freguesia da Sé of 1852.
47 Bylaws of the Society of the Montepio Jesus Maria José of 1844.
48 Elinor OSTROM: "Collective Action and the Evolution of Social Norms", *Journal of Economic Perspectives*, 14, 3 (2000), pp. 137–58. Retrieved from the internet (https://pubs.aeaweb.org/doi/10.1257/jep.14.3.137).
49 Bylaws of Montepio Firmeza of 1849.
50 Historical Archive of the Directorate-General for Trade and Industry. Process of the Associação dos Artistas de Bragança, 1865–1899.
51 Historical Archive of the Directorate-General for Trade and Industry. Process of the Associação dos Artistas e Classes Laboriosas de Setúbal de 1861–1891.
52 Bylaws of the Mutual Aid Montepio Association were installed in Lisbon on 30 September 1842.
53 Montepio Firmeza Bylaws of 1849.
54 Historical Archive of the Directorate-General for Trade and Industry. Process of the Montepio Artístico Tavirense de 1872–1899.
55 Historical Archive of the Directorate-General for Trade and Industry. Process of the Associação Protetora dos Artistas de Faro, 1855–1899.
56 Bylaws of the Montepio de S. António de Lisboa of 1843.
57 *Jornal do Centro Promotor dos Melhoramentos das Classes Laboriosas*, 16 May 1854.
58 Bylaws of the Sociedade Cooperativa e Caixa Económica do Porto, 15 May 1872.
59 Franz-Paul LANGHANS: *As corporações dos ofícios mecânicos: subsídios para a sua história: com um estudo do Prof. Doutor Marcello Caetano*, Lisboa, Imprensa Nacional, 1943.
60 Bylaws of the Cooperativa de Chapeleiros, *Diário do Governo,* 20 January 1876.
61 Bylaws of the Indústria Social, 11 September 1873.
62 Bylaws of the Caixa Económica Azambujense, 2 March 1878.

63 Bylaws of the Cooperativa de Produção e Consumo Silvense, 24 November 1886.
64 Process of the Montepio dos Pescadores da Vila do Seixal, 1851.
65 Bylaws of the Montepio dos Pescadores, Artistas e Agricultores da Póvoa do Varzim, 1872.
66 Bylaws of the Sociedade Cooperativa Montemorense, 11 January 1918.
67 Dulce FREIRE and Joana Dias PEREIRA: "Consumer Cooperatives in Portugal: Debates and Experiences from the Nineteenth to the Twentieth Century", in Mary HILSON, Silke NEUNSINGER and Greg PATMORE (eds.): *A Global History of Consumer Cooperation since 1850: Movements and Businesses*, Leiden Boston, BRILL, 1917, pp. 296–325.
68 José Silvestre RIBEIRO: *RIBEIRO, José Silvestre, 1807–1891 Historia dos estabelecimentos scientificos litterarios e artisticos de Portugal nos successsivos reinados da monarchia*, 19 vols, Lisboa, Academia de Ciências de Lisboa, 1871.
69 Maria Alexandre LOUSADA: "O "espírito de associação" em Portugal. Dinâmica social e legislação (1820–1926)", in Luisa VELOSO *et al.*: *Anarquismo, Trabalho e Sociedade. Livro de homenagem a João Freire*, Lisboa, Almedina, 2017, pp. 97–11.
70 Joana Dias PEREIRA: "O Pioneirismo do Associativismo Agrícola na Internacionalização da Ação Coletiva: O caso de estudo português no longo século XIX", *Revista Tempos Históricos*, 23, 1 (2019), pp. 472–492.
71 Decree of 15 January 1855, *Diário do Governo*, 15 January 1855, pp. 9–14.
72 José Silvestre ribeiro: *RIBEIRO, José Silvestre ...*
73 Available online at: https://purl.pt/17413.
74 Vasco ROSENDO: *O mutualismo em Portugal ...*; Álvaro GARRIDO and David PEREIRA: *A economia social ...*
75 Maria Elvira CASTANHEIRA: "Os annaes da Sociedade Promotora da Indústria Nacional", *População e Sociedade*, 5 (1999), pp. 425–441.
76 Maria Rita LINO GARNEL: "Portugal e as Conferências Sanitárias Internacionais (em torno das epidemias oitocentistas de cholera-morbus)", *Revista de História da Sociedade e da Cultura*, 9 (2009), pp. 229–251.
77 *Congrès international de bienfaisance de Londres. London: Bureau de l'Association Nationale pour les Progrès des Sciences Sociales*, VII.
78 Replies to the questionnaires sent out by the 28 November 1860 and 8 September 1866 circulars concerning the operation of mutual aid associations (1860–1872). BAHMOP. DGCI-RCI-1S.
79 Questionnaire addressed to the motorised rescue societies for 1869 (1869–1871). BAHMOP. DGCI-RCI-1S.
80 Christian TOPALOV (ed.): *Laboratoires du nouveau siècle: la nébuleuse réformatrice et ses réseaux en France, 1880–1914*, Paris, Ecole des hautes études en sciences sociales, 1999.
81 Joana Dias PEREIRA: "Fabricando consensos e conflitos: protagonistas e temas da primeira onda de congressos associativos em Portugal (1865–1934)", *Revista Brasileira de História*, 41, 88 (2021), pp. 331–355.
82 The newspaper *A Federação* published between October 1865 and February 1866 the names, public, or associative positions of the delegates to the weekly sessions of the congress.
83 *A Federação*, October 1865 to February 1866.
84 José COSTA GOODOLPHIM: *A Previdência: Associações de Socorros Mútuos* ... p. 117.

85 *Diário do Governo*, 31 March 1869.
86 Victor de SÁ: *A crise do Liberalismo e as primeiras manifestações das ideias socialistas em Portugal (1820–1852): Tese de Doutoramento*, 4th. ed., UMinho Editora, 2021. Retrieved from the internet (https://ebooks.uminho.pt/index.php/uminho/catalog/book/38).
87 *Coleção de documentos sobre sociedades cooperativas*, Lisboa, Impresa Nacional, 1981, pp. 17–18
88 Fernando FERREIRA DA COSTA: *As cooperativas na legislação portuguesa: Subsidios para o estudo do sector cooperativo portugues*, Lisboa, Livraria Petrony, 1976.
89 Coleção de documentos sobre sociedades cooperativas. Lisboa, Impresa Nacional, 1871.
90 Pinheiro chagas *et al.*: *Primeiro Congresso das Associções Portuguesas*, Lisboa, Typ. Universal, 1883.
91 UNKNOWN AUTHOR: *Protesto Operário,* 10 and 24 May 1885, pp. 1–2.
92 The Possibilist Congress was held in Paris during the Universal Exhibition of 1889. It argued for legislation protecting labour, which included the eight-hour working day, the right to holidays, the abolition of night work as far as possible for men and entirely for women and children, the total suppression of work by children under the age of 14 and the protection of children, employers' responsibility for accidents at work, workshops organised by workers with state subsidies, minimum wages, equal pay for women and men, among others. The Times reports in July 1889 on the "Possibilist" Congress, transcribed by Ted Crawford and available online: https://www.marxists.org/history/international/socialdemocracy/1889/workers-congress.htm.
93 UNKNOWN AUTHOR: "O Congresso das Associações de Socorros Mútuos", *O Protesto: periódico socialista,* 2 February 1890.
94 UNKNOWN AUTHOR: "O Congresso das Associações de Socorros Mútuos", *O Protesto: periódico socialista,* 9 February 1890.
95 UNKNOWN AUTHOR: "Medidas do governo", *O Protesto: periódico socialista*, 16 February 1890.
96 UNKNOWN AUTHOR: *Boletim da Federação Nacional das Asssociações de Socorros Mútuos*, August 1915.
97 UNKNOWN AUTHOR: "Representation of the Mutual Aid Associations of Porto, Coimbra and Gaia to the Minister of Promotion", *A Voz do Operário,* 14 May 1911, p. 1.
98 UNKNOWN AUTHOR: "As associações mutualistas e as ligas farmacêuticas", *A Voz do Operário*, 3 July 1910, p. 1.
99 Edouard DUQUENNE (ed.): *IVe Congrès international de la mutualité tenu à Roubaix du 19 au 22 octobre 1911: compte-rendu des travaux*, Lille, Imprimerie Liégeois-Six, 1912.
100 Michel DREYFUS: "Mutualité et organisations politiques et sociales internationales (1889–1939)", *Vingtième Siècle, revue d'histoire*, 48, 1 (1995), pp. 92–102.
101 Álvaro GARRIDO and David PEREIRA: *A economia social em movimento …*
102 José Ernesto DIAS DA SILVA (dir.): *1° Congresso Nacional de Mutualidade: relatório, theses, actas das sessões e documentos*, Lisboa, Imprensa Nacional, 1911, p. 532.
103 Julio Alexandre IRWIN: *Tese II: A ação da mutualidade na aquisição de meios de subsistência. Sobre o papel do Cooperativismo,* Lisboa, Imprensa Nacional, 1910.

104 *1° Congresso Nacional de Mutualidade: relatório, theses, actas das sessões e documentos*, Lisboa, Imprensa Nacional, 1911, p. 532.
105 Miriam HALPERN PEREIRA: *Do estado liberal ao estado-providência ...*
106 "Congresso Nacional das Mutualidades", *Boletim da Previdência Social*, October to December 1916.
107 Álvaro GARRIDO and David PEREIRA: *A economia social em movimento ...*
108 ANTT: *Minutes Books of the Board of Directors of the ISSOPG*, 1919, Box 7, book 1.
109 Miriam HALPERN PEREIRA: "As origens do Estado-providência em Portugal: as novas fronteiras entre o público e o privado", in Nuno SEVERIANO and António Costa PINTO (eds.): *A Primeira República Portuguesa: entre o Liberalismo e o Autoritarismo*, Lisboa, Colibri, 1999, pp. 47–76.
110 Dulce FREIRE and Joana Dias PEREIRA: "Consumer Cooperatives in Portugal ... ".
111 Acts of the International Labour Conferences are available at: https://labordoc.ilo.org/.
112 UNKNOWN AUTHOR: "The oligarchic collusion unmasked", *A Acção Cooperativa*, 31 January 1922, p. 4.
113 Directorate-General of Archives. Ministry of Labour, Institute of Compulsory Social Insurance and General Welfare, Directorate of Services of the Central Secretariat and External Services, Board of Directors, Minutes, Minute Books of the Board of Directors of the ISSOPG, 1919. Current Quota Box 7. Original Classification Book 1. Minute No. 5.
114 Políbio Artur GARCIA: "O cooperativismo sob o aspeto económico. The Thesis was Approved in the 1st National Congress of Cooperatives", *National Federation of Cooperatives*, 1921.
115 Bento CARQUEJA: "Alteração da lei relativa às cooperativas. Theses Approved at the 1st National Congress of Cooperatives", *National Federation of Cooperatives*, 1921.
116 Reis SANTOS: "A FNC nas suas relações com a situação atual da Sociedade Portuguesa. Theses Approved at the 1st National Congress of Cooperatives", National Cooperative Federation, 1921.
117 UNKNOWN AUTHOR: *A Ação Cooperativa*, 31 January 1922, pp. 1–2.
118 J. Andrade SARAIVA: "Especulação e subida de preços", *Boletim da Previdência Social* (October–May 1919), pp. 315–316.
119 The work of the National Federation of Cooperatives *in A Acção Cooperativa*, 6 January 1923, pp. 1–2.
120 Joana Dias PEREIRA, "Fabricando consensos ... ", pp. 331–355.

References

ALEXANDER, Robert S.: *Europe's Uncertain Path, 1814–1914: State Formation and Civil Society*, Chichester, John Wiley and Sons, 2012.

ANTT: *Minutes Books of the Board of Directors of the ISSOPG*, 1919, Box 7, book 1.

BAKER, Alan R.: *Fraternity among the French Peasantry: Sociability and Voluntary Associations in the Loire Valley, 1815–1914*, Cambridge, Cambridge University Press, 2004.

BATISTA, Virginia: "As Mulheres e o Mutualismo – do final da Monarquia ao Estado Novo", in Eduarda FERREIRA *et al.* (eds.): *Percursos Feministas: Desafiar os Tempos*, Lisboa, UMAR, 2014.
BELO, Miguel Maria, "Associações de Seguros de Gado", *Boletim do Ministério da Agricultura*, 1931.
BELTRAN TAPIA, F. J.: "Commons, Social Capital, and the Emergence of Agricultural Cooperatives in Early Twentieth Century Spain", *European Review of Economic History*, 16, 4 (2012), pp. 511–528.
CALHOUN, Craig J.: *The Roots of Radicalism: Tradition, the Public Sphere, and Early Nineteenth-century Social Movements*, Chicago; London, University of Chicago Press, 2012.
CARQUEJA, Bento: "Alteração da lei relativa às cooperativas. Theses Approved at the 1st National Congress of Cooperatives", *National Federation of Cooperatives*, 1921.
CASTANHEIRA, Maria Elvira: "Os annaes da Sociedade Promotora da Indústria Nacional", *População e Sociedade*, 5 (1999), pp. 425–441.
CHAGAS, Pinheiro *et al.*: *Primeiro Congresso das Associções Portuguesas*, Lisboa, Typ. Universal, 1883.
COSTA GOODOLPHIM, José: *A Associação*, Lisboa, Imprensa Nacional, 1876.
COSTA GOODOLPHIM, José: *A Previdência: Associações de Socorros Mútuos, Cooperativas, Caixas de Pensões e Reformas, Caixas Económicas*, Lisboa, Imprensa Nacional, 1889.
DE MOOR, Tine: "The Silent Revolution: A New Perspective on the Emergence of Commons, Guilds, and Other Forms of Corporate Collective Action in Western Europe", *International Review of Social History*, 53, S16 (2008), pp. 179–212.
DE MOOR, Tine; FARJAM, Mike; VAN WEEREN, René; BRAVO, Giangiacomo; FORSMAN, Anders; GHORBANI, Amineh and ALE EBRAHIM DEHKORDI, Molood: "Takingsanctioning Seriously: The Impact of Sanctions on the Resilience of Historical Commons in Europe", *Journal of Rural Studies*, 87 (2021), pp. 181–188. Retrieved from the internet (https://linkinghub.elsevier.com/retrieve/pii/S0743016721002333).
DIAS DA SILVA, José Ernesto (dir.): *1° Congresso Nacional de Mutualidade: relatório, theses, actas das sessões e documentos*, Lisboa, Imprensa Nacional, 1911.
DREYFUS, Michel: "Mutualité et organisations politiques et sociales internationales (1889–1939)", *Vingtième Siècle, revue d'histoire*, 48, 1 (1995), pp. 92–102.
DUQUENNE, Edouard (ed): *IVe Congrès international de la mutualité tenu à Roubaix du 19 au 22 octobre 1911: compte-rendu des travaux*, Lille, Imprimerie Liégeois-Six, 1912.
FERREIRA DA COSTA, Fernando: *As cooperativas na legislação portuguesa: Subsidios para o estudo do sector cooperativo portugues*, Lisboa, Livraria Petrony, 1976.
FREIRE, Dulce and PEREIRA, Joana Dias: "Consumer Cooperatives in Portugal: Debates and Experiences from the Nineteenth to the Twentieth Century", in Mary HILSON, Silke NEUNSINGER and Greg PATMORE (eds.): *A Global*

History of Consumer Cooperation since 1850: Movements and Businesses, Leiden; Boston, BRILL, 1917, pp. 296–325.

GARCIA, Políbio Artur: "O cooperativismo sob o aspeto económico. The Thesis Was Approved in the 1st National Congress of Cooperatives", *National Federation of Cooperatives*, 1921.

GARRIDO, Álvaro and PEREIRA, David: *A economia social em movimento: uma história das organizações*, 1st. ed., Lisboa, Tinta da China, 2018.

HALPERN PEREIRA, Miriam: "As origens do Estado-providência em Portugal: as novas fronteiras entre o público e o privado", in Nuno SEVERIANO and António Costa PINTO (eds.): *A Primeira República Portuguesa: entre o Liberalismo e o Autoritarismo*, Lisboa, Colibri, 1999, pp. 47–76.

HALPERN PEREIRA, Miriam: *Do estado liberal ao estado-providência: um século em Portugal*, Bauru; Lisboa, EDUSC; FCT, CEHC-IUL, 2012.

HOBSBAWM, E. J: *A era dos impérios: 1875–1914*, São Paulo, Paz e Terra, 2010.

IRWIN, Julio Alexandre: *Tese II: A ação da mutualidade na aquisição de meios de subsistência. Sobre o papel do Cooperativismo*, Lisboa, Imprensa Nacional, 1910

LANGHANS, Franz-Paul: *As corporações dos ofícios mecânicos: subsídios para a sua história: com um estudo do Prof. Doutor Marcello Caetano*, Lisboa, Imprensa Nacional, 1943.

LARGO JIMÉNEZ, Fernando: "Institutional factors in the decline of Spanish workers' mutualism. The case of Barcelona in the first third of the 20th century", *International Journal of the Commons*, 10, 2 (2016), p. 642.

LINO GARNEL, Maria Rita: "Portugal e as Conferências Sanitárias Internacionais (em torno das epidemias oitocentistas de cholera-morbus)", *Revista de História da Sociedade e da Cultura*, 9 (2009), pp. 229–251.

LOUSADA, Maria Alexandre: "O "espírito de associação" em Portugal. Dinâmica social e legislação (1820–1926)", in Luisa VELOSO *et al.* (eds.): *Anarquismo, Trabalho e Sociedade. Livro de homenagem a João Freire*, Lisboa, Almedina, 2017, pp. 97-11.

LUCASSEN, Jan; DE MOOR, Tine and VAN ZANDEN, Jan Luiten: "The Return of the Guilds: Towards a Global History of the Guilds in Pre-industrial Times", *International Review of Social History*, 53, S16 (2008), pp. 5–18. Retrieved from the internet (https://www.cambridge.org/core/product/identifier/S0020859008003581/type/journal_article).

MATTHEWS, Stephen: "Insurance and Plague in the Mid-Nineteenth Century", *The Agricultural History Review*, 2, 53 (2005), pp. 192–211.

MORENO RUIZ, Rafael: "La génesis del mutualismo moderno en Europa", *REVESCO: Revista de Estudios Cooperativos*, 72 (2000), pp. 199–214.

OSTROM, Elinor: *Governing the Commons: The Evolution of Institutions for Collective Action*, 1. Ed., Cambridge, Cambridge University Press, 1990. Retrieved from the internet (https://www.cambridge.org/core/product/identifier/9780511807763/type/book).

OSTROM, Elinor, "Collective Action and the Evolution of Social Norms", *Journal of Economic Perspectives*, 14, 3 (2000), pp. 137–158. Retrieved from the internet (https://pubs.aeaweb.org/doi/10.1257/jep.14.3.137).

PEREIRA, Joana Dias: *A Previdência: Associações de Socorros Mútuos, Cooperativas, Caixas de Pensões e Reformas, Caixas Económicas*, Lisboa, Imprensa Nacional, 1889

PEREIRA, Joana Dias: "Resilient Alliances: Portuguese Cooperative Movement in the Transition to Modern Times (1867–1933)", *REVESCO: Revista de Estudios Cooperativos*, 128 (2018), pp. 59–75.

PEREIRA, Joana Dias: "O Pioneirismo do Associativismo Agrícola na Internacionalização da Ação Coletiva: O caso de estudo português no longo século XIX", *Revista Tempos Históricos*, 23, 1 (2019), pp. 472–492.

PEREIRA, Joana Dias: "Fabricando consensos e conflitos: protagonistas e temas da primeira onda de congressos associativos em Portugal (1865–1934)", *Revista Brasileira de História*, 41, 88 (2021), pp. 331–355.

PINTO, António Costa and ALMEIDA, Pedro Tavares de: "On Liberalism and Civil Society in Portugal", in Nancy Gina BERMEO and Philip G. NORD (eds.): *Civil Society Before Democracy: Lessons from Nineteenth-century Europe*, Lanham, MD, Rowman & Littlefield Publishers, 2000, pp. 3–21.

PINTO, Virgilio Bugalho, *Do seguro mútuo de gado: estudo monográfico, estatístico e crítico das associações mútuas locais encontradas no distrito de Viana do Castelo em 1915*, Coimbra, Imprensa da Universidade, 1920.

PONS-PONS, Jerònia and CARPIO-ELÍAS, Juan: "Evolución de la gestión del riesgo en el sector agrario español: De la economía preindustrial a los seguros", *Historia Agraria Revista de agricultura e historia rural*, 2020. Retrieved from the internet (http://www.historiaagraria.com/FILE/articulos/RHA81_pons-carpio.pdf).

RAMELA, Franco: *Storiografia francese e italiana a confronto sul fenomeno associativo durante XVIII e XIX secolo. Atti delle giornate di studio promosse dalla Fondazione Luigi Einaudi (Torino, 6 e 7 maggio 1988)*, Turim, Fondazione Luigi Einaudi, 1990.

RIBEIRO, José Silvestre: *RIBEIRO, José Silvestre, 1807–1891 Historia dos estabelecimentos scientificos litterarios e artisticos de Portugal nos successsivos reinados da monarchia*, 19 vols., Lisboa, Academia de Ciências de Lisboa, 1871.

ROSENDO, Vasco: *O mutualismo em Portugal: dois séculos de história e suas origens*, Lisboa, Multinova, 1996.

SANTOS, Reis: "A FNC nas suas relações com a situação atual da Sociedade Portuguesa. Theses Approved at the 1st National Congress of Cooperatives", National Cooperative Federation, 1921.

SARAIVA, Andrade J.: "Especulação e subida de preços", *Boletim da Previdência Social* (October to May 1919), pp. 315–316.

SOBRAL NETO, Margarida: "A população de mira e a desamortização dos baldios na segunda metade do séc. XIX", *Revista Portuguesa de História Separata*, 19 (1982), pp. 15–58.

SOBRAL NETO, Margarida: "As estruturas agrárias: a força da tradição", *Revista de História*, X (1990), pp. 129–135.

SOBRAL NETO, Margarida: *O universo da comunidade rural: época moderna*, Coimbra, Palimage, 2010.

SOBRAL NETO, Margarida: "Propriedade e usos comunitários em Portugal", in Márcia MOTTA and Mónica PICCOLO (orgs.): *Domínio de outrem: Posse e propriedade na era moderna (Portugal e Brasil)*, *S. Luís do Maranhão, São Luís, Guimarães: Editora UEMA (Universidade Federal do Maranhão) & Nós Por Cá Todos Bem*, 2017, pp. 13–30. Recuperado de internet (http://hdl.handle.net/10316/84810).

SOUSA, Tude: *Costumes e Tradições Agrícolas do Minho: Regímen Pastoril dos Povos da Serra do Gerês*, Porto, Imprensa Portuguesa, 1908.

SOUSA, Tude: "Comunalismo na Serra", *Terra portuguesa: revista ilustrada de arqueologia artística e etnografia*, 32–33 (1922), pp. 99–100.

SIMÃO, Ana Catarina: "Introdução ao Estudo das Confrarias Corporativas do Porto", Unpublished Mestrado, Porto, Faculdade de Letras da Universidade do Porto, 1996. Retrieved from the internet (https://ler.letras.up.pt/uploads/ficheiros/2462.pdf).

sá, Victor de: *A crise do Liberalismo e as primeiras manifestações das ideias socialistas em Portugal (1820–1852): Tese de Doutoramento*, Braga, UMinho Editora, 2021. Retrieved from the internet (https://ebooks.uminho.pt/index.php/uminho/catalog/book/38).

TOPALOV, Christian (ed.): *Laboratoires du nouveau siècle: la nébuleuse réformatrice et ses réseaux en France, 1880–1914*, Paris, Ecole des hautes études en sciences sociales, 1999.

UNKNOWN AUTHOR: *Protesto Operário*, 10 and 24 May 1885, pp. 1–2.

UNKNOWN AUTHOR: "O Congresso das Associações de Socorros Mútuos", *O Protesto: periódico socialista*, 2 February 1890.

UNKNOWN AUTHOR: "O Congresso das Associações de Socorros Mútuos", *O Protesto: periódico socialista*, 9 February 1890.

UNKNOWN AUTHOR: "Medidas do governo", *O Protesto: periódico socialista*, 16 February 1890.

UNKNOWN AUTHOR: "As associações mutualistas e as ligas farmacêuticas", *A Voz do Operário*, 3 July 1910, p. 1.

UNKNOWN AUTHOR: "Representation of the Mutual Aid Associations of Porto, Coimbra and Gaia to the Minister of Promotion", *A Voz do Operário*, 14 May 1911, p. 1.

UNKNOWN AUTHOR: *Boletim da Federação Nacional das Asssociações de Socorros Mútuos*, August 1915.

UNKNOWN AUTHOR: "The Oligarchic Collusion Unmasked", *A Acção Cooperativa*, 31 January 1922, p. 4.

VAN LEEUWEN, Marco H. D.: *Mutual Insurance 1550–2015: From Guild Welfare and Friendly Societies to Contemporary Micro-Insurers*, London, Palgrave Macmillan, 2017.

ZIEMANN, Benjamin and MERGEL, Thomas (eds.): *European Political History 1870–1913*, Aldershot; Burlington, VT, Ashgate, 2007.

4 From Associationism to the Solidarity Economy

A Historical Perspective

Jean-Louis Laville

Today we are seeing the disintegration of the thought of the "second 19th century" – of that productivist perspective which belonged to the "age of capital and empire", according to Hobsbawm. This invites us to return to examine a social phenomenon that has hitherto been obscured: the associationism of the "first 19th century", "the age of revolution", again according to Hobsbawm.[1] The idea that guides this chapter is that this return can help us deal with the challenges of the future.

The chapter proceeds in three stages. First, it recalls what this associationism was and how it was distorted by the official version of events before being forgotten. Next, it shows how the start of the 21st century has been characterised by a multiplication of solidarity-based initiatives, in a strange way echoing the first 19th century. Finally, it suggests that the solidarity economy is a resurgence of associationism.

To understand what is associationism it is necessary to conceptualise political and economic spheres. The political sphere is not restricted to representative democracy which, according to Weber, has a monopoly over legitimate violence; it includes the power to determine the rules of being together which, according to Arendt, are based on collective deliberation and decision-making. The political domain thus encompasses the state, which exercises authority, as well as the public sphere, which rests on common action and dialogue between citizens about the polity. Democracy results from a delicate balance between these two poles of the state and the public sphere. Groups forming in the public sphere would begin to institute norms that they establish for themselves in order to stabilise the common world they want to see. But in order to do so, they need institutional coordination and approval from the state, resulting sometimes in cooperation, and sometimes in conflict.

As for the economic sphere, it is not limited to market, two definitions of the economy are possible as Polanyi points. The first, formal definition, refers to the calculation of interest by which each individual allocates the scarce resources at his disposal in order to "make the best" of them, thus

DOI: 10.4324/9781003439554-5

"maximising" or "economising" his efforts. The second, substantive definition, takes as its starting point "man's patent dependence for his livelihood upon nature and his fellows".[2] In order to satisfy his material needs, he interacts with his natural and social environment through an institutionalised process. In a substantive economy, the market coexists with reciprocity – which emerges through symmetry between groups; redistribution – which requires a central power; and householding – which refers to the relations within the basic group.[3] There is thus not just one form but many forms of economic integration; this allows us to move away from the "economistic fallacy"[4] that equates the economy with the market.

Solidarity associationism and its gradual obscuration

The solidarity-based innovation inherent to associationism lays in its ability to bypass traditional forms of tutelage. Occurring prior to the division between market economy and welfare state, its originality stemmed from its imbrication of the demand for free access to the public sphere, on the one hand, and the establishment of economic activities on the basis of egalitarian reciprocity, on the other. This demonstrates that democratic solidarity emerged before the protective state – something approaches that link the invention of the social[5] with the intervention of the state fail to recognise.

By forging social bonds anchored in the political freedom that had just been gained and remained to be expanded, solidarity-based associationism gave rise to concrete attempts to work together towards both protection and emancipation. Numerous re-interpretations of history have now told the story of these collective actions, which amounted to an extension of the power to act in the first 19th century in France, as this chapter shows, but also in England,[6] Italy,[7] Portugal, and Spain.[8]

Convergent experiences

Throughout Europe, associationism was brought about by the mass of small trades, but it was not therefore "a workerist hijacking of political action".[9] Self-government, mutual aid, and demand-making were brought together in initiatives that mixed together production governed by labour, activity in political clubs, mutual assistance, and protests in the streets.

Between 1780 and 1830, hundreds of machines were destroyed, with Luddism crystallising this "negotiation by riot" in England from 1810 onwards. This resistance was less a rejection of technology than a defence of dignity, as the workers advocated flexible and specialised modes of production within local systems that gained the approval of some public authorities.[10] Their enemy was mass production, which gave rise not just to deskilling but also to forms of pollution, which in turn generated other conflicts. Their goal was to ensure that work and nature were not made subject to the law of capital. In France, "in the 1820s, nearly 10% of trials in the rural cantons around Marseille concerned pollution"[11] and popular public spheres hummed with ideas about "the organisation of work" between 1830 and 1848. The collective effort to achieve emancipation from traditional forms of tutelage combined freely accepted self-discipline, a critique of religion and property owners, and street parades and festivals. In Paris alone, 39 trades developed associational projects.[12] While this proliferation came out of the professions, it was not confined within them; Deroin even mentions a "Fraternal and Solidarity Association of all associations" whose purpose was to "bring together the workers of both sexes from different professions".[13] In this period, industrialisation did not have the inevitability it would later be attributed, and workers proud of their skills saw the threat it posed to them. What they wanted to protect and improve was a moral economy,[14] because in their eyes it guaranteed fair pay and productive quality.

Their protest activity was inextricable from self-help. In England, the friendly societies had hundreds of thousands of members, as did the *società operare di mutuo soccorso* in Italy[15] and the *sociedades de socorro mutuo* in Spain.[16] The solidarity-based associationism present in production was thus also present in mutual assistance and more generally gave rise to increased sociability. All in all, as Estivill notes for Spain and Portugal, "a veritable mosaic of collective identities emerged out of the fabric of the domestic economy and the fight for survival". Craft work and self-production for consumption overlapped with "mutual assistance for sowing and harvesting, the informal economy, the non-monetary exchange of goods and services, collective work for common goods (wood cutting, land use, maintenance of roads and bridges, irrigation, fishing areas)". "To these should be added the networks of associations for education and leisure, the athénées encyclopédiques,[17] the rationalist circles, adult education courses, conferences, debate sessions, libraries and popular sports groups, choirs, town bands and music groups, republican fraternities, cafés and popular theatres. These are expressions of a solidarity economy before its time, and of a popular culture that was organised autonomously and almost always democratically, on the fringes and often against the spirit of profit".[18]

A forgotten message

Yet the message of solidarity-based associationism has been caricatured on the basis of a distinction, as fallacious as it is famous, between the utopian socialism it supposedly represented and the scientific socialism that supposedly succeeded it.[19] The idea of socialism was indeed born among the groups of proletarians confronted with the gap between the political recognition they had just obtained and the economic constraints they continued to suffer. But this original socialism cannot be equated with an infancy – with the immature expression of a social movement in the making that would only become meaningful at a later stage. This evolutionist illusion is dispelled as soon as we shift our attention to social practices. Several features can still be discerned from the trace they have left, even if this has been almost entirely erased.

Associationism set out to bridge the gap between democratic principles and everyday life. The different domains of the lifeworld were intertwined, and demands relating to the organisation of economic activity could not be detached from an extension of citizenship beyond those who paid tax, through universal suffrage. The issue of socio-economic inequality was not separated from that of political inequality; on the contrary, popular public spaces based on associations necessarily addressed socio-economic issues. In other words, social and economic issues did not contaminate politics; they fed it.

This multi-dimensionality proved to be associationism's characteristic feature when it was confronted with the test of reality. While associationism's foundations were prepared by intense intellectual activity, it crystallised around a pressing need for collective initiative. This need was fuelled by a rejection of violence: "it's not by means of arms that we want to succeed, it's by means of ideas", Payard declared.[20] Their modes of organisation did not correspond to those of an avant-garde movement ready to impose its views, nor did they make the success of the revolt conditional on a particular stage of development, nor were they paralysed by an unfavourable balance of power. On the contrary, it was the scale of inequalities that called for action. Their commitment was given meaning by their desire to emancipate themselves from control by the elites, and for this there was no available model – only the initiatives they took were able to pave the way. Disseminating ideas, words, and actions, the movement's participants did not get lost in abstract generalities; they analysed what they were doing and tried to draw out concrete suggestions to increase their room for manoeuvre. The reform texts they produced – on pay, jobs, old age, or sickness – may seem dated, but they deserve to be re-read as a valuable legacy of ideas submitted for deliberation by those who were gaining access to a public discourse of which they had been deprived.

In this respect, solidarity-based associationism was a protest against the monopoly of expression held by the elites. It resulted from the irruption into the debate of groups and individuals who had not been invited and who were reacting against their exclusion. But this irruption did not consist of the uncontrolled howling that the notables automatically attributed to a plebeian population they believed incapable of controlling itself. To the great surprise of observers, those involved in the "events" of 1848 did not behave like savage hordes sweeping through Paris and threatening civilisation. They staged "the peaceful but serious spectacle of workers united in a common thought: the immediate improvement of the lot of workers".[21] The assemblies increased in number but not in unruliness, releasing a "generous power" in the development of projects through exchanges between peers.[22]

What's more, this form of direct democracy did not envisage change occurring through its intervention alone. On the one hand, it drew support from the old guilds, which it changed into fraternal and mutual aid societies. On the other hand, it did not get carried away by the constant stream of new initiatives. A concern for action was combined with an awareness that it was essential to connect this action up with a transformation of existing institutional frameworks. The organisation of activities on the basis of professional skills was coupled with requests to legislators for the extension of rights. Advocates of associationism did not make the mistake of confusing autonomy with autarky. Recognising that becoming more egalitarian depended above all on the people concerned taking risks, they understood that, to succeed, associationism must be combined with other repertoires of action to reduce the negative discrimination that self-organisation alone could not eliminate. Unlike many intellectuals who mythologise revolutionary moments, succumbing to a fascination with their ephemeral brilliance and rapid destruction, the participants tried from the outset to make their contribution last.

For this reason, although the popular mobilisations of the first 19th century were inspired by utopian writers they shied away from any reference to a reconciled society. The workers distanced themselves from the kind of totalising conception typical of the doctrines of the time, according to which association alone would establish an order to replace the disorder produced by individualism. Not believing in attempts to create a perfect world, they preferred less idealised associations, exposed to the risks of experimentation without the help of providential figures. In short, they were both propagators and dissidents of utopian doctrines. Associationalist approaches sought human emancipation through the construction of collectives whose "impetus is fundamentally democratic insofar as we do not restrict democracy to a form of regime, but know how to perceive in it a specific form of socialisation".[23]

As we can now see, taking full account of the workers' movement precludes us from associating associationism with communitarian prophets. The latter, in their search for patrons and disciples, avoided questions of power, whereas associationism had from the outset the goal of deepening democracy. Its aim was to gradually achieve collective autonomy, and it therefore differed from the authoritarianism of the familistères and other colonies, which came up against the two faces of the utopian imaginary – an imaginary that was certainly fertile, but also misleading[24] when it turned into a dogmatic denial of reality. Implemented by workers and peasants immersed in conflictual social relations, associationism in no way claimed to create either a new type of human being or a new world. It instead more modestly advocated the linking together of professional traditions, egalitarian practices, and public policy. Professional allegiances were mobilised with a view to transferring them to a world of imagined equality. Initiatives that deliberately rejected forms of discrimination made it possible to formulate demands for institutional change. So it was not group egoism that was being created, but arduous attempts to maintain ways of life that coexisted with practices that broke through the norms of the institutional framework via the democratisation of collective action, which was itself affected by the laws and regulations enacted by the state. Associationism maintained that, to transition towards a fairer society, both transformative social practices and new legislative frameworks were necessary.

In short, there is a remarkable discrepancy between the picture that has been painted of pioneering associationism and its reality. Once we have stripped away a superficial interpretation that accuses it of naivety, we are able to see a reality that remains relevant today. Starting from the premise that all citizens should have free access to the public sphere, it seeks to expand political democracy into social life, thus running counter to any separation between politics and economics. This prolific associationism of the first 19th century promoted a popular economy and politics with a strong moral dimension, which Scott[25] also identified in the peasant world. Its characteristics, mentioned above, can be summarised as follows. First, as a reaction against charity and benevolence, it was based on a democratic understanding of solidarity, which presupposed equal rights for all those involved. Centred on mutual aid as much as on the articulation of demands, it combined self-organisation with a broader movement. Second, it closely linked significant political transformation to the use of social experimentation; far from relying on the virtues of isolated initiatives, it recognised the need to come together to press for changes in institutions and public action.

A gradual depoliticisation

The reference to utopian socialism in the early 19th century, which has become habitual, masks the originality of the pioneering associations, which lay in their concern to encourage emancipation through collective learning and the creation of institutions. This practical socialism was based both on the idea of democratic solidarity and on a project for social change that extended the political principles of freedom and equality into all spheres of life through the association of free citizens experiencing a sense of solidarity in their interactions.

After 1848, a symbolic date in Europe, repression was coupled with a devaluing of popular practices. The "external annexation" of colonised countries was mirrored by an "internal annexation"[26] that condemned activities perceived as "backward", unproductive, and wedded to the protection of old skills. The discourse that identified modernisation with the industrial revolution gained in strength, neutralising social and environmental critiques. Capital accumulation became a priority because it held out the promise of development and power.

The ideology of progress pointed to the market and the capital-owning society as evidence of the wealth of nations and their populations. As a result, poverty was seen as only a transitory problem, and the productive efficiency of capitalism was supposed to eradicate it in the long term. The logical consequence of this was a redefinition of solidarity. Confined to the need to contain pauperism, it now relied on the solicitude of the rich to relieve the poor, before economic development could bring them its benefits. The prospect of equality faded as paternalism reintroduced the tutelage of the elites, limiting relief to the most deserving. Previously, philanthropic societies had mixed together ideas borrowed from Christianity with notions of fraternity and of "social man". But now philanthropic solidarity regressed,[27] becoming a weapon against democratic solidarity.

The established powers set about delegitimising any reference to associationism, which they accused of being unrealistic. Frightened by the audacity of the people, who had dared to challenge the laws and rules established by tradition, conservatives emphasised the risk of an excess of democracy, which would disrupt the values that guaranteed the security provided by enduring hierarchies. The liberals, meanwhile, dismissed working-class views as archaic, arguing that they were out of touch with the modern individual and incompatible with the ideology of economic progress. From then on, the best way to "govern misery"[28] was through patronage and paternalism, which became inseparable from the symbolic invalidation and ongoing repression of autonomous forms of workers' organisation. The moral economy of associationism was replaced by an effort to moralise the poor. With Le Play, this effort identified itself as social economy, which was described by Marx as "vulgar" because it abandoned "the search for fundamental laws in favour of the pragmatic world of ad hoc reforms designed to maintain the existing order"[29] or even to reconcile classes. In this respect, the "creation of (the) social economy"[30] was not simply the recognition of legal statuses extracted from the associationalist "gangue"; it was also the renunciation of associationism's political project.

Although its French theorists, Fauquet,[31] Desroche,[32] and Vienney,[33] abandoned the moralistic prism, the fact remains that by making the cooperative its centre of gravity, social economy adopted an enterprise-focused perspective which led it to think of its development in terms of economic success and to restrict its democratic concerns to the internal functioning of these entities. In doing so, it abandoned any questioning of what the economy is beyond the market, and of what politics means beyond the formal equality of an organisation's members. Even though social economy was born out of associationism, its theorising endorsed the split between social movements and enterprises. This had damaging consequences for the future, since the link between the economic and political spheres was weakened in favour of a specialisation of human activities. The social economy is therefore marked by ambiguity between practices stemming from associationism and conceptions that are too exclusively focused on the enterprise. It separates into distinct entities (associations, cooperatives, mutual societies) what the latter wanted to bring together in a single movement that included actions to emancipate and protect workers. In its own way, it was writing an evolutionist history. While social economy was opposed to communism, it was aligned with it insofar as it retained only a summary and disorganised prefiguration of associationism, as if it too represented the progression to a mature stage of thought after the approximations of a stage that was confused because it was utopian.

Associationism's marginalisation entrenched the loss of a set of norms and reciprocal obligations that had been defended by the collectivity of workers because they expressed a shared way of life and a common pride and could link together trades and promote human rights. This collective heritage, rooted in tradition but transformed by the introduction of democratic goals, bore witness to a desire for emancipation that established interactions between ideas, initiatives, and institutional change.

The prioritisation of statism and productivism

In this context, during the second half of the 19th century, Marxism established itself as the unifying theory at the cost of simplifying its arguments. The acuity of its critique of capitalism coexisted with a twist in thinking about emancipation. By prioritising the overcoming of capitalism, it marginalised self-organisation and neglected access to the public sphere. Vilified, associationism faded away. The political sphere would increasingly be equated with the action of the state alone, providing a superstructure that legitimised the economic infrastructure. In line with this vision, the strategy of the working class focused on establishing state control over the economy, which was necessary to change the relations of production.

The pioneering associationism of the first half of the 19th century came up against economic determinism and the action of an enlightened avant-garde that could bring about the dictatorship of the proletariat. This tendency, which had been present since the Second International, was further accentuated with the Third International, which condemned humanists and democrats, advocating democratic centralism and obedience to clandestine leadership bodies. It turned violence into a veritable political "myth", following in Sorel's footsteps by making it the infallible sign of the proletarian force which, seizing the levers of power through revolution, could adopt legislation favourable to itself.

It was in a bid to counter this perspective that social democracy emerged. With its emphasis on public intervention, it defended the idea that the transition from a capitalist to a socialist society could be made smoothly. After 1945, it enjoyed a "golden age". Two features, however, put this success into perspective.

The first feature was the tendency to consider users of public services as passive recipients. This concentrated arbitration in the spheres of representative democracy (government, employers' representatives, and trade unions), where the voice of ordinary citizens was largely ignored. At the same time as Fordism reigned in companies, keeping workers out of decision-making in return for an increase in their incomes, providentialism, to use Bélanger and Lévesque's term,[34] developed in the welfare state: the recipients of social services remained far removed from their design, with this exclusion compensated for by virtually free access to them. Refusing to place its faith in avant-gardism, social democracy remained stuck in state fetishism and productivism, which it shared with Bolshevism. Although these two political tendencies clashed over how to act against capitalism – over whether expropriation or negotiation was the best course to take – paradoxically, they were united in the trust they placed in experts charged with mapping out the path to socialism. This elitism produced a conception of social change that left little room for advances coming from civil society.

The second striking feature was that redistributive solidarity remained dependent on market growth, which becomes increasingly restrictive when the slowdown in the growth rate deprives social democracy of some of its means of action. In the dominant conception of the economy, only the market economy is productive. This view has been internalised by social democrats, who see the market economy as the wealth-generating economy on which the state levies in order to redistribute.

Between civil society movements and neoliberal reaction

This fragility became apparent at the end of the 1960s with the emergence of "new" social movements. In addition to the social conflict arising from the confrontation between capital and labour, other issues were entering the public sphere. They challenged the certainties about production, consumption, and the role of the state that had bound society together around the ideology of progress. Thus both the merits of growth and the role of the state came into question. The coincidence between rising living standards and improved quality of life was no longer so obvious, nor that between state redistribution and the equalisation of living standards.

A democratic opening

Doubts were expressed about the hopes entertained during the post-war boom years of continuous economic and social progress. New demands criticised inequalities of power and called for a discussion of the development model that had been decided on by experts at a distance from citizens.

New movements formed around these issues of knowledge and participation, continuing a struggle over the control of historical action that was "positively oriented towards the collective appropriation of the means by which a society produces itself".[35] Together with feminism, the ecological movement was the most emblematic of this perspective. As mentioned above, in the first half of the 19th century, protests against the damage caused by progress made themselves heard. They did not disappear completely afterwards and were taken up by English back-to-nature socialism, the "German *Lebensreform* and certain French anarchist currents",[36] but the majority consensus suppressed them for a long time. The Club of Rome's Meadow Report in 1972 symbolised the new global awareness of environmental issues. It was born of the ecological collapse brought about by the Anthropocene, an era characterised by the human origin of major changes to the natural environment, the consequences of which can no longer be hushed up: climate change due to the accumulation of greenhouse gases, damage to the biosphere, and a drastic reduction in biodiversity, modification of "the bio-geochemical cycles of water, nitrogen and phosphate, all as essential as that of carbon", and the introduction of substances into ecosystems ("synthetic organic chemistry, hydrocarbon chemistry, plastics, endocrine disruptors, pesticides, radionuclides dispersed by nuclear testing, fluorinated gases, etc.").[37]

These problems reveal the neglect of nature among the founders of liberal economics, such as Say, but also in a Marxism that was enthraled by the development of the productive forces and predicted that this could be fully realised once the capitalist fetters had been thrown off. Moving away from demands in terms of living standards to broader demands in terms of quality of life, "post-industrial"[38] social movements, to use Bell's term, or even "post-materialist"[39] movements, to use Inglehart's, set themselves apart from the institutional left. They also exhibited a change in forms of engagement: disaffected with forms of delegation and decision-making perceived as too remote, they strengthened local activism. Thus the "activists", whose demise Ion[40] heralded, and who were supporters of widespread self-management, saw themselves being countered by the "alternativists", who were more focused on experimentation and "drip-by-drip self-management".[41]

In an echo of the democratic opening-up of the first half of the 19th century, the last quarter of the 20th century was a time of democratisation throughout Europe, amplified by the transition to democracy in Spain, Greece, and Portugal.

The neoliberal response

But the fall of the Berlin Wall reshuffled the world's geopolitical cards; it was presented as the triumph of capitalism, which was identified with the end of history. Like the 19th century, the 20th century ended with a call to order on the pretext of economics, with the advent of a political project based on prioritising competition. This project was explicitly conceived in opposition to the new social movements, particularly environmental and feminist ones.

Reformulating the conservative fears of the 19th century, the main theorists of neoliberalism, such as Hayek and Friedman, stoked panic about unlimited democracy and advocated warding it off by establishing a society purged of human will. For them, all teleological action was reprehensible – at the state level this meant eliminating the general will; at the collective level it meant the taming of popular associations into a functional third sector providing services at the lowest possible cost; and at individual level it meant that competition should govern relationships between individuals lacking a common goal, thus establishing a spontaneous or self-generated order.[42] For Friedman,[43] the market ensured freedom and diversity, and each individual could "vote, as it were, for the color of tie he wants and get it; he does not have to see what color the majority wants and then, if he is in the minority, submit". Behind this consumerist conception of diversity and freedom, neoliberalism is profoundly standardising, since it maintains that everyone is asking themselves what colour of tie they want. Hayek,[44] for his part, was lucid enough to recognise that the inhabitants of communist countries were on "the road to serfdom", but he inferred from this that any reference to a common good led to totalitarianism. For him, the decentralised arrangements that mark out the path to freedom result from a multitude of signals using which individuals orient themselves, guided by their interests. In short, generalised competition provides the reference points for collective life and is so important that it subordinates democracy. His ambition is clearly a limited democracy, as demonstrated by his idea of economic constitutionality. With this proposal, he justifies authoritarianism and moves away from liberalism by seeking to make the economy a domain removed from political deliberation.

This first wave of neoliberalism at the end of the 20th century triggered an upheaval. Most governments abandoned the Keynesianism urged by the Declaration of Philadelphia and adopted a monetarism that was given concrete expression in 1989 in the Washington Consensus, which asserted the need to restrict the scope of state intervention in order to restore competitiveness. The effects have been far-reaching, as the European Commission has sacrificed Europe's founding ideals of peace and social cohesion in order to follow these precepts of free and undistorted competition. Hence the popular opposition from Athens to Madrid has disrupted the neoliberal order.

The anxiety aroused among increasingly intertwined economic and political elites led to a second wave of neoliberalism, which sought to re-legitimise the capitalist system. Following the 2008 crisis and the Arab springs, neoliberalism was no longer able to stem the rise of opposition to austerity policies, so it adapted using a range of methods whose common reference point was private solidarity. Anticipating possible challenges to capitalism, this new wave was characterised by the narrative of the market rescuing the poor, taken up by international organisations on the basis of the Millennium Goals. The concept of social business is emblematic of this perspective. In the words of Yunus, one of its principal architects, it refers to a "company that is cause-driven rather than profit-driven", but that "in accordance with management principles just like a traditional PMB [profit-maximising business]"[45] and "aims for full cost recovery".[46] According to its other supporters,[47] "When the social-business concept becomes well known and begins to spread through all the free-market economies of the world, the flood of creativity that this new business channel will unleash has the potential to transform our world".[48] It is intended to form a system with corporate social responsibility and bottom-of-the-pyramid marketing,[49] confirming the system's renewed potential for self-regulation and heralding a "new capitalism" with a social purpose. Aiming to introduce "the advantages of free-market competition into the world of social improvement",[50] it is also adopting new means such as social impact bonds. The distinctive feature of these social impact investments is that they shift the financial risk in social services from the public sector to a private intermediary. This intermediary, funded by institutional investors, allocates funds to operators, associations, or companies. The evaluation of the results determines the payment, and the return to the remunerated investors, by the public authorities who only commit funds in the event of success. The project contains an entirely new philosophy of social action that has been disseminated internationally, with expansions into culture,[51] international solidarity, and development.[52]

This panoply of measures is supposed to promote a reconfiguration of solidarity in favour of private action that combines "managerialism" and venture philanthropy. It affirms the application of rigorous management and well-meaning compassion towards the poor, who should be both helped and educated.[53]

The persistence of resistance

But despite the two waves of neoliberalism, civil society initiatives – a legacy of the social movements – continue to spread. Since 2008 in particular, they have resulted in a "reconstruction of daily life around autonomous economic practices".[54] According to the all-too-rare data available, the spread of these alternative practices is far greater than is generally estimated. In Catalonia, for example, more than 300,000 people are involved in them, and a study of a statistically representative sample in Barcelona in 2012 showed that 97% of the population participates in at least one of them.[55] Many have joined because they find solutions here to the problems caused by the crisis as they become part of inter-personal networks. Others have joined as a logical extension of their participation in the "Indignados" revolts. The repertoire of protests is now interwoven with participation in short food supply chains, cooperatives, sharing schemes, and legal aid and rehousing services for people who have been evicted. Although these initiatives are scattered, many of them, as in Catalonia, identify with the term "solidarity economy", which defines the content of this alternative by highlighting three features that differentiate it from the social economy.

The first feature of this solidarity-based economy is its emphasis on the purpose of production; its objectives relate to the kind of society we live in (social justice, environmental preservation, cultural diversity, etc.) and as such are part of the challenge to the productivist ideology. The second salient feature is its political dimension, because these goals are to be achieved by relying on the actors' own ability to enact the rules, which depends on the quality of discussions both in the public spheres internal to the initiatives and in the external arenas and forums through which they make themselves known. Finally, the third feature is that the political dimension influences the economic model; hence the hybridisation of economic principles for socially useful projects that cannot self-finance on the market, since the collective benefits generated can only be maintained through reciprocity and redistribution. Each of these three features places the opposition to neoliberalism front and centre: a teleological perspective is accepted, the political dimension is affirmed, and the economic model does not restrict itself to the market.

A renewal of democratic solidarity

A struggle is playing out between solidarity organised by private actors and democratic solidarity. In this context, the intensification of cultural identities can become reactionary if it is disconnected from socio-economic issues. Hence the importance of the critique, mentioned earlier, of "claims for the recognition of identity and difference" that "overextend the critique of culture, while downplaying the critique of political economy",[56] and give in to a commodification seen as emancipation from statism. Here again, debates initiated in the Global South are illuminating. According to feminisms of the South, rebalancing the dimensions "of redistribution, recognition, and representation" requires an awareness of the influence of "professionals" and the "disproportionate voice" given "to English-speaking elites".[57]

Reticent about a cultural turn in social movements, feminist approaches have stressed the importance of political transformation through the interweaving of cultural, social, and economic issues. They theorise the close interweaving of the economic and political spheres.[58] Democratic solidarity restores the possibility of collective pride, but it requires a linking up of perspectives that have been compartmentalised in "hegemonic" feminism. As Guérin, Hillenkamp, and Verschuur conclude,[59] we must together design "alternative economic practices that at the same time attempt to influence politics, through what can be described as a cultural reinvention of politics" and "practices of protest and struggle, sometimes radical, that accompany the provision of concrete services".

The current picture is therefore mixed, as it combines the domination of neoliberalism and the strengthening of social resistance. Reforging a connection to associationism may prove decisive if contemporary initiatives are to avoid being instrumentalised.

The solidarity economy as a resurgence of associationism

Associationism provides evidence of the circulation between ideas and practices. It has given rise to another way of thinking and acting that may resonate with our present situation. As such, associationism is not just a field of practice; it is also an epistemology according to which the production of knowledge is not the prerogative of scholars.

The rejection of associationism and the rise of scientism

There was a link between the abandonment of the associationalist perspective and the spread of the "antiquated intellectual structure"[60] that is scientistic socialism. To understand the turn that occurred in the transition from the first to the second half of the 19th century, we must look back at the history of the First International. During its lifetime, from 1864 to 1872, the workers' movement faced growing hostility from the established powers, and thinking about emancipation underwent major changes.

In 1870, for example, the imperial lawyer in the trial of the Paris office of the International Workingmen's Association demanded a penalty because of the intrusion into the political arena of the group known as the "Gravilliers": "While the government had tolerated a Society that sought to solve economic problems through the association, cooperation and solidarity of workers, it had never tolerated an Association which, by raising political questions, appealing to the most ardent passions, rallying considerable forces in France, Europe and soon the whole world around hostile and disastrous doctrines, wanted to become a state within the state and was thus creating a permanent and organised danger for the government and for society".[61] The conference of the International from 16–23 September 1871, in London recalled in a resolution "that in the militant state of the working class, its economical movement and its political action are indissolubly united" and a comment by French socialist politician Édouard Vaillant concurred, recalling "that the political question and the social question are indissolubly united, that they are but the two sides of one and the same question".[62] These quotations show that the split between political, economic, and social issues was not a defect of the original socialism but resulted from the prosecution of associations that did not confine themselves to a single field. This acknowledgement that repression led to a separation between previously linked domains should not, however, conceal the fact that the groundwork for this split was laid by thinkers who moved away from the democratic orbit to tackle change by focusing on developments within the economic infrastructure.

The further the 19th century progressed, the more the involvement of the people in solving their own problems, so important in associationism, declined. Insurmountable walls were constructed between science and common sense. Soon, as Lefort noted, "the Communists [were] not expressing their own views; it [was] the world and history which [were] expressing themselves through them". As the Communist Manifesto claims, all they do is reveal "actual relations springing from an existing class struggle, from a historical movement going on under our very eyes".[63] In the relationship between this theory and practice, the former seizes on movements emanating from society that are moving in the direction that it indicates. It "apodictically" assumes the existence of "resistance movements", rather than "exploring reality" for them.[64] Saint-Simon, Owen, and Proudhon share the conviction that they are revealing the objective interests "of an oppositional movement already present in contemporary society" that "represent[s] the theorists' own ideals".[65] This "tendency to draw self-referential conclusions" was reinforced when, in Marx, moving away from his early works, understood the proletariat as a "unified subject" entirely turned towards revolution – one that "lends expression to the urgent desire of all human beings". Leaving little room for the "concrete feelings" of the various groups within the working class, the doctrine exonerates itself from verification since it is "bound to the virtually transcendent precondition of an already present social movement".[66]

The rejection of associationism and the rise of dirigisme

In this respect too, the history of the First International is instructive. The Inaugural Address of the Workers' Association in 1864 is an analysis of the transition that began at that time. In this text, Marx returned to the struggle between the "political economy of the working class" and that of the "bourgeois class". He saw in the legal limitation of working hours a success of the former, but this legislative change coincided with another "even more complete victory" of labour over property: the cooperative movement proved that "wage-labour was destined to disappear in the face of associated labour performed with spirit, joy and goodwill". Self-realisation through work became the ultimate goal. But for this to happen, it required "the seizure of political power, which had become the first duty of the working class". The multi-dimensionality of workers' actions remains, but Marx establishes a hierarchy between the tasks to be accomplished. Workers' main strength is their number, but they "only carry weight if they are united by association and guided by knowledge". Hence the idea of the International Association, coordinated by the Central Council, later called the General Council. The cooperative and mutualist principles specific to workers' associations remained pre-eminent at the Geneva Congress in 1866, but the intensification of social conflicts led to a preference, in substantive terms, for the collective appropriation of all the tools of work and forces of production, as well as a preference, in organisational terms, for centralisation. At the London Conference in 1871, Marx took the side of this decision against federalism, expressing his desire to establish the General Council as the governing body, with Engels adding that it needed an "unlimited number of delegates".[67] Two months later, the Jura Federation challenged "this unity that is being sought through centralisation and dictatorship",[68] with Marx and Engels retorting that their concern was to prevent sectarian drift. In 1872, dissension worsened over the location of the Council, the exclusion of Bakunin and Guillaume, the departure of the Blanquists, until finally the movement fell apart.

From then on, associationalist fraternity was mocked as if it meant class collaboration. Self-organisation and philanthropy were wrongly equated, as if they were one and the same movement, when in fact they were two antagonistic projects for society. This reduction of associationism to paternalism and moralisation was also apparent in Spain in relation to the *Ateneos populares*. It was not until the end of the 20th century that historians made a clear distinction between those that were part of an attempt to establish control by elites and those that were "building an active citizenry aware of its political, economic, social and cultural choices",[69] thanks to the egalitarianism of their members and the democratic functioning of their internal operation.

The authoritarian turn of the workers' movement was fuelled by a narrative in which associationism was merely a form of angelic romanticism that was opposed by centralising realism, which did not shy away from the use of force. The inevitable revolution was, according to Engels, and as repeated by Lenin, "certainly the most authoritarian thing that is possible. Revolution is the act whereby one part of the population imposes its will upon the other part by means of rifles, bayonets, and cannons, i.e. extremely authoritarian means. And the victorious party of necessity is compelled to maintain its rule by means of fear which its arms inspire in the reactionaries".[70] In other words, political naivety was imputed to all those accused of playing into the hands of reaction because they were reluctant to militarise workers' organisation.

This dirigisme had many consequences during the second half of the 19th century. One was that "the relationship between the socialist worker's movement and the emerging feminist movement remained tense and unhappy"[71] in countries like France and Germany. The virile characteristics that legitimised proletarian violence came to the fore with the Second and Third Internationals and intensified in Bolshevism. But even the socialist currents that accepted democratic rules remained prisoners of a conception of change as occurring via public intervention and national collective bargaining. Where the latter was weak, as it was in France, the elimination or correction of market capitalism seemed possible only through statism. Hence the tendency to see the state as the entity that could discipline and restore civil society.

In France, this tendency – which began with the Le Chapelier law and the d'Allarde decree – was confirmed in 1848 when a Council for the Encouragement of Workers' Associations was set up[72]; most of the projects submitted were rejected on various pretexts, and self-organised collectives were discriminated against in favour of alliances between capital and labour. Audigamme's slip of the tongue (1860) in referring to it as a "Council for the Improvement" of workers' associations is symptomatic, showing that the state aimed to reframe initiatives by forcing them to place themselves under a new form of supervision. The way it operated reveals that it was a veritable council of discouragement, telling workers why their experiments were not worthy of public support unless they had been corrected by a supervisory authority. Even if the French case is extreme in this respect, it shows the extent to which the welfare state generally distrusts civil society and imposes its own norms on it. Obsessed with protection to the detriment of emancipation, it hides a whiff of paternalism behind egalitarian rules, which feminists were quick to criticise at the end of the 20th century, citing gender inequalities and a failure to take account of users' views. More broadly, this tendency can be found in any form of statism masquerading as progressivism.

However, the salutary renunciation of state dirigisme should not encourage a form of plutocratic dirigisme[73] in which the beneficiaries of private compassion are dependent on their benefactors. As we have noted often enough, associationism, with its democratic roots, protects us from responses to social inequalities that rely on the goodwill of the powerful and leave power relations in the shadows. Indeed, it is because of this vigilance over inequalities that associationism is not only to be found by looking back at the past but can feature in a vision for the future.

The political dimension of the solidarity economy

Today's solidarity-based initiatives should "be considered, beyond their economic, social or political objectives, as places where public spheres are opened up – public spheres that are both hybrid and plural. Hybridity and pluralism are the prerequisites for non-institutional publicity, as a counterpoint to elective, trade-union and political representation. Not without their own ambiguities and paradoxes, these forms of socialisation and sociability, of engagement and public organisation, blur the established markers that separate the economic, social and political spheres, and reconfigure civil society's complicated relationship with the state and the market".[74]

What emerges, then, is the possibility of bringing together actions and research that take their meaning from the same opposition to a profoundly standardising neoliberalism. Just as necessary as biodiversity, it is economic and political plurality that is capable of constructing institutions in a way that restores the opportunity for democratic deliberation on the future of the economy, i.e. the antithesis of the Hayekian fantasy of constitutionalising the economy so that it becomes the preserve of experts.

It is worth noting the growing number of initiatives being carried out within civil society, without giving the impression that they are sufficient. The challenge of institutional change is a major one. Laclau[75] deserves to be heard when he warns against the "ultralibertarianism" that focuses all its attention on movements without seeing that their future depends on institutional construction. This warning is echoed by Mauss, who was prescient in this respect too, since he rejected such "brutal choices between two contradictory forms of society", preferring those "which are made and will be made by processes of constructing new groups and institutions alongside and on top of the old ones".[76] He assigns a role to the state that does not consist of driving change from above, but more modestly of "enhancing social practice", "sanctioning" it, and "enforcing" it[77] – in short, amplifying what this practice has already begun. It is changes to the institutional environment that can prevent "a kind of democracy of withdrawal, of enclosure", by encouraging "initiatives taken by citizens themselves, around the management of commons, around taking control of places, around community initiatives".[78]

"We are therefore faced with a real and potentially powerful movement, but one that is limited both by a political context of widespread despair and social fear, which does not make it easy to take up a bold position, and by the resistance of the actors of the old society, of the old politics, who are standing in the way of this movement's recognition".[79] While a dynamic of solidarity is perceptible, this needs to be reinforced if it is not to be diluted through either normalisation or marginalisation.

For a democratic experimentalism

In order to avoid these two pitfalls, we cannot evade discussion of the relationship with institutions – of either its necessity or its difficulty. There is no point denying it: it poses problems. Inventiveness in practice comes up against ignorance on the part of the state. While society resists and proposes, the policies pursued by most governments are obsessed with market approval. The current tragedy lies in the gulf between society and public policy. Solidarity-based initiatives are as wary of being co-opted by politicians as the parties are liable to neglect what emerges from civil society, which is paralysing the construction of power relations that can counteract the excesses of the new capitalism.[80]

Breaking out of this mutual distrust is all the more important as the desire for greater citizen participation is being expressed in many different ways. If it is not listened to, as in the 1930s so well depicted by Polanyi,[81] the risk is of an authoritarian turn emanating either from extremist demagogies or from reactionary elitism. As Dewey established, in the face of the quest for certainty inherent in modernity, which is now capable of underpinning regressive manipulations, the antidote lies not in reducing solidarity in favour of markets, but in reaffirming the democratic wager that "[t]he more those who are affected by a problem are involved in the search for solutions to that problem, the more such historical-social experiments will lead to better and more stable solutions".[82] From this perspective, we can explore realistic ways forward by deepening the associational dimension of civil society initiatives and recognising the complex interactions that can lead either to their being "tamed" or to "institutions being made savage".[83] In opposition to the ideology of partnership, it is in any case important to accept the virtues of the social conflictuality necessary for a living democracy. As Honneth puts it, socialism can only renew itself as historical experimentalism, that is, by adopting experimentation as a historical-practical method for "realizing the idea of social freedom" through the exploration of "various possibilities and potentials".[84] Democracy has not yet run out of steam, but we are at a crossroads: down one route, a loss of confidence in democracy that is fraught with danger; down the other, a demand for a better life by reembedding economy in social and ecological purposes. This last sustainable perspective has to take account of the solidarity economy, this new generation of associationism.

Notes

1 Eric HOBSBAWM: *The Age of Revolution: Europe 1789–1848*, London, Abacus, 1988; *The Age of Capital 1848–1875*, London, Abacus, 1977; *The Age of Empire 1975–1914*, New York, Vintage, 1989.
2 Karl POLANYI: *The Livelihood of Man*, London, Academic Press, 1977, p. 20.
3 *Ibid.*, pp. 38–42.
4 Economistic fallacy is an expression from Polanyi and the title of a chapter in *The Livelihood of Man.*
5 Jacques DONZELOT: *L'invention du social- Essai sur le déclin des passions politiques,* Paris, Fayard, 1984.
6 Edward Palmer THOMPSON: *The Making of the English Working Class*, London, Victor Gollancz, 1988.
7 Massimo PACI: "Il sistema di welfare italiano tra tradizione clientelarie e prospettiva di reforma", in Ugo ASCOLI: *Welfare state all'italiana,* Roma, Laterza, 1984.
8 For Portugal and Spain see the chapters of these books: Daniel MELO: *Bibliografia seleccionada e anotada do associacionismo voluntario portugues*, Lisbonne, Obs 15, 2005; Santiago CASTILLO (ed.): *Solidaridad desde abajo,* Madrid, Confederación Nacional de Entidades de Previsión, 1994; Jordi

ESTIVILL: "Le mouvement associatif en Espagne: permanence historique et ouverture démocratique", in Jean-Louis LAVILLE and Anne SALMON (eds.): *Associations et action publique,* Paris, Desclée de Brouwer, 2015; Pere SOLÀ: *Els ateneus obrers i la cultura popular a Catalunya (1900 - 1939),* Barcelona, La Magrana, 1978.

9 Alain FAURE and Jacques RANCIÈRE: *La parole ouvrière*, Paris, La Fabrique, 2007, p. 32.

10 Christophe BONNEUIL and Jean-Baptiste FRESSOZ: *L'évènement Antropocène*, Paris, Le Seuil, 2013, p. 230.

11 *Ibid.*, p. 235.

12 Henri DESROCHE: *Solidarités ouvrières 1. Sociétaires et compagnons dans les associations coopératives (1981–1900)*, Paris, Editions ouvrières, 1981, pp. 58–66.

13 Jeanne DEROIN: *L'opinion des femmes*, n°6, August 1849, cited by Michèle RIOT-SARCEY: *Le procès de la liberté. Une histoire sous-terraine du XIXe siècle en France*, Paris, La Découverte, 2016, pp. 48–49.

14 Edward Palmer THOMPSON: *Customs in Common: Studies in Traditional Popular Culture*, London, Penguin, 1993, pp. 251–428.

15 Massimo PACI: "Il sistema di … ".

16 Santiago CASTILLO (ed.): *Solidaridad desde …*

17 Pere SOLÀ: *Els ateneus obrers …*

18 Jordi ESTIVILL: "Le mouvement associatif … ", p. 356

19 Friedrich ENGELS: *Socialism: Utopian and Scientific,* London, George Allen & Unwin, 1950.

20 Cited by Michèle RIOT-SARCEY: *Le procès de …*, p. 18.

21 *Ibid.*, p. 29.

22 *Ibid.*, pp. 29–35.

23 Miguel ABENSOUR: *Le procès des maîtres rêveurs suivi de Pierre Leroux et l'utopie,* Arles, Sulliver, 2000, p. 17.

24 Eugène ENRIQUEZ: "Imaginaire social, refoulement et répression dans les organisations", *Connexions,* 3, 1950; Florence GIUST-DESPRAIRIES: *L'imaginaire collectif,* Toulouse, Erès, 2003.

25 James C. SCOTT: *The Moral Economy of the Peasant,* New Haven and London, Yale University Press, 1976.

26 Burkart LUTZ: *Le mirage de la croissance marchande,* Paris, Maison des sciences de l'homme, 1990.

27 Catherine DUPRAT: *"Pour l'amour de l'humanité": le temps des philanthropes. La philanthropie parisienne des Lumières à la monarchie de Juillet,* Paris, Edition du comité des travaux historiques et scientifiques, vol. I, 1993, p. 478.

28 Giovanna PROCACCI: *Gouverner la misère. La question sociale en France (1789–1848),* Paris, Le Seuil, 1998.

29 *Ibid.*, p. 71.

30 André GUESLIN: *L'invention de l'économie sociale,* Paris, Economica, 1987.

31 Georges FAUQUET: *Œuvres complètes* (1935), Paris, Éd. de l'Institut des études coopératives, 1965.

32 Henri DESROCHE: *Le projet coopératif,* Paris, Les éditions ouvrières, 1976.

33 Claude VIENNEY: *L'économie sociale,* Paris, La Découverte, 1994.

34 Paul BÉLANGER and Benoît LÉVESQUE: *La théorie de la régulation. Du rapport salarial au rapport de consommation,* Montréal, UQAM, 1990.

35 Alain TOURAINE: *Production de la société,* Paris, Le Seuil, 1973.

36 Christophe BONNEUIL and Jean-Baptiste FRESSOZ: *L'évènement ...*, p. 246.
37 *Ibid.*, pp. 20–33.
38 Daniel BELL: *The Cultural Contradictions of Capitalism*, New York, Basic Books, 1976.
39 Ronald INGLEHART: *The Silent Revolution. Changing Values and Political Styles among Western Democracies,* Princeton, Princeton University Press, 1977.
40 Jacques ION: *La fin des militants,* Paris, L'Atelier, 1977.
41 Daniel MOTHÉ: *L'autogestion goutte à goutte,* Paris, Editions du Centurion, 1980.
42 Jean-Louis LAVILLE and Anne SALMON (eds.): *Associations et ...*, pp. 552–558.
43 Milton FRIEDMAN: *Capitalism and Freedom,* Chicago, The University of Chicago Press, 2002, p. 15.
44 Friedrich HAYEK: *The Road to Serfdom*, London, Routledge, 2001 [1944].
45 Muhammad YUNUS: *Building Social Business, The New Kind of Capitalism That Serves Humanity's Most Pressing Needs*, New York, Public Affairs, 2010, pp. 52–53.
46 *Ibid.*, p. 54.
47 David BORNSTEIN: *How to Change the World: Social Entrepreneurs and the Power of New Ideas*, New York, Oxford University, 2007.
48 Muhammad YUNUS: *Creating a World Without Poverty, Social Business and the Future of Capitalism*, New York, Public Affairs, 2007, p. 37.
49 Coimbatore PRAHALAD: *The Fortune at the Bottom of the Pyramid, Eradicating Poverty Through Profits*, New Jersey, Prentice Hall, 2009.
50 Muhammad YUNUS: *Building Social Business ...*, p. 60.
51 Steve HEARN: *Développer l'entreprenariat culturel,* Paris, Rapport remis au ministère de la Culture et de la Communication et au ministère de l'Economie, du Redressement productif et du Numérique, 2014.
52 Emmanuel FABER and Jay NAIDOO: *Innover par la mobilisation des acteurs: une nouvelle approche de l'aide au développement,* Paris, Rapport pour le ministre délégué chargé du développement, 2014.
53 Laurence FONTAINE: *Le marché – Histoires et usages d'une conquête sociale*, Paris, Gallimard, 2014.
54 Manuel CASTELLS, Joao GARAÇA and Gustavo CARDOSA (eds.): *Aftermath. The Cultures of the Economic Crisis,* Oxford, Oxford University Press, 2012, p. 211.
55 *Ibid.*, pp. 210–248.
56 Nancy FRASER: *Fortunes of Feminism: From State-Managed Capitalism to Neoliberal Crisis*, London, Verso, 2013, p. 219.
57 *Ibid.*, pp. 213–223.
58 Florence DEGAVRE: "La pensée femmes et développement", in Isabelle GUERRIN, Madeleine HERSENT and Laurent FRAISSE: *Femmes, économie et développement,* Toulouse, Erès, 2011.
59 Isabelle GUÉRIN, Isabelle HILLENKAMP and Christine VERSCHUUR: "Economie solidaire et théories féministes: pistes pour une convergence nécessaire", *Revue d'économie solidaire*, 7 (2014), pp. 43–44.
60 Axel HONNETH: *The Idea of Socialism,* Cambridge, Polity, 2015, pp. 27–50.
61 Mathieu LEONARD: *L'émancipation des travailleurs. Une histoire de la Première Internationale,* Paris, La Fabrique éditions, 2011.
62 *Ibid.*, pp. 276–277.

63 Claude LEFORT: *Democracy and Political Theory,* translated by David Macey, Cambridge, Polity, 1988, p. 153.
64 Axel HONNETH: *The Idea … ,* p. 38.
65 *Ibid.*, pp. 37–38.
66 *Ibid.*, pp. 39–40.
67 Mathieu LÉONARD: *L'émancipation des …*, pp. 275–282.
68 James GUILLAUME: *L'Internationale. Documents et souvenirs (1864–1878)* tome 1, Genève, Grunauer, 1905, pp. 239–240.
69 Ramon ARNABAT and Xavier FERRÉ: *Ateneus: cultura y llibertat. Associacionisme a la Catalunya Contemporanià,* Federacio d'Ateneus de Catalunya, Barcelona, 2015, p. 209.
70 Vladimir Ilich LENIN: *The State and Revolution*, London, Penguin Books, 1992, p. 57.
71 Axel HONNETH: *The Idea of …*, pp. 159 n15.
72 Jean-François MARCHAT: *L'apprentissage de l'expérimentation sociale. Contribution à l'analyse et à la pédagogie institutionnelles de l'entreprise*, thèse de sciences de l'éducation, université Paris VIII, 1989.
73 Jean-Michel SERVET: "Les sociétés civiles entre risque ploutocratique de la philanthropie et alternatives solidaires: une lecture polanyenne", *Mondes en développement,* t. XL, CLIX, 3 (2012).
74 Daniel CEFAÏ: "L'association d'hier à aujourd'hui », in Philippe CHANIAL and Daniel CEFAÏ: *L'association comme politique*, Domont", Thierry Quinqueton, 2000, p. 64.
75 Ernesto LACLAU: "Logiques de la construction politique et identités populaires", in Jean-Louis Laville, Jose Luis Coraggio (dir.), 2016, *Les gauches du XXIe siècle – Un dialogue Nord-Sud*, Lormont, Le Bord de l'eau, 2016.
76 Marcel MAUSS: *Ecrits politiques,* Paris, Fayard, 1997, p. 265.
77 *Ibid.*, p. 553.
78 Loic BLONDIAUX: Interview with Philippe Frémeaux, in *Démocratiser l'économie,* volume 2, Paris, Institut pour le développement de l'information économique et sociale – Institut Veblen, 2018, pp. 14–15.
79 *Ibid.*, p. 15.
80 Ulrich BECK: *Risk Society: Towards a New Modernity*, translated by Mark Ritter, London, Sage Publications, 1992.
81 Karl POLANYI: *The Great Transformation: The Political and Economic Origins of Our Time*, Boston, Beacon Press, 2001 [1944].
82 Axel HONNETH: *The Idea of …*, p. 62.
83 NEVEU, pp. 196–209.
84 Axel HONNETH: *The Idea of …*, pp. 46–47.

References

ABENSOUR, Miguel: *Le procès des maîtres rêveurs suivi de Pierre Leroux et l'utopie*, Arles, Sulliver, 2000.

ARNABAT, Ramon and FERRÉ, Xavier: *Ateneus: cultura y llibertat. Associacionisme a la Catalunya Contemporanià*, Barcelona, Federacio d'Ateneus de Catalunya, 2015.

BECK, Ulrich: *Risk Society: Towards a New Modernity*, London, Sage Publications, 1992.

BÉLANGER, Paul and LÉVESQUE, Benoît: *La théorie de la régulation. Du rapport salarial au rapport de consommation*, Montréal, UQAM, 1990.

BELL, Daniel: *The Cultural Contradictions of Capitalism*, New York, Basic Books, 1976.
BLONDIAUX, Loic: "Interview with Philippe Frémeaux", in *Démocratiser l'économie*, volume 2, Paris, Institut pour le développement de l'information économique et sociale – Institut Veblen, 2018, pp. 14–15.
BONNEUIL, Christophe and FRESSOZ, Jean-Baptiste: *L'évènement Antropocène*, Paris, Le Seuil, 2013.
BORNSTEIN, David: *How to Change the World: Social Entrepreneurs and the Power of New Ideas*, New York, Oxford University, 2007.
CASTELLS, Manuel; GARAÇA, Joao and CARDOSA, Gustavo (eds.): *Aftermath. The Cultures of the Economic Crisis*, Oxford, Oxford University Press, 2012.
CASTILLO, Santiago (ed.): *Solidaridad desde abajo*, Madrid, Confederación Nacional de Entidades de Previsión, 1994.
CEFAÏ, Daniel: "L'association d'hier à aujourd'hui", in Philippe CHANIAL and Daniel CEFAÏ (eds.): *L'association comme politique*, Domont, Thierry Quinqueton, 2000.
DEGAVRE, Florence: "La pensée femmes et développement", in Isabelle GUERRIN, Madeleine HERSENT and Laurent FRAISSE (eds.): *Femmes, économie et développement*, Toulouse, Erès, 2011.
DEROIN, Jeanne: *L'opinion des femmes*, n°6, August 1849, cited by Michèle RIOT-SARCEY: *Le procès de la liberté. Une histoire sous-terraine du XIXe siècle en France*, Paris, La Découverte, 2016.
DESROCHE, Henri: *Le projet coopératif*, Paris, Les éditions ouvrières, 1976.
DESROCHE, Henri: *Solidarités ouvrières 1. Sociétaires et compagnons dans les associations coopératives (1981–1900)*, Paris, Editions ouvrières, 1981.
DONZELOT, Jacques: *L'invention du social- Essai sur le déclin des passions politiques*, Paris, Fayard, 1984.
DUPRAT, Catherine: *"Pour l'amour de l'humanité": le temps des philanthropes. La philanthropie parisienne des Lumières à la monarchie de Juillet*, Paris, Edition du comité des travaux historiques et scientifiques, vol. I, 1993.
ENGELS, Friedrich: *Socialism: Utopian and Scientific*, London, George Allen & Unwin, 1950.
ENRIQUEZ, Eugène: "Imaginaire social, refoulement et répression dans les organisations", *Connexions*, 3 (1950), 65–92.
ESTIVILL, Jordi: "Le mouvement associatif en Espagne: permanence historique et ouverture démocratique", in Jean-Louis LAVILLE and Anne SALMON (eds.): *Associations et action publique*, Paris, Desclée de Brouwer, 2015.
FABER, Emmanuel and NAIDOO, Jay: *Innover par la mobilisation des acteurs: une nouvelle approche de l'aide au développement*, Paris, Rapport pour le ministre délégué chargé du développement, 2014.
FAUQUET, Georges: *Œuvres complètes (1935)*, Paris, Éd. de l'Institut des études coopératives, 1965.
FAURE, Alain and RANCIÈRE, Jacques: *La parole ouvrière*, Paris, La Fabrique, 2008.
FONTAINE, Laurence: *Le marché - Histoires et usages d'une conquête sociale*, Paris, Gallimard, 2014.

FRASER, Nancy: *Fortunes of Feminism: From State-Managed Capitalism to Neoliberal Crisis*, London, Verso, 2013.
FRIEDMAN, Milton: *Capitalism and Freedom*, Chicago, The University of Chicago Press, 2002.
GIUST-DESPRAIRIES, Florence: *L'imaginaire collectif*, Toulouse, Erès, 2003.
GUÉRIN, Isabelle; HILLENKAMP, Isabelle and VERSCHUUR, Christine: "Economie solidaire et théories féministes: pistes pour une convergence nécessaire", *Coimbra, Revue d'économie solidaire*, 7 (2014), 4–43.
GUESLIN, André: *L'invention de l'économie sociale*, Paris, Economica, 1987.
GUILLAUME, James: *L'Internationale. Documents et souvenirs (1864–1878) tome 1*, Genève, Grunauer, 1905.
Hayek, Friedrich: *The Road to Serfdom*, London, Routledge, 2001 [1944].
HEARN, Steve: *Développer l'entreprenariat culturel*, Paris, Rapport remis au ministère de la Culture et de la Communication et au ministère de l'Economie, du Redressement productif et du Numérique, 2014.
HOBSBAWM, Eric: *The Age of Revolution: Europe 1789–1848*, London, Abacus, 1988; *The Age of Capital 1848–1875*, 1977, London, Abacus; *The Age of Empire 1975–1914*, 1989, New York, Vintage.
HONNETH, Axel: *The Idea of Socialism*, Cambridge, Polity, 2015.
INGLEHART, Ronald: *The Silent Revolution. Changing Values and Political Styles among Western Democracies*, Princeton, Princeton University Press, 1977.
ION, Jacques: *La fin des militants*, Paris, L'Atelier, 1977.
LACLAU, Ernesto: "Logiques de la construction politique et identités populaires", in Jean-Louis LAVILLE and Jose Luis CORAGGIO (dir.): *Les gauches du XXIe siècle – Un dialogue Nord-Sud*, Lormont, Le Bord de l'eau, 2016.
LEFORT, Claude: *Democracy and Political Theory*, translated by David Macey, Cambridge, Polity, 1988.
LENIN, Vladimir Ilich: *The State and Revolution*, London, Penguin Books, 1992.
LEONARD, Mathieu: *L'émancipation des travailleurs. Une histoire de la Première Internationale*, Paris, La Fabrique éditions, 2011.
LUTZ, Burkart: *Le mirage de la croissance marchande*, Paris, Maison des sciences de l'homme, 1990.
MARCHAT, Jean-François: *L'apprentissage de l'expérimentation sociale. Contribution à l'analyse et à la pédagogie institutionnelles de l'entreprise*, thèse de sciences de l'éducation, Université Paris VIII, 1989.
MAUSS, Marcel: *Ecrits Politiques*, Paris, Fayard, 1997.
MELO, Daniel: *Bibliografia seleccionada e anotada do associacionismo voluntario portugues*, Lisbonne, Obs 15, 2005.
MOTHÉ, Daniel: *L'autogestion goutte à goutte*, Paris, Editions du Centurion, 1980.
PACI, Massimo: "Il sistema di welfare italiano tra tradizione clientelarie e prospettiva di reforma", in Ugo ASCOLI (ed.): *Welfare state all'italiana*, Roma, Laterza, 1984.
POLANYI, Karl: *The Great Transformation: The Political and Economic Origins of Our Time*, Boston, Beacon Press, 2001 [1944].

POLANYI, Karl: *The Livelihood of Man*, London, Academic Press, 1977.
PRAHALAD, Coimbatore: *The Fortune at the Bottom of the Pyramid, Eradicating Poverty Through Profits*, New Jersey, Prentice Hall, 2009.
PROCACCI, Giovanna: *Gouverner la misère. La question sociale en France (1789–1848)*, Paris, Le Seuil, 1998.
SCOTT, James C.: *The Moral Economy of the Peasant*, New Haven and London, Yale University Press, 1976.
SERVET, Jean-Michel: "Les sociétés civiles entre risque ploutocratique de la philanthropie et alternatives solidaires: une lecture polanyenne", *Mondes en développement*, t. XL, CLIX, 3, 2012, 89–104.
SOLÀ, Pere: *Els ateneus obrers i la cultura popular a Catalunya (1900–1939)*, Barcelona, La Magrana, 1978.
THOMPSON, Edward Palmer, *The Making of the English Working Class*, London, Victor Gollancz, 1988.
THOMPSON, Edward Palmer: *Customs in Common: Studies in Traditional Popular Culture*, London, Penguin, 1993.
TOURAINE, Alain: *Production de la société*, Paris, Le Seuil, 1973.
VIENNEY, Claude: *L'économie sociale*, Paris, La Découverte, 1994.
YUNUS, Muhammad: *Building Social Business, The New Kind of Capitalism That Serves Humanity's Most Pressing Needs*, New York, Public Affairs, 2010.
YUNUS, Muhammad: *Creating a World Without Poverty, Social Business and the Future of Capitalism*, New York, Public Affairs, 2007.

5 Hybridisation, Social Innovation, and Commoning

The Experience of the Italian Cooperative Enterprises at the Turn of the Millennium

Patrizia Battilani

Introduction

Over the last decades, the international debate on cooperative enterprises has brought the attention to three main issues: the hybridisation/demutualisation of traditional cooperatives[1]; the ability of cooperatives to produce social innovations in urban and rural contexts[2]; and their being an alternative to the complete commodification of society fostering commons.[3]

Demutualisation became an issue at the end of the 1980s. In the command economies it was a key feature of the transition to a market economy and involved millions of people and thousands of undertakings. In the Western world it developed in parallel to the privatisation of State-owned enterprises and was both an answer to financial constraints and a way to ease mergers and acquisitions. In both cases demutualisation was the result of a managerial strategy aiming at supporting business growth and capturing benefits for the managers themselves.[4] The cultural framework in which demutualisation took shape both in Europe and the rest of the world is that of the conventional enterprise's supremacy over any other form of enterprise (State-owned, municipal, cooperatives) and the design of institutions according to the neo-liberal paradigm. In general, in the context of the third globalisation which included capital mobility and financial deepening, growth and competition with conventional enterprises became very challenging for cooperative enterprises. Often, the survival and the expansion abroad of cooperatives required some kind of hybridisation with the conventional enterprise, facilitating access to financial sources and foreign direct investment. In many countries, Italy among them, specific laws were approved making it possible for cooperatives to set up conventional companies and have access to private financial sources. This is what we usually defined as hybridisation, the emergence of a form of enterprise mixing the original cooperative features (democratic votes, open door, etc.) and the stock company ones. The scientific debate on the form and degree of

DOI: 10.4324/9781003439554-6

hybridisation accompanied the emergence of large cooperative groups in many European countries as well as the demutualisation of many financial and agricultural cooperatives, above all in the UK, the USA, and Australia.

In the meantime, a second strand of literature provided theoretical support to the development of new typologies of cooperatives focusing on innovation in the provision of services to the community. These undertakings shared features with non-profit organisations and could be considered a form of social enterprise. Their development was explained through different interpretations. Some scholars focused on the growing difficulties of Welfare State systems to provide the wide range of services needed by their citizens, above all after the oil crisis when the State budget constraint became an issue[5] and in parallel new concepts and forms of poverty and needs started to be identified.[6] The incapacity of conventional for-profit enterprises to elaborate their own business model in the field paved the way for the development of social enterprises which mixed paid work, volunteers, and local government engagement.[7]

Finally, due to the work of Eleonor Ostrom,[8] commons have received new attention. Originally, commons were understood as "the creations of nature and society that we inherit jointly and freely, and hold in trust for future generations",[9] as for instance the natural resources. However, some scholars introduced the concept of social commons (care services) or cultural commons (music, arts, scientific concepts).[10] Within this framework we can rethink the cooperative experience as a way of organising in commons (through the collective allocation of common resources and users' responsibility), for commons (by collective use), of commons (by collective production), as suggested by Valerie Fourier.[11] Furthermore, some cooperative principles seem to design an enterprise more based on commons than on private ownership.[12] Following Holder and Flessas 2008[13] we can define common property as the right of being not excluded from the use of a thing. For instance, the first principle of open membership aims at including in cooperatives anyone interested in them, within the rules and regulations of the cooperative bylaw. Also the concern for community (principle n°7), according to which cooperatives work for the sustainable development of their communities through policies approved by their members, can be interpreted as a way of keeping a link with commons. However, it is how cooperatives are regulated which makes them nearer or more distant to the idea of commons. The Italian regulation of demutualisation which required the transfer of part of the asset to the mutual funds organised by the cooperative umbrella organisations is based on the idea that cooperative assets belong to communities and also to future generations. In other words, part of their assets are commons.

Connecting the cooperative experience with the sociological and economic literature we can claim that in many countries cooperatives have experienced a sort of duality over the last five decades. From one side there has been a process of hybridisation stimulating cooperatives to acquire some features of the conventional enterprise and lose part of their identity. On the other side, they have been actively engaged in social innovation and "commoning" processes by focusing on the needs of local communities and sharing and producing resources for them.

In Italy this dualism has been particularly strong and contributed to the shape of a wide and variegated movement, which has played an important role in the economic and social life of the country. The Italian cooperative world is today characterised by a great variety in terms of enterprises' typology, size, and specialisation. Some cooperatives are very large, partly internationalised and play a pivotal role in their industry. The Conad and Consumer coop were respectively the number one and two in mass retailing; the CNS (National Services Consortium) and Coopservice led the facility management sector; Camst is one of the most important catering enterprises, Granarolo is the number one in the dairy sector in Italy, and Conserve Italia one of the largest food processing groups in Europe. This produces advantages and disadvantages. Their large size makes the involvement of members in strategic decisions very challenging; however the greater financial endowment increases the possibility to promote cultural and social projects at the local and national levels, keeping ties with the communities. Other cooperatives are very small with a heterogeneous membership fully focused on the community needs. This is the case for the social and community cooperatives. They try to revitalise the economic and social life of remote rural areas or provide services in an urban context. They are expressions of the needs and vitality of communities and participate in the production of social commons.

The aim of this essay is to investigate the connection between the evolution of cooperatives and the social and economic transformations which took place from the 1970s onwards, within the conceptualisation we introduced above: hybridisation, social innovation, commoning. Our research question is if cooperatives were able to be transformative in a context in which a new political and economic mainstream considered cooperatives a remnant of the past or if the adaptation process changed them so deeply that they lost their specificity.

To this aim we will analyse both the emergence of large and hybrid cooperative groups (section the hybridisation of cooperative) and the innovative experiences of the social and community cooperatives (section social innovation practices in the cooperative world and section from social innovation to communing). To understand the context of their evolution, section 1 will focus on the social and economic changes which took place in Italy from the 1970s onwards and their connection with the evolution of cooperation. Finally, the conclusion will try to answer our research question.

Cooperatives in a changing world: the case studies in Italy from 1970s to the present

Of the larger European countries, Italy is the one in which cooperatives are the most strongly rooted: proof of this was given by the data provided by Istat (the National Institute of Statistics), which reveals that in 2021, 6.1% of the total workforce were employed in cooperatives, and this figure rises to 11% if we only consider those enterprises with more than 250 employees (besides which, more than 12% of such enterprises are in fact cooperatives).[14] Furthermore, cooperatives lead the field in certain sectors, such as that of retail distribution (Conad and Coop Consumatori), fresh milk (Granarolo), vegetable preserves (Conserve Italia), and facility management (CNS and Coopservice). Furthermore, the Cooperative Monitor ranking of the 300 largest cooperatives in the world, counts 14 Italian undertakings.[15] This number is not high in comparison to Germany (42) and France (31) but needs to be framed in the Italian economy that is much more based on small and middle-sized enterprises than any other industrialised country.

As can be seen from Table 5.1, the 1970s represented a turning point in the history of Italian cooperative enterprises, marking the beginning of a long phase of expansion. Their number grew rapidly (from about 10,000 to more than 50,000), and the work force they employed grew from 2% to about 7% of the total. The growth was the result of a deep transformation in the traditional sectors (as for instance retailing and agriculture) and the setup of thousands of new undertakings, particularly in the service sector.

Table 5.1 Cooperatives and employees (1951–2021)

Year	*Coops*	*Employees*	*% of total employees*
1951	10,782	137,885	2
1961	12,229	192,008	2
1971	10,744	207,477	2
1981	19,900	362,435	3
1991	35,646	584,322	4
2001	53,393	935,239	6
2012	55,813	1,154,913	6.9
2018	56,516	1,193,252	6.8
2019	54,522	1,169,980	6.6
2020	51,116	1,108,650	6.4
2021	49,997	1,106,805	6.2

Source: ISTAT, Census of Industry, 1951–2001; I.stat, Imprese, 2012–2021.

In those decades, the cooperative movement was particularly able to understand and cater for the deep transformations undergoing in Italian economy and society.

It is indisputable that Italy in the last three decades of the twentieth century undertook a profound change. From the economic point of view, they witnessed the end of the economic miracle. With the 1973 oil crisis, the Italian economy ended a period of extraordinary growth and started a phase characterised by cyclical crises and, since the 1990s, even stagnation. Two changes influenced the economic performance of the country: the passage from a manufacturing to a service-based economy and the reorganisation of production with a decrease in company size and an increase in the demand for intermediate goods and services. Companies needed specialised skills, lower costs, and increased flexibility to compete in more and more competitive markets and reacted with the externalisation of the production of intermediate goods and services. This stimulated the boom in specialised suppliers (suppliers of goods and services) and often also the delocalisation of intermediate goods production.[16] The economic literature often uses the words outsourcing and offshoring to describe this reorganisation of the productive system.

In addition to that, the country started to fully experience the consumer society. Thanks to the rapid growth of the post war decades, Italian families could improve their living standard and buy a growing set of goods. The retailing sector underwent a deep change with the slow substitution of small shops with large supermarkets and hypermarkets. Also, the agricultural cooperatives tried to exploit the new opportunity by entering the food processing industry and designing their own brand for the supermarkets.[17]

In this context, middle- and working-class families could afford not only durable goods but also new services, such as the leisure and healthcare ones. Furthermore, the parallel rapid urbanisation and the re-organisation of the family structure and habits produced a growing demand for urban services from public transit to children care, from catering for white-collar and blue-collar workers during the workdays to cultural services.

The intersection of all these changes paved the way for the development of new industries and stimulated the opening of new enterprises. The Italian cooperative movement was ready to seize the opportunity. That said, it is not surprising that most new cooperatives set up from the 1970s onwards were focusing on the provision of services. Certain service industries, such as retail distribution and banking, may rightly be considered the cradle of cooperation. However, since the 1970s, cooperatives started to be set up also in other sectors.[18] As can be seen in Table 5.2 still today the presence of cooperatives is particularly strong in transport,

Table 5.2 Number of Italian enterprises and cooperatives in 2021

Industry	*Italian enterprises (sole proprietorship excluded)*	*Cooperatives*	*% of coops*
All industries	1,663,645	49,997	3.0
Mining	1,638	24	1
Manufacturing	212,432	3,964	2
Energy supply	10,835	154	1
Water supply	8,118	376	5
Construction	210,919	6,650	3
Retailing and wholesaling	383,313	4,562	1
Transportation	52,410	5,437	10
Accommodation and food service	169,473	2,495	1
Information and communication	64,205	2,027	3
Financial activities	29,632	600	2
Real estate	204,163	1,105	1
Professional, scientific, and technical activities	122,295	2,008	2
Administrative and support services	71,913	6,511	9
Human health and social works	35,791	8,528	24
Education	15,006	2,067	14
Arts and entertainment	27,829	1,789	6
Other services	43673	1700	4%

Source: I.Stat, Imprese; http://dati.istat.it/; last visit on 22 July 2023.

administrative and support services, human health and social work, arts and entertainment, and education.

Tracing the history of these sectors is very useful because it allows us to understand features and strategies which supported the great diffusion of cooperative enterprises from the 1970s onwards. Take for instance the transport service. After the Second World War, there was a rapid expansion in the numbers of trucks and truck drivers, who usually were the sons of peasant farmers in search of new jobs or former town cart drivers. Most of them had bought a second-hand truck and worked for themselves. During the 1960s, some of them organised "groups" or "associations" with the support of Trade Unions to improve their working conditions. Towards the end of the 1960s there were between 2,000 and 3,000 such unofficial organisations, generally of little economic importance. Their transformation into genuine cooperatives, capable of formulating proper strategies for growth, was one of the principal aims of the Italian umbrella organisations during the early 1970s, and this sector remains one of the most significant for the entire cooperative movement. Today there are both many cooperatives of truckers but also of taxi drivers.[19]

The history of cooperatives focusing on business services (facility management and other support services) was quite different. Their diffusion was very limited until the 1970s when the reorganisation of the productive system stimulated manufacturing (but also hospitals, schools, and supermarkets) to externalise cleaning or security services. Consequently, many new cooperatives emerged. Take for instance the Pulixcoop, set up in Forlì in 1975, by nine women, an all-female cleaning cooperative. Members' efforts produced positive results and made it possible to offer services also outside the cleaning sector. Its first contracts came from other cooperatives which were externalising cleaning services such as Edilcoop (in construction), Coop Consumatori, and Conad (in retailing). The umbrella organisations usually encouraged their members to support the new cooperatives operating in facility management. The first serious difficulties that it encountered were related to the transition from a small-scale enterprise to a larger, better organised business. It was necessary to improve the organisational form as well as to acquire know-how through the implementation of special training courses and by hiring new managers and professionals. Consequently, at the end of the 1980s, with around 300 members, the Pulixcoop was organised into five different divisions: the hygiene division (a new name for cleaning services); green space and gardening services; energy management; waste disposal; and logistics. During the 1990s a geographical expansion started with the acquisition of contracts all over Italy. To this end, Pulixcoop created a series of highly specialised subsidiaries in order to guarantee a more rational, orderly, but also prudent, involvement in the market. In 2001, it changed its name to Formula Servizi, which is currently a very important service supplier with 2,954 employees.[20]

Very similar was the history of Cooperativa Reggiana Pulizie which was set up in 1972 by a group of women in Reggio Emilia and that in 1991 merged with another cooperative (Coopsicurezza) to give birth to Coopservice, today one of the largest enterprises operating in this sector. Today it is a group with 16,782 employees, operating in nearly all of the Italian regions and also abroad.[21]

Cultural cooperatives have spread since the 90s, when a synergy with local authorities has developed which has allowed the flourishing of cooperatives for the cataloguing of cultural heritage, management of libraries, and exhibitions and events in general. Given the capacity to absorb the so-called "youth intellectual unemployment", the development of this sector was also promoted by the political world. The Ronchey Act of 1993 made it possible to outsource museum and cultural site services and also offer additional services, such as catering, bookshops, the organisation of events, and the production and sale of media and multimedia. This law created many new opportunities for cultural cooperatives. Take for instance the Codess Culture, set up in Venice in 2000, as a spin-off of a social cooperative dating back to 1979 and that since 1986 had been operating also in the cultural sector. Codess Culture had the responsibility for the management of important Venice museums, as the Jewish and the Civic ones. It also developed important relationships with the Venice Trade Fair Centre and other institutions such as the Venice Biennial and Palazzo Grassi. In 2010 it merged with another cooperative based in Rome, Pierreci, to set up Coop culture, which today has 1,987 employees and 1,050 members and manages some of the most important cultural sites in Italy such as the Colosseum and the Diocletian Bath in Rome or the Doge's Palace in Venice.[22]

Even more interesting is the history of cooperatives operating in social works and healthcare, whose diffusion stimulated the design of a new typology of cooperative, the social one. Due to their importance, we will deal with them in section 4.

The last category of cooperatives whose development was connected to the 1970s and 1980s transformation is the workers buyout. The reorganisation of production systems and the emergence of a global value chain accompanied a process of de-industrialisation in many European countries, Italy included. In this context, the closure or delocalisation of factories became more frequent. To cope with this phenomenon and provide a chance to workers, in 1985, the Italian parliament passed the Marcora law which promoted the workers buyout cooperatives (WBO). According to Eurofond the WBO is a restructuring process in which employees buy the majority or all of the ownership shares in their company and, in effect, become the owners.

The Marcora law aimed at promoting the acquisition of companies in difficulties (or branches of them) by their workers, through the creation of workers cooperatives. To make the process viable, the law envisaged the creation of a revolving fund and the setting up of Cooperazione Finanza Impresa (CFI), an institutional investor participated by the mutual funds of the Cooperative umbrella organisations,[23] the Ministry of Enterprises and Made in Italy and some 393 cooperatives. CFI is in charge of the feasibility and competitive analysis of the WBO and supervises financial schemes. Furthermore CFI, as an institutional investor, participates in the share capital, finances long-term investment plans, and assists workers in designing the industrial plan and in the start-up of the new cooperative.

The legal framework was then strengthened with two further laws: in 1991, the law n. 223 made it possible for workers to use their post-employment benefits (Indennità di fine rapporto) to finance the new cooperative; in 2013, the law 145 gave workers of the new cooperative the right of first refusal.

Until now the diffusion of WBO has been constant although quite limited. Since 1986, about 313 WBO have been set up, on average 8 per year (Figure 5.1). In general, they emerged from two different situations: the impossibility of carrying out the generational shift due to lack of a family successor or the risk of bankruptcy. Most of the rescued enterprises are middle size, and over the last year the percentage of small businesses has increased. Many of them operate in energy intense industries.[24]

In conclusion, the economic and social transformation which took place from the 1970s onwards represented a great opportunity for the Italian cooperative movement which stimulated the setup of new cooperatives, especially in the service sector. In this way the cooperative movement accompanied the transformation of the Italian economy from manufacturing to services. However, also manufacturing experienced the emergence of new cooperatives, through the WBO projects. As we will see in section 4, the cooperative reawakening of the last decades of the 20th century played an important role in designing the new cities providing answers to family and community needs.

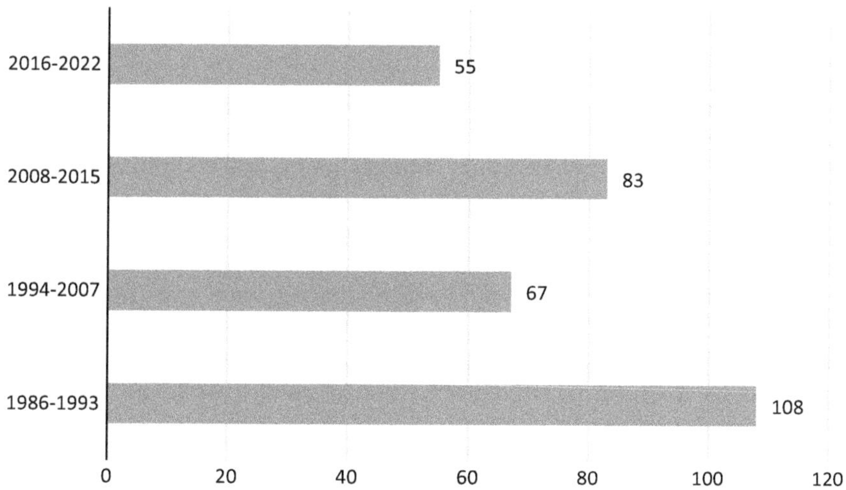

Figure 5.1 Workers buyout, 1985–2022.

Source: For the years 1986–2015: Paola DEMARTINI and Salvatore MONNI: *workers' buyout* … …,. For the years 2016–2022 Euricse dataset.

The hybridisation of the cooperative: the emergencc of cooperative groups

During the 1970s and 1980s, a new business culture gradually gained ground in the world of cooperation which provided invaluable support to the latter's expansion. From this point of view one of the most important changes was the building of large cooperative groups, comprising joint-stock companies as well.

Two laws created the precondition for this transformation. The first was no. 72 of 19 March 1983 (the so-called Visentini Law) which gave cooperatives the opportunity to become shareholders in joint-stock companies. The second was no. 59, passed in 1992, which introduced the figure of the financing member (socio sovventore). The combination of these two opportunities paved the way for the creation of cooperative groups.

In this way the laws stimulated the hybridisation of the cooperative models, introducing features of the conventional joint stock companies and making it possible to overcome the financial constraint to growth.

A survey carried out in 2004 by the Legacoop research centre showed that such groups were already quite widespread in 1998 and that they grew further during the following five years, increasing in number from 64 to 96. In 2010, there were 78 group among the 250 largest cooperatives.[25] The reasons for their development included the search for ways of expanding cooperative business abroad, the need for structures capable of managing different forms of business activity effectively, and the desire to distribute business risks.

To understand advantages and disadvantages we can analyse the Granarolo case study. The origin of this cooperative goes back to 1957. At the time, Italy had completed its reconstruction and entered a phase of sustained growth, which historians have identified with the name of economic miracle. In this context, one of the two most important cooperative apex organisations, Legacoop, identified in the creation of medium-large complexes in the field of land management and above all the processing of agricultural products, the most effective way to improve the living and working conditions of farmers and sharecroppers. The setup of Granarolo by a group of sharecroppers and small-scale tenant farmers, who grouped together to compete in a market dominated by previous "first movers", represented the most important element of this strategy. In the early years, the main obstacle to the development of the new cooperative was the shortage of financial resources, as in the best cooperative tradition. To overcome this issue the members' loans were decisive such as in 1960, when they exceeded the bank loans. Equally important was the credit that members were granted by accepting a delay in the payment of the delivered milk. It was not by chance that in 1961 in the Board of Directors report, it was claimed that the plant had already been paid at 80% thanks to the 15-day late payment of the milk that the partners have delivered. The second challenge was the conquest of a significant market share, which would allow for the best use of the purchased machinery. For this purpose, in January 1958 about 120 dairies were contacted (selected from among those belonging to relatives and friends of members or managed by milkmen culturally and politically left oriented) of which about 30 agreed to be supplied with the new milk as soon as it was marketed. At the end of the 1960s, Granarolo had risen to first place on the Bologna market and was able to offer a fairly wide range of products.

In 1972, the expansion from the local to the regional market was pursued through the setting up of a Consortium of five cooperatives called CERPL (Consortium of Milk Producers in Emilia Romagna) which could operate across the Emilia Romagna Region. In the second half of the 1980s, coinciding with a first change in the top management, a new strategy was elaborated which entrusted growth both to the development of the industrial brand (with new promotional and advertising campaigns and above all with the identification of innovative products) and to the acquisition of private companies operating in various Italian regions. For the first time Cerpl went beyond the borders of the cooperative world and also from the regional ones. However, the immediate results were not good, and in 1991, despite the increasing turnover, Granarolo faced a strong liquidity crisis due to the high rate of investment and enlargement of the previous decade. At the end of 1991 Granarolo executives started a wide rationalisation of plants, employees, and structural organisation of the group to cope with the deterioration of its financial situation. On this occasion the cooperative downsized its workforce. Until then, the undertaking had maintained the traditional structure, according to which the Consortium and the five cooperatives of milk producers owned factories and brand.

However, after restructuring, when a new phase of growth started, a deep change in the cooperative's architecture was carried out. At the time the two laws we mentioned before had already been passed. In this context, in 1993 the Consortium started the progressive transfer of all assets (that is factories and brand) to the Granarolo joint stock company, created in 1991 as part of a merger which then did not go through. Thus, this company became the place for defining the commercial and industrial strategies of the group. In 1998, the original cooperatives were grouped together in a new consortium named Granlatte, which was the majority stakeholder of Granarolo company. In this way it was possible to access bank loans and issue bonds following the procedures of conventional companies, without having disadvantages of any kind. In addition to that it became possible also to have minority shareholders providing capital. This is the case of Intesa San Paolo, one of the largest Italian banks, that in 2004 bought some 20% of the entire share capital. In this way it was possible to acquire one of the most important Italian companies producing yogurt, Yomo. At the end of the 1990s there was also the project to list Granarolo on the Milano Stock Exchange; however, it was never realised for reasons of contingency. In the new millennium, Granarolo launched its first foreign investment. To this aim they set up new companies: one for each market in which they decided to operate.

Overall, the group is now divided into three levels of which the first is made up of two cooperative consortia (Cooperlat and Granlatte), the National strategic fund (a state-owned fund supporting the long-term investment plans of profitable companies), Enpaia, (the National Mutual Fund for Agricultural Workers and Employees), and one bank (Intesa San Paolo), which directly owns the Granarolo company (Figure 5.2). The latter owns about 30 companies operating in the dairy sector in Italy, Europe, and the rest of the world. Some companies are specialised in the production of other types of food. Despite this complex architecture and the involvement of conventional banks and companies, the group maintains the characteristic of a cooperative whose members deliver and process milk.[26] The Granarolo Group is currently the largest Italian producer of fresh milk and yogurt, with about 2,600 employees, 14 factories in Italy and 9 abroad. The members who deliver milk are 637.[27]

The Granarolo case study shows that the growth strategies widely used the new instrument made available by the Italian legislation: both the entrance in new sectors as well as the expansion abroad were realised through the creation of conventional companies.

We can say that hybridisation was necessary for the cooperative growth. However, it was also a challenge. First of all, the growth itself made it more and more difficult for members to design or simply supervise the group strategies and the managers whose autonomy became extremely high. Second the concern for the community had to take a new shape due to the international dimension of the group. In order to maintain a role in the local communities in which the factories operate the group promoted social and cultural initiatives on a provincial or municipal base, as for instance the donated human milk bank project in Bologna or the Portobello one in Modena. The latter aims at helping the new poor, people who are not used to asking social services or parishes for help. In collaboration with the Modena voluntary associations and Conad (the main Italian retailer cooperative), Granarolo makes it possible for these new poor to go shopping by choosing the products and paying in "points" loaded on the tax code card and assigned according to the composition of

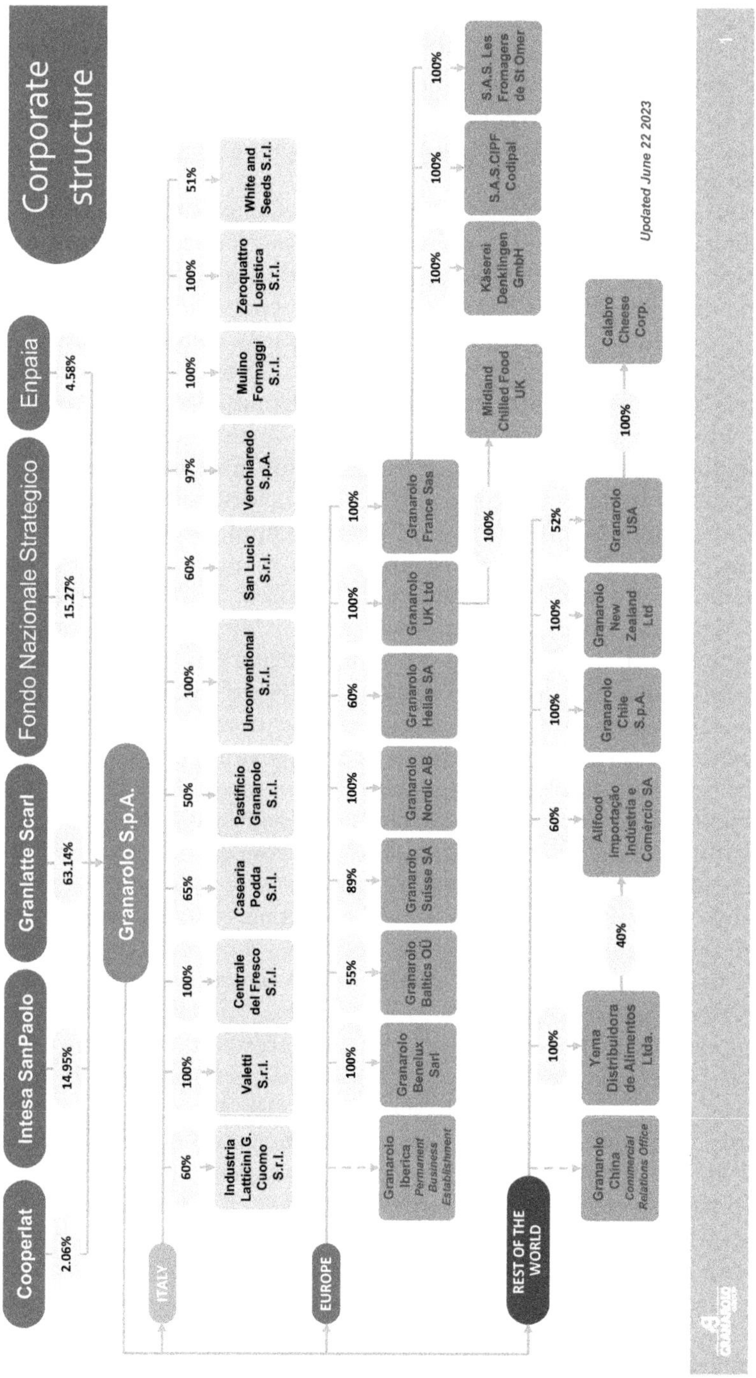

Figure 5.2 Granarolo cooperative group (2021).

the household for six months. To date there are 250 families who had accessed Portobello, for a total of 1,000 people. Other projects were developed abroad, such as that which permitted the opening of a milk factory in Tanzania which employs 800 people and provides free milk to 26,000 children; and the AfricHAnd project, aiming at building a milk value chain in Mozambique.

Granarolo is not an exception. Conad, Coop Consumatori, and many other leading cooperatives show a similar complex architecture to witness that this was the prevailing model of growth adopted by Italian cooperatives. And, they all tried to reconceptualise the cooperative principle of concern for community to make it suitable to the new context.[28]

We can ask ourselves if this hybridisation beyond facilitating the cooperatives growth has been a way to avoid demutualisation, which in Italy was extremely rare. It could be. However, we also need to highlight that the Italian legislation makes demutualisation extremely expensive. According to the Italian civil code (art. 2545) such transformation must be approved with the favourable vote of at least half of the members of the cooperative. However, when there are fewer than 50 members, the favourable votes of two-thirds of them are required. This is not really a deterrent. What can discourage demutualisation is the fact that it obliges to allocate the effective value of the assets (after deducting the paid-in and revalued capital) and the dividends not yet distributed (possibly increased up to the minimum amount of capital of the new company) at the transformation date to the mutual funds of the apex organisations so that they can be invested for the promotion and development of cooperation. It is worth highlighting that in this way the Italian legislation recognises the social function and the intergenerational pact of cooperatives, making the real owners of a cooperative not only the members but also the members of tomorrow. A cooperative is a common good that remains available to the community and to the generations to come. Cooperative members contribute to the creation of new wealth which benefits also those who will come after them.

In a context in which it is possible to finance growth through the same tools used by conventional enterprises and demutualisation is very expensive, it is not surprising that very few cooperatives have tried to demutualise. The most important case is Manutencoop, one of the most important Italian enterprises in the facility management sector, which announced its conversion to a conventional joint stock company in 2022. The cooperative had been established in 1938 by 16 workers to provide cleaning and maintenance services at the Bologna railway station. After the war its size was already remarkable. During the 1980s, a rationalisation process specialising the cooperative in the provision of cleaning services and energy management laid the foundation of a rapid expansion.

In 2003 Manutencoop employed more than 13,000 people. The growth required the organisation of a complex cooperative group, even more daring than the one put in place by Granarolo. In 2003 the Manutencoop Facility Management joint stock company was set up and progressively acquired all the assets. The original cooperative was the majority shareholder of the company, in a context in which various Private Equity funds bought part of the share capital (for a total share of 25%). In parallel also the number of members decreased, so that at the beginning of the new millennium there were 700 out of a total of over 12,000 employees.[29] The progressive departure from the cooperative model then led, in 2022, Manutencoop (which had been renamed Rekeep since 2018) to begin the demutualisation process.

A company note explained that "The adoption of the new legal form of the joint-stock company was motivated by the need to best support the national and international development path of the Rekeep Group. In a very polemical way, the note claimed that "the cooperative form, due to its rule of governance and remuneration of invested capital, has in fact proved over time to be unsuitable for coping with this process, which requires both capital contributions from members and the financial market and access to advanced financial instruments".[30]

In conclusion, between the 1980s and the 1990s a new legislative framework helped cooperative growth through the design of complex groups of enterprises. In this context demutualisation was a strategy not explored. So far only one of the large hybrid cooperative groups has demutualised despite the high cost of this procedure.

Social innovation practices in the cooperative world: the case study of social cooperatives

The 1970s were a turning point also in terms of social habits and urban life. As we mention in section 2, new needs emerged and the desire for higher living standards became stronger. Thus the demand for social and also cultural services increased. The new context was accompanied by important changes in the cultural and religious movements.

Between 1962 and 1965 the Second Vatican Council of the Catholic Church was held. The main aim was to redesign the link between the Church itself and a more secularised world by proposing changes in practices and doctrine. Among other things the Second Vatican Council marked a turning point in the social teaching of the Church by stimulating innovative interventions that could better contribute to a socially just world. An important follow-up was the birth in 1971 of the diocesan Caritas, which had the task of promoting the testimony of charity and became a driver of a multitude of initiatives to help families and people in need.

In parallel also in Italy the so-called youth revolution pushed young people into a stronger social protagonism, which during the 1970s took the shape of new associations and also cooperatives. In the same years Italy like other Western countries was experiencing the transition from elite to mass associationism. In this context a growing number of young people joined the associations promoting environmental protection, solidarity with people in need, or new forms of cultural entertainment. Finally, during the 1970s there was also the emergence of a new direction in psychiatry linked to Professor Franco Basaglia which contributed not only to an important reform in 1978 (the law 180 called Basaglia law, relating to the closure of psychiatric hospitals) but also to the setup of undertakings aiming at the reintegration of people with mental health problems.[31]

In this context the first solidarity cooperatives were expression of groups of citizens wishing to get involved directly in the production of social services. Thus, they resorted both to paid workers and voluntary members. We can mention the San Giuseppe cooperative dating back to 1963 in the province of Brescia or the Santa Gemma Galgani in 1966, in the Marche region. During the 1970s also the first integrated cooperatives aiming at reintroducing people with mental health issues in society were set up. The most famous of them were "Il posto delle fragole", set up in September 1979 in the park of the former Psychiatric Hospital of Trieste and the Cooperativa Lavoratori Uniti Franco Basaglia (CLUFB) in 1972 to manage the former psychiatric hospital's premises and grounds. The latter, bringing together psychiatrists, mental health workers, and those suffering from mental illness, represented a test case for the new approach to the treatment of mental illness, as it granted the title of worker to patients who in the past had worked only without pay within therapy schemes based on work. All these cooperatives still exist. Il posto delle Fragole counts 19 members who manage a restaurant bar and a hotel; the San Giuseppe actually manages a professional training centre, a primary school and a preschool; Santa Gemma Galgani manages a family-type community for minors in need; the CLUFB with its 189 members continues to re-integrate disadvantaged people by operating in disinfection, ecology, logistic, and other fields.

In the meantime, the development of care services stimulated the development of workers' cooperatives providing home assistance to the infirm, the elderly, and children. One of the most important was CADIAI, created in 1974 by 27 women in Bologna.[32]

In general we can say that these cooperatives were asked to help build the city of the future, a diverse type of city created on the basis of the reorganisation of public and welfare services and the management of leisure services. This new strategic vision of the future gave greater economic and political weight to the service-sector cooperatives than they had previously been granted. For many years all these experiences did not have a unified conceptualisation but remained simply the expression of the proactive attitude of large parts of Italian society who desired to help people in need and to improve the quality of life of industrial cities.

In 1987, a first survey provided a general picture of these experiences: the 496 surveyed cooperatives came from voluntary organisations (23%), associations (13%), had been set up thanks to the support of a public body (5%), and were a cooperative from the start (50%).

In 1991 the law 381 "Discipline of Social Cooperatives" tried to regulate this new typology of cooperatives. The main difference with the other cooperatives was the coexistence of different types of members: the workers, the users who receive the satisfaction of their needs through the activity specifically carried out by the cooperative, and the volunteers who lend their activity for free.

Their development in the following decades was astonishing, so that in 2016 there were 15,600 coops and almost 429,000 employees (Figure 5.3). They continued to design services for old and new situations of need. Take for instance the Azalea Coop founded in 1992 by a group of 40 members to manage home care services for people affected by HIV or with mental health problems and to organise transport services for people with disabilities. The diffusion of a new disease, HIV, created a new category of people in need and a new type of services to provide. Today Azalea Cooperativa Sociale has more than 400 working members who operate in the management of educational, social, and socio-health services.

Over the last years a consolidation process has started, with the reduction in the number of enterprises and the increase in total employees.

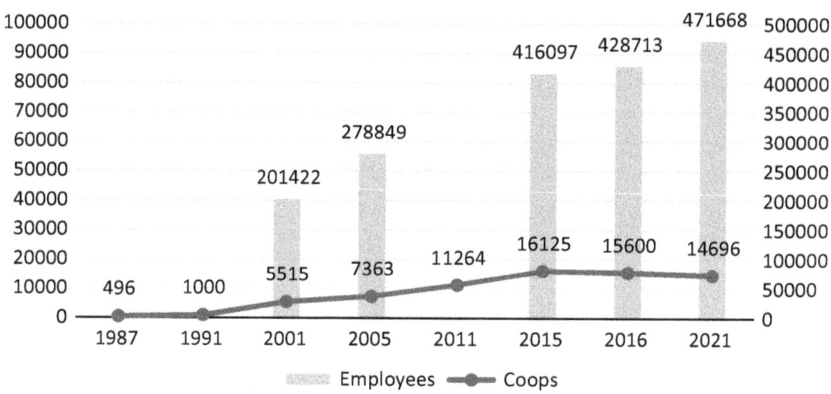

Figure 5.3 Social cooperatives (number and employees), 1987–2021.

Source: IstatDAta.

Social cooperatives have been one of the most interesting experiments of the Italian cooperative movement. They represent an innovative way to help disadvantaged people by integrating them into work and organising the care for different categories of people in need (elderly people, children, and young people in difficulty). They are one of the most successful examples of social innovation.

From social innovation to communing: the community cooperatives

The emergence of community cooperatives was the consequence of a double movement: residents started a bottom-up process by inventing new cooperatives in order to improve the quality of life in marginal areas; cooperative apex organisations and public administrations accompanied these attempts by providing a legal framework and supporting them in many ways. Attention to community cooperatives dates back to the 2008 crisis when the two most important umbrella organisations (Legacoop and Confcooperative) decided to strengthen the social impact of the Italian movement also by looking for new ideas and solutions to the problems which the crisis had exacerbated. At the time not only the cooperative movement but also some important institutions started to look for new policies and strategies fostering people's participation to cope with the social and economic consequences of the crisis.

The economic crisis not only hit Italy hard but also arrived 15 years after the greatest political scandal of the Republic's history, namely "Clean Hands", which had weakened the trust of citizens in traditional parties – some of them had completely disappeared – contributing to the development of new political forces basing their success on a negative view of politics and politicians. Overall, the degree of citizen involvement in the local and national political life strongly decreased and participation became a pressing issue. In this context a group of regions passed new laws stimulating residents' participation in the decision-making process. Tuscany was the first in 2007, then came Emilia Romagna in 2010, and finally the Apulia and Marche regions.

The Emilia Romagna region, traditionally considered a model of social cohesion and civic awareness, passed the law on "Rules for the definition, reorganisation and promotion of consultation procedures and participation in the elaboration of regional and local policies" in 2010 (Regional Law No. 3/2010), two years after the opening of a Participation Observatory, aiming at ensuring constant recognition of the participatory experiences throughout the region. In 2011 the Participation Observatory equipped itself with a web space which displayed all data on participatory experiences, thus also responding to the information and communication needs provided for by the 2010 law itself. Then in 2012 the first regional call for financing the participatory processes of local authorities was issued.

In addition to political and social issues, the 2008 crisis had also exacerbated the consequences of the hyper-urbanisation of the last decades, which had depopulated many small towns particularly in marginal areas, as for instance the mountain range of the Apennines. Consequently, shops, post offices, and recreational activities had closed down little by little, forcing the small communities living there to acquire goods and services elsewhere. In this context community cooperatives were conceived by the regions working to increase citizens participation a further tool binding together this issue with the challenges faced by marginal areas.

These regional policies intersected with the cooperative movement's reflection on innovative forms of cooperative enterprise. In Legacoop, the project was launched in 2010 as part of the strategies to overcome the economic crisis. Initially it was entrusted to Bruno Busacca who described it with these words: "The Community Cooperatives project, starting from the existing realities, wants to promote a network of cooperatives linked to specific communities and aimed primarily at satisfying the needs of citizens through the conservation and enhancement of the communities themselves. They can take the shape of user cooperatives, social cooperatives, labour cooperatives, mixed cooperatives, but they are always set up by the citizens of the community".[33]

Substantially, by providing services and generating jobs, these cooperatives could make possible the survival of communities living in marginal areas, where doing business was increasingly difficult. The search for a new type of cooperative found support in the successful experiences started in the previous decades, before anyone had conceptualised the idea of community cooperatives. Some of the most successful were the Cooperativa Valle dei Cavalieri and the Cooperativa I Briganti del Cerreto, respectively, set up in 1991 and 2003 in the Emilia Romagna Apennines. In both cases, the main aim of the cooperative was to support an area suffering from depopulation and resource depletion. The needs to which these cooperatives responded were manifold: work for young people, provision of social, health, school, commercial (bars, shops, fuel), communications (post, telephony, broadband), and environmental services, cultural revitalisation, and promotion of renewable energies. These cooperatives also pursued the enhancement of tourism (focusing on community tourism), the recovery of environmental and cultural heritage, the commercialisation of traditional products (agricultural, pastoral, craft), the preservation of cultural traditions, and the regeneration of their village in a more general sense.

To design and promote the new typology, Legacoop decided to identify the cooperatives that were already perceived by local communities as carriers of general interest, even though they have never named themselves a community cooperative. Many different experiences were recognised as the precursors of community cooperatives: the Cooperative Family (i.e. the consumer cooperative of Trentino), electric cooperatives (in Trentino), the cooperative clubs, and some housing cooperatives.

At the time, the two most important Apex organisations, Legacoop and Confcooperative, were working on the project to create a unitary federation of for all the Italian cooperatives, the Alleanza delle Cooperative Italiane (ACI). In this context, Confcooperative suggested to also share this project. It was then decided to make a coordinated work plan where Confcooperative was entrusted with the task of working on the concept of community cooperatives and Legacoop to produce an overview of the experiences already existing.[34]

An important contribution to the identification of community cooperatives came from Euricse, the European Research Institute on Cooperatives and Social Enterprises, based in Trento. In 2015, it dedicated part of its Annual Report to the "New frontier of cooperation", by focusing on three innovative experiences: the workers buyout, the cooperative management of the land confiscated from crime organisations (mafia), and finally the community cooperatives.[35] In this publication the appearance of community cooperatives was considered the beginning of a new phase in the movement's history. "This phenomenon is the culmination of a centuries-old evolution that has seen the progressive shift of the centre of gravity of cooperatives from particular social or professional groups to the entire society. While in the past cooperatives were concerned primarily with satisfying the needs of specific groups within society, often identified from the economic functions performed (workers, consumers, etc.), community cooperatives are at the service of an entire community".[36] Thus different stakeholders can play a crucial role in their development: workers, volunteers, public administration, and sometimes also other cooperatives (when they provided the business skills as well as the financial support).

In conclusion we can say that the cooperative movement supported their development also by building a new narrative and providing them with a past, a story. They were narrated as the natural development of the original cooperative feeling and the transformation of mountain consumer cooperatives, urban housing cooperatives, cooperatives providing electricity or managing pubs, and cultural associations.[37]

In 2021, a snapshot of community cooperatives was offered by AICCON, which mapped 188 of them. Almost two out of three were located in an internal area, but there was also a significant share in peri-urban areas. In the three-year period, 2018–2020, there was an "exponential" increase in the phenomenon driven above all by specific territorial areas (Tuscany and Abruzzo): more than half of the mapped cooperatives were born in this period (57%). The most widespread legal forms were the work cooperatives (44%); however also the social ones were quite widespread (20%). These organisations were multipurpose and provided a plurality of interventions in many different sectors: primarily tourism (60%), environmental conservation and protection of natural and cultural assets (47%), and agriculture (38%).[38]

The impact on local communities was variegated and involved multiple dimensions connected to the common good and the territory, for example through the creation of supply chains fostering the local economy and connecting tourism to the preservation of heritage to the agriculture to the well-being of local communities, especially in terms of social and community life.

If social cooperatives were regulated by a national law, community cooperatives remained a regional issue. Until now, their functioning has been regulated only by regional laws. The first to legislate on community co-ops was Puglia, which in 2014 defined a general framework which then was used also by other regions as Liguria and Sardinia. Emilia Romagna, which had the strongest cooperative movement in Italy, chose a different approach: its laws promoted community cooperatives, by financing start-ups or creating information points, but never defined them.

Even though there are still few community cooperatives in Italy, compared to other forms of cooperative, they are playing an important role in re-defining the role of the cooperative movement in the entire country by focusing on the production and organisation of commons.

Conclusion: are Italian cooperatives transformative?

Since their first appearance in the second half of the 19th century, Italian cooperatives shaped new forms of social promotion in the local community and functioned as a laboratory of participatory practices. According to some scholars, they contributed to the development of democratic regimes by getting people used to democratic rules. They were run according to the one member one vote rule, well before universal suffrage rooted in Italy. In addition to that, since the beginning they enlarged their aims to the cultural promotion of their members, in a context in which the open-door principle made it possible to welcome any member of the local community. There is a lot of documentary evidence of earlier cooperatives' social awareness. They organised many activities both for their members and for the rest of the community: libraries, meeting points, etc. In many cooperatives, economic and social activities overlapped so much that it became difficult to design precisely their economic boundary. They often put together people at the margins of society providing them not only a work but also the possibility to feel part of the community itself and contribute to local development. In many ways, they were an example of commoning.

This attitude did not diminish at the turn of the new millennium, when market competition forced cooperatives to become more business oriented, increase their size, and pay a growing attention to strategic management. The community awareness and the attention to members' needs continued to characterise also the largest cooperative groups, which, however, combined the business and the social dimensions by adopting renewal strategies based on ambidexterity. The "manager's ability to deal with contradictory dualities in their decision making" and "the organisation's capacity to do two different things equally well"[39] was extremely important to permit large groups to reconcile market competition with social awareness and concern for community.

However, in the meantime, the cooperative movement, the apex organisations, many non-profit associations, and their members worked to the emergence of new typologies of cooperatives in which social innovation and communing could be at the forefront. Thus, through a double process which mixed bottom-up and top-down aspects, the Italian cooperative movements experienced the development of social cooperatives and community cooperatives, suitable to cater for the needs of a society that was going through profound social and economic changes.

These comments bring us to the question we asked in the introduction, if Italian cooperatives have been transformative by pursuing social innovation and improving the quality of life of the community in which they are set up.

Even if it is not easy to provide an answer, we can certainly say that social awareness and concern for community have been at the forefront of cooperatives' strategies. Furthermore, the apex organisations have often stimulated an innovation aiming at contrasting poverty, social marginalisation, and promoting social mobility. And they often asked for a legislation which could strengthen the emergence of non-profit oriented undertakings. In the meantime, they also worked to support the growth and facilitate the emergence of large groups of enterprises, which were examples of hybridisation.

This duality had the advantage to make possible the accumulation of a managerial knowledge that in many situations was transferred from one cooperative to another. However, it raises also issues in terms of the real participation of members in the decision-making process. A second disadvantage was the hybrid image of the cooperation itself, that seemed much more oriented to business than to the economic and social promotion of members and communities.

However, it is undeniable that cooperatives have played a significant role in almost all the projects and programmes aiming at inclusion, accessibility, and social cohesion implemented at local or national level. Furthermore, many undertakings are a real example of commoning practices. In conclusion, we can say that cooperatives tried to implement their principles in a context in which the economy was going in another direction.

Notes

1 Greg PATMORE, Nikolas BALNAVE and Olivera MARJANOVIC: "Resistance Is Not Futile: Co-operatives, Demutualization, Agriculture, and Neoliberalism in Australia", *Business and Politics*, 23 (2022), pp. 510– 528; Jerker NILSSON, Anna KIHLEN and Lennart NORELL: "Are Traditional Cooperatives an Endangered Species? About Shrinking Satisfaction, Involvement and Trust", *International Food and Agribusiness Management Review*, 12 (2009), pp.101–122; Fabio CHADDAD and Michael L. COOK: "The Economics of Organization Structure Changes: An US Perspective on Demutualization", *Annales de l'Économie Publique, Sociale et Coopérative*, 75 (2004), pp. 575–594; Patrizia BATTILANI and Harm SCHROETER: "Demutualization and Its Problems", in Patrizia BATTILANI and Harm SCHROETER (eds.): *The Cooperative Business Movement, 1950 to the Present*, New York, Cambridge University Press, 2012, pp. 150–171.

2 Giovanna CAMPOPIANO and Gaia BASSANI: "Social Innovation: Learning from Social Cooperatives in the Italian Context", *Journal of Cleaner Production*, 291 (2021), pp. 1–11; Janina MACKE *et al.*: "Where Do We Go From Now? Research Framework for Social Entrepreneurship", *Journal of Cleaner Production,* 183 (2018), pp. 677–685; Amir RAHADARI, Sahar SEPASI and Mohammad MORADI: "Achieving Sustainability Through Schumpeterian Social Entrepreneurship: The Role of Social Enterprises", *Journal of Cleaner Production*, 137 (2016), pp. 347–360; Ermanno C. TORTIA, Florence DEGAVRE and Simone POLEDRINI: "Why Are Social Enterprises Good Candidates for Social Innovation? Looking for Personal and Institutional Drivers of Innovation", *Annals of Public and Cooperative Economics*, 91 (2020), pp. 1–19; Samuel BOSCARELLO: "La storia del movimento cooperativo come innovazione sociale", *Italia Contemporanea*, 25 (2022), pp. 155–167.

3 Valérie FOURNIER: "Commoning: On the Social Organisation of the Commons", *M@n@gement,* 16 (2013), pp. 433–453; Greig DE PEUTER and Nick DYER-WITHERFORD: "Commons and Cooperatives", *Affinities: A Journal of Radical Theory, Culture, and Action*, 4 (2010), pp. 30–56; Alexandre GUTTMANN: "Commons and Cooperatives: A New Governance of Collective Action", *Annals of Public and Cooperative Economics,* 92 (2021), pp. 33–53.

4 Patrizia BATTILANI and Harm SCHROETER: "Demutualization …", pp. 150–171.

5 Antonio THOMAS: "The Rise of Social Cooperatives in Italy", *Voluntas*, 15 (2004), pp. 243–263.

6 Alberto IANES: "La cooperazione sociale come storia di impresa", *Imprese e storia*, 37 (2009), pp. 85–130.

7 Ermanno C. TORTIA, Florence DEGAVRE and Simone POLEDRINI: "Why Are Social Enterprises … ", pp. 1–19.

8 Eleonor OSTROM: *Governing the Commons*, Cambridge, Cambridge University Press, 1990.
9 Stuart HODKINSON: "Housing in Common: In Search of a Strategy for Housing Alterity in England in the 21st Century", in Duncan FULLER, Andrew JONAS and Roger LEE (eds.): *Interrogating Alterity: Alternative Economic and Political Spaces,* Farnham, Ashgate, 2010, pp. 241–258.
10 Jane HOLDER and Tatiana FLESSAS: "Emerging Commons", *Social and Legal Studies*, 17 (2008), pp. 299–310; Donald NONINI "Introduction: The Global Idea of the 'Common'", *Social Analysis*, 50 (2006), pp. 164–177.
11 Valérie FOURNIER: "Commoning ... ", pp. 433–453.
12 Greig DE PEUTER and Nick DYER-WITHERFORD: "Commons and Cooperatives", *Affinities: A Journal of Radical Theory, Culture, and Action*, 4 (2010), pp. 30–56.
13 Jane HOLDER and Tatiana FLESSAS: "Emerging Commons", *Social and Legal Studies*, 17 (2008), pp. 299–310.
14 I.Stat, Imprese; http://dati.istat.it/; last visit on 22 July 2023.
15 WORLD COOPERATIVE MONITOR: Exploring the Cooperative Economy, Report 2022, Euricse-ICA, 2022. Available online https://monitor.coop/sites/default/files/2022-11/WCM_2022.pdf. Last visit 23 July 2023.
16 Patrizia BATTILANI and Francesca FAURI: "L'economia italiana dal 1945 a oggi", Bologna, Il Mulino, 2019[2]; ÍD.: "The Bel Paese and the transition to a service economy", *Journal of Modern Italian Studies*, 15 (2010), pp. 21–40.
17 Emanuela SCARPELLINI: *L'Italia dei consumi. Dalla Belle Époque al nuovo millennio*, Bari, Laterza, 2008; Stefano CAVAZZA, "Politica e consumi", in Stefano CAVAZZA and Emanuela SCARPELLINI (eds.): *I consumi*, Storia d'Italia, Annali 27, Torino, Einaudi, 2018; Patrizia BATTILANI: "Perché il brutto anatroccolo non è diventato un cigno: la mancata trasformazione del settore distributivo italiano", *Imprese e Storia*, 33 (2006), pp. 157–189.
18 Giuliana BERTAGNONI and Tito MENZANI: *Servizi, lavoro e impresa cooperativa Il terziario in Legacoop e nelle altre organizzazioni di rappresentanza (1975–2010)*, Bologna, Il Mulino, 2010.
19 Patrizia BATTILANI, Giuliana BERTAGNONI and Stefania VIGNINI: *Un'impresa di cooperatori, artigiani, camionisti: la Cta e il trasporto merci in Italia*, Bologna, Il Mulino, 2008.
20 Patrizia BATTILANI and Giuliana BERTAGNONI: *Cooperation, Network, Service. Innovation in Outsourcing*, Lancaster, Crucicle Book-Carnagie Book Production, 2010.
21 *Ibid.*
22 *Ibid.*
23 The mutual funds were established in 1992, with law n. 59. Their goal was the development and promotion of the cooperative movement with internally generated resources. Indeed, they obtain their resources from the payment of 3% of the profits of each cooperative, from the residual assets of the cooperatives put into liquidation, and, finally, from the funds' profits. The mutual funds of the three cooperative umbrella organisations are: Coopfond for Legacoop, Fondosviluppo for Confcooperative, and General Fund for AGCI.
24 Paola DEMARTINI and Salvatore MONNI: *Workers' buyout Corporate Governance e sistemi di controllo*, Roma, RomaTre press, 2017; Marcello VIETA and Sara DEPERI: "Le imprese recuperate in Italia", in EURICSE: *Terzo rapporto. Economia cooperativa. Rilevanza, evoluzione e nuove frontiere della cooperazione italiana*, Trento, Euricse, 2015: LEGACOOP AREA STUDI,

Le imprese recuperate in Italia, Nota 8, marzo 2020, https://areastudi.legacoop.coop/wp-content/uploads/2020/03/Nota-8-WBO_Le-imprese-recuperate-in-Italia.pdf.

25 LEGACOOP AREA STUDI: Lo sviluppo delle grandi imprese cooperative aderenti a Legacoop, 1998–2003, Legacoop 2004; LEGACOOP AREA STUDI: *Le grandi cooperative italiane nel 2010*, Legacoop 2012.

26 Giuliana BERTAGNONI (ed.): *Una storia di qualità. Il gruppo Granarolo fra volori etici e logiche di mercato*, Bologna, Il Mulino, 2004.

27 GRUPPO GRANAROLO: Annual Report, 2022.

28 Patrizia BATTILANI: "The Case of Coop Consumatori, Italy: Ambidexterity as a Way to Reconcile Social and Economics Dimensions", in John WILSON *et al.* (eds.): *The Consumer Cooperative Sector. International Perspectives on Strategic Renewal*, New York, Routledge, 2023.

29 Patrizia BATTILANI and Giuliana BERTAGNONI: *Cooperation ...*

30 REKEEP: *Annual Report at December 2022*, https://www.rekeep.com/pdf/Bilancio-Rekeep-2022-ENG.pdf. Last visit 23 July 2023.

31 Giuliana BERTAGNONI and Tito MENZANI: *Servizi, lavoro ... .*; Patrizia BATTILANI and Giuliana BERTAGNONI: *Cooperation, ...*

32 Lorenza MALUCCELLI: *Lavori di cura. Cooperazione sociale e servizi alla persona. L'esperienza di Cadiai*, Bologna, Il Mulino, 2007.

33 "Le cooperative di comunità: una esperienza che dall'Appennino reggiano si sta sviluppando in altre regioni", *Modena2000*, 30 September 2011.

34 Interview to Maurizio Davolio, realised by Patrizia Battilani, in April 2016.

35 EURICSE, *Terzo rapporto. Economia cooperativa.*

36 *Ibid.*

37 Pier Angelo MORI and Jacopo SFORZI (eds.): *Imprese di Comunità. Innovazione istituzionale, partecipazione e sviluppo locale*, Bologna, Il Mulino, 2019.

38 Paolo VENTURI and Serena MICCOLIS: *Economie di luogo: fotografia e dimensioni qualitative delle cooperative di comunità*, AICCON, 2021.

39 Kimmo KARHU and Paavo RITALA: "Towards a Cognitive Dimension: Organizational Ambidexterity Framework", in Aybars TUNCDOGAN *et al.*: *Strategic Renewal: Core Concepts, Antecedents, and Micro Foundations*, New York, Routledge, 2019.

References

BATTILANI, Patrizia: "Perché il brutto anatroccolo non è diventato un cigno: la mancata trasformazione del settore distributivo italiano", *Imprese e Storia*, 33 (2006), pp. 157–189.

BATTILANI, Patrizia: "The Bel Paese and the Transition to a Service Economy", *Journal of Modern Italian Studies*, 15 (2010), pp. 21–40.

BATTILANI, Patrizia and BERTAGNONI, Giuliana: *Cooperation, Network, Service. Innovation in Outsourcing*, Lancaster, Crucicle Book-Carnagie Book Production, 2010.

BATTILANI, Patrizia and FAURI, Francesca: *L'economia italiana dal 1945 a oggi*, Bologna, Il Mulino, 2019.

BATTILANI, Patrizia and SCHROETER, Harm: "Demutualization and Its Problems", in Patrizia BATTILANI and Harm SCHROETER (eds.): *The*

Cooperative Business Movement, 1950 to the Present, New York, Cambridge University Press, 2012, pp. 150–171.

BATTILANI, Patrizia; BERTAGNONI, Giuliana and VIGNINI, Stefania: *Un'impresa di cooperatori, artigiani, camionisti: la Cta e il trasporto merci in Italia*, Bologna, Il Mulino, 2008.

BATTILANI, Patrizia: "The Case of Coop Consumatori, Italy: Ambidexterity as a Way to Reconcile Social and Economics Dimensions", in John WILSON *et al.* (eds.): *The Consumer Cooperative Sector. International Perspectives on Strategic Renewal*, New York, Routledge, 2023.

BERTAGNONI, Giuliana (ed.): *Una storia di qualità. Il gruppo Granarolo fra volori etici e logiche di mercato*, Bologna, Il Mulino, 2004.

BERTAGNONI, Giuliana and MENZANI, Tito: *Servizi, lavoro e impresa cooperativa Il terziario in Legacoop e nelle altre organizzazioni di rappresentanza (1975–2010)*, Bologna, Il Mulino, 2010.

BOSCARELLO, Samuel: "La storia del movimento cooperativo come innovazione sociale", *Italia Contemporanea*, (25) (2022), pp. 155–167.

CAMPOPIANO, Giovanna and BASSANI, Gaia: "Social Innovation: Learning from Social Cooperatives in the Italian Context", *Journal of Cleaner Production*, 291 (2021), pp. 1–11.

CAVAZZA, Stefano: "Politica e consumi", in Stefano CAVAZZA and Emanuela SCARPELLINI (eds.), *I consumi*, Storia d'Italia, Annali 27, Torino, Einaudi, 2018.

CHADDAD, Fabio and COOK, Michael L.: "The Economics of Organization Structure Changes: An US Perspective on Demutualization", *Annales de l'Économie Publique, Sociale et Coopérative*, 75 (2004), pp. 575–594.

DE PEUTER, Greig and DYER-WITHERFORD, Nick: "Commons and Cooperatives", *Affinities: A Journal of Radical Theory, Culture, and Action*, 4 (2010), pp. 30–56.

DEMARTINI, Paola and MONNI, Salvatore: *Workers' buyout Corporate Governance e sistemi di controllo*, Roma, RomaTre press, 2017.

FOURNIER, Valérie: "Commoning: On the Social Organisation of the Commons", *M@n@gement*, 16 (2013), pp. 433–453.

GRUPPO GRANAROLO: Annual Report, 2022.

GUTTMANN, Alexandre: "Commons and Cooperatives: A New Governance of Collective Action", *Annals of Public and Cooperative Economics*, 92 (2021), pp. 33–53.

HODKINSON, Stuart: "Housing in Common: In Search of a Strategy for Housing Alterity in England in the 21st Century", in Duncan FULLER, Andrew JONAS and Roger LEE (eds.): *Interrogating Alterity: Alternative Economic and Political Spaces*, Farnham: Ashgate, 2010, pp. 241–258.

HOLDER, Jane and FLESSAS, Tatiana: "Emerging Commons", *Social and Legal Studies*, 17 (2008), pp. 299–310

IANES, Alberto: "La cooperazione sociale come storia di impresa", *Imprese e storia*, 37 (2009), pp. 85–130.

KARHU, Kimmo and RITALA, Paavo: "Towards a Cognitive Dimension: Organizational Ambidexterity Framework", in Aybars TUNCDOGAN *et al.*:

Strategic Renewal: Core Concepts, Antecedents, and Micro Foundations, New York, Routledge, 2019.

LEGACOOP AREA STUDI: Le imprese recuperate in Italia, Nota 8, marzo 2020, https://areastudi.legacoop.coop/wp-content/uploads/2020/03/Nota-8-WBO_Le-imprese-recuperate-in-Italia.pdf.

LEGACOOP AREA STUDI: Lo sviluppo delle grandi imprese cooperative aderenti a Legacoop, 1998-2003, Legacoop 2004.

LEGACOOP AREA STUDI: Le grandi cooperative italiane nel 2010, Legacoop 2012.

MACKE, Janina *et al.*: "Where Do We Go From Now? Research Framework for Social Entrepreneurship", *Journal of Cleaner Production*, 183 (2018), pp. 677–685.

MORI, Pier Angelo and SFORZI, Jacopo (eds.): *Imprese di Comunità. Innovazione istituzionale, partecipazione e sviluppo locale*, Bologna, Il Mulino, 2019.

MALUCCELLI, Lorenza: *Lavori di cura. Cooperazione sociale e servizi alla persona. L'esperienza di Cadiai*, Bologna, Il Mulino, 2007.

NILSSON, Jerker; KIHLEN, Anna and NORELL, Lennart: "Are Traditional Cooperatives an Endangered Species? About Shrinking Satisfaction, Involvement and Trust", *International Food and Agribusiness Management Review*, 12 (2009), pp. 101–122.

NONINI, Donald: "Introduction: The Global Idea of the 'Common'", *Social Analysis*, 50 (2006), pp. 164–177.

OSTROM, Eleonor: *Governing the Commons*, Cambridge, Cambridge University Press, 1990.

PATMORE, Greg; BALNAVE, Nikolas and MARJANOVIC, Olivera: "Resistance Is Not Futile: Co-operatives, Demutualization, Agriculture, and Neoliberalism in Australia", *Business and Politics*, 23 (2022), pp. 510–528.

RAHADARI, Amir; SEPASI, Sahar and MORADI, Mohammad: "Achieving Sustainability Through Schumpeterian Social Entrepreneurship: The Role of Social Enterprises", *Journal of Cleaner Production*, 137 (2016), pp. 347–360.

REKEEP: *Annual Report at December 2022*, https://www.rekeep.com/pdf/Bilancio-Rekeep-2022-ENG.pdf. Last visit 23 July 2023.

SCARPELLINI, Emanuela: *L'Italia dei consumi. Dalla Belle Époque al nuovo millennio*, Bari, Laterza, 2008.

THOMAS, Antonio: "The Rise of Social Cooperatives in Italy", *Voluntas*, 15 (2004), pp. 243–263.

TORTIA, Ermanno C.; DEGAVRE, Florence and POLEDRINI, Simone: "Why Are Social Enterprises Good Candidates for Social Innovation? Looking for Personal and Institutional Drivers of Innovation", *Annals of Public and Cooperative Economics*, 91 (2020), pp. 1–19.

UNKNOWN AUTHOR: "Le cooperative di comunità: una esperienza che dall'Appennino reggiano si sta sviluppando in altre regioni", Modena*2000*, 30 September 2011.

VENTURI, Paolo and MICCOLIS, Serena: *Economie di luogo: fotografia e dimensioni qualitative delle cooperative di comunità*, AICCON, 2021.

VIETA, Marcello and DEPERI, Sara: "Le imprese recuperate in Italia", in *EURICSE: Terzo rapporto. Economia cooperativa. Rilevanza, evoluzione e nuove frontiere della cooperazione italiana*, Trento, Euricse, 2015.

WORLD COOPERATIVE MONITOR: Exploring the Cooperative Economy, Report 2022, Euricse-ICA, 2022. Available online https://monitor.coop/sites/default/files/2022-11/WCM_2022.pdf. Last visit 23 July 2023.

6 Mutualism in Chile, 1848–1990[1]

Social Security, Sociopolitical Movement, and Space of Sociability in the Working Class

Fernando Venegas Espinoza

Introduction

The analysis of the validity of mutualism during the 20th century is relevant for two reasons: the first one is because the specialized literature has discussed that with the establishment of social security systems by the State, this historical phenomenon became involved in a crisis and irreversible decline. The second one is, consistent with the above, it has been ensured that mutualism also lost relevance as a social movement, compared to the role that trade syndicalism was going to assume. These ideas need to be reviewed.

In this chapter, in light of the study of the Chilean experience, it will be shown that although mutuality experienced a major crisis since the 1910s, it was able to recover and have a second cycle of expansion. This new cycle was projected until the 1970s to begin a new contractive cycle which extends to the present time. Consequently, the reasons for which the terminal depression of the mutuality has been explained have been nothing more than explanations for an unquestionable though circumstantial trance. Until now, the variables for which the importance it achieved as a cell of the social solidarity economy have not been understood or pondered. On the other hand, it is not known what is the role of mutualism within the expanding social fabric, its role in the social popular movement, and its association with the State.

In the case of Chilean historiography, the main explanations of the terminal crisis of mutualism since 1925 have been provided by Sergio Grez Toso. In the first place, there are the political and economic reasons related to the Act N°4054 of 1924, which created the Compulsory Insurance against Disease and Disability, as well as the amendment to that act in 1952, which established the compulsory nature of the national insurance. A second dimension that caused the crisis, as stated by Grez, in political and social terms was the impact that affected its own bosom as in the

DOI: 10.4324/9781003439554-7

relationship with trade syndicalism, the support that the leadership of mutualism granted to the dictatorship of Carlos Ibáñez del Campo.[2]

On his part, Enrique Fernández proposes that it was not the absence of the State that led to the emergence of mutuality but rather its exclusive nature that took a turn with the intervention of the military in politics in 1924. The objectives of the new State were social integration and regulation of the industrial relationships.[3] This resulted in the creation of a welfare policy in laws such as the creation of the Worker's Insurance and union policy. However, from the moment the State took charge of people's health, "creating a state national health structure, the Mutual Aid Associations, organized fundamentally around the need of people's health, such organizations lost a large part of the reason d'être".[4]

María Angélica Illanes argues that mutualism arises as a response to the lack of solidarity from the liberal State and is inspired by popular humanism and solidarity-based organization, rejecting charity.[5] However, in the 1920s, Illanes sees a crisis in mutualism due to the influence of anarchist-syndicalist ideas and the institutionalization of the Welfare State through an alliance between doctors and the military. The implementation of laws such as Act 4.054 of the Worker's Insurance (1924) and the Compulsory Unionization Law (1928) changes the dynamics of mutualism. She adds that despite the offensive of mutualism with the rise of the Popular Front to power in 1938, the idea prevails in Parliament that returning to voluntary mutualism would be a step backward.[6]

Gabriel Salazar has valued the management of the mutual fund, as it not only financed mutual aid but also "class unity". However, this autonomy was lost with the nationalization and semi-privatization of the funds.[7] Salazar emphasizes the importance of these resources in the construction of headquarters, schools, and educational and political activities. He also highlights the participation of mutualists in the constituent process of 1925. Regarding the appropriation of funds by the dominant class, it should be noted that less than 8% of the active population belonged to Mutual Aid Societies (MAS), and their funds and assets were not expropriated in 1924 and remained in force during the 20th century.[8]

From other perspectives, Juan Carlos Yáñez has been emphasizing on how a consensus was developed from the State in relation to the need to face the social problems derived from the "social question" before the 1920s. For Yáñez, the creation of the Labor Office in 1907 is framed in the "process of institutionalization of the State around social issues, specifically in the creation of a social intervention field ...".[9] In this context, mutuality is valued as an instance of social organization regarding the issue of social security, from which the political elites and businessmen were not oblivious.

On the other hand, the historiography that has studied the mutualist movement in both Latin America and Europe has coincided in arguing that when states assumed social security as part of their responsibilities, it had a short- and medium-term impact on mutualism. However, it has also been argued from a multi-causal perspective, such as in the study by Fernando Largo and Josep Pujol, who proposed for Spain that the decline was a consequence of the structure and networks of societies, their precarious economic situation, as well as the competition they faced from insurance markets and commercial companies.[10]

As a hypothesis, what is proposed is that mutuality, although, was affected by a multi-causal crisis since the second decade of the 20th century. Here, what impacted it seriously was the Great Depression that began in 1929. In the mid-1930s it was capable of initiating its recovery, being expanded until the 1970s. However, this time, new problems arising from the powers granted to the National Mutualist Confederation by the state and the actions of the Civic-Military Dictatorship will undermine mutualistic fraternity, although what seems to have been more decisive was the economic crisis of 1982, which marked the beginning of a new setback. This, despite the fact that mutualistic values have been put back into effect, in the current context of global environmental and economic crisis, has not been overcome.

This work was aimed to show and explain the expansion of mutualism between the two contractive cycles mentioned above (which began in 1929 and 1983, respectively). This is a work that combines perspectives of social, cultural, and economic history. Mutualism should be understood by following Van der Linden,[11] as organizations that could operate in democratic terms –with social and cultural purposes – and bureaucratic, in which those economic purposes predominated. However, differentiation will be made in relation to the multiple and emerging processes of the democratic societies – diseases, accidents, death, education, sociability, savings, and resistance – as opposed to those very limited ones – diseases, accidents, and death.

Methodology

In methodological terms, research on mutualism has predominantly been conducted within the field of social history, with a critical and contextualized approach to the available documentation. The main sources have been the press, archives of mutualist organizations, and publications from the Labor Office and the Labor Magazine. However, it has been observed that some of these sources provide limited information about mutualism, which has influenced the research outcomes. Although relevant data has been found in the minute books of certain organizations, their use in comprehensive studies is avoided due to their specificity. Overall, it is acknowledged that the availability and scope of documentary sources have influenced the direction and extent of research on the subject of mutualism.[12]

This research, along with a social historical approach has also incorporated some perspectives of cultural, political, and economic history. In terms of sources, the parliamentary sources were used in greater depth, although this has already been carried out by Angélica Illanes. In this sense, the most innovative in terms of sources corresponds to the bulletins of some mutualist organizations, and what is totally unpublished corresponded to the archives of the Chilean Mutualist Federation. This organization still keeps the information, despite its current difficult situation. These sources cover a period from 1963 and 1990, moment in which the State of Chile recognized it as a public entity (it was founded in 1939 by a decision of mutualist organizations). A great attribution was granted to this federation: To grant or not legal personality to those collectivities that were mutualists, with the exception of guilds and unions. This went hand in hand with the obligation of all Mutual Aid Association (MAS) institutions of integrating the Confederation. As result oof this responsibility given by the State, between 1963 and 1900 a list of 518 associations with a full record of their legal, social, and economic information, as well as a copy of their bylaws.

Additionally, records of those organizations whose legal personality, although requested, was not granted are kept. Correspondence between the Confederation and the provincial federations or MAS has also been preserved, as well as correspondence and official letters with authorities and information regarding the organization of mutualist congresses that were the leading organization of the mutuality since before it was recognized by the State. Furthermore, there is a very significant dossier of information in which it is stated how the head of the Confederation supported the military-civic dictatorship (1973–1989). Finally, there is also documentation of the period from 1990 onwards, where it is possible to monitor the crisis in which mutualism gradually descended.

Mutualism between the rise and fall of liberalism, 1848 and 1924

During the predominance of liberal ideas, in the transition from the 19th to the 20th century, the safety in which the ruling class was interested was that related was order, a central element that would guarantee progress. For this, the resources were directed toward police forces or the military spending from the War of the Pacific (1879–1884). Resources were also directed toward public works, although in an economic sense. On the one hand, the railroad to connect production spaces with consumption centers, or moves the production of mining centers to the ports.[13] These were other areas to which the investment of the liberal state was channeled, whereas public lighting, drinking water, and sewerage were abandoned for a long time by private companies. In the government of José Manuel Balmaceda an attempt to redirect the investment with a more social sense was observed, but after the Civil War of 1891, this action was localized and depended on the initiatives of the municipalities.[14] The main mechanism of state expansion was public education, though with the purpose of consolidating the idea of notion and disciplining the popular sectors. Under this frame, mutualism will emerge in Chile.

In general terms, the first feature that can be observed is that from 1848 until practically 1913, the growth of mutualism in Chile, in relation to the number of mutualist organizations, was exponential and even slightly above that trend between 1890 and 1899 (see Figure 6.1). When zooming on the lens, four phases can be differentiated.

The first one extends from 1848 to 1882 and corresponds to the time in which mutualism began its development, reaching 38 societies. It would be necessary to highlight the influence of immigrants in the diffusion of mutualist ideas, not at the level in Argentina,[15] but it is evident that they were significant both in the foundation of emblematic associations (as was the case of the Peruvian Víctor Laínez, one of the founders of the "Society of Typographers of Santiago" in 1853) and in the diffusion of the mutualist ideology. It is imperative to consider for almost a decade there were more foreign MAS than domestic ones. Furthermore, for an additional decade the national MAS barely exceeded those formed by immigrants.[16]

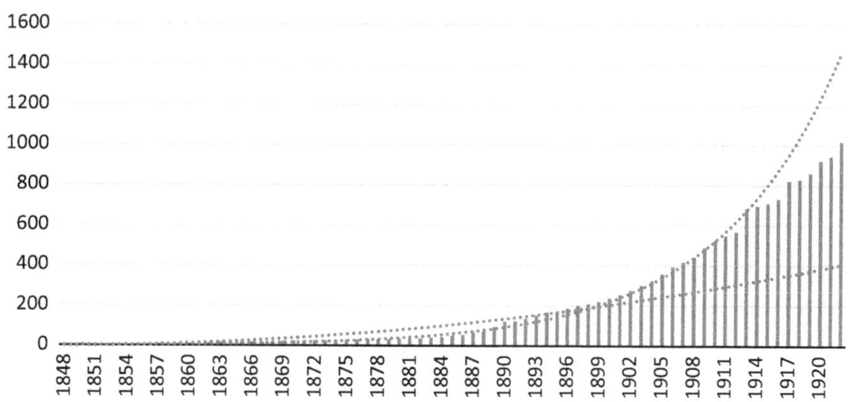

Figure 6.1 Mutualist organizations in Chile between 1848 and 1922 (exponential and potential trend).

Source: Own, from: ARNAD, Dirección del Trabajo, vols. 1–100; Memoriachilena.cl: Revista Sucesos (1902–1932); Diario La Unión (Valparaíso), 1920–1924; Sergio Grez Toso: De la 'regeneración del pueblo' a la huelga general; Illanes, Chile Des-centrado.

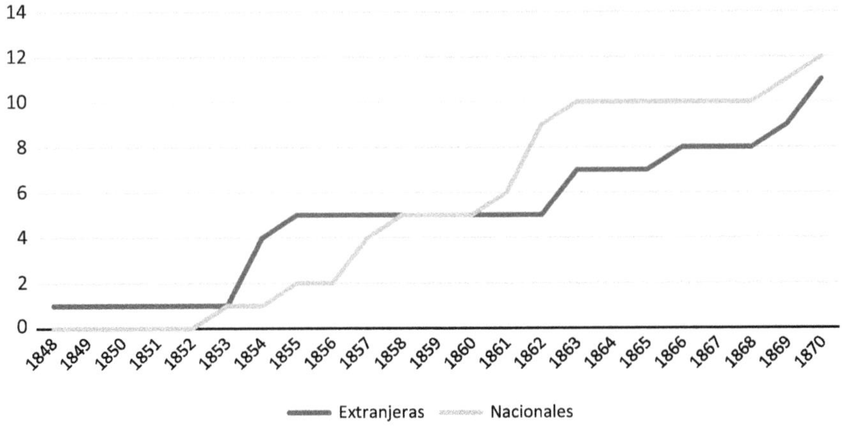

Figure 6.2 Expansion of mutualism in Chile between 1848 and 1870, confronting national and foreign societies.

Source: Own, from: ARNAD, Dirección del Trabajo, vols.1–100; Memoriachilena.cl: Revista Sucesos (1902–1932); Diario La Unión (Valparaíso), 1920–1924; Sergio Grez Toso: De la 'regeneración del pueblo' a la huelga general ...; Illanes, Chile Des-centrado.

The above is obviously related to the notion that mutualistic ideas were imported from Europe, where countries such as France and Great Britain had already reached a significant expansion for the mid-19th century.[17] However, as can be seen in Figure 6.2, that trend would be reversed *aposteriori*, in such a way that by 1900 there were 196 national and 43 foreign MAS.

Another aspect that characterized this period and would be a trend that persisted in the following one is that the majority of societies were founded in Valparaiso (37%, 14 SSM), in line with the cosmopolitanism that characterized the then-main port of Chile. The capital city, Santiago, was in second place, with 24% (9 MAS). The remaining 39% is divided into collectivities that were established in different locations. In central Chile, in the cities of Quillota, Melipilla, Concepción, Talca, Parral, Chillán, and Los Ángeles. In the north of the country, associations were founded in La Serena, Coquimbo, Copiapó, Iquique, and Tacna – space that would be in dispute with Perú until 1929.[18] Not all associations were capable of consolidating, and, on the contrary, they were subjected to different situations both internal and external. The latter, especially of political nature, was the case of the Society of Artisans of La Serena, which had to be reconstituted in 1869.[19]

The second phase ranges between 1883 and 1891 and corresponds to a relevant development of mutualism, spurred by the success and nationalist spirit that was present after the War of the Pacific and what was diminished by the Civil War of 1891.[20] During this period, MAS continued to be created, predominantly in central Chile, highlighting localities such as Talca, Concepción, as well as Santiago (20%) and Valparaíso (31%). These continued to be the cities in which these associations were founded. In northern Chile, MAS was founded in Antofagasta and Ovalle. In the southern zone of the country, the first associations were about to be created in Valdivia (1885).

During this period, the foundation of MAS for women in Santiago, Concepción, and especially Valparaíso is highlighted. The latter once again will be the most prominent city in this matter. Additionally, the first associations for personnel were founded in Iquique, Santiago, Talca, and Valparaíso. A "Ligue of Workers' Societies" was also founded in Valparaíso, which undoubtedly reflected the British influence present in that port, considering that it was in the United Kingdom where the *friendly societies*[21] were developed. A last aspect to be considered is that at this stage, Catholic MAS began to be founded, as well as those with the ascendancy of the Conservative party. These associations had a reactive nature to which the Democratic Party and the diverse liberal movements propitiated, without missing the influence of freemasonry. This is not contradictory to the fact that there was a sense of class on the part of the workers. This was also forged from sociability.

The third phase extended from 1892 to 1913. Here, an expansion in terms of foundations or organizations is observed, in total unity with the exponential trend. During this phase, the creation of 66 MAS: Valparaíso (20%) and Santiago (17%) was carried out, and these cities concentrated the largest amount of societies, although this time, the highest percentage of entities were established outside these cities. On the other hand, in intermediate cities and small towns of central Chile, 33% of MAS were created during those years, highlighting the cities of Linares, Quillota, Talca, Chillán, Talcahuano, and Concepción. The latter, with 39 MAS (17%), was the third city with the highest increase of instaurations in those years.

In regional terms, the southern zone of the country stands out, which in this stage reached 10% of those collective organizations. It corresponded to an economically dynamized space as a result of the migratory policies promoted from Santiago. Thus, Northern Europeans (Germans, Scandinavians, and Swiss) were brought, which in turn had an impact on the native indigenous populations of Mapuches and Huilliches and their territories.[22] With 22 societies, the city with the most associations was Valdivia, followed by Osorno and Temuco. A great dispersion occurred in intermediate cities or localities such as Ancud, Arauco, Lautaro, Mulchén, or La Unión.

In the case of the North Grand, a few decades before, it was only an "uninhabited desert." Due to the expansion associated with nitrate exploration, the area also experienced growth that reached 9% of the total, although much less disperse. The cities of Iquique (by far, with 24 associations set up in this period), Tocopilla, Antofagasta, and Taltal stand out. The small north continued to represent 8%, largely due to the development of mining and agricultural activity. In this region, mutualism reached importance in La Serena, Coquimbo, Ovalle, Vallenar, and Caldera. At that time, small coastal or Andean localities were adopting this type of sociability, such as the cases of Huasco, Vicuña, Elqui, or Mejillones. There is greater dispersion than concentration in the north of the country.[23]

As originally occurred in central Chile, mutualism arises due to the impulse of immigrants in the extreme south. Indeed, of the 21 MAS created in Punta Arenas in this period, 10 of them were foreign. They were also the first to emerge, and another two defined themselves as cosmopolitan. The presence of foreign societies in this macro-region was such that the first established national collectivity was baptized as "Chilean Society of Mutual Aid" (1898).

This period was characterized by the formation of unions that united the labor movement, advocating for mutual aid and resistance against the challenging labor conditions imposed by the advancement of capitalism. Despite state repression, mutualist organizations established connections that allowed their members to receive benefits in a network with other mutuals, especially in the case of lung diseases that required a change of environment.

The precarious social situation, with overcrowding and lack of hygiene, led to the proliferation of diseases and high infant mortality rates. Despite the adversities, the "mancomunales" and MAS in cities and regions played a key role in forging class consciousness.[24]

The state repression against the working class, symbolized by the massacre at the Santa María School in Iquique in 1907, and the economic crisis of the First World War, severely affected workers' organizations. However, the establishment of the Labor Office in 1907 marked a change in the state's disposition toward the labor movement.

Mutualism continued to evolve with the formation of the National Union and the Workers' Federation of Chile, but disaggregation prevailed in the mutualist system. International approaches were sought to resolve regional enmities, demonstrating the importance of collaboration among workers' organizations.

Although official statistics present modest figures, the exegesis of various sources reveals the rich history of workers' organizations in Chile and their struggle to improve living and working conditions.

The fourth phase, which spans from 1914 to 1923, was affected by the economic crisis resulting from the First World War and the postwar period. During this time, a total of 343 MAS were established, with 23% in Santiago and 22% in Valparaíso. Despite these two cities continuing to concentrate the largest number of foundations in the country, central Chile accounted for 21%, increasing to 15%, while the southern zone reached 10%, and the Small North had 8%. Cities such as Valdivia, Osorno, Temuco, Viña del Mar, Talcahuano, Coquimbo, Tacna, and Concepción stood out for the number of MAS founded.

During this short cycle, critical observations about the unnecessary multiplication of mutualist organizations increased. The reason is because they put their capacities at risk to ensure their affiliates and because it was considered a threat to democracy.[25] At the same time, it is observed that mutualist organizations created from the armed forces were those that acquired a bureaucratic nature, whereas the democratic mutualism – in the Van der Linden terminology – not only continued to expand. This followed the French experience and began to be taught in schools.[26] According to figures from the Labor Office, by 1923 the number of workers' associations implied 1,114 affiliate collectivities, with a total of 177,711 affiliates. In this universe, the organizations that were identified as mutualists were 338. The masculine ones were estimated at 302, with 93,147 associates. A total of 36 female MAS with 5,096 partners (5.1%).[27] Those figures were different from the 1,016 MAS estimated for a year earlier, from the consultation of different sources. However, the emphasis was on establishing the organizations that were founded and not on those that stopped doing so. It would be necessary to insist the figures of the Labor Office were far from being exact and with a high margin of error. However, the situation of the permanent economic crisis that was present in Latin America and in Chile in particular should not be ignored because there were organizations when this crisis worsened, they only operated nominally.[28] In addition to the aforementioned, it is very relevant to insist that during the liberal period, mutualists did not represent more than 8% of the economically active population, and female mutualism, in relation to the total universe, according to official figures, represented 5.1%, corresponding to 5,096 associates. These figures are important to take into consideration for the analysis that follows.[29]

Crisis of the MAS during the Great Depression (1929–1931)

As has already been pointed out, Chilean historiography put the tombstone on mutualism since the promulgation of the Workers' Insurance Law (1924), though the sources can be interpreted in another way. Mutualism, focused on mutual aid organizations, experienced a crisis during that decade, but the truly disruptive moment came with the Great Depression that began in 1929 and would last through the early 1930s.

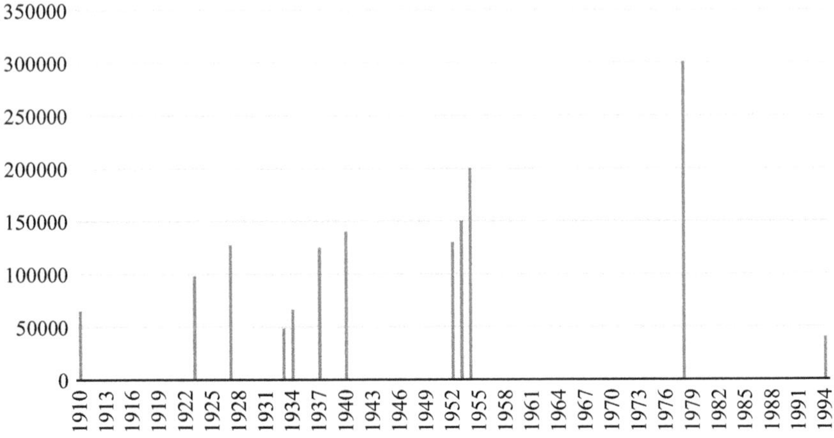

Figure 6.3 Mutual aid societies in Chile, 1920–1994.

Source: Own from BN, Boletín de la Oficina del Trabajo, N°1 (Enero/marzo 1911) – N°15; BN, Revista del Trabajo, abril, mayo, junio 1938; Sesiones de los cuerpos legislativos: Sesión 23, 5 de julio de 1944; Sesión 3, 5 de octubre de 1954; Sesión 62, 16 de septiembre de 1959. Archivo Dirección del Trabajo, vols. 100–200; Archivo Confederación Mutualista de Chile, 1966–2010.

Then, a recovery would come to be contracted again from the economic crisis of 1982 (see Figure 6.3).

In this long-term view that we are constructing on mutualism in Chile and, more specifically, on MAS, a fifth stage is situated from 1924 to 1933. However, contrary to what has been sustained until now, social laws did not immediately mean a decrease in associates. In fact, in 1923 there were 98,237 mutualists, and in 1927, with the Workers' Insurance already created, 127,090 associates were summoned to the "Congreso Social Obrero". These data are highly relevant because they challenge the thesis that mutualism began to decline irreversibly by then.[30] An undeniable topic present in this period is that Act N° 4,054 was resisted by mutualists.[31] This was visualized as a threat, which had to be reinforced by the fact that although it allowed them not to contribute to the new institutionality and continue doing so in their own MAS. This could not be possible due to associated bureaucratic demands.[32]

Illanes' work highlights that the 1928 law that regulated unionism in Chile incorporated mutuality in the health of its members as one of the priorities of the unions, leading to the institutionalization of mutual aid in factories.[33] Although some leaders of mutualist organizations supported the dictatorship of Carlos Ibáñez del Campo, this did not significantly affect the number of members, which remained around 8% of the active Chilean population. Statistics from the Labor Directorate show that the real turning point for mutualities occurred around 1933, when their membership reached 48,615 people. The Great Depression had a strong impact on these mutualist associations, exacerbated by the retirement benefits they had incorporated, which increased their financial obligations and depleted their funds. In retrospect, this explanation seems more coherent for understanding the crisis of the mutualities, rather than attributing it to a political decision, as its roots were in cultural and social aspects. Additionally, governmental and municipal support was always scarce and relied more on their networks of relationships than on public policies.

In summary, the economic crisis specifically and regionally affected MAS. The departure of Tacna from Chilean territory and the decline in nitrate production had an impact on these organizations. In October 1931, the number of unemployed reached significant figures. Valparaíso, once a mutualist hub, experienced a significant decrease in its societies. The depression of the port and restrictive measures influenced the decline of mutual aid. However, the bureaucratic mutual aid associated with armed forces continued to function while the State regulated employer-organized mutual aid through the Superintendence of Insurance Companies.

New mutualist expansion during the National Populism, between 1934 and the 1970s

After the First World War and its wake of successive crisis, fascist regimes would emerge in Europe, as well as the national socialism. In Latin America, National Populism emerged, with charismatic leaders who questioned traditional politics. These leaders strengthened the role of the State and promoted social policies.[34] In Chile, this was expressed in a package of social policies issued from the end of the government of Arturo Alessandri, which included laws on labor contracts, work accidents, union organization, and worker's insurance, having the German social security model as a reference. However, as already has been evidenced, this greater presence of the State was not capable to imply a terminal crisis of mutualism. At the same time, it meant a scarce regulation or control from the State to mutuality.

Once the economic debacle after the collapse of the New York Stock Market in 1929 and its consequent political and social effects, the mutualist societies became alive again, beginning what could be characterized as a sixth phase, of unquestionable development. Obviously, this was a complex process. When the crisis was over, many societies disappeared for not having the capacity to sustain themselves in an economic way, whereas others merged. This made their survival valuable, being established in some cases, as mixed collectivities. Throughout this process, patrimony – especially in its property nature – that had forged

MAS in the liberal period was fundamental. By itself, this should be considered as a matter of investigation.

In 1933 the associates had reached 48,615 people, though a new statistical analysis of the Labor Directorate corresponded to 1938 detailed 561 mutual organizations, with a total of 118,758 associates[35] (see details in Table 6.1). It should be noted that in this figure there were 6.711 mutualist women, corresponding to 5.3%. Later data recorded 125,00 mutualists in 1940, rising to 200,000 in 1954.[36] A relevant detail is that FOCH that had a double dimension both mutualist and union was dissolved in 1936 when the Confederation of Chilean Workers was formed. This organization grouped union organizations of anarcho-syndicalist, socialist, and communist ideas.[37] Regardless of its directions,

Table 6.1 Mutualism in Chile, 1933–1937

Years	*1933*		*1938*		*1966–1989*	
Provinces	Societies	Members	Societies	Members	Societies	Members
Tarapacá	80	10.468	49	4,383	20	3,989
Antofagasta	52	5.184	63	7,827	34	14,981
Atacama	15	869	21	2,074	17	5,878
Coquimbo	35	4.397	35	3,816	31	4,409
Aconcagua	–	–	7	790	7	2,687
Valparaíso	50	8.027	77	14,400	128	29,186
Santiago	20	5.294	62	57,838	101	99,928
O'Higgins	–	–	7	586	20	16,479
Colchagua	5	412	4	277	2	598
Curicó	–	–	5	404	5	818
Talca	7	1.625	7	1,174	13	3,723
Maule	9	669	18	1.388	3	254
Ñuble	10	982	23	2.296	13	3,935
Concepción	38	4.467	55	9,492	35	8,414
Arauco	–	–	3	425	–	–
Biobío	13	1.359	19	2,126	7	1,738
Malleco	–	–	–	–	6	1,265
Cautín	13	1.110	39	3,317	13	2,972
Valdivia	15	875	36	2,991	20	3,702
Llanquihue	–	–	–	–	20	2,502
Chiloé	9	312	12	548	–	–
Magallanes	17	2.565	18	2,753	4	354
Total	388	48.615	561	118,758	499	207,812

Source: Own from: BN, Labor Office Bulletin, N°1 (January/March 1911) – N°15; BN, Labor Magazine, April, May, June 1938; Sessions of the Legislative Bodies: Session 23, July 5, 1944; Session 3, October 5, 1954; Session 62, September 16, 1959. Labor Directorate Archives: vols. 100–200; Mutualist Confederation of Chile Archive, 1966–2010.

the State was concerned with generating an active regulation of its operation, in contrast to what had took place and would continue to occur with the MAS.

According to documentation preserved by the Chilean Mutualist Confederation (CMCh), in the period 1966–1989, a total of 207,812 mutualists were registered. This is the number recorded at the time of obtaining legal personality because, according to the CMCh itself, by the end of 1970, mutualists were around 300,000 people.[38] These data, in addition to confirming the validity of the SSM, show that the decline of Valparaiso also affected its mutualist social fabric, although we need to analyze these data comparatively in relation to other organizations. What is evident is that Santiago began to have the largest number of mutualist organizations by the end of the 1930s, and this was maintained until the end of the 1980s. The cities of Concepción and Antofagasta followed in importance. Out of the five hundred companies that were in operation by then, 274 were founded after 1925. If we group them by decades, these are the indicators: 1925 to 1934, 34 SSM; 1935 to 1944, 50 SSM; 1945 to 1954, 64 SSM; 1955 to 1964, 59 SSM; 1965 to 1974, 47 SSM; and finally, from 1975 to 1985, only 18 SSM were founded.[39] The figures for the creation of societies are quite homogeneous and only show a considerable downward trend in the years of the Civic Military Dictatorship.

Of the total universe of MAS and mutualists registered, 30 societies declared themselves mixed, with a total of 4,490 people, who corresponded to 2.1% of the total. Another 164 societies declared themselves female and totaled 10,906 women, corresponding to 5.2%. These figures are similar to the historical percentages, though by adding the female presence in mixed societies, it should have been at least 1% more. In other words, around 6% of those who were part or organized the MAS corresponded to women. Although it is true, when considering the mixed mutuality, the percentages are slightly higher than those in the previous cycle and up to triple, according to official figures. The numbers of mutualist women were the highest in all history. This was reflected not only in sociability but also in leaderships since women were projected from all communal federations to the very heart of the Chilean Mutualist Federation, in Santiago.

On the other hand, where a new phenomenon can be dimensioned, is in the expansion of mutualism of retirees from the Armed Forces" to this one: "A new phenomenon during this period was the expansion of mutualism among retirees from the Armed Forces, what reinforces the explanation that one of the main reasons for associating lay in the meager pensions or simply their inexistence. Indeed, during the liberal period after the War of the Pacific (1879–1884), the Veterans Associations of 1897 were created. These organizations had a democratic profile and by 1938 a total of eight were in force between Coquimbo and Victoria, congregating 397 associates. In 1918 the Mutuality of Carabineros was created, which by 1922 had 3,500 associates. The Army and Navy Mutuality was created in 1919 and by 1922 had 8,000 associates. According to the universe of associates of that time, they represented about 12% of the total. In 1930, Army and Navy Mutuality had about 15,00 insured persons and had reserve funds for $11,500.000, "diligently invested in first-class properties". This organization was not exclusive for the military as it had been opened to civilians.[40] A similar situation corresponded to the Carabineros Mutuality.[41] On the other hand, the bureaucratic mutuality also reached other areas, such as universities. In these cases, associations focused on the well-being of their lecturing and administrative staff were formed, although others were established as cooperatives.[42] Around the 1970s, there were 63 armed forces societies, totaling 62,036 members, this is to say 29.7% of the total. Of these figures, 40,000 people, 19% corresponded to the Army and Air Force, founded in 1917. This organization corresponded to a bureaucratic mutualism. These numbers need to be analyzed in depth and should lead to further research.

Regarding mutualism in the Armed Forces, the bureaucratic type had been consolidated to such an extent that after the coup d'état, during the civic-military dictatorship, it was protected by the State. As it is known, the Chilean Armed Forces pension system was not integrated into the individual capitalization of the Pension Funds Association, created in 1980. Additionally, it is worth noting that around 20,000 former military personnel grouped together in democratic mutuals, and this would have sociopolitical projections. Although their problem was pensions, these organizations were with the Pinochet dictatorship and their influence was expressed in the Mutualist Confederation of Chile and in their own organization: the Confederation of Pensioners and Benefits of the National Defense, erected on 8 October 1942.[43]

As part of the expansive moment that was experienced during those years, mutualist people began to unite and they were going to achieve it in a way that they had not been achieved until then, in a trajectory of more than 100 years. In 1931, once the National Workers' Congress had concluded, the MAS developed a national convention in Santiago. Here, delegates from all over the country decided to form a Nation Confederation of Mutual Aid Societies. In 1936, the Society of Union of Typographers in Santiago promoted the establishment of the Mutualist Central of Chile, whose objective was to unite all the MAS in the country and face the difficulties of Law 4054, by which mutualists had to pay double fees (to both the Worker's Insurance and their respective mutual aid society). The following year, by the initiative of the Workers' Societies of Valparaíso, the Third National Mutualist Congress of Valparaíso, in which the National Central Mutualist of Chile was constituted. This organization would be formed by all MAS of the country that had legal personality. The purpose was to develop a "national front of mutuality in order to study and solve general and urgent issues".[44] Through this organization and its multiple local dimensions, the mutuality as it had done in the past raised its voice before the authorities to request different matters.

All these articulations came together in the formation of the Chilean Mutualist Confederation in 1939, which would bring together more than 500 MAS from all over the country.[45] This whole movement reached its climax when, in 1953, on the occasion of its centenary, the First Latin American Mutualist International Congress was held in Santiago de Chile.[46]

What is undeniable is that the mutualist movement organized within the Chilean Mutualist Confederation was associated with extraordinary associative vitality. Outside the capital Santiago, there were male, female, and mixed associations, which articulated communal federations. A network of sociability and support flowed from each one of them, despite the adverse economic context due to inflation and the double fee from the Workers' Insurance Saving banks and the mutualist fund. This was not new, because during the liberal period, a relevant percentage of workers who joined a mutualist organization were enrolled in more than one MAS. At the local level and in some spaces, the convergence between mutualism and syndicalism was even more evident and permanent. Many times, they had the same leaders and of course, the same purposes such as public health, education, and housing problems.[47] They also shared the spaces of sociability. In contextual terms, the difference was in the fact that the associative frame had become remarkably dense by then.

Despite the context of the time, it has been mentioned that the recovery of mutualism was not related to greater support from the State. Its main role, through Congress – and according to the provisions of the civil code – was to authorize the conservation of the acquired goods (headquarters, mausoleums, etc.).[48] On the other hand, what interested the mutualist organizations was the obtaining of subsidies since unlike the unions, they received no permanent economic support. However, it was just an occasional aid whose obtaining depended on the procedures they could make to the Congress. Among congressmen and senators, there were those who, from these demands that arose from the mutualist organizations themselves, promoted the initiatives tending to provide greater prominence to the MAS as spaces of social security, preventing their associates from paying an extra fee to the Workers' saving bank or to the different social fund organizations that were emerging. They did so, convinced that mutualism offered greater certainties than the system created by the State, which they claimed was bankrupt due to a lack of financing. They also characterized it as a cold system, which contrasted with the warmth of the mutuality. Nonetheless, for leftist sectors, mutualism was an overcome stage, and going back to it would be considered a setback. They were convinced that now was the time of syndicalism.[49] Therefore, the interpretation that has prevailed in the historiography of a declining mutualism versus an expanding unionism has been the result of what contemporaries thought should happen, but this was very far from reality.

If there were no political decisions that allowed for the revival of mutualism, and on the contrary, there were rather moves to install it within the unions but not necessarily to strengthen it as an instance of social security, what explains the persistence of democratic mutualism? First, as has already been pointed out, the Caja del Seguro Obrero (CSO) – a pension system financed by the contributions of workers, employers, and the state – responsible for providing protection to the majority of the working population, granted very limited benefits for a long time. The number of registered individuals in the CSO was estimated at 614,000 for 1930–31, corresponding to 44.7% of the active population at that time.[50] The other pension funds that were created accommodated an additional percentage of workers, but it did not exceed 10%.[51] In the early years, social security from the state was essentially "health insurance for medical care and subsidies while on work incapacity".[52] Both old-age and disability pensions only had a relatively significant reach around the 1950s. Most of the income was absorbed by sickness and maternity benefits, so the CSO was underfunded to cover pensions. The Law of Preventive Medicine (1938) expanded the demand for primary care, with an emphasis on "comprehensive health for the insured".[53] The gender imbalance observed in mutualism was also reflected in the CSO, although in 1945, out of 275,884 male affiliates, there were 144,589 insured women.[54]

On the other hand, for mutualist organizations, the health of their affiliates continued to be their main concern. On the occasion of a motion presented by a group of representatives in 1954 for the National Mutualist Confederation to be recognized by the State, it was argued that additionally, the MAS provided its associates the medical services and subsidies in case of illnesses. Then, extra aids were provided in cases of unemployment and orphanhood. Subsequently, these organization could set up medical and dental offices, where services such as minor surgery procedures were provided. Likewise, X-ray equipment, ultraviolet light, and diathermy equipment were also provided. Therefore, a "noble gesture of the mutual clinics, which keep their doors open to attend free of charge with doctors and practitioners to the families of the neighborhood and to indigent people were highlighted". The concern of the MAS rests "on hospitalizing its associates affected by chronic diseases, in order to submit them to complete examinations and treatments".[55] On the other hand, the health commissions "surrounded their patients with all kinds of care, whether by providing them specialist doctors or by taking them to modern hospitals or laboratories. All this so that these patients would not lack at any time, the indispensable means to recover their health or save their lives, with alacrity and opportunity, in serious or desperate cases".[56] Other commissions were in charge to visit sick associates, bringing them medicines, resources, and even food if required. Those visits to the homes comforted families and if a death occurred, the deceased associate received "all services that the Institution has arranged: coffin, chapel, wake, funeral honors, solemn burial in the niche of the social mausoleum". They also added: "A heterogeneous procession of leaders and affiliates, headed by a mourned social banner arrives at the cemetery to offer a merciful burial. On occasions, when it comes to the death of an outstanding mutualist leader, there are hundreds of associates and countless social insignia of various corporations that accompany the body to his last resting place".[57] Finally, the mortuary quota was highlighted. This was formed by the obligatory and extraordinary contribution of all the associates and the fact that, if there were orphaned children, there was the concern of obtaining scholarships so that they could continue with their professional education.

The fact that mutuality was part of the culture of public issues of the working class should be added.[58] This was one of the quintessential spaces of sociability, in its own or leased headquarter. Whether on the occasion of the anniversaries of the society or mutuality, or the visit to a sick associate, the members shared and talked. Those societies that acquired their own corporate headquarters became the spaces in which trade unionists, guilds, neighborhood associations, and sport clubs usually performed their meetings. This way of relating was part of the culture of the working class, regardless of other spaces for sociability, such as theaters, movies, or sport fields, which were also opened up to mass culture.[59]

The appreciation of mutual aids could be renewed from childhood when it was decided to teach it during the 1920s.[60] By 1928–1929 and following the ideas by John Dewy of educating in democracy from the praxis, school communities were formed. This linked society even more with schools. Therefore, it was not easy for mutualism to stop being valued as a solidary and social experience.[61] In turn, education had been and continued to be one of the main concerns of the mutuality. Indeed, in their social buildings there were "primary night schools, technical and professional institutes. There were also learning and improvement courses in aspects such as mechanics, electricity, radiotelephony, line drawing, carpentry, furniture, crafts, motor mechanics, commercial education in all its topics, fashion courses, clothing, trousseau, shirts, artificial flowers, etc."[62] Thus, in Santiago three educational organizations still stood out in the mid-20th century: the Victorino Laínez Technical Institute, in the

Union of Typographers; the Fermín Vivaceta Technical Institute, in the Society of Artisans La Unión, and the Augusto Villanueva Technical and Commercial Institute, of the Dávila Baeza Society. Libraries were still in force, being public in many cases. The MAS also stood out by promoting sports, such as the case of the female basketball team of the Dávila Baeza Society of Santiago, "whose members have performed with unsurpassed mastery to the point of appearing as South American champions and vice-champions in memorable international competitions".[63] Summarizing, these communities had brigades of boy scouts, girl guides, rover scouts, soccer teams, cycling, musical ensembles, and artistic performances.

The Chilean Mutualist Confederation (CMCh) as a public entity: new challenges and problems

During the 1950s, the so-called mutual law began to be discussed, which in March 1963 became Law 15,177. Thus, the CMCh founded in 1939 began to be recognized as a public institution.[64] In 1966, the regulations for the operation of CMCh were approved. On this occasion, it was established that the main task was "to study and solve the problems of Chilean mutualism, according to its attributions and economic resources available, especially related to assistance, education and cooperative activities".[65] In other words, the State, in a time which has always been based on the premise that it had a greater presence, it was limited to establishing a regulatory framework of the mutuality, but without interfering directly in its operation. Where this situation became even more evident was in the task that was entrusted to the Confederation to "organize and keep up to date the national registry of mutual entities", reports on the requests for legal personality, approval or reform of statutes and review the requests for reconsideration of cancellations of legal personality were also indicated.[66] The most relevant aspect at this point was the obligation established to all mutualist societies in order to belong to the CMCH.[67] Indeed, in Article 5 of the regulation it was established "that it is compulsory for all mutual aid organizations to be registered in the National Registry of Mutual Entities, within ninety days from the date of publication of the decree that grants them legal personality".[68] Mutual aid institutions or entities were defined as "organizations, institutions, corporations, associated circles, and, in general, any entity that sustains and practices the principles of cooperation and mutual assistance among its associates, in accordance to their respective statutes".[69] However, syndicates and other forms of union associations were not considered.

The fact that an attribution that corresponded to the State was granted to the CMCh in the terms in which it was carried out caused many problems. The first was resources because as the procedures had to be performed by lawyers, payments were required, which were not cheap. In addition, secretarial and stationery expenses also increased. These expenses were added to those already assumed by the Confederation for the maintenance of its headquarters and a mutualist home, which could be used by anyone who traveled to Santiago and clearly accredited by their respective provincial federations. Moreover, directors and the board of directors were forced to meet at the capital. The expenses were attempted to be covered with the sale of a mutual card, discs with the anthem, as well as the membership fees that the societies affiliated to the confederation had to pay annually. However, the income was well below the expenses. Probably, one of the main problems was that the MAS that joined the CMCh never paid their dues on time. It is necessary to return to the time of the mutual again and think how difficult was for them to support themselves, especially for those that lacked a place to meet. Consequently, paying an annual fee was not easy. In order to counteract these difficulties, boards carried out multiple efforts and managed to double subvention in times of Popular Unity. However, this was insufficient because the inflationary context made everything more expensive very quickly.

The second problem that was generated, and it was even more serious, was that the bureaucratization of the CMCh transformed it into a field of dispute. At present, it is difficult to distinguish the political background of the differences and in the documentation of the Confederation, only the conflicts were evidenced as an organizational problem. Confronting personal egos for institutional purposes was also considered a problem. These conflicts erupted with force in 1969, when the outgoing president Marcial Cáceres Ugarte challenged the entire incoming presidency before the Ministry of Justice, six months after being elected. This generated a true internal earthquake in the Confederation, which was resolved on the one hand, with the resolution of no considering the opinion of the Ministry and, on the other, with the unanimous decision of the councilors to expel Cáceres from the Confederation. Among those who supported Cáceres was Miguel Ernesto Gil Núñez, who would assume the CMCh after the 1973 coup d'état.

Although this period requires a specific study, it is possible to ascertain certain key ideas. In the first place, the impact of the dictatorial repression on the society in motion and social movements was not new. Specifically, Sergio Grez points out that the premises of the Mutualist Confederation were raided and a great amount of their books and archives were burned.[70] The president of the institution, a socialist militant, was forced to resign; the vice president of the organization assumed the direction, who was also very resisted both in Santiago and Valparaíso for being involved in the attempt of Marcial Cáceres to retake the presidency through a coup d'état in 1969: Miguel Gil Núñez. This person hurriedly gave support to the dictatorship, obviously without consulting the base, and used the coercion of the regime to overcome the resistance of the federations of Valparaíso and Santiago to affiliate with CMCh. Prior to the coup, the Confederation had managed to get a bill introduced to get a provisional subvention to ensure adequate financing to its functions. This was repressed in 1976. This situation caused a major problem. On the one hand, the societies that had to be affiliated had to assume the costs involved in their inscription. In addition, they had to pay the fee again on an annual basis. Belonging to the Confederation only represented obligations and problems, but without benefits. The reductions of rights in the cemeteries obtained during the Popular Unit ceased to be applied. Additionally, it was not too comfortable to stay in the mutualist home of Santiago, which increasingly deteriorated because of the lack of maintenance.

The public support to the regime allowed the CMCh once again to organize the National Mutualists Congresses. The last one was held in Osorno, in April 1973. In 1976, The XII Mutualist Congress was held in Antofagasta and then they continued to be organized successively every three years, according to was established in the law that had created the Confederation. Conflicts between the CMCH and the federations of Santiago and Valparaíso, among others, were active during the 1970s and the relations only seemed to have relaxed in the following decade. For Sergio Grez, the decree N°3.341 of 1980 that granted "freedom" to mutualist organizations to affiliate or disaffiliate the CMCh was the coup de grace for mutualist organizations, since it meant to apply the method of "divide to rule", applied to the union movement and the entire civil society.[71] The effect this measure had on the Confederation becomes undeniable and what is appreciated is the fact that the conflicts were intense and had dragged on practically since its creation as a public entity for the reasons indicated above. These can be synthesized by the fact that it was given a great responsibility with limited resources and the political disputes that caused its bureaucratization.

The dictatorship did not solve the economic problems of the CMCh, and the discrepancies between the leaders, who were in Santiago openly in favor of the regime, and the societies throughout the country and in the capital itself began to resume their activities, under the surveillance of military delegates, became unsustainable. Some federations and mutuals supported the Confederation, while others distanced themselves openly. The idea that religious and political differences were not allowed within mutualism was an important argument to sustain mutual aid, but that did not prevent some of its members, who had participated in the Unidad Popular, from being persecuted. While thousands of mutualists had retired from the Armed Forces and therefore felt close to the dictatorship, in the halls of other mutuals in the country, such as the Juan Martínez de Rozas

Society in Concepción or the Artisans Society of Limache in the Valparaíso region, "peñas" were organized, cultural resistance spaces against the dictatorship.[72] Therefore, Decree No. 3.341, which stripped the CMCh of control of all mutuals in the country, contrary to Sergio Grez's argument, could have been rather a decompressor, an oxygen tank, so that mutualism could recover again.

But that was far from happening, and once again, what explains it, more than political reasons, is of an economic and cultural nature, in addition to certain changes in the long term. First, the functions fulfilled by the SSM (forecasting, education, and socio-political organization) gradually began to be taken over by other entities, as these communities had projected and built themselves upon all these areas because none of them had been assumed by either the State or the businessmen. In the case of forecasting, social security, and mutual insurance had expanded to achieve increasingly greater coverage, which made the role of the SSM increasingly less relevant. In 1941, those contributing to the Social Security Funds amounted to 1,516,161 people, far from the 125,000 of the mutual insurance.[73] But in the 1960s, the incorporation into the Social Security Service (created in 1952) deepened, reaching 2,194,000 people, 66% of its universe.[74] All of the above was reflected in indicators such as infant mortality, which reached 82 per thousand births in 1970. Since 1925, for those who had been and wanted to continue being mutualists, contributing to the workers' insurance or a Fund was not a problem, if they could afford it. But the working classes who entered the labor market in the 1960s, with an increasingly present State in matters of forecasting, did not consider it an option. It should also be weighed the efforts – albeit limited by the lack of resources – that began to be made in the field of preventive medicine and in relation to work accidents, which in turn led to the forecasting becoming a very broad field, in which, as has been demonstrated for other realities, the insurance market also made headway.[75]

A debate that opened in the 1960s was about the survival of employer mutual insurance companies. For some parliamentarians, it was an outdated modality that could undermine the financing of social insurance in relation to work accidents and occupational diseases. From other points of view, it was advisable to maintain these insurance forms, as they were considered to have had good results.[76] In 1967, with the discussion of the bill about professional diseases and work accidents, the existence of these mutualist organizations was hotly debated. At that time, there were three of them: The Chilean Security Society and the ASIVA Safety Institute, both created in 1962. Subsequently, The Corporation for Safety and Work Accident Prevention was founded in 1965. These were organisation managed by employers and workers, whose control was in the hands of the National Health Service, and whose supervision was responsibility of the Superintendence of Social Security. According to Senator José Foncea, in 1965 Chile was one of the countries with the highest density and frequency of work accidents. In the same way, these type of mutualist organizations "through various security and control measures",[77] had managed to lower the rate, so that whereas in the Work Accident Saving Bank, during that year the average number of injured persons attended had been 22.7%, in the mutual insurance or employers' associations, the accident rate reached 10.3%. In other words, "this was less than half of the average indicated above, despite its their attention is related to one of the activities with the greatest risk, which is construction".[78] There was an information that out of those mutualist organizations of recent foundation, two of them had hospitals. Finally, of the 2,800,000 workers in Chile, 572,00 were insured against risks of professional diseases and accidents, though that figure could continue to increase, also by considering the fact that that benefit was planned to extend to students and independent workers. Therefore, the universe of insured workers could reach 3,200.000 or 3,400,000 people. For Salvador Allende, who would become President of the Republic, the history of the employers' mutualist organization was related to the fact they went bankrupt before fulfilling their commitments with the affiliates. He was suspicious that they could take charge of the recovery and rehabilitation of the injured person, since not even the accident insurance companies could do it. If the accident rate of the Work Accident Fund (of the State) was higher, it was because it had to cover the risks of agriculture, livestock, and mining, whose indices were more dangerous and frequent.[79] Furthermore, at the time and according to Senator María Elena Carrera, these mutualist societies had no more than 40,000 insured workers.[80] However, it is important to take them into consideration, because of the remarkable growth they would have due to the establishment of compulsory social insurance against Risks of Accidents at Work and Occupational Diseases in 1968.[81]

In the field of education, the significant investments carried out from the 1930s, especially during the radical party governments, should be highlighted. During these governments, both infrastructure and coverage were increased. In the case of primary education, the system increased from 327,000 to 1,670,000 schoolchildren. On the other hand, in secondary education, the increase changed from 53,000 to 982,500 students. The same occurred with university education, which increased from 2,900 students in 1911 to 119,500 in 1982. All these changes associated with the strengthening of public education led to a notable increase in student enrollment and channeled through the national education system. On the other hand, the education offered to the working class by the mutualist organizations began to lose the importance it used to have, despite the fact that subsidies continued to be requested for some of their schools. These were definitely suppressed. Moreover, although for a long time, the labor structure was dominated by workers and employees, the growing professionalization began to cause cultural changes that very slowly would impact on the working class and labor dynamics. By the 1960s, trade unionism had expanded noticeably, and that growth would deepen during that decade, when peasant unionization is authorized. It is already clear that mutuality was one of their functions and that this had been regulated by the State, for which they were the main and essential form of organization of the working class. Already in 1940, it became clear that the authorities had little interest in supervising the functioning of the MAS, which was even more evident with Law 15.177. Trade unionism became the main space for the struggle of the working class gathered in the CUT (Single Union of Workers).[82]

During the government of Eduardo Frei (1964–1970), legislation also passed on neighborhood associations, and the creation of mothers' centers was promoted. In other words, new forms of associativity and sociability were added to the already existing sport organizations, syndicates, social clubs, parents' centers, school colonies, religious organizations, and, of course, mutualist associations. Consequently, and although the society of that time participated in multiple groups, it is clear that the MAS ceased to have the central role they used to have until at least the 1920s.

Economic crisis of 1982: cultural and definitive changes of the civic-military dictatorship

The world economic crisis of 1982 shuddered the country and its dictatorship. The debacle meant the closure of many companies, increase in unemployment, and the beginning of protests to overthrow the regime. Although the dictatorship capsized, it was forced to open up to civilians and consider a part of the opposition. At this time, deep changes had been driven, which ensured the projection in both culture and population. The dismantling of the State was followed by an opening of the economy and the privatization of health and pensions. In just a few decades, a society that had been deeply associative and collectivist became individualist and consumerist.[83]

From the present point of view, when considering the tension and ruptures that the decree N°3,341 meant for the CMCh, what explains the second crisis of mutuality was the brutal impact of the crisis on the economy, society, and cultural changes. The saving banks of a number of mutualist organizations were not capable to sustain themselves and cover the medical expenses and death insurances. Thus, with the changes that were performed in the health and welfare systems, in the field of education and culture, it ceased to make less and less sense to associate with mutualist purposes. The main threat of any organization was present in this last phase. This final crisis began with the crisis of 1983 and which is projected to the present: the non-renewal of its age groups. It is interesting to note how in time, with the memory of what happened, particularly in the 1970s, the confederation was seen more as a source of problems and interference than as a commonwealth. Indeed, in its memory of the activities carried out between 1992 and 1994, the board of the Confederation explained that a cadastre had been prepared and distributed throughout the country. This information circled among all organizations enrolled in the national register of mutualist entities totaled 518. Only 99 institutions responded, 19.1%: "The remaining organizations considered that the Confederation was misusing its powers and wanted to become part of the Societies, which are Private Law Institutions. Instead, it was intended to fulfill a mandate by a National Mutualist Congress to know exactly, how many societies and how many members has this solidary movement throughout the country".[84]

According to the numbers reviewed, mutualist by then throughout the country and not only those that responded to the surveys – were about 40,000. Today, affiliated to the CMCh there are just over a thousand members. However, although it is enigmatic, this is far from specifying that the mutualist idea is not valid, because since the beginning of the 1920s, it was projected in other areas: from the armed forces and law enforcement to the associations of school teachers; in the case of bureaucratic mutualism; the so-called employers' mutualism; and the mutualism as part of the dimensions of guilds and syndicates. Finally, what is clear is that the convergence between mutualism and society in motion is weakened.

Conclusions

In this chapter, we demonstrate that mutualism experienced two expansive cycles between two moments of crisis, the first in 1929 and the second in 1982. Although in both circumstances, political contexts of authoritarian governments and political decisions impacting the internal and external social dynamics of MAS converged, the common denominator was primarily economic crises that weakened the funds of mutualist societies and resulted in a significant decline in the number of members. However, there was a substantial difference that marked a profound difference in how each of these contraction cycles took place. In the first case, social and cultural transformations, although entering the dynamics of mass culture, did not mean the destruction of the social fabric but its strengthening. In Chile and Latin America, associability and sociability around the public sphere probably reached its golden age between the 1930s and 1970s. But the thickening of the social fabric did not weaken mutualism because organizations at the time did not necessarily compete with each other. There was room for everyone in them: unions, mutuals, sports clubs, public service collectives, advancement centers for progress, school colonies, parent and guardian centers, guilds, and social clubs. While it is true that during this period, the State had a greater presence in certain areas; it did not mean that society contracted.

The scenario of the second economic crisis that devastated Latin America and Chile (1982) and consequently, the MAS, was completely different. This time, in addition to the impact on mutual savings, deep cultural transformations were being promoted, which also projected onto educational, health, and pension institutions. The fundamental principle that was sown is the efficiency of the private sector versus the public sector, and of the individual versus the collective. In that context, the retreat of this type of associationism and its related sociability seemed inevitable.

Regardless of the moment in which Chilean mutualism began its definitive decline, starting in the 1930s, the question is whether it returned to occupy the central place in the popular movement that characterized it during the liberal period. According to the research conducted, the moment of the greatest expansion of mutual aid occurred between the 1930s and 1970s, that is, the period in which it had been systematically maintained until now when it had entered a terminal crisis. That said, regardless of the expansion that mutual aid had, historiography has shown the central role that unions, especially those of an industrial nature, came to play in the popular movement. These received significant resources for their operation from companies based on gratuities provided by law. However, as already mentioned, it is also true that during this period, the social fabric "thickened" as never before, and in its density, it sometimes becomes very difficult to distinguish the preeminence of one type of association over another. In that case, perhaps the most appropriate thing is to say that until the 1920s, the leadership of mutualism over the social movement was unquestionable and that from the 1930s, it was not a type of organization that predominated but rather the society in motion or as a social movement, with the prominent role that women, peasants, and students had at different times.

References cited

Links

Udec.cl/asociacion/index.php?glb=asocper#angen.

Confar.cl

Bcn.cl/portal

Files consulted

Archivo Confederación Mutualista de Chile.

Archivo Nacional de la Administración.
Inspección del Trabajo.
Boletín de la Oficina del Trabajo, 1–22

Magazines
Sucesos: 1903–1919
Revista del Trabajo:1930–1950

Notes

1 This work is part of the Regular Fondecyt project N° 1190308. We appreciate Wilson Lermanda´s comments. We also appreciate the support of the project *Historia de la Catalunya Subalterna Contemporánea: alternativas solidarias y cooperativas*. Reference: PID2019–109560GB-I00, convocatoria 2019 *proyectos de I+D+i* del Ministerio de Ciencia e Innovación- Gobierno de España.
2 Sergio GREZ: "La trayectoria histórica del mutualismo en Chile (1853–1990)", *Mapocho: Revista de Humanidades y Ciencias Sociales*, 35 (1994), pp. 293–315; ÍD: *De la 'regeneración del pueblo' a la huelga general. Génesis y evolución histórica del movimiento popular en Chile (1810–1910)*, 2nd. ed., Santiago, Dirección de Bibliotecas, Archivos y Museos, Centro de Investigaciones Diego Barros Arana-RIL Editores, 2007. For a full and recent review of the state of the art, please see: Fernando VENEGAS and Sergio GREZ: "Historiografía del mutualismo chileno, 1853–1990: análisis crítico y nuevas perspectivas", *Izquierdas*, 50 (2021), pp. 1–30.
3 Enrique FERNÁNDEZ: *El ocaso de las sociedades de socorros mutuos en el cambio de siglo (1915–1932). De la exclusión estatal a la búsqueda de la integración social*, Tesis para optar al grado de Magíster, Pontificia Universidad Católica de Chile, 1995, p. 97.
4 *Ibid*., p. 107.
5 Mª Angélica ILLANES: *En el nombre del Pueblo, del Estado y de la Ciencia. Historia Social de la Salud Pública. Chile, 1880–1973 (Hacia una historia social del siglo XX)*, Santiago, Ministerio de Salud, 2010, p. 35.
6 *Ibid*., pp. 326–339.
7 Gabriel SALAZAR: *Movimientos sociales en Chile: trayectoria histórica y proyección política*, Santiago, Uqbar, 2012.
8 Fernando VENEGAS: "Mutualismo y economía ...", pp. 309–353.
9 Juan YÁÑEZ: *La intervención social en Chile. Y el nacimiento de la sociedad salarial, 1907–1932*, Santiago, RiL editores, 2008, p. 24.
10 Fernando LARGO and Josep PUJOL-ANDREU: "Desarrollo y crisis del mutualismo de trabajadores en España en el siglo XX: nueva aproximación desde el capital social", *Scripta Nova*, vol. XX, 540 (2016). A comprehensive vie won sociability in Spain: Ramon ARNABAT: *Asociaos y seréis fuertes. Sociabilidades, modernizaciones y ciudadanías en España, 1860–1930*, Zaragoza, Prensas de la Universidad de Zaragoza, 2019.
11 Marcel VAN DER LINDEN (ed.): *Social Security Mutualism. The Comparative History of Mutual Benefit Societies*, Berne, Peter Lang AG, European Academic Publishers, 1996. For conceptual accuracy, please see: Fernando VENEGAS: "Mutualismo y economía ...", pp. 309–353.

12 However, this appreciation is relative because it has been a study carried out from those sources that has come to question the notion that mutualism entered into an irreversible crisis in the mid-1920s. Please see: Fernando VENEGAS: "Las posibilidades para el renacimiento del mutualismo en Chile entre 1930 y 1960. Estudio de un caso, Limache", *Historia 396*, 2 (2014), pp. 319–349.

13 Regarding this issue, please see: Carlos IBARRA: "Construcción del ramal Talcahuano-Chillán (1869–1874): una mirada desde la historia ambiental", *Historia*, vol. II, 55 (2022), pp. 149–174; Wilson LERMANDA: "De entrepôt a puerto comercial del Pacífico Sur: Talcahuano (Chile), 1872–1914", *Revista Austral de Ciencias Sociales*.

14 On this issue, please see: Fernando VENEGAS: *Estado y Sociedad. Construcción de Espacios en contextos locales. Limache, 1860*–1960, vol. 1 and 2, Valparaíso, Ediciones Universitarias de la PUCV, 2019.

15 About the importance of immigrants in Argentine mutualism, please see: Roberto DI STEFANO *et al.*: *De las Cofradías a las Organizaciones de la Sociedad Civil. Historia de la iniciativa asociativa en Argentina. 1776–1990*, Buenos Aires, Edilab Editora, 2002.

16 This aspect is developed mainly in: Fernando VENEGAS: "Mutualismo en Chile Central: la clase trabajadora y la seguridad social (1848–1922)", *Revista de Historia*, 28, 2 (2021), pp. 334–391. However, more examples could be provided throughout the country of how transcendental foreign influence was, as befitting the case of Magellan. Please see: Mateo MARTINIC: *Historia de la Región Magallánica,* vol. III, Punta Arenas, Ediciones de la Universidad de Magallanes, 2006.

17 Juan José GARRIDO: *El mutualismo privado en la Europa del siglo XX*, Madrid, Ed. Mapfre, 1994.

18 Please see: Fernando VENEGAS: "Trayectoria mutualista en el Norte de Chile: expansión del socorro mutuo durante el predominio liberal (1862–1922)", *Estudios Atacameños*, 68 (2022), pp. 11, 19, and 21; Fernando VENEGAS and Wilson LERMANDA: "Socorro Mutuo en la zona sur de Chile, 1885–1922: previsión social, patrimonio y ahorro", in Mathias ÓRDENES (ed.): *Sujetos sin voz en el sur de Chile y Argentina. Frontera, colonización, marginalidad y organización popular chilena en los siglos XIX y XX*, Santiago, Lom Ediciones, 2022, pp. 353–419.

19 Archivo Nacional de la Administración (en adelante ARNAD), Inspección del Trabajo (IT), vol. 86, 1922.

20 Deepen in: Fernando VENEGAS: "Mutualismo en Chile Central ...", pp. 354–356.

21 Juan José GARRIDO: *El mutualismo privado ...* , pp. 19–21. This aspect has been previously addressed in Fernando VENEGAS: "Mutualismo en Chile Central ...", p. 356.

22 Regarding this subject, please see: Jorge VERGARA and Aldo MASCAREÑO: "La propiedad y conflictos de tierras indígenas en la provincia de Valdivia" in Jorge VERGARA, Aldo MASCAREÑO and Rolf FOERSTER: *La propiedad huilliche en la provincia de Valdivia*, Santiago, Corporación Nacional de Desarrollo Indígena (CONADI), 1996; Jorge PINTO and Mathias ÓRDENES: *Chile, una economía regional en el siglo XX: La Araucanía, 1900–1960*, Temuco, Ediciones Universidad de la Frontera, 2012; Martín CORREA: *La Historia del despojo. El origen de la propiedad particular en el territorio mapuche*, Santiago, Pehuen & Ceibo, 2021.

23 Fernando VENEGAS: "Trayectoria mutualista en el Norte de Chile ...", pp. 1–32.
24 There are important studies about these organizations: we recommend the following: Julio PINTO: "En el camino de la mancomunal: organizaciones obreras en la provincia de Tarapacá, 1880–1895", *Cuadernos de Historia*, 14 (1994), pp. 81–135; Eduardo DEVÉS: *Los que van a morir te saludan. Historia de una masacre. Escuela Santa María, Iquique, 1907*, Santiago, Ediciones Documentas, 1988; Pablo ARTAZA: "El Impacto de la matanza de Santa María de Iquique. Conciencia de clase, política popular y movimiento social en Tarapacá", *Cuadernos de Historia*, 181 (1998), pp. 169–227; Pablo ARTAZA: *Movimiento social y politización popular en Tarapacá, 1900–1912*, Concepción, Ediciones Escaparate, 2006.
25 Fernando VENEGAS: "Mutualismo y economía ...", p. 333.
26 Óscar PARRAO: "La Mutualidad en Chile", *Boletín de la Oficina del Trabajo*, Imprenta Santiago, Santiago de Chile, 1924, pp. 11–29.
27 "Asociaciones obreras en 1923", *Boletín de la Oficina del Trabajo*, 22 (1924), pp. 214–221.
28 For an analysis of the situation of the Chilean economy in the period, please see: Mario matus: *Precios y salarios reales en Chile durante el ciclo salitrero, 1880–1930*, Tesis doctoral, Universidad de Barcelona, 2009.
29 Fernando VENEGAS, "Mutualismo y economía ...", p. 317.
30 Jorge ROJAS: *La Dictadura de Ibáñez y los sindicatos (1927–19231),* Santiago, Dirección de Bibliotecas Archivos y Museos & Biblioteca Nacional, 1994, pp. 117–121
31 Wilson LERMANDA: "*¡A los obreros del país ... por qué rechazamos la ley 4.054!". Resistencias y recepciones hacia la Caja del Seguro Obrero (Chile, 1924–1938),* chapter of his unpublished and under development doctoral thesis at the Doctors Program, University of Concepción.
32 Sergio GREZ: "La trayectoria histórica del mutualismo ...", pp. 308–309.
33 Mª Angélica ILLANES: *En el nombre del Pueblo ...*, p. 238.
34 Concept taken from: Armando DE RAMÓN, Juan COUYOUMDJIAN and Samuel VIAL: *Historia de América. 2. América Latina en búsqueda de un nuevo orden (1870–1990),* Santiago, Andrés Bello, 1992.
35 Taken from: BN: *Revista del Trabajo*, 4 (1938), pp. 85–87; ÍD: *Revista del Trabajo*, 5 (1938), pp. 63–73; and ÍD: *Revista del Trabajo*, (June 1938), pp. 71–75.
36 Session of 7 April 1954. Retrieved from the internet (bcn.cl/portal).
37 Mario GARCÉS and Pedro MILOS: *FOCJ CTCH CUT: las centrales Unitarias en la historia del sindicalismo chileno*, Santiago, Educación y Comunicaciones (ECO), 1988.
38 Mutualist Confederation of Chile Archive (onwards ACMCh). Without classification.
39 *Ibid.*
40 BN: *Revista del Trabajo*, 8 (1932), p. 47.
41 Session of 29 August 1944. Retrieved from the internet (bcn.cl/portal).
42 In the University of Concepción, this association was created on 17 October 1943. Retrieved on 15 January 2023: http://www2.udec.cl/asociacion/index.php?glb=asocper#angen.
43 Retrieved on 15 January 2023. Retrieved from the internet (www.Confar.cl).
44 Session of 16 September 1953. Retrieved from the internet (bcn.cl/portal).
45 Sergio GREZ: "La trayectoria histórica del mutualismo ...", p. 312.

46 Session of 16 September 1953. Retrieved from the internet (bcn.cl/portal).
47 Fernando VENEGAS: *Estado y Sociedad ...* , vol. 2, pp. 59–90.
48 Multiple examples of grants are found in parliamentary sessions, although there are also complaints that they were not being delivered. Revise: Session of 31 December 1930. Retrieved from the internet (bcn.cl/portal); Session of 29 December 1941. Retrieved from the internet (bcn.cl/portal) and Sitting of 28 December 1949. Retrieved from the internet (bcn.cl/portal).
49 This discussion can be followed in: Session of 18 August 1937. Retrieved from the internet (bcn.cl/portal); Session of 29 November 1939. Retrieved from the internet (bcn.cl/portal) and Session of 27 August 1940. Retrieved from the internet (bcn.cl/portal).
50 Francisca RENGIFO: "El Estado de seguridad social chileno y la institucionalización desigual del bienestar", in Iván JAKSIC and Francisca RENGIFO (eds.): *Historia política de Chile, 1810–2010. Tomo II. Estado y sociedad*, Santiago, Fondo de Cultura Económica, 2017, pp. 410–411.
51 Francisca Rengifo estimates it between 20% and 30% additional, but we believe that was a lower percentage than what was observed from: DIRECCIÓN GENERAL DE ESTADÍSTICA: *Veinte años de Legislación social*, 1945.
52 Francisca RENGIFO, "El Estado de seguridad social chileno ...", p. 411.
53 *Ibid.*, p. 412.
54 *Ibid.*, p. 413.
55 *Íd.*
56 *Íd.*
57 *Íd.*
58 In this aspect, it is important to take into consideration the analysis carried out by Richard SENNETT: *El declive del hombre público*, Barcelona, Anagrama, 2011.
59 Stefan RINKE: *Cultura de masas: reforma y nacionalismo en Chile, 1910–1931*, Santiago, Dirección de Bibliotecas, Archivos y Museos, Centro de Investigaciones Diego Barros Arana, 2002.
60 Fernando VENEGAS: "Acercar la vida a las escuelas y los liceos: las comunidades escolares como ámbitos de convergencia entre la sociedad y la educación. La experiencia desde las regiones. Chile, 1928–1952", in Benjamín SILVA (Compilator): *Historia Social de la Educación Chilena. Tomo* 6, Santiago, Ediciones Universidad Tecnológica Metropolitana, 2020, pp. 101–146.
61 *Íd.*
62 Session of 30 August 1956. Retrieved from the internet (bcn.cl/portal).
63 *Íd.*
64 Law 15.177. Promulgated on 6 March 1963. Retrieved from the internet (bcn.cl/portal).
65 Decree 215. Regulations for the application of the law 15.177, bcn.cl/portal
66 *Íd.*
67 Article 3 of the 1966 regulations indicated: "The Mutual Confederation of Chile will be part of the mutual aid institutions of the country that have legal personality in force or that obtain it in the future and that are registered in the Register of Affiliated Mutual Entities". Íd.
68 ACMCh: *Carta a los presidentes de las federaciones provinciales*, 15 April 1970.
69 Law 15.177, issued on 6 March 1963, bcn.cl/portal. Article 4.
70 Sergio GREZ: "La trayectoria histórica del mutualismo ...", p. 314.

71 *Ibid.*, p. 314.
72 Regarding this, please refer to: Gabriela BRAVO and Cristian GONZÁLEZ: *Ecos del tiempo subterráneo. Las peñas de Santiago durante el régimen militar (1973–1983)*, Santiago, Lom Ediciones, 2009.
73 DIRECCIÓN GENERAL DE ESTADÍSTICA: *Veinte años de Legislación social*, 1945.
74 Francisca RENGIFO: "El Estado de seguridad social chileno ...", p. 418.
75 Mª Teresa SÁNCHEZ: "El mutualismo de previsión social en España", *CIRIEC-España: Revista de Economía pública, social y cooperativa*, 57 (2007), pp. 225–248.
76 Session of 1 August. Retrieved from the internet (bcn.cl/portal).
77 Session of 26 July 1967. Retrieved from the internet (bcn.cl/portal).
78 *Íd.*
79 *Íd.*
80 Session of 17 October 1967. Retrieved from the internet (bcn.cl/portal).
81 Law 16.744, 1 February 1968, bcn.cl/portal.
82 Mario GARCÉS and Pedro MILOS: *FOCJ CTCH CUT: las centrales ...*
83 Tomás MOULIAN: *El consumo me consume*, Santiago, LOM Ediciones, 1988.
84 ACMCh: *Memory of the Board of Directors of the Mutual Aid Confederation of Chile*, 1994.

References

ARNABAT, Ramon: *Asociaos y seréis fuertes. Sociabilidades, modernizaciones y ciudadanías en España, 1860–1930*, Zaragoza, Prensas de la Universidad de Zaragoza, 2019.

ARTAZA, Pablo: "El Impacto de la matanza de Santa María de Iquique. Conciencia de clase, política popular y movimiento social en Tarapacá", *Cuadernos de Historia*, 18 (1998), pp. 169–227.

ARTAZA, Pablo: *Movimiento social y politización popular en Tarapacá, 1900–1912*, Concepción, Ediciones Escaparate, 2006.

ARTAZA, Pablo and GONZÁLEZ, Sergio: *A noventa años de los sucesos de la escuela Santa María de Iquique*, Santiago, Dirección de Bibliotecas Archivos y Museos, Lom Ediciones, Universidad Arturo Prat, 1998.

BRAVO, Gabriela and GONZÁLEZ, Cristian: *Ecos del tiempo subterráneo. Las peñas de Santiago durante el régimen militar (1973–1983)*, Santiago, Lom Ediciones, 2009.

CAVIERES, Eduardo: "Grupos intermedios e integración social: la Sociedad de Artesanos de Valparaíso a comienzos del siglo XX", *Cuadernos de Historia*, 6 (1986), pp. 33–47.

CORREA, Martín: *La Historia del despojo. El origen de la propiedad particular en el territorio mapuche*, Santiago, Pehuen & Ceibo, 2021.

DE RAMÓN, Armando; COUYOUMDJIAN, Juan and VIAL, Samuel: *Historia de América. 2. América Latina en búsqueda de un nuevo orden (1870–1990)*, Santiago, Andrés Bello, 1992.

DEVÉS, Eduardo: *Los que van a morir te saludan. Historia de una masacre. Escuela Santa María, Iquique, 1907*, Santiago, Ediciones Documentas, 1988.

DI STEFANO, Roberto *et al.*: *De las Cofradías a las Organizaciones de la Sociedad Civil. Historia de la iniciativa asociativa en Argentina. 1776–1990*, Buenos Aires, Edilab Editora, 2002.

FERNÁNDEZ, Enrique: "El ocaso de las sociedades de socorros mutuos en el cambio de siglo (1915–1932)", *De la exclusión estatal a la búsqueda de la integración social*, Tesis para optar al grado de Magíster, Pontificia Universidad Católica de Chile, 1995.

FERNÁNDEZ, Marcos *et al.*: *Alcohol y trabajo. El alcohol y la formación de las identidades laborales. Chile siglo XIX y XX*, Osorno, Editorial Universidad de Los Lagos, 2008.

GARCÉS, Mario and MILOS, Pedro: *FOCJ CTCH CUT: las centrales Unitarias en la historia del sindicalismo chileno*, Santiago, Educación y Comunicaciones (ECO), 1988.

GARRIDO, Juan José: *El mutualismo privado en la Europa del siglo XX*, Madrid, Ed. Mapfre, 1994.

GREZ, Sergio: "La trayectoria histórica del mutualismo en Chile (1853–1990)", *Mapocho: Revista de Humanidades y Ciencias Sociales*, 35 (1994), pp. 293–315.

GREZ, Sergio: *La 'cuestión social' en Chile. Ideas y debates precursores (1804–1902)*, Santiago, Dirección de Archivos, Bibliotecas y Museos, Centro de Investigaciones Diego Barros Arana, 1995.

GREZ, Sergio: *De la 'regeneración del pueblo' a la huelga general. Génesis y evolución histórica del movimiento popular en Chile (1810–1910)*, 2nd ed., Santiago, Dirección de Bibliotecas, Archivos y Museos, Centro de Investigaciones Diego Barros Arana-RIL Editores, 2007.

IBARRA, Carlos: "Construcción del ramal Talcahuano-Chillán (1869–1874): una mirada desde la historia ambiental", *Historia*, vol. II, 55 (2022), pp. 149–174.

ILLANES, Mª Angélica: *Chile Des-centrado. Formación sociocultural republicana y transición capitalista (1810–1910)*, Santiago, Lom Ediciones, 2003.

ILLANES, Mª Angélica: *En el nombre del Pueblo, del Estado y de la Ciencia. Historia Social de la Salud Pública. Chile, 1880–1973 (Hacia una historia social del siglo XX)*, Santiago, Ministerio de Salud, 2010.

LARGO, Fernando and PUJOL-ANDREU, Josep: "Desarrollo y crisis del mutualismo de trabajadores en España en el siglo XX: nueva aproximación desde el capital social", *Scripta Nova: revista electrónica de Geografía y Ciencias Sociales*, vol. XX, 540 (2016).

LERMANDA, Wilson: "*¡A los obreros del país ... por qué rechazamos la ley 4.054!*", *Resistencias y recepciones hacia la Caja del Seguro Obrero (Chile, 1924–1938)*, Tesis Doctoral, Universidad de Concepción, Chapter of His Unpublished and Under Development Doctoral Thesis at the Doctors Program, University of Concepción.

LERMANDA, Wilson: "De entrepôt a puerto comercial del Pacífico Sur: Talcahuano (Chile), 1872–1914", *Revista Austral de Ciencias Sociales*.

MARTINIC, Mateo: *Historia de la Región Magallánica. Tomo III*, Punta Arenas, Ediciones de la Universidad de Magallanes, 2006.

MATUS, Mario: *Precios y salarios reales en Chile durante el ciclo salitrero, 1880–1930*, Tesis doctoral, Universidad de Barcelona, 2009.

MOULIAN, Tomás: *El consumo me consume*, Santiago, LOM Ediciones, 1988.

PARRAO, Óscar: "La Mutualidad en Chile", *Boletín de la Oficina del Trabajo*, 21 (1924), pp. 11–29.

PINTO, Jorge and ÓRDENES, Mathías: *Chile, una economía regional en el siglo XX: La Araucanía, 1900–1960*, Temuco, Ediciones Universidad de la Frontera, 2012.

PINTO, Julio: "En el camino de la mancomunal: organizaciones obreras en la provincia de Tarapacá, 1880–1895", *Cuadernos de Historia*, 14 (1994), pp. 81–135.

RENGIFO, Francisca: "El Estado de seguridad social chileno y la institucionalización desigual del bienestar", in Iván JAKSIC and Francisca RENGIFO (eds.): *Historia política de Chile, 1810–2010. Tomo II. Estado y sociedad*, Santiago, Fondo de Cultura Económica, 2017, pp. 397–423.

RINKE, Stefan: *Cultura de masas: reforma y nacionalismo en Chile, 1910–1931*, Santiago, Dirección de Bibliotecas, Archivos y Museos, Centro de Investigaciones Diego Barros Arana, 2002.

ROJAS, Jorge: *La Dictadura de Ibáñez y los sindicatos (1927–19231)*, Santiago, Dirección de Bibliotecas Archivos y Museos & Biblioteca Nacional, 1994.

SALAZAR, Gabriel: *Movimientos sociales en Chile: trayectoria histórica y proyección política*, Santiago, Uqbar, 2012.

SÁNCHEZ, Mª Teresa: "El mutualismo de previsión social en España", *CIRIEC-España. Revista de Economía pública, social y cooperativa*, 57 (2007), pp. 225–248.

SENNETT, Richard: *El declive del hombre público*, Barcelona, Anagrama, 2011.

VAN DER LINDEN, Marcel (ed.): *Social Security Mutualism. The Comparative History of Mutual Benefit Societies*, Berne, Peter Lang AG, European Academic Publishers, 1996.

VENEGAS, Fernando: "Las posibilidades para el renacimiento del mutualismo en Chile entre 1930 y 1960. Estudio de un caso, Limache", *Historia 396*, 2, (2014), pp. 319–349.

VENEGAS, Fernando: *Estado y Sociedad. Construcción de Espacios en contextos locales. Limache, 1860–1960, vol. 1 and 2*, Valparaíso, Ediciones Universitarias, 2019.

VENEGAS, Fernando: "Acercar la vida a las escuelas y los liceos: las comunidades escolares como ámbitos de convergencia entre la sociedad y la educación. La experiencia desde las regiones. Chile, 1928–1952", in Benjamín SILVA (Compilator): *Historia Social de la Educación Chilena: Tomo 6. Estado docente con crecientes niveles de responsabilidad en sus aulas. Chile 1920–1973. Regiones, pueblos originarios y emergencias educativas*, Santiago, Ediciones Universidad Tecnológica Metropolitana, 2020, pp. 101–146.

VENEGAS, Fernando: "Mutualismo en Chile Central: la clase trabajadora y la seguridad social (1848–1922)", *Revista de Historia (Concepción)*, vol. 28, 2 (2021), pp. 334–391.

VENEGAS, Fernando: "Mutualismo y economía social solidaria. Chile, 1910–1930", *Cuadernos de Historia*, 57 (2022), pp. 309–353

VENEGAS, Fernando: "Trayectoria mutualista en el Norte de Chile: expansión del socorro mutuo durante el predominio liberal (1862–1922)", *Estudios Atacameños*, 68 (2022), pp. 1–32.

VENEGAS, Fernando and GREZ, Sergio: "Historiografía del mutualismo chileno, 1853–1990: análisis crítico y nuevas perspectivas", *Izquierdas*, 50 (2021), pp. 1–30.

VENEGAS, Fernando and LERMANDA, Wilson: "Socorro Mutuo en la zona sur de Chile, 1885–1922: previsión social, patrimonio y ahorro", in Mathias ÓRDENES (ed.): *Sujetos sin voz en el sur de Chile y Argentina. Frontera, colonización, marginalidad y organización popular chilena en los siglos XIX y XX*, Santiago, Lom Ediciones, 2022.

VERGARA, Jorge and MASCAREÑO, Aldo: "La propiedad y conflictos de tierras indígenas en la provincia de Valdivia", in Jorge VERGARA, Aldo MASCAREÑO and Rolf FOERSTER: *La propiedad huilliche en la provincia de Valdivia*, Santiago, Corporación Nacional de Desarrollo Indígena (CONADI), 1996, pp. 15–241.

YÁÑEZ, Juan: *La intervención social en Chile. Y el nacimiento de la sociedad salarial, 1907–1932*, Santiago, RiL editores, 2008.

7 From Cooperation to Workers' Control[1]

"Defending Sources of Employment" in Argentina

Mirta Zaida Lobato

Beatrice and Sidney Webb wrote in 1891 that: "Democracies of producers ..., whether in the form of the 'self-governing workshop' or in the wider organizations of Trade Unions or Professional Associations, have hitherto failed, with almost complete uniformity, whenever they have themselves sought, either to own the instruments of production or to organize and direct the industries and services in which their members work. And this, as we have mentioned, has not been for want of trying. The experiment has been carried out in literally thousands of instances, extending over nearly a century, in almost every occupation, in various countries, often under apparently the most promising conditions. Even the most enthusiastic believers in this form of democracy would be hard put to it hard to find, in the entire range of industry and commerce, a single lasting success. In the relatively few cases in which such enterprises have not eventually succumbed to business concerns, they have ceased to be democracies of producers, themselves managing their own work; and have become, in effect, associations of capitalists on a small scale capitalist, some of them continuing also to work at their trade—making profit for themselves by the employment at wages of workers outside their association".[2]

They were interested in understanding the key features of English industrial society in the hope of putting an end to poverty and the exploitation of capital. In their reflections, the theme of workers' cooperative organizations and their limitations reveal the difficulties faced by these associations and by "economic democracy". Images of urban poverty, hallmarks of which are unemployment, instability, and job insecurity, have only multiplied in contemporary societies.

In Argentina, recurring economic and political crises have made it impossible to maintain the levels of economic activity that were observed during the first half of the twentieth century. As a result, unemployment, poverty, and job insecurity now encapsulate the complex set of circumstances faced by the working classes and call into question the steps that

DOI: 10.4324/9781003439554-8

are taken to alleviate a growing and persistent problem in the capitalist world.

Given this social, political, economic, and cultural dilemma, I aim to analyze how individuals, trade unions, political organizations, and the State have proposed organizational solutions to mitigate unemployment at different historical moments that take into account instances of conflict, negotiation, and social experimentation. To do so, I examine cooperative associations as a discontinuous trend in the long term and the emergence of new and challenging forms of organization of production such as the recovered factories movement.

More specifically, in this text, I try to explore whether workers' cooperatives were organized in the early twentieth century and if so who their promoters were. I also analyze several examples of workers' cooperatives mainly from the 1960s, reflect on cooperatives created thanks to State subsidies to the unemployed after the 2001 crisis, and examine a variety of issues associated with recovered factories in this latter historical era. Throughout this extensive period spanning from the early 20th century to the present, I examine the ideas on which the cooperatives were based, the distinguishing characteristics of their workers' involvement, and the limitations they faced in relation to the following questions: Are cooperatives and recovered factories based on similar principles, notions, and practices? Which actors participated in this self-management process? And what role does the State play in supporting some of these practices?

In Argentina, the drive to establish cooperative organizations has been a fundamental foundation of socialism since the beginning of the twentieth century. As we will see in the first section, entitled *Cooperation: Organization, Education, and Solidarity. First Manifestations of Organization,* socialism focused its efforts on organizing consumer, housing, and credit cooperatives. Insufficient information makes it impossible to observe the path taken by any specific workers' cooperative, but we do know that the Socialist Party did not prioritize such organizations. Its limitations and problems notwithstanding, the cooperative movement's initial organizational experiences took place at a time in the country's labor history that was characterized by both excess demand for workers and competitive wages. It is important to note that Argentina at that time was competing with Canada, Australia, and New Zealand to attract immigrants, mainly from Europe.

This context would change in the second half of the 20th century when economic difficulties were forcing factories to close. For that reason, in the second section of this chapter, entitled *Companies in crisis: workers' cooperatives*, I analyze two cases of cooperatives that were required to manage the suspension of their work-related activities. From the crisis of 2001 – a key moment in the country's history – until the present factory closures have encouraged collective action aimed at defending sources of employment. This stage is analyzed in the third section of this chapter, which is entitled *Crisis in the work-based society: recovering companies and organizing cooperatives.* Two experiences are important here. First, under the designation "recovered factories", several forms of self-management were proposed, and a debate was formulated, mainly by left-wing groups, centered on the notion of "workers' control". And second, the establishment of state subsidies to social organizations for the unemployed expanded the use of cooperatives as a way to organize the required considerations.

In the first section of this chapter, I reflect on the dissemination of the concepts of cooperation and their distinguishing characteristics between the late nineteenth and early twentieth centuries. In the second section I analyze two experiences of workers' cooperatives while examining their practices and the difficulties they experienced in the 1960s. Finally, in the third section I consider the complex web woven since the 2001 economic, political, and social crises in two settings around the recoveries of failing factories, including some recovered by fraudulent means, and the formation of cooperatives based on government subsidies. The wider context considers these experiences as responses to the uncertainty and vulnerability of the general population when capital abandons their communities.[3]

Cooperation: organization, education, and solidarity. First manifestations of organization

The meaning of the term "cooperation" has a long history and has changed depending on when and how it has been used. In the nineteenth century, authors such as Charles Fourier, Robert Owen, and Louis Blanc regarded cooperation as a voluntary association with the basic assumption that the principle of solidarity could help resolve social and economic inequality. Cooperation promotes organization, education, solidarity, and mutual assistance without seeking to make a profit.[4]

In Argentina, the cooperative movement is part of the dissemination of associative ideas, whose principles of organization, solidarity, and fairness are rooted in liberal thought and socialist traditions.[5] References to utopian and republican socialist thinkers abound in tales of workers' associationism. Indeed, in the early twentieth century, it was the socialists who promoted one of the first cooperative projects. Juan B. Justo, one of socialism's most prominent leaders, considered the cooperative movement fundamental to providing a political alternative and improving the living conditions of working people.

With an eye on Europe, Justo proposed establishing a close interrelationship between cooperative associations, political organizations, and trade unions, though he also understood that cooperativism possessed a broader political scope because it included those who were not necessarily socialist. He believed that cooperation should be fashioned without partisan purposes, considering it further proof of the capacity and education of the working classes and a symbol of the country's modernization and progress.[6]

This proposal for cooperation with socialism was important for cementing the principles of solidarity and organization. It was also important for raising the cultural level of workers and their families since cooperatives usually had a library, organized conferences, and promoted theatrical activities. Women and children were to be actively included in a cooperative movement that was largely made up of men, so notes were published on "how a child can be a good cooperator" and how an "intelligent mother" should acquire "the customs of order and economy", which were considered the bases for their "moral education". Socialist women, who were also feminist militants, encouraged the formation of cooperatives and urged other women to join as partners (specifically, the El Hogar Obrero cooperative), but did not become leaders of those cooperatives. Cooperative and trade union associations were content to be viewed as environments of male sociability that partially excluded female and feminist militancy. Worker and socialist cooperatives and the problems associated with their organization populated the pages of the socialist press via *La Vanguardia, La Cooperación Libre, and Vida Feminina.*[7]

The socialists of the late nineteenth and early twentieth centuries sought to "achieve an economic democracy [that] would bring about the attainment of a political democracy", as Aricó has argued,[8] as well as greater social and gender equality.[9] Juan B. Justo, Nicolás Repetto, Enrique Dickmann, Ángel Giménez, and others promoted the establishment of cooperatives, the most important of which was the above-mentioned El Hogar Obrero, which was founded in 1905.[10] As Dora Barrancos has pointed out, Argentinian socialists, particularly Justo, viewed Belgian socialism as the model for developing cooperativism, creating labor exchanges, and promoting different forms of popular education.[11]

El Hogar Obrero has a long history specializing in mortgage credit, home construction projects, and cooperativism aimed at encouraging consumption.[12] Initially, it opened warehouses that incorporated the production of goods such as bread in an effort to reduce costs. By the 1930s these warehouses were packaging oil and manufacturing bleach and other products and had expanded the range of goods it supplied. It could be said that socialism's cooperative initiatives regarded workers as partner-consumers, though they attempted to appeal to a wider audience from both the working and middle classes. Consumption that could improve the quality of life of families was the key.[13] Since services such as electricity were included in the range of consumable goods, members of the socialist movement were also among the founders of electric cooperatives such as the one in Zárate.[14] Socialists and the El Hogar Obrero cooperative thus propagated the ideas behind cooperation and helped to effect the formation of numerous organizations in Buenos Aires and places such as Zárate, Bahía Blanca, Santa Fe, Córdoba, and La Pampa.

Cooperative institutions grew in number and size and began to diversify the range of products they offered consumers, whom they also needed to educate. They therefore created a School of Cooperation in 1922, published brochures, and gave lectures to disseminate their ideas.[15] In 1919 they organized a conference for cooperatives that had been set up outside Buenos Aires.[16] They also proposed the formation of a League of Cooperatives and an Institute of Statistics.[17] The idea of consumption, the availability of goods, and the methods of advertising transcended the various social classes, and while discursive tensions over the relationship between goods and classes can be clearly followed in *La Vanguardia*, such tensions cannot overshadow the fact that the main interest was to raise the social and moral standing of working people.[18]

The history of El Hogar Obrero is long and complex due both to political ebbs and flows within the Argentine socialist movement and to the country's economic fluctuations. Such turmoil did not have an equal impact on all associations though it did affect the financial capacity of this particular cooperative. Nevertheless, this socialist cooperative managed to sustain itself over time, becoming a significant enterprise with hundreds of partners and employees after entering the world of commerce in the 1960s through large supermarkets which in the 1970s became popular under the name "Supercoop". However, since Argentina is a country that has been under constant threat of inflation throughout the second half of the twentieth century and into the present, the cooperative accumulated debts, especially with savers, and had to deal with a lack of credit, a rigid labor system, and currency devaluations. The coup de grâce came in 1991 when it declared itself insolvent, only managing to survive with financial and legal problems.

The socialists promoted the formation of various types of cooperatives and participated in the creation of consumer, credit, and electricity cooperative organizations. However, they did not put the same effort into organizing workers' cooperatives except as a component of consumer organizations and as a means for producing inexpensive marketable goods for their sales outlets.

The debate on cooperative organization filled many pages of the workers' and trade union press as parts of various projects aimed at disseminating ideas, education, organization, and actions intended to improve living and working conditions.[19] This debate revolved around two main ideas. On one hand, the socialists believed that cooperativism would help to improve working people and emancipate them, while the anarchists and revolutionary trade unionists believed the exact opposite, i.e. that it could distance workers from the revolution. Despite these differences, print cooperatives were formed that published brochures, newspapers, and almanacs. Between 1896 and 1901, for example, a publishers' cooperative edited *La Vanguardia, El Pintor* and *L'Emigrato.* In 1857 the "People's Bakery Association" was founded in Paraná in the province of Entre Ríos.[20] Then a blacksmiths' cooperative was registered in 1904 and a builders' cooperative was formed in 1905, though no information is available about either organization. In 1928, "La Edilicia", which comprised 170 workers in both the private and public sectors, was founded in Pergamino in the province of Buenos Aires.

Scholars of the types of cooperation implemented in Argentina make no reference to labor cooperativism before the 1950s due to insufficient information. Workers' newspapers would need to be thoroughly scrutinized to find any data, which would be highly fragmentary in any case. Nor do their studies provide any explanation for the poor dissemination of worker cooperatives in Argentina at that time.

Note also that while certain agrarian cooperatives were known as production cooperatives because they produced or industrialized raw materials from their associates, their basic problem was that their wage-earning staff did not normally participate in running the company. Organizing a workers' cooperative is a complex task since cooperatives are governed by the fundamental principle that they aim to free workers from being dependent on a wage-based system and to free themselves from being subordinate to capital because they do not aim to "profit from anyone's labor". Workers' cooperatives need an amount of capital that will enable them to purchase tools and a complex organization that will allow them to market their products. Although the cooperative organization of credit, housing, and consumption was greater in Argentina than in other Latin American countries, the capital available to workers in general was not sufficient to form workers' cooperatives. Wage earners were mainly immigrants who had settled in the coastal regions (which were those most associated with the dynamic export-driven economy) and native workers employed as unskilled laborers and day workers. Any capital investment had to be sustained over time to obtain a surplus that could be distributed among the partners. Starting a cooperative was a difficult undertaking because workers and their families had to live.

Also bear in mind that in Argentina, a fluid labor market, at least between the late nineteenth and early twentieth centuries, undermined the notion of sacrifice associated with an enterprise of this nature. We also know that wages remained high and were competitive internationally.[21]

Certain disruptions notwithstanding, until 1914 the expanding economy guaranteed workers employment[22] before fluctuations became a fact of working life. The 1930 recession created high levels of unemployment before rapid recovery enabled workers to re-enter the labor market. It could be said that work flowed during the first half of the twentieth century. In the second half of the century, however, when the economy stagnated for long periods of time and numerous companies went out of business, unemployment began to rise. It was then that workers began to view cooperative organizations as a way to maintain their sources of income.

This might explain why consumer cooperatives such as those run by socialists (e.g. El Hogar Obrero) and others created by groups of immigrants and other workers prospered in the first half of the twentieth century. In 1885, for example, Welsh immigrants created the Mercantile Company in Chubut and French immigrants set up a consumer cooperative, while in 1921 railway workers organized their own cooperative. The remarkable expansion in agriculture saw the creation of several agricultural cooperatives, including the Israelita de Basabilbaso cooperative in the province of Entre Ríos in 1900 and SANCOR in 1938.[23] Cooperatives in the telephone, electricity, and transportation industries were also formed.

These cooperatives were driven by workers and political activists, with the State intervening by establishing a legal framework. Study of this legislation goes far beyond the scope of this chapter. However, I would point out that a law on "The legal regime of cooperative societies" was passed in 1926 and has since been subject to numerous modifications.[24]

Companies in crisis: workers' cooperatives

As I mentioned earlier, the creation of workers' cooperatives was not studied in depth until this form of organization multiplied after the 2001 crisis. However, at least one exception arises in the gap between studies of the early experiences of cooperative formation and those formed in the 1960s. In 1949, Jorge del Río, a lawyer specializing in cooperativism, asserted in an investigation into workers' cooperatives that only 3.9% of cooperative entities created between 1928 and 1950 were workers' cooperatives.[25] This is a paltry percentage compared to the multitude of agricultural and electricity cooperatives that existed practically throughout the country.

The new political scenario, which became consolidated after the 1946 election of Juan Domingo Perón as president, saw several debates on cooperativism. From the political perspective, a new national constitution was passed in 1949 while from the economic perspective, a second five-year plan was drafted, and a Congress on Productivity was held.[26]

The influence of Jorge del Río's research permeated the 1953 Economic Plan, appearing as a theme in the sections on the Forecasts,[27] Education,[28] Housing,[29] and, especially, Agrarian Cooperative Action[30] programs. The chapter on the presentation of State investments, however, did not provide for any allocation of funds for cooperation, while the chapter on Employment made no mention of this form of organization.[31] Under Perón's first and second governments (1946–1955), the issue of labor cooperativism was more rhetorical than the result of effective policies aimed at promoting this form of organization. Moreover, unemployment had not yet become a real problem for many Argentines, let alone for a government that advocated full employment and sought to guarantee one's Right to Work.

Jorge del Río names numerous workers' cooperatives in a book he published in 1966. He mentions, for example, that in 1954, at the initiative of the Federation of Workers' Cooperatives of the Automotive Transport Sector, Cinematografia San Miguel and Trabajadores Unidos de la República Argentina assembled 18 workers' cooperatives with the aim of forming a federation.[32] The institutions that participated in this meeting included numerous film production cooperatives that the author's research on the film industry mentions as film companies.[33] It could be suggested that these companies may have operated as cooperatives in order to socialize costs even though they were not constituted as such. This was a fairly common practice in cinema and theater. Del Río also mentions the San Antonio Metallurgical Production Cooperative, created in 1962, and the Work, Production, and Consumption Cooperative of the Meat Industry and its Derivatives of Cordoba, also created in 1962 by employees of the municipal meat-processing plant.[34]

We also know that in 1957, after Perón had been overthrown in a military coup in 1955, a group of workers from the company Alea, which had gone into liquidation that year, formed the COGTAL printers' cooperative. Though the history of this cooperative has not yet been written, it is often mentioned because Raymundo Ongaro, a well-known trade union leader with revolutionary Peronist tendencies worked there between 1958 and 1963. COGTAL remains a functioning enterprise that has printed newspapers such as *La Vanguardia* and *El Cronista Comercia*, different types of magazines, and party political voting papers.

Without thorough basic research, it is therefore impossible to further examine the creation of workers' cooperatives in the 1950s and early 1960s. However, to explain the complexities involved in the process behind the formation of workers' cooperatives in the late 1960s, I will analyze two experiences that involved workers and trade union leaders. These experiences fundamentally concern economic activities that were in crisis at the time, i.e. the textile and meat industries, both of which were showing signs of exhaustion and required significant investment. These two cooperatives, located in the province of Buenos Aires, were defensive experiences aimed at mitigating the threat of unemployment.

The Berisso textile workers' cooperative

The Berisso textile workers' cooperative was founded in July 1969. In the late 1960s, the economic and employment situation in the town was challenging. The Armour meat-processing plant had closed down, and the Patent Knitting company had gone into liquidation.[35] In 1925 a spinning mill had opened in Berisso to produce yarns, fabric for hosiery, cloth for packaging meats for export, and surgical gauze. Since the production of stockinettes for meat coverings connected the local textile industry to large meat companies such as Swift and Armour, when the crisis intensified in those industries and the Armour meat-processing plant closed down, the textile industry's difficulties intensified.

La Textil was a medium-sized cotton spinning mill whose operations in Argentina had begun with an expansion of their production during the First World War when this industrial sector experienced important growth. According to a report produced by the National Department of Labor, the textile industry was transformed between 1914 and 1935 as new plants were built, existing ones were expanded, and modern machinery was installed.[36] The Patent Knitting company was one of several small and medium-sized factories located in various neighborhoods of Buenos Aires and the surrounding districts. Aided by state protection and a gradual increase in consumption, especially among the poorer sectors of society, many of these small and medium-sized enterprises grew, thus increasing opportunities for trade and production. However, when the economy began to shrink in the 1950s, many companies began to face insurmountable difficulties. In addition to these sectoral difficulties, the Berisso spinning mill was impacted by transformations in the meat industry, which bought much of its production of gauze and fabrics, since that industry was affected by plant obsolescence and financial mismanagement that culminated in the fraudulent bankruptcy of the Swift-Deltec group. These changes made it difficult for the company to resist competition from the larger textile companies that controlled production and marketing. Exacerbating this critical situation in the textile industry was the impact of labor conflicts that arose in the 1950s: strikes, walkouts, and increasing state intervention undermined the authority of entrepreneurs and reduced their ability to reorganize production by making new investments. Also involved in these labor disputes were the political and ideological struggles of the trade unions themselves.

When the company announced its definitive closure in 1968, the provincial government was in the hands of federal administrators because the national government was being run by the military after the overthrow of the elected president, Arturo Illía, in another coup d'état. In addition, some unions were divided by political differences and their relationships with Perón and the military. These divisions were felt in numerous industries. Specifically, in the case of the textile industry, administration of the local branch of the Asociación Obrera Textil (AOT, or Textile Workers Association) was taken over by the union's national authorities. In the Berisso branch, however, the union leaders had a good relationship with the government of Juan Carlos Onganía, leader of the 1966 military coup. These differences weighed heavily when it came to choosing the best policy for maintaining employment. Critical situations in the sector, union disputes, changes in the consumption of certain goods, and tensions within the Peronist trade union movement (divided between sectors open to dialogue with the military government and those more critical of it) help to define the complex background to the formation of worker's cooperatives in the late 1960s.

In the Berisso textile workers' cooperative, the relationship between the leadership of the textile union and the formation of the cooperative is clear. According to José Manuel dos Santos, leader of the Textile Workers Association and president of the Cooperative, the spinning mill was founded twice for its workers. Obviously, the first time was when it was founded by its owners, while the second time, which they considered the most important, was in July 1969 when the company's workers resolved to keep the facilities open.

Dos Santos asserted that: "Thanks to our people's efforts and determination, the initial distressing situation has been overcome. We have experienced some horrific moments that have tested the courage and decisiveness of our comrades. In those initial moments, we had to make a titanic effort ... But all that is now behind us and, as a reward for the sacrifice and efforts of everyone ... our factory is now playing a hugely important role in the domestic market. This not only vindicates our workers but also destroys the myth that [workers] are incapable of managing the means of production and running the commercialization of the company".[37]

The labor union was an area of male sociability, though its leaders spoke on behalf of the whole working community. This was mostly made up of women though they occupied a marginal place in both union and cooperative.[38] Photographs of the demonstrations that were held to keep the factory open, however, show them on the front line of public rallies and marches. At the same time, workers (both male and female) with responsibilities in the organization acted on several fronts, negotiating the agreement on a share package with the company, persuading the provincial authorities to endorse those negotiations and award a subsidy to allow the agreement to go ahead, and bargaining with the workers themselves.[39] However, because not every worker had set their hopes on the cooperativization process, State resources also provided compensation for those who were left out of the project. State provisions were also fundamental to putting the plant back into operation. Indeed, they are a distinctive feature of the creation of workers' and production cooperatives and recovered factories as a whole. Dependence on the State continues to this day. In November 2020, for example, the cooperative was visited by the provincial employment minister, who referred to the *Preservar Trabajo* (Preserve Work) program which, though designed to help preserve jobs affected by the COVID-19 pandemic, could also be used to support the cooperative, which is always in need of financial assistance.[40]

The participation of workers and union leaders was vital, though it was generally the union representatives who ended up controlling the cooperative. An example is that of José Manuel dos Santos, a union leader who became president of the Board of Directors on numerous occasions.[41] Dos Santos, a son of Portuguese immigrants, was born in Berisso in 1924. He had entered the textile industry at the age of 15 as an apprentice before becoming a weaver. He joined the Peronist movement and in 1946 was elected a delegate in his section. In 1949 he became a committee member of the union's local branch. In the difficult moments of the company's liquidation and cooperativization, dos Santos was one of the leaders who had mobilized into action. Now he was Chairman of the Board of Directors of the newly formed Cooperativa Textil de Trabajo Limitada, with one of his sons as collaborator. Male and female workers whom I interviewed referred to him as the owner of the cooperative.[42]

As I mentioned earlier, the Berisso Textile Cooperative is still in operation. However, it is constantly plagued by a lack of resources and, since its main buyer is the provincial authority, it is always seriously impacted by the critical situations that affect both the State and the province. Newspaper headlines such as *The future of the Berisso textile cooperative 'hangs by a thread'* are common as its main activity is the production of gauze for public hospitals and its main client is the Ministry of Health in the Province of Buenos Aires. As a result, today, the lives of 130 families in its workforce are marked by uncertainty and anxiety.[43]

The Martín Fierro Cooperative in Zárate

The Martín Fierro Cooperative in Zárate, whose fate was similar to that of the Berisso Textile Cooperative, closed down 20 years after its foundation. This cooperative had been created in 1965 when purchase of the premises and machinery of the former Smithfield meat-processing plant from Corporación Argentina de Carnes (CAP) enabled it to continue operating as an abattoir, thus preventing it from completely closing down and dismissing its entire workforce.

The origins of the Cooperative are rooted in the difficulties faced by the meat industry after the Second World War. Large, vertically integrated establishments were unable to solve the problems associated with transformations in meat marketing and were much less able to carry out the capital investments required to maintain the rhythm of work and production.

Smithfield was one of three establishments installed in the town of Zárate. The first of these was the Las Palmas Produce Company (1886), which later transferred to Union Cold Storage and then to the English and Dutch Meat Company. The second was the Smithfield meat-processing plant, construction of which began in 1903. When it began its operations in 1905, it became the town's main employer.[44] The third establishment, the Anglo meat-processing plant, which was founded in 1916, consolidated the British oligopoly that operated in the area.[45]

The Smithfield meat-processing plant was the establishment that lasted the longest and exerted the greatest influence in the local area. Although research is ongoing in this regard, its closure has been related to the dynamics of the relationships between businessmen and local political forces in the town and province. Complaints of collusion between businesses and politicians (both conservative and radical) were rife in times of elections.[46] Socialists and communists, though few, were active in trade union organizations,[47] while Peronism would later come to dominate union leadership. The testimonies of Tilio Fernández,[48] Pablo Toledo,[49] and María Stanisio[50] and the accounts of José Peter are eloquent commentaries on issues such as long working hours, low wages, and poor working conditions.[51]

The words of Moisés Lyntridis are especially vivid when he discusses the impetus the socialists gave to the organization of labor unions and cooperatives:[52] "The labor unions focused not only on union issues but also on cultural and cooperative matters, so we also founded the electricity cooperative. Also, when the José Ingenieros library was founded, it was frequented by workers. Over time, however, it became a library that provided textbooks for students. We collected empty bottles, newspapers and magazines and sold them to buy educational materials so that secondary students could consult all the books they needed".[53]

The cultural objective of this recycling culture, the aim of which was to improve the lives of young people morally and socially, was thus introduced many decades before the familiar appearance of the urban recycler as an occupation intended to ensure daily subsistence. Moisés Lyntridis also asserted that: "After the Second World War, employment levels dropped dramatically and Smithfield was taken over by Corporación Argentina de Productores de Carne (CAP). However, the injustices did not abate; in fact, more injustices were committed than by the previous English owners".[54]

Corporación Argentina de Productores de Carne controlled the company until it sold it to the workers who had set up the Martín Fierro Cooperative. CAP had originally been founded in 1934 to process and market meat in local and international markets.[55] This was not a voluntary association but a public sector company whose actions were the topic of frequent debate. Cattle farmers were involved in the Corporación, but their involvement was compulsory and withholdings from the sector were used to reinvest in it.[56] In 1947, CAP acquired Smithfield, a company with which it had already been conducting business in the cattle market. Like other companies in the sector, the meat-processing plant was now obsolete and by the 1950s required large capital investment to enable it to modernize and maintain adequate production levels. In truth, CAP was more interested in the livestock business than industrial activities so, in view of the difficulties faced by the meat-processing industry, in 1965 it sold Smithfield to the Martín Fierro Cooperative, which had been set up by workers of the company with the participation of Alfredo Ciliberti, leader of the meat union, who was elected president.[57]

Despite the efforts of its workers, the Cooperative was unable to maintain its animal slaughter activity and attempted to diversify by using its cold storage facilities to preserve fruit and vegetables, which they sold directly to the public. However, as its Achilles heel was a lack of funds, numerous demonstrations were held to request official loans. One of these demonstrations was a march to Buenos Aires in January 1970.[58] Additionally, there was no shortage of internal differences among its leaders, one of which was between its president Alfredo Ciliberti and the trustee Dr Juan Carlos Deghi.[59] The cooperative finally closed down and its former facilities and the land that surrounds it are now under threat of seizure.[60]

The Berisso Textile Cooperative and the meat-processing plant in Zárate clearly illustrate the difficulties, due to lack of capital for modernizing machinery, price competition, the nature of the goods produced, and administrative difficulties, involved in setting up workers' cooperatives. Other important issues were internal conflicts due to differences in their partners' decision-making authority and to political or ideological discrepancies.

Although both of these cooperatives made strenuous efforts to survive, their final closures appear to support Beatrice and Sidney Webb's assertion stated in the quote on the first page of this chapter that workers' cooperatives do not endure over time. Today they are components of a deindustrialized urban landscape that have sometimes become places of memory. Workers, their descendants, local historians, and those interested in the industrial past encourage processes that aim to remember those who spent their lives within the confines of factories and create spaces in websites and museums.[61]

Crisis in the work-based society: recovering companies and organizing cooperatives

In my opinion, the impact of unemployment in the final quarter of the twentieth century is the key to understanding why workers' organizations expanded in a different direction from those of earlier eras. When the country was governed by Peronist Carlos Saúl Menem (1989–1999), neoliberal economic and social policies were introduced that led to the liquidation of companies, the privatization of State-run enterprises, and the closure of railway branch lines, all of which impacted people's living and working conditions. Entrepreneurs upheld the long-standing practice of becoming importers in unfavorable circumstances to maintain production or engaged in highly profitable short-term financial transactions. Moreover, the Convertibility Law, which pegged the Argentine peso to the US dollar, made industrial production increasingly difficult, though it is also true that not all economic activities were affected to the same degree.

In this context, the government implemented strategies aimed at mitigating the unemployment situation. For example, the privatization of Yacimientos Petrolíferos Fiscales (YPF) in Patagonia generated a large sector of self-employed workers and micro-enterprises, but these were unable to survive for a long time. The State also designed a series of short-term policies intended to cushion the impact of the crisis, though without much success.[62]

The economic, political, and social chaos of 2001 intensified protests staged by the unemployed, those with savings, and the middle classes. In this heterogeneous group of social actors, the unemployed represented an inescapable manifestation of the huge societal transformation that was taking place. Unemployed men and women were forced to accept a new working world marked by precariousness and casual labor. This new framework led to the recovered companies movement and the formation of cooperatives based on State-formulated welfare plans and local and provincial initiatives.[63]

The socio-historical literature on this subject has generally studied cooperativism after 2001 and the recovered factories movement in the context of workers' collective action. Mobilized by the loss of their sources of employment and lower living standards, male and female wage earners demonstrated, protested, occupied streets and factories, and attempted to find mechanisms that would allow the factories to remain open. This situation no doubt provides a rich foundation on which to study the forms of protests that were employed in the late twentieth century. However, it is also worth considering their organizational dynamics, and especially the long-term perspective, to understand the moment in which they arose as well as their difficulties and limitations.[64]

To analyze the formation of cooperatives that were linked to government aid programs, relevant data are as follows. Between 2009 and 2015, 2,224 cooperatives were created under the Programa Argentina Trabaja with 60,000 beneficiaries; by 2015 the number of cooperatives had almost doubled to 5,142 while, according to data from the Ministry of Economy and Public Finance, the number of beneficiaries had almost quadrupled to 218,070.[65] According to data from Argentina's National Institute of Associativism and Social Economy, in June 2019 there were 8,618 active cooperatives. Of the total number of cooperatives created under government programs, 62% are located in the coastal regions (mainly in the Buenos Aires conurbation), while 22% are located in the northwest of the country. These are the two regions with the highest rates of poverty. According to studies carried out in 2021 by INDEC, the percentage of households below the poverty line was 31.2%, while 8.2% of them were below the indigence line.[66]

The creation of workers' cooperatives by unemployed workers as a result of State-sponsored aid programs indicates that such programs were diverse and dependent on at least two ministries. According to the database of the INAES (National Institute of Associativism and Social Economy of the Ministry of Productive Development), these programs consisted of the Water + Work Plan, the Federal Housing Plan, Community Integration Centers, the Manos a la Obra (Let's Get to Work) Plan, the Ingreso Social con Trabajo (Social Income through Work) Plan, and the Social Investment Program (Pris) (without the participation of municipalities). Cooperatives were also requested by municipalities and provincial agencies. In all cases, the territorial dimension must also be considered due to the tensions between social organizations and municipalities.[67] Also implemented were programs that focused on women, which suggests that State policies were also mindful of the gender dimension. The Ellas Hacen ("Women Do") program, for example, seeks to empower women in their role as mothers through educational and employment opportunities and the creation of workers' cooperatives for women in situations of poverty. This is significant given the above-mentioned poverty and indigence rates and important for those who experience domestic violence.[68] These types of cooperatives are currently under pressure due to a lack of resources, which is why demonstrations take place, mainly on the streets of Buenos Aires, to demand more programs and more resources.

There are few examples of cooperativism resulting from initiatives other than State welfare plans. One example, which has not yet been the topic of research, is the La Juanita cooperative. This cooperative was founded by the La Matanza Movement of Unemployed Workers (MTD) after the 2001 crisis when its members chose to reject the government's plans and work jointly on their productive and educational ventures.[69] Another is the Arañitas Hilanderas workers' cooperative, an enterprise created and run by women in 2007 in the town of Belén in the province of Catamarca. This cooperative, which has incorporated women from the local rural environment into its solidarity-based organization, aims to recover the province's spinning and artisanal weaving traditions.[70] Studying Arañitas Hilanderas sheds light on the lives of these women, who became organized to look after themselves and each other, were alone supporting their children, and, in the words of María Rosa Usqueda, were "in desperate need". Also important were their know-how and the transfer of their knowledge to the new generations, thus converting this workers' cooperative into an educational environment based on knowledge and solidarity.

Another type of experience is the cooperativization of companies that have fallen into liquidation. Case studies illustrate the complexity of recovery procedures since workers, political and labor union leaders, the State, and employers all intervene in the process.[71] The closure of the Gatic footwear and clothing factory is an interesting example as this company supplied fabrics and synthetic leather to global manufacturers of sneakers such as Adidas, New Balance, and Le Coq Sportif. Gatic also manufactured the official football for the 1978 World Cup and had factories in the provinces of Buenos Aires, La Rioja, and Corrientes.[72] In 1987 it employed 4,500 workers of both sexes but was impacted by the opening up of the import market in the 1990s and problems created by a drop in demand. When the company's financial worries increased, it even incurred debts in European bonds.[73] In 2000, its debts to workers, banks, and bondholders accumulated. As bankruptcy loomed, the workers reacted with mobilizations to challenge their deteriorating living conditions. And when layoffs were implemented at several plants, the working families' anxiety increased. Participants in the events increased in number with the intervention of political parties and municipal authorities after closure of the company's subsidiaries created local conflicts in those regions. The interests of the local authorities were visible in every town and city where a factory closed down. In addition, the National Movement of Recovered Enterprises, which already had experience in helping to recover factories that had closed down, also generally intervened.

The number of companies recovered by workers has multiplied since 2001. The best-known of these are the metallurgical company IMPA, the

Yaguane meat-processing plant, Grissinopoli, La Baskonia, Brukman,[74] Zanón,[75] and Bauen.[76] A pattern associated with the recovery of such enterprises has emerged: the workers become mobilized and occupy the facilities, posters are put up denouncing business fraud, and the police and legal profession intervene. Sometimes violent evictions take place. Less visible are the negotiations that take place with employers and the State to render the occupation legitimate. Once they are formalized, the recovered factories have to overcome complex economic challenges that are alleviated with help from other social, political, and cultural organizations. Although men and women are involved in the entire process, women play an important care-giving role, often at the expense of concealing their own distress, by providing emotional support, collecting and preparing food, and organizing community meals – all without compromising their participation in assemblies and committees. [77]

According to Florencia Partenio, recovered companies and cooperatives must overcome numerous challenges, including restoring and planning production, recovering formulas and protocols according to the type of activity involved, ensuring safety standards, obtaining capital, choosing where to invest and what technology to use, providing professional training for workers, distributing surplus resources, selecting the approaches for hiring new workers, and establishing relationships with stakeholders.[78] Since no single approach has existed (or exists), all these challenges imply a need for political discussion on management methods. The dilemma over workers' control in the management of a company was openly raised, for example, at the Zanón factory by left-wing activists and their organizations. Raúl Godoy, a worker at Zanón and a Trotskyist militant in the Socialist Workers' Party (PTS), presented this problem when he wrote: "There were other autonomy-focused alternatives that contemplated 'self-managed experiences' on the fringes of the system. These experiences occurred in small businesses or ventures that soon clashed with capitalist pressures and relationships. While fighting side by side on many fronts against attacks from employers and the State, we were also engaged in debates with all the factions. Because, although integrating cooperatives into a capitalist system in crisis was the best road to self-exploitation, it was impossible to conceive of a 'liberated' autonomous factory because autonomy only lasts until the gas and electricity bills arrive, that is, until it has to be commercialized. That is when we observe the laws of the capitalist market, which can't be evaded. All these debates within the recovered factory movement were taking place at the same time as we had to face attempts to evict us and deal with the pressures of employers, bureaucracy and the justice system."[79]

The proposal to introduce a system of workers' management that would be autonomous from employers and the State pitted this left-wing faction against groups linked to Peronism, provincial and municipal leaders, and Peronist union leaders.[80] In some ways it updated the confrontation with "union bureaucracy" that was only possible in the context of the formalized labor market.[81] "Factories without bosses" was an aspiration that could refute the notion that "When you lose your job, you lose everything" – a phrase often repeated by male and female workers alike.[82] But the experience of putting self-managed companies into practice is enmeshed in a web of actions that include grassroots assemblies, the democratic election and continuous supervision of representatives, the organization of production and marketing processes, and the impact of those companies on society. The proposal for workers' control in Zanón was both a response to the social crisis and a reclamation by left-wing movements of ideas that had been forgotten or obscured. It is this position that made it a novel concept.

The recovered factories movement coexists as an experience with the cooperatives, which are supported by the government's social welfare policies but threatened by a lack of funding, organizational difficulties, links to municipal, provincial, and national governments, the vicissitudes of changes in those governments, and the danger of becoming mere administrators of state subsidies.

A possible epilogue

One main idea permeates this chapter: the creation of worker's cooperatives was more intense when the closure of companies exposed workers, both male and female, to the specter of unemployment and job insecurity. That specter began to appear in the 1960s but grew more ominous and repetitive with the reforms introduced by the government of Carlos Menem and the crisis of 2001. It could be suggested that the process to recover enterprises and form worker's cooperatives that has occurred in Argentina's recent history reveals two distinct paths. One taken by those who believed it was possible to take the autonomous route to resolve the dilemmas of a restructured capitalism, and the other taken by those who followed the State social programs route as a way of maintaining sources of employment and promoting social inclusion. The first group believes that recovered companies and workers' cooperatives are an alternative employment option and a collective and supportive lifestyle project for working people. The second group has higher expectations for the State's role as a promoter of cooperative work, though the limits of its role emerge when state intervention comes to an end.

Cooperative developments that seek to maintain their autonomy – a complex task in the context of the country's structural crisis – may recognize their roots in the principles of solidarity, equity, and mutual support integral to the socialist-driven cooperative association movement of the late nineteenth and early twentieth centuries, though they emanated from an entirely different work environment. The cooperatives that were formed in the early decades of the twentieth century, which focused on improving the consumption and living conditions of the working classes, created a few workers' cooperatives to provide cheap goods for consumer cooperatives. Those that were formed in the 1960s revealed the limits of their ability to sustain themselves after the initial efforts that were made to establish them.

The cooperatives associated with State social policies have managed to construct ties of solidarity but rely on State resources and are subject to the fluctuations of politics and the economy. Since they depend on income-transfer programs, they oblige us to reflect on the relationship between the State and social organizations and the restructuring of that relationship, though it is also true that they demand actions to prevent cooperative organizations from becoming "merely a social plan". As a document that appears on the blog of one social organization says: "We at the AGTCAP have long demanded a proactive attitude to make substantial amendments to a program **we wish to prevent from becoming a mere social plan and instead to prioritize it as a genuine work program** for important national public works and production projects that provide decent wages in accordance with the employment agreement for each activity, guarantee sufficient monthly working hours to support a family and safeguard the social rights of every worker".[83] The expression "we wish to prevent from becoming a mere social plan" is a warning that limits the dream, as one worker put it, of working "without controlling anyone" and "without being controlled".

Maintaining sources of employment was a goal articulated in the 1960s and is also expressed today in emotional and dramatic tones and precise terms: "we are defending our sources of work", "losing our jobs is losing our dignity", "it is bread for our children", "working is all we know how to do". However, the dilemma lies in knowing how to address the challenges of acquiring knowledge, obtaining resources, maintaining production, and designing forms of distribution that promote solidarity rather than competition.

Both paths are influenced and challenged by gender relations. Although I have not discussed the subject in great detail, I have highlighted the presence (albeit in a subordinate position to that of men) of socialist feminist militants in the cooperative movement of the early twentieth century. In both the formation of workers' cooperatives in the 1960s and the recovered factories movement at the time of the 2001 crisis, women participated actively and autonomously, for example, in the formation of the Las Arañitas Hilanderas cooperative and in their mobilization to recover the Brukman textile company. While it is true that they had to combine those efforts with looking after their children and families (which did not necessarily involve their male counterparts), both genders converged on the key point of interest, i.e. defending work is essential to ensuring the survival of working families.

From the historiographical point of view, the increased number of studies on the Socialist Party and consumer, credit, electricity, and agrarian cooperatives has broadened our knowledge of this subject. The same has occurred with regard to the recent history of the formation of cooperatives since such studies are now abundant and have entered the debate on State social policies and forms of collective action.[84] On the other hand, historical perspectives on workers' cooperatives are scarce as well as documents available for historical research.

The success of some recovered companies over time has led scholars to reflect, from the economic and sociological perspectives, on both the solidarity economy and alternatives to the capitalist system.[85] In practice, these companies are helping modestly to alleviate the current structural crisis facing Argentina.

Notes

1 I am grateful to Andrea Andújar for her comments and to Daniel Plotinsky for helping me access bibliographic material. This paper is part of the project *Historia de la Catalunya Subalterna Contemporánea: alternativas solidarias y cooperativas (History of Contemporary Subordinate Catalonia: Supportive and Cooperative Alternatives)*. Reference: PID2019–109560GB-I00. 2019 call for RDI projects of the Spanish Ministry of Science and Innovation.

2 Beatrice and Sydney WEBB: *The Consumers' Co-operative Movement*, Longmans, Green and Co., 1921, pp. 463–464 (the original text dates from 1891).

3 Mirta Zaida LOBATO: ""Lo que el capital se llevó": fábricas cerradas, memoria e historia reciente", *Anuario del Instituto de Historia Argentina*, 21-1 (2021), p. 135. https://doi.org/10.24215/2314257Xe135.

4 A classic text on socialist thought is George Douglas Howard COLE: *A History of Socialist Thought*, I Leviatán. ePub base rl. 1.2. In the English tradition, Owen is considered the founder of cooperativism. Another form of cooperativism is rooted in Christianity.

5 Roberto DI STEFANO, Hilda SABATO, Luis Alberto ROMERO and José LUIS MORENO: *De las cofradías a las organizaciones de la sociedad civil. Historia de la iniciativa asociativa en Argentina, 1776–1990*, Buenos Aires, Edilab editora 2002, pp. 193–196. On socialists and cooperativism, see Verónica RONCHI: *La cooperación integral. Historia de "El Hogar Obrero"*, Buenos Aires, Ediciones Fabro, 2016; María Natalia RABASA: "El Partido socialista y El Hogar Obrero. Un análisis de las primeras experiencias cooperativas en el cambio de siglo", in *Archivos de historia del movimiento obrero y la izquierda*, 19 (September 2021–February 2022), pp. 133–155. The literature on the ideas and practice of Argentinian socialism is much more

extensive. On cooperativism, see Daniel PLOTINSKY: *Historia del cooperativismo 1, Idealistas y realizadores: el cooperativismo argentino hasta la sanción de la Ley de Sociedades Cooperativas*, 2009, available at: http://www.centrocultural.coop/blogs/cooperativismo/2009/06/18/historia del cooperativismo 1/ and *Cooperativismo y dictaduras*, 2011, available at: http://www.centrocultural.coop/blogs/cooperativismo/2011/03/21/cooperativismo-y-dictaduras/.

6 Juan B. JUSTO: "Cooperación Obrera", *La Vanguardia*, 29 January 1897.

7 On *Vida femenina* see Ana Lía REY: "Palabras y proyectos de mujeres socialistas a través de sus revistas (1900–1956)", *Mora (Buenos Aires)*, 17-1 (2011), accessed on 31 March 2023 from http://www.scielo.org.ar/scielo.php?script=sci_arttext&pid=S1853-001x2011000100009&lng=es&tlng=es.

8 José ARICÓ: *La hipótesis de Justo. Escritos sobre el socialismo en América Latina*, Buenos Aires, Sudamericana, 1999, pp. 126–127.

9 Mirta Zaida LOBATO: "Los socialistas y los derechos sociales y políticos de las mujeres, Argentina 1890–1930", *Labrys, Estudos feministas*, August–December 2005, Labrys.net.br.; Marina BECERRA: *Marxismo y feminismo en el primer socialismo argentino, Enrique del Valle Iberlucea*, Rosario, Prohistoria, 2009.

10 Verónica RONCHI: *La cooperación* ... pp. 200–221; María Natalia RABASA: *El Partido Socialista* ... , pp. 133–155.

11 Dora BARRANCOS: *La escena iluminada. Ciencia para Trabajadores, 1890–1930*, Buenos Aires, Plus Ultra, 1996, p. 37.

12 According to Verónica RONCHI, the El Hogar Obrero cooperative progressively added services such as healthcare, cooperative pharmacies, a savings bank, cooperative education institutes, libraries, courses on cooperation, and the construction of kindergartens close to housing: *La Cooperación integral* ... , p. 89.

13 Jeremy ADELMAN: "El Partido Socialista argentino", in Mirta Zaida LOBATO (dr.): *El progreso, la modernización y sus límites, 1880–1916*, Vol. 3, Buenos Aires, 2000, pp. 261–290; Juan BUONOME: "El partido de los consumidores. Publicidad, consumo y cultura de clase en la prensa socialista argentinas, entre el Centenario y la Gran Depresión", *Desarrollo Económico*, 16, 219 (September–December 2016), pp. 245–276.

14 Andrea LLUCH and Laura SÁNCHEZ: *De movimiento popular a empresa. El cooperativismo eléctrico en La Pampa (1925–1950)*, Santa Rosa, Fondo Editorial Pampeano, 2002.

15 Roberto DI STEFANO, Hilda SABATO, Luis Alberto ROMERO and José Luis MORENO: *De las cofradías* ... , p. 193.

16 Verónica RONCHI: *La cooperación integral* ... , p. 89.

17 *Ibid.*, p. 90.

18 Juan BUONOME, "El partido de los ... ", pp. 245–276.

19 Mirta Zaida LOBATO: *La prensa obrera, Buenos Aires y Montevideo, 1890–1958*, Buenos Aires, EDHASA, 2009.

20 Daniel PLOTINSKY: *Orígenes y consolidación del cooperativismo en la Argentina. Instituto de la Cooperación*, IDELCOOP, 2015. Available at: https://www.idelcoop.org.ar/sites/www.idelcoop.org.ar/files/revista/articulos/pdf/revista-215-con- membretes-origenes_y_consolidacion_del_cooperativismo_en_la_argentina.pdf.

21 Roberto CORTES CONDE: *El Progreso Argentino, 1880–1914,* Buenos Aires, Sudamericana, 1979.

22 *Ibid.*, pp. 204–209.
23 Andrés RUGGERI: *Autogestión y revolución. De las primeras cooperativas a Petrogrado y Barcelona*, Buenos Aires, Callao, 2018; Daniel PLOTINSKY: "Argentina: políticas públicas y cooperativismo (1976–2015)", *IX Rulescoop International Congress* "Respuesta de la Universidad a las necesidades de la economía social ante los desafíos del mercado", 2015. For example, Sancor Cooperativas Unidas Ltda. is a federation of dairy industry cooperatives that brings together dairy producers from the provinces of Córdoba and Santa Fe. The Unión de Cooperativas Chaqueñas acts as the central sales agency for the cotton producers of Chaco, while the associates of the Federación de Cooperativas Agrarias de Misiones produce yerba mate, tung, and tobacco. Jorge del RIO: *Las cooperativas de trabajo,* Buenos Aires, Librería Jurídica Abeledo, 1949, pp. 112–122.
24 Alicia KAPLAN DE DRIMER and Bernardo DRIMER: *Las Cooperativas*, Buenos Aires, INTERCOOP, 1975.
25 Jorge DEL RÍO: *Las cooperativas de trabajo ...*; ID.: "Cooperativas de Trabajo", *Revista Hechos e Ideas*, 97 (April 1952), Buenos Aires, Argentina; ID.: "El cooperativismo en el Segundo Plan Quinquenal", *Hechos e Ideas*, pp. 106–109.
26 Presidencia de la Nación. Subsecretaria de Informaciones, *Segundo Plan Quinquenal*, Buenos Aires, 1953.
27 *Ibid.*, p. 71.
28 *Ibid.*, p. 89.
29 *Ibid.*, p. 140.
30 *Ibid.*, p. 173.
31 *Ibid.*, pp. 50–61
32 Jorge DEL RÍO: *Cooperativismo. Cooperativas de Trabajo*, Buenos Aires, Ediciones del autor, 1966, pp. 118–122.
33 Fernando PEÑA: *Cien años de cine argentino,* Buenos Aires, Biblos, 2012; Clara KRIGER: *Cine y peronismo. El estado en escena*, Buenos Aires, Siglo XXI, 2009; Rocío ESPÍNOLA, Sebastián MATTIA, Ariel NAVARRO and Maximiliano PONCE: "Entre plátanos y melodramas: historia y memoria de los Estudios San Miguel", *Imagofagia, Revista de la Asociación Argentina de Estudios de Cine y Audiovisual,* 19 (2019), which contains a photograph of the film-production team of the San Miguel cooperative and mentions Miguel Machinandiarena as founder and owner, pp. 565 and 573.
34 Jorge DEL RÍO: *Cooperativismo ...* , pp. 178–181 and 183–196.
35 Mirta Zaida LOBATO: "El trabajo en la industria textil de Berisso", *Revista de Historia Bonaerense,* Instituto y Archivo Histórico de Morón, Año XVIII, 38 (September 2011).
36 Industria Textil, Capacidad Normal de Trabajo de los Obreros de la Industria Textil, especialmente mujeres y menores, *Departamento Nacional del Trabajo*, Buenos Aires, 12 June 1939, p. 2.
37 José Manuel dos Santos, leader of the Asociación Obrera Textil, president of the Cooperativa Berisso, 12 April 1991. *El Día* (La Plata), 13 July 1979, "A diez años de una experiencia exitosa". Also see Claudio PANELLA: "Así nació la Cooperativa Textil de Berisso", in Claudio PANELLA (ed.): *Berisso: Escenas de su historia*, La Plata, Archivo Histórico de la Provincia de Buenos Aires "Dr. Ricardo Levene", 2003, pp. 105–111.
38 Only one woman, Ángela de Sincak, was on the cooperative's board of directors.

39 *El Día*, La Plata, 29 May, 24, 26, and 27 June, 6 September, and 21 October 1969.
40 *El Mundo de Berisso,* Berisso, 13 November 1920.
41 "Murió un histórico del peronismo local", *El mundo de Berisso,* 31 October 2012. Also *El día*, La Plata, 31 October 2012.
42 José Manuel dos Santos, interview conducted in Berisso, 5 August 1990. Also, *El Día* (La Plata), 13 July 1979 and *El mundo de Berisso*, 17 March 1988.
43 *Info Berisso,* 20 March 2018; *La izquierda diario*, 29 December 2021.
44 *El Debate,* Zárate, 21 November 1920.
45 *El Debate,* Zárate, 20 May, 1 and 12 August 1920, and 22 November 1923.
46 *El Debate*, 17 November 1918, for example, denounced the radical influence of Manuel Besasso.
47 *El Debate*, Zárate, 24 March 1918. On the Anglo meat-processing plant and communist influence, see José PETER: *Crónicas proletarias*, Buenos Aires, Editorial Sfera, 1968.
48 Interview with Tilio Fernández, Zárate, 19 July 1985.
49 Conversation with Pablo Toledo, Zárate, 13 June 1985.
50 Interview with María Stanisio, Zárate, 21 June 1985.
51 José PETER: *Crónicas proletarias …*
52 Interview with Moisés Lyntridis, Zárate, December 1984. Lyntridis was a Greek immigrant who worked as a mattress maker until 1972, when he retired. He had arrived in Argentina in 1924. His father had arrived in 1920 and worked in the local port as a machine greaser for a ferry. Moisés had joined his father in that occupation, but both became unemployed when the ship sank.
53 Interview with Moisés Lyntridis, Zárate, December 1984.
54 *Ibid.*
55 José María SACCOMANO: *Los ganaderos argentinos y el frigorífico nacional. El caso de la CAP (1934–1976)*, Master's degree thesis, Postuate in History, Universidad Torcuato Di Tella, March 2014, p. 1. See also *Corporación Argentina de Productores de Carnes, CAP y la Economía Ganadera Argentina*, Buenos Aires, Estudio de la Empresa, 1967.
56 *Ibid.*, p. 2.
57 The Cooperativa de Trabajo, Consumo, Vivienda, Producción de Carnes y Afines, Comercialización Interna y/o Internacional "Martín Fierro" Limitada was established on 25 October 1965. Its first day of operation was 28 January 1966. https://www.diariolavozdezarate.com/2021/07/07/se-cumplen-50-anos-de-la-entrega-de-la-escritura-a-la-cooperativa-martin-fierro/. See also Jorge DEL RÍO: *Cooperativas …* , pp. 197/205.
58 Archivo General de La Nación, Film material, Alfredo Ciliberti enters Government House to speak to president Onganía, 3 January 1970. http://www.difilm-argentina.com/detalle_film_archivo.php?id=21460&show=54&sel=0&page=18.
59 https://www.diariolavozdezarate.com/2016/04/23/la-cooperativa-martin-fierro-creo-una-comision-investigadora/ and *La cooperativa* Martín Fierro, https://www.youtube.com/watch?v=iRj4y6yZ5nY.
60 *La Voz de Zárate,* Zárate, 23 Abril 2016 and *La Voz*, regional newspaper, 11 June 2021.
61 See Asociación Amigos del Museo de Zárate/Quinta Jovita-Ituzaingó 278, Tel. (03487) 422038 amigosmuseozarate@yahoo.com.ar / lajovita@argentina.com.ar. For the 1871 Berisso Museum of the working class community, visit http://

museo1871berisso.org.ar/. Mirta Zaida LOBATO: *Comunidades: historia local e historia de pueblos. Huellas de su formación*, Buenos Aires, Prometeo, 2020.

62 Daniel MÁRQUEZ and Mario PALMA GODOY: *Distinguir y comprender. Aportes para pensar la sociedad y la cultura en Patagonia*, Comodoro Rivadavia, Chubut, Ediciones Proyección Patagónica, 1995.

63 LOBATO and SURIANO: *La protesta ...* , pp. 145–155: Florencia PARTENIO, Verónica GARCÍA ALLEGRONE and María Inés FERNÁNDEZ ÁLVAREZ: "Las recuperaciones de fábricas: apuntes para una reflexión a la luz de las experiencias de ocupación en la historia argentina", *Estudios del trabajo*, 28 (July–December 2004), pp. 29–55; Andrés RUGGERI: *¿Que son las empresas recuperadas?*, Buenos Aires, Continente, 2014; Alejandro BROCATO: *Cooperativas de trabajo. Algunos elementos para su análisis*, Buenos Aires, Argentina: Pronatass-Ministerio de Economía y Obras y Servicios Públicos-Secretaría de Industria-INAC, 1994; Mirta VUOTTO: "El cooperativismo de trabajo en la argentina. Contribuciones para el diálogo social", *Programa Regional para la Promoción del Diálogo y la Cohesión Social en América Latina*, OIT, Serie Documentos de Trabajo, 217 (2011), Lima, Peru, pp. 1–96. Available at: http://dialogosocial.oit.org.pe/?p=1301; Cecilia CROSS and Matías BERGER: *La producción del trabajo asociativo. Condiciones, experiencias y prácticas de la economía social*, Buenos Aires, Ediciones Ciccus-Ceil Piette, 2010.

64 Mirta Zaida LOBATO and Juan SURIANO: *La protesta social en Argentina*, Buenos Aires, FCE, 2003.

65 Cynthia MANGO FERRARI: "La política pública y sus elementos constitutivos: una mirada desde el Programa Ingreso Social con Trabajo - Argentina", *Trabajo y Sociedad*, Issue 33 (2019), pp. 349–369, Universidad Nacional de Santiago del Estero, Facultad de Humanidades y Ciencias Sociales, INDES.

66 Ministerio de Economía, Instituto Nacional de Estadísticas y Censos (INDEC): *Incidencia de la pobreza y la indigencia en 31 aglomerados urbanos, primer semestre de 2021*, Informes técnicos, Vol. 5, no. 182, 2021, pp. 5–7.

67 The bibliography and documents available for this period are extensive. They include: Denise KASPARIAN: *Lucha ¿sin patrón? La conflictividad de trabajo en empresas recuperadas y cooperativas del Programa Argentina Trabaja*, Buenos Aires, Teseo-Universidad de Buenos Aires, Facultad de Ciencias Sociales, 2020; Ministerio de Desarrollo Productivo, Instituto Nacional de Asociativismo y Economía Social (INAES): *Mapeo cooperativo de Datos Estadísticos*, Informe Nacional Ara, Programa ACI-UE, International Co-operative Alliance, Cooperativa de las Américas, Región de la Alianza Cooperativa Internacional, September 2020, p. 9; Ana NATALUCCI: "Políticas sociales y disputas territoriales ¿La recreación de un nuevo estado protector y el caso del Programa Argentina Trabaja", *Revista de perspectivas de políticas públicas*, Año II, 3 (July–December 2012), UNLA, pp. 126–147.

68 Mercedes BASCO CARACCIOLO and María del Pilar FOTI: *Las mujeres en la economía social y solidaria, experiencias rurales y urbanas en Argentina*, Buenos Aires, Asociación Lola Mora, UNSAM-IDAES-UNIFEM, 2010.

69 Its team and projects can be followed at http://www.cooperativalajuanita.org/us.html. Toti FLORES: *Cuando con otros somos nosotros: el experiencia associativa del Movimiento de Trabajadores Desocupados de La Matanza*, Buenos Aires, Ediciones Continente, 2007.

70 https://www.facebook.com/aranitashilanderasok/?locale=es_LA, Cooperativa Arañitas Hilanderas en Belén, provincia de Catamarca, Banco de Proyectos

comunitarios rurales, https://www.bancodeproyectos.org.ar/node/74, Documental *Arañitas Hilanderas,* Directora Mariel BOMCZUK, Catamarca, Argentina, and interviews conducted by the author of this article in November 2022.

71 María Inés FERNÁNDEZ ÁLVAREZ: "La productividad en cuestión. La formación de cooperativas en el proceso de recuperación de empresas en la ciudad de Buenos Aires", in Cecilia CROSS and Matías BERGER: *La producción del trabajo asociativo. Condiciones, experiencias y prácticas de la economía social,* Buenos Aires, Ediciones Ciccus-Ceil Piette, 2010, pp. 19–39.

72 Andrés RUGGERI, Luciana BOURLOT, Fernando MARINO and Pablo PELÁEZ: *Cooperativa textiles Pigue. Historia de la recuperación de una fábrica de Gatic,* Buenos Aires, Peña Lillo-Ediciones Continente, 2014.

73 *Ibid*, pp. 26–29.

74 Brukman was a textile company that in 1995 began to experience difficulties in paying the salaries of its employees. In late 2001 it entered into a formal process with its creditors. Rumors of imminent closure began to multiply, and the workers occupied the factory. When the owners tried on several occasions to evict them, the solidarity shown by social, political, and student groups heightened, which led to the factory being surrounded in 2003. In the same year, the Legislature of the City of Buenos Aires approved the company's expropriation, but it was not until October 2013 that bankruptcy was officially declared. *La Nación*, 30 October 2002; Silvina PASCUCCI: "Brukman por dentro", *Razón y Revolución,* 1 September 2004.

75 Zanón was one of the first companies to be recovered. The company was founded in 1971 in the city of Neuquén by an entrepreneur of Italian origin who was attracted by the industrial promotion plan implemented in the region. The factory, which produced ceramics, is under workers' control after becoming a cooperative (FASINPAT = FÁbrica SIN PATrones, or "factory without bosses") in 2004. Under workers' control, the factory received endorsements and support from artists, intellectuals, students, and Mapuche organizations. Numerous projects to recover the collective memory were also organized. The extensive literature on this cooperative includes: Fernando AIZICSON: "Trayectorias de politización: la estrategia del sindicato ceramista neuquino, 2001–2003", *Revista Contenciosa,* 6 (2016); ID.: "FASINPAT como modelo de autonomía obrera. Del derecho al trabajo a la disputa por la autogestión", *Revista Nuestra América,* 7, 14 (July–December 2019); ID.: *Zanón una experiencia de lucha obrera*, Buenos Aires, Herramienta, 2009; Orietta FAVARO and Fernando AIZICSON: "Al filo de la cornisa. La resistencia obrera en la fábrica Zanón, Neuquén", *Realidad Económica*, 197 (2000), Buenos Aires, pp. 40–58; Esteban MAGNANI: *El cambio silencioso,* Buenos Aires, Prometeo, 2003; Jorgelina FREIRE: "Mujeres y participación en las fábricas recuperadas: el caso de la cerámica FASINPAT (ex Zanón), Neuquén, 2000–2006", *Historia Regional*, 27 (2009), Año XXII, Villa Constitución, pp. 29–53. On Zanón and Brukman numerous documents are available on the internet, the best-known of which are *La Toma* by Avi LEWIS and Naomi KLEIN (2004) and *Memorias del saqueo* by Fernando SOLANAS (2004).

76 The golden age of the Bauen Hotel, located in Callao Street in the center of Buenos Aires 360 meters from the National Congress, was the 1980s. In March 2003 some 38 employees occupied the building. After a long process of occupations and judicial interventions, the Cooperativa Hotel de Buenos Aires

Una Empresa Nacional (COOP. HOTEL B.A.U.E.N.) was created, thus called because they were prohibited from using the BAUEN brand. In October 2020 the cooperative closed down. Andrés RUGGERI, Emiliano BALAGUER and Desiderio ALFONSO: *Bauen. El hotel de los trabajadores*, Buenos Aires, Callao Cooperativa, Peña Lillo and Ediciones Continente, 2017.

77 Raúl GODOY: *Militante sin patrones: el rol de los trotskistas*, Argentina, Ediciones IPS, 2020, pp. 22–23. Godoy is a Zanón worker who actively participated in the process of recovering the company.

78 Florencia PARTENIO: "Interconexiones entre justicia económica, ecológica y de género: herramientas para re-pensar la sostenibilidad en los procesos autogestivos", in *Simposio N° 6: Trabajo, economía del cuidado y desigualdades: desafíos y alternativas desde las intersecciones de trabajo y género en experiencias de asociatividad laboral, IV ENCUENTRO INTERNACIONAL DE INVESTIGACION DE GÉNERO*, Universidad Nacional de Luján, 2016, pp. 173–98. Also in Raúl GODOY: *Militante sin patrones* ..., p. 79.

79 Raúl GODOY: *Militante sin patrones* ... p. 197.

80 Fernando AIZICZON: "Teoría y práctica del control obrero: el caso de cerámica Zanón, Neuquén, 2002–2005", *Revista Herramienta*, 31 (March 2002), https://herramienta.com.ar/?id=351.

81 Daniel JAMES: *Resistencia e Integración. El peronismo y la clase trabajadora argentina*, Buenos Aires, Sudamericana 1990, pp. 62–128 and 219–330.

82 The phrases appear frequently mentioned in the interviews cited by Raúl GODOY: *Militante sin patrones* ... p. 16 onwards, in the leftist press and in the workers' testimonies from Zanon, Brukman, and cooperatives such as the textile company in Berisso and the Smithfield meatpacking houses in Zárate.

83 Asociación Gremial de Trabajadores Cooperativistas Autogestivos y Precarizados (AGTCAP) integrada por el Movimiento de Trabajadores desocupados Aníbal Verón Nueva Fuerza, Organización Popular y Rebelde Villa Hidalgo, Frente de Organizaciones en Lucha, Agrupación Barrial Víctor Choque, Movimiento Teresa Rodríguez por Democracia Directa, Movimiento 8 de abril, Tierra y Libertad, Frente Popular Darío Santillán y Fogoneros y la Confederación de Trabajadores de la Economía Popular (CTEP). http://cooperativistasenlucha.blogspot.com. The bold font in the quotation is mine.

84 José Luis CORAGGIO: "Las políticas públicas participativas: ¿Obstáculo o requisito para el Desarrollo Local?", *Seminario Nacional: Fortaleciendo la relación Estado-Sociedad Civil para el Desarrollo Local*, Buenos Aires, Argentina, 2, November 2003, Retrieved from http://www.coraggioeconomia.org/jlc/archivos%20para%20descargar/ponencia%20CENOC%202.pdf; Malena HOPP: "Identidades laborales de destinatarios del Programa Ingreso Social con Trabajo Argentina Trabaja", *Trabajo y Sociedad*, 24 (2015), pp. 207–223. Retrieved from http://www.scielo.org.ar/scielo.php?script=sci_arttext&pid=S1514-68712015000100011: ID.: "El trabajo cooperativo en cuestión: "Desafíos en el nuevo contexto argentino". *Revista Ciencias Sociales*, 93 (2017), pp. 102–107. Retrieved from http://www.sociales.uba.ar/wp-content/blogs.dir/219/files/2017/05/REVISTA-93-102-HOPP.pdf; Malena Victoria HOPP and Eliana LIJTERMAN: "Trabajo, derechos sociales y protección social en argentina de la reconstrucción neoliberal", *R. Katal*, Florianópolis, V. 22, 1 (Jan/Abr, 2019), pp. 66–79. Retrieved from https://www.scielo.br/j/rk/a/dVGCsKYMn58dqRTW6bMZtNt/?format=pdf&lang=es

85 Floreal FORNI and Nicolás DZEMBROWSKY: "La economía social en Europa y en América Latina", in Cecilia CROSS and Matías BERGER: *La producción del trabajo asociativo* ... , pp. 339–355.

References

ADELMAN, Jeremy: "El Partido Socialista argentino", in Mirta Zaida LOBATO (ed.): *El progreso, la modernización y sus límites, 1880–1916*, Vol. 3, Buenos Aires, Sudamericana, 2000, pp. 261–290.

AIZICSON, Fernando: "Teoría y práctica del control obrero: el caso de cerámica Zanón, Neuquén, 2002–2005", *Revista Herramienta*, 31 (March 2002). https://herramienta.com.ar/?id=351.

AIZICSON, Fernando: *Zanón una experiencia de lucha obrera*, Buenos Aires, Herramienta, 2009.

AIZICSON, Fernando: "FASINPAT como modelo de autonomía obrera. Del derecho al trabajo a la disputa por la autogestión", *Revista Nuestra América,* 7, 14 (July–December 2019).

AIZICSON, Fernando: "Trayectorias de politización: la estrategia del sindicato ceramista neuquino, 2001–2003", *Revista Contenciosa*, 6 (2016).

ARICÓ, José: *La hipótesis de Justo. Escritos sobre el socialismo en América Latina*, Buenos Aires, Sudamericana, 1999.

BARRANCOS, Dora: *La escena iluminada. Ciencia para Trabajadores, 1890–1930*, Buenos Aires, Plus Ultra, 1996.

BECERRA, Marina: *Marxismo y feminismo en el primer socialismo argentino, Enrique del Valle Iberlucea*, Rosario, Prohistoria, 2009.

BROCATO, Alejandro: *Cooperativas de trabajo. Algunos elementos para su análisis*, Buenos Aires, Argentina, Pronatass-Ministerio de Economía y Obras y Servicios Públicos-Secretaría de Industria- INAC, 1994.

BUONOME, Juan: "El partido de los consumidores. Publicidad, consumo y cultura de clase en la prensa socialista argentinas, entre el Centenario y la Gran Depresión", *Desarrollo Económico*, 16, 19 (September–December 2016), pp. 245–276.

BASCO CARACCIOLO, Mercedes and FOTI, María del Pilar: *Las mujeres en la economía social y solidaria, experiencias rurales y urbanas en Argentina*, Buenos Aires, Asociación Lola Mora, UNSAM-IDAES-UNIFEM, 2010.

COLE, George Douglas Howard: *Historia del pensamiento socialista*, I Leviatán. ePub base rl.1.2.

CORAGGIO, José Luis: "Las políticas públicas participativas: ¿Obstáculo o requisito para el Desarrollo Local?", *Seminario Nacional: Fortaleciendo la relación Estado-Sociedad Civil para el Desarrollo Local*, Buenos Aires, Argentina, 2 November 2003, Retrieved from http://www.coraggioeconomia.org/jlc/archivos%20para%20descargar/ponencia%20CENOC%202.pdf.

CORTES CONDE, Roberto: *El Progreso Argentino, 1880–1914*, Buenos Aires, Sudamericana, 1979.

CROSS, Cecilia and BERGER, Matías: *La producción del trabajo asociativo. Condiciones, experiencias y prácticas de la economía social*, Buenos Aires, Ediciones Ciccus-Ceil Piette, 2010.

DEL RIO, Jorge: *Las cooperativas de trabajo*, Buenos Aires, Librería Jurídica Abeledo, 1949, pp. 112–122.

DEL RIO, Jorge: "Cooperativas de Trabajo", *Revista Hechos e Ideas*, 97 (April 1952), Buenos Aires, Argentina.

DEL RIO, Jorge: "El cooperativismo en el Segundo Plan Quinquenal", *Hechos e Ideas*, (1954), pp. 106–109.

DEL RIO, Jorge: *Cooperativismo. Cooperativas de Trabajo*, Buenos Aires, Ediciones del autor, 1966, pp. 118–122.

DI STEFANO, Roberto; SABATO, Hilda; ROMERO, Luis Alberto and MORENO, José Luis: *De las cofradías a las organizaciones de la sociedad civil. Historia de la iniciativa asociativa en Argentina, 1776–1990*, Buenos Aires, Edilab editora, 2002.

ESPÍNOLA, Rocío; MATTIA, Sebastián; NAVARRO, Ariel and PONCE, Maximiliano: "Entre plátanos y melodramas: historia y memoria de los Estudios San Miguel", *Imagofagia, Revista de la Asociación Argentina de Estudios de Cine y Audiovisual*, 19 (2019).

FAVARO, Orietta and AIZICSON, Fernando: "Al filo de la cornisa. La resistencia obrera en la fábrica Zanón, Neuquén", *Realidad Económica*, 197 (2000), Buenos Aires, pp. 40–58.

FERNÁNDEZ ÁLVAREZ, María Inés: "La productividad en cuestión. La formación de cooperativas en el proceso de recuperación de empresas en la ciudad de Buenos Aires", in Cecilia CROSS and Matías BERGER (eds.): *La producción del trabajo asociativo. Condiciones, experiencias y prácticas de la economía social*, Buenos Aires, Ediciones Ciccus-Ceil Piette, 2010, pp. 19–39.

FLORES, Toti: *Cuando con otros somos nosotros: la experiencia asociativa del Movimiento de Trabajadores Desocupados de La Matanza*, Buenos Aires, Ediciones Continente, 2007.

FORNI, Floreal and DZEMBROWSKY, Nicolás: "La economía social en Europa y en América Latina", in Cecilia CROSS and Matías BERGER (eds.): *La producción del trabajo asociativo ...*, pp. 339–355.

FREIRE, Jorgelina: "Mujeres y participación en las fábricas recuperadas: el caso de la cerámica FASINPAT (ex Zanón), Neuquén, 2000–2006", *Historia Regional*, 27 (2009), Año XXII, Villa Constitución, pp. 29–53.

GODOY, Raúl: *Militante sin patrones: el rol de los trotskistas*, Argentina, Ediciones IPS, 2020.

HOPP, Malena: "Identidades laborales de destinatarios del Programa Ingreso Social con Trabajo Argentina Trabaja. Trabajo y Sociedad", 24 (2015), pp. 207–223. Retrieved from http://www.scielo.org.ar/scielo.php?script=sci_arttext&pid=S1514-68712015000100011:

HOPP, Malena: "El trabajo cooperativo en cuestión: "Desafíos en el nuevo contexto argentino"", *Revista Ciencias Sociales*, 93 (2017), pp.102–107. Retrieved from http://www.sociales.uba.ar/wp-content/blogs.dir/219/files/2017/05/REVISTA-93-102-HOPP.pdf.

HOPP, Malena Victoria and LIJTERMAN, Eliana: "Trabajo, derechos sociales y protección social en argentina de la reconstrucción neoliberal", *R. Katal,*

Florianópolis, 22, 1 (Jan/Abr 2019), pp. 66–79. Retrieved from https://www.scielo.br/j/rk/a/dVGCsKYMn58dqRTW6bMZtNt/?format=pdf&lang=es

JAMES, Daniel: *Resistencia e Integración. El peronismo y la clase trabajadora argentina*, Buenos Aires, 1990.

KAPLAN DE DRIMER, Alicia and DRIMER, Bernardo: *Las Cooperativas*, Buenos Aires, INTERCOOP, 1975.

KASPARIAN, Denise: *Lucha ¿sin patrón? La conflictividad de trabajo en empresas recuperadas y cooperativas del Programa Argentina Trabaja*, Buenos Aires, Teseo-Universidad de Buenos Aires, Facultad de Ciencias Sociales, 2020.

KRIGER, Clara: *Cine y peronismo. El estado en escena*, Buenos Aires, Siglo XXI, 2009.

LOBATO, Mirta Zaida: "Los socialistas y los derechos sociales y políticos de las mujeres, Argentina 1890–1930", *Labrys, Estudos feministas*, August–December, 2005, Labrys.net.br.

LOBATO, Mirta Zaida: *La prensa obrera, Buenos Aires y Montevideo, 1890–1958*, Buenos Aires, EDHASA, 2009.

LOBATO, Mirta Zaida: "El trabajo en la industria textil de Berisso", *Revista de Historia Bonaerense*, Instituto y Archivo Histórico de Morón, Año XVIII, 38 (September 2011).

LOBATO, Mirta Zaida: *Comunidades: historia local e historia de pueblos. Huellas de su formación*, Buenos Aires, Prometeo, 2020.

LOBATO, Mirta Zaida: ""Lo que el capital se llevó": fábricas cerradas, memoria e historia reciente", *Anuario del Instituto de Historia Argentina*, 21-1 (2021), e135. 10.24215/2314257Xe135.

LOBATO, Mirta Zaida and SURIANO, Juan: *La protesta social en Argentina*, Buenos Aires, FCE, 2003.

LLUCH, Andrea and SÁNCHEZ, Laura: *De movimiento popular a empresa. El cooperativismo eléctrico en La Pampa (1925–1950)*, Santa Rosa, Fondo editorial pampeano, 2002.

MAGNANI, Esteban: *El cambio silencioso*, Buenos Aires, Prometeo, 2003.

MANGO FERRARI, Cynthia: "La política pública y sus elementos constitutivos: una mirada desde el Programa Ingreso Social con Trabajo-Argentina", *Trabajo y Sociedad*, Issue 33 (2019), pp. 349–369, Universidad Nacional de Santiago del Estero, Facultad de Humanidades y Ciencias Sociales, INDES.

MÁRQUEZ, Daniel and PALMA GODOY, Mario: *Distinguir y comprender. Aportes para pensar la sociedad y la cultura en Patagonia*, Comodoro Rivadavia, Chubut, Ediciones Proyección Patagónica, 1995.

NATALUCCI, Ana: "Políticas sociales y disputas territoriales ¿La recreación de un nuevo estado protector y el caso del Programa Argentina Trabaja", *Revista de perspectivas de políticas públicas*, Año II, 3 (July–December 2012), UNLA, pp. 126–147.

PANELLA, Claudio: "Así nació la Cooperativa Textil de Berisso", in Claudio PANELLA (ed.): *Berisso: Escenas de su historia*, La Plata, Archivo Histórico de la Provincia de Buenos Aires "Dr. Ricardo Levene", 2003.

PARTENIO, Florencia: "Interconexiones entre justicia económica, ecológica y de género: herramientas para re-pensar la sostenibilidad en los procesos autogestivos", in *Simposio N° 6: Trabajo, economía del cuidado y desigualdades: desafíos y alternativas desde las intersecciones de trabajo y género en experiencias de asociatividad laboral, IV ENCUENTRO INTERNACIONAL DE INVESTIGACION DE GÉNERO*, Universidad Nacional de Luján, 2016, pp. 173–198.

PARTENIO, Florencia; GARCÍA ALLEGRONE, Verónica and FERNÁNDEZ ÁLVAREZ, María Inés: "Las "recuperaciones de fábricas: apuntes para una reflexión a la luz de las experiencias de ocupación en la historia argentina", *Estudios del trabajo*, 28 (July–December 2004), pp. 29–55.

PASCUCCI, Silvina: "Brukman por dentro", *Razón y Revolución*, 1 (September 2004).

PEÑA, Fernando: *Cien años de cine argentino*, Buenos Aires, Biblos, 2012.

PETER, José: *Crónicas proletarias*, Buenos Aires, Editorial Esfera, 1968.

PLOTINSKY, Daniel: *Historia del cooperativismo 1*, Idealistas y realizadores: el cooperativismo argentino hasta la sanción de la Ley de Sociedades Cooperativas, 2009, accessed at: http://www.centrocultural.coop/blogs/cooperativismo/2009/06/18/historia del cooperativismo 1/.

PLOTINSKY, Daniel: *Cooperativismo y dictaduras*, 2011, accessed at: http://www.centrocultural.coop/blogs/cooperativismo/2011/03/21/cooperativismo-y-dictaduras/.

PLOTINSKY, Daniel: *Orígenes y consolidación del cooperativismo en la Argentina. Instituto de la Cooperación*, IDELCOOP, 2015. Available at: https://www.idelcoop.org.ar/sites/www.idelcoop.org.ar/files/revista/articulos/pdf/revista-215-con- membretes-origenes_y_consolidacion_del_cooperativismo_en_la_argentina.pdf, 2015.

PLOTINSKY, Daniel: "Argentina: políticas públicas y cooperativismo (1976 – 2015)", *IX Rulescoop International Congress Respuesta de la Universidad a las necesidades de la economía social ante los desafíos del mercado*, 2015.

RABASA, María Natalia: "El Partido socialista y El Hogar Obrero. Un análisis de las primeras experiencias cooperativas en el cambio de siglo", in *Archivos de historia del movimiento obrero y la izquierda*, 19 (September 2021–February 2022), pp. 133–155.

REY, Ana Lía: "Palabras y proyectos de mujeres socialistas a través de sus revistas (1900–1956)", *Mora (Buenos Aires)*, 17-1 (2011). Accessed on 31 March 2023 at http://www.scielo.org.ar/scielo.php?script=sci_arttext&pid=S1853-001X2011000100009&lng=es&tlng=es.

RONCHI, Verónica: La cooperación integral. Historia de "El Hogar Obrero", Ediciones Fabro, Buenos Aires 2016.

RUGGERI, Andrés: *¿Que son las empresas recuperadas?*, Buenos Aires, Continente, 2014

RUGGERI, Andrés: *De las primeras cooperativas a Petrogrado y Barcelona*, Buenos Aires, Callao, 2018.

RUGGERI, Andrés; BALAGUER, Emiliano and ALFONSO, Desiderio: *Bauen el hotel de los trabajadores*, Buenos Aires, Callao Cooperativa, Peña Lillo y Ediciones Continente, 2017.

RUGGERI, Andrés; BOURLOT, Luciana; MARINO, Fernando and PELÁEZ, Pablo: *Cooperativa textiles Pigue. Historia de la recuperación de una fábrica de Gatic*, Buenos Aires, Peña Lillo-Ediciones Continente, 2014.

SACCOMANO, José María: *Los ganaderos argentinos y el frigorífico nacional. El caso de la CAP (1934–1976)*, Master's degree thesis, Posgraduate in History, Universidad Torcuato Di Tella, March 2014.

VUOTTO, Mirta: "El cooperativismo de trabajo en la argentina. Contribuciones para el dialogo social", Programa Regional para la Promoción del Diálogo y la Cohesión Social en América Latina. OIT, *Serie Documentos de Trabajo*, 217 (2011), Lima, Perú, pp. 1–96. Available at: http://dialogosocial.oit.org.pe/?p=1301.

WEBB, Beatrice and WEBB, Sydney: *The Consumers' Co-operative Movement*, Longmans, Green, 1921 (the original is from 1891).

8 Mutual Benefit Societies in Spain from the Ancien Régime to 1936[1]

Three Decades of Studies

Santiago Castillo

The initial years (1990–1992)

In 1990, the general situation of studies on mutual benefit societies [*sociedades de socorros mutuos*, hereinafter SSMs] in Europe could be summarised as follows: "Much has been written about these organizations [...] However, the historiography is uneven: some countries have been relatively well studied (e.g. Great Britain, France, and Italy) while for others, the information is so far negligible".[2]

There was little doubt that the author of the above words considered Spain to be one of the countries with little information available. At the time, there was no general work in Spain dealing with SSMs in particular, or mutualism in general, as a specific object of study in the 19th and 20th centuries.

It is true that the non-existence of work of this type does not mean that there were no important texts produced in the field of social history in general and of the workers' movement in particular, or that the so-called sociability studies[3] and monographs on some specific societies[4] had not opened up new perspectives of analysis. But it is clear that we were lagging a long way behind most European countries in this respect. We were still a long way from being able to provide a picture, even a general one, of the vicissitudes of mutualism in our country or to outline its most significant stages and incidents in the 19th and 20th centuries.

We were faced with an object of study that had hitherto been almost invisible to researchers.

This was the general outlook when the news was received that an international conference was to be held in Paris under the expressive title of Mutualités de tous les pays: un passée riche d'avenir, which was to be attended by researchers from 50 countries from all over the world. Along with the news came the invitation to prepare and present at the conference a report on the state of affairs in Spain.

It was worth replying and insisting on the little that had been published so far and pointing out the irrelevance of the subject in our recent

DOI: 10.4324/9781003439554-9

historiography. But, on reflection, I decided to convene and organise a previous scientific meeting on the subject in Spain.

1992: *First International Meeting on Workers' Mutual Benefits Societies in Spain*, 19th and 20th centuries[5]

The objective was twofold: on the one hand, to stimulate possible research on aspects that had not yet been analysed and to encourage people to take a different look at topics that had already been researched, thus making SSMs visible and relevant to ongoing research on related topics; and on the other, closely related to the above, to encourage collective discussion of existing knowledge.

In both cases, results were very positive. The 35 papers presented and discussed at the meeting considerably expanded the existing bibliography and, more importantly, the knowledge on the subject. They also made it possible to adopt an initial overall approach to the phenomenon. But, above all, they meant that, for the first time, contemporary mutual provident societies were the specific object of collective reflection in our country and, as such, an initial general assessment could be presented to the Paris Conference.[6]

The importance of this outcome did not go unnoticed. The same author who, two years earlier, had regarded Spain as one of the countries with insignificant studies on mutualism, now had the following to say about our meeting: "The papers presented at this gathering brought Spanish achievements in this area of historical recearch up to international standards".[7]

The publication of the proceedings of the meeting – the book *Solidaridad desde abajo*[8] – documented this leap forward in Spain and was noted in the report to the Parisian congress.

The 32 papers published in the book outlined the object of study: they gave an initial general picture of the evolution of mutualism in our country, both in terms of legislation and the underlying political vicissitudes; they suggested general lines in the development of the different types of mutuality, from the workers' to the popular with its different variants; the quantitative evolution of mutual societies was dealt with by analysing the different and disparate sources; there was no shortage of analyses of the effective implementation of some societies or of the types of benefits desired or actually provided by some of them; nor was there any shortage of initial approaches by regions: Asturias, Catalonia, Galicia, the Basque Country, etc.[9]

What was achieved? What remained uncertain? We will come back to this later. Let us now return to the chronological sequence.

Three decades of uneven road

The start was promising and it suggested that now the first step had been taken – Spanish mutualism had been turned into an attractive object of study – we had to keep momentum going by encouraging greater complexity in our approaches to the subject. With this in mind, in 1995 we convened the 2nd International Meeting on "Mutualism and Social Protection in 20th Century Spain".[10]

This time, the primary objectives underlying the call for papers were different. The aim was to reconstruct the roles played and the relations between private mutualism and the institutions of public social protection set up at the beginning of the 20th century. This period covered from the beginning of social insurance to the welfare systems in Spain at the end of the 20th century, and the analysis focused on their actual situation and the possible and/or desirable evolution.

We therefore conceived the second meeting as an important occasion to encourage researchers, actors, and managers of public and private social welfare to reflect collectively on the recent past, the present, and the possible future of an issue that was as burning as it was basic in all advanced contemporary societies.[11]

Sixteen papers were presented, which together served as an initial approach to some of the key issues on the fulfilment of the aims of mutual societies, their functionality from the times that they were almost the only social welfare institutions to when they entered into unequal competition with the emerging public social welfare institutions, the resulting challenges, and the eventual assumption of a complementary role.[12]

Unfortunately, this brought our cycle of meetings to an end,[13] and I am not aware of any other initiatives to promote collective discussion of the phenomenon of voluntary mutuality in the years that immediately followed. However, of course, some worthwhile work was still published, to which we will refer later on. There was also the opportunity to discuss specific topics in international colloquia or publications.[14] There was even the opportunity to make an overall reflection on the first decade after the book *Solidaridad* ....[15]

But, to my knowledge, the collective discussion on mutualism was not taken up again for some considerable time.

6th Social History Conference on "Social Protection in History" 2008

The centenary of the creation of the Instituto Nacional de Previsión (INP) (National Welfare Institute) was used by the Asociación de Historia Social (Social History Association) not only to compile various specific studies[16] but also to commission three papers of a total of more than a hundred pages for the period under consideration here up to the Civil War[17] and another hundred pages for the period of the Franco dictatorship.[18] This work once again included reflections on the whole, taking stock of what had been published to date, starting from the end of the Ancien Régime and finishing with the period of mutualism in modern-day Spain.[19] The path taken at the 2nd Meeting 13 years earlier was thus extended and updated, and the private and public welfare systems were revisited in their conflicting, solidarity-based, complementary relations.

This path has been marked by three major milestones and has been widened in subsequent years with an intermittent but continuous trickle of publications on different aspects and periods of mutuality. These include a study on the spirit of cooperation and mutualism in the Valencian Country, 1834–1936, the entire period covered here[20]; a book on the most important federation of the period 1896–1936 – the Federation of Mutualities of Catalonia – written from the novel perspective of social capital[21]; a mosaic of studies by various authors on private social protection in the Basque Country in the 19th, 20th, and 21st centuries, and involving cattle brotherhoods, mining mutual insurance companies, and mounts of piety of municipal employees.[22]

Likewise, some work touched on aspects that had been little discussed up to that point, such as the degree of effectiveness and efficiency offered by mutual societies in the social coverage of risks in general and more particularly the risk of illness in the 20th century,[23] and overall assessments of the state of the art in mutuality studies.[24] These latter authors have recently added a complete study on employers' mutual insurance companies for accidents at work from their beginnings to the present day, 1900–2019.[25]

Last but by no means least is the Base de datos del asociacionismo catalán contemporáneo [BDACC] (Database of Contemporary Catalan Associations) created by the ISOCAC research group of the Universitat Rovira i Virgili, Tarragona, which we will discuss below.[26]

We will return to several of the topics outlined above in the following pages, but for now, let us conclude this panoramic journey through the evolution of studies on Spanish mutualism as a way of fulfilling our first purpose.

Let us now move on to highlight some of the contributions in terms of approaches and results accumulated over the last 30 years. To do so, we will return to part of the outline of significant themes that we used at the beginning of the 1990s.[27]

Let us begin, then, by defining what we mean when we refer to mutual benefit societies and/or mutual societies.

Mutual benefit societies and/or mutuals

Mutuals are associations whose purpose is essentially to insure their members. It is therefore appropriate, as a first step, to place them in the context of the other existing insurance institutions.

As is well known, the essence of insurance is that several insured people share the economic value of the loss suffered by one of them as a result of a fortuitous but calculable event. It therefore involves the association of several people who are exposed to identical risks. Its effectiveness stems from the fact that the combined contributions of the insured people allow those that suffer a loss as a result of fortuitous events to which they are all exposed to be compensated financially. Its basic function is therefore to distribute among many the economic losses suffered by some in a system of equal rights and duties for all.

The insurance entities can take various forms:

- *Mutual societies:* voluntary associations in which the policyholders are their own managers and administrators; they know each other, as they carry out all operations together and are therefore both policyholders and insurers at the same time. Any profits belong to all members and are distributed in accordance with statutes or regulations.
- *Commercial insurance companies (or mutual insurance companies):* companies that administer or manage the insurance of the whole group of insured people with the aim of obtaining a lawful profit from the capital they use for this purpose. The policyholders have no relationship with each other, and the company is responsible for all obligations by means of a guarantee capital.
- The *State:* can set itself up as an insurer and even directly manage welfare institutions.

We shall refer to the other types only to the extent necessary for a better understanding of the former. In terms of what is insured – i.e. the type of risk covered – two main groups should be distinguished: *personal risk* (sickness, old age, unemployment, accident, disability, death, etc.) and *property risk* (houses, fire, crops, livestock, etc.). Our discussion will be limited to personal risk insurance.[28] On the other hand as far as their composition is concerned, different groups or social collectives have set up personal insurance entities, their greater or lesser permanence being made possible by their capacity for periodic savings. The studies on which we will focus are limited to those trials in which workers, labourers, or wage earners in general participated, either in their totality or in a significant way. Let us summarise: here we refer mainly to voluntary mutual insurance companies for personal risk insurance with significant employee participation, which, over time, have been called SSMs, Montepíos, Mutualidades de Previsión Social.[29]

We shall use the following terms to further define SSMs or mutuals:

Workers' mutuals are those made up of salaried workers. They can be further subdivided as *general* or *territorial* (that is to say, they admit workers at a national or local level); *trade* or *professional* (the workers are from the same profession or branch); *workshop* or *company* (the workers are from a given industrial establishment or company).

Popular mutuals are those that do not require members to belong to a specific social or professional group. Therefore, they could and generally did tend to include wage earners of any level and profession or trade, self-employed artisans, small landowners, etc., and even the higher strata of the population. By definition, then, they are interclass.

We will also use the term *welfare* to describe those workers' or popular mutual societies that *depend* to a greater or lesser degree on the support and action of external notables who finance them and/or supervise and control them.[30]

Finally, insurance is the fundamental overt function of SSMs, but not the only one. The people who join one of these societies also seek a certain type of companionship or solidarity and often even share explicit ideological, religious, or political-party conceptions, which are the emblem or rallying cry of the society in question. On the other hand, as has been pointed out by many authors, SSMs play an important role in the accumulation of experience in managing their own affairs. Moreover, mutuality, as Van der Linden recalls, "taught workers some essential virtues in bourgeois society, such as voluntary discipline and long-term thinking". There are, therefore, many reasons for studying the mutual societies we are discussing here. A number of them have in fact been addressed in the studies that will be referenced.

Contemporary Spain 1836–1936

The process of building mutual societies was already 100 years old by the beginning of this period. However, although we may refer to this initial period below, the bulk of our considerations will focus on contemporary Spain, and we take as our starting point the changes that began after the death of Ferdinand VII (1833) which, as is commonly accepted, marked a definitive break with the Ancien Régime in our country.

Soon after Ferdinand's death, a series of measures were implemented that would give shape to the bourgeois liberal revolution and lay the foundations for the development of capitalism. These measures were in the same direction as contemporary European processes of change, but they had different effects in different countries. In the case of Spain, one of these effects was that industrial development was late and slow.

As far as workers' associations were concerned, the foundations for the implementation of the liberal system began to be laid in December 1836 with the definitive abolition of guilds as the institutions responsible for regulating professional practice. A little more than two years later (Royal Order of 28 February 1839), the conditions established at the end of the 18th century for the free association of all those who sought to "help each other in their misfortunes, illnesses, etc., or to save together to meet their future needs" – whether they were workers or not – were improved. In other words, mutual aid associations now had a legal channel that was much more suited to their needs. Implicitly, what would soon become known as "societies of resistance [to capital]" (that is to say, trade unions) were excluded because no legislation was passed on specific associations of workers entrusted with regulating professional practice.

In this respect, the Spanish liberal system also took the same path as most neighbouring countries: the principles of individualist liberalism entailed opposition to the organisation of workers' unions, and the State abstaining from regulating labour relations and developing compulsory welfare institutions. The modifications made to these three intertwined and complementary aspects of the new system would, to a large extent, be indicators of the degree of evolution and development of Spanish society.

As far as trade unionism was concerned, and as in other countries, the situation would end up changing when it became clear that it was impossible to contain trade union development with a repressive policy. The trade unions were legalised in Spain, after the parenthesis of the revolutionary six-year period (1868–73), with the Law of Associations of 1887. This law already provided a suitable legal channel for all associations, trade unions included, although the effective recognition of their instruments of collective action – striking and collective bargaining – was still decades away.[31]

As for the modification of the State's abstentionist attitude towards social issues, this was to come somewhat later. It was not until 1900 that a real process of legal intervention by the State in social issues began in Spain. The turn of the century saw the beginning of a process of shaping a new system of labour relations, soon complemented by the beginning of State-promoted social welfare which, via the INP, would lead to the first compulsory insurance policies in the 1920s. This would be systematised and unified in the 1930s.[32]

Along the way, the State regulated the general framework of insurance, especially as regards commercial companies, in the 1908 law. However, it ignored mutuality from a legislative point of view to such an extent that in 1936, it was still possible to write: "Legislation on the free and spontaneous mutualist phenomenon has not yet been drafted [...] Spain lacks a general legislation on mutuality".[33] From the very first studies on mutuality in Spain, then, it has been clear that, unlike in other countries, state modification of the legislation governing the framework and the possibilities of action of the mutualities did not play a major role in the stages in the history of mutuality until the civil war.[34]

We will return later to some of the reasons for this lack of specific State legislation, but first we should point out, at least briefly, some of the features of the evolution of mutualism in this historical period. Under the name of Sociedades de Socorros Mutuos or Mutualidades, they gradually became established in Spain as a welfare system. At first they were almost unique, but subsequently, they coexisted and competed with the mercantile Mutual Societies and then with State insurance.

Quantification and sources

To address the mutualist phenomenon in contemporary Spain, it was clearly necessary to be able to faithfully quantify volume and evolution over time.

In the search for the basic sources on which to build this picture, it soon became apparent that there was a lack of general data for more than three quarters of the 19th century. In fact, in order to work on the actual accounts or statistics of associations, and therefore on the mutual benefits, we could only go as far back as 1882, when data were collected but not published, and only partially preserved in the documents provided by 19 provinces. Five years later, another statistical report was compiled and published, but not without serious imperfections.[35] The following reports were the two compiled for 1904 by the Institute of Social Reforms and the Census of Associations on 30 June 1916.[36]

After studying the different sources available at the time and analysing and comparing official statistics, three decades ago we predicted the following probable evolution of mutualist associations in Spain: 1887, 1,200 societies; 1904, 2,500; 1916, 5,500. These figures were quite different from the official ones: 664, 1,691, and 4,517 for the same years.[37] Our estimates, we noted at the time, were tentative. They were in line with the state of research on the subject.

The situation has certainly evolved. In recent years, as a result of collective initiatives such as those of research teams and/or groups such as those set up in both Castiles[38] or personal research, studies have brought to light new data from local and provincial archives, civil governments, private or public libraries, the press, etc., in provincial or regional areas such as Valladolid, Valencia, and Galicia, to name but a few.[39]

The most recent and ambitious initiative is the creation of the *Contemporary Catalan Associations Database* (BDACC) by the ISOCAC research group of the Universitat Rovira i Virgili.[40]

The new contributions since our initial prediction suggest that we can cautiously maintain those estimates as we expressed them at the time. We will have to wait for the results of new research to be added to the global estimates of the phenomenon.

Then as now, however, quantification was not the only major problem we faced. Largely due to the sources available, many of the studies on SSMs are largely based on analyses of the statutes and by-laws of the societies, which are kept in archives, libraries, or governmental agencies. From these sources, it is rarely possible to obtain information on the balance sheets of members, the income and expenditure of the mutual societies, or the types and amounts of benefits they actually give, all of which is essential if we wish to understand what these societies really were and not to what they claimed to be in their statutes and programmes. It is clear that the fact that this problem continues to hover over numerous studies is not due to the inability of researchers but to a fundamental problem of sources. As sources are located, or become available, analyses are carried out and our knowledge is enriched.[41]

It is obvious, we said then and we maintain today, that the approach must at the very least involve finding and exploiting more complementary sources and regrouping and serialising the knowledge that is being produced. In the meantime, the current state of research certainly does not allow us to make more than generic considerations on certain issues.

Evolution of Spanish mutualism

Among the first questions to be answered when beginning the study of the period were: what types of associations specifically or primarily dedicated to mutual aid existed prior to the Royal Order of 1839, and what new types of societies were created afterwards?

In *Solidaridad desde abajo* we began by noting a certain proliferation of "mutualism" at the end of the Ancien Régime. At the First Encuentro a study was presented[42] that followed in the wake of previous studies[43] and showed that in Madrid at the end of the 17th century and especially in the 18th century a new type of association had been created: the Hermandades de Socorro [HSs] (mutual aid brotherhoods). Composed fundamentally, but not exclusively, of artisans and craftsmen, HSs were different from the guilds and/or religious confraternities from which they originated in various key aspects: among other things, they were voluntary, which allowed them to bring together people from different trades and occupations, although some HSs were set up for a single trade or for women only; they provided relief in different ways to all their members, and depending on what they contributed; and they systematically applied relief for illness. Other innovative aspects of the HSs were the restriction of access to membership on the basis of economic capacity; a progressive tendency to introduce age limits for entry and the exclusion of those suffering from chronic illnesses; the disciplined payment of dues; and penalties for non-participation in collective events. In other words, they had features that until then we had generally assumed would be the prerogative of 19th-century SSMs.

Such a singular associative phenomenon had characteristics that went beyond their role as a mere precedent of the modern SSMs from the 19th century onwards. We wondered whether the movement was restricted and marginal or, on the contrary, generalised throughout Spain. At the time, we concluded that the latter was probable, "although we still need more research to be able to support such a hypothesis".[44]

And the new research was not long in coming. Today, of course, there is little room for doubt in this respect. If Sánchez de Madariaga[45] spoke of the creation of no fewer than 80 *hermandades de socorros* in 18th century Madrid, according to Zarzoso Orellana, in Barcelona there were between 55 and 60 in 1787, and 31 more were authorised to be set up or had their ordinances modified between 1792 and 1804, and this number increased by a further 33 between 1805 and 1820.[46] For his part, Barnosell wrote that in Barcelona "by the mid-1830s a dense network of societies dedicated to applied relief (death and illness) had been consolidated", and according to his data, some 50 societies were formed between 1810 and 1845, and that by the end of this period, there were a total of about 70 societies with 9,000 members.[47]

As well as those cited above, there are other studies of merit on the subject[48] and the splendid synthesis by Fernando Díez[49] at the 7th Congress of the AHS is worthy of particular mention. Analysing the works cited and his own, Díez considers that the change from confraternities to relief brotherhoods, as specialised associations for mutual aid in the event of illness and/or death, is "undoubtedly the main innovation in the field of popular associations before the 19th century". He compares the stages, characteristics, and specificities of the process in Spain and England and discusses the action taken by the Bourbon monarchy to channel it.

This new view of the *hermandades de socorros* suggests that we need to discard our initial idea that they were the precedents of a modern trade union movement, the advent of which would give them their true meaning. And this is not even to begin by biasing the following question, which is about how the *hermandades de socorro* (which became *sociedades de socorros mutuos* or *montepíos* after the Bourbon reform at the end of the previous century) would fit in with the new ways in which the workers were organised, fundamentally as the resistance societies or trade unions as soon as these began to take shape in the 1940s.

Under the 1839 regulations in Catalonia, an industrial region par excellence, the Weavers' Society and the Weavers' Mutual Association of Barcelona came into being. Both organisations, historiography tends to point out, were two sides of the same coin: "The first was a trade union for protest purposes, while the second was apparently set up to solve social welfare problems (forced unemployment, illness, invalidity, etc.), but, as a charitable association, was designed to replace the first if it was banned", under the protection of the Royal Order of 1839.[50]

The first textile trade unions are key to the history of Catalan workerism. They were the beginnings of the modern workers' movement in a geographical area where development generated a large mass of industrial workers. The fact that this sort of early trade unionism entailed some kind of mutualist activity or relief in response to contingencies of the labour process and the labour market – accidents at work, unemployment – was not a peculiarly Spanish phenomenon.

However, this was not the only claim. It was also claimed that mutualism by its very nature was instrumental, subordinate, and coexistent. This is certainly true, but it was claimed, not documented. In the first decades of the 19th century, there was no research directly addressing the subject. But very soon there was a serious and documented study on the characteristics of the first resistance societies in the years 1810–1845 in Catalonia.[51] And shortly afterwards, a comparison was made of the mutual aid societies and trade unions in Barcelona for the same period by the same author [Barnosell, 2009]. His conclusions could not have been more categorical. He notes the existence of "important differences in terms of structure, functions, target audience, internal democracy, supra-local action and public image between both types of societies, so in Barcelona in the first half of the 19th century both types of societies responded to quite different demands and actions, but we cannot say that the mutual benefit societies were simply a screen for the resistance societies, or that the latter were a simple evolution of the former".[52]

Contemporary mutualism, therefore, had not been vicariously created by new workers' structures as a screen for – or a subordinate shield to – new essentially vindictive structures. They were autonomous creations. So rather than focusing on the evolution from mutual to trade union, we had to analyse how some mutual and/or trade union institutions were related or intertwined on the long and complex path from the dissolution of the guilds to the creation of the new resistance structures. Likewise, we also had to analyse how the functions of mutualist societies and trade unions could, or could not, be exercised by institutions that were only of one type or the other.

These issues have also been addressed in the city of Valencia. It should be remembered that, by law, the guilds lost their capacity for the corporate control of production in 1836. From then on, they had to adapt to the new situation of freedom of industry and recruitment imposed by the liberal system. And this meant coping with highly complex problems, as Martínez Gallego pointed out decades ago in the case of Valencia. Sometimes, the leading members of guilds who were setting themselves up to become entrepreneurs used the transformation of guild regulations to get rid of the guild's patrimony (farms, tools, etc.) so that the distribution of the profits would have an impact on their private capitalisation. On other occasions, craftsmen in the process of proletarianisation fought to maintain the guild's patrimony in order to establish cooperatives for the supply of raw materials or even for production and to maintain the provision of mutual aid.[53]

This was an important part of the general process of organising Valencian workers, which would crystallise in a variety of associations – resistance societies, cooperatives, mutual societies – the evolution and peculiarities of which have been extensively analysed by Martínez-Gallego in the period up to 1936. According to him, the conditions of the liberal system in general and the conditions of some governments in particular meant that between 1834 and 1868, and "from 1874 onwards, many resistance societies had to camouflage themselves as friendly societies". In the 19th century, still in Valencia, there was "an extraordinary parallelism between the constitution of friendly societies by industrial workers and the emergence of societies of resistance to capital. The protagonist of the two stories is the same, and the chronological synchrony seems to mean that they are not antagonistic entities. Sometimes the mutualist society gives way to the resistance society; sometimes it is the other way around. Either way, the coexistence of both is perfectly possible".[54] This situation differs from what has been observed in Barcelona and its province, at least in the first decades of the 19th century.

Unfortunately, there are no studies such as those available for Barcelona or Valencia for other Spanish regions. With regard to the transformation of guilds or the resulting creation of mutual benefit societies [SSMs] for other places, we have little data. We know, for example, that in Santander the three SSMs existing in the mid-19th century arose out of guilds and survived until the beginning of the 20th century; that in the mining area of Cartagena, in 1848, there were about 20 mutual societies that had also arisen out of guilds; that some of the first SSMs in Palma de Mallorca had their origins in guilds; and that in Zaragoza in the 1880s a large number of SSMs were still being set up for purposes of trade.[55]

However, these are only references to the genesis and emergence of these companies, and, generally speaking, there is no information about their members and the services they provided during the period of their existence, assuming that this went beyond the date of their formal incorporation, which is sometimes unknown.

Further research will shed new light and nuances on these issues and may be able to determine which SSMs originated from transformations to trade unions and which were parallel initiatives – retaining their name but changing their composition and aims – or ex novo. It is clear that only specific case studies will make this possible.

The predominance of popular mutual societies

We have devoted a great deal of space to considerations about trade unions and mutual societies, so we should not forget that in Spain, as in Europe, a large number of public welfare associations rapidly emerged alongside workers' mutual societies from the beginning of the 19th century. As we pointed out at the beginning of this text, these associations were by definition interclass.

From the data available to us, from the beginning of the 19th century these associations became progressively more important in most places than the workers' mutualism described. Their primacy was total in Vitoria and San Sebastian in the Basque Country, in Asturias, Galicia, Salamanca, La Rioja, Majorca, etc.[56]

It is reasonably clear that popular mutualism, and perhaps even welfare, was predominant in the middle years of the 19th century, that this trend was confirmed in "the transition from the nineteenth to the twentieth century"[57] and that it progressively established itself in the first decades of the 20th century. It is therefore very necessary to study the evolution, extent, and types of welfare, and the function pursued and/or achieved by the notables with their patronage. To this end, it is also essential to study a large number of specific societies, so that we can move from conjectures and/or presumptions to documented affirmations. To our knowledge, no significant steps have been taken in this direction in recent decades.

Some of the characteristics of Spanish mutualism

As far as we know, from the mid-19th century onwards, the most common forms of assistance in most societies – popular, employers' or workers', linked to one political party or another – were for illness or accident, or death (funeral expenses and/or the amount paid to the widow or orphans). At the beginning of the 20th century, with the decline in accident benefit after the law of 1900, the predominant mutual aid in Spain was sickness benefit and the associated medical and apothecary expenses (i.e. health care and pharmaceutical expenses).[58] Although these expenses were not always paid, as the rising cost of pharmaceuticals and medical care, particularly from the beginning of the 20th century, meant that this type of benefit was often limited to the inspection and monitoring of the patient's progress, and the treatment itself and the drugs were often not covered. In the 1920s, various sources indicate that the priority, and sometimes the sole purpose, was to provide the ill with financial support for a maximum generally of three to six months, with a decreasing amount every month.[59]

In this situation, there were various alternatives. They ranged from ceasing to pay such benefits – due to the material impossibility of providing them – thus leaving their members without, or resorting to affiliation with private commercial companies so that they could still offer benefits to their members and families through joint mutualist initiatives, as some companies did, especially in Catalonia.[60]

But undoubtedly the most singular reaction was that of the Madrid socialists, who created a new structure in 1904 The Workers' Mutual Medical, Pharmaceutical and Funeral Co-operative for Associated Workers.

La Mutualidad Obrera Cooperativa Médico-farmacéutica y de Enterramientos de Trabajadores Asociados[61]

The socialist aim was to provide workers with an alternative to the only courses of action available to them: recourse to charity as paupers or contracting the substandard services of private companies that supplied uncertain drug formulas in their pharmacies. The idea was to create an institution of its own capable of providing effective medical care for members and their families, as well as the medicines they might need in the event of illness, and a dignified burial in the event of death. However, this could not be done if each trade union worked independently. Rather they all had to work together, to have a sufficiently large group of potential mutual members and enough income to be able to face any fluctuations caused by adverse situations in any of the trades. For this reason, the indispensable condition for membership was to be a member of one of the trade unions of the Centre of Workers' Societies in Madrid.

There were two types of members: individual members, who paid a membership fee of 1.15 pesetas, and family members, whose monthly membership fee was 2.25 pesetas. In addition to the member, family members could include his or her partner and their children, as well as parents who lived in the same household and were dependent on the member, provided that the number of family members did not exceed five.[62]

The benefits offered were burial in case of death, and medical, surgical, and pharmaceutical services covering all kinds of diseases.

Elsewhere we have referred to the Mutua's development in terms of instruments – dispensaries, medical, nursing, and pharmaceutical staff recruited on a competitive basis, with a scale and social incentives – and its preventive medicine campaigns. But there was still a long way to go, with many crises before it was finally able to create its own Social Centre and Clinic, with two operating theatres and 22 hospital beds. In 1936, the Mutua had 12 surgeries and 13 pharmacies to satisfy the demands of the 12,000 associated families – i.e. it covered some 60,000 people – and in the same year it attended more than 150,000 people for issues of general medicine, surgery, otorhinolaryngology, dermatology, ophthalmology, gynaecology, and paediatrics. Meanwhile, more than 4,500 major surgical operations were performed at its clinic, as well as gynaecology, ophthalmology, and dentistry. In the same year, the Mutua's pharmacies served nearly 250,000 free prescriptions to its members. Indeed the benefits were considerable, much higher than those provided, for example, by the municipal charities and at a much lower cost.

And all this was provided at such a high level of quality that their services could be compared with those of other institutions in our country and it could be claimed, not without reason, that there was no other mutualist organisation in Spain at the time capable of offering its members the same service, in the same way and in the same conditions.

According to the socialist leaders, all this had many salutary effects for the Centro de Sociedades Obreras. The dual membership – trade union and mutualist – contributed to the maintenance and development of the resistance societies. Another effect, undoubtedly not negligible, was to largely prevent desertions as a result of strikes.

Other mutual benefits

We have already pointed out in our discussion of the Mutualidad Obrera socialista de Madrid that the most common forms of assistance from the mid-19th century onwards were sickness, medical and pharmacy expenses, and burial. However, numerous societies proposed other benefits such as permanent disability or retirement, but this seems to have been little more than a declaration of a deep desire or a lure to attract members, and in most cases they had to abandon the idea before or soon after implementation.

However, there are some exceptions to this generalisation. Let us take two examples. The first is the AGEOFE[63] (General Association of Employees and Workers of the Spanish Railways) which rejected sickness benefits from the outset and opted for invalidity and retirement as key benefits which began to be granted progressively and steadily from 1894 onwards. This exception was of particular importance, as the railwaymen's association, with its 17,300 members at the beginning of the century, already accounted for more than 20% of the total number of members, 84,426, of all the SSMs in Spain, and continued to grow until it reached 71,131 in 1935. The annual amount spent on pensions also grew: the 117,520 pesetas paid out in 1900 increased to 12,449,546 in 1935.[64]

The second of our examples is the *El Trabajo* society in Alcoy, which since it was founded in 1882 spent a large part of its budget on what it calls *invalids*, i.e. those who "can no longer work because they have contracted a chronic illness or are too old". Between 1909 and 1942 this amount exceeded the amount spent on sickness benefits. And the Alcoy society was not one of the least important of the popular societies, as at the beginning of the 20th century it had 1,500 members.[65] It is advisable, therefore, to consider our generalisations only within the context of the current level of knowledge. Even less is known about the mutualist implementation of other benefits. For example, although some data is available on mutual unemployment benefits, as we pointed out a decade ago, the field is still largely unexplored in our country.[66]

There remains, therefore, a vast unexplored territory for research on mutualism in the period being considered here.

Some topics have been studied so little that it is only possible to venture generalisations such as that in the early days women tended to be marginalised by statutes and/or practice and that from the 20th century onwards, female-only societies began to increase in number but were overseen totally or partially by men.

It is illustrative what we know about the first female-only society, born in September 1900, in the heart of the Círculo Obrero Ilicitano (founded in March 1885 and controlled from the beginning by the socialists), La Sociedad Feminista La Unión (The Unión Feminist Society) of a popular character with a working class predominance. The aim of the Union was to give women an opportunity in a centre that was male-dominated, working class-based, and under socialist leadership. It was both a resistance and a friendly society, with a board of directors of women and a board of trustees of men. When it was founded, it had 1,200 members. In its resistance role, it was involved in conflicts. In 1903, it separated the resistance from the relief organisations, giving rise to the union Despertar Femenino (Women's Awakening). The Union continued as a mutual benefit society, oscillating between 1,400 and 1,200 members, and in 1908 it established assistance for illness, childbirth, invalidity, and old age.[67]

Control was stricter in Catholic women's mutual societies, which, as in Catholic associations in general, were governed by the ecclesiastical offices of the Circle itself and its protective members, generally people of high social standing, whose contributions generally made the survival of the mutual society possible but also gave them almost total control.[68]

However, about other aspects, we know considerably more.

The size of the mutuals

All available estimates suggest that the average size of an SSM was between 100 and 250 members depending on the time. However, the variability was enormous. For example, in the references collected in *Solidarity from below*, we can see that from a sample of 100 Valencian societies in 1921, the average is 352 members, but the societies ranged from 20 to 1,800 members. For Barcelona, the average size in 1914 was 211, although of the 127 societies analysed, 8 had fewer than 50 members, another 30 had fewer than 100 members, 9 had between 500 and 1,000 members, and 1 had more than 1,000. The 23 SSMs registered in Asturias in 1900 had 3,687 members, i.e. an average of 160 members, but in fact half of them had no more than 100 members, and some even had as few as 25 and 26.[69]

The persistence of a large number of small SSMs meant that as a financial entity it was weak and there was no technical structure to cope with negative eventualities even as predictable as the simple ageing of the initial partners.[70]

One of the ways of reducing the financial burden was to federate or join forces. This was the case of the Unión y Defensa de los Montepíos de Barcelona y sus afueras, founded in 1896, which included mounts of piety, SSMs, benefit societies, and mutual societies. It had 554 member societies and 124,916 members in 1911, 747 and 167,623 in 1915, and, 10 years after its name changed in 1918 to Federación de Sociedades de Socorros Mutuos de la provincia de Barcelona, it reached 827 societies and 289,773.[71]

But this case was more than exceptional; it was unique. During the first third of the 20th century, the capacity of Spanish mutuals to federate was very limited at the provincial level and non-existent at the national level. In line with this, empiricism and the lack of application of actuarial techniques were the norm. Likewise, most SSMs rarely applied modern management techniques, if at all.[72] These issues will be discussed below.

The role played by the state with regard to mutualism

The characteristics of the Spanish mutualist movement discouraged the State's from legislating it. Mutual societies were left out of the insurance law of 1908, because, as we have already indicated, neither the requirements that it demanded nor the control instruments that it put in place were in line with those presumably required of mutual societies in general, and even less so with those of Spanish mutual societies in particular.[73]

The Insurance Act 1908

A few months after the INP was created, an insurance law was passed. It was the first time in Spain that the sector was regulated by a specific general law.

The State established an official register that required all companies to fulfil a series of requirements. Among others, those operating in the life insurance branch had to present the complete tariff of the categories of premiums, and mortality and survival tables on which they based their calculations of the mathematical reserves. In addition to companies having to make a large prior deposit, the Insurance Inspectorate was also set up to supervise the companies' compliance with the law and to avoid any administrative irregularity that could "compromise the interests of the insured" or involve "dangerous management contrary to the technical principles of insurance".

In other words, insurance companies were inspected and supervised, and policyholders were protected. Registration gave companies full rights to conduct the insurance business for which they were registered, as long as they operated in accordance with their statutes and in compliance with legal requirements.

The Insurance Act regulated only insurance companies. It was designed to respond to a market that had been growing since the end of the century.

It therefore expressly excluded from its scope "mounts of piety, SSMs and, in general, those constituted for exclusively charitable purposes provided that their funds are used solely for such purposes, except for administrative expenses" and "mutual associations without fixed premiums or fees of a local, municipal or provincial nature whose purpose is not to make a profit but exclusively to indemnify members for damages or risks that they may suffer to their property".

Mutual societies were still governed, as before, by the generic criteria of the 1887 Law on Associations.[74]

Of course, the insurance law was not designed for them. Neither the requirements it laid down nor the control instruments it put in place were in line with those presumably demanded of mutuals in general, and even less so of Spanish mutuals in particular.

The characteristics of the Spanish mutualist movement continued to make it impossible to legislate, even at times when it might have been in the State's interest to have its support (for example, when the introduction of compulsory social insurance was being considered).

The draft SSM law of 1922

In 1919–21, the Workers' Retirement Scheme marked the beginning of compulsory social insurance in Spain. The regulations were the result of a conference convened by the government in October 1917 to inform the public authorities about compulsory social insurance and to draw up a plan for its implementation. In 1922, the INP organised another conference to study not only maternity insurance but also sickness and disability insurance, which it considered to be directly linked.[75] Maternity insurance was finally approved in 1929.[76]

As early as the 1917 Conference, it had been suggested that if they were to retain a role in the new system, mutual insurance companies needed to be refined "by adapting themselves to the technical requirements of modern insurance and abandoning the empirical procedures which have had such disastrous results in practice". It was even proposed that in order for the mutual societies to be the basis for health insurance, a "law on mutual aid was needed to sanction, regulate and perfect their operation, establishing the requirements they must meet in order to be accepted for the purposes of health insurance, both voluntary and compulsory". After they had heard the mutual societies, qualified people asked the INP to prepare a draft law on mutual benefit societies.

The 1922 Conference, then, opened up new perspectives. The mutualists themselves understood the major role they had been asked to play in the preparations. They were directly involved in two of the general topics of discussion: "Legal and economic claims of the SSM. Whether the SSM and similar institutions should be used for the administration of these insurances and what cooperation they could provide".

A large group of mutualist advocates signed the paper on these issues. It included a preliminary draft law which was to be approved by the Conference.

Leaving aside other aspects, we should point out that the fundamental aspects of the draft law tended to correct or avoid the basic deficiencies that we have been discussing. For example, in addition to the essential requirements of mutual societies – non-profit making, self-management, personal and non-capitalist structure, and democratic participation – other requirements were added regarding the tables or rules used to establish the contributions, the need to demand sufficient contributions to establish reinsurance for their members against the risk of the entity's disappearance, exchange of members, maternity, long illnesses, etc. Reinsurance for which the law obliged the provincial federations to be established when the corresponding bodies were set up.

This obligation to federate at the provincial or regional level was also a key feature of the law. In addition to the function of guaranteeing reinsurance, the federations were constituted as instruments of supervision and control of the mutuals in their geographical areas and as an obligatory channel for their relations with the Higher Council of Mutuality, composed of 13 mutual and 13 government representatives, and the ultimate guarantor of the implementation and observance of the law.

As we have seen, the full introduction of actuarial techniques, compulsory federation in order to enable the reinsurance of obligations, and the monitoring and inspection of compliance with them were issues that had been discussed for a long time. However, although the proposal was accepted without discussion and became part of the conclusions of the Conference, the preliminary draft would not become law in the future[77] because this was not possible at the national level. The disconnection between mutuals and the distrust of external control, together with the characteristics of the movement described above – small size, poor technical and actuarial skills – made any global initiative from the mutualist collective itself impossible and discouraged the possible initiatives of the State in a situation that was by no means favourable to the insurance to which it wanted to commit itself.

Spanish mutual insurance in the 1930s was therefore weak and precarious, largely because it was part of a context in which its competitors, state social security and private insurance companies, also showed shortcomings and limitations.[78]

In this scenario, as we have pointed out above, only one provincial Federation had attended the Conference. In collaboration with political institutions such as the Commonwealth of Catalonia and private bodies such as the Caja de Pensiones, this Federation had been working in favour of mutuality in Catalonia, where the drafters of the law themselves recognised that mutuality was regarded as being "innate in social life, as an indispensable element for the normal functioning of the working-class family".

Thus, the confluence of the most important mutualist movement in Spain with its own government institutions (Generalitat) made Catalonia the first Spanish region in the 1930s to have specific legislation on mutual societies.

Indeed, in the new legality opened up by the Second Republic, the autonomous government of Catalonia legislated on cooperation and mutualism. The first of these laws dealt with cooperatives, mutual societies, and agricultural unions and was "a true regulatory norm for the social economy in Catalonia". Proof of the modernity of the Catalan law is that many of its precepts were practically reproduced in the subsequent legal regulations of Spanish mutuality.[79]

In any case, the scope of application of these two laws was limited to Catalan territory, and they did not remain in force for long. On 5 April 1939, the Franco government, victor of a civil war, annulled the legislation of the Catalan Parliament among many other things.

As far as the text of the Francoist legislation is concerned, it was a continuation of the Republican legislation of Catalonia, but the socio-political situation in which it operated, however, was radically different. Francoism, therefore, ushered in a new period, which would be brought to an end by the 1984 law, part of a new stage of democratic reformulation that would regulate the global scope of private insurance in a new and different way, and end up being consolidated in 1995 with the new law for its regulation and supervision. Although the role of private mutualism in the different stages of both periods, Francoism and democracy, has been sketched out, it is still a field wide open to research.[80,81]

Notes

1 We conceive our text as a complementary update of three previous balance sheets: Santiago CASTILLO: "Las Sociedades de Socorros Mutuos en la España contemporánea", in Santiago CASTILLO (ed.): *Solidaridad desde abajo*, Madrid, Centre of Historical Studies, UGT, 1994, pp. 1–29; ID.: "En torno al mutualismo español contemporáneo. Solidaridad desde abajo revisited", in Elena MAZA (coord.): *Asociacionismo en la España contemporánea*, Valladolid, Universidad de Valladolid, 2003, pp. 61–88; ID.: *Mundo del trabajo y asociacionismo en España:*, 1836–1936. Varias cuestiones, algunas respuestas", pp. 171–205, in Actas VII congreso de la Asociación de Historia Social, Madrid, La Catarata, 2014, thus providing clear continuity and, of course, recurrent ideas.

2 Marcel VAN DER LINDEN: "The Comparative History of Mutual Benefit Societies. Some Queries and Suggestions", Amsterdam, *working paper* préparatoire du *Colloque International sur l'Histoire de la Mutualité: un passé riche d'avenir*, París, 1 a 3 décembre de 1992.

3 Michel RALLE: "El montepío obrero ¿anacronismo o modelo?", *Estudios de Historia Social*, Madrid, 30 (1984), pp. 7–21; Josefina CUESTA: "Las Sociedades de Socorros Mutuos en la España de los años 20. Un silencio en el reformismo social", in VVAA: *El reformismo social en España. La Comisión de Reformas Sociales*, Córdoba, 1987, pp. 301–330; Gérard BREY: "Le mutualisme populaire en Espagne au XIX siècle: l'exemple de Galicie", *Revue de l'Economie Sociale*, March, 1989, pp. 151–159; Feliciano MONTERO and Mariano ESTEBAN DE VEGA: "Aproximación tipológica al mutualismo popular y obrero en España: el mutualismo asistencial", in Santiago CASTILLO (ed.): *La Historia social en España. Actualidad y perspectivas*, Madrid, Siglo XXI, 1991, pp. 457–470.

4 Mercedes LLORENTE ROMERA: *Salud y condición obrera. La sociedad de socorros mutuos de obreros de Soria (1880–1949)*, Soria, Centre of Sorian Studies, 1987; Rafael HERNÁNDEZ: *La Sociedad Cooperativa El Trabajo, 1880–1942*, Alicante, Instituto Juan Gil-Albert, 1988.

5 Faculty of Political Science and Sociology, Complutense University, Madrid, 25–27 June 1992.

6 Santiago CASTILLO: *Las Sociedades de Socorros Mutuos en España. Del Antiguo Régimen a la dictadura de Franco*. Report to the International Conference in Paris, Madrid; ID.: *Les sociétés de Secours Mutuels en Espagne: de l´Ancien Régime à la dictature de Franco,* Paris; ID.: *Mutual Benefits Societies in Spain: from the Ancien Régime to Franco´s Dictatorship*, Amsterdam, 1992.

7 Marcel VAN DER LINDEN: *Social Security Mutualism. The Comparative History of Mutual Benefit Societies*, Berna, Peter Lang, 1996, p. 12.

8 Santiago CASTILLO: *Solidaridad desde abajo. Trabajadores y Socorros Mutuos en la España Contemporánea*, Madrid, Centre of Historical Studies-UGT, *NationalConfederation of Private Mutual Societies*, 1994.

9 In the bibliography, we indicate the authors and titles of the papers contained in the cited volume.

10 Julián Besteiro School, Madrid 17–19 November 1995.

11 Researchers and scholars discussed their work with representatives of the public Social Security, including its Secretary of State, and the leaderships of the *Spanish Confederation of Private Mutual Societies.*

12 In the bibliography, we list the authors and titles of the texts presented, which were not published collectively this time.

13 A third meeting was prepared but did not materialise due to lack of funding.

14 Santiago CASTILLO: “La mutualité et la construction du système de protection sociale en Espagne”, in Comité d´Histoire de la Sécurité Sociale, *Un siècle de protection sociale en Europe*, Paris, Documentation Française, 2001, pp. 103–123; ID.: “Mutualité et santé dans l’Espagne Contemporaine, 1839–2002”, in Dominique ASSAYAG; François GUEDJ, and Patricia TOUCAS-TRUYEN (coord.): *La santé in Europe. Entre marché et solidarité. Complémentaire santé. Entre logique mutualiste et logique assurantielle*, Paris, Les Éditions de l’Atelier, 2003, pp. 29–41; Elena MAZA: “Mutualité et protection sociale en Espagne, 1887–1936”, *Histoire et Sociétés*, 16 (2005), pp. 44–54.

15 Santiago CASTILLO: “En torno al mutualismo español contemporáneo. Solidaridad desde abajo revisited”, in Elena MAZA (coord.): Asociacionismo en la España contemporánea, Valladolid, Universidad de Valladolid, 2003, pp. 61–88.

16 Genís BARNOSELL: “Las Sociedades de Socorros Mutuos en Barcelona 1810–1845. Una comparación con el sindicalismo”, and Pilar LEÓN: “Higienismo y previsión social a través de una Sociedad de Socorros Mutuos: el Consultorio de Niños de Pecho de La Conciliación (1905–1916)”, in Santiago CASTILLO and Rafael RUZAFA (coord.): La previsión social en la historia, Madrid, AHS, 2009 (CD edition).

17 Fernando DÍEZ: “La previsión social en la España del siglo XVIII. Realidad, reforma e historia comparada”, in Santiago CASTILLO and Rafael RUZAFA (coord.): *La previsión social en la Historia*, Actas del VI Congreso de Historia Social, Madrid, Siglo XXI, 2009, pp. 67–98; Francesc Andreu MARTÍNEZ-GALLEGO: “Tocata y fuga de la fábrica urbana. Colisión artesana y disciplina obrera (Valencia, 1840–1880)”, in *Sociología del Trabajo*, 19 (1993), pp. 123–141; Santiago CASTILLO and Rafael RUZAFA (coord.): *La previsión social en la Historia*, Actas del VI Congreso de Historia Social, Madrid, Siglo XXI, 2009; Elena MAZA: “El mutualismo en España, 1900–1941. Ajustes e interferencias”, in Santiago CASTILLLO and Rafael

RUZAFA (coord.): *La previsión social en la Historia*. Actas del VI Congreso de Historia Social, Madrid, Siglo XXI, 2009, pp. 333–368.

18 The papers from the Franco period are not included in the final bibliography, as they go beyond the time frame of this chapter.

19 Santiago CASTILLO and Rafael RUZAFA (coord.): *La previsión social en la Historia*, Actas del VI Congreso de Historia Social, Madrid, Siglo XXI, 2008, CD edition; *La previsión social ....*

20 Francesc Andreu MARTÍNEZ-GALLEGO: *Esperit d'associació: cooperativisme i mutualisme laics entre 1834 i 1936*, Valencia, PUV, 2010.

21 Fernando LARGO JIMÉNEZ: *Mutualismo y capital social. El papel de la Federación de mutualidades de Cataluña, 1896–1936*, Barcelona, Universidad Autónoma de Barcelona, 2017.

22 Rafael RUZAFA ORTEGA and Rocío GARCÍA ABAD: "Formas de previsión social en la zona minera vizcaína. Siglos XIX–XX", in Rafael RUZAFA (ed.): *De las Hermandades a la Seguridad Social*, Madrid, Catarata, 2018, pp. 43–71.

23 Margarita VILAR RODRÍGUEZ: "La cobertura social al margen del Estado: asociacionismo obrero y socorros mutuos en Galicia (c. 1839–1935)", *IX Congreso Internacional de la AEHE*, Murcia, 2008; "La cobertura social a través de los socorros mutuos obreros, 1839–1935. ¿Una alternativa al Estado para afrontar los fallos del mercado?", in Jerònia PONS and Javier SILVESTRE (eds.): *Los orígenes del Estado del Bienestar en España, 1900–1945: los seguros de accidentes, vejez, desempleo y enfermedad*, Zaragoza, Universidad de Zaragoza, 2010, pp. 85–122.

24 Margarita VILAR RODRÍGUEZ and Jerònia PONS: "El papel de las sociedades de socorro mutuo en la cobertura del riesgo de enfermedad en España (1870–1942)", Universidad Pablo Olavide, Carmona (Sevilla), *X Congreso Internacional de la AEHE*, September, 2011. The paper of Margarita VILAR: "La cobertura social ...", pp. 85–122, allows us to appreciate his approach to the social coverage of mutual societies in parallel to the deployment of such coverage by the State for the period 1900–1945.

25 Jerònia PONS and Margarita VILAR-RODRÍGUEZ: *La gestión del seguro de accidentes del trabajo en España: De mutuas patronales a entidades colaboradoras de la seguridad social 1900–2019*, Madrid, Tesorería G. de la Seguridad Social, Ministerio de Inclusión, Seguridad Social y Migraciones, 2020.

26 See text and note 17 in this same contribution.

27 Santiago CASTILLO: "Las Sociedades de Socorros ...", pp. 1–29.

28 It is by no means a question of ignoring the importance of property risks. They are even fundamental in the world of agricultural work. The issue is that, as far as we know, there is a lack of work on the subject.

29 For a schematic reference to the evolution of these terms from the 19th century to the present, see Santiago CASTILLO: "La mutualité et la construction ...", pp. 104–106.

30 These concepts are clearly fragile and require multiple nuances. They are used for two fundamental reasons: they have been in conventional use since the subject was first discussed in writing, and we believe them to be sufficient for the type of considerations we will be making here.

31 Antonio MARTÍN VALVERDE: *La legislación social en la historia de España: de la revolución liberal a 1936*, Madrid, Congreso de los Diputados, 1987.

32 Elena MAZA: "El mutualismo en España, 1900–1936: ajustes e interferencias", in Santiago CASTILLO and Rafael RUZAFA (eds.): *La previsión social*

en la historia. Comunicaciones, Madrid, Asociación de Historia Social, 2008, pp. 333–367, CD edition.

33 Alejandro GALLART FOLCH: *Derecho Español del Trabajo*, Barcelona, Labor, 1936, p. 355.

34 Santiago CASTILLO: *Solidaridad desde abajo …*; Josefina CUESTA: "Las Sociedades de …", pp. 301–330.

35 For extensive analyses of these statistics: Feliciano MONTERO: *Los seguros sociales en la España del siglo XX. Orígenes y antecedentes de la previsión social*, Madrid, Ministerio de Trabajo, 1988; Jean Louis GUEREÑA: "Fuentes para la historia de la sociabilidad en la España Contemporánea", *Estudios de Historia Social,* 50-51 (1989), pp. 273–305; Elena MAZA: "Hacia una interpretación del mutualismo español decimonónico: peculiaridades y polivalencias", in Santiago CASTILLO (ed.): *Solidaridad desde abajo*, Madrid, UGT, Centre of Historical Studies, 1994, pp. 392–407.

36 IRS: *Estadística de la Asociación Obrera en 1° de noviembre de 1904*, Madrid, IRS, 1907; ID.: *Estadística de las Instituciones de ahorro, cooperación y previsión en 1° de noviembre de 1904*, Madrid, IRS, 1908; ID.: *Estadística de Asociaciones. Censo electoral de Asociaciones profesionales para la renovación de la parte electiva del Instituto y de las Juntas de Reformas Sociales y relación de las Instituciones no profesionales de ahorro, cooperación y previsión in 30 de noviembre de 1916*, Madrid, IRS, 1917.

37 Santiago CASTILLO: *Las Sociedades de Socorros Mutuos …*; ID.; *Solidaridad desde abajo …*; ID.: "En torno al …", pp. 61–88. We could not extend these estimates to later periods because, on the one hand, the official figures for 1915–1925 posed serious problems of interpretation and, on the other, the number of existing studies or research on the 1920s and 1930s was still limited. Esteban RODRÍGUEZ OCAÑA: "La asistencia médica colectiva en España hasta 1936", in VVAA: *Historia de la acción social pública en España. Beneficencia y previsión*, Madrid, Ministerio de Trabajo, 1990, pp. 322–359; INP: *La cuestión del seguro de Enfermedad ante la X^a reunión de la Conferencia Internacional del Trabajo (Ginebra, mayo 1927)*, Madrid, INP, 1927; Elena MAZA: "La horizontalidad de las solidaridades. El mutualismo en la España contemporánea", *Ayer*, 25 (1997), pp. 73–102.

38 A balance sheet for the first year of the research team on Castilla y León: Elena MAZA: *Sociabilidad en la España Contemporánea. Historiografía y problemas metodológicos*, Valladolid, Universidad de Valladolid, 2002. For Castilla-La Mancha: GEAS: *España en sociedad. Las asociaciones a finales del siglo XIX*, Cuenca, Ediciones Universidad de Castilla-La Mancha, 1998; Francisco ALÍA and Rafael VILLENA: "Asociacionismo sociabilidad en Castilla-La Mancha. Nuevas fuentes, nuevas aportaciones", in Elena MAZA (coord.): *Sociabilidad en la España*, "…" pp. 77–101.

39 Elena MAZA: "Preferencias y destinatarios del asociacionismo vallisoletano en su rodaje contemporáneo", in Elena MAZA (coord.): *Asociacionismo en la España contemporánea: vertientes y análisis interdisciplinar*, Valladolid, Universidad de Valladolid, 2003, pp.147–174; Francesc Andreu MARTÍNEZ-GALLEGO: *Esperit d'associació …*; Margarita VILAR RODRÍGUEZ: "La cobertura social al margen … ; "La cobertura social …", pp. 85–122.

40 Searchable database at: https://www.irmu.org/base-de-dades-associacionisme. Popular associationism is understood as that which broadly organises the working classes of the countryside and the city, and any overarching system, even if it is of an interclass type. The characteristics of the BDACC are explained

in Ramon ARNABAT and Agustí AGRAMUNT: "Eines metodològiques: la Base de dades de l'associacionisme català contemporani", in Montserrat DUCH, Ramon ARNABAT, and Antoni GAVALDÀ (eds.): *La Catalunya asociada (1868–1938)*, Valencia, PUV, 2020, pp. 39–49.

41 For example the following studies: Mercedes LLORENTE ROMERA: *Salud y condición obrera …*; Rafael HERNÁNDEZ: *La Sociedad Cooperativa …*; Jordi IBARZ: "El Montepío de San Pedro Pescador y las Sociedades de Socorros Mutuos de los estibadores de Barcelona (1890–1939)", in Santiago CASTILLO (ed.): *Solidaridad desde abajo*, Madrid, UGT, Centre of Historical Studies, 1994, pp. 107–123; Antonio Javier SÁNCHEZ CASTRO: "La Sociedad de Obreros Amigos de la villa de Vegadeo", in Santiago CASTILLO (ed.): *Solidaridad desde abajo*, Madrid, UGT, Centre of Historical Studies, 1994, pp. 285–305; Pere FULLANA and Antoni MARIMÓN: *Història del "Montepío" de Previsió de l'Arraval de Santa Catalina. Centenario, 1894–1994*, Palma de Mallorca, Escola Natzaret, 1994; Miguel José GARCÍA GONZÁLEZ: *Historia de la Obrera de Ponferrada*, Ponferrada, Publicación del autor y La Obrera, 2004; Pilar LEÓN SANZ: "La concertación de la asistencia en la enfermedad en La Sociedad de Obreros *La Conciliación* (1902–1919)", in *Navarra: Memoria e Imagen*, Pamplona, Eunate, 2006, vol. II, pp. 97–108; ID.; "Creando identidad. Educación y recreación en *La Conciliación*, 1902–1933", in Santiago CASTILLO (coord..): *Comunicaciones a VII congreso de la Asociación de Historia Social de España. Mundo del trabajo y asociacionismo in España. Collegia, gremios, mutuas, sindicatos …* Madrid, Asociación de Historia Social, 2013, CD edition.

42 Elena SÁNCHEZ DE MADARIAGA: "De la caridad fraternal al Socorro Mutuo. Las Hermandades de Socorro de Madrid en el siglo XVIII", in Santiago CASTILLO (ed.): *Solidaridad desde abajo*, Madrid, UGT, Centre of Historical Studies, 1994, pp. 31–50.

43 Antonio RUMEU DE ARMAS: *Historia de la Previsión social en España. Cofradías, Gremios, Hermandades, Montepíos*, Madrid, Revista de Derecho Privado, 1944; Fernando DÍEZ: *Viles y mecánicos. Trabajo y sociedad en la Valencia preindustrial*, Valencia, IVEI, 1990.

44 Santiago CASTILLO: "Las Sociedades de Socorros …", pp. 1–29.

45 Elena SÁNCHEZ DE MADARIAGA: "De la caridad fraternal …", pp. 31–50.

46 Alfons ZARZOSO ORELLANA: *La pràctica mèdica a la Catalunya del segle XVIII*, Doctoral thesis, Institut Universitari d'Història Jaume Vicens Vives, Universitat Pompeu Fabra, Barcelona, 2003; ID.: "El fenómeno asociativo y la preocupación por la salud entre las clases trabajadoras de Barcelona en el tránsito del siglo XIX", in Santiago CASTILLO and Rafael RUZAFA (coords.): *La previsión social en la historia*, Madrid, Siglo XXI, 2009 (CD edition).

47 Genís BARNOSELL: "Las Sociedades de Socorros Mutuos en Barcelona 1810–1845. Una comparación con el sindicalismo", in Santiago CASTILLO and Rafael RUZAFA (coord.): *La previsión social en la historia*, Madrid, AHS, 2009 (CD edition).

48 Gloria Ángeles FRANCO RUBIO: "Asociacionismo femenino en la España del siglo XVIII: las hermandades de socorro de mujeres", *Cuadernos de Historia Moderna*, 16 (1995), pp. 179–199; Elena SÁNCHEZ DE MADARIAGA: "Solidaridad popular femenina: las hermandades de socorro de mujeres en el Madrid del siglo XVIII", in Pilar PÉREZ CANTÓ and Elena POSTIGO (eds.): *Autoras y protagonistas*, Madrid, Universidad Autónoma, 2000.

49 Fernando DÍEZ: "La previsión social ...", pp. 67–98.
50 Miguel IZARD: *Industrialización y obrerismo: las Tres Clases de Vapor, 1869–1913*, Barcelona, Ariel, 1973, p. 94.
51 Genís BARNOSELL: *Orígens del sindicalisme català*, Vic, Eumo, 1999.
52 Genís BARNOSELL: "Las Sociedades de Socorros Mutuos ...".
53 Francesc Andreu MARTÍNEZ-GALLEGO: "Disolución gremial y constitución societaria. Los términos del vínculo. Valencia 1834–1868", in Santiago CASTILLO (ed.): Solidaridad *desde abajo*, Madrid, UGT, Centre of Historical Studies, 1994, pp. 51–69; *Esperit d'associació ...* , p. 47.
54 Francesc Andreu MARTÍNEZ-GALLEGO: *Esperit d'associació ...* , p. 78 and p. 119.
55 José Ignacio BARRÓN: *Historia del socialismo in Cantabria. Los orígenes 1887–1905*, Santander, Partido Socialista de Cantabria, 1987; Juan Bautista VILAR et al.: *El movimiento obrero en el distrito de Cartagena-La Unión (1840–1930)*, Murcia, Biblioteca murciana de Bolsillo, 1987, pp. 84–86; Pere FULLANA: "Las sociedades de socorros mutuos en Mallorca en la segunda mitad del siglo XIX (1836–1900)", in Santiago CASTILLO (ed.): *Solidaridad desde abajo*, Madrid, UGT, Centre of Historical Studies, 1994, pp. 347–371; Carlos SOLÁ AYAPE: "Dos ejemplos de Sociedades de Socorros Mutuos en la Zaragoza de mediados del siglo XIX: La Sociedad de Horneros de San Miguel y el Centro Industrial o el asociacionismo de los fabricantes zaragozanos", in Santiago CASTILLO (ed.): *Solidaridad desde abajo*, Madrid, UGT, Centre of Historical Studies, 1994, pp. 307–317; Juan Jaime LÓPEZ GONZÁLEZ and José GARCÍA LASAOSA: *Orígenes del movimiento obrero en Aragón (1854–1890)*, Zaragoza, Diputación de Zaragoza e Institución Fernando el Católico, 1982.
56 Antonio RIVERA: "Desarrollo y crisis del modelo de sociedad de socorros (Vitoria, 1849–1938)", pp. 135–143; M. Ascensión MARTÍNEZ MARTÍN: "Las sociedades de socorros mutuos en Guipúzcoa: 1880–1936", pp. 155–175; Juan Jesús RODRÍGUEZ GONZÁLEZ: "Las sociedades de socorros mutuos en Asturias, 1859–1900", pp. 189–203; Jorge URÍA: "Mutualismo y sociedades de socorros mutuos en Asturias. Una visión de conjunto (1898–1936)", pp. 225–243; Jean Louis GUEREÑA: "El espacio mutualista en la sociabilidad popular de la Restauración (1875–1900). El ejemplo asturiano", pp. 205–223; Gérard BREY: "Mutualismo popular y mutualismo obrero en Galicia (1841–1916)", pp. 245–255; Carmen FERNÁNDEZ CASANOVA: "La situación del asociacionismo mutualista de trabajadores de El Ferrol y Santiago, 1884–1903", pp. 257–283, All the texts cited up to this point in Santiago CASTILLO (ed.): Solidaridad desde abajo, Madrid, UGT, Centre of Historical Studies, 1994; Mª José LACALZADA: *La Rioja 1852–1902. Un eslabón entre la tradición y el progreso,* Zaragoza, Libreria Central, 19, pp. 52–55; Jerònia PONS: *El sector seguros en Baleares: Empresas y empresarios en los siglos XIX y XX*, Palma de Mallorca, El Tall Editorial, 1998, pp. 81–99 and 116–127; Pere FULLANA: "Las sociedades de socorros ...", pp. 347–371; Pere FULLANA and Antoni MARIMÓN: *Història del "Montepío" ...*
57 Feliciano MONTERO and Mariano ESTEBAN DE VEGA: "Aproximación tipológica ...", pp. 457–470.
58 Álvaro LÓPEZ NÚÑEZ: *El seguro obrero en España*, Madrid, IRS, 1908; Santiago CASTILLO: *Solidaridad desde abajo ...*

59 Luis JORDANA DE POZAS: "Las Sociedades de Socorros Mutuos en el reino de Valencia", in *Actas de la Conferencia sobre el seguro de enfermedad e invalidez*, Barcelona, 1922, pp. 279–321; Esteban RODRÍGUEZ OCAÑA: "La asistencia médica ...", pp. 322–359; Margarita VILAR RODRÍGUEZ and Jerònia PONS: "El papel de las sociedades ...".

60 We are referring to the creation of the *Cooperative Pharmacy* for the *Union and Defence of the Montepíos of Barcelona*, the embryo of the Catalan Federation of Mutual Societies, to which we shall return.

61 In this section we summarise what has been developed in Santiago CASTILLO: "La Mutualidad obrera Médico-farmacéutica y el socialismo madrileño en el primer tercio del siglo XX", in MORAL (coord.): *Catálogo de la exposición conmemorativa del Centenario de la Casa del Pueblo de Madrid*, 1908–2008, Madrid, UGT-SECC, 2008, pp. 243–249.

62 Through family members, the Mutualidad extended its benefits beyond *manual workers*. Journalists, employees of private offices, banks, and the various public administrations soon enjoyed its benefits. Many small industrialists, as well as retired military personnel, also received benefits and even provided burial services for priests.

63 Asociación General de Empleados y Obreros de los Ferrocarriles de España

64 Santiago CASTILLO: "Las Sociedades de Socorros ...", pp. 1–29.

65 Rafael HERNÁNDEZ: *La Sociedad Cooperativa* ..., p. 42.

66 Santiago CASTILLO: "En torno al ...", pp. 78–79.

67 Francisco MORENO SÁEZ: *El movimiento obrero en Elche (1890–1931)*, Alicante, Instituto Alicantino de Cultura, 1987, pp. 169–170.

68 Amelia GARCÍA CHECA: "Ideología y práctica del mutualismo católico femenino", in Santiago CASTILLO (ed.): *Solidaridad desde abajo*, Madrid, UGT, Centre of Historical Studies, 1994, pp. 125–134.

69 Santiago CASTILLO: "Las Sociedades de Socorros ...", pp. 1–29; Jean Louis GUEREÑA: "El espacio mutualista ...", pp. 205–223; Pere SOLÁ I GUSSINYER: "El mutualismo contemporáneo en una sociedad industrial. Anotaciones sobre el caso catalán (1880–1939)", pp. 71-85, in Santiago CASTILLO (ed.): *Solidaridad desde abajo*, Madrid, UGT, Centre of Historical Studies, 1994.

70 Luis JORDANA DE POZAS: "Las Sociedades de Socorros ...", pp. 279–321.

71 Marcel MORETA I AMAT: "Cataluña en el movimiento mutualista de Previsión Social en España", in Santiago CASTILLO (ed.): *Solidaridad desde abajo*, Madrid, UGT, Centre of Historical Studies, 1994, pp. 503–539; Pere SOLÁ I GUSSINYER: "El mutualismo ...". The in-depth study of the role played by this institution, maintained after numerous vicissitudes up to the present day as *Federació de Mutualitats de Catalunya,* is a key element in the pending tasks of research on Spanish mutualism. Fortunately, this lack is beginning to diminish, see in the bibliography of Fernando LARGO JIMÉNEZ: "Capital social y mutualismo: la Federación de Sociedades de Socorros Mutuos de Cataluña, 1896–1946", in Santiago CASTILLO (coord.): *Comunicaciones VII Congreso de Historia Social. Mundo del trabajo y asociacionismo en España*, Madrid, Asociación de Historia Social, 2013, CD edition; ID.: "La sociabilidad como instrumento del mutualismo. El caso de la Federación de Sociedades de Socorros Mutuos de Cataluña, 1896–1936", in Santiago CASTILLO and Montserrat DUCH (coord.): Comunicaciones al *VIII Congreso de Historia Social. Sociabilidades en la Historia,* Madrid, Asociación de Historia Social, 2015, CD edition; ID.: *Mutualismo y capital social* ...

72 Among the exceptions is AGEOFE, which, as early as the end of 1900, was already considering the application of actuarial principles, which meant that it had to adapt its income levels and profitability in advance to the foreseeable calculated costs, and, to this end, it made the necessary statutory and technical changes.

73 Santiago CASTILLO: "La Charte de la Mutualité et la loi de 1908 en Espagne", in Michel DREYFUS, Bernard GIBAUD and André GUESLIN (ed.): *Démocratie, Solidarité et Mutualité. Autour de la loi de 1898*, Paris, Economica, 1999, pp. 220–232.

74 The Insurance Act, however, required mutuals to submit their statutes or regulations, a sample of their policies, and copies of their annual balance sheets to the General Insurance Inspectorate but ... no penalty was established in the case of non-compliance.

75 INP: *Conferencia de Seguros Sociales. Celebrada en Madrid los días 24 a 31 de octubre de 1917*, Madrid, INP, 1917; ID.: *Conferencia Nacional de Seguros*, Vol. I, *Ponencias. Actas. Conclusiones*,Vol. II, *Documentos de información*, Madrid, INP, 1922.

76 The bibliography on the implementation of social insurance in this period is very extensive, ranging from the pioneering books by Feliciano MONTERO: *Los seguros sociales ...*; Josefina CUESTA: *Hacia los seguros sociales obligatorios. La crisis de la Restauración*, Madrid, Ministerio de Trabajo y de la Seguridad Social, 1988; Mercedes SAMANIEGO: *La unificación de los seguros sociales a debate. La Segunda República*, Madrid, Ministerio de Trabajo y Seguridad Social, 1988, to more recent views such as those contained in Santiago CASTILLO (ed.): *Solidaridad, seguridad, bienestar. Cien años de protección social in España*, Madrid, Ministerio de Trabajo e Inmigración, 2008; Santiago CASTILLO and Rafael RUZAFA: *La previsión social ...*; Jerònia PONS and Javier SILVESTRE (eds.): *Los orígenes del Estado del Bienestar en España, 1900–1945: los seguros de accidentes, vejez, desempleo y enfermedad*, Zaragoza, Prensas U. de Z, 2010.

77 INP: *Conferencia Nacional de Seguros de enfermedad, invalidez y maternidad. Barcelona, noviembre de 1922*, Madrid, S. de la S de M. Minuesa de los Ríos, 2 vols, 1925.

78 Margarita VILAR RODRÍGUEZ: "La cobertura social ...", pp. 85–122.

79 *Ley de Mutualidades*, de la Generalitat, 22 March 1934. A not inconsiderable number of fundamental aspects of this law "were practically reproduced by The Spanish Law of 1941" its regulation of 1943 and *Ley de Ordenación de los seguros privados* of 2 August 1984, and *Ley de Ordenación y Supervisión de los seguros privados* of 5 October 1995. José Mª ANTRÁS: "La ley de Mutualidades de Cataluña de 22 de marzo de 1934", [presented at the 2nd *Encuentro Internacional*] in *Mutual*, 2 (June 1996), pp. 15–16.

80 An overview of both periods in Santiago CASTILLO: "La mutualité et la construction ...", pp. 119–123. Broader and more detailed views: Luis Miguel AVALOS MUÑOZ and Jerónimo SANZ VALDÉS: "Las Mutualidades de previsión social: Antecedentes, situación actual y perspectivas", in Santiago CASTILLO: *Solidaridad desde abajo*, Madrid, UGT, Centre of Historical Studies, 1994, pp. 87–105 and pp. 541–567; Cristobal SARRIAS: "Las Mutualidades de Previsión social in España, 1939–2008", in Santiago CASTILLO and Rafael RUZAFA (coord.): *La previsión social en la historia*, Madrid, Siglo XXI, 2009, pp. 369–399; José Antonio AJURIA: "La Previsión

Social Complementaria in Euskadi, 1970–2008", pp. 401–436 in Santiago CASTILLO and Rafael RUZAFA (coord.): *La previsión social en la historia*, Madrid, Siglo XXI, 2009.

81 The bibliography only includes titles of works used in the preparation of this text.

References

AJURIA, José Antonio: "La Previsión Social Complementaria in Euskadi, 1970–2008", in Santiago CASTILLO and Rafael RUZAFA (coord.): *La previsión social en la historia*, Madrid, Siglo XXI, 2009 (CD edition), pp. 401–436.

ALÍA, Francisco and VILLENA, Rafael: "Asociacionismo, sociabilidad en Castilla-La Mancha. Nuevas fuentes, nuevas aportaciones", in Elena MAZA (coord.): *Sociabilidad en España*, Valladolid, Universidad de Valladolid, 2002, pp. 77–101.

ALONSO OLEA, Eduardo José: "El mutualismo patronal en Vizcaya. La Sociedad de Seguros mutuos de Vizcaya sobre accidentes de trabajo, 1930–1936", *[Presented at the 2nd Encuentro Internacional]*, Bilbao, Mutua Vizcaya Industrial, 1995.

ANTRÁS, José Mª: "La ley de Mutualidades de Cataluña de 22 de marzo de 1934", *[Presented at the 2nd Encuentro Internacional] in Mutual*, 2 June 1996, pp. 26–34.

ARNABAT MATA, Ramon: "Las sociedades de socorros mutuos in la Catalunya rural 1879–1939", in Santiago CASTILLO (ed.): *Solidaridad desde abajo*, Madrid, UGT, Centre of Historical Studies, 1994, pp. 87–105.

ARNABAT MATA, Ramon: *Asociaros y seréis Fuertes. Sociabilidades, modernizaciones y ciudadanías en España, 1860–1930*, Zaragoza, Prensas Universitarias de Zaragoza, 2019.

ARNABAT, Ramon and AGRAMUNT, Agustí: "Eines metodològiques: la base de dades de l'associacionisme català contemporani", in Montserrat DUCH, Ramon ARNABAT, and Antoni GAVALDÀ (eds.): *La Catalunya asociada (1868–1938)*, Valencia, PUV, 2020, pp. 39–49.

ARTOLA SAN MIGUEL, Asier: "'Por vía de hermandad y buena amistad. Una aproximación al mutualismo guipuzcoano desde Tolosa y su comarca (1840–1936)", in Rafael RUZAFA (ed.): *De las Hermandades a la Seguridad Social*, Madrid, Catarata, 2018, pp. 72–106.

AVALOS MUÑOZ, Luis Miguel and SANZ VALDÉS, Jerónimo: "Las Mutualidades de previsión social: Antecedentes, situación actual y perspectivas", in Santiago CASTILLO: *Solidaridad desde abajo*, Madrid, UGT, Centre of Historical Studies, 1994, pp. 87–105 and pp. 541–567.

BARNOSELL, Genís: *Orígens del sindicalisme català*, Vic, Eumo, 1999.

BARNOSELL, Genís: "'Salir de esta ciudad, no siendo fuera del Principado. Organizaciones locales y socorros regionales (Barcelona y Cataluña, 1800–1845)", *Actas del X Simposio de Historia Económica. Análisis de Redes en la Historia Económica*, Bellaterra, 2005 (CD edition).

BARNOSELL, Genís: "Relaciones conflictivas. Maestros y mancebos en Barcelona (1820–1856)", in Vicent SANZ and José PIQUERAS (ed.s): En *el nombre del oficio. El trabajador especializado: corporativismo, adaptación y protesta*, Madrid, Biblioteca Nueva, 2005, pp. 23–46.

BARNOSELL, Genís: "Las Sociedades de Socorros Mutuos en Barcelona 1810–1845. Una comparación con el sindicalismo", in Santiago CASTILLO and Rafael RUZAFA (coord.): *La previsión social en la historia*, Madrid, Siglo XXI, 2009 (CD edition).

BARRÓN, José Ignacio: *Historia del socialismo in Cantabria. Los orígenes 1887–1905*, Santander, Partido Socialista de Cantabria, 1987.

BERRIOCHOA, Pedro: "Auzolan y Hermandades de ganado en el caserío vasco en los siglos XIX y XX", in Rafael RUZAFA (ed.): *De las Hermandades a la Seguridad Social. Estudios sobre previsión social en el País Vasco, siglos XIX-XXI*, Madrid, La Catarata, 2018, pp. 17–42.

BERZAL, Enrique: "Educación católica versus escuela laica durante la IIª República. La Mutualidad de padres de familia de Valladolid, 1933–36", [Presented at the 2nd *Encuentro Internacional*] 1995.

BREY, Gérard: "Le mutualisme populaire en Espagne au XIX siècle: l'exemple de Galicie", *Revue de l'Economie Sociale*, March, 1989, pp. 151–159.

BREY, Gérard: "Histoire du secours mutuel en Espagne", *Bulletin d'Històire Contemporaine de l'Espagne*, 17–18 (1993), pp. 96–107.

BREY, Gérard: "Mutualismo popular y mutualismo obrero en Galicia (1841–1916)", in Santiago CASTILLO (ed.): *Solidaridad desde abajo*, Madrid, UGT, Centre of Historical Studies, 1994, pp. 245–255.

CANAL, Jordi: "La sociabilidad en los estudios sobre la España contemporánea. Una revisión", in Elena MAZA (ed.): *Sociabilidad en la España contemporánea. Historiografía y problemas metodológicos*, Valladolid, Universidad de Valladolid, 2002, pp. 35–55.

CARASA SOTO, Pedro: "El mutualismo en los sindicatos agrícolas y en las Cajas rurales en el primer tercio del siglo XX", in Santiago CASTILLO (ed.): *Solidaridad desde abajo*, Madrid, UGT, Centre of Historical Studies, 1994, pp. 447–467.

CASTILLO, Santiago: *Las Sociedades de Socorros Mutuos en España. Del Antiguo Régimen a la dictadura de Franco. Report to the International Conference in Paris, Madrid, 1992; Les sociétés de Secours Mutuels en Espagne: de l´Ancien Régime à la dictature de Franco, Paris, 1992; Mutual Benefits Societies in Spain: From the Ancien Régime to Franco's Dictatorship*, Amsterdam, 1992.

CASTILLO, Santiago (ed.) *Solidaridad desde abajo. Trabajadores y Socorros Mutuos en la España Contemporánea*, Madrid, Centre of Historical Studies-UGT-Confederación Nacional de Entidades de Previsión, 1994.

CASTILLO, Santiago: "Las Sociedades de Socorros Mutuos en la España contemporánea", in Santiago CASTILLO (ed.): *Solidaridad desde abajo*, Madrid, Centre of Historical Studies, UGT, 1994, pp. 1–29.

CASTILLO, Santiago: "Les sociétés de Secours Mutuels in Espagne Contemporaine", in Michel DREYFUS and Bernard GIBAUD (drs.): *Mutualités de tous les pays. Un passé riche d'avenir*, Mutualité Française, 1995, pp 141–152.

CASTILLO, Santiago: "Mutual Benefits Societies in Spain in the Nineteenth and Twentieth Centuries", in Marcel VAN DER LINDEN (ed.): *Social Security Mutualism*, Peter Lang, 1996, pp. 273–286.

CASTILLO, Santiago: "La Charte de la Mutualité et la loi de 1908 en Espagne", in Michel DREYFUS, Bernard GIBAUD, and André GUESLIN (eds.): *Démocratie, Solidarité et Mutualité. Autour de la loi de 1898*, Paris, Economica, 1999, pp. 220–232.

CASTILLO, Santiago: "La mutualité et la construction du système de protection sociale en Espagne", in *Comité d'Histoire de la Sécurité Sociale, Un siècle de protection sociale en Europe*, París, Documentation Française, 2001, pp. 103–123.

CASTILLO, Santiago: "Mutualité et santé dans l'Espagne Contemporaine, 1839–2002", in Dominique ASSAYAG, François GUEDJ, and Patricia TOUCAS-TRUYEN (coord.): *La santé in Europe. Entre marché et solidarité. Complémentaire santé. Entre logique mutualiste et logique assurantielle*, Paris, Les Éditions de l'Atelier, 2003, pp. 29–41.

CASTILLO, Santiago: "En torno al mutualismo español contemporáneo. Solidaridad desde abajo revisited", in Elena MAZA (coord.): *Asociacionismo en la España contemporánea*, Valladolid, Universidad de Valladolid, 2003, pp. 61–88.

CASTILLO, Santiago: "Mutualidad y salud en la España contemporánea, 1839–2002", in *Mutual*, 14 (2005), pp. 11–18 [Spanish versión of Santiago Castillo, 2003].

CASTILLO, Santiago: "La Mutualidad obrera Médico-farmacéutica y el socialismo madrileño en el primer tercio del siglo XX", in Enrique MORAL (coord.): *Catálogo de la exposición conmemorativa del Centenario de la Casa del Pueblo de Madrid, 1908–2008*, Madrid, UGT-SECC, 2008, pp. 243–249.

CASTILLO, Santiago (ed.): *Solidaridad, seguridad, bienestar. Cien años de protección social in España*, Madrid, Ministerio de Trabajo e Inmigración, 2008.

CASTILLO, Santiago (coord) : *Comunicaciones a VII congreso de la Asociación de Historia Social de España. Mundo del trabajo y asociacionismo in España. Collegia, gremios, mutuas, sindicatos ...* Madrid, CD edition, Asociación de Historia Social, 2013.

CASTILLO, Santiago (coord) : *Mundo del trabajo y asociacionismo en España: Colegia, gremios, mutuas, sindicatos ...* Actas VII congreso de la Asociación de Historia Social, Madrid, La Catarata, 2014.

CASTILLO, Santiago: "Mutualismo de trabajadores en España, 1836–1936. Varias cuestiones. Algunas respuestas", in Santiago CASTILLO (coord.): *Mundo del trabajo y asociacionismo en España*, Madrid, La Catarata, 2014, pp. 171–205.

CASTILLO, Santiago and DUCH, Montserrat (coord.): *Comunicaciones al VIII Congreso de Historia Social. Sociabilidades en la Historia*, Madrid, Asociación de Historia Social, 2015, CD edition.

CASTILLO, Santiago and ORTIZ DE ORRUÑO, José Mª (coord.): *Estado, protesta y movimientos sociales. Actas del III Congreso de Historia Social*, Vitoria, Universidad del País Vasco-EHU, 1998.

CASTILLO, Santiago and RUZAFA, Rafael (coord.): *La previsión social en la Historia. Comunicaciones*, Madrid, Asociación de Historia Social, 2008, CD edition.

CASTILLO, Santiago and RUZAFA, Rafael (coord.): *La previsión social en la Historia. Actas del VI Congreso de Historia Social*, Madrid, Siglo XXI, 2009.

CASTILLO, Santiago and URÍA, Jorge (coord.): *Comunicaciones a Sociedades y Culturas. Treinta años de la Asociación de Historia Social. IX Congreso*, Madrid, Asociación de Historia Social, 2019, CD edition.

CUESTA, Josefina: "Las Sociedades de Socorros Mutuos en la España de los años 20. Un silencio en el reformismo social", in VVAA (ed.): *El reformismo social en España. La Comisión de Reformas Sociales*, Córdoba, 1987, pp. 301–330.

CUESTA, Josefina: *Hacia los seguros sociales obligatorios. La crisis de la Restauración*, Madrid, Ministerio de Trabajo y de la Seguridad Social, 1988.

CUESTA, Josefina: "Las Sociedades de Socorros Mutuos en el primer tercio del siglo XX: Sociedad sin Estado. Una relación fallida", in Santiago CASTILLO (ed.): *Solidaridad desde abajo*, 1994, pp. 409–421.

DE DIEGO GARCÍA, Emilio: "Una forma de sociabilidad: las sociedades de socorros mutuos en el Madrid del siglo XIX", in Enrique MARTÍNEZ (coord.): *Vínculos y sociabilidades en España e Iberoamérica: siglos XVI-XX*, Madrid, Puertollano, 2005, pp. 221–242.

DÍEZ, Fernando: *Viles y mecánicos. Trabajo y sociedad en la Valencia preindustrial*, Valencia, IVEI, 1990.

DÍEZ, Fernando: "La previsión social en la España del siglo XVIII. Realidad, reforma e historia comparada", in Santiago CASTILLO and Rafael RUZAFA (coord.): *La previsión social en la Historia. Actas del VI Congreso de Historia Social*, Madrid, Siglo XXI, 2009, pp. 67–98.

DÍEZ, Fernando: "Oficios y artesanos en la crisis del gremialismo a finales del siglo XVIII y principios del siglo XIX", in Santiago CASTILLO (coord.): *Mundo del trabajo y asociacionismo en España: Colegia, gremios, mutuas, sindicatos ...*Actas VII congreso de la Asociación de Historia Social, Madrid, La Catarata, 2014, pp. 53–95.

DREYFUS, Michel and GIBAUD, Bernard (drs.): *Mutualités de tous les pays. Un passé riche d'avenir*, Paris, Mutualité Française, 1995 [Proceedings of the 1992 Paris Conference, with abbreviated versions of 29 reports from participating countries, including the one referring to Spain].

DUCH PLANA, Montserrat: "Les societats de protecció mútua de Tarragona al segle XIX", *Universitas tarraconensis*, 5 (1982), pp.121–131.

DUCH PLANA, Montserrat: *La Cooperativa Obrera Tarraconense (1904–1965). Consum, treball i lleure*, Tarragona: El Médol, 1993.

DUCH PLANA, Montserrat: "Societarismo catalán de previsión social: identidades y pertenencias", in Santiago CASTILLO and Rafael RUZAFA (coord.): *La previsión social en la Historia. Comunicaciones*, Madrid, Asociación de Historia Social, 2008, CD edition.

DUCH, Montserrat; ARNABAT, Ramon and FERRÉ, Xavier (eds.): *Sociabilitats a la Catalunya contemporània. Temps i espais en conflicte, Barcelona*, Barcelona, PAM, 2015.

DUCH, Montserrat; ARNABAT, Ramon and GAVALDÀ, Antoni (eds.): *La Catalunya asociada (1868–1938)*, Valencia, PUV, 2020.
ESTEBAN DE VEGA, Mariano: "La asistencia liberal española: beneficencia pública y previsión particular", *Historia Social*, 13 (1992), pp. 123–138.
ESTEBAN DE VEGA, Mariano: "Las Sociedades de Socorros Mutuos en la provincia de Salamanca en el último cuarto del siglo XIX", in Santiago CASTILLO (ed.): *Solidaridad desde abajo*, Madrid, UGT, Centre of Historical Studies, 1994, pp. 339–345.
FERNÁNDEZ CASANOVA, Carmen: "La situación del asociacionismo mutualista de trabajadores de El Ferrol y Santiago, 1884–1903", in Santiago CASTILLO (ed.): *Solidaridad desde abajo*, Madrid, UGT, Centre of Historical Studies, 1994, pp. 257–283.
FERNÁNDEZ-CORDERO AZORÍN, Concepción: "La primera sociedad de socorros mutuos en Alicante 1870. (El obrerismo en Alicante durante el sexenio democrático 1868–1874)", in Santiago CASTILLO (ed.): *Solidaridad desde abajo*, Madrid, UGT, Centre of Historical Studies, 1994, pp. 319–337.
FRANCO RUBIO, Gloria Ángeles: "Asociacionismo femenino en la España del siglo XVIII: las hermandades de socorro de mujeres", *Cuadernos de Historia Moderna*, 16 (1995), pp. 179–199.
FULLANA, Pere and MARIMÓN, Antoni: *Història del "Montepío" de Previsió de l'Arraval de Santa Catalina. Centenario, 1894–1994*, Palma de Mallorca, Escola Natzaret, 1994.
FULLANA, Pere: "Las sociedades de socorros mutuos en Mallorca en la segunda mitad del siglo XIX (1836–1900)", in Santiago CASTILLO (ed.): *Solidaridad desde abajo*, Madrid, UGT, Centre of Historical Studies, 1994, pp. 347–371.
GABRIEL, Pere: "Sociabilidad obrera y popular y vida política en Cataluña 1868–1923", *Bulletin d'històire Contemporaine de l'Espagne*, 17–18 (1993), pp. 145–156.
GALLART FOLCH, Alejandro: *Derecho Español del Trabajo*, Barcelona, Labor, 1936.
GARAU LLOMPART, Isabel: "La Confianza y otras sociedades de ahorro y de socorros mutuos de Llucmajor (siglos XIX y XX)", in *Estudis Balèarics*, 25 (1987), pp. 17–30.
GARCÍA CHECA, Amelia: "Ideología y práctica del mutualismo católico femenino", in Santiago CASTILLO (ed.): *Solidaridad desde abajo*, Madrid, UGT, Centre of Historical Studies, 1994, pp. 125–134.
GARCÍA GALINDO, Juan Antonio: "Las primeras sociedades españolas de periodistas: entre el socorro mutuo, los intereses profesionales y la libertad de expresión", in Santiago CASTILLO (ed.): *Solidaridad desde abajo*, Madrid, UGT, Centre of Historical Studies, 1994, pp. 469–489.
GARCÍA GONZÁLEZ, Miguel José: *Historia de la Obrera de Ponferrada*, Ponferrada, Publicación del autor y La Obrera, 2004.
GEAS: *España en sociedad. Las asociaciones a finales del siglo XIX*, Cuenca, Ediciones Universidad de Castilla-La Mancha, 1998.

GONZÁLEZ GÓMEZ, Santiago: "La cotización sindical a base múltiple: puerta de integración del mutualismo obrero en el primer sindicalismo socialista madrileño", in Santiago CASTILLO (ed.): *Solidaridad desde abajo*, Madrid, UGT, Centre of Historical Studies, 1994, pp. 437–445.
GONZÁLEZ, Ángeles: "Una aproximación al mutualismo obrero en la ciudad de Sevilla, 1900–1923", 1995 [Presented at the 2nd International Meeting].
GRABULEDA, Carles: "Industrialización y previsión popular. Sociedades de Socorros Mutuos en un suburbio de Barcelona: Sant Martí de Provençals", in Santiago CASTILLO and José Mª ORTIZ DE ORRUÑO (coord.): *Estado, protesta y movimientos sociales. Actas del III Congreso de Historia Social*, Vitoria, Universidad del País Vasco-EHU, 1998, pp. 385–398.
GUEREÑA, Jean Louis: "Fuentes para la historia de la sociabilidad en la España Contemporánea", *Estudios de Historia Social*, 50–51 (1989), pp. 273–305.
GUEREÑA, Jean Louis: "El espacio mutualista en la sociabilidad popular de la Restauración (1875–1900). El ejemplo asturiano", in Santiago CASTILLO (ed.): *Solidaridad desde abajo*, Madrid, UGT, Centre of Historical Studies, 1994, pp. 205–223.
GUIMERÁ, Carmen: "Les associacions religioses de laics a la Barcelona de la segona meitat del segle XVIII", in *Actes del primer Congrés d'Historia Moderna de Catalunya*, 2°, (1987), pp. 501–506, Barcelona, Universitat de Barcelona.
HERNÁNDEZ, Rafael: *La Sociedad Cooperativa El Trabajo, 1880–1942*, Alicante, Instituto Juan Gil-Albert, 1988.
IBARZ, Jordi: "Sociedades y Montepíos. Asociacionismo laboral de los cargadores y descargadores del puerto de Barcelona, 1884–1931", in *Sociología del Trabajo*, 18 (1993), pp. 119–138.
IBARZ, Jordi: "El Montepío de San Pedro Pescador y las Sociedades de Socorros Mutuos de los estibadores de Barcelona (1890–1939)", in Santiago CASTILLO (ed.): *Solidaridad desde abajo*, Madrid, UGT, Centre of Historical Studies, 1994, pp. 107–123.
IBARZ, Jordi: "La protección social en el puerto de Barcelona durante la segunda República y el primer Franquismo. Un estudio comparativo", 1995 [Presented at the 2nd International Meeting].
Ier *Encuentro Internacional* sobre *las Sociedades de Socorros Mutuos de los Trabajadores in España. Siglos XIX y* XX, Facultad de CC. Políticas y Sociología, Universidad Complutense de Madrid, 25–27 June, 1992.
II° Encuentro Internacional sobre *Mutualismo y protección social in la España del siglo XX*, Escuela sindical Julián Besteiro, Madrid, 1995.
IRS: *Estadística de la Asociación Obrera en 1° de noviembre de 1904*, Madrid, IRS, 1907.
IRS: *Estadística de las Instituciones de ahorro, cooperación y previsión en 1°° de noviembre de 1904*, Madrid, IRS, 1908.
IRS: *Estadística de Asociaciones. Censo electoral de Asociaciones profesionales para la renovación de la parte electiva del Instituto y de las Juntas de Reformas Sociales y relación de las Instituciones no profesionales de ahorro, cooperación y previsión in 30 de noviembre de 1916*, Madrid, IRS, 1917.

INP: *Conferencia de Seguros Sociales. Celebrada en Madrid los días 24 a 31 de octubre de 1917*, Madrid, INP, 1917.

INP: *Conferencia Nacional de Seguros, Vol. I, Ponencias. Actas. Conclusiones; Vol. II, Documentos de información*, Madrid, INP, 1922.

INP: *Conferencia Nacional de Seguros de enfermedad, invalidez y maternidad. Barcelona, noviembre de 1922*, Madrid, S. de la S de M. Minuesa de los Ríos, 2 Vols, 1925.

INP: *La cuestión del seguro de Enfermedad ante la X[a] reunión de la Conferencia Internacional del Trabajo (Ginebra, mayo 1927)*, Madrid, INP, 1927.

IZARD, Miguel: *Industrialización y obrerismo: las Tres Clases de Vapor, 1869–1913*, Barcelona, Ariel, 1973.

IZQUIERDO GOIKOETXEA, Luis Carlos: "La previsión social en Euskadi: Antecedentes y situación actual", in Rafael RUZAFA (ed.): *De las Hermandades a la Seguridad Social*, Madrid, Catarata, 2018, pp. 130–155.

JORDANA DE POZAS, Luis: "Las Sociedades de Socorros Mutuos en el reino de Valencia", in *Actas de la Conferencia sobre el seguro de enfermedad e invalidez*, Barcelona, 1922, pp. 279–321.

LACALZADA, M[a] José: *La Rioja 1852–1902. Un eslabón entre la tradición y el progreso*, Zaragoza, Libreria Central, 1986.

LARGO JIMÉNEZ, Fernando: "Capital social y mutualismo: la Federación de Sociedades de Socorros Mutuos de Cataluña, 1896–1946", in Santiago CASTILLO (coord.): *Comunicaciones VII Congreso de Historia Social. Mundo del trabajo y asociacionismo en España*, Madrid, Asociación de Historia Social, 2013, CD edition.

LARGO JIMÉNEZ, Fernando: "La sociabilidad como instrumento del mutualismo. El caso de la Federación de Sociedades de Socorros Mutuos de Cataluña, 1896–1936", in Santiago CASTILLO and Montserrat DUCH (coord.): *Comunicaciones al VIII Congreso de Historia Social. Sociabilidades en la Historia*, Madrid, Asociación de Historia Social, 2015, CD edition.

LARGO JIMÉNEZ, Fernando: *Mutualismo y capital social. El papel de la Federación de mutualidades de Cataluña, 1896–1936*, thesis, Barcelona, Universidad Autónoma de Barcelona, 2017.

LARGO JIMÉNEZ, Fernando and PUJOL-ANDREU, Josep: "Desarrollo y crisis del mutualismo de trabajadores en España en el siglo XX: Nueva aproximación desde el capital social", *Barcelona, Scripta Nova*, vol. XX, 540 (15 July 2016), p. 25.

LARRINAGA, Carlos and LÁZARO, Carmen: "Los inicios del seguro privado en Guipúzcoa: De las Sociedades de Socorros Mutuos a las primeras compañías (1852–1914)", *Espacio tiempo y forma, Historia Contemporánea*, 9 (1966).

LEÓN SANZ, Pilar: "La concertación de la asistencia en la enfermedad en La Sociedad de Obreros La Conciliación (1902–1919)", in *Navarra: Memoria e Imagen, Pamplona, Eunate*, 2006, vol. II, pp. 97–108.

LEÓN SANZ, Pilar: "Professional Responsibility and the Welfare System in Spain at the Turn of the 19th Century", *Hygiea Internationalis*, 1 (2006), pp. 575–590.

LEÓN SANZ, Pilar: "Higienismo y previsión social a través de una Sociedad de Socorros Mutuos: el Consultorio de Niños de Pecho de *La Conciliación* (1905–1916)", in Santiago CASTILLO and Rafael RUZAFA (coords.): *La previsión social en la Historia. Actas del VI Congreso de Historia Social*, Madrid, Siglo XXI, 2008, CD edition.

LEÓN SANZ, Pilar: "Los relatos de los enfermos: análisis de las quejas de los socios en una Sociedad de Socorros Mutuos (1902–1919)", in VV. AA (coord.): *La experiencia de enfermar en perspectiva histórica*, Granada, Universidad de Granada, 2008, pp. 51–54.

LEÓN SANZ, Pilar: "Networking and Interaction between a Mutual Assistance Association and Other Agencies (Pamplona, 1902–1919)", in *Hygiea internationalis*, 8-1 (2009), pp. 31–50.

LEÓN SANZ, Pilar: "Private Initiatives Against Social Inequalities and Health Vulnerabilities: The Case of La Conciliación (Pamplona, 1902–1920)", in Patrice BOURDELAIS and John CHIRCOP (eds.): *Vulnerabilities, Social Inequalities and Health*, Évora, Ediçoes Colibri, 2010, pp. 93–108.

LEÓN SANZ, Pilar: "Medical Assistance Provided by La Conciliación, a Pamplona Mutual Assistance Association (1902–84)", in Bernard HARRIS (ed.): *Welfare and Old Age in Europe and North America: The Development of Social Insurance*, London, Pickering and Chatto, 2012, pp. 137–166.

LEÓN SANZ, Pilar: "Creando identidad. Educación y recreación en *La Conciliación*, 1902–1933", in Santiago CASTILLO (coord.): *Comunicaciones a VII congreso de la Asociación de Historia Social de España. Mundo del trabajo y asociacionismo in España. Collegia, gremios, mutuas, sindicatos ...* Madrid, Asociación de Historia Social, 2013, CD edition.

LLORENTE ROMERA, Mercedes: *Salud y condición obrera. La sociedad de socorros mutuos de obreros de Soria (1880–1949)*, Soria, Centre of Sorian Studies, 1987.

LÓPEZ GONZÁLEZ, Juan Jaime and GARCÍA LASAOSA, José: *Orígenes del movimiento obrero en Aragón (1854–1890)*, Zaragoza, Diputación de Zaragoza e Institución Fernando el Católico, 1982.

LÓPEZ NÚÑEZ, Álvaro: *El seguro obrero en España*, Madrid, IRS, 1908.

LUENGO TEIXIDOR, Félix: "Las Sociedades de Socorros Mutuos en Rentería, 1890–1930", in Santiago CASTILLO (ed.): *Solidaridad desde abajo*, Madrid, UGT, Centre of Historical Studies, 1994, pp. 177–187.

LEÓN SANZ, Pilar: "Sociabilidad y socorros mutuos: las Sociedades de Socorros Mutuos en Rentería (1890)–1930)", *Bilduma*, 9 (1995).

MAESTRO, Manuel: *Formación del mercado español de seguros, 1908–1960*, Madrid, INESE, 1993.

MARÍN CASADO, Guillermo: "Florecimiento y ocaso de una tipología asociativa: Socorros mutuos de artesanos en Vitoria (1849–1949)", *Sancho el Sabio*, 38 (2015), pp. 243–262.

MARÍN CASADO, Guillermo: "Un modelo particular de previsión social: El Montepío de empleados municipales del Ayuntamiento de Vitoria", in Rafael RUZAFA (ed.): *De las Hermandades a la Seguridad Social*, Madrid, Catarata, 2018, pp. 107–129.

MARÍN CASADO, Guillermo: "Tipologías asociativas y espacios productivos: el caso de la *Sociedad de Socorros a Enfermos* de la fábrica de naipes de Heraclio Furnier", in Santiago CASTILLO and Jorge URÍA (coord.): *Comunicaciones a Sociedades y Culturas. Treinta años de la Asociación de Historia Social. IX Congreso*, Madrid, Asociación de Historia Social, 2019, CD edition, pp. 447–474.

MARTÍN VALVERDE, Antonio: *La legislación social en la historia de España: de la revolución liberal a 1936*, Madrid, Congreso de los Diputados, 1987.

MARTÍNEZ MARTÍN, Mª Ascensión: "Las sociedades de socorros mutuos en Guipúzcoa: 1880–1936", in Santiago CASTILLO (ed.): *Solidaridad desde abajo*, Madrid, UGT, Centre of Historical Studies, 1994, pp. 155–175.

MARTÍNEZ MARTÍN, Mª Ascensión: "La Previsión social en Guipúzcoa, 1900–1936", 1995 [Presented at the 2nd International Meeting].

MARTÍNEZ MARTÍN, Mª Ascensión: *Guipúzcoa en la vanguardia del reformismo social: beneficencia ahorros, previsión (1876–1936)*, San Sebastián, Fundación Social y Cultural Kutxa, 1996.

MARTÍNEZ, F: "La Seguridad Social en la etapa preconstitucional: referencia especial a los sistemas complementarios", 1995 [Presented at the 2nd International Meeting].

MARTÍNEZ-GALLEGO, Francesc Andreu: "Tocata y fuga de la fábrica urbana. Colisión artesana y disciplina obrera (Valencia, 1840–1880)", *Sociología del Trabajo*, 19 (1993), pp. 123–141.

MARTÍNEZ-GALLEGO, Francesc Andreu: "Disolución gremial y constitución societaria. Los términos del vínculo. Valencia 1834–1868", in Santiago CASTILLO (ed.): *Solidaridad desde abajo*, Madrid, UGT, Centre of Historical Studies, 1994, pp. 51–69.

MARTÍNEZ-GALLEGO, Francesc Andreu: *Esperit d'associació: cooperativisme i mutualisme laics entre 1834 i 1936*, Valencia, PUV, 2010.

MARTÍNEZ-GALLEGO, Francesc Andreu and RUZAFA, Rafael: "Los socorros mutuos y la cooperación en la España del siglo XIX: actitudes de los poderes públicos y soluciones populares", in Santiago CASTILLO and Rafael RUZAFA (coord.): *La previsión social en la historia*, Madrid, Siglo XXI, 2009, pp. 101–135.

MAZA, Elena: "El mutualismo y su polivalente papel en la España del siglo XIX (1839–1887)", *Investigaciones Históricas*, 11 (1991), pp. 173–198.

MAZA, Elena: "*Hacia una interpretación del mutualismo español decimonónico: peculiaridades y polivalencias*", in Santiago CASTILLO (ed.): *Solidaridad desde abajo*, Madrid, UGT, Centre of Historical Studies, 1994, pp. 392–407.

MAZA, Elena: "Especialización funcional y decantación social en la España del siglo XX (primer tercio): fuentes y rasgos dominantes", 1995 [Presented at the 2nd International Meeting].

MAZA, Elena: "La horizontalidad de las solidaridades. El mutualismo en la España contemporánea", *Ayer*, 25 (1997), pp. 73–102.

MAZA, Elena: "Sociabilidad e historiografía en la España contemporánea", *Ayer*, 42 (2001), pp. 241–252.

MAZA, Elena: *Sociabilidad en la España Contemporánea. Historiografía y problemas metodológicos*, Valladolid, Universidad de Valladolid, 2002.

MAZA, Elena: "Sociabilidad in la España del interior. Castilla y León. A modo de balance", in Elena MAZA (coord.): *Sociabilidad en la España Contemporánea. Historiografía y problemas metodológicos*, Valladolid, Universidad de Valladolid, 2002, pp. 103–131.
MAZA, Elena: *Asociacionismo en la España contemporánea: vertientes y análisis interdisciplinar*, Valladolid, Universidad de Valladolid, 2003.
MAZA, Elena: "Preferencias y destinatarios del asociacionismo vallisoletano en su rodaje contemporáneo", in Elena MAZA (coord.): *Asociacionismo en la España contemporánea: vertientes y análisis interdisciplinar*, Valladolid, Universidad de Valladolid, 2003, pp. 147–174.
MAZA, Elena: "Mutualité et protection sociale en Espagne, 1887–1936", *Histoire et Sociétés*, 16 (2005), pp. 44–54.
MAZA, Elena: "El mutualismo en España, 1900–1936: ajustes e interferencias", in Santiago CASTILLO and Rafael RUZAFA (eds.):*La previsión social la Historia. Comunicaciones*, Madrid, Asociación de Historia Social, 2008, pp. 333–367, CD edition.
MOLERO, Jorge; JIMÉNEZ, Isabel and TABERNERO, Carlos: "La 'acción directa' y el mutualismo en el seno de la Confederación Nacional del Trabajo: la *Obra Popular Antituberculosa de Cataluña*, 1931–1932", in Santigo CASTILLO (coord.): *Comunicaciones a VII congreso de la Asociación de Historia Social de España. Mundo del trabajo y asociacionismo in España. Collegia, gremios, mutuas, sindicatos* … Madrid, Asociación de Historia Social, 2013, CD edition.
MONTERO, Feliciano: *Los seguros sociales en la España del siglo XX. Orígenes y antecedentes de la previsión social*, Madrid, Ministerio de Trabajo, 1988.
MONTERO, Feliciano and ESTEBAN DE VEGA, Mariano: "Aproximación tipológica al mutualismo popular y obrero en España: el mutualismo asistencial", in Santiago CASTILLO (ed.): *La Historia social en España. Actualidad y perspectivas*, Madrid, Siglo XXI, 1991, pp. 457–470.
MORALES, Manuel: "El mutualismo popular y obrero en la comarca de Antequera (1853–1936)", *Revista de Estudios Antequerano*, 2 (1994).
MORALES, Manuel: "Cofradías y Pósitos de pescadores en la provincia de Málaga, 1924–1943", 1995 [Presented at the 2nd International Meeting].
MORENO SÁEZ, Francisco: *El movimiento obrero en Elche (1890–1931)*, Alicante, Instituto Alicantino de Cultura, 1987.
MORETA I AMAT, Marcel: "Cataluña en el movimiento mutualista de Previsión Social en España", in Santiago CASTILLO (ed.): *Solidaridad desde abajo*, Madrid, UGT, Centre of Historical Studies, 1994, pp. 503–539.
PONS, Jerònia: *El sector seguros en Baleares: Empresas y empresarios en los siglos XIX y XX*, Palma de Mallorca, El Tall Editorial, 1998.
PONS, Jerònia and SILVESTRE, Javier (eds.): *Los orígenes del Estado del Bienestar en España, 1900–1945: los seguros de accidentes, vejez, desempleo y enfermedad*, Zaragoza, Prensas U. de Z, 2010.
PONS, Jerònia and VILAR-RODRÍGUEZ, Margarita: *La gestión del seguro de accidentes del trabajo en España: De mutuas patronales a entidades colaboradoras de la seguridad social 1900–2019*, Madrid, Tesorería G. de la Seguridad Social, Ministerio de Inclusión, Seguridad Social y Migraciones, 2020.

RALLE, Michel: "El montepío obrero ¿anacronismo o modelo?", *Estudios de Historia Social, Madrid*, 30 (1984), pp. 7–21.

RALLE, Michel: "La cultura política del primer socialismo español", *Anales de Historia de la Fundación Pablo Iglesias*, 1 (1986), pp. 55–85.

RALLE, Michel: "La función de la protección mutualista en la construcción de una identidad obrera, (1870–1910)", *Sociología del Trabajo*, 16 (1992), pp. 143–163.

RALLE, Michel: "La función de la protección mutualista en la construcción de una identidad obrera, (1870–1910)", in Santiago CASTILLO (ed.): *Solidaridad desde abajo*, Madrid, UGT, Centre of Historical Studies, 1994, pp. 423–435.

Resumen de las Sociedades de todas clases existentes en España en el día 1 de enero de 1887 con expresión de su objeto según los datos oficiales facilitados a esta Dirección General [de Seguridad]. Clasificación y objeto. [National Historical Archive, file 575].

RIVERA, Antonio: "Desarrollo y crisis del modelo de sociedad de socorros (Vitoria, 1849–1938)", in Santiago CASTILLO (ed.): *Solidaridad desde abajo*, Madrid, UGT, Centre of Historical Studies, 1994, pp. 135–143.

RODÓN, Assumpta: *Inventari de les associacions polítiques, sindicals i obreres inscrites en el Govern Civil de Barcelona des de l'any 1887 fins 1936*, Barcelona, 1982.

RODRÍGUEZ OCAÑA, Esteban: "La asistencia médica colectiva en España hasta 1936", in VVAA: *Historia de la acción social pública en España. Beneficencia y previsión*, Madrid, Ministerio de Trabajo, 1990, pp. 322–359.

RODRÍGUEZ GONZÁLEZ, Juan Jesús: "Las sociedades de socorros mutuos en Asturias, 1859–1900", in Santiago CASTILLO (ed.): *Solidaridad desde abajo*, Madrid, UGT, Centre of Historical Studies, 1994, pp. 189–203.

RUMEU DE ARMAS, Antonio: *Historia de la Previsión social en España. Cofradías, Gremios, Hermandades, Montepíos*, Madrid, Revista de Derecho Privado, 1944.

RUZAFA, Rafael (ed.): *De las Hermandades a la Seguridad Social. Estudios sobre previsión social en el País Vasco, siglos XIX–XXI*, Madrid, Asociación de Historia Social-Catarata, 2018.

RUZAFA, Rafael: "Tradiciones, imposición patronal y auto organización. Mutualismo obrero en Vizcaya en el siglo XIX", in Santiago CASTILLO and José Mª ORTIZ DE ORRUÑO (coord.): *Estado, protesta y movimientos sociales. Actas del III Congreso de Historia Social*, Vitoria, Universidad del País Vasco-EHU, 1998, pp. 371–384.

RUZAFA, Rafael: "El mutualismo obrero en Vizcaya en el siglo XIX", in *Vizcaínos rurales, vizcaínos industriales. Estudios de historia social contemporánea*, Librería S. Antonio, Barakaldo, 2002, pp. 105–137.

RUZAFA ORTEGA, Rafael and GARCÍA ABAD, Rocío: "Formas de previsión social en la zona minera vizcaína. Siglos XIX-XX", in Rafael RUZAFA (ed.): *De las Hermandades a la Seguridad Social*, Madrid, Catarata, 2018, pp. 43–71.

SALOMÓN, Pilar: "Anticlericalismo y beneficencia: hacia la secularización de la Previsión social en España, 1900–1936", 1995 [Presented at the 2nd International Meeting].

SAMANIEGO, Mercedes: *La unificación de los seguros sociales a debate. La Segunda República*, Madrid, Ministerio de Trabajo y Seguridad Social, 1988.

SÁNCHEZ CASTRO, Antonio Javier: "La Sociedad de Obreros Amigos de la villa de Vegadeo", in Santiago CASTILLO (ed.): *Solidaridad desde abajo*, Madrid, UGT, Centre of Historical Studies, 1994, pp. 285–305.

SÁNCHEZ COLLANTES, Sergio: "La participación de los republicanos en el asociacionismo local de Oviedo desde el periodo isabelino a comienzos del siglo XX: mutuas, cooperativas, colegios profesionales y otras sociedades", in Santiago CASTILLO (ed.): *Comunicaciones a VII congreso de la Asociación de Historia Social de España. Mundo del trabajo y asociacionismo in España. Collegia, gremios, mutuas, sindicatos ...* Madrid, Association of Social History, 2013, CD edition.

SÁNCHEZ DE MADARIAGA, Elena: "De la caridad fraternal al Socorro Mutuo. Las Hermandades de Socorro de Madrid en el siglo XVIII", in Santiago CASTILLO (ed.): *Solidaridad desde abajo*, Madrid, UGT, Centre of Historical Studies, 1994, pp. 31–50.

SÁNCHEZ DE MADARIAGA, Elena: "Una forma de sociabilidad del Antiguo Régimen en trasformación: las cofradías madrileñas", in Javier DONEZAR and Manuel PÉREZ LEDESMA (eds.): *Antiguo Régimen y liberalismo. Homenaje a Miguel Artola*, Madrid, Alianza, 1994.

SÁNCHEZ DE MADARIAGA, Elena: *Cofradías y sociabilidad en el Madrid del Antiguo Régimen*, Madrid, UAB, 1997.

SÁNCHEZ DE MADARIAGA, Elena: "Cultura religiosa y sociedad: las cofradías de laicos", *Historia Social*, 35 (1999), pp. 23–42.

SÁNCHEZ DE MADARIAGA, Elena: "Solidaridad popular femenina: las hermandades de socorro de mujeres en el Madrid del siglo XVIII", in Pilar PÉREZ CANTÓ and Elena POSTIGO (eds.): *Autoras y protagonistas*, Madrid, Universidad Autónoma, 2000.

SANTALLA, M: "El Ministerio de Marina y la Previsión social en los arsenales del Estado: El arsenal y el astillero de Ferrol, 1900–1936", 1995 [Presented at the 2nd International Meeting].

SANTANA MORRO, Manel: *El forjament de la solidaritat. Mutualisme, cooperatives, societats obreres i recreatives a Mallorca (1868–1936)*, Palma, Cort, 2002.

SARRIAS, Cristobal: "Las Mutualidades de Previsión social in España, 1939–2008", in Santiago CASTILLO and Rafael RUZAFA (coord.): *La previsión social en la historia*, Madrid, Siglo XXI, 2009 (CD edition).

SOLÁ AYAPE, Carlos: "Dos ejemplos de Sociedades de Socorros Mutuos en la Zaragoza de mediados del siglo XIX: La Sociedad de Horneros de San Miguel y el Centro Industrial o el asociacionismo de los fabricantes zaragozanos", in Santiago CASTILLO (ed.): *Solidaridad desde abajo*, Madrid, UGT, Centre of Historical Studies, 1994, pp. 307–317.

SOLÁ AYAPE, Carlos: "La Sociedad de Socorros mutuos de empleados municipales de Pamplona", 1995 [Presented at the 2nd International Meeting].

SOLÁ AYAPE, Carlos: "Asociacionismo mutualista en el Vínculo de Pamplona: del Montepío a la Sociedad de Socorros Mutuos (1832–1870)", *Príncipe de Viana*, 217 (1999).

SOLÁ I GUSSINYER, Pere: *Historia del associanime catalá contemporani. Barcelona i les comarques de la seva demarcació (1874–1966)*, Barcelona, Generalitat de Catalunya, 1993.

SOLÁ I GUSSINYER, Pere: "El mutualismo contemporáneo en una sociedad industrial. Anotaciones sobre el caso catalán (1880–1939)", in Santiago CASTILLO (ed.): *Solidaridad desde abajo*, Madrid, UGT, Centre of Historical Studies, 1994, pp. 71–85.

SOLÁ I GUSSINYER, Pere: "Industrialización y previsión. Sociedades de Socorros Mutuos en un suburbio de Barcelona: Sant Martí de Provençals", in Santiago CASTILLO and José Mª ORTIZ DE ORRUÑO (coord.): *Estado, protesta y movimientos sociales. Actas del III Congreso de Historia Social*, Vitoria, Universidad del País Vasco-EHU, 1998, pp. 385–398.

SOLÁ I GUSSINYER, Pere: *Itineraris per la sociabilitat meridional catalana: l'Associacionisme i la cultura popular a la demarcació de Tarragona (1868–1964)*, Tarragona, Diputació de Tarragona, 1998.

SOLÁ I GUSSINYER, Pere: "Asociacionismo en la España periférica: tipología y rasgos dominantes", in Elena MAZA (coord.): *Asociacionismo en la España contemporánea: vertientes y análisis interdisciplinar*, Valladolid, Universidad de Valladolid, 2003, pp. 89–146.

SOLÁ I GUSSINYER, Pere: "El mutualismo y su función social: Sinopsis histórica", *CIRIEC-España, Revista de Economía Pública, Social y Cooperativa*, 44 (2003), pp. 175–198.

SUÁREZ BOSA, Miguel: "Las sociedades de socorros mutuos en las Canarias orientales entre finales del siglo XIX y principios del XX", in Santiago CASTILLO (ed.): *Solidaridad desde abajo*, Madrid, UGT, Centre of Historical Studies, 1994, pp. 373–389.

URÍA, Jorge: "Mutualismo y sociedades de socorros mutuos en Asturias. Una visión de conjunto (1898–1936)", in Santiago CASTILLO (ed.): *Solidaridad desde abajo*, Madrid, UGT, Centre of Historical Studies, 1994, pp. 225–243.

URÍA, Jorge: "Los lugares de la sociabilidad. Espacios, costumbre y conflicto social", in Santiago CASTILLO and Roberto FERNÁNDEZ (coords.): *Historia social y ciencias sociales*, Lleida, Milenio, 2001, pp. 201–224.

URZAINQUI BIEL, Carlos: "Sociedades de socorros mutuos: entre dos conceptos de sociedad", in Alberto SABIO ALCUTÉN and Carlos FORCADELL (coords.): *Las escalas del pasado. IV Congreso de Historia Local de Aragón*, Barbastro, Instituto de Estudios Altoaragoneses, 2005, pp. 367–378.

VAN DER LINDEN, Marcel: "The Comparative History of Mutual Benefit Societies. Some queries and suggestions", Amsterdam, working paper préparatoire du *Colloque International sur l'Histoire de la Mutualité: un passé riche d'avenir*, Paris, 1–3 December 1992.

VAN DER LINDEN, Marcel: *Social Security Mutualism. The Comparative History of Mutual Benefit Societies*, Berna, Peter Lang, 1996 [Proceedings of the 1992 Paris Conference with Abbreviated Versions of 26 of the Reports from Participating Countries, Including Spain].

VILAR RODRÍGUEZ, Margarita: "La cobertura social al margen del Estado: asociacionismo obrero y socorros mutuos en Galicia (c. 1839–1935)", *IX Congreso Internacional de la AEHE*, Murcia, 2008.

VILAR RODRÍGUEZ, Margarita: "La cobertura social a través de los socorros mutuos obreros, 1839–1935. ¿Una alternativa al Estado para afrontar los fallos del mercado?", in Jerònia PONS and Javier SILVESTRE (eds.): *Los orígenes del Estado del Bienestar en España, 1900–1945: los seguros de accidentes, vejez, desempleo y enfermedad*, Zaragoza, Prensas U. de Z, 2010, pp. 85–122.

VILAR RODRÍGUEZ, Margarita and PONS, Jerònia: "El papel de las sociedades de socorro mutuo en la cobertura del riesgo de enfermedad en España (1870–1942)", Universidad Pablo Olavide, Carmona (Seville), *X Congreso Internacional de la AEHE*, September, 2011.

VILAR, Juan Bautista et al.: *El movimiento obrero en el distrito de Cartagena-La Unión (1840–1930)*, Murcia, Biblioteca Murciana de Bolsillo, 1987, pp. 84–86.

ZARZOSO ORELLANA, Alfons: *La pràctica mèdica a la Catalunya del segle XVIII*, Doctoral thesis, Institut Universitari d'Història Jaume Vicens Vives, Universitat Pompeu Fabra, Barcelona, 2003.

ZARZOSO ORELLANA, Alfons: "El fenómeno asociativo y la preocupación por la salud entre las clases trabajadoras de Barcelona en el tránsito del siglo XIX", in Santiago CASTILLO and Rafael RUZAFA (coord.): *La previsión social en la historia*, Madrid, Siglo XXI, 2009 (CD edition).

9 Associationism, Mutualism, and Cooperativism in Catalonia, 1868–1938[1]

Montserrat Duch-Plana and Ramon Arnabat-Mata

During the nineteenth century and the first third of the twentieth century, social relationships based on capitalism spread throughout Catalonia as a result of specialisation in the wine sector and industrialisation. At the same time, an increasingly urbanised society emerged in which popular associations set up to protect the rural and urban working classes from capitalist exploitation proliferated. These popular associations supplanted the state, which made no provision for social protection and education, and provided the working classes with collective protection, education, and recreational opportunities.[2]

In the contemporary history of Catalonia, the movement giving rise to associations of this type began in the 1830s, with the creation of workers' cooperative and resistance associations, workers' and farmers' mutual benefit societies, and workers' athenaeums. This was a multifunctional form of associationism that experienced significant growth during periods of transition to democracy: 1854–1856 (the two years of progress) and 1868–1874 (the six years of revolution), before growing exponentially following the passage of the 1887 Association Law and during the first four decades of the twentieth century.

This text examines popular associationism in general, and particularly the mutualist and cooperative forms in the 70 years between 1868 and 1938. 'Popular associationism' is understood to be community engagement through associations organised by and including the rural and urban working classes in a broad sense and encompasses associations of an interclass nature. The data referenced in this text is from the Base de Datos del Asociacionismo Catalán Contemporáneo (Database of Contemporary Catalan Associationism, or BDACC).[3]

Popular associationism

Timeline

Contemporary Catalan popular associationism, which dates back to the 1840s, experienced significant growth in the number of associations, with

DOI: 10.4324/9781003439554-10

an increasing variety of types in a wider range of locations, between the years 1887 and 1922, and during the republican years of 1931–1938. An average of 251 entities were created each year between 1868 and 1938. However, after the Association Law came into force in 1887, the average number of new associations per year exceeded this figure (Table 9.1).[4] Over the 70 years studied, Catalan popular associations accounted for one-third of Spanish associations, despite the fact that only 11% of the population lived in Catalonia.[5]

In addition to the absolute data, the ratio of the number of associations to the resident population in each period is also of interest. The concept of AOD was employed to establish the ratio of associations to population expressed as an annual average of the number of associations per 10,000 inhabitants (Table 9.2).[6] From 1887 onwards, the annual AOD was between 1.4 and 2.4 associations per 10,000 inhabitants, with the highest figure (2.4) occurring during the Second Republic (1931–1938).

The timeline of Catalan associationism clearly shows the stimulus of the 1887 Association Law. After the law was enacted, associationism spread to every political culture and corner of Catalonia, impacting all aspects of people's lives. In his study of Catalonia's early twentieth-century economy and society, French economist Édouard Escarra wrote, 'although resistance associations, the true bodies of action and defence for Catalonia's working class, are of relative importance in Catalonia; however, it is clear that consumer cooperatives, mutual aid and assistance societies, educational and recreational associations, etc. are quite numerous and generally enjoy considerable prosperity', concluding that 'it should be noted that Catalans associate with great ease, if not for purely economic reasons, then at least for political, musical, literary, etc. reasons'.[7] It was this network of workers' and popular associations that helped to foster social cohesion among the workers and the emergence of a basic working-class culture.

The evolution of popular associationism in Catalonia during the last third of the nineteenth century was closely linked to the expansion of the republican and anarchist political cultures. The spearheads were the workers' athenaeums, mutual societies, and consumer cooperatives.[8] Cooperation between workers and the educated sections of the middle class fostered the creation of workers' athenaeums and similar institutions in various Catalan municipalities and cities. The *Ateneu Català de la Classe Obrera* (1861) and the *Ateneu Igualadí de la Classe Obrera* (1863) are good examples. These organisations sought to promote cultural, educational, and leisure activities for the working class within the framework of the political cultures of federal republicanism and anarchism. The convergence of the world of work with the world of culture found expression in the *Certámenes Socialistas* held in Reus (1885) and Barcelona (1889).

Table 9.1 Popular associations created in Catalonia, 1868–1938

Types	*Before 1887*	*1887–1900*	*1901–1922*	*1923–1930*	*1931–1938*	*1868–1938*	%
Cooperatives	29	86	422	123	105	765	4.5
Cultural and instructional	180	291	450	201	300	1,422	8.0
Recreational	547	933	750	547	488	3,265	18.5
Mutual assistance	270	653	1.369	193	217	2,765	16.0
Political	27	269	509	254	2.577	3,636	20.5
Religious	246	207	615	260	126	1,454	8.0
Unions	83	716	1,806	724	833	4,099	23.5
Other	8	36	51	31	35	161	1.0
Total	1,390	3,191	5,972	2,333	4,681	17,567	100
Annual average	70	228	271	291	585	251	

Source: Created by the authors based on BDACC data.

Table 9.2 Associations by period, Catalonia, 1868–1938

Types	*Before 1887*	*1887–1900*	*1901–1922*	*1923–1930*	*1931–1938*	*1868–1938*
Cooperatives	29	93	445	234	164	965
Cultural and instructional	180	336	534	334	384	1,768
Recreational	547	1,070	1,017	801	688	4,123
Mutual assistance	270	784	1,565	584	363	3,566
Political	27	276	578	398	2,677	3,956
Religious	246	269	682	431	234	1,862
Union	83	674	1,974	1,218	1,137	5,086
Other	8	38	61	46	46	199
Total	1,390	3,540	6,856	4,046	5,693	21,525
Population	1,752,033	1,843,549	2,084,868	2,791,292	2,921,216	
AOD	8	19	33	14.5	19.5	
AOD/year	0.2	1.4	1.5	1.8	2.4	

Source: Created by the authors based on BDACC data.

The rise of popular associationism in the second half of the nineteenth century led the ruling classes and the Catholic Church to establish associations of their own in order to maintain or regain control of the working classes. This reaction led to the emergence of interclass and Catholic associations that sought to meet the leisure, cultural, and social protection needs of the working classes. These were interclass associations with a social project that aimed to prevent the 'revolutionary derailment of the workers', in the light of the founding of the International Workingmen's Association (1864) and the revolutionary experience of the Paris Commune (1871).

The Catholic civil associations took various names: Catholic centres, Catholic circles, parish centres, various boards, mutual aid societies, cooperatives, and trade unions. Although they claimed to be 'apolitical', they were part of a conservative political culture and had a particularly significant impact among women and farmers. The strength of Catholic associationism and its informal forums of socialisation in the first third of the twentieth century, even during the republican years, was considerable.[9]

In the first third of the twentieth century, three factors combined to give a decisive boost to Catalonia's association movement: the arrival of thousands of young immigrants, the assimilation of young people into the movement, and the desire for emancipation among various women's groups. A considerable proportion of the half a million immigrants who came from different parts of Spain and settled in urban and industrial areas quickly joined the community of Catalan associations, in the fields of labour (trade unions) and community (cooperation, culture, and recreation), although this process was not free of tensions.[10]

In a society that gave young people a more significant role, they gradually joined the association movement, became more active, and assumed more responsibilities. This took the form of both the creation of sections for young adults within existing associations and the formation of specific associations.[11]

The Catalan association movement during the nineteenth century was predominantly male and left little room for the participation of women, when not explicitly prohibited. Women's participation in the association movement went hand in hand with suffragism and incipient feminism, social Catholicism, republicanism, the labour movement, and the complex world of spiritualism.[12] However, it was not until the last decades of the nineteenth century that some women organised themselves into their own associations, such as the *Sociedad Autónoma de Mujeres* (1889) and the *Sociedad Progresiva Femenina* (1898).[13] Women's social engagement expanded considerably during the first decades of the twentieth century, as shown by the examples of the *Biblioteca Popular de la Dona* (1909), which was later renamed the *Institut de la Cultura i Biblioteca Popular de la Dona* (1910), and the *Club Femení i d'Esports* (1928). However, it was not until the Second Republic that women took an active role in the existing associations, forming their own sections in some of them and creating their own associations, such as the *Lyceum Club de Cataluña* (1931).

Types and locations

The world of popular associationism and formal socialisation is very broad, complex, and heterogeneous. For this reason, beyond the specific name of each organisation, the functions of each organisation and the opportunities for socialisation it provided in its specific location must be considered, as well as the time this took place.[14] In the period studied, production and consumer cooperatives often took on cultural, educational, or recreational functions; athenaeums and *casinos* (social clubs) developed mutual benefit or consumer cooperative sections; religious entities offered mutual, cultural, and/or recreational activities; and agricultural unions acted as cultural and leisure centres.

As Tables 9.1 and 9.2 show, among Catalan associations between 1868 and 1938, trade union and professional associations were very strongly represented, with 4,099 associations (23.5% of the total); followed by political associations, with 3,633 (20.5%); recreational associations, with 4,309 (18.5%); and mutual benefit associations, with 2,765 (16%). Three out of every four Catalan popular associations set up in this period were one of these four types. These were followed by religious associations (8%), cultural and educational associations (8%), and cooperatives (4.5%).

Catalan popular associations in the period 1868–1938 can be classified into four main groups, based on their function: cultural, educational, and recreational associations to satisfy cultural and recreational needs (27%); mutual benefit and cooperative associations to meet social, production, and consumer needs (20%); political and religious associations for political and social action (29%); and trade union and professional associations to address problems related to labour and professional relations (24%).

If the annual averages of the four main types are disaggregated, the timelines of their development are seen to be almost parallel (Figure 9.1). Two important factors to note are the large increase in political associations during the republican period and the slowdown in mutual aid and cooperative associations from the dictatorship of Primo de Rivera onwards.

Over the 70 years covered by this study, popular associations were formed in 833 of the 947 Catalan municipalities (88% of the total), the types of associations becoming more diverse: trade union, mutual and cooperative, professional, educational, and instructive, recreational, cultural, political, and religious.

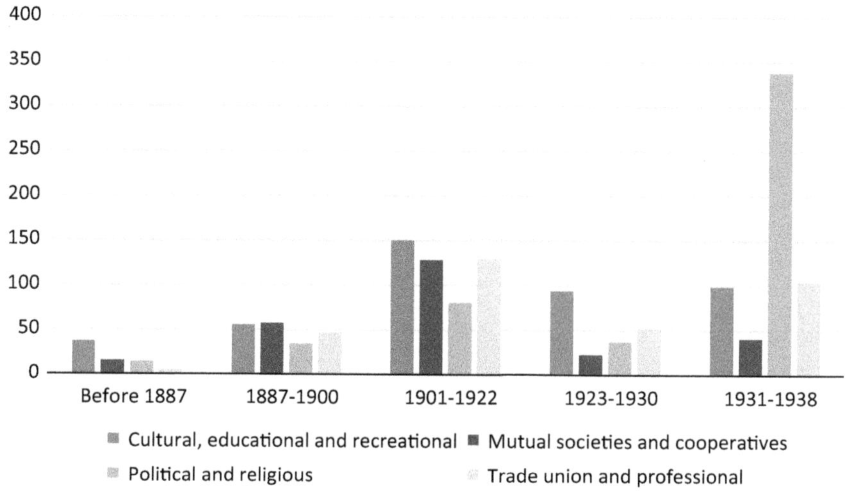

Figure 9.1 Evolution of associations by type: annual averages.

Source: Created by the authors based on Table 9.1.

Popular associations took root in all of the counties of Catalonia, albeit to a varying extent, which led to different degrees of association opportunity and density (AOD). For the entire period analysed, the highest AODs were found in 14 counties: eight of them in the Province of Barcelona (Maresme, Anoia, Vallès Occidental, Vallès Oriental, Bages, Berguedà, Moianès, and Osona) and six in the Province of Tarragona (Baix Penedès, Tarragonès, Baix Camp, Alt Camp, Conca de Barberà, and Priorat – see Table 9.2 and Figure 9.2). These 14 counties, which represent a third of the total, are home to 28% of the Catalan population and 57% of its popular associations, with an association density of 17 associations per 1,000 inhabitants in 1868–1938. The average for Catalonia as a whole was nine, just over half. Furthermore, 344 of the 378 municipalities in these counties (91%) had registered associations.

Most of the counties with a high density of associations in the period analysed are typified by growing specialisation in the wine sector (Tarragona counties), industrial development (Barcelona counties), and increasingly urbanised populations (both). During the 1920s, half of the Catalan working class lived in the 14 counties with the highest association density, 60% of their land was occupied by vineyards, and 30% of the population lived in towns with more than 10,000 inhabitants. Literacy increased by almost 40% during the first three decades of the twentieth

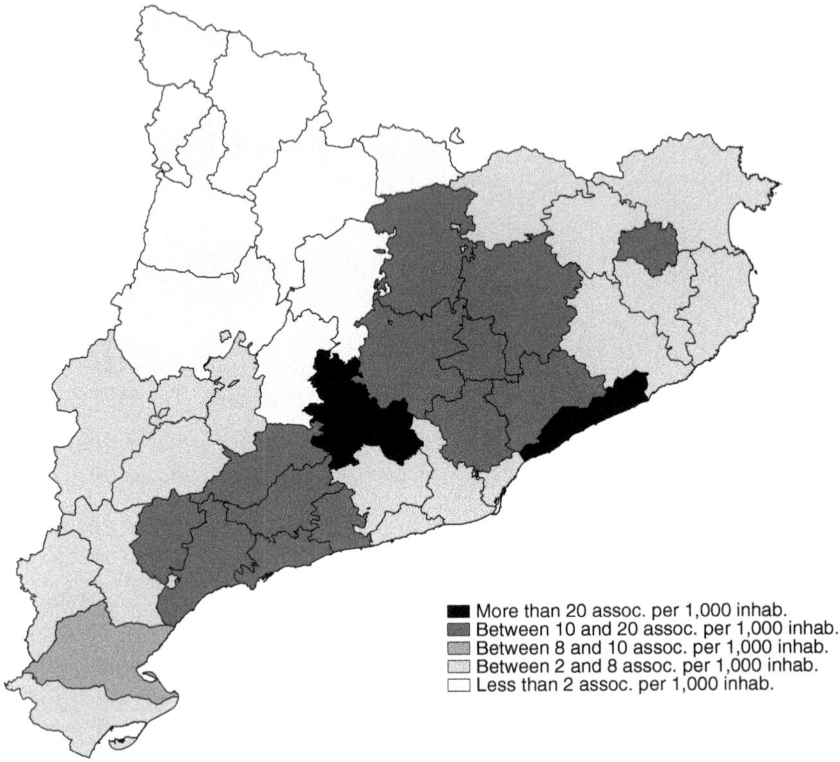

Figure 9.2 Density of popular associations by county, Catalonia, 1868–1938.
Source: Created by Agustí Agramunt based on BDACC data.

century. Furthermore, 91.5% of the associations were in municipalities with a railway station or within a 10 km radius of one.

One characteristic of the Catalan popular association movement was its strong presence in medium-sized towns and cities of between 5,000 and 30,000 inhabitants. These account for 41 municipalities (4.4% of the total), where 20% of the Catalan population lived, and where 34% of the popular associations were found, leading to a density of 11–15 associations per 1,000 inhabitants. From these towns and cities, most of which were county capitals, ideas and practices spread and ended up being implemented in the small and medium-sized municipalities of the respective counties, once they were proven to work and offer advantages. Another feature of the contemporary Catalan popular association model was the distribution of municipal associations, with an average of 53% of associations found in municipalities that were not county capitals, compared to 47% in county capitals.

Popular associationism and politicisation

During the six democratic years, from 1868–1874, there was a strong but not complete correlation between the republican vote and the density of regional associations, with four nuclei standing out: the area comprised of the counties of Barcelonès, Baix Llobregat, and Vallès; Segrià County; the counties of Camp de Tarragona, Priorat, and Baix Ebre; and Empordà County.

During the Restoration (1875–1923), republicanism extended its sphere of action, although it continued to revolve around four nuclei: Empordà and Gironès; Penedès, Vallès, Barcelonès, and Baix Llobregat; Camp de Tarragona, Priorat, Terra Alta, and Baix Ebre; and Pallars Jussà and La Noguera. Meanwhile, the Carlist vote was concentrated where it had a strong network of associations: Garrotxa, Osona, Gironès, Baix Empordà, and Berguedà. Meanwhile, the Catalan regionalist vote was primarily from the inland and northern regions of the country: Alt Urgell, Solsonès, Bages, Berguedà, Cerdanya, Anoia, Moianès, Osona, Garrotxa, and some of the coastal counties (Selva, Maresme, and Garraf). Despite the socioeconomic and demographic differences between the counties where republicanism, Carlism, and Catalanism received most of their votes, most of the counties had a high density of associations.

During the first third of the twentieth century, popular associations became politicised mainly at the local level, and an increasing number of non-political associations adopted names that recognised their affiliation with a particular political culture. This trend intensified during the years of Primo de Rivera's dictatorship (1923–1930) and the Second Republic (1931–1938), as a logical consequence of the increasing intensity of the social and political conflicts that had begun in the second decade of the twentieth century.[15]

The growing politicisation of Catalan associations occurred in parallel with the consolidation of the political cultures of republicanism, anarchism, Catalanism, socialism, communism, and social Catholicism, and with the political socialisation and politicisation of the urban and rural working classes, as evidenced in local and county studies of the Second Republic.[16] Analysis of voting by county in the 1931–1936 period does not show a strong correlation between the left-wing vote and counties with high association density, since, although this occurred in most of the counties of Girona and Tarragona, it did not occur in the counties of Barcelona or Lleida. This provides a good example of how all of the political cultures, progressive and conservative, had a strong network of associations and socialisation forums that enabled them to consolidate their support.

Politicisation went hand in hand with the polarisation of associations. In most municipalities of fewer than 5,000 inhabitants, a two-tiered pattern of socialisation was created: 'high' society and 'low' society; the society of the rich and the society of the poor; the society of landowners and strike-breakers; the society of workers and farmers; the society of Catholics and the society of the laity; and the society of the right and the society of the left. In these municipalities, the forums where this two-tiered socialisation occurred were shared by the different political cultures within each of the blocs (conservative and progressive). Traditionalists, liberals, monarchists, and conservative Catalanists came together in the landowners' associations, and republicans, anarchists, socialists, and left-wing Catalanists came together in popular associations.

Polarisation and two-tiered associations led to political, social, and cultural conflicts in many Catalan municipalities. In towns and cities with more than 5,000 inhabitants, polarisation did not imply a reduction to two umbrella organisations. Rather, it was a polarisation that affected all types of organisations, attracting existing associations to one or the other of the two poles (conservative or progressive).

In modern Catalonia, the heterogeneous popular association movement was widely distributed geographically and involved many sectors, which allowed the rural and urban working classes as well as the dominated or subaltern classes to have horizontal groups and opportunities for socialisation as an alternative to the traditional vertical ones and the modern interclass associations supported by the Catholic Church and landowners. The popular association network provided the subordinate classes with forums for horizontal socialisation, and from these they developed a symbolic-cultural framework that enabled them to interpret social and political reality and situate themselves within it while formulating actions to change it.

The popular association network gave the lower classes experience in organisation, cooperation, and solidarity that was instrumental in dealing with the serious political, economic, and social crises of the 1920s and 1930s. It was in these associations that democratic and transformative political cultures from republicanism to anarchism spread and gained strength. It was here that large sections of the Catalan working class strengthened their identities and their autonomy and equipped themselves with material and immaterial resources to face political, social, and productive life. It was here that social mobilisation emerged to confront the wealthy classes, the state, and the Catholic Church, who also developed a strong network of associations linked to Catholicism, Carlism, and Catalanism.

Mutualism

The many hardships that affected the working classes during Catalonia's contemporary history are a key factor in explaining the proliferation of Mutual Insurance Societies and the expansion of the solidarity culture. The development of this culture, seen as one organised horizontally among equals, becomes unintelligible unless the connections between these two phenomena are considered. They are, therefore, the social foundation that made the mutualist experience and the historiographical debate on Catalan distinctiveness possible, determining the popularity of the movement and the way it was organised on the federal level from 1890 to 1936.

One consideration that cannot be ignored, based on the current state of the literature, is the absence of women. Women were not welcomed until quite late; widows were treated as subordinates when they entered men's spaces. Women were highly active in Catalan industry and had their traditional seasonal bond with the agricultural cycle, both subject to the discourse of domesticity.[17] The numerous mutual insurance companies founded in Catalonia reflect the mentality of the time in their statutes and practices, as they perpetuate the myth of the family wage and the discourse of the male provider in society, which are shaped by relationships of power, production, and experience that pay homage to the gendered social contract of their time.

The Historical Statistics of Spain offer an approximate distribution of family consumption: between 1900 and 1939, consumption was predominantly foodstuffs (65.7 and 60.1), clothing and footwear (6.2 and 9.4), housing (10 and 14.6), household expenses (11.2 and 8.5), and miscellaneous (6.9 and 7.4).[18] Was there enough for the mutual quota? Was it a question of disposable family income or lifestyle? The close relationship between the amount and regularity of wages and living and working conditions should clearly be considered.[19]

A central aspect of the role of mutual insurance societies in social history is their solidity against a background of widespread wage precariousness, or, more exactly, people's standard of living, since the relatively high cost of the aid system was a serious obstacle to strengthening popular and workers' mutualism in comparison with other European societies. The Barcelona Social Museum estimated in 1917 that 70% of wages were spent on food, and Morato concluded a few years earlier, in 1909, that there was a correlation between lower standards of living and 'higher mortality, higher morbidity, earlier ages of disability, more disability and earlier disability, and that low wages presuppose job insecurity, which makes compulsory unemployment relief extremely difficult'.[20]

In some cases, this situation led to these services being discontinued with users resorting to affiliation to the services of private companies and collective mutual initiatives, which some companies did, particularly in Catalonia, where the *Farmacia Cooperativa de la Unión y la Defensa de los Montepíos* was founded in Barcelona in 1896, the precursor of the *Federacio de Mutualitats de Catalunya*, a pharmaceutical association whose merit would be confirmed in 1935. The most common benefits were cash benefits for illness starting on the third day, medical care, pharmaceutical support, and death and disability benefits.[21]

The predominance of popular mutualism marks a trend that was reaffirmed in the transition from the nineteenth to the twentieth century, although studies of the evolution, degree, and types of aid, as well as the role pursued or achieved by prominent individuals through their patronage, are still lacking and can only be advanced through the study of individual associations. In Catalonia, progress still needs to be made in local research on these issues. Pere Solà dissected the nature of Catalan mutualism, which has a cohesive social function and an economic *raison d'être*, which, at first sight, reveals a confusion of purposes between groups, trade societies (descendants of the guilds), trade unions, cooperatives, charities, and popular mutual societies.[22] As such, 'the social function of "mutual aid" can only be studied as a whole, taking into account the type of production relations and the character of the whole associative fabric.'[23] The lower middle class used the mutualist model, in some cases imbued with a secular spirituality.[24]

Social welfare and popular socialisation

Insurance is the main overt function of mutual benefit societies, but not the only one. Those who join these societies also seek and often find a certain kind of camaraderie and solidarity and frequently share specific ideological, religious, party, or political views that are the emblem or standard of the society they belong to.[25] Mutual benefit societies play an important role in garnering experience in managing one's own affairs; they offer forums to learn and exercise the condition of citizenship from the bottom up. It is important to bear in mind that mutualism 'taught workers some essential values in bourgeois society, such as voluntary discipline and long-term thinking'.[26] Its ritual functions are also worth considering. In all human cultures, the function of ritual is to alleviate and dispel anxiety by turning people towards the outside world through shared symbolic actions. Secular rituals, particularly those that have cooperation as their purpose, have been shown to be too weak to provide this. However, the expansive mutualist network undoubtedly offered forums and opportunities to forge and celebrate the dynamics of belonging that ritual reinforced. This is reiterated in the popular memory.

At the beginning of the twentieth century, the number of mutual societies in Catalonia was comparable to that in Great Britain, France, or

Belgium and much greater than in Spain as a whole.[27] There were mutual benefit societies in 153 municipalities in 1890 (16.3%), in 382 in 1910 (40.6%), and in 424 in 1930 (45% of the 939 municipalities).

The heterogeneity, complexity, and variability over time of the mutualist phenomenon lends itself to the use of various different typological criteria. Three basic types emerge: the Catholic model (defined as overprotective, paternalistic, more charitable and welfare-oriented than preventive, and with a significant presence of patrons); the popular model (which requires no affiliation with a specific occupation and which gives rise to a wide array of associations); and worker-based welfare mutualism (associated with specific production sectors and geographical areas and arising from the initiative of workers or employers).[28]

Official statistics are unreliable, due to the failure to register 36% of societies in the 1904 census, or, as happened with the 1924 and 1928 Corporate Electoral Censuses, they are not useful for analysing the evolution of solidarity associations, due to attitudes of indifference, suspicion, or neglect.[29] One of the aspects of Catalonia's multifaceted mutual associationism is reflected in the fact that it is a solidarity-based and more or less cohesive manifestation of popular socialisation, which, faced with ineffective initiatives on the part of the state, basically sought protection from contingencies that could upset the balance of daily life.[30]

The phenomenon of mutual and cooperative associationism is neither secondary nor peripheral. Until the second decade of the twentieth century, it represented the first form of formal socialisation, an effort from below to coordinate responses to misfortune through solidarity. They were extraordinarily flexible groups, which could change from mutual aid groups to agricultural cooperatives. Consumer cooperatives also developed mutual insurance sections.[31] So, we can speak of pure, impure, or versatile mutual societies, or, with Van der Linden, of societies based on mutual associations established for personal, voluntary mutual insurance for employees and to provide members with financial assistance in case of need.[32] The historical cause behind the establishment of mutual benefit societies or workers' societies for resistance to capital is the same. Mutual benefit societies, with greater structural and ideological diversity, aspired to offer medical, pharmaceutical, pension, and death coverage. In 1900, as Hobsbawm wrote, two social strata emerged in the social arena: the old, comprising all the mercantile producers whose social position was undermined by the advance of capitalism (the artisans); and the new, the product of the confluence of the organisation of the state and the advance of capitalism. If the old had played the leading role in defensive mutualism throughout the nineteenth century, the new played the leading role in adaptive mutualism in the first third of the twentieth century. An examination of the mutual aid societies founded by craftsmen and tradesmen in the nineteenth century reveals their desire for emancipation, while those created by the new middle classes emphasised the imperative need to adapt to new living and working conditions.[33]

Multifunctionality and small-scale mutualism

The fact that the available sources prefer to quantify mutual benefit societies has not helped us to know their members' numbers or the mutual societies' incomes and expenditures, types, and levels of benefits, which are central to understanding what these associations really were rather than what they claimed to be in their statutes. The studies available indicate that the average size of mutual benefit societies was between 100 and 250 members, although they varied enormously.[34] 'The continued existence of numerous small mutual benefit societies meant they lacked the financial resources and technical capacity to deal with negative events as predictable as the simple ageing of the original members'.[35] One way to reduce expenditure was to federate or unite, as was the case with *Unión y Defensa de los Montepíos de Barcelona y sus Afueras*. The entity was founded in 1896 and included assistance funds, mutual benefit societies, charitable societies, etc. in Barcelona and the surrounding area. It had 554 member associations and 124,916 members in 1911, and 747 associations with 167,623 members in 1915. It changed its name in 1918 to *Federación de Sociedades de Socorros Mutuos de la Provincia de Barcelona*, reaching a total of 827 federated mutual benefit societies and 289,773 members ten years later.[36] Discussion of the state's failure to take part in developing social legislation, doubtless attributable to many factors, must take account of its fiscal capacity and public expenditure. In 1920, state expenditure as a percent of national income was 32% in France, 26% in the United Kingdom, and 8% in Spain.[37]

Spanish mutualism in the 1930s was weak and precarious and 'was able to remain so largely because it operated in a context in which its competitors, state social security and private insurance companies, also had shortcomings and limitations', resulting in a substantial number of workers without coverage, since private insurance did not take hold among the working classes due to the combined effects of their standard of living and mentality.[38] Spain lagged behind in adopting public policies and was unable to emulate the different solutions applied in the German, Belgian, and Italian models. During the passage of the 1933 law on workplace accidents, it was recorded that there was only one provincial federation, Barcelona's, represented at the 1922 conference, which had been able to work with political institutions of regional self-government, such as the Commonwealth of Catalonia (*la Mancomunitat*), and private bodies such as the *Caja de Pensiones*, that were working to promote mutuality. The drafters of the law recognised that mutualism was considered 'an innate part of social life, an indispensable facet of the normal functioning of the working-class family' in Catalonia.[39]

The 1920s were the heyday of Catalan civil mutualism but also a time of crisis for it, as shown by the densely packed timeline of the Federation of Mutual Aid Societies, starting in 1896 with the acts of mutualist affirmation, the conferences in Barcelona on Social Security, and the creation of the *Refugio Mutual* in 1913.[40] The Federation of Mutual Aid Societies had no public funding but did have some 800 associations and 200,000 members in 1924 and was headed by Joan Colominas Maseras, a politician of the Radical Republican Party.[41] In 1925, the Vilanova 'pact' between mutual benefit societies and cooperatives was signed, according to which 'Catalan mutualism in its threefold expression of mutual aid, cooperation and medical care, has embarked on the path to its full potential with a sure step'.[42] The statistics show an increase in their social and economic representation in terms of their number of associated entities and members, and the volume of subsidies, so much so that half the working population in the Province of Barcelona belonged to federated mutual societies in 1923, a profoundly revealing fact. Solà argues that, prior to 1936, Catalonia had the quantitative and qualitative foundation (associative and organic) for civil mutualism that was not directly controlled by the state, as well as relatively mature welfare and assistance services in response to capitalist exploitation.

The case of Sabadell is illustrative in that, in a textile manufacturing environment with a trade unionist working class, a *Federació de Germandats* had existed since 1922. It was comprised of 22 mutual benefit societies and had 12,245 members, which represented more than a quarter of the city's population. An expert like Pere Solà would thus conclude that 'the network of Catalan mutual benefit societies of the Restoration would have been in line with the small-scale industry of the region where it developed'.

The location of the mutual benefit societies followed patterns quite similar to those of industrial facilities. In England, Daniel Defoe noted in 1697 that friendly societies were already widespread in urban areas and that the system was growing stronger and acquiring new functions in response to the decline of charitable organisations.[43] These organisations were taking on previously unknown functions with new implications, teaching immigrants arriving in the city about insurance, saving, and future planning in an uncertain context. The use of these associations to channel welfare subsidies under the National Insurance Act of 1911 meant that their membership was compulsory.[44]

In Catalonia, the newly created social welfare associations were the result of an urbanised environment that was economically dependent on the secondary sector and the establishment of a class structure and wage composition that, although stable, did not grow at the same rate as the industrial sector itself. In rural Catalonia, meanwhile, rural-urban migration led to a comparative improvement in wages due to the lack of labour, an improvement that became particularly evident as automation advanced in rural areas.[45]

We hold that this was related to greater diversity in industrialisation and socioeconomic structure, society becoming hyper-specialised, with a more equitable structure of cities and municipalities. This was the model that would eventually spread throughout rural Catalonia, from Priorat and Terres de l'Ebre to Garrigues and Urgell, and from Osona to Gironès. At the beginning of the twentieth century, the old areas of concentration also began to disperse, which reduced the ratio of inhabitants to mutual benefit societies. In 1930, mutualism was widespread in the populated areas of Catalonia, with a map that was as urban and industrial as it was rural and agricultural. We are, therefore, dealing with an archetypal process of the dissemination of ideas and innovations that first take root in urban environments and are subsequently transferred to rural areas, which emulate them.[46]

Comparison by territory

In terms of the number of associations, the Catalan provinces accounted for 24.3% of all associations in Spain, the province of Barcelona accounting for 60.5% of them. With regard to mutual benefit societies, Catalonia accounted for 11% of the total with 10.6% of the population, a symmetrical situation. Twelve years later, in 1916, the situation had changed. Catalonia accounted for 13.7% of workers' associations. This was due to the increase in such associations throughout Spain, which reduced the relative weight of Catalonia, although it had been a pioneer in the field and had well-established organisations.

An examination of 1916 statistics on distribution by type shows a notable prominence of mutual benefit societies, which accounted for 50% of savings, cooperation, and welfare societies. In 1916, the 1,779 Catalan welfare societies represented 50% of the Spanish total. In 1915, 73.4% of mutual benefit societies were formed in Catalonia. By 1925, however, the proportion had fallen slightly to 65.3%, while in the same decade, the percentage of members rose from 56.3% to 61.9%. Although Catalonia's predominance is clear, the movement was also relatively small, since there were approximately 81,017 members in Catalonia in 1915 and 246,854 ten years later, while Spain as a whole had 143,993 and 398,999 ten years later, according to official statistics on 'the question of health insurance' (1927).[47]

A monograph on social cooperatives in Italy compares the creation and development of cooperativism in Northern Italy and Catalonia, in 'the most Protestant areas of Catholic countries'.[48] In other words, it was where the first signs of capitalism appeared; where a bourgeoisie that was becoming more industrialised and modernised grew; where the entrepreneurial spirit associated with hard work, diligence, and merit gained a stronger foothold; and where the middle and lower classes were able to organise themselves and start all kinds of societies and associations of a mutual, social, or cultural nature. Both areas had diversified social stratification and an urban fabric that structured the territory, opposed to a state with a centralist, anachronistic, and often despotic tradition. However, this did not prevent them from becoming engines of considerable economic growth that linked them to the rest of Europe and made them a gateway for Nordic ideas and movements.[49] In Greece, Portugal, Italy, and Spain, southern European countries with common characteristics, mutual assistance seemed to play a leading role in the beginning, and the Catholic and Orthodox Churches marked their territories by relegating the state to a complementary role. Labour legislation therefore precedes social legislation in southern European societies, which also had their own type of protection, since the first compulsory insurance was that covering work-related accidents.

In the Catalan and perhaps also in the Mediterranean cases, these networks were informal forums of solidarity centred on kinship, what in studies of political cultures has been called 'familism'.[50] Even in its evolution, one sees similarities with the Rochdale pioneers, who created the first cooperative in 1843 and 20 years later a welfare society for health and burial relief. The prevention of accidents impacting members also appears in Catalonia's powerful (agricultural and consumer) cooperativism.[51] The comparison of Northern Italy and Catalonia shows similarities in the introduction of capitalism, the dialectic of the construction of the liberal state between the modernising bourgeoisie and the traditional agrarian oligarchy, as well as the presence and power of the church, which had a monopoly on private welfare.[52] The church was an obstacle to mutualism, but it also provided an incentive for workers to organise.[53] Finally, the large amount of social capital from the old guild structures and organisations helped to promote its development, indicators that Sennet outlined in *Juntos. Rituales, placeres y política de cooperación* (Together: Rituals, Pleasures and the Politics of Cooperation).

The social relations of resistance to the living conditions of capitalism are manifested in collective mentalities that promote trust between people, reciprocity, social networks, and a sense of belonging to a community. These were present in Catalan society in the last decades of the nineteenth century and the first decades of the twentieth century. They largely promoted organisation and mutual aid among workers. In 1910, mutual benefit societies existed in 637 municipalities and in 661 municipalities in 1930. This strong presence was found in most counties, with the exception of the areas of Lleida and the Pyrenees, while the concentration was even higher in Barcelona, Tarragona, and Reus.

I would venture to argue that mutualism was an important facet of Catalan social history that overcame the rural-urban, agrarian-industrial dichotomy. Despite their differences, the grassroots response to comparable needs was uniform: the establishment of risk protection for the citizenry. Analysis of the ratio of inhabitants to mutual benefit societies shows greater density and capacity for risk coverage from 1910 onwards.

Ramon Arnabat's analysis of rural mutual insurance in the Penedès concluded that contributions represented 1% of salary and benefits 50–75% of salary, with very high levels of coverage, about 80% of adult workers and 75% of workers in companies. He states that associationism was gradually cutting the ties that bound workers to key socioeconomic stakeholders and the church, while increasing their autonomy. In the context of a severe agrarian crisis, coverage was combined with other functions: acquisition of experience in solidarity and organisation skills that would be reflected in the peasant movement of the 1920s and 1930s, especially in the wine-growing counties.[54]

Richard Sennett refers to the bonds that liberated workers in Boston as a social triangle comprised of earned authority, mutual respect, and cooperation in times of crisis.[55] In the social space of mutual benefit societies, rituals were practised that provided relief from experiences of anxiety and offered a sense of belonging. And to the extent they belonged to multifunctional entities such as cooperatives or republican organisations, they constituted their own 'home'.[56] Mutual benefit societies help to shape collective identity by cultivating values such as self-organisation and responsibility while simultaneously shaping geographical and/or professional community identities. It is perhaps more about belonging and security than real risk protection: symbolic and emotional returns that outweigh the material ones.

Future studies should focus on understanding why the network of Catalan mutual benefit societies, especially in the coastal provinces, grew so strong in the 1880s, how this network was linked to labour organisation and resistance to capitalism, what influences came from French mutual benefit societies, and how the trade guilds and religious guilds provided a kind of substratum for Catalan industrial mutual benefit societies in the late nineteenth century.[57]

Cooperativism

Consumer and production cooperatives became one of the mainstays of popular associationism in Catalonia with the twofold aim of resolving the immediate consumption and production needs of workers and farmers, and constructing alternatives aimed at social transformation.

The process of industrialisation and urbanisation in Catalonia from the 1830s until the Civil War (1936–1939) led to significant migration from the countryside to the cities and a consequent increase in the urban population. The majority of the population were workers who crowded into industrial towns and cities, lived on the edge of subsistence, and were exposed to precarious working conditions.

Awareness of their situation, the spread of democratic, republican, and pro-worker political cultures, and short periods of political freedom led to the emergence of solidarity and cooperative associative practices among the working classes. Despite their diversity, all these practices were based on cooperation and mutual aid to protect the common good and collective well-being.[58]

In industrial and semi-industrial urban environments, the majority of the population depended on private businesses for the acquisition of consumer goods such as foodstuffs, basic household goods, and clothing. Low wages and the need to buy good quality products at low prices led to the creation of consumer cooperatives among the working classes.[59] At the same time, the lack of work led to the creation of production cooperatives. Later on, credit, housing, and medical-pharmaceutical cooperatives were formed.[60]

A global vision

Between 1840 and 1938, a total of 622 cooperatives were created in Catalonia, of which the majority were consumer cooperatives (472 or 76%), followed by production cooperatives (114 or 18%), and housing cooperatives (56 or 6%), as shown in Table 9.3.

In the entire period analysed, an average of eight cooperatives were founded per year. The first third of the twentieth century stands out, with

Table 9.3 Creation of cooperatives in Catalonia, 1840–1938

	Total	*Consumer*	*%*	*Production*	*%*	*Housing*	*%*	*Per year*
Before 1887	27	25	92.6	2	7.4	0	0.0	1
1887–1900	77	66	85.7	11	14.3	0	0.0	5.5
1901–1922	330	263	79.7	53	16.1	14	4.2	15
1923–1930	102	59	57.8	23	22.5	20	19.6	13
1931–1938	86	59	68.6	25	29.1	2	2.3	11
Total	622	472	75.9	114	18.3	36	5.8	8

Source: Created by the authors based on BDACC data.

an annual average of 11–15. The period 1901–1922 was particularly fruitful: 330 new cooperatives were created, at an annual average of 15.

The distribution of cooperatives in the counties was very heterogeneous. The counties with the most cooperatives were in the coastal and pre-coastal areas, the interior industrial areas, and the wine-producing areas of Camp de Tarragona and Penedès (Figure 9.3). These 13 counties (31% of the total), where 58% of the Catalan population lived, had 501 cooperatives, 80.5% of the total. In the cities, Barcelona, Mataró, Terrassa, Sabadell, Tarragona, Igualada, Vic, Valls, Manlleu, Badalona, Manresa, Olot, Torelló, Palafrugell, and Girona had the most cooperatives, a total of 320, or 51.5% of the total.

The highest density, or ratio of cooperatives to inhabitants of a county, is found in Priorat, Osona, Maresme, Anoia, Berguedà, Alt Camp, Baix Penedès, and Vallès Occidental. These counties have significant industrial

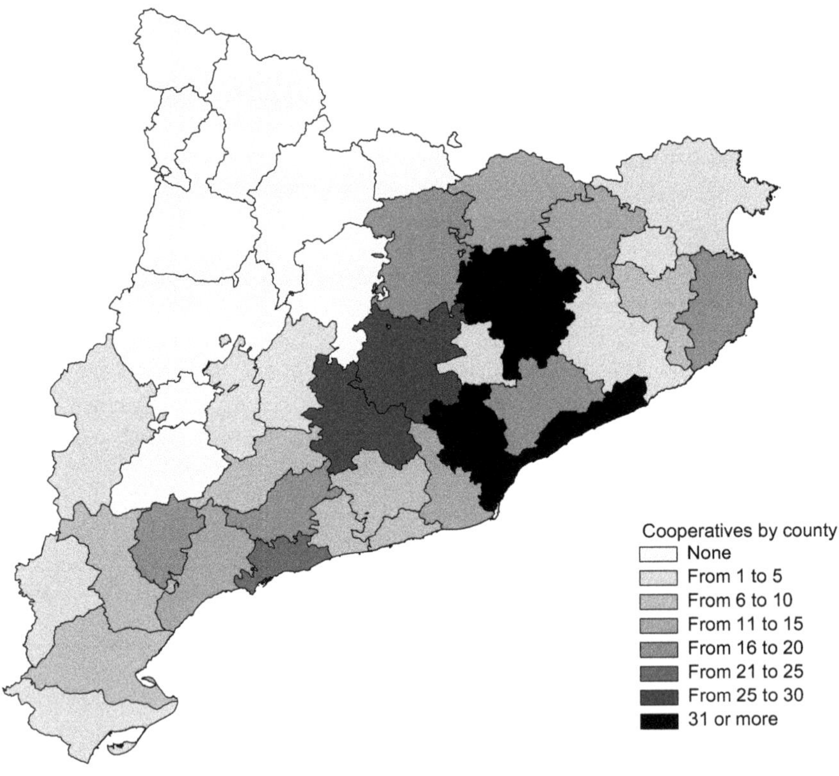

Figure 9.3 Cooperatives by county, Catalonia 1868–1938.

Source: Created by Agustí Agramunt based on BDACC data.

development and/or wine-growing activity and a high degree of urban concentration.[61]

Cooperatives came to have a strong presence in the working-class neighbourhoods of the city of Barcelona. This is the case of Sants, where, between 1870 and 1939, ten workers' and popular consumer cooperatives were formed.[62] And one of the city's most important consumer cooperatives, *La Flor de Maig* (1890), was based in the Poblenou neighbourhood.[63] In 1935 there were 57 workers' consumer cooperatives in Barcelona, with such symbolic names as *La Constancia, La Fraternidad, La Lealtad, La Amistad, Paz y Justicia*, and *La Igualitaria*. There were also five second-degree cooperatives that manufactured charcoal, soup pasta, soap, chocolate, and carbonated water.[64]

According to the Institute of Social Reform, in 1904 there were 241 cooperatives with 40,366 members registered in Catalonia. Of these, 17 were production cooperatives (4,920 members), 42 were credit cooperatives (6,502 members), and 182 were consumer cooperatives (40,366 members).[65] Catalonia was home to 40% of the cooperatives in Spain and 21% of their members, despite accounting for only 11% of the population.[66]

The first steps (1840–1900)

The first Catalan cooperatives were production cooperatives set up between 1840 and 1843 by the basket makers, shoemakers, and weavers of Barcelona, their aim being to provide work for unemployed members.[67] However, it was not until the 1860s that cooperativism definitively took root in Catalonia, promoted by the work of the republicans Fernando Garrido and Joan Josep Tutau, who had been to Rochdale, England, in 1862 to learn about cooperativism at first hand.[68] The two men shared their experience of the English cooperative system and advocated the Rochdale model, which was based on open and voluntary membership, economic democracy (one member, one vote), and returning a portion of the cooperative's annual profits to members.[69]

Cooperativist ideas made an impression on federal democrats and republicans, and on the Catalan working classes, leading to the establishment of production cooperatives: *La Textil Obrera Mataronense* (1864) and *La Propagadora del Trabajo* (1865) and consumer cooperatives *La Económica Palafrugellense* (1865); *la Companyia de Canet de Mar* (1865); *L'Antiga del Camp de l'Arpa* (1866); and *La Constancia Martinenca* (1868).[70]

The rise of cooperativism coincided with the efforts of Catalan workers to organise and was an active facet of the various workers' conferences between 1866 and 1870. However, the initial consensus on cooperativism fractured in the 1870s, when the anarchist – and to a lesser extent Marxist and socialist – political culture took root in Catalonia. At the 1870 First Spanish Workers' Congress, one of the most contentious issues was cooperativism, a subject on which two opposing points of view emerged. The cooperativists advocated cooperatives as the centrepiece of the strategy for workers' emancipation, while the Bakuninists championed the creation of trade unions both for the daily struggle of workers and for social transformation.

Despite the ideological divergences, cooperatives, predominantly consumer cooperatives, continued to proliferate and expand geographically, especially after the 1887 Association Law. These included the *Associació Cooperativa de Reus* (1870), *La Constancia* (Tarragona, 1871), *Teixidors a Mà* (Gràcia, 1876), *Artesana del Poblenou* (1876), *Obrera Sabadellense* (1877), *L'Andreuenca* (Sant Andreu del Palomar, 1878), *La Fraternidad* (Barcelona, 1879), *Sabadellenca* (1881), *La Economía* (Sant Feliu de Guíxols, 1885), *La Regeneradora* (Llagostera, 1886), *La Equitativa* (Palamós, 1887), *La Flor de Maig* (1890), *La Guixolenca* (Sant Feliu de Guíxols, 1898), and *La Redemptora* (Sants, 1899).[71] The production and consumer cooperative *Sociedad Cooperativa La Obrera Sabadellense* (Sabadell, 1877) offers an illustrative example. It also operated as a mutual benefit society and savings bank, with the aim of 'building factories and workshops where members without work would take preference; supplying members with quality food products at reasonable prices; ensuring decent subsistence for members who are unable to work through illness, and establishing a savings bank' (1899).[72]

The cooperatives were created by pooling small contributions from members. Their primary mission was to avoid intermediaries by purchasing basic necessities (mainly foodstuffs) directly and in bulk, which they then sold to their members. The annual profits were used for collective funds for education, culture, and mutual assistance. Little by little, small cooperative shops expanded, and new buildings were built to serve as schools, theatres, and cafés, offering social spaces for members.

In 1898, the First Assembly of Catalan Cooperatives was held in Badalona, attended by 37 delegates. A regional committee was appointed, and the *Revista Cooperativa Catalana* journal was founded.[73] The following year, in 1899, the First Catalan-Balearic Cooperative Congress was held in Barcelona. Of the 110 existing cooperatives, 48 took part, representing 7,000 families. At the congress, delegates agreed to establish the Regional Chamber of Catalan-Balearic Cooperatives and the Office of Business Relations to make joint purchases through a central purchasing warehouse. The following year, the Catalan cooperative movement decided to join the International Cooperative Alliance.

The Second Catalan-Balearic Cooperative Congress (1902) was attended by 81 cooperatives. Debates focused on the model of cooperativism to be adopted (whether cooperativism should be individualistic or collective), whether the aim of the Chamber should be cooperation ('cooperation is association') or cooperatism ('cooperation developed as a system of social emancipation)'. The relationship between the cooperatives and the unions was also discussed. It was agreed that 'Catalan and Balearic cooperatives are recognised as part of the general workers' movement, whose objectives they share in full'.[74]

The congresses served to focus attention on obstacles to the development of cooperatives and to demand greater involvement on the part of the public authorities through exemptions from certain taxes and the enactment of a cooperative law, which would not come into force until the Second Republic.[75] They also served to help the cooperatives expand to new regions and fostered cooperation among them.[76]

The roots of cooperativism (1904–1920)

From the beginning of the twentieth century, representatives of the cooperativist movement (*Cámara Regional de Cooperativas*) and mutualism (*Unión y Defensa de los Montepíos*) worked closely together to benefit their members, who in many cases were the same people. This cooperation led to a number of initiatives, such as the founding of the *Sociedad Cooperativa de Farmacias Populares in Barcelona* in Barcelona (1904), Mataró (1909), and other cities. The experience was so successful that by the 1930s *Farmacias Populares* had 87 associated mutual and cooperative organisations. In addition, the *La Alianza* health village (1904) developed into a leading health service. It founded several hospitals to care for the growing number of individual and collective members (e.g. associated cooperatives).[77]

Another focus of the cooperative movement was providing decent, affordable housing when the arrival of thousands of immigrants in Catalonia led to a housing shortage. Several cooperatives used the 1911 and 1921 Affordable Housing Acts to implement housing projects, although most initiatives came from professional groups (military, civil servants, journalists, railwaymen, and architects).[78]

The 1914 Annual Social Statistics Report on Catalonia records 308 consumer cooperatives, with some 50,000 members and 26.1 billion pesetas in sales,[79] while the preliminary version of the Institute of Social Reform 1915 Census of Associations showed a total of 298 workers' cooperatives in Catalonia, of which 242 were consumer cooperatives (81%), 33 had multiple functions (consumption and production or savings, representing 11% of the total), 13 were credit and savings cooperatives (4.5%), 5 were production cooperatives, 4 were low-cost housing cooperatives, and 1 was a medical-pharmaceutical cooperative.[80]

In 1916, a new Assembly of Catalan Cooperatives was held, in which 97 organisations took part, representing 16,500 families.

Francisco J. Medina and Josep Pujol Andreu point out that consumer cooperatives 'contributed significantly to nutritional transition in two ways: they promoted more stable access to basic foodstuffs of good quality and a more diverse diet by selling new products'.[81]

As cooperativism took root, the 'praxis of cooperativism' was reaffirmed, as opposed to simple cooperation, since the former was an economic and ethical ideology that offered a socioeconomic model based on the cooperative organisation of consumers.[82] This model was presented as a social alternative that aimed to replace capitalism. To a large extent, it was based on the economic programme developed by Charles Gide in Nîmes (1899) for comprehensive cooperativisation of the economy and society, based on the needs of consumers.[83]

Education and training were among the priorities of Catalan cooperativism from the beginning, although this was emphasised even more after the Second Congress of 1902.[84] The aim was to end the high illiteracy rates among the working classes and women. To achieve this, many cooperatives earmarked part of their surpluses for educational funds.[85] The cooperatives also promoted cultural groups that organised talks, lectures, and other activities, which were coordinated through the *Agrupació Cultural Cooperatista*, chaired from 1928 by Josep Joan Domènech, a member of the *Confederació Nacional del Treball* and president of the *Unió Cooperatista Barcelonesa*. Concern for education and culture was one of the main links between cooperativeists and trade unionists.

Catalan women who were members of the cooperatives were a minority among the minorities. However, there were exceptions, one of the most notable being cooperativist, feminist, and socialist Micaela Chalmeta, who helped create the consumer cooperative *La Economía Social* (1904) and later the cooperative *Modelo del Siglo XX* (1925).[86] Chalmeta saw cooperatives as 'a weapon to root out one of the sources of dominant capitalism' and a forum for socialisation, education, and organisation outside the domestic sphere to help bring about women's emancipation, because the cooperative was to be the embryo of the 'society of the future'.[87] Also worthy of mention are María Palomera, Dolors Abelló, Rosa Forment, Antonia Sancho, Ángela Graupera, Teresa Canalda, María Soriano, Josefa Bosque, Regina Lamo, among others.

Women's cooperation developed from working-class feminism, which advocated equality, autonomy, and the economic and social emancipation of women through education and work. They promoted the view that social emancipation and women's emancipation were closely linked and that the cooperative idea was a useful tool.[88]

The consolidation of cooperativism (1920–1938)

In 1919, the Regional Chamber of Catalan-Balearic Cooperatives was dissolved and replaced in 1920 by the Regional Federation of Cooperatives of Catalonia, a result of agreements reached at the Fourth Regional Cooperative Congress. Although, as Eladi Gardó pointed out, the main enemy of cooperativism was its *esperit de capelleta*[89] (its 'little chapel' spirit, meaning a tendency to associate only with a select group), it continued to advance in Catalonia and to organise itself on the regional level by creating the provincial federations of Barcelona, Tarragona, and Girona (1921). It also made progress at the national level and in 1928 the National Federation of Cooperatives of Spain was set up, both federations presided over by Joan Ventosa i Roig.

For their part, women continued to be invisible in the Catalan cooperative movement, and, although in 1916 the Assembly of the Regional Chamber of Cooperatives approved a ruling allowing women cooperative members to be full members of organisations, it was not effectively applied until 1929, when it was included in the new regulations of the cooperative *La Flor de Maig*.

During the 1920s, the consolidation of various local consumer cooperatives into one single cooperative was encouraged to increase their economic power. In accordance with the economic paradigm of consolidated cooperativism, in 1920, the Regional Federation of Cooperatives also established the Union of Cooperatives for the Manufacture of Pasta for Soup, which distributed production among approximately 100 cooperatives.

The 1931 Republican Law on Cooperatives and subsequent regulations clearly defined the term cooperative as 'an association of natural or legal persons whose purpose is to meet a common need by seeking the social and economic progress of its members through joint action in a collective project'. The Government of Catalonia also enacted the Law on Cooperation and the Specific Cooperative Law, which were markedly collectivist and made cooperativism an integral part of government by creating a Supreme Council for Cooperation, composed of representatives of all the federations and reporting to the Catalan Economic Council.

Republican legislation promoted the expansion of cooperativism, and consumer cooperatives increased in number and tripled their membership between 1931 and 1936 from 166 cooperatives and 27,718 members to 241 cooperatives and 84,300 members.[90] The 1932–1933 annual report indicated that a total of 592 cooperatives were registered, of which 205 were consumer cooperatives, 101 were housing cooperatives, and 110 were agricultural cooperatives.[91] In 1935, the Federation of Cooperatives became the Confederation of Cooperatives and undertook the constitution of the Central Purchasing Cooperative, a wholesale warehouse meant to supply the Catalan cooperative movement in the future.

For the first time, the cooperative movement was working in close cooperation with the government to promote cooperativism in all its different forms and at all possible levels (local, municipal and regional), while maintaining its autonomy.[92] All of this was in keeping with the guidelines set out by the International Cooperative Alliance and the French experience, which led to the creation of the *Caja de Crédito Agrícola y Cooperativo* (1933) and various cooperative factories making soap (1933), soft drinks (1934) and chocolates (1936).

During the Second Republic, autonomous production and worker cooperatives founded by employees and independent of consumer cooperatives flourished to a degree unknown in previous decades. In 1934, the *Subfederación de Cooperativas de Producción y Trabajo* brought together 125 entities with 7,200 members and an annual turnover of 27.3 million pesetas.[93] Anarcho-syndicalist and cooperativist Joan Peiró, founder of *Cristalleries de Mataró*, pointed out that production cooperativism was both a way to solve the practical problems of workers in the present and a way to build a proletarian identity with an alternative approach to the radical transformation of society.[94]

During the republican period, women's groups appeared within the cooperatives, aiming to promote the participation of women in the cooperative movement and increase their visibility. The first women's groups formed were *La Moral de Badalona, La Atrevida Martinenca,* and *La Unión Cooperatista Barcelonesa*. Subsequently, in October 1931, the women's groups that had appeared in the different cooperatives became an integral part of the Cooperative Federation, as part of the Propaganda Department. The body was known as the *Grup Femení de Propaganda*. The following year, the group became the *Agrupació Femenina de Propaganda Cooperativista*, with the aim of 'fostering cooperativism among women'.[95]

In addition to their propaganda work, women cooperativists worked hard to educate and train women. They organised all kinds of workshops, courses, and lectures and published Honora Enfield's booklet, *El poder de la cesta de la compra* (The Power of the Market Basket, translated by Micaela Chalmeta).[96] Another battleground of cooperative feminism was the struggle for the inclusion of women in all organisational spheres of the cooperative world, although it was not until 1936 that the first women joined the board of the *Centro Obrero Aragonés* cooperative.

According to Rafael Celada's study, at the beginning of the Spanish Civil War, 2,235 cooperatives had been set up in Catalonia, of which 911 were consumer cooperatives (41%), 889 were agricultural cooperatives (40%), 270 were production cooperatives (12%), and 165 (7%) were of various other types.[97] These more than 2,000 cooperatives show the strength of the cooperative movement in Catalonia. Cooperativism and the Catalan social economy had come of age thanks to institutional support in the form of legislation; specialisation and diversification in the movement itself and the federative bodies' capacity to adapt to this diversity; the development of second-degree industrial cooperatives based on consumer cooperatives; and the founding of the Central Purchasing Cooperative to make collective purchases; and, above all, thanks to the internalisation of cooperative principles among the working classes in Catalonia after decades of propaganda in the cooperative press, without which none of this would have been possible.

The outbreak of the Civil War posed new challenges for Catalan cooperativism. On the one hand, the emergence of industrial collectives affected production cooperatives, and on the other, the centralisation and control of the distribution of supplies affected consumer cooperatives, leading to a process of concentration. Examples include the merging of 45 cooperatives in the *Unió de Cooperadors de Barcelona*; the integration of second-tier cooperatives in consumer cooperatives under the *Productes Coop.* seal; and the fact that the *Federación de Cooperativas de Producción y Trabajo* brought 365 organisations together under one roof.

Notes

1 This text is part of the research project *Historia de la Catalunya Subalterna Contemporánea: alternativas solidarias y cooperativas* (History of Contemporary Subaltern Catalonia: Solidarity and Cooperative Alternatives), PID2019–109560GB-I00, funded by the Ministry of Science and Innovation of the Government of Spain.

2 For contemporary Catalan associationism, see Pere SOLÀ: *Cultura popular, educació i societat al Nord-Est Català (1887–1959)*, Girona, University of Girona, 1983; ID.: *Història de l'Associacionisme català contemporani: Barcelona i comarques de la Seva Demarcació (1874–1966)*, Barcelona, Government of Catalonia, 1993; ID.: *Itineraris per la sociabilitat meridional catalana: l'Associacionisme i la cultura popular a la demarcació de Tarragona (1868–1964)*, Tarragona, Provincial Council of Tarragona, 1998; Ramon ARNABAT and Xavier FERRÉ: *Ateneus. Cultura i llibertat. Associacionisme a la Catalunya contemporània*, Barcelona, Federació d'Ateneus de Catalunya, 2015; Montserrat DUCH, Ramon ARNABAT, and Xavier FERRÉ (eds.): *Sociabilitats a la Catalunya contemporània. Temps i espais en conflicte*, Barcelona, PAM, 2015; Montserrat DUCH, Ramon ARNABAT, and Antoni GAVALDÀ (eds.): *La Catalunya asociada (1868–1938)*, València, PUV, 2020.

3 Prepared by the ISOCAC research group of Rovira i Virgili University and available at: https://www.irmu.org/base-de-dades-associacionisme. See Ramon ARNABAT and Agustí AGRAMUNT: "Eines metodològiques: la Base de dades de l'associacionisme català contemporani", in Montserrat DUCH, Ramon ARNABAT, and Antoni GAVALDÀ (eds.): *La Catalunya asociada ...*, pp. 39–49.

4 Ramon ARNABAT: *"L'associacionisme popular: una mirada de conjunt"*, in Montserrat DUCH, Ramon ARNABAT and Antoni GAVALDÀ (ed.), *La Catalunya asociada ...*, pp. 293–366.

5 Jean-Louis GUEREÑA (ed.): *Cultura, ocio, identidades. Espacios y formas de sociabilidad en la España de los siglos XIX y XX*, Madrid, Biblioteca Nueva, 2018; Ramon ARNABAT: *Asociaos y seréis fuertes. Sociabilidades, modernizaciones y ciudadanías en España, 1860–1930*, Zaragoza, PUZ, 2019.
6 Active entities in each period are calculated as entities created in the current period plus 20% from the previous period.
7 Édouard ESCARRA: *El desarrollo industrial de Cataluña (1900–1908)*, Barcelona, Grijalbo, 1970 [1908], p. 92.
8 Ramon ARNABAT: "Notes sobre l'associacionisme cultural a Catalunya: de la revolució liberal a la guerra civil (1835–1936)", in Ignasi CUADROS and Héctor ISIDRO (ed.): *Associacionisme cultural: entre el mosaic i les xarxes*, Valls, CCEPC-IRMU-Cossetània, 2022, pp. 13–35.
9 Montserrat DUCH: "Mundo, demonio y carne. Proceso de secularización, feminización de la religión y sociabilismo católico en la diócesis de Tarragona (1932)", *Feminismo(s)*, 28 (2016), pp. 269–292.
10 José L. OYON (ed.): *Vida obrera en la Barcelona de entreguerres 1918–1936*, Barcelona, CHCC, 1998; José L. OYON and Juan J. GALLARDO: *El cinturón rojinegro. Radicalismo cenetista y obrerismo en la periferia de Barcelona (1918–1939)*, Barcelona, Carena, 2004.
11 Enric UCELAY-DA CAL (dir.): *La joventut a Catalunya al segle XX*, 2 vol., Barcelona, Provincial Council of Barcelona, 1987.
12 Dolors MARÍN: *Esperitistes i lliurepensadores. Dones pioneres en la lluita pels drets civils*, Barcelona, Angle Editorial, 2018.
13 Mary NASH (ed.): *Més enllà del silenci: les dones a la historia de Catalunya*, Barcelona, Government of Catalonia, 1998.
14 Maurice AGULHON: "¿Es la sociabilidad un objeto histórico?", in Maurice AGULHON: *Política, imágenes, sociabilidades. De 1789 a 1989* [edited by Jordi CANAL], Zaragoza, PUZ, 2016, pp. 103–118.
15 Ramon ARNABAT: *Asociaos y seréis fuertes* ..., pp. 316–383; ID.: "L'associacionisme popular ...", pp. 326–341.
16 Ramon ARNABAT, Òscar JANÉ, and Carles SANTACANA (coord.): *La Segona República. Balanç historiogràfic des dels estudis locals*, Barcelona, Afers-CCEPC, 2019.
17 Mary NASH: *Mujeres en el mundo*, Madrid, Alianza Editorial, 2012.
18 Albert CARRERAS and Xavier TAFUNELL (coords.): *Estadísticas Históricas de España, ss. XIX-XX*, Bilbao, Fundación BBVA, 2005; Pedro María PÉREZ CASTROVIEJO: *Clase obrera y niveles de vida en las primeras fases de la industrialización vizcaína*, Madrid, Ministry of the Presidency, 1992.
19 Rafael LUQUE FERNÁNDEZ: *La ratlla de la precarietat. Condicions de vida de les famílies obreres a una ciutat industrial catalana, Sabadell 1919–1923*, Sabadell, Caixa Sabadell, 1996.
20 Santiago CASTILLO: *Trabajadores, ciudadanía y reforma social en España: Juan José Morato (1864–1938)*, Madrid, Editorial siglo XXI and Fundación Largo Caballero, 2005.
21 Josefina CUESTA: "El proceso de expansión de los seguros sociales obligatorios. Las dificultades, 1919–1931", in VV. AA: *Historia de la acción social pública en España. Beneficencia y Previsión*, Madrid, Ministry of Labour, 1990, pp. 287–321.
22 Jordi IBARZ: "Oficios y cualificaciones en el trabajo portuario. El caso de Barcelona en la primera mitad del siglo XX", *Historia Social*, 45 (2003), pp. 119–138.

23 Pere SOLÀ: "El mutualismo contemporáneo en una sociedad industrial. Anotaciones del caso catalán (1880–1939)", in Santiago CASTILLO (ed.): *Solidaridad desde abajo,* Madrid, Centro de Estudios Históricos-UGT, 1994.
24 Montserrat DUCH PLANA: *Quimeres. Sociabilitats i memòries col·lectives a la Catalunya del segle XX,* Tarragona, Rovira i Virgili University, 2013.
25 *Ibid.*, pp. 33–35; Santiago CASTILLO and Rafael RUZAFA: *La previsión social en la Historia,* Madrid, Siglo XXI, 2009.
26 Marcel VAN DER LINDEN: *Social Security Mutualism. The Comparative History of Mutual Benefit Societies,* Paris, Paris Conference, 1992; Richard SENNET: *Juntos. Rituales, placeres y política de cooperación,* Barcelona, Editorial Anagrama, 2012; Jean JAURÉS: *Movimiento obrero y sindicalismo,* Barcelona, Yulca Editorial, 2016.
27 Pedro TRINIDAD: *Historia de la acción social pública en España. Beneficencia y previsión,* Madrid, Ministry of Labour, 1990.
28 Feliciano MONTERO and Mariano ESTEBAN DE VEGA: "Aproximación tipológica al mutualismo popular y obrero en España: el mutualismo asistencial", in Santiago CASTILLO (coord.): *La Historia Social en España. Actualidad y perspectivas,* Madrid, Siglo XXI, 1991.
29 Margarita VILAR: "La cobertura social a través del as sociedades de socorro mutuo, 1839–1935. ¿Una alternativa al Estado para afrontar los fallos del mercado?", in Jerònia PONS PONS and Javier SILVESTRE RODRÍGUEZ (eds.): *Los orígenes del estado de bienestar en España, 1900–1945. Los seguros de accidente, vejez, desempleo y enfermedad,* Zaragoza, Zaragoza University Press, 2010, pp. 106–108.
30 Montserrat DUCH, Ramon ARNABAT and Xavier FERRÉ (coords.): *Sociabilitats ...*; Santiago CASTILLO and Montserrat DUCH (coords.): *Sociabilidades en la historia,* Madrid, Catarata, 2015; Maurice AGULHON and Maryvonne BODIGUEL: *Les associations politiques au village,* Le Paradou, Actes sud, 1981; Jordi CANAL: "Maurice Agulhon. Historia y compromiso republicano", *Historia Social*, 29 (1997), pp. 47–72.
31 Montserrat DUCH: *La Cooperativa Obrera Tarraconense*, Tarragona, Edicions el Mèdol, 1993; Marc DALMAU and Ivan MIRÓ: *Les cooperatives obreres de Sants: autogestió proletària en un barri de Barcelona (1870–1939),* Barcelona, La Ciutat Invisible, 2010.
32 Marcel VAN DER LINDEN: *Social Security ...*
33 Montserrat DUCH: *Quimeres ...*; Fernando LARGO JIMÉNEZ: "Capital social y mutualisme: la Federación de Sociedades de Socorros Mutuos de Cataluña, 1896–1946", *Comunicaciones presentades al VII Congreso de la AHS,* Madrid, Catarata, 2015.
34 Josefina CUESTA: "El proceso de expansión ...", pp. 287–319.
35 Santiago CASTILLO: "Mutualismo de trabajadores en España (1836–1936). Varias cuestiones, algunas respuestas", in Santiago CASTILLO (coord.): *Mundo del trabajo y asociacionismo en España. Collegia, gremios, mutuas, sindicatos ... ,* Madrid, Catarata, 2014, pp. 171–205.
36 Fernando LARGO JIMÉNEZ: "Capital social y mutualismo ...".
37 Albert CARRERAS and Xavier TAFUNELL (coord.): *Estadísticas ...*, pp. 837–966.
38 Santiago CASTILLO: "Mutualismo de ...", p. 197; Sergio ESPUELAS, *La evolución del gasto social público en España, 1850–2005*, Madrid, Bank of Spain, 2013.

39 Alfred PÉREZ BASTARDAS: *Els inicis de les assegurances socials modernes a Catalunya: 1917–1937,* Barcelona, Arxiu Històric de la Ciutat, 2004; Jordi NADAL and Carles SUDRIÀ: *Història de la Caixa de Pensions,* Barcelona, Edicions 62, 1981.

40 Marcel·lí MORETA AMAT: "Cataluña en el movimiento mutualista de previsión social en España", in Santiago CASTILLO (ed.): *Solidaridad desde abajo* ..., pp. 437–489.

41 Maria Teresa MARTÍNEZ DE SAS and Pelai PAGÈS BLANCH: "Colominas Maseras, Joan", in *Diccionari biogràfic del moviment obrer als Països Catalans,* Barcelona, Publicacions Abadia de Montserrat, 2000; Cèlia CAÑELLAS and Rosa TORAN: *Els governs de la ciutat de Barcelona (1875–1930): eleccions, partits i regidors. Diccionari biogràfic,* Barcelona, Ajuntament de Barcelona, 2013; Pere SOLÀ: "El mutualismo y su función social: sinopsis histórica", *CIRIEC – España. Revista de Economía Pública,* 44 (2003), pp. 175–198; José ÁLVAREZ JUNCO: *El emperador del paralelo: Lerroux y la demagogia populista,* Madrid, RBA Libros, 2012; Joan CULLA: *El republicanisme lerrouxista a Catalunya (1901–1923),* Barcelona, Curial, 1987.

42 Pere SOLÀ: "El mutualismo contemporáneo ...", p. 80.

43 C. BROWN and J. TAYLOR: *Friendly Societies,* Cambridge, Cambridge University Press, 2014; Simon CORDERY: *British Friendly Societies, 1740–1914*, New York, Palgrave Macmillan, 2003.

44 *Ibid.*, pp. 22, 23, and 123.

45 Jordi NADAL, Josep M. BENAU, and Carles SUDRIÀ: *Atles de la industrialització de Catalunya. 1750–2010,* Barcelona, Vicens Vives, 2010; Ángel GARCÍA SANZ: "Jornales agrícolas y presupuesto familiar en España a mediados del siglo XIX", *Anales de CUNEF,* 1979, pp. 50–71; Jorge MARTÍNEZ CARRIÓN: *El nivel de vida en la España rural, siglos XVIII–XX,* Alacant, Publicacions de la Universitat d'Alacant, 2002.

46 Jane JACOBS: *La economia de las ciudades,* Barcelona, Ediciones Península, 1971.

47 Josefina CUESTA: "Las sociedades de Socorros Mutuos en el primer tercio del siglo XX: sociedad sin Estado, una relación fallida", in Santiago CASTILLO (ed.): *Solidaridad desde abajo* ..., pp. 331–332.

48 Joan BERNEY and Jordi ESTIVILL: *Las cooperativas sociales en Italia,* Barcelona, Editorial Hacer, 1993.

49 Borja RIUS: *El mutualisme: una opció diferent. Anàlisi comparativa entre el mutualisme a Itàlia i a Espanya*, Barcelona, Agrupació Mútua, 2002.

50 Familism generally refers to the increasingly widespread belief in the importance of the family and so the need to develop programmes to support and defend the institution of the family.

51 Maurizio ANTONIOLI and Jorge TORRE: "La creación de un modelo sindical territorial: Las 'Camere del lavoro' in Lombardía, 1891–1914", *Historia Social,* 68 (2010), pp. 115–133; Ramon ARNABAT and Antoni GAVALDÀ: "Sociabilidad y asociacionismo como factores de movilización social: el mundo rural catalán entre 1870 y 1980", in Santiago CASTILLO and Montserrat DUCH (coords.): *Sociabilidades* ..., pp. 169–193; Marc DALMAU and Ivan MIRÓ, *Les cooperatives obreres* ...

52 Josefina CUESTA: "Las sociedades ...", pp. 409–422; Pere SOLÀ: "El mutualismo ...", p. 85.

53 A prime example is Catholic mutuality for women with its functions of submission and social control. Amelia GARCÍA CHECA: "Ideología y práctica

del mutualismo católico femenino en Cataluña, 1900–1930", in Santiago CASTILLO (ed.): *Solidaridad desde abajo* ..., 1994, pp. 125–135; Maria Jesús ESPUNY: "La protección a la maternidad en el textil catalán", Actas del VI Congreso de Historia Social, 14° Simposio del Instituto Valentín de Foronda: *La previsión social en la historia,* Vitoria, 2008; Jerònia PONS PONS and Javier SILVESTRE RODRÍGUEZ (eds.): *Los orígenes del estado* ...; María José BERNUZ BENÉITEZ and Manuel CALVO GARCÍA: *La eficacia de los derechos sociales,* Valencia, Tirant lo Blanch, 2014.

54 Ramon ARNABAT: "Las sociedades de socorros mutuos en la Catalunya rural 1879–1939", in Santiago CASTILLO (ed.): *Solidaridad desde abajo* ..., pp. 87–105; Ramon ARNABAT and Antoni GAVALDÀ: "Sociabilidad y asociacionismo ...", pp. 174–189.

55 Richard SENNET: *Juntos* ... , p. 212.

56 Montserrat DUCH and Joaquim NADAL (eds.): *Els Ateneus a Catalunya. Sociabilitat i catalanisme popular*, Girona, Catalan Institute for Cultural Heritage, 2018.

57 Pere SOLÀ: "El mutualismo contemporáneo ...", p. 86.

58 Juan REVENTÓS CARNER: *El movimiento cooperativo en España*, Barcelona, Ariel, 1960; Albert PÉREZ BARÓ: *Les cooperatives a Catalunya,* Barcelona, Institut d'Estudis Catalans, 1972; Rafael CELADA: *Aproximació a l'Atlas Cooperatiu de Catalunya fins 1936*, Barcelona, Government of Catalonia, 1989; Gabriel PLANA: *El cooperativisme català o l'economia de la fraternitat*, Barcelona, University of Barcelona, Ferrer i Guàrdia Foundation and Roca i Galés Foundation, 1998; Joan AYMERICH: *Las cooperativas y las colectivizaciones obreras en Catalunya como modelos de gestión colectiva. Proceso de regulación legal (1839–1939),* unpublished doctoral thesis, Barcelona, University of Barcelona, 2008; Susana MARTÍNEZ RODRÍGUEZ: *Catalunya un país de cooperatives*, Barcelona, Government of Catalonia, 2010; Ignasi FAURA: *L'economia social catalana als inicis del segle XX. Cooperació, solidaritat i valors,* Lleida, Pagès Editors, 2016; Miguel GARAU: *Entre la utopía y la supervivencia. El desarrollo y la diversidad de las cooperativas de producción y trabajo en la Catalunya urbana e industrial (1864–1936)*, unpublished doctoral thesis, Barcelona, University of Barcelona, 2016; Marc DALMAU and Antoni GAVALDÀ: *Catalunya terra cooperativa*, Barcelona, Roca i Galès Foundation, 2019; Jordi ESTIVILL and Iván MIRÓ: *L'Economia Social i Solidària a Catalunya*, Barcelona, Icària, 2020. The collection of biographies 'Cooperativistes Catalans', directed by Antoni GAVALDA and published by the Roca Galés Foundation merits special mention: https://www.rocagales.cat/publicacions/col%C2%B7leccio-biografies/

59 Horace MELLER KALLEN: *The Decline and Rise of the Consumer: A Philosophy of* Consumer Cooperation, New York, D. Appleton-Century Co., 1936; Mercè RENOM (ed.): *Abastecer Barcelona. El Municipio y la alimentación de la Ciudad*, 1329–1930, Barcelona, MUHBA, 2019, pp. 229–427.

60 According to Alicia KAPLAN DE DRIMER and Bernardo DRIMER: *Manual de Cooperativas*, Buenos Aires, Intercoop, 1977.

61 Ramon ARNABAT: "L'associacionisme popular ...", pp. 320–326; Josep CASANOVAS: *El cooperativisme a Osona,* Vic, Eumo, 1998; Joan TORRENTS and Gerard VALLEJO: *La història del cooperativisme a la Catalunya Central*, Manlleu, Museu del Ter, 2021.

62 Marc DALMAU and Iván MIRÓ: *Les cooperatives obreres ...*; Marc DALMAU: *Gràfica cooperativa en Barcelona. Iconografia del cooperativisme obrer (1875–1939)*, Barcelona, Montaber, 2018.
63 Dolors MARÍN: "De 1890 a 1939. La Cooperativa La Flor de Maig", in VV.AA: *Flor de Maig: del cooperativisme al servei als municipis*, Barcelona, Provincial Council of Barcelona, 2006, pp. 19–70; Marc DALMAU: *Un barri fet a cops de cooperació. El cooperativisme obrer al Poblenou*, Barcelona, La Ciutat invisible, 2015.
64 Iván MIRÓ and Jordi GARCÍA: *Cooperativisme BCN, 1842–1939. Guia d'història urbana*, Barcelona, MUHBA, 2012.
65 *Boletín del Instituto de Reformas Sociales*, 47 (May 1908), pp. 1,103–1,119.
66 Ramon ARNABAT: *Asociaos y seréis fuertes ...*, pp. 122–139.
67 Josep M. OLLÉ: *Els moviments socials a Catalunya, 1840–1843*, Barcelona, Nova Terra, 1973, pp. 49–57.
68 Beatrice POTTER WEBB: *Cooperative. Movement in Great Britain*, London, Hesperides Press, 2013 [1891]; Antonio GASCÓN MARIMÓN: *Historia de los cooperadores de la Rochdale*, Madrid, Sobrinos de la Sucesora de M. Muniesa de los Ríos, 1923.
69 Fernando GARRIDO: *Historia de las Asociaciones Obreras en Europa o las clases trabajadoras regeneradas por la Asociación*, Barcelona, Imprenta y Librería de Salvador Manero, 1864, vol. I, pp. 83–336; Juan TUTAU: "Asociaciones cooperativas", *Almanaque democrático para el año (bisiesto) de 1864*, Barcelona, I. López editor, 1864, pp. 60–68.
70 Albert PÉREZ BARÓ: "El cooperativismo de consumo en Cataluña", *Estudios Cooperativos*, 21 (1970), pp. 35–54; Federación Regional de Cooperativas de Cataluña: *La Cooperación de Consumo*, Barcelona, 1928, reproduced by Santiago JOAQUINET: "Historia del Movimiento Cooperativo en Cataluña", *Estudios Cooperativos*, 8 (1965), pp. 3–20, pp. 6–7.
71 Marc DALMAU and Iván MIRÓ: *Catalunya terra ...*, pp. 17–22.
72 "Reglamento orgánico de la Sociedad cooperativa La Obrera Sabadellense", Sabadell, 31 January 1877. National Historical Archive of Spain. FC Ministry of the Interior. File 2808, dossier 20. Ver Ellen FURLOUGH and Carl STRIKWERDA (eds.): *Consumer Against Capitalism?*, London, Rowman & Littlefield Publishers, 1999.
73 The magazine changed its name on several occasions. Starting in 1905, it was published every two weeks with the title *El Cooperador Cooperativista.* In 1911, it adopted the name *El cooperatista.* In 1915, it changed its name to *Cooperatismo,* and again in 1920, it changed to *Acción Cooperatista*, which was published until 1938. The changes of the name on the masthead were in response to ideological and doctrinal debates among intellectuals of the cooperative movement.
74 Reproduced by Susana MARTÍNEZ-RODRÍGUEZ: *Catalunya, un país ...*, p. 32.
75 Juan REVENTÓS: *El movimiento cooperativo ...*, pp. 105–113; Baldomero CERDÁ RICHART: *Cooperativas en sus relaciones con el Estado*, Barcelona, Bosch, 1938.
76 "La Cooperativa Central de Cataluña y Baleares (Proyecto de constitución)", *Revista Cooperativa Catalana*, 38 (June 1902), pp. 1–4.
77 Gabriel PLANA: *El cooperativisme ...*, pp. 148–156; Ignasi FAURA: *L'economia social ...*, pp. 63–64.
78 Joan AYMERICH: *Las cooperativas ...*, pp. 121–174.
79 MUSEO SOCIAL OF BARCELONA: *Anuari d'Estadística Social de Catalunya*, Barcelona, 1914, pp. 164–165; *Cooperativismo*, 36 (1 August 1916), pp. 230–232.

80 INSTITUTO DE REFORMAS SOCIALES. SECCIÓN TERCERA: *Avance al Censo de Asociaciones del Instituto de Reformas Sociales*, Madrid, Imprenta de la Sucesora de M. Minuesa de los Ríos, 1915.
81 Francisco J. MEDINA-ALBADALEJO and Josep PUJOL-ANDREU: "Cooperativas de consumo y niveles de vida, España 1865–1939: Una primera aproximación", *Scripta Nova. Revista Electrónica de Geografía y Ciencias Sociales,* [online], University of Barcelona, XVIII-494 (2014), http://www.ub.es/geocrit/sn/sn-494.htm.
82 Joan SALAS: "La obra de la Cámara Regional debe ser de cooperación o de cooperatismo", *Revista Cooperativa Catalana,* 37 (mayo de 1902), p. 2.
83 See, for example, the reproduction in *El Socialista*, 4,477 (15 June 1923), p. 4, in the article "La economía de la cooperación" by Charles GIDE published in *Bulletin Coopératif International.*
84 *Revista Cooperativa Catalana*, 39 (April 1902), p. 35.
85 *Revista Cooperativa Catalana*, 39 (April 1902), pp. 35–40
86 Montserrat DUCH: *Micaela Chalmeta*, Valls, Cossetània, 2009.
87 *Ibid.*, pp. 23–40; Temma KAPLAN: "Female Consciousness and Collective Action: The Case of Barcelona, 1910–1918", *Signs*, 7–3 (1982), pp. 545–566.
88 *Acción Cooperatista*, 208 (April 1927), p. 2.
89 Eladi GARDÓ: *La cooperación catalana: Recopilación histórica (1898–1926)*, Barcelona, Gráficas Funes, 1927.
90 Jason GARNER: "La Segona República (1931–1936), ¿època daurada del cooperativisme català?", *Cooperació Catalana*, 332 (2010), p. 25.
91 Juan REVENTÓS: *El movimiento cooperativo ...*, pp. 219–221.
92 "En el Ateneo Politechnicum. Duran i Guardia conference on social policies of the Barcelona City Council", *Acción Cooperatista*, 476 (17 June 1932), p. 3.
93 Miguel GARAU: *Entre la utopía ...*, pp. 300–302.
94 Miguel GARAU: "Un reto desconocido de Joan Peiró i Belis: integrar cooperativismo, cultura y revolución social", *Cercles*, 13 (2010), pp. 201–220.
95 *Acción Cooperatista*, 463 (18 March 1932), p. 3, and 466 (8 April 1932), p. 2. This body was recently studied by Marc DALMAU and Mar MASIP: *El moviment feminista cooperatiu. L'Agrupació Femenina de Propaganda Cooperatista (1931–1939)*, Valls, Cossetània, 2022.
96 Honora ENFIELD: *El poder de la cesta de la compra, Barcelona*, Agrupació Femenina de Propaganda Cooperatista, 1932 (4ª).
97 Rafael CELADA: *Aproximació a l'Atlas ...*, p. 16.

References

AGULHON, Maurice: "¿Es la sociabilidad un objeto histórico?", in Maurice AGULHON (ed.): *Política, imágenes, sociabilidades. De 1789 a 1989* [edited by Jordi CANAL], Zaragoza, PUZ, 2016, pp. 103–118.

AGULHON, Maurice and BODIGUEL, Maryvonne: *Les associations politiques au village*, Le paradou, Actes sud, 1981.

ÁLVAREZ JUNCO, José: *El emperador del paralelo: Lerroux y la demagogia populista*, Madrid, RBA Libros, 2012.

ANTONIOLI, Maurizio and TORRE, Jorge: "La creación de un modelo sindical territorial: Las 'Camere del lavoro' in Lombardía, 1891–1914", *Historia Social*, 68 (2010), pp. 115–133.

ARNABAT, Ramon: "Las sociedades de socorros mutuos en la Catalunya rural 1879–1939", in Santiago CASTILLO (ed.): *Solidaridad desde abajo*, Madrid, Centro de Estudios Históricos-UGT, 1994, pp. 87–105.

ARNABAT, Ramon: *Asociaos y seréis Fuertes. Sociabilidades, modernizaciones y ciudadanías en España, 1860–1930*, Zaragoza, PUZ, 2019.

ARNABAT, Ramon: "L'associacionisme popular: una mirada de conjunt", in Montserrat DUCH, Ramon ARNABAT, and Antoni GAVALDÀ (eds.): *La Catalunya asociada (1868–1938)*, València, PUZ, 2020, pp. 293–366.

ARNABAT, Ramon: "Notes sobre l'associacionisme cultural a Catalunya: de la revolució liberal a la guerra civil (1835–1936)", in Ignasi CUADROS and Héctor ISIDRO (eds.): *Associacionisme cultural: entre el mosaic i les xarxes*, Valls, CCEPC-IRMU-Cossetània, 2022, pp. 13–35.

ARNABAT, Ramon and AGRAMUNT, Agustí: "Eines metodològiques: la Base de dades de l'associacionisme català contemporani", in Montserrat DUCH, Ramon ARNABAT, and Antoni GAVALDÀ (eds.): *La Catalunya asociada (1868–1938)*, València, PUZ, 2020, pp. 39–49.

ARNABAT, Ramon and FERRÉ, Xavier: *Ateneus. Cultura i llibertat. Asociacionisme a la Catalunya contemporània*, Barcelona, Federació d'Ateneus de Catalunya, 2015.

ARNABAT, Ramon and GAVALDÀ, Antoni: "Sociabilidad y asociacionismo como factores de movilización social: el mundo rural catalán entre 1870 y 1980", in Santiago CASTILLO and Montserrat DUCH (coords.): *Sociabilidades en la historia*, Madrid, Catarata, 2015, pp. 169–193.

ARNABAT, Ramon; JANÉ, Òscar and SANTACANA, Carles (Coord.): *La Segona República. Balanç historiogràfic des dels estudis locals*, Barcelona, Afers-CCEPC, 2019.

AYMERICH, Joan: *Las cooperativas y las colectivizaciones obreras en Catalunya como modelos de gestión colectiva. Proceso de regulación legal (1839–1939)*, unpublished doctoral thesis, Barcelona, Universitat de Barcelona, 2008.

BERNEY, Joan and ESTIVILL, Jordi: *Las cooperativas sociales en Italia*, Barcelona, Editorial Hacer, 1993.

BERNUZ BENÉITEZ, María José and CALVO GARCÍA, Manuel: *La eficacia de los derechos sociales*, Valencia, Tirant lo Blanch, 2014.

BROWN, C.H.L. and TAYLOR, J.A.G.: *Friendly societies*, Cambridge, Cambridge University Press, 2014.

CANAL, Jordi: "Maurice Agulhon. Historia y compromiso republicano", *Historia Social*, 29 (1997), pp. 47–72.

CAÑELLAS, Cèlia and TORAN, Rosa: *Els governs de la ciutat de Barcelona (1875–1930): eleccions, partits i regidors. Diccionari biogràfic*, Barcelona, Ajuntament de Barcelona, 2013.

CARRERAS, Albert and TAFUNELL, Xavier (coord.): *Estadísticas Históricas de España, ss. XIX–XX*, Bilbao, Fundación BBVA, 2005.

CASANOVAS, Josep: *El cooperativisme a Osona*, Vic, Eumo, 1998.

CASTILLO, Santiago: *Trabajadores, ciudadanía y reforma social en España: Juan José Morato (1864–1938)*, Madrid, Editorial siglo XXI & Fundación Largo Caballero, 2005.

CASTILLO, Santiago: "Mutualismo de trabajadores en España (1836–1936). Varias cuestiones, algunas respuestas", in Santiago CASTILLO (coord.): *Mundo del trabajo y asociacionismo en España. Collegia, gremios, mutuas, sindicatos ...*, Madrid, Catarata, 2014, pp. 171–205.

CASTILLO, Santiago and DUCH, Montserrat (coord.): *Sociabilidades en la historia*, Madrid, Catarata, 2015.

CASTILLO, Santiago and RUZAFA, Rafael: *La previsión social en la Historia*, Madrid, Siglo XXI, 2009.

CELADA, Rafael: *Aproximació a l'Atlas Cooperatiu de Catalunya fins 1936*, Barcelona, Generalitat de Catalunya, 1989.

CERDÁ RICHART, Baldomero: *Cooperativas en sus relaciones con el Estado*, Barcelona, Bosch, 1938.

CORDERY, Simon: *British friendly societies, 1740–1914*, New York, Palgrave Macmillan, 2003.

CUESTA, Josefina: "El proceso de expansión de los seguros sociales obligatorios. Las dificultades, 1919–1931", in VV.AA: *Historia de la acción social pública en España. Beneficencia y Previsión*, Madrid, Ministerio de Trabajo, 1990, pp. 287–321.

CUESTA, Josefina: "Las sociedades de Socorros Mutuos en el primer tercio del siglo XX: sociedad sin Estado, una relación fallida", in Santiago CASTILLO (ed.): *Solidaridad desde abajo*, Madrid, Centro de Estudios Históricos-UGT, 1994, pp. 409–422.

CULLA, Joan: *El republicanisme lerrouxista a Catalunya (1901–1923)*, Barcelona, Curial, 1987.

DALMAU, Marc: *Un barri fet a cops de cooperació. El cooperativisme obrer al Poblenou*, Barcelona, La Ciutat invisible, 2015.

DALMAU, Marc: *Gràfica cooperativa en Barcelona. Iconografia del cooperativisme obrer (1875–1939)*, Barcelona, Montaber, 2018.

DALMAU, Marc and GAVALDÀ, Antoni: *Catalunya terra cooperativa*, Barcelona, Fundació Roca i Galès, 2019.

DALMAU, Marc and Masip, Mar: *El moviment feminista cooperatiu. L'Agrupació Femenina de Propaganda Cooperatista (1931–1939)*, Valls, Cossetània, 2022.

DALMAU, Marc and MIRÓ, Iván: *Les cooperatives obreres de Sants: autogestió proletària en un barri de Barcelona (1870–1939)*, Barcelona, La Ciutat Invisible, 2010.

DUCH, Montserrat: *La Cooperativa Obrera Tarraconense*, Tarragona, Edicions el Mèdol, 1993.

DUCH, Montserrat: *Micaela Chalmeta*, Valls, Cossetània, 2009.

DUCH, Montserrat: *Quimeres. Sociabilitats i memòries col·lectives a la Catalunya del segle XX*, Tarragona, Universitat Rovira i Virgili, 2013.

DUCH, Montserrat: "Mundo, demonio y carne. Proceso de secularización, feminización de la religión y sociabilismo católico en la diócesis de Tarragona (1932)", *Feminismo(s)*, 28 (2016), pp. 269–292.

DUCH, Montserrat; ARNABAT, Ramon and FERRÉ, Xavier (eds.): *Sociabilitats a la Catalunya contemporània. Temps i espais en conflicte*, Barcelona, PAM, Barcelona, 2015.

DUCH, Montserrat; ARNABAT, Ramon and GAVALDÀ, Antoni (eds.): *La Catalunya asociada (1868–1938)*, València, PUZ, 2020.
DUCH, Montserrat and NADAL, Joaquim (eds.): *Els Ateneus a Catalunya. Sociabilitat i catalanisme popular*, Girona, Institut Català de Recerca en Patrimoni Cultural, 2018.
ENFIELD, Honora: *El poder de la cesta de la compra, Barcelona*, Agrupació Femenina de Propaganda Cooperatista, 1932 (4ª).
ESCARRA, Édouard: *El desarrollo industrial de Cataluña (1900–1908)*, Barcelona, Grijalbo, 1970 [1908].
ESPUELAS, Sergio: *La evolución del gasto social público en España, 1850–2005*, Madrid, Banco de España, 2013.
ESPUNY, Maria Jesús: "La protección a la maternidad en el textil catalán", Actas del VI Congreso de Historia Social, 14ºº Simposio del Instituto Valentín de Foronda: *La previsión social en la historia,* Vitoria, 2008.
ESTIVILL, Jordi and MIRÓ, Iván: *L'Economia Social i Solidària a Catalunya*, Barcelona, Icària, 2020.
FAURA, Ignasi: *L'economia social catalana als inicis del segle XX. Cooperació, solidaritat i valors*, Lleida, Pagès Editors, 2016.
FEDERACIÓN REGIONAL DE COOPERATIVAS DE CATALUÑA: *La Cooperación de Consumo*, Barcelona, 1928 [reproduced by Santiago JOAQUINET: "Historia del Movimiento Cooperativo en Cataluña", *Estudios Cooperativos*, 8 (1965), pp. 3–20].
FURLOUGH, Ellen and STRIKWERDA, Carl (eds.): *Consumer against capitalism?*, Londres, Rowman & Littlefield Publishers, 1999.
GARAU, Miguel: "Un reto desconocido de Joan Peiró i Belis: integrar cooperativismo, cultura y revolución social", *Cercles*, 13 (2010), pp. 201–220.
GARAU, Miguel: *Entre la utopía y la supervivencia. El desarrollo y la diversidad de las cooperativas de producción y trabajo en la Catalunya urbana e industrial (1864–1936)*, unpublished doctoral thesis, Barcelona, Universitat de Barcelona, 2016.
GARCÍA CHECA, Amelia: "Ideología y práctica del mutualismo católico femenino en Cataluña, 1900–1930", in Santiago CASTILLO (ed.): *Solidaridad desde abajo*, Madrid, Centro de Estudios Históricos-UGT, 1994, pp. 125–135.
GARCÍA SANZ, Ángel: "Jornadas agrícolas y presupuesto familiar en España a mediados del siglo XIX", *Anales de CUNEF*, 1979, pp. 50–71.
GARDÓ, Eladi: *La cooperación catalana: Recopilación histórica (1898–1926)*, Barcelona, Gráficas Funes, 1927.
GASCÓN MARIMÓN, Antonio: *Historia de los cooperadores de la Rochdale*, Madrid, Sobrinos de la Sucesora de M. Muniesa de los Ríos, 1923.
GARRIDO, Fernando: *Historia de las Asociaciones Obreras en Europa o las clases trabajadoras regeneradas por la Asociación*, Barcelona, Imprenta y Librería de Salvador Manero, 1864.
GUEREÑA, Jean-Louis (ed.): *Cultura, ocio, identidades. Espacios y formas de sociabilidad en la España de los siglos XIX y XX*. Madrid, Biblioteca Nueva, 2018.

IBARZ, Jordi: "Oficios y cualificaciones en el trabajo portuario. El caso de Barcelona en la primera mitad del siglo XX", *Historia Social*, 45 (2003), pp. 119–138.

Instituto de Reformas Sociales. Sección Tercera: *Avance al Censo de Asociaciones del Instituto de Reformas Sociales*, Madrid, Imprenta de la Sucesora de M. Minuesa de los Ríos, 1915.

JACOBS, Jane: *La economia de las ciudades*, Barcelona, Ediciones Península, 1971.

JAURÉS, Jean: *Movimiento obrero y sindicalismo*, Barcelona, Yulca Editorial, 2016.

KAPLAN, Temma: "Female Consciousness and Collective Action: The Case of Barcelona, 1910–1918", *Signs*, 7–3 (1982), pp. 545–566.

KAPLAN DE DRIMER, Alicia and DRIMER, Bernardo: *Manual de Cooperativas*, Buenos Aires, Intercoop, 1977.

LARGO JIMÉNEZ, Fernando: "Capital social y mutualisme: la Federación de Sociedades de Socorros Mutuos de Cataluña, 1896–1946", *Comunicaciones presentades al VII Congreso de la AHS*, Madrid, Catarata, 2015.

LUQUE FERNÁNDEZ, Rafael: *La ratlla de la precarietat. Condicions de vida de les famílies obreres a una ciutat industrial catalana, Sabadell 1919–1923*, Sabadell, Caixa Sabadell, 1996.

MARÍN, Dolors: "De 1890 a 1939. La Cooperativa La Flor de Maig". in VV.AA: *Flor de Maig: del cooperativisme al servei als municipis*, Barcelona, Diputació de Barcelona, 2006, pp. 19–70.

MARÍN, Dolors: *Esperitistes i lliurepensadores. Dones pioneres en la lluita pels drets civils*, Barcelona, Angle Editorial, 2018.

MARTÍNEZ CARRIÓN, Jorge: *El nivel de vida en la España rural, siglos XVIII–XX*, Alacant, Publicacions de la Universitat d'Alacant, 2002.

MARTÍNEZ DE SAS, Maria Teresa and PAGÈS BLANCH, Pelai: "Colominas Maseras, Joan", in *Diccionari biogràfic del moviment obrer als Països Catalans*, Barcelona, Publicacions Abadia de Montserrat, 2000.

MARTÍNEZ RODRÍGUEZ, Susana: *Catalunya un país de cooperatives*, Barcelona, Generalitat de Catalunya, 2010.

MEDINA–ALBADALEJO, Francisco J. and PUJOL-ANDREU, Josep: "Cooperativas de consumo y niveles de vida, España 1865–1939: Una primera aproximación", *Scripta Nova. Revista Electrónica de Geografía y Ciencias Sociales*. [Online]. Barcelona, Universidad de Barcelona, XVIII–494 (2014), http://www.ub.es/geocrit/sn/sn-494.htm.

MELLER KALLEN, Horace: *The Decline and Rise of the Consumer: A Philosophy of Consumer Cooperation*, New York, D. Appleton-Century Co., 1936.

MIRÓ, Iván and GARCÍA, Jordi: *Cooperativisme BCN, 1842–1939. Guia d'història urbana*, Barcelona, MUHBA, 2012.

MONTERO, Feliciano and ESTEBAN DE VEGA, Mariano: "Aproximación tipológica al mutualismo popular y obrero en España: el mutualismo asistencial", in Santiago CASTILLO (coord.): *La Historia Social en España. Actualidad y perspectivas*, Madrid, Siglo XXI, 1991.

MORETA AMAT, Marcel·lí: "Cataluña en el movimiento mutualista de previsión social en España", in Santiago CASTILLO (ed.): *Solidaridad desde abajo*, Madrid, Centro de Estudios Históricos-UGT, 1994, pp. 437–489.

MUSEO SOCIAL DE BARCELONA: *Anuari d'Estadística Social de Catalunya*, Barcelona, 1914.

NADAL, Jordi; BENAU, Josep M. and SUDRIÀ, Carles: *Atles de la industrialització de Catalunya. 1750–2010*, Barcelona, Vicens Vives, 2010.

NADAL, Jordi and SUDRIÀ, Carles: *Història de la caixa de pensions*, Barcelona, Edicions 62, 1981.

NASH, Mary (ed.): *Més enllà del silenci: les dones a la historia de Catalunya*, Barcelona, Generalitat de Catalunya, 1998.

NASH, Mary: *Mujeres en el mundo*, Madrid, Alianza Editorial, 2012.

OLLÉ, Josep M.: *Els moviments socials a Catalunya, 1840–1843*, Barcelona, Nova Terra, 1973.

OYON, José L. (ed.): *Vida obrera en la Barcelona de entreguerres 1918–1936*, Barcelona, CHCC, 1998.

OYON, José L. and GALLARDO, Juan J.: *El cinturón rojinegro. Radicalismo cenetista y obrerismo en la periferia de Barcelona (1918–1939)*, Barcelona, Carena, 2004.

PLANA, Gabriel: *Josep Roca i Galès*, Valls, Cossetània, 2017.

PÉREZ BARÓ, Albert: "El cooperativismo de consumo en Cataluña", *Estudios Cooperativos*, 21 (1970), pp. 35–54.

PÉREZ BARÓ, Albert: *Les cooperatives a Catalunya*, Barcelona, Institut d'Estudis Catalans, 1972.

PÉREZ BASTARDAS, Alfred: *Els inicis de les assegurances socials modernes a Catalunya: 1917–1937*, Barcelona, Arxiu Històric de la Ciutat, 2004.

PÉREZ CASTROVIEJO, Pedro María: *Clase obrera y niveles de vida en las primeras fases de la industrialización vizcaína*, Madrid, Ministerio de la Presidencia, 1992.

PLANA, Gabriel: *El cooperativisme català o l'economia de la fraternitat*, Barcelona, Universitat de Barcelona, Fundació Ferrer i Guàrdia & Fundació Roca i Galés, 1998.

PONS PONS, Jerònia and SILVESTRE RODRÍGUEZ, Javier (eds.): *Los orígenes del estado de bienestar en España, 1900–1945. Los seguros de accidente, vejez, desempleo y enfermedad*, Zaragoza, Prensas Universitarias de Zaragoza, 2010.

RENOM, Mercè (ed.): *Abastecer Barcelona. El Municipio y la alimentación de la Ciudad, 1329–1930*, Barcelona, MUHBA, 2019.

REVENTÓS CARNER, Juan: *El movimiento cooperativo en España*, Barcelona, Ariel, 1960.

RIUS, Borja: *El mutualisme: una opció diferent. Anàlisi comparativa entre el mutualisme a Itàlia i a Espanya*, Barcelona, Agrupació Mútua, 2002.

SENNET, Richard: *Juntos. Rituales, placeres y política de cooperación*, Barcelona, Editorial Anagrama, 2012.

SOLÀ, Pere: *Cultura popular, educació i societat al Nord-Est Català (1887–1959)*, Girona, Universitat de Girona, 1983.

SOLÀ, Pere: *Història de l'Associacionisme català contemporani: Barcelona i comarques de la Seva Demarcació (1874–1966)*, Barcelona, Generalitat de Catalunya, 1993.

SOLÀ, Pere: "El mutualismo contemporáneo en una sociedad industrial. Anotaciones del caso catalán (1880–1939)", in Santiago CASTILLO (ed.): *Solidaridad desde abajo*, Madrid, Centro de Estudios Históricos-UGT, 1994.

SOLÀ, Pere: *Itineraris per la sociabilitat meridional catalana: l'Associacionisme i la cultura popular a la demarcació de Tarragona (1868–1964)*, Tarragona, Diputació de Tarragona, 1998.

SOLÀ, Pere: "El mutualismo y su función social: sinopsis histórica", *CIRIEC – España. Revista de Economía Pública*, 44 (2003), pp. 175–198.

TORRENTS, Joan and VALLEJO, Gerard: *La història del cooperativisme a la Catalunya Central*, Manlleu, Museu del Ter, 2021.

TRINIDAD, Pedro: *Historia de la acción social pública en España. Beneficencia y previsión*, Madrid, Ministerio de Trabajo, 1990.

TUTAU, Juan: "Asociaciones cooperativas", *Almanaque democrático para el año (bisiesto) de 1864*, Barcelona, I. López editor, 1864, p. 60–68.

UCELAY DE CAL, Enric (dir.): *La joventut a Catalunya al segle xx*, 2 vol., Barcelona, Diputació de Barcelona, 1987.

VAN DER LINDEN, Marcel: *Social Security Mutualism. The Comparative History of Mutual Benefit Societies*, Paris, Paris Conference, 1992.

VEGA, Eulàlia: *Entre revolución i reforma: la CNT a Catalunya, 1930–1936*, Lleida, Pagès, 2004.

VILAR, Margarita: "La cobertura social a través de las sociedades de socorro mutuo, 1839–1935. ¿Una alternativa al Estado para afrontar los fallos del mercado?", in Jerònia PONS PONS and Javier SILVESTRE RODRÍGUEZ (eds.): *Los orígenes del estado de bienestar en España, 1900–1945. Los seguros de accidente, vejez, desempleo y enfermedad*, Zaragoza, Prensas Universitarias de Zaragoza, 2010, pp. 106–108.

WEBB, Beatric Potter: *Cooperative. Movement in Great Britain*, London, Hesperides Press, 2013 [1891].

10 Origins and Diversity of Cooperative Practices Between Pupils in France

Towards a Didactics of Cooperation

Sylvain Connac

France has historically had a strong school system that welcomes all children regardless of their origins. In fact it can be said that it has succeeded in democratising schooling, with every family being able to send their children to school free of charge, with teachers trained for this purpose. However, it has not yet succeeded in democratising educational success, with many pupils (around 80,000 each year)[1] leaving the education system without a diploma and finding themselves challenged when they enter the workplace. It is therefore a major challenge for French schools to drastically reduce this proportion of failing pupils, who, moreover, come overwhelmingly from socially, economically, and culturally deprived families. "France is still one of the OECD countries in which social origin has the greatest impact on educational outcomes".[2] Tu put in a nutshell, the priority of French schools is currently to accompany pupils as far as possible in their studies, avoiding drop-out strategies, whatever their profiles and despite the heterogeneous nature of the classes accommodating them.

Getting pupils to cooperate is a paradoxical practice in France because it is both widespread and little known. It is widespread because all teachers regularly get their pupils to cooperate: often through help or group work. It is encouraged by school leaders because it has the potential to develop useful skills outside school, particularly in preparation for the world of work, and because it promises to contribute, at least in theory, to a positive accommodation of student diversity, with cooperative classes becoming learning communities. However, it remains little known because its origins are often ignored and because people are rarely aware of the slides associated with insufficiently thought-out cooperation.

Indeed, without special care, getting pupils to cooperate can quickly become counterproductive and prevent them from learning.

We have known for a long time that it is not enough to put pupils around a table for cooperation to take place and for everyone to benefit. Meirieu[3] already explained this in his thesis in educational sciences.

DOI: 10.4324/9781003439554-11

Without any specific preparation, students spontaneously organise themselves by dividing up into four unfair functions: designers (those who think about solving the task), implementers (those who put into practice the ideas brought by the designers), idlers (those who stand back and wait for the work to be done), and troublemakers (those who do not accept passivity and parasitise their group or the class). This problem becomes even more acute when we realise that it is the students from the poorest families who most often adopt the postures of idlers and troublemakers.

More broadly, we have been able to identify that students who are led to cooperate without prior training and without any pedagogical organisation provided for this purpose are likely to be confronted with four major families of slides:[4]

- Attentional slide: because students are allowed to talk and move around, the space becomes too noisy and hectic to facilitate concentration;
- a fusional slide: some students use strategies known as "consensus of convenience" to avoid conflicts of ideas, for example, by tacitly agreeing with a classmate so as not to enter into a conflict of ideas with them;
- productivist: with a confusion between the cooperative organisation (how we work) and the learning expectations (what we have to learn);
- differentiating: the most academically advanced pupils investing in the most mobilising cooperative functions (e.g. to help someone or to carry out an instruction as a designer).

It is therefore because of the presence of this series of slides that it is appropriate both to specify what is meant by cooperative pedagogies and to indicate what pedagogical research has been able to highlight so that these pedagogies can benefit all pupils. To do this, after defining the notion of cooperation, we will provide the main historical landmarks that led to cooperation between pupils in France, before describing the main variations. In particular, this will be an opportunity to distinguish between cooperation, competition, and collaboration, three interrelated practices that are not all compatible with the requirements of a pedagogy oriented towards democratised learning.

What is cooperative behaviour?

In the living world, cooperative action has three different and complementary characteristics.[5] Cooperative action is what corresponds to a combined action (it is not possible to cooperate with oneself), what is the result of an intention (one does not cooperate on orders, it is a voluntary process), and what leads each of the cooperators to derive a personal benefit (not necessarily identical or of the same intensity). Thus, in order to cooperate, it is necessary to carry out an action with several people, in the same space, which is accepted and which allows each person to learn from it.

In education, cooperation occurs in all situations where pupils act or learn together (with, through, and for others), in order to grow individually. Cooperation between pupils is therefore neither a teaching method nor a specific pedagogical trend. It is rather an additional pedagogical "kit" that is added to teaching practices to give more importance to the social dimension of learning. Learning would thus correspond to the paradox "alone – with": on the one hand, a subject can only learn by himself, by an effort to appropriate information present in his environment; on the other hand, it would be easier to learn with, by, and for others. It is this second part of the paradox which underlines the social dimension of the act of learning and which fully justifies the use of cooperative pedagogies (Table 10.1).

On the other hand, excessive individualism, i.e. egocentricity, is the opposite of cooperation because of its refusal to relate. Competition has surprisingly many links with cooperation. It can be defined as exchanges with negative interference, aimed at particular interests, because "the attainment of the goal by an adversary constitutes an obstacle to be avoided for the attainment of the same goal by oneself".[6] Cooperation and competition are therefore not synonymous. Both to adapt to it and to influence it, cooperation would consist in exploiting or facilitating the activity of one's partner, whereas "competition would like to avoid or counteract it".[7] However, the segments of these two interactive forms must be put into perspective, when groups act cooperatively within a competitive logic: a group develops a strong cohesion to become better than its competitors. So-called competition strategies are also developing,[8] with small structures joining forces to act better against large entities seeking appropriate monopolies. In addition, other cooperative activities emerge from competitive contexts, for example in the world of sport: between an athlete and their coach, between training or team partners and even during individual opposition (as in tennis) when opponents show each other what can subsequently be the subject of new efforts to improve their performance[9] (Table 10.2).

Table 10.1 Cooperation

Combined action	*Intent*	*Individual benefit*

Table 10.2 Competition

Combined action	*Performance*	*Commitment*

In this respect, it is very interesting to distinguish cooperation from collaboration,[10] especially because pedagogical consequences are important. Cooperation, as we have just explained, corresponds to a combined action, intentional and with individual benefits. A collaboration, even if it is similar to the combination of actions (by an interdependence between the actors, each one needing the other to succeed), is rather translated by the sharing of the same project (collaborators have a common goal) and an organisation of work by division of tasks (each one engaging in the activities for which he is the most competent).

Collaboration is not the only way of organising production work, but it seems to be suitable for optimising individual talents: after consultation, if each partner takes on a share of the work they are capable of doing, the combination of all these actions seems more effective than if each person tries the same thing individually. This is what happens in a school team when teachers deal with pupils divided into "classes" and, in secondary schools, according to teaching subjects.

However, this collaboration, which seems to be valid for a production or a project, is not suitable for learning. Indeed, it is very risky to rely on a division of tasks because, ultimately, learning requires cognitive activity in the exact area of what one wishes to help learn. In other words, cooperation that is useful for learning needs to prevent all forms of student withdrawal (such as the postures of performer, idler, or troublemaker), because otherwise it could only satisfy the interests of those who think the most and best (the designers). This is why all forms of pedagogy that focus on doing and producing (performance goals)[11] are risky: especially group work and teamwork. Conversely, group work (seeking the confrontation of ideas) and teamwork (inducing the construction of skills), because they are oriented towards learning (mastering goals), have more place in pedagogy. Otherwise, because cognitive interaction between peers rarely occurs, insufficiently designed cooperation can lead to an inequitable differentiation of positions, through a division of workload between designers, implementers, idlers, and troublemakers (Table 10.3).

Often, the adage associated with cooperation is: "alone we go fast, together we go far". However, in education, when faced with a difficulty, alone you get stuck. Moreover, when you find yourself working with others who are primarily pursuing selfish goals, together you stay still or

Table 10.3 Collaboration

Combined action	*Common goal*	*Division of labour*

progress more slowly than alone. This adage is therefore particularly limited in education. It is easier to prefer this equally paradoxical adage: "cooperate to learn better alone".

The origins of cooperation

The idea of formal cooperation between humans is first described with the social experiments of Etienne Cabet – the self-managing fraternity (1788–1856), Charles Fourier – the phalanstery (1772–1837), Jean-Baptiste André Godin – the familistères (1817–1888), Pierre-Joseph Proudhon – mutualism (1809–1865), or Robert Owen (1771–1858). The latter's work was carried out in Scotland, in the business world, to propose a critical alternative to capitalism. As a gifted young industrialist, he found no interest other than financial in running businesses that operated through a division of labour, which he saw as "blind and soulless" (Sennett, 2014, p. 64). To replace it, he set up worker cooperative communities, from which he derived the "six Rochdale principles": open door to all (equal employment), one man-one vote (workplace democracy), distribution of trade margins (profit sharing), cash trade (no abstract debt), political and religious neutrality (tolerance of differences in the workplace), promotion of education (vocational training linked to employment). These realities led to the development of consumer and production cooperatives: "we will consider co-operative as collective actors and their structures as containers of social capital based on trust, inherited from ancient craft and communal solidarities".[12] For example, in Portugal, they were encouraged by the law of 2 July 1867, which recognises "spontaneous and free association, cooperation of individual wills and forces, based on mutuality or reciprocity of services".[13]

In the social field, cooperation seems to have emerged through Saul Alinski's (1909–1972) method of community organisation. An American writer and sociologist, he engaged in a social struggle against various forms of control and discrimination through a method that aimed to bring different people together: it consisted of getting to know the streets of a community, chatting with people, bringing them together, and hoping for the best. He never told them what to do, but encouraged the shy ones to talk, himself providing factual information when necessary. The community organiser has no fixed timetable or set questions. The demands are always changing, the situation fluctuating and shifting, and the goal to be achieved often does not materialise in hours of work or in increased wages.[14] By bringing together people who have never really spoken to each other, by providing them with elements they did not know (because they were usually left out of the backstage negotiation spaces), and by suggesting other contacts, the community organiser hopes to maintain a dialogic discussion.[15] The ambition is to create peaceful, if imperfect, verbal connections between people who have little or no experience of meeting each other and who may hold opposing views. "Assist, do not lead" (the rule deduced by Charlotte Towle) is the informal logic of this approach. Personalities such as Barack Obama and Hilary Clinton have directly built on Alinski's approach.

Where does cooperation in education come from?

The practice of cooperation between pupils is not new. The oldest traces can be found in the Latin schools of the late Middle Ages, when children could take on certain functions: "officer" to help other pupils to read and write or "prefect" to control and train fellow pupils in religious exercises. This principle of functions is found in John Baptist de la Salle, founder of the Brothers of the Christian Schools (1651–1719), with children as "prayer reciters", "bowsers", or "inspectors", to replace the teacher in his absence. They are also mentioned by J.A. Comenius (1592–1670) about students who could benefit from teaching each other. The practices of school cooperation developed especially from the 19th century onwards, in the logic of putting pupils into participative and reciprocal activity (F. Pawlet at the Ecole des Orphelins de Paris from 1774 onwards) and of mutual teaching (J. Lancaster, A. Bell, and G. Girard), as an alternative to individual methods and simultaneous teaching.

They also go back to the first forms of *self-government*, in England with the Bedales School (opened in 1893), in the United States (W. Gill's *School City* from 1887), in Germany with the Odenwald School (from 1910) directed by P. Geheeb or in Russia with M. Pistrak, and the Labour Schools (from 1917), in Catalonia with Francesc Ferrer i Guàrdia (from 1901) who founded the modern school, with a cooperative organisation of work.

In France, they evolved notably through the notion of the school cooperative, attributed to Barthélémy Profit, Emile Bugnon, and Célestin Freinet. "Institutionally, it was in 1922 that the Commission nationale de l'enseignement de la coopération appeared, then in 1929 the Office Central de la Coopération à l'École (OCCE), which is still very active today".[16] These school cooperatives are associations for children, with cash flow, so that they can collect money through charity actions and spend it on class projects. School cooperatives also served to prepare children for adult mutualism, which we now use when we take out mutual insurance or insurance policies to be covered in case of life difficulties. Work at school thus becomes the greatest factor of social integration: solidarity, situated between liberal individualism and collectivist socialism, justifies the obligation to work, but it makes students feel the joys of working together. "Through mutual aid and cooperation, students should experience the benefits of the division of labour and the happiness of belonging to a collective".[17]

The Freinet movement, under the impetus of Elise and Célestin Freinet, has also greatly contributed to the development of cooperation: those who cooperate increase their capacity for action, as well as that of their group.[18] It is the opposite of individualism and competition. Cooperation in Freinet pedagogy is first and foremost that is established between teachers, within collectives. "They did not only establish this cooperation in their classroom, they also established it beyond themselves".[19] It is also translated between pupils: they are offered the opportunity to learn by interacting with their peers, on the one hand as receivers of information and, above all, on the other, by adopting the teaching posture. By cooperating, children develop knowledge-producing relationships. "In a collective perspective, this leads to looking together for what we cannot yet do or say. The promise of another becoming, which converts alienated work into an adventure".[20]

C. Freinet drew on the writings of the first socialists (Fourrier, Owen, Saint Simon, Louis Blanc, Proudhon, etc.) for ideas of cooperation and social solidarity. It was first as an adult co-operator that he became involved, and then, alongside Barthélemy Profit, he developed them for pupils, in particular through "school co-operatives". It is a question of cooperating to produce, create, acquire know-how, learn together, draw up and apply rules of life, share responsibilities, resolve conflicts, propose and carry out a project, organise partnerships, communicate with people outside the classroom, organise themselves, build a culture, and evaluate and assess themselves.[21]

The intention is to actively contribute to the development of socialisation, generosity, and solidarity among children. "Through school cooperation, the children effectively take in hand the organisation of the activity, work and life of their school. That, and only that, is important".[22] Thus, a Freinet pedagogy offers a political alternative to the dominant ideology which relies on the need of the masses to have a master or a leader. Students develop these skills in communities at their level: cooperative classes. It is "a community which the child serves and which serves them".[23] Roger Cousinet pioneered another approach, a "method of free work in groups". The children meet spontaneously in groups of four or five. A group leader takes charge of a notebook in which the pupils write the texts they have worked out together. These texts often depend on the projects that each group is involved in: the history of a costume, life in a distant country, a new technology, etc. It is from this pool that collective sessions are organised, which gives each group new work.

These approaches to cooperation differ from the one promoted by J. Dewey, which gave life to the so-called *cooperative learning*[24] consisting of learning with others, by others, for others, and not alone against others.

These cooperative practices are part of the broad dynamics of Education Nouvelle, structured through the International League for New Education (LIEN), founded on 6 August 1921, and mediated by the Revue "Pour l'Ere Nouvelle", an international journal of new education. One of its rallying principles is stated in its n°11 (July 1924): Selfish competition must disappear from education and be replaced by cooperation which teaches the child to put his individuality at the service of the community.

In France, the educational sciences have also taken an interest in cooperative pedagogies, mainly on the initiative of studies conducted by Philippe Meirieu on group work,[25] by Alain Marchive on mutual help,[26] by Marie-Anne Hugon on interactive pedagogy,[27] by Maria Pagoni[28] and Jean Le Gal[29] on cooperative student councils, by Jacques Saury on the links between cooperation and competition,[30] or by Alain Baudrit on cooperative learning,[31] collaborative learning,[32] and on tutoring.[33] In particular, P. Meirieu has shown that cooperation between pupils, contrary to what one might expect, is not systemically relevant and effective: it often happens that pupils who are members of a group are confined to the roles of observers and "little hands", while others carry out the bulk of the intellectual activity required (see the slides described above concerning collaboration for learning). M.-A. Hugon (with CRESAS) has studied the manifestations of such cooperation within small groups of children of heterogeneous levels, conceived as one of the pedagogical forms most likely to encourage interaction. According to his work, it is not enough to have three pupils sit around the same table and propose a stimulating activity for the children to "engage in interesting and mutually beneficial controversies in a democratic and cooperative climate".[34]

The contribution of psychologists

Cooperation also owes much to the contributions of social constructivism. These are inputs that justify group work and, more broadly, cooperation between students for the social nature of the interactions it generates. However, it appears that this reference is partly misleading, mainly because it is not about interacting with peers to "build knowledge". We see this as a consequence of an important misunderstanding (knowledge is not constructed at the level of students, who rather construct knowledge and skills – learning), which we propose to develop.

The function of conflict is expressed through the exchange of opinions, methods, and reasoning between partners in order to bring about reciprocal decentration and the need for cognitive reconfiguration.[35] This question of the link between thinking, learning, and the environment was first addressed by J. Dewey (1938/1968). For him, it is the interaction between the organism and the environment (experience) that is ontologically primary.[36] It is thought-provoking because it is presented as incomplete and needs to be developed: the subject then takes charge of the imbalance caused and tries to reduce it.

Thus, interactive experience is not problematic from the outset, but becomes so through investigation. It is because the situation is dubious and confused that it does not hold and that it requires investigation: "there is only a problem for a subject who takes it on".[37] This would be the way projects would be born, namely, anticipations, programmes of experience. Knowledge would then only have meaning in reference to the problems, the sources of these projects.[38] It would be, through learning, what would take the place of doubt. It is during these investigations that proposals are formulated, in order to be tested and evaluated. The fact that they are subject to discussion (for validation or refutation) would constitute a central element of its treatment. The situation that motivates the investigation would never be problematic from a subjective point of view; it would become so through social processing.[39]

In the 1960s, this social conception of learning emerged through three psychological theories.

Social learning and vicariance

Albert Bandura emphasises the importance of observation of others in learning. He explains human behaviour in terms of continuous interactions between cognitive, behavioural, and environmental determinants: individuals and their environments are "reciprocal determinants".[40] The mere observation of a behaviour in others may be sufficient to produce the same learning effect in oneself. This is the channel of observation and imitation that is also found in the theory of vicariousness, designating all the mechanisms, attitudes, or devices that make the observation of others and their actions a learning circuit. "All direct experiential learning phenomena occur on a vicarious basis, i.e. by observing the behaviour of others and the resulting consequences for them. Being able to learn by observation enables people to acquire large and coordinated behavioural repertoires, without having to develop them gradually in the laborious process of trial and error".[41]

This is the main reason why potentially dangerous situations are not taught through experience but through observation of competent models. Later, this information serves as a guide for action. "As a general rule, if one sees that a behaviour adopted by others is successful, it increases the tendency to behave in the same way, while conversely seeing a behaviour punished decreases the tendency to reproduce that behaviour".[42]

From socio-cognitive to cognitive conflicts

W. Doise, A.N. Perret-Clermont, G. Mugny ... criticise J. Piaget for having given too little importance to social interactions. Their approach pursues the theories of enquiry and the project of J. Dewey by considering relational partners in the environment. The latter would participate in the questioning process, during which the subject would question the conditions of the problem because they are lacking,[43] as well as in the critical examination of the proposals. It then appears that subjects who have to solve problems would learn more quickly and in a more lasting way during interactions with peers through socio-cognitive conflicts: "such a conflict arises between the contradictory conceptions of two (or more) children made manifest during their communicative interactions".[44]

The notion of socio-cognitive conflict recognises that it is not easy for a teacher, in charge of a group of 25–30 students, to accompany the emergence of cognitive conflicts as a tutor might do in a dual relationship. It also recognises that it would be an illusion to be satisfied with a correct answer from a few pupils in order to convince themselves of an equal understanding by all their classmates. Socio-cognitive conflict corresponds to the opportunity given by a teacher to their pupils, through group work, to confront their ideas on the same problem. Having an opinion and not sharing it with classmates, whom one otherwise values, leads to doubts about one's ideas. "What if they were right? The outcome of a socio-cognitive conflict, a cognitive conflict, is a state of doubt arising from a disagreement with peers. The other is interesting because it allows me to question what seems obvious and, if necessary, to learn what I am missing. With a cognitive conflict, doubt comes from the recognition of the insufficiency of one's knowledge. It arises from "the ability to hear the legitimacy of the other's point of view to the point of making it one's own and being wrong against oneself".[45] During a socio-cognitive conflict, this doubt arises from a disagreement with peers, which is pedagogically easier to establish.

One of the experiments on socio-cognitive conflict focused on the exercise of conservation of equal lengths:[46] two bars of the same length are used, one of them is shifted and asked if one is longer than the other. A panel of 53 children, chosen because they were identified as "non-conservative", i.e. responding that the bars were not the same length, were grouped in pairs. One claims that the high bar is the longest, the other that it is the low bar. An experimenter is present so that the children can discuss their disagreements without agreeing on a complacent agreement (for a relational regulation of their conflict): "How come you can try to agree?".[47] If one child agrees with their partner, the experimenter reiterates their initial reverse position. If both children agree that the bars are equal, the experimenter says nothing. If both children agree on the prevalence of a single bar, the experimenter gives and argues the correct answer. These situations are compared to exchanges where children immediately agree on the same incorrect answer, where there is no conflict between them. The results of these experiments, ten days after the session, are that:

- when the answer is given by the experimenter, all the children conclude with a response of equality: "these are obvious effects".[48] Note that not all the arguments provided by the children are similar to those given by the experimenter;
- when the two children disagree, 15 out of 20 subjects come to the equality response, which they then discard when the experimenter makes incorrect counter-arguments. In the end, one child in two concludes that the two bars are equal;
- when children agreed on an incorrect answer from the outset, no one changed their mind and no one raised the issue of equality.

The aim of a socio-cognitive conflict is therefore not a dialectical conversation (aiming to establish a common ground between opposing ideas) but rather a dialogical conversation (so that the partners, through the confrontation of opposing ideas, come to deepen their mutual understandings). It is this doubt, born of the heterogeneity of the answers, which would lead the subject to try new answers, strategies, techniques ... The more intense the conflict and the more it cannot be avoided, the stronger the doubt and the more marked the cognitive restructuring. These controversies would lead to an increase in individual investment, cognitive benefits, the development of interpersonal skills and epistemic curiosity, a motivation to understand and acquire new knowledge.[49] Socio-cognitive conflict thus presents itself as a necessary condition for intellectual decentration. By thinking in pairs, students would come to explore wider areas of their ideas and, in this way, could reconsider their efficiency based on the feedback provided by the opinion of peers. The divergence of views would allow for an increase in critical thinking, and thus creativity, by exploring more possibilities, including those not initially supported.[50]

It appears that if the pupil is already capable of carrying out the test proposed to them alone, "he will probably not do it much better in a group".[51] There would also be no natural socio-cognitive conflicts, in the sense that groups would naturally aspire to an agreement: conflicts of ideas would not come about spontaneously because of an apprehension of peer evaluation, social laziness, and a quest for conformity.[52] These contributions would therefore legitimise pedagogical intervention, both to make students feel secure and to encourage them to "battle" intellectually with their peers.

However, even if socio-cognitive conflicts can be relevant to learning, pupils may be tempted to avoid them: either to avoid reliving a painful cognitive imbalance (strategies for avoiding thinking),[53] or to remain in a phase of equilibrium whose reconfiguration does not meet a need. Several strategies have thus been identified, in the form of fusional and productivist slides of group work:[54] the opinion of another may be delegitimised (it is not listened to) or, on the contrary, being a totem (it is blindly accepted); priority may be given to what needs to be done, which dispenses with having to worry about what should be thought (and which is the subject of an attribution to another pupil, most of the time, recognised as competent). In other words, conflicts between peers are not always beneficial, due to avoidance of controversy, non-cooperation between partners, or defensive reactions of the pupils.[55] Often, these impediments would come from a misdirection of the pupils' achievement goals: they would tend more towards performance goals (to highlight their own skills or the achievement of a production) than towards mastery goals (signs of learning). However, it would be primarily the search for mastery goals that would lead to a constructive regulation of conflicts. Performance goals, on the other hand, would favour relational regulation, avoiding the focus on solving the task and favouring social comparison, the affirmation of one's skills or complacency.[56]

Learning from others

The theory developed by the Russian Lev S. Vygotski argues that learning develops through two types of cognitive experiences: first through collective and social activities (interpsychic), and second through individual thinking activity (intrapsychic). "The development of thought depends on language, the means of thought and the child's socio-cultural experience".[57] It presupposes the use of resources (material and/or human) that exercise a cultural mediation function. It thus rehabilitates the role of the third party in development and learning.

Learning is therefore social because it proceeds from collective realities and because it requires an interaction between the learner and a third party, more advanced than them in the mastery of the skill to be learned. School content is transmitted through situations designed for this purpose, during which pupils are led to ask themselves new questions: learning is constructed in response to needs, based on pupils' spontaneous conceptions. The teacher plays the role of mediator who makes knowledge accessible to pupils: "teaching the child what he is not capable of learning is as sterile as teaching him what he already knows how to do on his own".[58]

These theories were later taken up by J.S. Bruner, for whom learning is above all a co-construction of meaning, inscribed in a particular context, requiring the acquisition of codes allowing access to the culture of belonging. This trend develops teaching methods which encourage social interaction between peers and also between learner and tutor. It refers to the tutoring process as "the means by which an adult or specialist helps someone who is less of an adult or specialist than they are".[59] Further on, he mentions the term monitor: " ... practical work in which the monitor alone knows how to do it".[60] Through the mediation of the adult, the child acquires a framework for interpreting their experience and learns a common language that serves to negotiate meaning, in particular, to learn to speak, to anticipate the intentions of the others, and to enter a culture.

Interaction and mediation are conceived as necessary for the intellectual and social development of the subject. This is the notion of scaffolding: the masonry metaphor of a provisional structure useful "to consolidate or support a construction but which it will eventually have to do without".[61] Learners are accompanied and guided by someone more experienced (a tutoring interaction) who leads them to participate in shared experiences (enrolment), so that they can interpret and make sense of them, through simplification of tasks that discards what is secondary, presentations of models that provide sources and examples of improvement, and feedback that indicates the gap between what has been achieved and what is expected. These scaffolding strategies consist of protecting the child from distractions (by ensuring a focus of attention), relating the means used by the child to the goals, limiting the difficulty of the task to the level accessible to the child, and maintaining conventions of interaction.[62]

The main experiment that led him to such conclusions involved a group of 30 children, aged between 3 and 5, from the small and middle classes of Cambridge (Massachusetts). These children were presented with a problem situation, chosen to be "exciting, provocative, accessible, complex" and relating to a block that could be overcome by means of knowledge to be appropriated. The aim was to build a pyramid from blocks to be assembled. "They can only be formed by assembling the appropriate pairs in the correct direction since each block has a quarter of these large junctions".[63] After a period of individual trial and error, each child received interventions from a tutor-experimenter, in the form of verbal instructions or gestures shown, when they observed a difficulty or deviation from the initial task. If the children succeeded in building the assembly on their own, the tutor did not intervene. The analysis of the correlations between children's success and adult support reveals several functions of support:[64]

- Enrolment: engaging children's interest and commitment to the proposed research activity (and not another)
- Reduction of degrees of freedom: simplifying the task by focusing on essential activities

- Maintaining orientation: towards the pursuit of the defined objective, in particular by acting on the motivation to show one's achievements and to make them progressively evolve
- Signposting of defining features: highlighting the elements that are crucial for the task to be carried out
- Frustration control: to make people realise that solving a problem is less risky with a tutor than alone, without creating dependency
- Demonstration: using the solutions partially provided by the children, present models, examples, and techniques which, when observed and imitated, enable them to acquire new and effective ways of carrying out the task.

The transmitting teacher thus becomes the mediating teacher between the pupil and knowledge, the one who organises encounters with knowledge, where the context gives it meaning.

The zone of proximal development is "the distance between the current level of development as determined by how the child solves problems alone and the level of potential development as determined by how the child solves problems when assisted by the adult or collaborating with other more advanced children".[65] In other words, current development marks what an individual has already mastered on their own, the type and level of cognitive functioning that they are able to apply independently to solve a problem. This is what can be mobilised by working "at one's own pace". The zone of proximity, on the other hand, marks what can be learnt "from one's needs": what can constitute the next stage of one's current development if social interaction (with an adult or peers) is initiated. The child moves from what they can do to what they cannot yet do but which lies within their potential capacity. Therefore, a child can only be taught what they already capable of learning. The consequence of the mediation activity in the zone of proximal development, if it is well conducted, is to enable the learner to function jointly with others at a higher level than they were able of doing alone and, in a second phase, to function alone at the level reached in a group.

Towards a didactics of cooperation

It is on the basis of these psychological markers of the social dimension of learning that cooperative pedagogies can continue to be developed. At this stage of our research, three main families of precautions appear to be necessary to organise cooperation for the learning of all pupils:

- distinguishing cooperative arrangements,
- organising reciprocity,
- training students.

This is the paradigm of cooperation didactics.

Indeed, cooperative practices correspond to a myriad of variations, comparable to a toolbox available to teachers according to the needs they encounter. There are a large number of these variations. It is important to emphasise that each cooperative variation corresponds to specific intentions and that one should not be used for the other (like a craftsman does not use a trowel for a hammer) (Table 10.4).

Help (between students)

Pupil-to-pupil assistance is a cooperative situation in which a pupil, who recognises their ability, comes to contribute their knowledge and skills to a pupil who has expressed a need for them. To avoid the risk of devaluation through stigmatising labelling, it is best carried out on the initiative of the

Table 10.4 Cooperative variations and specific intentions

	Description	*Priority objectives*
Help – tutoring	Response to a request for help from a pupil who is blocked by an instruction or a situation	Fighting against school blocking and isolation Multiplying the sources of support in the group
Mutual aid	Association of pupils facing the same difficulty together	
Group work	Situation of confrontation of ideas in the resolution of a problem situation	Raising questions through socio-cognitive conflict
Workshop work	Activity space around specific materials and with other pupils	Promoting vicariousness: learning by observation and imitation
Teamwork	Carrying out a project approach in a group	Developing *soft skills* Improving the transfer of learning
Cooperative councils	Democratic meeting to involve children in classroom decisions that affect them	Learning democracy through direct participation
Cooperative games	Challenging games, but without losers or winners	Building friendship and mutual trust within a group
Democratic discussions	Democratic organisation of an exchange around a common question (philosophical, literary, scientific ...)	Learning to think for oneself (reflexively)
Knowledge fairs	Organisation of stands to exchange knowledge	Valuing students and developing a sense of self-efficacy

person who requests it.[66] In other words, rather than imposing help on a pupil who seems to be in difficulties, it seems more cautious to let them take the initiative to ask for help from a fellow pupil whom they trust.

Mutual aid

Mutual aid is a cooperative situation in which two or more students decide to get together to try to solve a problem or difficulty that they encounter jointly.[67] A potential by-product of mutual aid is a decrease in investment when students choose to associate themselves with a partner whom they expect to carry out the required activity alone. This avoidance strategy can be rendered null and void by prior training in mutual aid and by individual finalisation of the learning situation.

Tutoring (peer-to-peer)

A tutorial corresponds to an organised system of assistance given between students.[68] A tutor is a voluntary student who has been trained in the gestures of support and explanation. They master what is asked of them or know how to refer to someone skilful. A tutor is a pupil who expresses the need to obtain occasional support, more or less long term, from a tutor. In order to avoid increasing inequalities between pupils (if some pupils are never tutors), a reciprocal link is necessary between tutors and tutees. Reciprocity in pedagogy is the principle which translates into an alternation, according to needs, between the function of tutor and that of the tutee. No one is systematically a tutor, no one is systematically a tutee, everyone can occupy, at different times, one and the other of these functions. It is this reciprocity which distinguishes tutoring from monitoring, an instructor necessarily being a student recognised as an expert in transmitting content.[69]

Group work

Group work is a cooperative and didactic situation, organised by the teacher, so that the pupils explore, in groups, a problem situation that they have previously studied individually. Group work aims at the emergence of a socio-cognitive conflict, in the form of a dispute between the pupils, so that the initial representations of each one are tested, then increased by a formalisation of knowledge. In other words, group work seeks to create disagreements between pupils so that each of them comes to doubt their own opinions (relating to the problem situation studied), so that sufficient appetite for knowledge is created, which is thus presented as an answer to the questions that arise.[70]

Teamwork

In pedagogy, whereas a group prioritises confrontation and disagreements, a team is always looking for agreements to achieve a work, a project, or a production. Teamwork is therefore a cooperative situation organised by the teacher, within the framework of a project approach,[71] to put them in a position of enquiry and surprise.[72] Pupils come together to choose, think, implement, communicate, and evaluate a project, over a long period of time. The main vigilance is to ensure that students do not turn their work into collaboration too much, through an unfair and unjust division of tasks. For this reason, the finalisation of teamwork deserves an individual dimension (to avoid some students accepting a withdrawal that is harmful to their learning).

Workshop work

A workshop corresponds in pedagogy to a grouping of pupils around the same activity. These workshops can be organised by the teacher (composition and nature of the activities) or be initiated by the pupils (permanent workshops). Rotating workshops consist of a rotation of groups according to the activities: at the end of the cycle, all the pupils have completed all the workshops. The permanent workshops correspond to centres of activity towards which the pupils orientate themselves independently according to their individual work. The main advantage of workshop work is that there are several pupils: they can then learn by vicariance.[73]

Cooperative council

It is a democratic meeting that seeks to harmonise the life of the group by involving the participants: taking stock of personal or collective projects, modifying the rules of the class, dealing with proposals, problems, the cooperative, congratulations, but also everything that concerns the symbolic in the class (permits, certificates, belts, responsibilities, etc.). A cooperative council is the keystone of the exercise of cooperation between pupils.[74] It is partly ritualised by master words (recurring formulas that mark out the exchanges) and allows members of the class freedom of expression. However, it differs from a children's court in that it avoids publicly addressing conflicts between individuals. The use of devices such as "clear messages"[75] makes it possible to reserve the councils for the study of the rules of operation and the organisation of projects within the group. They thus become instruments of education for democracy through the exercise of participatory democracy and participate in the monitoring and encouragement of students' projects.

Democratic and philosophical discussion

A discussion with a democratic and philosophical purpose (DVDP) is a meeting in which exchanges are organised democratically (all participants have equal access to the floor) in order to address a specific question or subject philosophically. To do this, the participants are guided by the facilitator to articulate reflective thinking processes: problematisation, argumentation, and conceptualisation.[76] DVDPs aim to develop self-reflection and group speaking skills. As such, they contribute to citizenship education. Other forms of democratic discussion exist: literary interpretation debates, scientific debates, etc., which serve to problematise teaching content, educate reflective thinking, and develop citizenship skills.

Cooperative game

The principle of a cooperative game is physical or intellectual engagement, intense but without winners or losers, without competition or violence, with the aim of achieving a challenge or beating a previously established record. Regular practice of cooperative games, in addition to the development of prosocial skills, is associated with the construction of a serene and secure relationship climate. Cooperative games present themselves as solid alternatives for dealing with tensions within a group of students. In this sense, they are instruments of peace education.[77]

Knowledge fairs

Knowledge fairs (or reciprocal knowledge exchange networks) are cooperative forms where student-offerers pass on knowledge to student-receivers. The starting point is that everyone has and is able to make available knowledge that may be of interest to others. It turns out that it is the offerers who benefit most from knowledge markets. Therefore, the main precaution is to establish a reciprocity[78] that obliges the providers to become receivers and, above all, all participants to take on the role of provider. It is on this condition that knowledge fairs can help all students to maintain their sense of self-efficacy (or their sense of competence) and to more easily accept the functions of student tutors.

Specific attention was needed in the implementation of these cooperative variations. For the cooperative councils, do not publicly address conflicts between a few children so as not to ostracise a pupil within their group. For knowledge fairs, make sure that everyone has a stall (even if it means helping them to find an idea), in order to educate reciprocity. For help and tutoring, let students take the initiative to ask for help (do not do it for them, even "for their own good"). Give priority to tutoring over monitoring because tutoring allows reciprocity by encouraging the function of a tutor for all students (and not only for experts, which is the characteristic of monitoring). For self-help, explain why it is not effective to partner with a student who will do the work for you. For group work, warn students that the most important thing is to disagree, not to try to reach a consensus. For teamwork, inform them that the most important thing is not to succeed in the project at all costs, but rather that everyone has an important place in its realisation. For workshop work, the children are not alone. For cooperative games, they are a regular part of the class timetable.

These attentions are worked on with the pupils, based on observations of cooperative behaviour. They can be discussed over the course of a school year through the cooperative council, which serves as a keystone for the functioning of the class.

These attentions can also be the object of an awareness-raising of the pupils, by a preliminary training, which seeks to avoid those who are farthest from the school culture to fall into the slides described previously. It also helps children to understand why they cooperate (and how) and sometimes why it is better not to cooperate. In other words, this initial training helps to remove implicit assumptions and make explicit the real priorities of cooperative situations: cooperative games are not about having fun, but about creating trust in the group; student councils are not about discussing, but about finding decisions collectively so that everyone feels in the best conditions to learn; group work is not a time out, but helps students, through the confrontation of ideas, to question their certainties; tutoring is not an opportunity to succeed in exercises, but to have support when one is no longer able, alone, to carry out one's work in order to learn …

This training prior to cooperative actions, consisting of exercises highlighting specific aspects of cooperation that we want pupils to be aware of,[79] does not need to be long. It "costs" a few hours at the beginning of the year and, over the course of the months, a few reminders if it is noticed that habits seem to be forgotten or that problematic gestures are emerging. This time devoted to training students quickly becomes a time-saving lever, which avoids having to deal with problems and fight against the traps into which some have fallen.

Thus, through the dual intermediary of these student training situations and rigorous structuring of their work by the teacher, they are more likely to evolve within a serene social functioning and to engage in deep and effective learning.[80]

The values of cooperation

In France, the official texts rather advocate a conception of cooperation between pupils as a means to help them learn better. It is much less an end in itself. In other words, the principle is more about learning through cooperation than learning to cooperate. However, the recurrence of cooperative situations experienced by the pupils contributes at least indirectly to the development of cooperative values. By cooperating to learn, they learn to cooperate. This is why several educational intentions are pursued through the cooperative organisation of pupils' work.

First, to take into account the diversity of pupils, considering their differences as assets. This means that introducing a cooperative organisation within a class is a lever for pedagogical differentiation. Indeed, with group or teamwork, pupils can be enrolled in collective activities and thus benefit from the common momentum and ideas exchanged. With help, mutual aid, or tutoring, they have several ways of working and learning: alone, with others around the same problem, asking for help when blocked, giving help (and thus reusing what has been learned), working in a small group with the teacher or even individually with the teacher. This wide range of working methods gives pupils the opportunity to choose the one that seems to suit them and for teachers to no longer be the only resource person in the classroom to meet individual needs.

Second, to develop prosocial skills. By working at school through cooperation, pupils also learn to cooperate. In France, this is not an objective required by school curricula, but it is nevertheless recognised as a transversal skill, valid in different disciplines and outside school environments. For example, they can develop their communication skills, learn to work in a team (integrate, coordinate a dynamic, show rigour, reliability, and empathy, take into account feedback from partners, etc.), learn to manage conflicts (through active listening, mediation, and objective fact-finding) or learn the art of negotiation (to show influence, persuasion, diplomacy, and perseverance).

Finally, to bring human and civic values to life. The motto of the French Republic states three of them: liberty, equality, and fraternity. By cooperating at school, pupils learn the uses of those types of freedom that end where those of others begin. They work together so that everyone can make equal progress, with no child left behind and discouraged from making an effort. They see the classroom as a community of brotherhood where the strengths of some are at the service of the difficulties of others, so that the collective becomes a structure of mutual enhancement and support. This is certainly a hope for education in the principle of secularism. Thus, without great speeches, a cooperative class is a space of values in action, where pupils live them instead of just hearing about them.

Cooperative practices in France have thus been the subject of many years of development and study. We have attempted to show the diverse range of forms they can take, as well as the theoretical levers on which they can be justified and supported. There remains the major problem of democratising them among teachers: many say that they make their pupils cooperate, but few have been really trained in this, for example, to distinguish cooperation from collaboration. This is therefore the major pedagogical task of the years to come: to give the didactics of cooperation between pupils a status equivalent to that of the disciplinary didactics, which are predominant in the training of French teachers. If this project can be undertaken, we will be able to collectively hope for a school that is tailored to the needs of each child, capable of participating in the challenges of our contemporary societies.

Notes

1 Source INSEE https://www.insee.fr/fr/statistiques/3281681?sommaire=3281778
2 Jean-Paul DELAHAYE: *Pour une école républicaine et fraternelle*, Lormont, Editions Le bord de l'eau, 2022, p. 10.
3 Philippe MEIRIEU: *Itinéraire des pédagogies de groupe – Apprendre en groupe*, Lyon, Chronique Sociale, 1996.
4 Sylvain CONNAC: "Impact de la coopération entre élèves sur leurs performances scolaires en 6e", *Les Sciences de l'Éducation pour l'Ere Nouvelle, 51*/4 (2018), pp. 31–62. DOI: 10.3917/lsdle.514.0011
5 Pablo SERVIGNE and Gauthier CHAPELLE: *L'entraide - L'autre loi de la jungle*, Paris, Les liens qui libèrent, 2017.
6 Jacques SAURY: "La coopération dans les situations d'intervention, de performance et d'apprentissage en contexte sportif", *Note de synthèse en vue de l'habilitation à diriger des recherches en sciences de l'éducation*, Université de Nantes, 2008, p. 107.
7 *Ibid.*, p. 142.
8 Adam BRANDENBURGER and Barry NALEBUFF: *Co-opetition*, New York, First Currency Paperback Edition, 1998.
9 Jacques SAURY: La coopération dans les situations ...
10 Eloi LAURENT: *L'impasse collaborative – Pour une véritable économie de la cooperation*, Paris, Les liens qui libèrent, 2018.
11 Céline DARNON, Céline BUCHS, and Fabrizio BUTERA: "Buts de performance et de maîtrise et interactions sociales entre étudiants: la situation particulière du désaccord avec autrui", *Revue française de pédagogie*, 155 (2006), pp. 35–44. DOI: 10.4000/rfp.84
12 Dulce FREIRE and Joana DIAS PEREIRA: "Consumer Co-operatives in Portugal: Debates and Experiences from the Nineteenth to the Twentieth Centuy", in Mary HILSON, Sike NEUNSINGER, and Greg PATMORE: *A Global History of Consumer Co-operation since 1850*, Leiden, Brill., 2017, p. 297.
13 *Ibid.*, p. 299.
14 Saul D. ALINSKI: *Rules for Radicals*, New York, Random House, 1969, p. 66.
15 Richard SENNETT: *Ensemble, pour une éthique de la cooperation*, Paris, Albin Michel, 2014, p. 73.
16 Malini SUMPUTH and François FOURCADE: *Oser la pédagogie coopérative complexe*, Lyon, Chronique Sociale, 2013, p. 38.
17 Marie-Claude BLAIS: *La solidarité, histoire d'une idée*, Paris, Gallimard, 2007, p. 294.

18 Sylvain CONNAC, Bruce DEMAUGÉ-BOST, Bernadette GUIENNE, Isabelle HUCHARD, and Isabelle QUIMBETZ: *Les Pédagogies Freinet – Origines, concepts et outils pour tous*, Paris, Editions Eyrolles, 2019.
19 Nadine GIAUQUE and Chantal TIÈCHE CHRISTINAT: *La Pédagogie Freinet – Concepts, valeurs, pratiques de classe*, Lyon, Chronique Sociale, 2015, p. 3 and p. 49.
20 LRC: Éléments de théorisation de la pédagogie Freinet – Une approche complexe des apprentissages, Nantes, Editions ICEM, 2013, p. 19.
21 Catherine CHABRUN: *Entrer en pédagogie Freinet*, Montreuil, Libertalia, 2015, p. 94.
22 Célestin FREINET: "Coopérative scolaire et pédagogie Freinet", *L'Educateur*, 34–35 (1968), p. 4.
23 Célestin FREINET: *Para uma escola do povo*, Lisboa, Presença, 1969, p. 18.
24 David W. JOHNSON, Roger T. JOHNSON, and Edythe J. HOLUBEC: *El Aprendizaje cooperativo en el aula*, Barcelona, Paidós, 1999, sometimes translated as "cooperative pedagogy" - Yann VOLPÉ et Céline BUCHS: "Pédagogie coopérative: pratiques déclarées et facteurs d'appropriation", *Revue Suisse des Sciences de l'éducation,* 41(1) (2019), pp. 99–120, or "cooperative work" – Joan RUÉ I DOMINGO: "L'immigrant a l'escola. La metodologia del treball cooperatiu com a via d'integració social i acadèmica dels alumnes d'origen immigrant", *Educar*, 22–23 (1998), pp. 285–294.
25 Philippe MEIRIEU: *Itinéraire des pedagogies …*
26 Alain MARCHIVE: *L'entraide entre élèves à l'école élémentaire. Relations d'aide et interactions pédagogiques entre pairs de six classes du cycle trois*, Thèse de doctorat en sciences de l'éducation, Université de Bordeaux II, 1995.
27 Marie-Anne HUGON: *Vers une approche coopérative des apprentissages à l'école, en formation et dans la recherche pédagogique. Note de synthèse pour une HDR*, Université Paris-Ouest Nanterre La Défense, 2003.
28 Maria PAGONI: "La pratique de conseil de classe et son genre scolaire: la règle scolaire", *Les cahiers Théodile,* 6 (2005), pp. 91–113.
29 Jean LE GAL: *Les droits de l'enfant à l'école, pour une éducation à la citoyenneté*, De Boeck et Belin, 2002.
30 Jacques SAURY: La coopération dans les situations …
31 Alain BAUDRIT: *L'apprentissage coopératif: origine et évolution d'une méthode pédagogique*, Bruxelles, De Boeck, 2005.
32 Alain BAUDRIT: *L'apprentissage collaboratif …*
33 Alain BAUDRIT: *Tuteur: une place, des fonctions, un métier?,* París, PUF, 1999; ID.: "Cross-cultural Peer Tutoring: Ethnographic Observations of Two Dyads", *Irish Educational Studies,* 21, 3 (2002), pp. 93–109.
34 Marie-Anne HUGON: *Vers une approche cooperative …*, p. 116.
35 Céline DARNON, Fabrizio BUTERA, and Gabriel MUGNY: *Des conflits pour apprendre*, Grenoble, PUG, 2008.
36 Michel FABRE and Etiennette VELLAS: *Situations de formation et problématisation,* Bruxelles, De Boeck Supérieur, 2006.
37 John DEWEY: *Expérience et education*, Paris, Armand Colin, 1968, p. 171.
38 *Ibid.*
39 *Ibid.*
40 Albert BANDURA: *L'apprentissage social*, Bruxelles, Editions Pierre Mardaga, 1976, p. 8.
41 *Ibid.,* p. 20.
42 *Ibid.,* p. 11.

43 Michel FABRE and Etiennette VELLAS: *Situations de formation* ..., p. 29.
44 Willem DOISE and Gabriel MUGNY: *Le développement social de l'intelligence*, Paris, Interéditions, 1981, p. 40.
45 Philippe MEIRIEU: *La riposte – Pour en finir avec les miroirs aux alouettes*, Paris, Editions Autrement, 2018, p. 206.
46 *Ibid.*, pp. 92–116.
47 *Ibid.*, p. 99.
48 *Ibid.*, p. 100.
49 Céline BUCHS, Céline DARNON, Alain QUIAMZADE, Gabriel MUGNY, and Fabrizio BUTERA: "Conflits et apprentissage: régulation des conflits sociocognitifs et apprentissage", *Revue française de pédagogie,* 163 (2008), pp. 109.
50 *Ibid.*, p. 107.
51 Willem DOISE and Gabriel MUGNY: *Le développement* ..., p. 16.
52 Céline BUCHS, Céline DARNON, Alain QUIAMZADE, Gabriel MUGNY, and Fabrizio BUTERA: "Conflits et apprentissage ... ", p. 108.
53 Serge BOIMARE: *Retrouver l'envie d'apprendre*, Paris, Dunod, 2019.
54 Philippe MEIRIEU: *Itinéraire des pedagogies* ...
55 Céline BUCHS, Céline DARNON, Alain QUIAMZADE, Gabriel MUGNY, and Fabrizio BUTERA: "Conflits et apprentissage ... ", p. 106.
56 *Ibid.*, p. 116.
57 Lev S. VYGOTSKI: *Pensée et langage*, Paris, La dispute, 1997, p. 197.
58 *Ibid.,* p. 370.
59 Jerome BRUNER: *Savoir faire, savoir dire*, Paris, PUF, 2011, p. 5 and p. 261.
60 *Ibid.*
61 Philippe MEIRIEU: *La riposte* ..., p. 193.
62 Jerome BRUNER: *Savoir faire* ..., p. 289.
63 *Ibid.*, p. 267.
64 *Ibid.*, pp. 277–278.
65 Lev S. VYGOTSKI: *Pensée et langage* ... cited by Jerome BRUNER: *Savoir faire* ..., p. 287.
66 Minna PUUSTINEN: *La demande d'aide chez l'élève – Avancées conceptuelles, méthodologiques et nouvelles données*, Paris, L'Harmattan, 2013.
67 Alain MARCHIVE: *L'entraide entre élèves à l'école* ...
68 Alain BAUDRIT: *Education et formation dans les sociétés contemporaines - Le don/contre-don toujours d'actualité?*, Montpellier, Presses Universitaires de la Méditerranée, 2018.
69 Florianne OURSEL: "Du monitorat au tutorat", *Education permanente, 206/ 2016-1* (2016), pp. 11–18.
70 Philippe MEIRIEU: *Itinéraire des pedagogies* ...; Céline BUCHS, Céline DARNON, Alain QUIAMZADE, Gabriel MUGNY, and Fabrizio BUTERA: "Conflits et apprentissage ... ".
71 Michel HUBER: *Apprendre en projets*, Lyon, Chronique Sociale, 1999; Dominique COTTEREAU: *Alterner pour apprendre – Entre pédagogie de projet et pédagogie de l'écoformation*, Paris, Réseau Ecole et Nature, 2007.
72 Joris THIEVENAZ: *De l'étonnement à l'apprentissage – Enquêter pour mieux comprendre*, Bruxelles, De Boeck Supérieur, 2017.
73 Albert BANDURA: *L'apprentissage social* ...
74 Maria PAGONI: "La pratique de conseil ... ", pp. 91–113.
75 Danielle JASMIN: *Le Conseil de coopération, un outil pédagogique pour l'organisation de la vie de classe et la gestion des conflits*, Montréal, Chenelière /McGraw-Hill, 1994.

76 Michel TOZZI: *Nouvelles pratiques philosophiques*, Lyon, Chronique Sociale, 2012.
77 Mildred MASHEDER: *Jeux coopératifs pour bâtir la paix*, Lyon, Chronique Sociale, 2005.
78 Claire HÉBER-SUFFRIN: *Apprendre par la réciprocité – Réinventer ensemble les démarches pédagogiques*, Lyon, Chronique Sociale, 2016.
79 Sylvain CONNAC: *La coopération, ça s'apprend*, Paris, ESF Editeur – Collection « Je me lance », 2020.
80 Céline BUCHS: "Inclure tous les élèves", *Cahiers Pédagogiques, 576* (2022), pp. 16–17.

References

ALINSKI, Saul D.: *Rules for Radicals*, New York, Random House, 1969.

BANDURA, Albert: *L'apprentissage social*, Bruxelles, Editions Pierre Mardaga, 1976.

BAUDRIT, Alain: *Tuteur: une place, des fonctions, un métier?* París, PUF, 1999.

BAUDRIT, Alain: "Cross-cultural Peer Tutoring: Ethnographic Observations of Two Dyads", *Irish Educational Studies*, 21, 3 (2002), pp. 93–109.

BAUDRIT, Alain: *L'apprentissage coopératif: origine et évolution d'une méthode pédagogique*, Bruxelles, De Boeck, 2005.

BAUDRIT, Alain: *Education et formation dans les sociétés contemporaines - Le don/contre-don toujours d'actualité?*, Montpellier, Presses Universitaires de la Méditerranée, 2018.

BLAIS, Marie-Claude: *La solidarité, histoire d'une idée*, Paris, Gallimard, 2007.

BOIMARE, Serge: *Retrouver l'envie d'apprendre*, Paris, Dunod, 2019.

BRANDENBURGER, Adam and NALEBUFF, Barry: *Co-opetition*, New York, First Currency Paperback Edition, 1998.

BRUNER, Jerome: *Savoir faire, savoir dire*, Paris, PUF, 2011.

BUCHS, Céline: "Inclure tous les élèves", *Cahiers Pédagogiques*, 576 (2022), pp. 16–17.

BUCHS, Céline; DARNON, Céline; QUIAMZADE, Alain; MUGNY, Gabriel and BUTERA, Fabrizio: "Conflits et apprentissage: régulation des conflits sociocognitifs et apprentissage", *Revue française de pédagogie*, 163 (2008), pp. 105–125.

CHABRUN, Catherine: *Entrer en pédagogie Freinet*, Montreuil, Libertalia, 2015.

CONNAC, Sylvain: *Enseigner sans exclure – La pédagogie du colibri*, Paris, ESF Editeur – Collection Références, 2017.

CONNAC, Sylvain; DEMAUGÉ-BOST, Bruce; GUIENNE, Bernadette; HUCHARD, Isabelle and QUIMBETZ, Isabelle: *Les Pédagogies Freinet - Origines, concepts et outils pour tous*, Paris, Editions Eyrolles, 2019.

CONNAC, Sylvain: "Impact de la coopération entre élèves sur leurs performances scolaires en 6e", *Les Sciences de l'Éducation pour l'Ere Nouvelle*, 51/4 (2018), pp. 31–62. DOI: 10.3917/lsdle.514.0011

CONNAC, Sylvain: *La coopération, ça s'apprend*, Paris, ESF Editeur – Collection « Je me lance », 2020.

CONNAC, Sylvain and IRIGOYEN, Albert: "Apprentissage coopératif ou pédagogies coopératives?", *Education et Socialisation*, 73 (2023), en ligne: https://journals.openedition.org/edso/22840

COTTEREAU, Dominique: *Alterner pour apprendre – Entre pédagogie de projet et pédagogie de l'écoformation*, Paris, Réseau Ecole et Nature, 2007.

DARNON, Céline; BUCHS, Céline and BUTERA, Fabrizio: "Buts de performance et de maîtrise et interactions sociales entre étudiants: la situation particulière du désaccord avec autrui", *Revue française de pédagogie*, 155 (2006), pp. 35–44. DOI: 10.4000/rfp.84

DARNON, Céline; BUTERA, Fabrizio and MUGNY, Gabriel: *Des conflits pour apprendre*, Grenoble, PUG, 2008.

DELAHAYE, Jean-Paul: *Pour une école républicaine et fraternelle*, Lormont, Editions Le bord de l'eau, 2022.

DEWEY, John: *Expérience et education*, Paris, Armand Colin, 1968.

DOISE, Willem and MUGNY, Gabriel: *Le développement social de l'intelligence*, Paris, Interéditions, 1981.

FABRE, Michel and VELLAS, Etiennette: *Situations de formation et problématisation*, Bruxelles, De Boeck Supérieur, 2006.

FREINET, Célestin: *Para uma escola do povo*, Lisboa, Presença, 1969, p. 18.

FREIRE, Dulce and DIAS PEREIRA, Joana: "Consumer Co-operatives in Portugal: Debates and Experiences from the Nineteenth to the Twentieth Century", in Mary HILSON, Sike NEUNSINGER and Greg PATMORE: *A Global History of Consumer Co-operation since 1850*, Leiden, Brill., 2017, pp. 296–325.

GIAUQUE, Nadine and TIÈCHE CHRISTINAT, Chantal: *La Pédagogie Freinet – Concepts, valeurs, pratiques de classe*, Lyon, Chronique Sociale, 2015.

HÉBER-SUFFRIN, Clair: *Apprendre par la réciprocité – Réinventer ensemble les démarches pédagogiques*, Lyon, Chronique Sociale, 2016.

HUBER, Michel: *Apprendre en projets*, Lyon, Chronique Sociale, 1999.

HUGON, Marie-Anne: *Vers une approche coopérative des apprentissages à l'école, en formation et dans la recherche pédagogique. Note de synthèse pour une HDR*, Université Paris-Ouest Nanterre La Défense, 2003.

JASMIN, Danielle: *Le Conseil de coopération, un outil pédagogique pour l'organisation de la vie de classe et la gestion des conflits*, Montréal, Chenelière /McGraw-Hill, 1994.

LAURENT, Eloi: *L'impasse collaborative – Pour une véritable économie de la cooperation*, Paris, Les liens qui libèrent, 2018.

LRC: *Éléments de théorisation de la pédagogie Freinet - Une approche complexe des apprentissages*, Nantes, Editions ICEM, 2013.

MARCHIVE, Alain: *L'entraide entre élèves à l'école élémentaire. Relations d'aide et interactions pédagogiques entre pairs de six classes du cycle trois*, Thèse de doctorat en sciences de l'éducation, Université de Bordeaux II, 1995.

MASHEDER, Mildred: *Jeux coopératifs pour bâtir la paix*, Lyon, Chronique Sociale, 2005.

MEIRIEU, Philippe: *Itinéraire des pédagogies de groupe – Apprendre en groupe*, Lyon, Chronique Sociale, 1996.

MEIRIEU, Philippe: *La riposte – Pour en finir avec les miroirs aux alouettes*, Paris, Editions Autrement, 2018.

OURSEL, Florianne: "Du monitorat au tutorat", *Education permanente*, 206/ 2016-1 (2016), pp. 11–18.

PAGONI, Maria: "La pratique de conseil de classe et son genre scolaire: la règle scolaire", *Les cahiers Théodile*, 6 (2005), pp. 91–113.

PERRET-CLERMONT, Anne-Nelly: *Approches psychosociologiques de l'apprentissage en situation collective. Séminaire de psychologie appliquée*, Neuchâtel, Université de Neuchâtel, 1981.

PUUSTINEN, Minna: *La demande d'aide chez l'élève – Avancées conceptuelles, méthodologiques et nouvelles données*, Paris, L'Harmattan, 2013.

RUÉ I DOMINGO, Joan: "L'immigrant a l'escola. La metodologia des treball cooperatiu com a via d'integració social i acadèmicadels alumnes d'origen immigrant", *Educar*, 22–23 (1998), pp. 285–294.

SAURY, Jacques: La coopération dans les situations d'intervention, de performance et d'apprentissage en contexte sportif, *Note de synthèse en vue de l'habilitation à diriger des recherches en sciences de l'éducation*, Université de Nantes, 2008.

SENNETT, Richard: *Ensemble, pour une éthique de la cooperation*, Paris, Albin Michel, 2014.

SERVIGNE, Pablo et CHAPELLE, Gauthier: *L'entraide - L'autre loi de la jungle*, Paris, Les liens qui libèrent, 2017.

SMITH, Adam: *Recherche sur la nature et les causes de la richesse des Nations*, Paris, Gallimard, 1976.

SUMPUTH, Malini and FOURCADE, François: *Oser la pédagogie coopérative complexe*, Lyon, Chronique Sociale, 2013.

THIEVENAZ, Joris: *De l'étonnement à l'apprentissage – Enquêter pour mieux comprendre*, Bruxelles, De Boeck Supérieur, 2017.

TOZZI, Michel: *Nouvelles pratiques philosophiques*, Lyon, Chronique Sociale, 2012.

VOLPÉ, Yann and BUCHS, Céline: "Pédagogie coopérative: pratiques déclarées et facteurs d'appropriation", *Revue Suisse des Sciences de l'éducation*, 41(1) (2019), pp. 99–120.

VYGOTSKI, Lev S.: *Pensée et langage*, Paris, La dispute, 1997.

WEIXLER, Frédérique: *L'orientation scolaire, paradoxes, mythes et défis*, Boulogne-Billancourt, Berger Levrault, 2020.

11 Cooperation Between Pupils, a Comparative View[1]

Spain, France, and Italy

Albert Irigoyen[2]*, Josep M. Pons-Altés, and Carole Gauthié*

Introduction

The current competitive and unequal system of neo-liberal hegemony is advancing, endangering the good of the majority (standard of living, rights, and freedoms) for the benefit of a few, while justifying austerity, injustice, and precariousness as lesser evils of infinite progress.[3] We live in a "burnout society", where we are saturated by multitasking, overexposed, prisoners of social media, and disproportionately concerned with immediate performance and constant activity, leading to the self-exploitation of the individual.[4] In short, the social, political, and economic situation exposes the limitations of the capitalist system[5] and reveals the need for a social system based on cooperation, responsibility, and generosity.

In this context, if the cooperative movement hopes to develop new economic and social relationships, it must transcend the economic and social order so it can play its part in education, fostering cooperative education as a driver of change. One of the distinguishing features of the cooperative movement and, in general, initiatives linked to the social and solidarity economy is the importance attributed to education. To the extent that they share the aim of a more or less profound social transformation, they assign a fundamental role to education that also contributes to this transformation and improves people's participatory and critical capacity. This desire has often been manifested in schools through activities related to the organisation and management of cooperatives, or to educational projects dealing with social justice and environmental sustainability.

As we discuss below, in recent decades there has been a substantial increase in proposals for implementing cooperative learning (CL) in schools in many countries. However, although the predominant version allows pupils to work on values, it is not related to projects for social change. It has no relationship with the foundations of the social and solidarity economy.

DOI: 10.4324/9781003439554-12

And these social movements in turn do not identify with CL practices that do not fully incorporate cooperative values but appear closer to other traditions such as the critical didactic model or libertarian pedagogy.

Within this general framework, we aim to reflect on the conceptualisation and impact of the Anglo-Saxon approach to CL, which clearly predominates in Spanish and Italian schools that apply cooperation between pupils, and contrast it with the francophone concept *pédagogies coopératives* (*PC*). To conclude, we will examine areas in which cooperative learning could converge with the social and solidarity economy.

The expansion of CL in recent decades

Although its increasing importance in recent years may suggest otherwise, CL is not a new concept in education. It can be traced back to the early and mid-twentieth century and the work of John Dewey and Morton Deutsch, and has been the subject of research[6] that demonstrates its effectiveness for performance, motivation, self-esteem, critical thinking, social skills, and social cohesion in pupils compared with competitive and individualistic structures.[7] More specifically, one of these studies, involving an in-depth review of the scientific literature concludes that CL: 1) helps to increase pupils' level of achievement; 2) contributes to improving intrinsic motivation towards learning; 3) helps to create a positive attitude to learning; 4) has a positive correlation with higher levels of self-esteem; 5) makes pupils responsible for their involvement in learning; 6) improves group cohesion and treats differences as a positive aspect of heterogeneous groups; 7) facilitates social integration and the inclusion of pupils with special educational needs; 8) reduces aggressive behaviour by providing democratic mechanisms for decision making; and 9) promotes independent, responsible critical thinking, thus increasing pupil satisfaction.[8]

In order to understand the conditions under which CL has the aforementioned positive effects, in 2014 Slavin proposed that four mutually complementary theoretical perspectives should be taken into account:[9] 1) the motivational perspective, which focuses on the goal structure developed by teachers in the tasks assigned, as this is what motivates pupils to learn;[10] 2) the social cohesion perspective, which suggests that the relationships established among the members of the group enable them to help each other to learn;[11] 3) the cognitive perspective, which claims that to learn, pupils need to carry out a cognitive restructuring of new content and CL helps in this process;[12] 4) the developmental perspective, according to which the interaction between pupils with different levels of development in different aspects stimulates the ability of individuals more than if they work alone.[13]

CL is thus currently seen as a methodological tool that can meet the differing needs of twenty-first century individuals.[14] This also applies to university education, where an appreciation of the importance of cooperative work for the development of competencies has led to an increase in the use of cooperative group work as a basis for learning.[15] It must be understood that cooperating is not a simple action: learning cooperatively requires the teaching-learning situation to be designed with the context in mind,[16] especially if we are to train teachers so they can apply it in their future classes.

Finally, we should note that CL is not the only way for pupils to cooperate in class. In recent years, in France *PC* have become very influential. They constitute a concept of cooperation between pupils more in line with the French *Éducation nouvelle*, an approach that is now beginning to take off in small pockets in Spain and Italy.

Semantic clarification and approaches to cooperation between pupils in Spain, Italy, and France

There are various concepts of cooperation in learning and numerous ways of implementing it. Since the early twentieth century different cultures of application have emerged, which can be grouped under two main headings: CL, which has Anglo-Saxon roots, and *PC*, which has francophone roots.[17] These approaches do not conflict or compete with one another but are systems based on different traditions for promoting learning that, in some ways, complement each other.[18]

The concept of CL

CL, so-called since its origins in the United States and known internationally by this term, is a widespread approach to classroom work. It has been translated into Spanish as *aprendizaje cooperativo* and into Italian as *apprendimento cooperativo*, using a similar form and structure. However, in Italy "CL" is often used untranslated, to distinguish this specific way of working from the Italian expression *apprendimento cooperativo*, which is considered to have a more general meaning.[19]

In France, publications about cooperation between pupils are not altogether clear, as "CL" has been translated into French as *apprentissage coopératif*, but also as *pédagogie coopérative*.[20] Of the two possible French translations, Rouiller and Howden adopt the second, *pédagogie coopérative*.[21] Lerhaus and Rouiller argue that this translation of "CL" makes it possible in Europe to establish links with Freinet's approach and complement it in areas it did not initially consider.[22] For their part, Connac and Irigoyen use *apprentissage coopératif*, which is closer to the forms used in other Romance languages, avoiding the suggestion of a direct relationship between Freinet and CL,[23] and distinguishing it clearly from *pédagogies coopératives* (in the plural).[24]

CL has a long history, dating back to the work of Dewey,[25] Lewin,[26] and Thelen.[27] Lewin influenced Deutsch,[28] and subsequently Deutsch influenced Aronson and Johnson. Elliot Aronson created the Jigsaw classroom, while, starting in the 1970s and 1980s, David W. Johnson and his brother, Roger T. Johnson, laid the foundations of social interdependence theory and established the theoretical and practical principles of the Learning Together, the essential basis of CL. Studies by researchers such as Slavin, Sharan and Sharan, and Kagan and Kagan appeared in the same period. All of them argue for a series of cooperative methods and simple techniques. The theory constantly evolved, and the approach was increasingly applied in the United States and Canada, while the study and practice of CL also began to grow in Israel, the Netherlands, Norway, and the United Kingdom, each with its own specific characteristics, and subsequently spread on a smaller scale to Italy, Sweden, and Spain.

But what exactly do we mean by CL? CL is a generic term, an umbrella concept that includes a range of methods and simple techniques that originated in Anglo-Saxon countries and that organise teaching in schools implemented via cooperative interaction between pupils, most of whom work in groups. The most widely used cooperative methods include: Learning Together, developed by David W. Johnson and Roger T. Johnson; the Jigsaw classroom, developed by Elliot Aronson; Jigsaw II, developed by Robert E. Slavin; Student Team Learning, developed by David De Vries, Keith Edwards, and Robert E. Slavin; Group Investigation, developed by Shlomo Sharan and Yael Sharan; the Structural Approach developed by Miguel Kagan and Spencer Kagan; Complex Instruction by Elizabeth G. Cohen; and the Collaborative Approach developed by Helen Cowie. All these cooperative methods differ in practical aspects and their organisational structure, but they share some essential features and are designed to transform group work into a cooperative activity.[29] They all reject competitive and individualistic learning.[30] However, it should be pointed out that views on the links between cooperation and competition vary, as some of the proponents of CL defend competition between groups, while others maintain that it should be avoided. The myth of competition, which has a strong presence in the United States, has led these proponents to tend, to a greater or lesser extent, to introduce a competitive aspect in their models.[31]

Generally speaking, the programmes designed to apply CL and proposals for assessing its implementation adapt the ideas put forward by Slavin and his associates in "Learning to cooperate, cooperating to learn". CL serves two purposes: 1) pupils will learn more and better (cooperating to learn: cooperative group work as a resource); 2) they will learn to work as a team (learning to cooperate: cooperative group work as another part of course content that they must learn).

Important studies from French-speaking countries include the research published by Buchs, Howden, Rouiller, Lerhaus, and Baudrit. CL features strongly in the scientific literature in Spanish thanks to publications by researchers such as Ovejero, Rué, Pujolàs, Lago, Zariquiey, Duran, Iglesias, Fernández-Río, Gavaldà, Torrego, Negro, Serrano, Cañabate and Colomer, and many others.[32]

Spanish authors all refer to the Anglo-Saxon approach (CL), taking Johnson and Johnson as a model. Pere Pujolàs, for example, structures CL teams by developing notebooks and team plans as a mechanism for configuring the team and for its self-regulation, adapting the team-assisted individualisation (TAI) technique, developed by Slavin in 1984, which combines individualised, or rather personalised, work with teamwork. There is no inter-group or inter-individual competition of any kind, and emphasis is placed on cooperative strategies, such as Jigsaw classroom (developed by Aronson). David Duran is a member of the *Grup de Recerca sobre Aprenentatge entre Iguals* (GRAI), which conducts research and trains teachers with the aim of introducing peer learning as a standard methodological practice on three levels: 1) among pupils: promoting teaching by peers and enabling pupils to learn based on their differences; 2) among teachers: by forming pairs in the same school who learn from each other, putting new ideas into practice together; 3) among schools: through encounters between pairs of groups from different schools, support via an online classroom, and exchange visits. Antoni Gavaldà is interested in transmitting the principles of cooperativism to schools and specifies what cooperative values are essential to tackle and structure learning-teaching situations in class. Cooperative group work thus not only ensures the assimilation of knowledge but also the acquisition of social competence in the learning process, maintaining the cooperative groups used in the CL but based on the principles of cooperativism.

In Italy, where translations of the seminal studies (Johnson brothers, Slavin, etc.) are available, the most notable researcher is Mario Comoglio.[33] This highly respected researcher has attempted to synthesise the trends in CL, as reflected in the innovative educational projects undertaken in Turin, which treat CL as more than a simple teaching method.[34] He admits that CL is not a "thing" that can be defined precisely, although in very general terms it could be understood as a form of learning achieved through cooperation with other members of the class (and not excluding individual work or competitive activities).[35]

For practical reasons, Italian schools tend to adopt the most readily applicable and more technical approaches from the Anglo-Saxon tradition, and there is a remarkably extensive bibliography in Italian, apart from the key works of Mario Comoglio,[36] as well as specific studies of the usefulness of CL in tackling the challenges of cultural diversity.[37]

However, in Italy, as in France, there is also a tradition that is more concerned with examining the critical sense that education should have, with a more social and psychological component (for example, the *Movimento di Cooperazione Educativa*, which follows the work of Célestin Freinet).[38]

In Italy as a whole, the relationship between CL and the cooperative movement (and initiatives related to the social and solidarity economy) is not as close as one might have expected, and support from the cooperative movement for educational projects is relatively limited considering its strength in certain regions.

There are notable precedents, such as Comincioli and Gheza, who significantly referred to the "didactics of cooperation" in a project promoted by the cooperative movement, which aimed to educate young people about the cooperative way of life and cooperative values.[39] But educational initiatives coming from the cooperative world are usually limited to activities designed for pupils to form cooperatives or prepare sustainable cooperative projects. It would seem that schemes that are politically and socially more ambitious, with a stronger desire to bring about change, are normally associated with another type of institution or cultural cooperative: the FARE cooperative in Umbria, for example, does not even mention CL.[40]

The concept of PC

PC are mainly the work of educationalists and educational movements associated with the *Éducation Nouvelle* and scientific research into the social dimension of learning. They do not promote the acquisition of cooperative skills or cooperative values but correspond more closely to the principle of "cooperating to learn". This is the axiological framework in which leading French educationalists have presented cooperation between pupils, including Célestin and Élise Freinet with school cooperation, Roger Cousinet with free work in groups, Barthélémy Profit with school cooperatives, Fernand Oury with institutional pedagogy, and Philippe Meirieu with differentiated pedagogy and group learning. They have all contributed to the development of different approaches to education, encouraging cooperation between pupils in different forms and for different reasons. All these studies have become available thanks to educational movements such as ICEM-Pédagogie Freinet, the OCCE, the AGSAS, the GFEN, the AVPI, the CRAP, the RERS, the ICEM-34 group, and the PIDAPI teaching association.[41]

In addition to these developments, university disciplines such as educational science have explored the social dimension of learning.[42] They are generally based on constructivist theories of learning, which see cognitive obstacles as sources of epistemic development. In the *PC* framework, therefore, interpersonal relationships are regarded as vectors of three types of cooperative interaction: support in dealing with a problem, diversification of individual ideas, and inter-personal conflict (through the expression of differing opinions).[43]

The *PC* are consolidated today thanks to the tireless work of Sylvain Connac, who brings together under the *PC* umbrella a wide range of variants of cooperating to learn, including help (*aide*), mutual help (*entraide*), tutoring (*tutorat*), group work (*travail en groupe*), and teamwork (*travail en équipe*), plus other forms of cooperation to build together, such as cooperative councils (*conseils coopératifs*), discussions with democratic and philosophical purposes (*discussion à visée démocratique et philosophique*), cooperative games (*jeux coopératif*), balances (*bilan*), and knowledge markets (*marché de connaissances*).

A comparison of CL and *PC* in Spain, Italy, and France

These two forms of cooperation between pupils, CL and *PC*, both contribute to academic success and the well-being of pupils, although they generate different pedagogical paradigms. For the purposes of this study, we examine them from three perspectives: axiological, epistemological, and praxeological:[44]

- The axiological aspect of cooperative organisations emphasises the philosophical and political purposes they pursue.
- The epistemological aspect focuses on the theories on which the approach is based and its historical origins.
- The praxeological aspect deals with the practical realities of the classroom. We shall try to show how these cooperative practices apply to pupils and examine the positions taken by teachers.

Axiology: The values of cooperation

CL is not merely a teaching resource but a type of content that pupils learn.[45] It allows equal rights to become equal opportunities, revealing the value of working and engaging together in a setting that promotes cooperation.[46] Cooperative groups have a dual purpose: 1) to teach pupils course content; 2) to teach teamwork as part of the course content. Participants also have two responsibilities: they have to learn themselves, and they have to help their fellow pupils to learn.[47]

Many researchers identify CL as a specific way of developing a cooperative climate in the classroom and fostering social skills such as sharing materials and resources, the ability to ask for and offer help, the ability to listen to others and respect them, etc.[48] Values are thus transmitted through positive interdependence, shared leadership, and individual responsibility combined with group responsibility.[49] CL is therefore backed by values such as solidarity, mutual help, and respect for differences.

Howden and Rouiller refer to a precise matrix of values that are developed: respect, mutual help, commitment, openness to others, the right to be different, solidarity, trust, sharing, pleasure, autonomy, equity, and empathic listening.[50]

The Spanish "Cooperar para Aprender/Aprender a Cooperar" ("Cooperating to Learn/Learning to Cooperate (CA/AC)") programme, created by Pere Pujolàs and José Ramón Lago in 2018, focuses on the development of two conditions: 1) recognising and connecting with people who are very different at a cognitive-emotional level[51]; and 2) ensuring that those whose inclusion is assured are not indifferent to exclusion and the suffering of those who are at risk of exclusion.[52] The cooperative structure of these activities focus, therefore, on inclusion and equity.

In the French-speaking world, *PC* have various educational purposes. First, they accommodate pupil diversity, considering their differences an asset that can help them to succeed. The class is organised along cooperative lines to allow differentiated teaching approaches to be applied, based on personalised designs.[53] Working in groups or teams, pupils can take part in collective activities and benefit from a common effort and the exchange of ideas. With assistance, mutual help, and tutoring, they have various ways of working and learning: alone, with others dealing with the same problem, asking for help when they are stuck, offering help (and, by so doing, reusing what they have learnt), working in a small group, or even individually, with the teacher.[54] The wide range of options available in PC means pupils can choose what seems most suitable for them, and teachers are no longer the only human resource available in the classroom to meet individual needs.

Another educational aim of cooperative organisation is to promote human and civic values. Three of them feature in the motto of the French Republic: liberty, equality, and fraternity. By cooperating at school, pupils learn how to use freedoms that end where those of others begin. They work together so that they can all make equal progress: nobody gets left behind or becomes discouraged. This way of working turns the class into a community where the strengths of some are drawn on to help overcome the difficulties of others, so that the group becomes a structure characterised by appreciation and mutual support.[55] A cooperative classroom (one where the pupils can learn with, from, and for others) is thus a space where values are put into action, where pupils experience values rather than just hearing about them.

These values are closely related to the ideals of fraternity, and in this sense, cooperation can contribute to pupils' well-being, ensuring they do not feel isolated. This form of cooperation is not so much about solidarity, which is based on the cold logic of well-understood mutual interests,[56] but is more closely related to the idea of collaboration.[57] The humanistic aspect of fraternity makes it richer and also more demanding, as it requires giving unconditional attention to others.[58] Cooperation between pupils is not, therefore, based on solidarity but on generosity, understood as disinterested giving of oneself.[59]

In an interview published in the journal *Comunicació Educativa*,[60] Sylvain Connac argued that educational research into cooperation is fundamental: 1) to allow for diversity; 2) to study how and in what areas a cooperative organisation can advantageously replace normal practices of educational differentiation, which tend to discourage pupils and increase distances within the class.

Epistemology: Theories of learning

The basic theories on which CL and *PC* are based are widely known. In recent decades, the most prominent psychological and pedagogical theories highlight the benefits and effectiveness of interaction with others for learning, albeit from various perspectives.

PC have been influenced by various sources. First, the *Éducation Nouvelle* movement, particularly the ideas of French educationalists such as Célestin and Elise Freinet, Roger Cousinet, Barthélémy Profit, Fernand Oury and Philippe Meirieu. The Freinets were the source of major developments in education, leading to the creation of the *Institut Coopératif de l'École Moderne* (ICEM). The Freinet approach is founded on five pillars: pupils' freedom of expression, experimental trial and error, educational techniques, democratic participation, and cooperation.[61] Roger Cousinet developed a "free group-work method",[62] which tended to encourage, through mutual help in the class, the moral development of pupils, based on rejecting blind obedience to the binding forms of solidarity imposed by communities. Barthélémy Profit, motivated by the idea of mutualism as an educational tool for civic commitment, was one of the founders of the *Office Central de la Coopération à l'École* (OCCE), promoting the creation of school cooperatives, democratically organised and managed by and for children.[63] Fernand Oury and his brother Jean Oury were at the forefront of educational groups based on the Freinet movement, but they emphasised the unconscious dimension of educational relationships,[64] thereby developing the institutional pedagogy movement. For example, we might consider the cooperative life of a class within a pupil council, a structure empowered to establish rules and create new educational institutions.[65] Philippe Meirieu's contributions in the field of differentiated instruction and group learning, for example, also inspired various educational reforms.[66]

Second, the development of *PC* was based on theories of learning explored through numerous works on psychology, initially based on research carried out by Jean Piaget. They were then further defined by the social constructivist school of thought.[67] Mugny, Doise, and Perret-Clermont have described how disagreements between pupils' ideas (social-cognitive conflict) could develop into states of doubt and uncertainty (cognitive conflict).[68] These questions are the source of a need to learn that can be satisfied by a formal relationship with the content of teaching (like an answer to the questions pupils ask themselves). Vygotsky drew attention to the importance of the social dimension of learning in his definition of the zone of proximal development. The concept was further explored by Bruner through different approaches to scaffolding and through giving the pupils themselves a role in teaching.[69] Another aspect of social learning was identified by Bandura: vicarious learning. He pointed out that we can learn through a double process of observing and then imitating a third party.[70] All these approaches have been extensively studied in the field of educational sciences, which examine them in the light of sociological and philosophical concerns.

CL is also based on theories built on the work of Piaget and Vygotsky, and Mugny, Doise, and Perret-Clermont. The neo-Piagetian notion of "socio-cognitive conflict", i.e., cognitive imbalance and restored balance, brought about by social interaction,[71] is as important as the notion of "shared intentionality" in cooperation,[72] and the role of (interdependent) dialogue – but not conversation – as a vehicle by which to generate the above phenomena.[73] And the contributions of Bruner and Bandura should not be disregarded.

Even so, unlike PC, the origins of CL are to be found in John Dewey's work on learning as a social and democratic process and Kurt Lewin's studies of group dynamics, followed by Morton Deutsch, who defined it on the basis of social relationships and the theory of social interdependence. In the 1970s and 1980s, the Johnson brothers gave further support to the theory of social interdependence, as described in the work of Morton Deutsch and Kurt Lewin.[74]

The theory of social interdependence holds that the way it is structured within the group determines the interaction between members and the results of learning. According to the type of interaction, there are three types of interdependence:

- Positive interdependence (cooperation)
- Negative interdependence (competition)
- Absence of interdependence (individualistic efforts)

Setting the goal for pupils to both learn themselves and to ensure that the other members of the group learn gives rise to positive interdependence.[75]

To promote positive interdependence it is therefore necessary to establish group objectives or goals (interdependent goals) as well as other forms of interdependence: tasks, roles, resources, etc.[76] But it is important to point out that interdependence is not the only element that needs to be present for cooperative interaction to work. Scientists agree on the five essential elements for any work structure in a cooperative group. They come from the Learning Together Method, proposed by Johnson and Johnson, which is the model most often applied by teachers.[77] These are 1) positive interdependence, 2) individual accountability, 3) promotive interaction, 4) social skills, and 5) group processing.

However, other authors have added further criteria. For example, in the Spanish literature, Ovejero includes equitable participation, equal opportunities for success, heterogeneity, and shared leadership.[78] In the Italian literature, La Prova refers to Johnson and Johnson's five characteristics but adds two more: contemporaneous actions and distributed leadership.

In the literature in French, Buchs argues that positive interdependence and individual responsibility are the keys to cooperation and that a small number of pupils per group (two to five) makes individual face-to-face interaction possible.[79] Staquet lists six principles for CL: 1) a climate favourable to cooperation; 2) work teams; 3) positive interdependence and empowerment; 4) social and cognitive skills for cooperation; 5) consideration of group dynamics; 6) a teacher who can be consulted and acts as a facilitator.[80] Connac, meanwhile, defines Learning Together as: 1) working in small teams; 2) individual responsibility; and 3) positive interdependence.[81]

So, it is clear that merely putting pupils together and allowing them to interact is not enough to automatically obtain favourable results,[82] and it is also clear that the decisive factor is not the amount of interaction but rather the nature of that interaction.[83] Increasing awareness of this reality has led educationalists to intensify their efforts to identify forms of social organisation in learning activities that favour interaction between pupils.

Praxeology: The most common cooperative practices

CL is an effective approach to ensuring that pupils acquire the specific and generic competences defined for each level and subject area and to establish a way of doing, being, and living together in class. It is not only an end in itself, it is also a way of supporting learning: pupils learn through cooperation and learn to cooperate, while the teacher oversees "the conditions for constructive interaction".[84] It also involves training pupils in the social skills necessary for their school work.[85]

But it is important to recognise that developing cooperative structures (methods and simple techniques) is a complex process, and one which is even difficult to classify.[86] Although teachers can use CL according to their teaching philosophies and practices, each has its own features and peculiarities and uses specific cooperative strategies. It therefore seems fundamental that teachers should know some of these structures well and especially understand the conceptual principles on which CL is based, so they can choose the option that best suits their circumstances.

Over the years, to assist in the implementation of CL, much advice has been given and many programmes have emerged within major research projects that promote CL as a tool to improve learning, increase social cohesion, and foster inclusion. Generally, they view cooperation both as educational content (learning to cooperate) and as a resource for learning (cooperating to learn). For example, the schemes proposed by Pujolàs and Lago in Spain and by La Prova in Italy pay special attention to inclusion, equity, social cohesion, and harmony in the school.[87] We thus see that these educational approaches can be directed towards the contributions that cooperation makes in building learning, not only as a strategy for cognitive development but also as a methodology for interaction, a way of organising work that favours metacognitive habits and self-assessment, and a strategy for socialisation.[88] By and large, the principles of CL are applied in schools: pupils work in small groups (from two to six members, although four heterogeneous members is the recommended number for the creation of stable groups) with specific responsibilities (coordinator, spokesperson, organiser, and secretary, for example) and with common objectives for which the members depend on each other. In these small groups, with the guidance, support, instruction, and assessment of the teacher, pupils help each other, evaluate ideas, discuss, reach consensus, and break away from traditional individualistic and competitive teaching-learning models.

Cooperating to learn through cooperative methods can be a complex and often difficult task. Because cooperating is not a simple action, learning through cooperation requires the design of the teaching-learning situation to take the context into account. This demands rigour in the conditions under which it is applied. Teachers cannot be mere technicians who apply a method. They must internalise the method and adapt it to the real situation in the class, modifying the organisational structure if necessary, and designing cooperative techniques to guide learning.[89] The role of the teacher is fundamental for guaranteeing the participation of all the pupils, and cooperative activities must be structured so as to promote simultaneous interaction between pupils and ensure they participate on an equal footing. The teacher is also responsible for explaining the reasons for cooperation and clarifying the nature of interdependence.[90]

Although these approaches call for the application of highly structured cooperative programmes, it must be pointed out that research into cooperation in education and its practical application is at an early stage, and while we are seeing progress in schools, it is not always along the right lines.[91]

In the case of *PC*, we need to specify the nature of the (very diverse) organisations involved and, for each type, determine what specific measures are necessary for cooperation to contribute to their progress. It is in this sense that didactic techniques of cooperation between students are currently being developed,[92] detailing practices such as help, mutual help, peer tutoring, group work, teamwork, workshops, games, cooperative advice, and knowledge markets. These can be presented in two ways: the requirement to cooperate (as a formal teacher initiative or an informal pupil initiative) and their relationship with knowledge (symmetrical or asymmetrical).

These first forms of *PC* are intended to help pupils to succeed academically. Other forms pay more attention to their well-being and the conditions in which they learn, by constructing a non-threatening work environment, where pupils feel relaxed. They include cooperative councils,[93] cooperative games,[94] knowledge markets (or knowledge exchange networks),[95] and democratic discussion (especially of a philosophical nature).[96]

Possible areas of convergence between CL and the foundations of the social and solidarity economy

There is substantial evidence to suggest that social alternatives based on the social and solidarity economy are viable and that cooperative systems are often more stable and effective than those based on individual interest.[97] Cooperatives are an alternative to capitalist corporations that can operate and succeed in a market economy, and they have a positive influence on the well-being of societies.[98]

However, Ovejero points out that the original purpose of CL was exclusively to increase the efficiency of American schools and improve pupils' learning so that they could compete more effectively with other countries. He adds that, even today, Johnson and Johnson do not see a single criticism of an economic, social, and cultural system that makes people individualistic, selfish, and competitive.[99]

However, when CL is applied with a view to introducing pupils to cooperative principles, it cannot be entirely divorced from the ideologies of associationism and cooperativism. In recent years CL has evolved from being a method for teaching and learning to a much wider, richer educational movement that respects cultural and educational diversity and points towards greater social justice and increased opportunities together with an ethical, sustainable view of life.[100]

As Ovejero has stated, teachers should not be mere technicians who apply CL methods, but engineers who are familiar with their foundations and the reasons for their effectiveness. Nor should teachers limit themselves to working with a particular technical content. They should have a social purpose: cooperative learning should not be merely an educational technique, and its aim should not only be for pupils to learn more and better but also to learn to think for themselves, independently and critically. Schools should lead the way in developing relationships based on cooperation and mutual help, to help build a society that is more cooperative, more democratic, and more supportive. This approach has been referred to as "critical cooperative learning".[101]

The need to establish the link between cooperative values and CL can thus be seen as essential and urgent, if we do not want to distort the meaning of cooperation.[102] There are specific approaches that do create this link for schools. A good strategy is to base teaching on the traditional values of the cooperative movement as expressed by the International Cooperative Alliance (ICA): 1) Bring the social economy into the classroom; 2) democratic management; 3) economic participation; 4) autonomy and independence; 5) education, training, and information; 6) cooperation among cooperatives; 7) and concern for community.

Seeking to incorporate these values in education, Antoni Gavaldà established nine cooperative reference values for schools.[103] They are: 1) valuing divergent ideas; 2) the need for dialogue and consensus; 3) commitment to freedom; 4) sharing in equality; 5) responsible participation; 6) contributing to democracy; 7) a desire to learn; 8) social regulation of the economy; 9) constant, persistent reflection. In Table 11.1 we give a definition for each of them[104]:

Nevertheless, these nine values do not constitute an educational panacea. The frantic pace of day-to-day classroom activity, a fear of tackling topical issues, and the uneasiness that criticism can cause may inhibit efforts to introduce the values we want to pass on to pupils. There may also be reticence about, first, the implications of cooperative values that question individualism and selfishness as drivers of social development and as the basis of our social and economic system, and second, about the need to decode power structures and make them intelligible to improve the quality of our democracies.

Teachers must therefore equip themselves with arguments and be able to explain the advantages of applying these values. And be able to show, without prioritising work on the values of cooperation, CL is practically a contradiction in terms. Teachers not only need to teach pupils so that they do well in society, they also need to teach them to improve it. Pupils need to be taught about and involved in the transformation of society in order to promote the values of freedom, responsibility, equality, and generosity.

Table 11.1 Cooperative values for schools

1 Valuing divergent ideas	The social context influences ideas that are being developed, and we must accept that differences will arise if we want to improve and advance. This means we must look for solid foundations to justify our convictions and be able to contrast our ideas with others.
2 The need for dialogue and consensus	When a group has thought about and discussed an issue, the members need to seek agreement. They need to understand the difficulty of defending absolute truths and accept the changing nature of ideas and the possibility of revising previous, possibly conflicting, opinions.
3 Commitment to freedom	This implies that individuals have a right to express opinions and make decisions, without coercion. This right has been fought for historically and must still be defended against threats of erosion.
4 Sharing in equality	This is not uniformity. The equality of human rights and duties is a fundamental achievement in a democratic society, although it is difficult for the principle to be fully implemented, as legal equality and real equality are not equivalent. To avoid an excessively rigid interpretation, the concept of "equity" is needed.
5 Responsible participation	This implies that assuming responsibility is a sign of democratic and civic maturity. Schools must foster this sense of responsibility and combat nihilist and passive attitudes.
6 Contributing to democracy	This is fundamental in the cooperative and social solidarity movements through values that involve negotiation and the ability to handle possible rejections of what one believes and defends.
7 A desire to learn	This implies that there is an imperious need to instil in pupils a demand for knowledge and foster their intellectual curiosity, so that they can progress individually and socially.
8 Social regulation of the economy	This is indispensable to prevent greater social inequality and to ensure certain elites and businesses do not abuse their privileged status in free markets.
9 Constant, persistent reflection	This is necessary to access knowledge and construct sound projects. In pupils it is fundamental to emphasise personal effort as a way of achieving goals.

Notes

1 This text is part of the research project *Historia de la Catalunya Subalterna Contemporánea: alternativas solidarias y cooperativas* (History of Contemporary Subaltern Catalonia: Solidarity and Cooperative Alternatives), PID2019–109560GB-I00, funded by the Ministry of Science and Innovation of the Government of Spain.

2 Albert Irigoyen is a pre-doctoral researcher in FI-SDUR training with the support of the Secretariat of Universities and Research of the Department of Business and Knowledge of the Generalitat of Catalonia.

3 Josep FONTANA: *Capitalismo y democracia. 1756–1848. Cómo empezó este engaño*, Barcelona, Crítica, 2019.

4 Byung-Chul HAN: *La sociedad del cansancio*, Barcelona, Herder, 2022; Sebastian FRIEDRICH, Felix KLOPOTEK, Lars DISTELHORST, Detlef HARTMANN, Greta WAGNER, Mark FISHER, Sarah DIEHL and Volker SCHÜRMANN: *La sociedad del rendimiento. Cómo el neoliberalismo impregna nuestras vidas*, Pamplona, Katakrak Liburuak, 2018.

5 Eric HOBSBAWM: *Historia del siglo XX*, Barcelona, Crítica, 2011.

6 The benefits of cooperative learning have been demonstrated in seven theoretical reviews conducted by the University of Minnesota, which identify the most significant advances in research in this field in the twentieth century. For an analysis of these reviews, see Mª del Mar GARCÍA CABRERA, Ignacio GONZÁLEZ LÓPEZ and Rosario MÉRIDA SERRANO: "Validación del cuestionario de evaluación ACOES. Análisis del trabajo cooperativo en educación superior", *Revista de Investigación Educativa*, 30 (2012, 1), pp. 87–109, https://doi.org/10.6018/rie.30.1.114091.

7 David W. JOHNSON and Roger T. JOHNSON: *Cooperation and Competition: Theory and Research*, Interaction Book Company, 1989; Robyn M. GILLIES: "Developments in Cooperative Learning: Review of Research", *Anales de Psicología*, 30 (2014, 3), pp. 792–801, http://dx.doi.org/10.6018/analesps.30.3.201191; Eva KYNDT, Elisabeth RAES, Bart LISMONT, Fran TIMMERS, Eduardo CASCALLAR and Filip DOCHY: "A Meta-analysis of the Effects of Face-to-face Cooperative Learning. Do Recent Studies Falsify or Verify Earlier Findings?", *Educational Research Review*, 10 (2013), pp. 133–149; Robert E. SLAVIN: "Cooperative Learning and Academic Achievement: Why Does Groupwork Work?", *Anales de Psicología*, 30 (2014, 3), pp. 785–791, http://dx.doi.org/10.6018/analesps.30.3.201201; José Manuel SERRANO and Rosa M. PONS: "Cooperative Learning: We Also Do It Without Task Structure", *Intercultural Education*, 18 (2007, 3), pp. 215–230, https://doi.org/10.1080/14675980701463562.

8 Mª del Mar GARCÍA CABRERA, Ignacio GONZÁLEZ LÓPEZ and Rosario MÉRIDA SERRANO. "Validación del cuestionario ... ", pp. 87–109, https://doi.org/10.6018/rie.30.1.114091.

9 Robert E. SLAVIN: "Cooperative Learning and ... ", pp. 785–791, http://dx.doi.org/10.6018/analesps.30.3.201201.

10 David W. JOHNSON and Roger T. JOHNSON: "An Educational Psychology Success Story: Social Interdependence Theory and Cooperative Learning", *Educational Researcher*, 38 (2009), pp. 365–379.

11 Elizabeth G. COHEN: *Designing Groupwork: Strategies for the* Heterogeneous Classroom (2nd ed.), New York, Teachers College Press, 1994.

12 Dale H. SCHUNK: *Learning* Theories: An Educational Perspective (6th ed.), Boston, Allyn and Bacon, 2012.
13 William DAMON: "Peer Education: The Untapped Potential", *Journal of Applied Developmental Psychology*, 5 (1984), pp. 331–343, https://doi.org/10.1016/0193-3973(84)90006-6.
14 David W. JOHNSON and Roger T. JOHNSON: "Cooperative Learning in 21st Century", *Anales de Psicología*, 30 (2014, 3), pp. 841–851, http://dx.doi.org/10.6018/analesps.30.3.201241.
15 Dolors CAÑABATE and Jordi COLOMER (coord.): *El aprendizaje cooperativo en la universidad del siglo XXI. Propuestas, estrategias y reflexiones*, Barcelona, Graó, 2020.
16 Rosa COLOMINA and Javier ONRUBIA: "Interacción educativa y aprendizaje escolar: la interacción entre alumnos", in César COLL, Jesús PALACIOS and Álvaro MARCHESI (comps.): *Desarrollo psicológico y educación*, Madrid, Alianza Editorial, 2004 (vol. 2), pp. 415–436.
17 Albert IRIGOYEN and Sylvain CONNAC: "L'aprenentatge cooperatiu i les "pédagogies coopératives": dues concepcions diferents de treballar en grup cooperatiu", *Comunicació Educativa,* 36 (2023).
18 Sylvain CONNAC and Albert IRIGOYEN: "Apprentissage coopératif ou pédagogies coopératives?", *Éducation et socialisation*, 67 (2023), https://doi.org/10.4000/edso.22840.
19 Mario MARTINELLI: *In gruppo si impara*, Turin, SEI, 2004, p. 66; Mario COMOGLIO and Miguel Angel CARDOSO: *Insegnare e apprendere in gruppo. Il Cooperative Learning*, Rome, LAS, 1996, p. 4.
20 R. LOUIS: "Les facteurs qui influent sur l'adoption par l'enseignante d'une nouvelle approche pédagogique: le cas de la pédagogie coopérative", *Vie pédagogique*, 96 (1995), pp. 47–50; Jim HOWDEN and Marguerite KOPIEC: *Ajouter aux compétences: enseigner, coopérer et apprendre au secondaire et au collégial*, Montréal, Chenelière Education, 2000; Yviane ROUILLER and Katia LERHAUS: "Pédagogie coopérative: de l'expérience et de la science", *Éducateur*, 5 (2003), pp. 24–26.
21 Yviane ROUILLER and Jim HOWDEN: *La pédagogie coopérative. Reflets de pratiques et approfondissements*, Montréal, Chenelière Éducation, 2010, p. 13.
22 Katia LERHAUS and Yviane ROUILLER (dir.): *Vers des apprentissages en coopération: rencontres et perspectives*, Peter Lang, 2008.
23 We should point out that Freinet did not implement cooperative learning, but cooperation in school.
24 Sylvain CONNAC and Albert IRIGOYEN: "Apprentissage coopératif … "
25 John DEWEY: *The School and Society*, Chicago, The University of Chicago Press, 1915.
26 Kurt LEWIN: (1945). "The Research Center for Group Dynamics", *Sociometry*, 8 (1945, 2), pp. 126–136. https://doi.org/10.2307/2785233.
27 Herbert THELEN: *Dynamics of Groups at Work*, Chicago, University of Chicago Press, 1954.
28 Morton DEUTSCH: "A Theory of Cooperation and Competition", *Human Relations*, 2 (1949), pp. 129–152; Morton DEUTSCH: "Cooperation and Trust: Some Theoretical Notes", in Marshall R. JONES (ed.), *Nebraska Symposium on Motivation*, Lincoln, Univer. Nebraska Press, 1962, pp. 275–320.
29 Neil DAVIDSON: "L'apprentissage coopératif et en collaboration - une tentative d'unification", in Jacqueline S. THOUSAND, Richard A. VILLA

and Ann I. NEVIN (eds.): *La créativité et l'apprentissage coopératif*, Montréal, Les Editions Logiques, 1998, pp. 63–101.

30 David W. JOHNSON, Roger T. JOHNSON and Edythe J. HOLUBEC: *El Aprendizaje cooperativo en el aula*, Barcelona, Paidós, 1999.

31 Alain BAUDRIT: *L'apprentissage coopératif – Origines et évolutions d'une méthode pédagogique*, Brussels, De Boeck, 2005, p. 23.

32 Alain BAUDRIT: *L'apprentissage coopératif ...*; Céline BUCHS: "Preparar a los estudiantes para cooperar y organizar interacciones para apoyar el aprendizaje en la universidad", in Dolors CAÑABATE and Jordi COLOMER (coords.): *El aprendizaje cooperativo en la universidad del siglo XXI. Propuestas, estrategias y reflexiones*, Barcelona, Editorial Graó, 2020, pp. 51–59; Dolors CAÑABATE and Jordi COLOMER (coord.): *El aprendizaje cooperativo en la universidad del siglo XXI. Propuestas, estrategias y reflexiones*, Barcelona, Graó, 2020; David DURAN GISBERT and Carles MONEREO FONT: *Entramado. Métodos de aprendizaje cooperativo y colaborativo*, Barcelona, Horsori editorial, 2012; Antoni GAVALDÀ (coord.): *El treball cooperatiu. Una estratègia per ensenyar i aprendre des de les ciències socials*, Tarragona y Vic, Universitat Rovira i Virgili i Universitat de Vic, 2016; Jesús C. IGLESIAS MUÑIZ, Laura F. GONZÁLEZ-GARCÍA and Javier FERNÁNDEZ-RÍO: *Aprendizaje cooperativo: Teoría y práctica en las diferentes áreas y materias del currículum*, Madrid, Pirámide, 2017; Katia LERHAUS and Yviane ROUILLER (dir.): *Vers des apprentissages en coopération: rencontres et perspectives*, Peter Lang, 2008; Anastasio OVEJERO: *Aprendizaje cooperativo crítico. Mucho más que una eficaz técnica pedagógica*, Madrid, Pirámide, 2018; Pere PUJOLÀS and José Ramón LAGO: *Aprender en equipos de aprendizaje cooperativo. El Programa CA/AC (Cooperar para aprender/Aprender a cooperar)*, Barcelona, Octaedro, 2018; Yviane ROUILLER and Jim HOWDEN: *La pédagogie coopérative. Reflets de pratiques et approfondissements*, Montréal, Chenelière Éducation, 2010; Yviane ROUILLER and Katia LERHAUS: "Pédagogie coopérative: de l'expérience et de la science", *Éducateur, 5* (2003); Joan RUÉ: *El treball cooperatiu. L'organització social de l'ensenyament i l'aprenentatge*, Barcelona, Barcanova, 1991; José Manuel SERRANO and Rosa M. PONS: "Cooperative Learning: We Also Do It Without Task Structure", *Intercultural Education, 18* (2007, 3), pp. 215–230, https://doi.org/10.1080/14675980701463562; Juan Carlos TORREGO and Andrés NEGRO (coords.): *Aprendizaje cooperativo en las aulas*, Madrid, Alianza Editorial, 2012; Francisco ZARIQUIEY BIONDI: *Cooperar para aprender. Transformar el aula en una red de aprendizaje cooperativo*, Spain SM, 2016.

33 His key works include Mario COMOGLIO and Miguel Ángel CARDOSO: *Insegnare e apprendere ...* ; Mario COMOGLIO: *Il Cooperative Learning. Strategie di sperimentazione*, in "Quaderni di Animazione e Formazione – Animazione Sociale", Turin, Edizioni Gruppo Abele, 1999; and, above all, ÍD.: *Educare insegnando. Apprendere ad applicare il Cooperative Learning*, Rome, LAS, 1998.

34 http://www.apprendimentocooperativo.it.

35 Mario COMOGLIO and Miguel Angel CARDOSO: *Insegnare e apprendere ...*, pp. 5–6. In the same year, Comoglio suggested a more precise definition: "È un metodo di apprendimento-insegnamento in cui la variabile significativa è la cooperazione tra gli studenti. È un metodo di conduzione della classe che mette in gioco, nell'apprendimento, le risorse degli studenti. Così inteso, si distingue dai metodi tradizionali che puntano invece sulla qualità e sull'estensione delle

conoscenze didattiche e di contenuto dell'insegnante. Infatti, diversamente da questi ultimi, questo metodo permette di gestire e organizzare esperienze di apprendimento condotte dagli stessi studenti e, insieme, sviluppare obiettivi educativi di collaborazione, solidarietà, responsabilità e relazione, riconosciuti efficaci anche per una migliore qualità dell'apprendimento" (Mario COMOGLIO: "Verso una definizione del cooperative learning", *Animazione Sociale*, 4 (1996).

36 For example, Alberto AGOSTI: *Gruppo di lavoro e lavoro di gruppo. Aspetti pedagogici e didattici*, Milán, Franco Angeli, 2006; Giorgio CHIARI, *Il Cooperative Learning nelle scuole italiane: Apprendimento e Democrazia*, Trento, Università degli Setudi di Trento, 2003; A. GARDIN, M. AZZINI and R. VERRI: "Il Cooperative Learning: teoria e prassi di insegnamento attraverso la cooperazione", *Psicologia e Scuola*, 86–89 (1997–1998); Anna LA PROVA: *Apprendimento cooperativo in pratica. Proposte operative per attività di grupo in classe*, Trento, Edizioni Centro Studi Erickson, 2015; ID.: *Apprendimento cooperativo e differenze individuali*, Trento, Edizioni Erickson, 2008; Claudia MATINI: *Cooperative Learning: istruzioni per l'uso*, Perugia, Editrice La Fonte, 2019; Rinaldo RIZZI: *La cooperazione nell'educazione*, Bari, Laterza, 1991.

37 Stefania LAMBERTI: *Apprendimento cooperativo e educazione interculturale. Percorsi e attività per la scuola primaria*, Trento, Erickson, 2010; Isabella PESCARMONA: *Innovazione educativa tra entusiasmo e fatica. Un'etnografia dell'apprendimento cooperativo*, Rome, CISU, 2012.

38 www.mce-fimem.it .This group, which is more involved in school teaching than academic research, has published documents of great interest such as the journal *Cooperazione Educativa*. See: Rinaldo RIZZI: *La "cooperazione educativa" per una "pedagogia popolare". Una storia del MCE*, Parma, Edizioni Junior, 2021.

39 Giacomo COMINCIOLI and Franco GHEZA: *Didattica della cooperazione*, Brescia, Editrice La Scuola, 1989.

40 https://www.cooperativafare.it/.

41 ICEM: Institut coopératif de l'école moderne, http://www.icem-pedagogie-freinet.org/; OCCE: Office central de la coopération a l'école, http://www2.occe.coop/; AGSAS: Association des groupes de soutien au soutien, http://agsas.fr/; GFEN: Groupe français d'éducation nouvelle, http://www.gfen.asso.fr/fr/accueil; AVPI: Association vers la pédagogie institutionelle, http://avpi-fernand-oury.fr/; CRAP: Cercle de recherche et d'action pédagogiques, http://www.cahiers-pedagogiques.com/Presentation-du-CRAP; RERS: Réseaux d'échanges réciproques de savoirs, https://www.rers-asso.org/; ICEM34 – Pédagogie Freinet: Institut Coopératif de l'École Moderne de l'Hérault (34) – Pédagogie Freinet: https://www.icem34.fr/; PIDAPI: Parcours Individualisé des Apprentissages in Pédagogie Institutionnelle, https://www.pidapi-asso.fr/.

42 Alain BAUDRIT: "Le tutorat: un enjeu pour une pratique pédagogique devenue objet scientifique? (Note de synthèse)". *Revue française de pédagogie*, 132 (2000), pp. 125–153; Céline DARNON, Fabrizio BUTERA and Gabriel MUGNY: *Des conflits pour apprendre*, Grenoble, Presses universitaires de Grenoble, 2008.

43 Sylvain CONNAC and Albert IRIGOYEN: "Apprentissage coopératif ou …", 67 (2023), https://doi.org/10.4000/edso.22840.

44 Philippe MEIRIEU: *La riposte – Pour en finir avec les miroirs aux alouettes*, Paris, Editions Autrement, 2018.
45 Clara MIR (coord.): *Cooperar en la escuela. La responsabilidad de educar para la democracia*, Barcelona, Graó, 1998; Pere PUJOLÀS: *9 ideas clave. El aprendizaje cooperativo*, Barcelona, Graó, 2008.
46 Ramón FERREIRO and Margarita CALDERÓN: *El ABC del aprendizaje cooperativo. Trabajo en equipo para enseñar y aprender*, Méjico, Editorial Trillas, 2006; Anna LA PROVA: *Apprendimento cooperativo in pratica. Proposte operative per attività di grupo in classe*, Trento, Edizioni Centro Studi Erickson, 2015, pp. 17–22.
47 Pere PUJOLÀS: "Cooperar per aprendre i aprendre a cooperar: el treball en equips cooperatius com a recurs i com a contingut", *Suports: revista catalana d'educació especial i atenció a la diversitat*, 12 (2012), pp. 21–37; Pere PUJOLÀS and José Ramón LAGO: *Aprender en equipos de aprendizaje cooperativo. El Programa CA/AC (Cooperar para aprender/Aprender a cooperar)*, Barcelona, Octaedro, 2018.
48 Mario COMOGLIO: "Che cos'è il Cooperative Learning", *Orientamenti Pedagogici*, 43 (1996), pp. 259–293; Mario COMOGLIO and Miguel Angel CARDOSO: *Insegnare e apprendere …*; Maurizio GENTILE and Carlo PETRACCA: *Apprendimento cooperativo: Spunti per l'innovazione didattica*, Turin, Elmedi; Anna LA PROVA: *Apprendimento cooperativo e differenze individuali*, Trento, Erickson, 2008; Anna LA PROVA: *Apprendimento cooperativo …*, 2015.
49 Philip C. ABRAMI, Bette CHAMBERS, Catherine POULSEN, Christina DE SIMONE, Sylvia D'APOLLONIA and James HOWDEN: *Classroom connections: Understanding and using cooperative learning*, Toronto, Harcourt-Brace, 1995; Robert E. SLAVIN: *Aprendizaje cooperativo. Teoría, investigación y práctica*, Argentina, Aique, 1999; David W. JOHNSON and Roger T. JOHNSON: "Theoretical Approaches to Cooperative Learning". In Robyn M. GILLIES (ed.), *Collaborative Learning: Developments in Research and Practice*, New York, Nova Science Publishers, 2015, pp. 17–46.
50 Yviane ROUILLER and Jim HOWDEN: *La pédagogie coopérative …*, 2010.
51 Roland G. THARP, Peggy ESTRADA, Stephanie S. DALTON and Lois A. YAMAUCHI, L. A: *Transformar la enseñanza. Excelencia, equidad, inclusión y armonía en las aulas y las escuelas*, Barcelona, Editorial Paidós, 2002.
52 Roger SLEE: *La escuela extraordinaria. Exclusión, escolarización y educación inclusiva*, Madrid, Ediciones Morata, 2012.
53 Sylvain CONNAC: "Pour différencier: individualiser ou personnaliser?", *Education et Socialisation*, 59 (2021), https://journals.openedition.org/edso/13683.
54 Sylvain CONNAC: *La coopération entre élèves*, Futuroscope, Editions Canopé, 2017.
55 Sylvain CONNAC and Albert IRIGOYEN: "Apprentissage coopératif ou … "
56 Sylvain CONNAC: *La coopération, ça s'apprend*, Paris, ESF Editeur, 2020.
57 Eloi LAURENT: *L'impasse collaborative – Pour une véritable économie de la cooperation*, Paris, Les liens qui libèrent, 2018.
58 Christian BUDEX: *Éduquer à la fraternité par la pratique de la philosophie à l'école (primaire et collège): enjeux et conditions de possibilités*, Doctoral thesis, Université de Nantes, 2020.

59 Abdennour BIDAR: *Quelles valeurs partager et transmettre aujourd'hui?*, París, Albin Michel, 2016; Nicolas GO: "Approche coopérative et complexe en éducation", in Malini SUMPUTH and François FOURCADE: *Oser la pédagogie coopérative complexe*, Chronique Sociale, 2013, pp. 47–80.
60 Albert IRIGOYEN: "Entrevista a Sylvain Connac", *Comunicació Educativa*, 34 (2021), pp. 7–51. https://doi.org/10.17345/comeduc20217-51.
61 Sylvain CONNAC *et al.*: *Les Pédagogies Freinet - Origines, concepts et outils pour tous*, Paris, Editions Eyrolles, 2019.
62 Louis RAILLON: "Roger Cousinet". *Perspectives: revue trimestrielle d'éducation comparée*, vol. XXIII, 1–2 (1993), pp. 225–236.
63 Jean VUILLET: *La coopération à l'école*, Paris, Presses Universitaires de France, 1968.
64 Jacques PAIN: *Pédagogie institutionnelle*, Encyclopedia Universalis, 2005, http://www.jacques-pain.fr/jacques-pain/Definition_PI.html.
65 Maria PAGONI: "Conceptualisation des règles scolaires et éducation à la citoyenneté au sein des conseils de coopérative". *Carrefours de l'éducation*, 31 (2011, 1), pp. 177–192.
66 Website of Philippe Meirieu: http://meirieu.com/; Albert IRIGOYEN: "Entrevista a Philippe Meirieu", *Comunicació Educativa*, 35 (2022), pp. 9–57. https://doi.org/10.17345/comeduc20229-57.
67 Willem DOISE and Gabriel MUGNY: *Le développement social de l'intelligence*, Paris, Interéditions, 1981.
68 Céline BUCHS *et al.*: "Conflits et apprentissage: régulation des conflits sociocognitifs et apprentissage", *Revue française de pédagogie*, 163 (2008), pp. 105–125.
69 Jerome BRUNER: *Savoir faire, savoir dire*, Paris, PUF, 2011.
70 Albert BANDURA: *L'apprentissage social*, Brussels, Editions Pierre Mardaga, 1976.
71 Gabriel MUGNY and William DOISE: *La construcción social de la inteligencia*, Méjico, Trillas, 1983.
72 Michael TOMASELLO: *A Natural History of Human Thinking*, Harvard University Press, 2014.
73 David H. JONASSEN (2009). "Reconciling a Human Cognitive Architecture", in S. TOBIAS and T.-M. DUFFY (eds.): *Constructivist Theory Applied to Instruction: Success or Failure?*, London, Routledge.
74 The Johnson brothers claim that the theory of social interdependence dates back to the early twentieth century and the work of Kurt Koffka, one of the founders of the Gestalt school. Koffka's colleague, Kurt Lewin, further refined his ideas in the 1920s. Deutsch is considered a disciple of Lewin and continued his work on social interdependence, and David W. Johnson is considered a disciple of Deutsch. Information taken from the Johnson and Johnson website: http://www.co-operation.org/what-is-cooperative-learning.
75 Jesús C. IGLESIAS MUÑIZ, Laura F. GONZÁLEZ-GARCÍA and Javier FERNÁNDEZ-RÍO: *Aprendizaje cooperativo: Teoría y práctica en las diferentes áreas y materias del currículum*, Madrid, Ediciones Pirámide, 2017, p. 46.
76 David W. JOHNSON, Roger T. JOHNSON and Edythe Johnson HOLUBEC: *El Aprendizaje cooperativo* ..., pp. 73–80; Pere PUJOLÀS and José Ramón LAGO: *Aprender en equipos* ..., pp. 71–77.
77 Anna LA PROVA: *Apprendimento cooperativo* ... , p. 11.
78 Anastasio OVEJERO: *Aprendizaje cooperativo crítico. Mucho más que una eficaz técnica pedagógica*, Madrid, Pirámide, 2018, pp. 67–70.

79 Céline BUCHS: "Preparar a los estudiantes ... "
80 Christian STAQUET: *Une classe qui coopère – Pourquoi? Comment?*, Lyon, Chronique Sociale, 2007, p. 17.
81 Sylvain CONNAC: *La coopération, ça* ..., pp. 69–70.
82 Albert IRIGOYEN: "Entrevista a Philippe Meirieu ... "
83 César COLL: "Estructura grupal interacción entre alumnos y aprendizaje escolar", *Infancia y Aprendizaje*, 27/28 (1984), pp. 119–138.
84 Céline BUCHS: "Preparar a los estudiantes ... ", p. 52.
85 Christian STAQUET: *Une classe qui coopère* ... , 2007; Yviane ROUILLER and Jim HOWDEN: *La pédagogie coopérative* ... , 2010; Céline BUCHS, Ingrid GILLES, Jean-Philippe ANTONIETTI and Fabrizio BUTERA: "Why Students Need Training to Cooperate: A Test in Statistics Learning at University", *Educational Psychology*, 36 (2016, 5), pp. 956–974.
86 David DURAN GISBERT and Carles MONEREO FONT: *Entramado. Métodos de aprendizaje cooperativo y colaborativo*, Barcelona, Horsori editorial, 2012.
87 Pere PUJOLÀS and José Ramón LAGO: *Aprender en equipos* ..., 2018; Anna LA PROVA: *Apprendimento cooperativo* ..., 2015.
88 Joan RUÉ: "El aula: un espacio para la cooperación", in Clara MIR (coord.): *Cooperación en la escuela. La responsabilidad de educar para la democracia*, Barcelona, Graó, 1998, pp. 17–50.
89 Albert IRIGOYEN: "El treball cooperatiu en l'educació: peça clau per a la construcció d'un futur més democràtic i de participació responsable", in Josep M. PONS-ALTÉS (coord.), *Ciutadania compromesa i educació. Propostes per al foment de la memòria democràtica*, Tarragona, Publicacions URV, 2021, pp. 11–26. http://llibres.urv.cat/index.php/purv/catalog/book/483.
90 Céline BUCHS: "Comment organiser l'apprentissage des élèves par petits groupes?". En *Conférence Différenciation pédagogique: comment adapter l'enseignement pour la réussite de tous les élèves?*, Paris, Conseil national d'étude des systèmes scolaires (Cnesco)/Institut Français de l'Education (Ifé), 2017.
91 Albert IRIGOYEN: "Entrevista a Antoni Gavaldà", *Comunicació Educativa*, 33 (2020), pp. 7–28. https://doi.org/10.17345/comeduc20207-28.
92 Sylvain CONNAC: "L'école française et les pédagogies coopératives pour apprendre". *Revue Internationale d'éducation de Sèvres – CIEP*, 90 (2022), pp. 53–62, https://journals.openedition.org/ries/12745.
93 Jean LE GAL: *Les droits de l'enfant à l'école, pour une éducation à la citoyenneté*, Brussels, De Boeck et Belin, 2002; Claude LAPLACE: *Pratiquer les conseils d'élèves et les assemblées de classes*, Lyon, Chronique Sociale, 2008; Claude PIÉTRONS: *Pratiquer les conseils de la classe*, Lyon, Chronique Sociale, 2022.
94 Mildred MASHEDER: *Jeux coopératifs pour bâtir la paix*, Lyon, Chronique Sociale, 2005.
95 Claire HÉBER-SUFFRIN: *Apprendre par la réciprocité – Réinventer ensemble les démarches pédagogiques*, Lyon, Chronique Sociale, 2016.
96 Michel TOZZI: *Nouvelles pratiques philosophiques*, Lyon, Chronique Sociale, 2012.
97 Yochai BENKLER: *El Pingüino y el Leviatán. Por qué la cooperación es nuestra arma más valiosa para mejorar el bienestar de la sociedad*, Barcelona, Deusto, 2012.

98 Stefano ZAMAGNI and Vera ZAMAGNI: *Cooperative Enterprise. Facing the Challenge of Globalization*. Cheltenham, Edward Elgar, 2010.
99 Anastasio OVEJERO: *Aprendizaje cooperativo crítico …* , pp. 56–63.
100 Dolors CAÑABATE and Jordi COLOMER (coord.): *El aprendizaje cooperativo …*, 2020.
101 Anastasio OVEJERO: *Aprendizaje cooperativo crítico …*
102 Josep M. PONS-ALTÉS and Albert IRIGOYEN: "¿Aprendizaje cooperativo sin valores cooperativos? Análisis de manuales escolares", in Juan Carlos BEL MARTÍNEZ, Juan Carlos COLOMER RUBIO and Nicolás DE ALBA FERNÁNDEZ (eds.), *Repensar el currículum de Ciencias Sociales: prácticas educativas para una ciudadanía crítica*, Valencia, Tirant Lo Blanch, 2022, pp. 889–897.
103 Antoni GAVALDÀ: "Com abordar valors cooperatius a l'ensenyament?", *Cooperació Catalana*, 226 (2000), pp. 14–17.
104 Irigoyen and Pons-Altés have studied how these values are structured in the teaching of social sciences in: Albert IRIGOYEN and Josep M. PONS-ALTÉS: "Formación de docentes, didáctica de la historia contemporánea y aprendizaje cooperativo" in Francisco ACOSTA, Àngel DUARTE, Elena Lázaro and María J. RAMOS ROVI (eds.): *La Historia habitada. Sujetos, procesos y retos de la Historia Contemporánea del siglo XXI*, Córdoba, UCOPress Editorial, Universidad de Córdoba, 2023b, pp. 1687–1697; Albert IRIGOYEN & Josep M. PONS-ALTÉS: "Aprendizaje cooperativo y Objetivos de Desarrollo Sostenible (ODS): formación de docentes a partir de problemas sociales relevantes", in María E. CAMBIL HERNÁNDEZ, Antonio R. FERNÁNDEZ PARADAS and Nicolás DE ALBA FERNÁNDEZ (coords.): *La Didáctica de las Ciencias Sociales ante el reto de los ODS*, Madrid, Narcea, 2023c, pp. 779–787; Albert IRIGOYEN and Josep M. PONS-ALTÉS: "Els valors cooperatius: àncora de la cooperació entre alumnes a l'aula", in T. ABELLÓ *et al.* (coords.): *Herències/Legacies*. Secció d'Història Contemporània i Món Actual de la UB i Ventall Edicions, 2023, pp. 336–347; Josep M. PONS-ALTÉS and Albert IRIGOYEN: "¿Aprendizaje cooperativo sin … ", 2022, pp. 889–897; Albert IRIGOYEN: "El treball cooperatiu … ", 2021, pp. 11–26.

References

ABRAMI, Philip C.; CHAMBERS, Bette; POULSEN, Catherine; DE SIMONE, Christina; D'APOLLONIA, Sylvia and HOWDEN, James: *Classroom Connections: Understanding and Using Cooperative Learning*, Toronto, Harcourt-Brace, 1995.

AGOSTI, Alberto: *Gruppo di lavoro e lavoro di gruppo. Aspetti pedagogici e didattici*, Milan, Franco Angeli, 2006.

BANDURA, Albert: *L'apprentissage social*, Brussels, Editions Pierre Mardaga, 1976.

BAUDRIT, Alain: "Le tutorat: un enjeu pour une pratique pédagogique devenue objet scientifique? (Note de synthèse)". *Revue française de pédagogie*, 132 (2000), pp. 125–153.

BAUDRIT, Alain: *L'apprentissage coopératif – Origines et évolutions d'une méthode pédagogique*, Brussels, De Boeck, 2005.

BAUDRIT, Alain: *Education et formation dans les sociétés contemporaines - Le don/contre-don toujours d'actualité?*, Montpellier, Presses Universitaires de la Méditerranée, 2018.

BENKLER, Yochai: *El Pingüino y el Leviatán. Por qué la cooperación es nuestra arma más valiosa para mejorar el bienestar de la sociedad*, Barcelona, Deusto, 2012.

BIDAR, Abdennour: *Quelles valeurs partager et transmettre aujourd'hui?*, París, Albin Michel, 2016.

BRUNER, Jerome: *Savoir faire, savoir dire*, Paris, PUF, 2011.

BUDEX, Christian: *Éduquer à la fraternité par la pratique de la philosophie à l'école (primaire et collège): enjeux et conditions de possibilités*, Doctoral thesis, Université de Nantes, 2020.

BUCHS, Céline: "Comment organiser l'apprentissage des élèves par petits groupes?". En *Conférence Différenciation pédagogique: comment adapter l'enseignement pour la réussite de tous les élèves?*, Paris, Conseil national d'étude des systèmes scolaires (Cnesco)/Institut Français de l'Education (Ifé), 2017.

BUCHS, Céline: "Preparar a los estudiantes para cooperar y organizar interacciones para apoyar el aprendizaje en la universidad", in Dolors CAÑABATE and Jordi COLOMER (coords.), *El aprendizaje cooperativo en la universidad del siglo XXI. Propuestas, estrategias y reflexiones*, Barcelona, Editorial Graó, 2020, pp. 51–59.

BUCHS, Céline; DARNON, Céline; QUIAMZADE, Alain; MUGNY, Gabriel and BUTERA, Fabrizio: "Conflits et apprentissage: régulation des conflits sociocognitifs et apprentissage", *Revue française de pédagogie*, 163 (2008), pp. 105–125.

BUCHS, Céline; GILLES, Ingrid; ANTONIETTI, Jean-Philippe and BUTERA, Fabrizio: "Why Students Need Training to Cooperate: A Test in Statistics Learning at University", *Educational Psychology*, 36 (2016, 5), pp. 956–974.

CAÑABATE, Dolors and COLOMER, Jordi (coord.): *El aprendizaje cooperativo en la universidad del siglo XXI. Propuestas, estrategias y reflexiones*, Barcelona, Graó, 2020.

CHIARI, Giorgio: *Il Cooperative Learning nelle scuole italiane: Apprendimento e Democrazia*, Trento, Università degli Setudi di Trento, 2003.

COHEN, Elizabeth G.: *Designing Groupwork: Strategies for the* Heterogeneous Classroom (2nd ed.), New York, Teachers College Press, 1994.

COLL, César: "Estructura grupal interacción entre alumnos y aprendizaje escolar", *Infancia y Aprendizaje*, 27/28 (1984), pp. 119–138.

COLOMINA, Rosa and ONRUBIA, Javier: "Interacción educativa y aprendizaje escolar: la interacción entre alumnos", in César COLL, Jesús PALACIOS and Álvaro MARCHESI (comps.): *Desarrollo psicológico y educación*, Madrid, Alianza Editorial, 2004 (vol. 2), pp. 415–436.

COMINCIOLI, Giacomo and GHEZA, Franco: *Didattica della cooperazione*, Brescia, Editrice La Scuola, 1989.

COMOGLIO, Mario: "Che cos'è il Cooperative Learning", *Orientamenti Pedagogici*, 43 (1996), pp. 259–293.

COMOGLIO, Mario: *Educare insegnando. Apprendere ad applicare il Cooperative Learning*, Rome, LAS, 1998.
COMOGLIO, Mario: *Il Cooperative Learning. Strategie di sperimentazione*, in "Quaderni di Animazione e Formazione – Animazione Sociale", Turin, Edizioni Gruppo Abele, 1999.
COMOGLIO, Mario: "Verso una definizione del cooperative learning", *Animazione Sociale*, 4 (1996).
COMOGLIO, Mario and CARDOSO, Miguel Angel: *Insegnare e apprendere in gruppo. Il Cooperative Learning*, Rome, LAS, 1996.
CONNAC, Sylvain: *La coopération entre élèves*, Futuroscope, Editions Canopé, 2017.
CONNAC, Sylvain: *La coopération, ça s'apprend*, ESF Sciences Humaines, 2020.
CONNAC, Sylvain: "Pour différencier: individualiser ou personnaliser?", *Education et Socialisation*, 59 (2021), https://journals.openedition.org/edso/13683.
CONNAC, Sylvain and IRIGOYEN, Albert: "Apprentissage coopératif ou pédagogies coopératives?", *Éducation et socialisation*, 67 (2023), 10.4000/edso.22840.
CONNAC, Sylvain; DEMAUGÉ-BOST, Bruce; GUIENNE, Bernadette; HUCHARD, Isabelle and QUIMBETZ, Isabelle: *Les Pédagogies Freinet - Origines, concepts et outils pour tous*, Paris, Editions Eyrolles, 2019.
DAMON, William: "Peer Education: The Untapped Potential". *Journal of Applied Developmental Psychology*, 5 (1984), pp. 331–343, 10.1016/0193-3973(84)90006-6.
DARNON, Céline; BUTERA, Fabrizio and MUGNY, Gabriel: *Des conflits pour apprendre*, Grenoble, Presses universitaires de Grenoble, 2008.
DAVIDSON, Neil: "L'apprentissage coopératif et en collaboration - une tentative d'unification", in Jacqueline S. THOUSAND, Richard A. VILLA and Ann I. NEVIN (eds.), *La créativité et l'apprentissage coopératif*, Montréal, Les Editions Logiques, 1998, pp. 63–101.
DEUTSCH, Morton: "A Theory of Cooperation and Competition", *Human Relations*, 2 (1949), pp. 129–152.
DEUTSCH, Morton: "Cooperation and Trust: Some Theorical Notes", in Marshall R. JONES (ed.), *Nebraska Symposium on Motivation*, Lincoln, NE, Univer. Nebraska Press, 1962, pp. 275–320.
DEWEY, John: *The School and Society*, Chicago, IL, The University of Chicago Press, 1915.
DOISE, Willem and MUGNY, Gabriel: *Le développement social de l'intelligence*, Paris, Interéditions, 1981.
DURAN GISBERT, David and MONEREO FONT, Carles: *Entramado. Métodos de aprendizaje cooperativo y colaborativo*, Barcelona, Horsori editorial, 2012.
FERREIRO, Ramón and CALDERÓN, Margarita: *El ABC del aprendizaje cooperativo. Trabajo en equipo para enseñar y aprender*, Méjico, Editorial Trillas, 2006
FONTANA, Josep: *Capitalismo y democracia. 1756-1848. Cómo empezó este engaño*, Barcelona, Crítica, 2019.

FRIEDRICH, Sebastian; KLOPOTEK, Felix; DISTELHORST, Lars; HARTMANN, Detlef; WAGNER, Greta; FISHER, Mark; DIEHL, Sarah and SCHÜRMANN, Volker: *La sociedad del rendimiento. Cómo el neoliberalismo impregna nuestras vidas*, Pamplona, Katakrak Liburuak, 2018.

GARCÍA CABRERA, Mª del Mar; GONZÁLEZ LÓPEZ, Ignacio and MÉRIDA SERRANO, Rosario: "Validación del cuestionario de evaluación ACOES. Análisis del trabajo cooperativo en educación superior", *Revista de Investigación Educativa*, 30 (2012, 1), pp. 87–109, 10.6018/rie.30.1.114091

GARDIN, A.; AZZINI, M. and VERRI, R.: "Il Cooperative Learning: teoria e prassi di insegnamento attraverso la cooperazione", *Psicologia e Scuola*, 86–89 (1997-1998).

GAVALDÀ, Antoni: "Com abordar valors cooperatius a l'ensenyament?", *Cooperació Catalana*, 226 (2000), pp. 14–17.

GAVALDÀ, Antoni (coord.): *El treball cooperatiu. Una estratègia per ensenyar i aprendre des de les ciències socials*, Tarragona and Vic, Universitat Rovira i Virgili y Universitat de Vic, 2016.

GENTILE, Maurizio and PETRACCA, Carlo: *Apprendimento cooperativo: Spunti per l'innovazione didattica*, Turin, Elmedi.

GILLIES, Robyn M.: "Developments in Cooperative Learning: Review of Research", *Anales de Psicología*, 30 (2014, 3), pp. 792–801, 10.6018/analesps.30.3.201191.

GO, Nicolas: "Approche coopérative et complexe en éducation", in Malini SUMPUTH and François FOURCADE (eds.): *Oser la pédagogie coopérative complexe*, Chronique Sociale, 2013, pp. 47–80.

HAN, Byung-Chul: *La sociedad del cansancio*, Barcelona, Herder, 2022.

HÉBER-SUFFRIN, Claire: *Apprendre par la réciprocité – Réinventer ensemble les démarches pédagogiques*, Lyon, Chronique Sociale, 2016.

HOBSBAWM, Eric: *Historia del siglo XX*, Barcelona, Crítica, 2011.

HOWDEN, Jim and KOPIEC, Marguerite: *Ajouter aux compétences: enseigner, coopérer et apprendre au secondaire et au collégial*, Montréal, Chenelière Education, 2000.

IGLESIAS MUÑIZ, Jesús C.; GONZÁLEZ-GARCÍA, Laura F. and FERNÁNDEZ-RÍO, Javier: *Aprendizaje cooperativo: Teoría y práctica en las diferentes áreas y materias del currículum*, Ediciones Pirámide, 2017.

IRIGOYEN, Albert: "Entrevista a Antoni Gavaldà", *Comunicació Educativa*, 33 (2020), pp. 7–28. 10.17345/comeduc20207-28.

IRIGOYEN, Albert: "Entrevista a Sylvain Connac", *Comunicació Educativa*, 34 (2021), pp. 7–51. 10.17345/comeduc20217-51.

IRIGOYEN, Albert: "El treball cooperatiu en l'educació: peça clau per a la construcció d'un futur més democràtic i de participació responsable", in Josep M. PONS-ALTÉS (coord.), *Ciutadania compromesa i educació. Propostes per al foment de la memòria democràtica*, Tarragona, Publicacions URV, 2021, pp. 11–26. http://llibres.urv.cat/index.php/purv/catalog/book/483.

IRIGOYEN, Albert: "Entrevista a Philippe Meirieu", *Comunicació Educativa*, 35 (2022), pp. 9–57. 10.17345/comeduc20229-57.

IRIGOYEN, Albert and CONNAC, Sylvain: "L'aprenentatge cooperatiu i les "pédagogies coopératives": dues concepcions diferents de treballar en grup cooperatiu", *Comunicació Educativa*, 36 (2023).

IRIGOYEN, Albert and PONS-ALTÉS, Josep M.: "Els valors cooperatius: àncora de la cooperació entre alumnes a l'aula", in Teresa ABELLÓ *et al.* (coords.): *Herències/Legacies*. University of Barcelona Contemporary History and the World Today section and Ventall Edicions, 2023, pp. 336–347.

IRIGOYEN, Albert and PONS-ALTÉS, Josep M.: "Formación de docentes, didáctica de la historia contemporánea y aprendizaje cooperativo" in Francisco ACOSTA, Àngel DUARTE, Elena Lázaro and María J. RAMOS ROVI (eds.): *La Historia habitada. Sujetos, procesos y retos de la Historia Contemporánea del siglo XXI*, Cordoba, UCOPress Editorial, University of Cordoba, 2023, pp. 1687–1697.

IRIGOYEN, Albert and PONS-ALTÉS, Josep M.: "Aprendizaje cooperativo y Objetivos de Desarrollo Sostenible (ODS): formación de docentes a partir de problemas sociales relevantes", in María E. CAMBIL HERNÁNDEZ, Antonio R. FERNÁNDEZ PARADAS and Nicolás DE ALBA FERNÁNDEZ (coords.), *La Didáctica de las Ciencias Sociales ante el reto de los ODS*, Madrid, Narcea, 2023, pp. 779–787.

JOHNSON, David W. and JOHNSON, Roger T.: *Cooperation and Competition: Theory and Research*, Interaction Book Company, 1989.

JOHNSON, David W. and JOHNSON, Roger T.: "An Educational Psychology Success Story: Social Interdependence Theory and Cooperative Learning". *Educational Researcher*, 38 (2009), pp. 365–379.

JOHNSON, David W. and JOHNSON, Roger T.: "Cooperative Learning in 21st Century". *Anales de Psicología*, 30 (2014, 3), pp. 841–851, 10.6018/analesps.30.3.201241.

JOHNSON, David W. and JOHNSON, Roger T.: "Theoretical Approaches to Cooperative Learning". In Robyn M. GILLIES (ed.), *Collaborative Learning: Developments in Research and Practice*, New York, Nova Science Publishers, 2015, pp. 17–46.

JOHNSON, David W.; JOHNSON, Roger T. and HOLUBEC, Edythe J.: *El Aprendizaje cooperativo en el aula*, Barcelona, Paidós, 1999.

JONASSEN, David H. (2009): "Reconciling a Human Cognitive Architecture", in S. TOBIAS and T.-M. DUFFY (eds.): *Constructivist Theory Applied to Instruction: Success or Failure?*, London, Routledge.

KYNDT, Eva; RAES, Elisabeth; LISMONT, Bart; TIMMERS, Fran; CASCALLAR, Eduardo and DOCHY, Filip: "A Meta-analysis of the Effects of Face-to-face Cooperative Learning. Do Recent Studies Falsify or Verify Earlier Findings?", *Educational Research Review*, 10 (2013), pp. 133–149.

LAMBERTI, Stefania: *Apprendimento cooperativo e educazione interculturale. Percorsi e attività per la scuola primaria*, Trento, Erickson, 2010.

LAPLACE, Claude: *Pratiquer les conseils d'élèves et les assemblées de classes*, Lyon, Chronique Sociale, 2008.

LAURENT, Eloi: *L'impasse collaborative – Pour une véritable économie de la cooperation*, Paris, Les liens qui libèrent, 2018.

LA PROVA, Anna: *Apprendimento cooperativo e differenze individuali*, Trento, Erickson, 2008.

LA PROVA, Anna: *Apprendimento cooperativo in pratica. Proposte operative per attività di grupo in classe*, Trento, Edizioni Centro Studi Erickson, 2015.

LE GAL, Jean: *Les droits de l'enfant à l'école, pour une éducation à la citoyenneté*, Brussels, De Boeck et Belin, 2002.

LERHAUS, Katia and ROUILLER, Yviane (dir.): *Vers des apprentissages en coopération: rencontres et perspectives*. Peter Lang, 2008.

LEWIN, Kurt: "The Research Center for Group Dynamics". *Sociometry*, 8 (1945, 2), pp. 126–136. 10.2307/2785233.

LOUIS, R.: "Les facteurs qui influent sur l'adoption par l'enseignante d'une nouvelle approche pédagogique: le cas de la pédagogie coopérative". *Vie pédagogique*, 96 (1995), pp. 47–50.

MARTINELLI, Mario: *In gruppo si impara*, Turin, SEI, 2004.

MASHEDER, Milfred: *Jeux coopératifs pour bâtir la paix*, Lyon, Chronique Sociale, 2005.

MATINI, Claudia: *Cooperative Learning: istruzioni per l'uso*, Perugia, Editrice La Fonte, 2019.

MEDINA-ALBALADEJO, Francisco J. et al.: "Local Constraints and Knowledge Transfer in the Formation and Development of Cooperatives: Catalonia, 1860-1939", *Documentos de trabajo (DT-AEHE) de la Asociación Española de Historia Económica*, 1808 (2018).

MEIRIEU, Philippe: *La riposte – Pour en finir avec les miroirs aux alouettes*, Paris, Editions Autrement, 2018.

MIR, Clara (coord.): *Cooperar en la escuela. La responsabilidad de educar para la democracia*, Barcelona, Graó, 1998.

MUGNY, Gabriel and DOISE, William: *La construcción social de la inteligencia*, Méjico, Trillas, 1983.

OVEJERO, Anastasio: *Aprendizaje cooperativo crítico. Mucho más que una eficaz técnica pedagógica*, Madrid, Pirámide, 2018.

PAGONI, Maria: "Conceptualisation des règles scolaires et éducation à la citoyenneté au sein des conseils de coopérative". *Carrefours de l'éducation*, 31 (2011, 1), pp. 177–192.

PAIN, Jacques: *Pédagogie institutionnelle*. Encyclopedia Universalis, 2005, http://www.jacques-pain.fr/jacques-pain/Definition_PI.html.

PESCARMONA, Isabella: *Innovazione educativa tra entusiasmo e fatica. Un'etnografia dell'apprendimento cooperativo*, Rome, CISU, 2012.

PIÉTRONS, Claude: *Pratiquer les conseils de la classe*, Lyon, Chronique Sociale, 2022.

PONS-ALTÉS, Josep M. (coord.): *Ciutadania compromesa i educació. Propostes per al foment de la memòria democràtica*, Tarragona, Publicacions Universitat Rovira i Virgili, 2021. http://llibres.urv.cat/index.php/purv/catalog/book/483.

PONS-ALTÉS, Josep M. and IRIGOYEN, Albert: "¿Aprendizaje cooperativo sin valores cooperativos? Análisis de manuales escolares", in Juan Carlos BEL MARTÍNEZ, Juan Carlos COLOMER RUBIO and Nicolás DE ALBA FERNÁNDEZ (eds.), *Repensar el currículum de Ciencias Sociales: prácticas educativas para una ciudadanía crítica*, Valencia, Tirant Lo Blanch, 2022, pp. 889–897.

PUJOLÀS, Pere: *9 ideas clave. El aprendizaje cooperativo*, Barcelona, Graó, 2008.

PUJOLÀS, Pere: "Cooperar per aprendre i aprendre a cooperar: el treball en equips cooperatius com a recurs i com a contingut", *Suports: revista catalana d'educació especial i atenció a la diversitat*, 12 (2012), pp. 21–37.

PUJOLÀS, Pere and LAGO, José Ramón: *Aprender en equipos de aprendizaje cooperativo. El Programa CA/AC (Cooperar para aprender/Aprender a cooperar)*, Barcelona, Octaedro, 2018.

RAILLON, Louis: "Roger Cousinet". *Perspectives: revue trimestrielle d'éducation comparée*, vol. XXIII, 1-2 (1993), pp. 225–236.

RIZZI, Rinaldo: *La "cooperazione educativa" per una "pedagogia popolare". Una storia del MCE*, Parma, Edizioni Junior, 2021.

RIZZI, Rinaldo: *La cooperazione nell'educazione*, Bari, Laterza, 1991.

ROUILLER, Yviane and HOWDEN, Jim: *La pédagogie coopérative. Reflets de pratiques et approfondissements*, Montréal, Chenelière Éducation, 2010.

ROUILLER, Yviane and LERHAUS, Katia: "Pédagogie coopérative: de l'expérience et de la science". *Éducateur*, 5 (2003), pp. 24–26.

RUÉ, Joan: "El aula: un espacio para la cooperación", in Clara MIR (coord.): *Cooperación en la escuela. La responsabilidad de educar para la democracia*, Barcelona, Graó, 1998, pp. 17–50.

RUÉ, Joan: *El treball cooperatiu. L'organització social de l'ensenyament i l'aprenentatge*, Barcelona, Barcanova, 1991.

SCHUNK, Dale H.: *Learning theories: An educational perspective* (6th ed.), Boston, Allyn and Bacon, 2012.

SERRANO, José Manuel and PONS, Rosa M.: "Cooperative Learning: We Also Do It Without Task Structure". *Intercultural Education*, 18 (2007, 3), pp. 215–230, 10.1080/14675980701463562.

SLAVIN, Robert E.: *Aprendizaje cooperativo. Teoría, investigación y práctica*. Argentina, Aique, 1999.

SLAVIN, Robert E.: "Cooperative Learning and Academic Achievement: Why Does Groupwork Work?", *Anales de Psicología*, 30 (2014, 3), pp. 785–791, 10.6018/analesps.30.3.201201.

SLEE, Roger: *La escuela extraordinaria. Exclusión, escolarización y educación inclusiva*, Madrid, Ediciones Morata, 2012.

STAQUET, Christian: *Une classe qui coopère – Pourquoi? Comment?*, Lyon, Chronique Sociale, 2007.

THARP, Roland G.; ESTRADA, Peggy; DALTON, Stephanie S. and YAMAUCHI, Lois A: *Transformar la enseñanza. Excelencia, equidad, inclusión y armonía en las aulas y las escuelas*, Barcelona, Editorial Paidós, 2002.

THELEN, Herbert: *Dynamics of Groups at Work*, Chicago, University of Chigaco Press, 1954.

TOMASELLO, Michael: *A Natural History of Human Thinking*, Harvard University Press, 2014.

TORREGO, Juan Carlos and NEGRO, Andrés (coords.): *Aprendizaje cooperativo en las aulas*, Madrid, Alianza Editorial, 2012.

TOZZI, Michel: *Nouvelles pratiques philosophiques*, Lyon, Chronique Sociale, 2012.
VUILLET, Jean: *La coopération à l'école*, Paris, Presses Universitaires de France, 1968.
ZAMAGNI, Stefano and ZAMAGNI, Vera: *Cooperative Enterprise. Facing the Challenge of Globalization*, Cheltenham, Edward Elgar, 2010.
ZARIQUIEY BIONDI, Francisco: *Cooperar para aprender. Transformar el aula en una red de aprendizaje cooperativo*, Spain SM, 2016.

Contributors

Montserrat Duch-Plana is a professor of contemporary history at Rovira i Virgili University. She has been the coordinator of the consolidated research group ISOCAC (Ideologies and Society in Contemporary Catalonia) since 2010. She is the director of the Atenea series of studies on women, gender, and feminism (2005–present). She has published 18 books and articles in publications such as *Historia Social*, *Historia Contemporánea*, *Historia del presente*, *Ayer*, *Alcores,* and *Studia historica*. She is the principal investigator of the Ministry of the Economy's research projects "The spaces and memory of popular sociability in contemporary Catalonia" (2011–2013), "Sociabilities: spaces for constructing citizenship in Catalonia (1868–1938)" (2014–2018), and "Historia de la Cataluña subalterna: alternativas solidarias y cooperativas" (2020–2024). She is also a member of the MEFRO Project funded by Europe for citizens Programme of the European Union (2015–2017). Her main lines of research are the social history of the 20th century, memory policies and the public uses of history and the history of women.

Josep M. Pons-Altés is a professor at Rovira i Virgili University. He holds a PhD in history from Pompeu Fabra University of Barcelona, and he has taught at the University of Lleida, the University of Murcia, Jaume I University in Castelló, the National University of Paraguay in Asunción, and the Open University of Catalonia. Some of his publications include the books *Moderats i progressistes a la Lleida del segle XIX* (2002); *Lluís Companys, els orígens d'un símbol* (2005); and *Pere Boldú i Tilló. Cooperació i formació* (2013), and he has contributed to *El treball cooperatiu. Una estratègia per ensenyar i aprendre des de les ciències socials* (2016). He has also edited the books *Didàctica, història, cooperació i justícia social. Reconeixement al doctor Antoni Gavaldà* (2021) and *Ciutadania compromesa i educació. Propostes per al foment de la memòria democràtica* (2021). He has also published in *Investigación* *en la Escuela, Íber. Didáctica de las Ciencias Sociales, Geografía e Historia, Historia Social, Storia e Futuro. Rivista di storia e storiografia,* or *International Journal of Iberian Studies.*

Jordi Estivill is a sociologist, economist, and cooperativist. He is a member of the *Xarxa d'economia solidària* (XES) (Catalonia Solidarity Economy Network) and founder of RIPESS Europe. He is a professor emeritus at the University of Barcelona and directs one of the International Labor Organization's international programs on reducing social exclusion. He currently teaches a course on history and principles of the social and solidarity economy at the University of Lisbon's ICSTE. He is the author of numerous works on local development, social exclusion, and the solidarity economy. His work has been published in various countries, with a special focus on the history of the social and solidarity economy in Catalonia and Portugal.

Pedro Hespanha is a sociologist and founding member of the Center for Social Studies and retired Professor of the Faculty of Economics, both at the University of Coimbra. His main research is on the areas of rural studies, social policies, and solidarity economy. He has been a visiting professor at several universities in Europe, Brazil, and Angola. He participated as main researcher in several national and international research projects and research networks, dealing with active social policies, social exclusion and poverty, and non-capitalist economies, such as the economy of the commons. Since 2008, he coordinates the Research Group on Solidarity Economy (ECOSOL/CES).

Joana Dias Pereira is an integrated PhD researcher and member of the Institute of Contemporary History board. She has a position in the Faculty of Social Sciences and Humanities of the New University of Lisbon under the program to stimulate scientific employment of the Foundation for Science and Technology. She wrote several books, chapters, and articles dedicated to associationism and social movements in Portugal during the contemporary period. She collaborates with the national associative federations. Recently, she published two books, *Free Associationism: A History of Fraternity and Progress* (2020) and *The Origins of Mutualism in Portugal* (2021) with the Confederation of Culture, Recreation and Sports Associations and the Union of Portuguese Mutual Societies, respectively.

Jean-Louis Laville holds the chair in Solidarity Economy at Conservatoire national des arts et métiers (Cnam – Paris). He is also associated to CRISES (Canada), Cridis (Louvain-la-Neuve, Belgique), and Universidad Federal de Bahia (UFBA, Brasil). He is a founding member of EMES, International Research Network and of Riless. At the beginning of the 21st century, he has organized a multidisciplinary and international network in order to publish a first collection of works trying to present the social and solidarity economy realities and other aspects of the «other economy»: *Dictionnaire de l'autre économie* (2006); *Diccionario de la otra Economía* (2013); *Reinventar la izquierda en el siglo XX. Hasta un dialogo Norte-Sur* (2014); *La izquierda del siglo XXI* (2018). Some other publications are *Economia social y historia social* (2020) and *La economia solidaria* (2016).

Patrizia Battilani is a full professor of economic history at the University of Bologna. Since 2017, she sits on the Scientific Board of the Postgraduate Master in Economia della Cooperazione and in 2018–2021 she was the Director of the Center for Advanced Studies in Tourism. She has been a visiting scholar at the University of Sidney (2013) and Glasgow (2018 and 2019). Her primary research interests are business history and the history of tourism. She has published articles in many journals such as *Business History*, *Journal of Sustainable Tourism*, *Journal of Historical Research in Marketing*, and *Journal of Tourism History* and books with the Cambridge University Press and Il Mulino.

Fernando Venegas Espinoza is a scholar affiliated with the University of Concepción (UdeC) in Chile, and he holds a PhD from the University of Chile. His research is focused on social and cultural history and, more recently, environmental history. He is the director of the UdeC doctoral program in history and editor of the UdeC History Journal (https://revistas.udec.cl/index.php/historia/index). Among other activities, he is currently the principal investigator for the Mutualism in Chile, 1925–1990 project (Fondecyt research grant no. 1190308).

Mirta Zaida Lobato holds a PhD in history from the University of Buenos Aires. She is an adjunct professor in the Department of Philosophy and Letters at that same university and a researcher at the Interdisciplinary Gender Studies Institute (IIEGE). Her research is focused on the working world (national labor institutions, worker culture, gender relationships, and worker communities). She is the founder and a member of the editorial boards of the *Entrepasados* history journal and the journal *Mora* published by the Interdisciplinary Gender Studies Institute. She has received various awards and recognitions, including a Guggenheim Fellowship (2006). She has taught at universities in Argentina and in various other countries, with numerous articles published in local and international journals. Her books include *Infancias Argentinas* (2019); *La prensa obrera* (2009); *¿Tienen derechos las mujeres? Política y ciudadanía en la argentina del siglo XX* (2008); *Historia de las trabajadoras en la Argentina, 1869–1960* (2007); *La vida en las fábricas. Trabajo, protesta y política en una comunidad obrera,*

Berisso (1904–1970) (2001 and 2004); and *María Eva Duarte de Perón. Evita (1919–1952)* (2003).

Santiago Castillo is a professor emeritus in political science at the Complutense University of Madrid (UCM). He is the author of various books and articles on mutual associations, trade unions, politics, government, and processes of social reform in Spain since the 19th century. He is president of the *Social History Association* and codirector of the journal *Sociología del Trabajo* (*Sociology of Work*). His publications include *Historia del socialismo español, 1870–1909* (1989); (ed.) *Solidaridad desde abajo. Trabajadores y Socorros Mutuos en la España Contemporánea* (1994); (ed.) *Solidaridad, Seguridad, Bienestar. Cien años de protección social en España* (2008); (ed.) *Historia de la UGT* (2008–2012), 6 vols.; (ed.) *Centenario del Ministerio de Trabajo, 1920–2020* (2020).

Ramon Arnabat-Mata holds a PhD in history and is a professor of contemporary history at Rovira i Virgili University. He has also been involved in a variety of past and present research projects as a member of that university's Catalan History, Society, Politics, and Culture (ISOCAC) research group. His research activities have focused on studying revolution and counterrevolution during the 19th century, contemporary sociability and social movements, and the Spanish Second Republic, civil war, and Francoist periods. He has made presentations on these subjects at national and international conferences, published various articles in specialized journals as well as several books, and directed research and knowledge transfer projects.

Sylvain Connac is a teacher-researcher in education sciences. He works at the Paul-Valéry University in Montpellier and is a member of the Interdisciplinary Research Laboratory in Didactics, Education, and Training (LIRDEF). His research focuses on the professional skills of teachers in taking into account the diversity of students. For this reason, he guides teaching teams from kindergarten to high school who develop cooperation projects between students. He is the author of several books and scientific articles on cooperative pedagogies and the personalization of learning. He is a member of several educational groups: ICEM34, PIDAPI, Cahiers Pédagogiques, and OCCE.

Albert Irigoyen is a predoctoral researcher at Rovira i Virgili University with funding from the FI_SDUR 2021 program, and he has also taught there as an adjunct professor. He has degrees in Primary Education and History, and a master's degree in Secondary Education Teacher Training (Geography and History) from the same university. His doctoral thesis is currently in progress on the subject of teaching social sciences through cooperation during teacher training. He directs the journal *Educació Comunicativa* and is a member of Network of Teaching Innovation for Cooperative Learning (XINTERAC) and the Catalan History, Society, Politics, and Culture (ISOCAC) research group. He has also completed a doctoral study exchange with the LIRDEF research group at the Paul-Valéry University in Montpellier, France.

Carole Gauthié is a professor of French literature at the Paul Valéry University in Montpellier. She holds a PhD in education sciences from the Jean Jaurès University in Toulouse and has worked for 18 years in the fields of primary education and teacher training. Her research is focused on teacher versatility, and she works with two research groups, LIRDEF in Montpellier and EFTS in Toulouse. At her university, she teaches versatility, digital teaching, and French in the Education Sciences bachelor's and master's degree programs.

For Product Safety Concerns and Information please contact our EU representative GPSR@taylorandfrancis.com
Taylor & Francis Verlag GmbH, Kaufingerstraße 24, 80331 München, Germany

www.ingramcontent.com/pod-product-compliance
Ingram Content Group UK Ltd.
Pitfield, Milton Keynes, MK11 3LW, UK
UKHW022347190926
475702UK00015B/2155
* 9 7 8 1 0 3 2 5 7 4 8 0 6 *